D0723111

MATHEMATICS

FOR ECONOMICS AND BUSINESS

Pearson

At Pearson, we have a simple mission: to help people make more of their lives through learning.

We combine innovative learning technology with trusted content and educational expertise to provide engaging and effective learning experiences that serve people wherever and whenever they are learning.

From classroom to boardroom, our curriculum materials, digital learning tools and testing programmes help to educate millions of people worldwide – more than any other private enterprise.

Every day our work helps learning flourish, and wherever learning flourishes, so do people.

To learn more, please visit us at **www.pearson.com/uk**

MATHEMATICS

FOR ECONOMICS AND BUSINESS

IAN JACQUES

NINTH EDITION

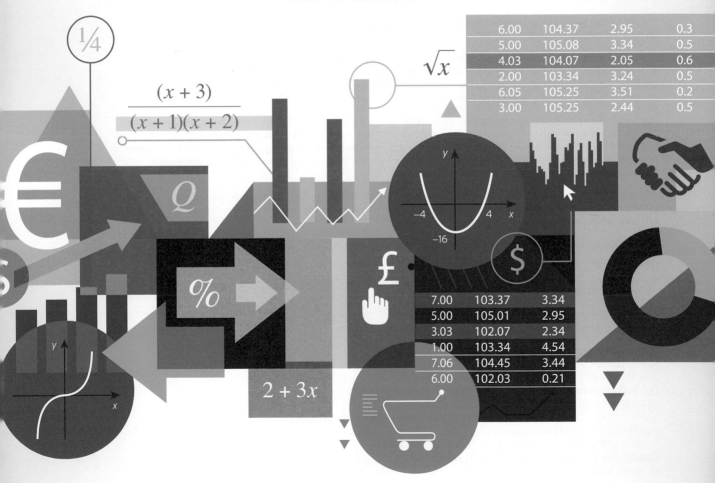

6.00	104.37	2.95	0.3
5.00	105.08	3.34	0.5
4.03	104.07	2.05	0.6
2.00	103.34	3.24	0.5
6.05	105.25	3.51	0.2
3.00	105.25	2.44	0.5

$$\frac{(x+3)}{(x+1)(x+2)}$$

$\sqrt{x}$

$2 + 3x$

7.00	103.37	3.34
5.00	105.01	2.95
3.03	102.07	2.34
1.00	103.34	4.54
7.06	104.45	3.44
6.00	102.03	0.21

Pearson

Harlow, England • London • New York • Boston • San Francisco • Toronto • Sydney • Dubai • Singapore • Hong Kong
Tokyo • Seoul • Taipei • New Delhi • Cape Town • São Paulo • Mexico City • Madrid • Amsterdam • Munich • Paris • Milan

PEARSON EDUCATION LIMITED
KAO Two
KAO Park
Harlow CM17 9NA
United Kingdom
Tel: +44 (0)1279 623623
Web: www.pearson.com/uk

First published 1991 (print)
Second edition published 1994 (print)
Third edition published 1999 (print)
Fourth edition published 2003 (print)
Fifth edition published 2006 (print)
Sixth edition published 2009 (print)
Seventh edition published 2013 (print and electronic)
Eighth edition published 2015 (print and electronic)
Ninth edition published 2018 (print and electronic)

© Addison-Wesley Publishers Ltd 1991, 1994 (print)
© Pearson Education Limited 1999, 2009 (print)
© Pearson Education Limited 2013, 2015, 2018 (print and electronic)

The right of Ian Jacques to be identified as author of this work has been asserted by him in accordance with the Copyright, Designs and Patents Act 1988.

The print publication is protected by copyright. Prior to any prohibited reproduction, storage in a retrieval system, distribution or transmission in any form or by any means, electronic, mechanical, recording or otherwise, permission should be obtained from the publisher or, where applicable, a licence permitting restricted copying in the United Kingdom should be obtained from the Copyright Licensing Agency Ltd, Barnard's Inn, 86 Fetter Lane, London EC4A 1EN.

The ePublication is protected by copyright and must not be copied, reproduced, transferred, distributed, leased, licensed or publicly performed or used in any way except as specifically permitted in writing by the publishers, as allowed under the terms and conditions under which it was purchased, or as strictly permitted by applicable copyright law. Any unauthorised distribution or use of this text may be a direct infringement of the author's and the publisher's rights and those responsible may be liable in law accordingly.

All trademarks used herein are the property of their respective owners. The use of any trademark in this text does not vest in the author or publisher any trademark ownership rights in such trademarks, nor does the use of such trademarks imply any affiliation with or endorsement of this book by such owners.

Pearson Education is not responsible for the content of third-party internet sites.

ISBN: 978-1-292-19166-9 (print)
 978-1-292-19170-6 (PDF)
 978-1-292-19171-3 (ePub)

British Library Cataloguing-in-Publication Data
A catalogue record for the print edition is available from the British Library

Library of Congress Cataloging-in-Publication Data
Names: Jacques, Ian, 1957– author.
Title: Mathematics for economics and business / Ian Jacques.
Description: Ninth edition. | Harlow, United Kingdom : Pearson Education,
  [2018] | Includes bibliographical references and index.
Identifiers: LCCN 2017049617| ISBN 9781292191669 (print) | ISBN 9781292191706
  (pdf) | ISBN 9781292191713 (epub)
Subjects: LCSH: Economics, Mathematical. | Business mathematics.
Classification: LCC HB135 .J32 2018 | DDC 512.024/33—dc23
LC record available at https://lccn.loc.gov/2017049617

10 9 8 7 6 5 4 3 2 1
22 21 20 19 18

Front cover image © Getty Images

Print edition typeset in 10/12.5pt Sabon MT Pro by iEnergizer Aptara®, Ltd.
Printed in Slovakia by Neografia

NOTE THAT ANY PAGE CROSS REFERENCES REFER TO THE PRINT EDITION

To Victoria, Lewis and Celia

CONTENTS

PREFACE

This text is intended primarily for students on economics, business studies and management courses. It assumes very little prerequisite knowledge, so it can be read by students who have not undertaken a mathematics course for some time. The style is informal, and the text contains a large number of worked examples. Students are encouraged to tackle problems for themselves as they read through each section. Detailed solutions are provided so that all answers can be checked. Consequently, it should be possible to work through this text on a self-study basis. The material is wide ranging and varies from elementary topics such as percentages and linear equations to more sophisticated topics such as constrained optimisation of multivariate functions. The text should therefore be suitable for use on both low- and high-level quantitative methods courses.

This text was first published in 1991. The prime motivation for writing it then was to try to produce a text that students could actually read and understand for themselves. This remains the guiding principle when writing this ninth edition.

One of the main improvements is the inclusion of over 200 additional questions. Each chapter now ends with both multiple choice questions and a selection of longer examination-style questions. Students usually enjoy tackling multiple choice questions since they provide a quick way of testing recall of the material covered in each chapter. Several universities include multiple choice as part of their assessment. The final section in each chapter entitled "Examination Questions" contains longer problems which require knowledge and understanding of more than one topic. Although these have been conveniently placed at the end of each chapter it may be best to leave these until the end of the academic year so that they can be used during the revision period just before the examinations.

Ian Jacques

INTRODUCTION
Getting Started

NOTES FOR STUDENTS: HOW TO USE THIS TEXT

I am always amazed by the mix of students on first-year economics courses. Some have not acquired any mathematical knowledge beyond elementary algebra (and even that can be of a rather dubious nature), some have never studied economics before in their lives, while others have passed preliminary courses in both. Whatever category you are in, I hope that you will find this text of value. The chapters covering algebraic manipulation, simple calculus, finance, matrices and linear programming should also benefit students on business studies and management courses.

The first few chapters are aimed at complete beginners and students who have not taken mathematics courses for some time. I would like to think that these students once enjoyed mathematics and had every intention of continuing their studies in this area, but somehow never found the time to fit it into an already overcrowded academic timetable. However, I suspect that the reality is rather different. Possibly they hated the subject, could not understand it and dropped it at the earliest opportunity. If you find yourself in this position, you are probably horrified to discover that you must embark on a quantitative methods course with an examination looming on the horizon. However, there is no need to worry. My experience is that every student is capable of passing a mathematics examination. All that is required is a commitment to study and a willingness to suspend any prejudices about the subject gained at school. The fact that you have bothered to buy this text at all suggests that you are prepared to do both.

To help you get the most out of this text, let me compare the working practices of economics and engineering students. The former rarely read individual books in any great depth. They tend to skim through a selection of books in the university library and perform a large number of Internet searches, picking out relevant information. Indeed, the ability to read selectively and to compare various sources of information is an important skill that all arts and social science students must acquire. Engineering students, on the other hand, are more likely to read just a few books in any one year. They read each of these from cover to cover and attempt virtually every problem en route. Even though you are most definitely not an engineer, it is the engineering approach that you need to adopt while studying mathematics. There are several reasons for this. First, a mathematics text can never be described, even by its most ardent admirers, as a good bedtime read. It can take an hour or two of concentrated effort to understand just a few pages of a mathematics text. You are therefore recommended to work through this text systematically in short bursts rather than to attempt to read whole chapters. Each section is designed to take between one and two hours to complete, and this is quite sufficient for a single session. Secondly, mathematics is a hierarchical subject in which one topic follows on from the next. A construction firm building an office block is hardly likely to erect the fiftieth storey without making sure that the intermediate floors and foundations are securely in place. Likewise, you cannot 'dip' into the middle of a mathematics text and expect to follow it unless you have satisfied the prerequisites for that topic. Finally, you actually need to do mathematics yourself before you can understand it. No matter how wonderful your lecturer is, and no matter how many problems are discussed in class, it is only by solving problems yourself that you are ever going to become confident in using and applying mathematical techniques. For this reason, several problems are interspersed within the text, and you are encouraged to tackle these as you go along. You will require writing paper, graph paper, pens and a calculator for this. There is no need to buy an expensive calculator unless you are feeling particularly wealthy at the moment. A bottom-of-the-range **scientific** calculator should be good enough. Answers to every question are printed at the back of this text so that you can check your own answers quickly as you go along. However, please avoid the temptation to look at them until you have made an honest attempt at each one. Remember that in the future you may well have to sit down in an uncomfortable chair, in front of a blank sheet of paper, and be expected to produce solutions to examination questions of a similar type.

At the end of each section there are two parallel exercises. The non-starred exercises are intended for students who are meeting these topics for the first time and the questions are designed to consolidate basic principles. The starred exercises are more challenging but still cover the full range so that students with greater experience will be able to concentrate their efforts on these questions without having to pick-and-mix from both exercises. The chapter dependence is shown in Figure I.1. If you have studied some advanced mathematics before, you will discover that parts of Chapters 1, 2 and 4 are familiar. However, you may find that the sections on economics applications contain new material. You are best advised to test yourself by attempting a selection of problems from the starred exercise in each section to see if you need to read through it as part of a refresher course. Economics students in a desperate hurry to experience the delights of calculus can miss out Chapter 3 without any loss of continuity and move straight on to Chapter 4. The mathematics of finance is probably more relevant to business and accountancy students, although you can always read it later if it is part of your economics syllabus.

At the end of every chapter you will find a multiple choice test and some examination questions. These cover the work of the whole chapter. We recommend that you try the multiple choice questions when you have completed the relevant chapter. As usual, answers

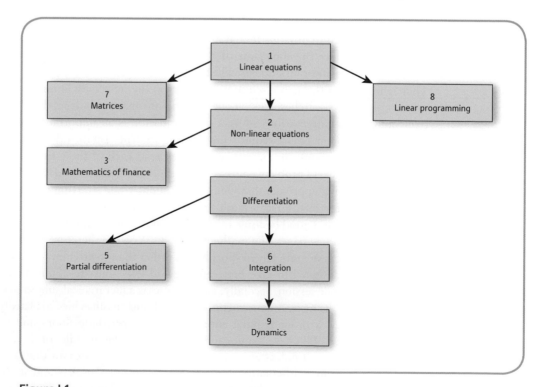

Figure I.1

are provided at the back of the book so that you can check to see how well you have done. If you do get any of the questions wrong, it would be worth re-doing that question perhaps writing down full working so that you can spot your mistake more easily. The final section contains several examination-style problems which are more challenging. They tend to be longer than the questions encountered so far in the exercises and require more confidence and experience. We recommend that you leave these until the end of the course and use them in your build-up to the final exams.

I hope that this text helps you to succeed in your mathematics course. You never know, you might even enjoy it. Remember to wear your engineer's hat while reading the text. I have done my best to make the material as accessible as possible. The rest is up to you!

CHAPTER 1

Linear Equations

The main aim of this chapter is to introduce the mathematics of linear equations. This is an obvious first choice in an introductory text, since it is an easy topic which has many applications. There are seven sections, which are intended to be read in the order that they appear.

Sections 1.1, 1.2, 1.3, 1.4 and 1.6 are devoted to mathematical methods. They serve to revise the rules of arithmetic and algebra, which you probably met at school but may have forgotten. In particular, the properties of negative numbers and fractions are considered. A reminder is given on how to multiply out brackets and how to manipulate mathematical expressions. You are also shown how to solve simultaneous linear equations. Systems of two equations in two unknowns can be solved using graphs, which are described in Section 1.3. However, the preferred method uses elimination, which is considered in Section 1.4. This algebraic approach has the advantage that it always gives an exact solution and it extends readily to larger systems of equations.

The remaining two sections are reserved for applications in microeconomics and macroeconomics. You may be pleasantly surprised by how much economic theory you can analyse using just the basic mathematical tools considered here. Section 1.5 introduces the fundamental concept of an economic function and describes how to calculate equilibrium prices and quantities in supply and demand theory. Section 1.7 deals with national income determination in simple macroeconomic models.

The first six sections underpin the rest of the text and are essential reading. The final section is not quite as important and can be omitted at this stage.

SECTION 1.1
Introduction to algebra

Objectives

At the end of this section you should be able to:

- Add, subtract, multiply and divide negative numbers.
- Understand what is meant by an algebraic expression.
- Evaluate algebraic expressions numerically.
- Simplify algebraic expressions by collecting like terms.
- Multiply out brackets.
- Factorise algebraic expressions.

ALGEBRA IS BORING

There is no getting away from the fact that algebra *is* boring. Doubtless there are a few enthusiasts who get a kick out of algebraic manipulation, but economics and business students are rarely to be found in this category. Indeed, the mere mention of the word 'algebra' is enough to strike fear into the heart of many a first-year student. Unfortunately, you cannot get very far with mathematics unless you have completely mastered this topic. An apposite analogy is the game of chess. Before you can begin to play a game of chess, it is necessary to go through the tedium of learning the moves of individual pieces. In the same way it is essential that you learn the rules of algebra before you can enjoy the 'game' of mathematics. Of course, just because you know the rules does not mean that you are going to excel at the game, and no one is expecting you to become a grandmaster of mathematics. However, you should at least be able to follow the mathematics presented in economics books and journals as well as to solve simple problems for yourself.

Advice

If you have studied mathematics recently, then you will find the material in the first few sections of the text fairly straightforward. You may prefer just to try the questions in the starred exercise at the end of each section to get yourself back up to speed. However, if it has been some time since you have studied this subject, our advice is very different. Please work through the material thoroughly even if it is vaguely familiar. Make sure that you do the problems as they arise, checking your answers with those provided at the back of this text. The material has been broken down into three subsections:

- negative numbers;
- expressions;
- brackets.

You might like to work through these subsections on separate occasions to enable the ideas to sink in. To rush this topic now is likely to give you only a half-baked understanding, which will result in hours of frustration when you study the later chapters of this text.

1.1.1 Negative numbers

In mathematics numbers are classified into one of three types: positive, negative or zero. At school you were probably introduced to the idea of a negative number via the temperature on a thermometer scale measured in degrees centigrade. A number such as -5 would then be interpreted as a temperature of 5 degrees below freezing. In personal finance a negative bank balance would indicate that an account is 'in the red' or 'in debit'. Similarly, a firm's profit of $-500\,000$ signifies a loss of half a million.

The rules for the multiplication of negative numbers are

$$\text{negative} \times \text{negative} = \text{positive}$$

$$\text{negative} \times \text{positive} = \text{negative}$$

It does not matter in which order two numbers are multiplied, so

$$\text{positive} \times \text{negative} = \text{negative}$$

These rules produce, respectively,

$$(-2) \times (-3) = 6$$

$$(-4) \times 5 = -20$$

$$7 \times (-5) = -35$$

Also, because division is the same sort of operation as multiplication (it just undoes the result of multiplication and takes you back to where you started), exactly the same rules apply when one number is divided by another. For example,

$$(-15) \div (-3) = 5$$

$$(-16) \div 2 = -8$$

$$2 \div (-4) = -1/2$$

In general, to multiply or divide lots of numbers it is probably simplest to ignore the signs to begin with and just to work the answer out. The final result is negative if the total number of minus signs is odd and positive if the total number is even.

Example

Evaluate

(a) $(-2) \times (-4) \times (-1) \times 2 \times (-1) \times (-3)$ **(b)** $\dfrac{5 \times (-4) \times (-1) \times (-3)}{(-6) \times 2}$

Solution

(a) Ignoring the signs gives

$$2 \times 4 \times 1 \times 2 \times 1 \times 3 = 48$$

There are an odd number of minus signs (in fact, five), so the answer is -48.

(b) Ignoring the signs gives

$$\frac{5 \times 4 \times 1 \times 3}{6 \times 2} = \frac{60}{12} = 5$$

There are an even number of minus signs (in fact, four), so the answer is 5.

> ### Advice
>
> Attempt the following problem yourself both with and without a calculator. On most machines a negative number such as −6 is entered by pressing the button labelled (−) followed by 6.

> ### Practice Problem
>
> 1. **(1)** Without using a calculator, evaluate
>
>   **(a)** $5 \times (-6)$ **(b)** $(-1) \times (-2)$ **(c)** $(-50) \div 10$
>
>   **(d)** $(-5) \div (-1)$ **(e)** $2 \times (-1) \times (-3) \times 6$ **(f)** $\dfrac{2 \times (-1) \times (-3) \times 6}{(-2) \times 3 \times 6}$
>
>   **(2)** Confirm your answer to part (1) using a calculator.

To add or subtract negative numbers it helps to think in terms of a number line:

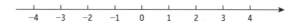

If b is a positive number, then

$$a - b$$

can be thought of as an instruction to start at a and to move b units to the left. For example,

$$1 - 3 = -2$$

because if you start at 1 and move 3 units to the left, you end up at −2:

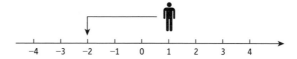

Similarly,

$$-2 - 1 = -3$$

because 1 unit to the left of −2 is −3.

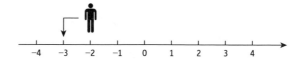

On the other hand,

$$a - (-b)$$

is taken to be $a + b$. This follows from the rule for multiplying two negative numbers, since

$$-(-b) = (-1) \times (-b) = b$$

Consequently, to evaluate

$$a - (-b)$$

you start at a and move b units to the right (that is, in the positive direction). For example,

$$-2 - (-5) = -2 + 5 = 3$$

because if you start at -2 and move 5 units to the right, you end up at 3.

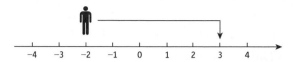

Practice Problem

2. **(1)** Without using a calculator, evaluate

     (a) $1 - 2$ **(b)** $-3 - 4$ **(c)** $1 - (-4)$

     (d) $-1 - (-1)$ **(e)** $-72 - 19$ **(f)** $-53 - (-48)$

    (2) Confirm your answer to part (1) using a calculator.

1.1.2 Expressions

In algebra, letters are used to represent numbers. In pure mathematics the most common letters used are x and y. However, in applications it is helpful to choose letters that are more meaningful, so we might use Q for quantity and I for investment. An algebraic expression is then simply a combination of these letters, brackets and other mathematical symbols such as $+$ or $-$. For example, the expression

$$P\left(1 + \frac{r}{100}\right)^n$$

can be used to work out how money in a savings account grows over a period of time. The letters P, r and n represent the original sum invested (called the principal – hence the use of the letter P), the rate of interest and the number of years, respectively. To work it all out, you not only need to replace these letters by actual numbers, but you also need to understand the various conventions that go with algebraic expressions such as this.

In algebra, when we multiply two numbers represented by letters, we usually suppress the multiplication sign between them. The product of a and b would simply be written as ab without bothering to put the multiplication sign between the symbols. Likewise, when a number represented by the letter Y is doubled, we write $2Y$. In this case we not only suppress the multiplication sign but adopt the convention of writing the number in front of the letter. Here are some further examples:

$P \times Q$ is written as PQ

$d \times 8$ is written as $8d$

$n \times 6 \times t$ is written as $6nt$

$z \times z$ is written as z^2 (using the index 2 to indicate squaring a number)

$1 \times t$ is written as t (since multiplying by 1 does not change a number)

In order to evaluate these expressions it is necessary to be given the numerical value of each letter. Once this has been done, you can work out the final value by performing the operations in the following order:

Brackets first	(B)
Indices second	(I)
Division and Multiplication third	(DM)
Addition and Subtraction fourth	(AS)

This is sometimes remembered using the acronym BIDMAS, and it is essential to use this ordering for working out all mathematical calculations. For example, suppose you wish to evaluate each of the following expressions when $n = 3$:

$2n^2$ and $(2n)^2$

Substituting $n = 3$ into the first expression gives

$$2n^2 = 2 \times 3^2 \quad \text{(the multiplication sign is revealed when we switch from algebra to numbers)}$$
$$= 2 \times 9 \quad \text{(according to BIDMAS, indices are worked out before multiplication)}$$
$$= 18$$

whereas in the second expression we get

$$(2n)^2 = (2 \times 3)^2 \quad \text{(again, the multiplication sign is revealed)}$$
$$= 6^2 \quad \text{(according to BIDMAS, we evaluate the inside of the brackets first)}$$
$$= 36$$

The two answers are not the same, so the order indicated by BIDMAS really does matter. Looking at the previous list, notice that there is a tie between multiplication and division for third place, and another tie between addition and subtraction for fourth place. These pairs of operations have equal priority, and under these circumstances you work from left to right when evaluating expressions. For example, substituting $x = 5$ and $y = 4$ in the expression, $x - y + 2$, gives

$$x - y + 2 = 5 - 4 + 2$$
$$= 1 + 2 \quad \text{(reading from left to right, subtraction comes first)}$$
$$= 3$$

Example

(a) Find the value of $2x - 3y$ when $x = 9$ and $y = 4$.

(b) Find the value of $2Q^2 + 4Q + 150$ when $Q = 10$.

(c) Find the value of $5a - 2b + c$ when $a = 4$, $b = 6$ and $c = 1$.

(d) Find the value of $(12 - t) - (t - 1)$ when $t = 4$.

Solution

(a) $2x - 3y = 2 \times 9 - 3 \times 4 \quad$ (substituting numbers)

$\qquad\qquad = 18 - 12 \qquad\qquad$ (multiplication has priority over subtraction)

$\qquad\qquad = 6$

(b) $2Q^2 + 4Q + 150 = 2 \times 10^2 + 4 \times 10 + 150$ (substituting numbers)

$= 2 \times 100 + 4 \times 10 + 150$ (indices have priority over multiplication and addition)

$= 200 + 40 + 150$ (multiplication has priority over addition)

$= 390$

(c) $5a - 2b + c = 5 \times 4 - 2 \times 6 + 1$ (substituting numbers)

$= 20 - 12 + 1$ (multiplication has priority over addition and subtraction)

$= 8 + 1$ (addition and subtraction have equal priority, so work from left to right)

$= 9$

(d) $(12 - t) - (t - 1) = (12 - 4) - (4 - 1)$ (substituting numbers)

$= 8 - 3$ (brackets first)

$= 5$

Practice Problem

3. Evaluate each of the following by replacing the letters by the given numbers:

(a) $2Q + 5$ when $Q = 7$.

(b) $5x^2y$ when $x = 10$ and $y = 3$.

(c) $4d - 3f + 2g$ when $d = 7, f = 2$ and $g = 5$.

(d) $a(b + 2c)$ when $a = 5, b = 1$ and $c = 3$.

Like terms are multiples of the same letter (or letters). For example, $2P$, $-34P$ and $0.3P$ are all multiples of P and so are like terms. In the same way, xy, $4xy$ and $69xy$ are all multiples of xy and so are like terms. If an algebraic expression contains like terms which are added or subtracted together, then it can be simplified to produce an equivalent shorter expression.

Example

Simplify each of the following expressions (where possible):

(a) $2a + 5a - 3a$

(b) $4P - 2Q$

(c) $3w + 9w^2 + 2w$

(d) $3xy + 2y^2 + 9x + 4xy - 8x$

Solution

(a) All three are like terms since they are all multiples of a, so the expression can be simplified:

$2a + 5a - 3a = 4a$

(b) The terms $4P$ and $2Q$ are unlike because one is a multiple of P and the other is a multiple of Q, so the expression cannot be simplified.

(c) The first and last are like terms since they are both multiples of w, so we can collect these together and write

$$3w + 9w^2 + 2w = 5w + 9w^2$$

This cannot be simpified any further because $5w$ and $9w^2$ are unlike terms.

(d) The terms $3xy$ and $4xy$ are like terms, and $9x$ and $8x$ are also like terms. These pairs can therefore be collected together to give

$$3xy + 2y^2 + 9x + 4xy - 8x = 7xy + 2y^2 + x$$

Notice that we write just x instead of $1x$ and also that no further simplication is possible since the final answer involves three unlike terms.

Practice Problem

4. Simplify each of the following expressions, where possible:

(a) $2x + 6y - x + 3y$ (b) $5x + 2y - 5x + 4z$ (c) $4Y^2 + 3Y - 43$

(d) $8r^2 + 4s - 6rs - 3s - 3s^2 + 7rs$ (e) $2e^2 + 5f - 2e^2 - 9f$ (f) $3w + 6W$

(g) $ab - ba$

1.1.3 Brackets

It is useful to be able to take an expression containing brackets and rewrite it as an equivalent expression without brackets, and vice versa. The process of removing brackets is called 'expanding brackets' or 'multiplying out brackets'. This is based on the **distributive law**, which states that for any three numbers a, b and c

$$a(b + c) = ab + ac$$

It is easy to verify this law in simple cases. For example, if $a = 2$, $b = 3$ and $c = 4$, then the left-hand side is

$$2(3 + 4) = 2 \times 7 = 14$$

However,

$$ab = 2 \times 3 = 6 \quad \text{and} \quad ac = 2 \times 4 = 8$$

and so the right-hand side is $6 + 8$, which is also 14.

This law can be used when there are any number of terms inside the brackets. We have

$$a(b + c + d) = ab + ac + ad$$
$$a(b + c + d + e) = ab + ac + ad + ae$$

and so on.

It does not matter in which order two numbers are multiplied, so we also have

$$(b + c)a = ba + ca$$
$$(b + c + d)a = ba + ca + da$$
$$(b + c + d + e)a = ba + ca + da + ea$$

Example

Multiply out the brackets in

(a) $x(x - 2)$

(b) $2(x + y - z) + 3(z + y)$

(c) $x + 3y - (2y + x)$

Solution

(a) The use of the distributive law to multiply out $x(x - 2)$ is straightforward. The x outside the bracket multiplies the x inside to give x^2. The x outside the bracket also multiplies the -2 inside to give $-2x$. Hence

$$x(x - 2) = x^2 - 2x$$

(b) To expand

$$2(x + y - z) + 3(z + y)$$

we need to apply the distributive law twice. We have

$$2(x + y - z) = 2x + 2y - 2z$$
$$3(z + y) = 3z + 3y$$

Adding together gives

$$2(x + y - z) + 3(z + y) = 2x + 2y - 2z + 3z + 3y$$
$$= 2x + 5y + z \quad \text{(collecting like terms)}$$

(c) It may not be immediately apparent how to expand

$$x + 3y - (2y + x)$$

However, note that

$$-(2y + x)$$

is the same as

$$(-1)(2y + x)$$

which expands to give

$$(-1)(2y) + (-1)x = -2y - x$$

Hence

$$x + 3y - (2y + x) = x + 3y - 2y - x = y$$

after collecting like terms.

> ### Advice
>
> In this example the solutions are written out in painstaking detail. This is done to show you precisely how the distributive law is applied. The solutions to all three parts could have been written down in only one or two steps of working. You are, of course, at liberty to compress the working in your own solutions, but please do not be tempted to overdo this. You might want to check your answers at a later date and may find it difficult if you have tried to be too clever.

Practice Problem

5. Multiply out the brackets, simplifying your answer as far as possible.

    (a) $(5 - 2z)z$ **(b)** $6(x - y) + 3(y - 2x)$ **(c)** $x - y + z - (x^2 + x - y)$

Mathematical formulae provide a precise way of representing calculations that need to be worked out in many business models. However, it is important to realise that these formulae may be valid only for a restricted range of values. Most large companies have a policy to reimburse employees for use of their cars for travel: for the first 50 miles they may be able to claim 90 cents a mile, but this could fall to 60 cents a mile thereafter. If the distance, x miles, is no more than 50 miles, then travel expenses, E (in dollars), could be worked out using the formula $E = 0.9x$. If x exceeds 50 miles, the employee can claim \$0.90 a mile for the first 50 miles but only \$0.60 a mile for the last $(x - 50)$ miles. The total amount is then

$$E = 0.9 \times 50 + 0.6(x - 50)$$
$$= 45 + 0.6x - 30$$
$$= 15 + 0.6x$$

Travel expenses can therefore be worked out using two separate formulae:

- $E = 0.9x$ when x is no more than 50 miles
- $E = 15 + 0.6x$ when x exceeds 50 miles.

Before we leave this topic, a word of warning is in order. Be careful when removing brackets from very simple expressions such as those considered in part (c) in the previous worked example and practice problem. A common mistake is to write

$$(a + b) - (c + d) = a + b - c + d \qquad \text{This is NOT true}$$

The distributive law tells us that the -1 multiplying the second bracket applies to the d as well as the c, so the correct answer has to be

$$(a + b) - (c + d) = a + b - c - d$$

In algebra, it is sometimes useful to reverse the procedure and put the brackets back in. This is called **factorisation**. Consider the expression $12a + 8b$. There are many numbers which divide into both 8 and 12. However, we always choose the biggest number, which is 4 in this case, so we attempt to take the factor of 4 outside the brackets:

$$12a + 8b = 4(? + ?)$$

where each ? indicates a mystery term inside the brackets. We would like 4 multiplied by the first term in the brackets to be $12a$, so we are missing $3a$. Likewise, if we are to generate an $8b$, the second term in the brackets will have to be $2b$.

Hence

$$12a + 8b = 4(3a + 2b)$$

As a check, notice that when you expand the brackets on the right-hand side, you really do get the expression on the left-hand side.

Example

Factorise

(a) $6L - 3L^2$

(b) $5a - 10b + 20c$

Solution

(a) Both terms have a common factor of 3. Also, because $L^2 = L \times L$, both $6L$ and $-3L^2$ have a factor of L. Hence we can take out a common factor of $3L$ altogether.

$$6L - 3L^2 = 3L(2) - 3L(L) = 3L(2 - L)$$

(b) All three terms have a common factor of 5, so we write

$$5a - 10b + 20c - 5(a) - 5(2b) + 5(4c) - 5(a - 2b + 4c)$$

Practice Problem

6. Factorise

(a) $7d + 21$ (b) $16w - 20q$ (c) $6x - 3y + 9z$ (d) $5Q - 10Q^2$

We conclude our discussion of brackets by describing how to multiply two brackets together. In the expression $(a + b)(c + d)$ the two terms a and b must each multiply the single bracket $(c + d)$, so

$$(a + b)(c + d) = a(c + d) + b(c + d)$$

The first term $a(c + d)$ can itself be expanded as $ac + ad$. Likewise, $b(c + d) = bc + bd$. Hence

$$(a + b)(c + d) = ac + ad + bc + bd$$

This procedure then extends to brackets with more than two terms:

$$(a + b)(c + d + e) = a(c + d + e) + b(c + d + e) = ac + ad + ae + bc + bd + be$$

Example

Multiply out the brackets

(a) $(x + 1)(x + 2)$ **(b)** $(x + 5)(x - 5)$ **(c)** $(2x - y)(x + y - 6)$

simplifying your answer as far as possible.

Solution

(a) $(x + 1)(x + 2) = x(x + 2) + (1)(x + 2)$
$$= x^2 + 2x + x + 2$$
$$= x^2 + 3x + 2$$

(b) $(x + 5)(x - 5) = x(x - 5) + 5(x - 5)$
$$= x^2 - 5x + 5x - 25$$
$$= x^2 - 25 \qquad \text{the xs cancel}$$

(c) $(2x - y)(x + y - 6) = 2x(x + y - 6) - y(x + y - 6)$
$$= 2x^2 + 2xy - 12x - yx - y^2 + 6y$$
$$= 2x^2 + xy - 12x - y^2 + 6y$$

Practice Problem

7. Multiply out the brackets.

   (a) $(x + 3)(x - 2)$
   (b) $(x + y)(x - y)$
   (c) $(x + y)(x + y)$
   (d) $(5x + 2y)(x - y + 1)$

Looking back at part (b) of the previous worked example, notice that

$$(x + 5)(x - 5) = x^2 - 25 = x^2 - 5^2$$

Quite generally

$$(a + b)(a - b) = a(a - b) + b(a - b)$$
$$= a^2 - ab + ba - b^2$$
$$= a^2 - b^2$$

The result

$$a^2 - b^2 = (a + b)(a - b)$$

is called the **difference of two squares** formula. It provides a quick way of factorising certain expressions.

Example

Factorise the following expressions:

(a) $x^2 - 16$ (b) $9x^2 - 100$

Solution

(a) Noting that

$$x^2 - 16 = x^2 - 4^2$$

we can use the difference of two squares formula to deduce that

$$x^2 - 16 = (x + 4)(x - 4)$$

(b) Noting that

$$9x^2 - 100 = (3x)^2 - (10)^2$$

$$(3x)^2 = 3x \times 3x$$
$$= 9x^2$$

we can use the difference of two squares formula to deduce that

$$9x^2 - 100 = (3x + 10)(3x - 10)$$

Practice Problem

8. Factorise the following expressions:

   (a) $x^2 - 64$ (b) $4x^2 - 81$

Advice

This completes your first piece of mathematics. We hope that you have not found it quite as bad as you first thought. There now follow a few extra problems to give you more practice. Not only will they help to strengthen your mathematical skills, but also they should improve your overall confidence. Two alternative exercises are available. Exercise 1.1 is suitable for students whose mathematics may be rusty and who need to consolidate their understanding. Exercise 1.1* contains more challenging problems and so is more suitable for those students who have found this section very easy.

Key Terms

Difference of two squares   The algebraic result which states that $a^2 - b^2 = (a + b)(a - b)$.

Distributive law   The law of arithmetic which states that $a(b + c) = ab + ac$ for any numbers, a, b, c.

Factorisation   The process of writing an expression as a product of simpler expressions using brackets.

Like terms   Multiples of the same combination of algebraic symbols.

Exercise 1.1

1. Without using a calculator, evaluate

   (a) $10 \times (-2)$ **(b)** $(-1) \times (-3)$ **(c)** $(-8) \div 2$ **(d)** $(-5) \div (-5)$

   (e) $24 \div (-2)$ **(f)** $(-10) \times (-5)$ **(g)** $\dfrac{20}{-4}$ **(h)** $\dfrac{-27}{-9}$

   (i) $(-6) \times 5 \times (-1)$ **(j)** $\dfrac{2 \times (-6) \times 3}{(-9)}$

2. Without using a calculator, evaluate

   (a) $5 - 6$ **(b)** $-1 - 2$ **(c)** $6 - 17$ **(d)** $-7 + 23$

   (e) $-7 - (-6)$ **(f)** $-4 - 9$ **(g)** $7 - (-4)$ **(h)** $-9 - (-9)$

   (i) $12 - 43$ **(j)** $2 + 6 - 10$

3. Without using a calculator, evaluate

   (a) $5 \times 2 - 13$ **(b)** $\dfrac{-30 - 6}{-18}$ **(c)** $\dfrac{(-3) \times (-6) \times (-1)}{2 - 3}$ **(d)** $5 \times (1 - 4)$

   (e) $1 - 6 \times 7$ **(f)** $-5 + 6 \div 3$ **(g)** $2 \times (-3)^2$ **(h)** $-10 + 2^2$

   (i) $(-2)^2 - 5 \times 6 + 1$ **(j)** $\dfrac{(-4)^2 \times (-3) \times (-1)}{(-2)^3}$

4. Simplify each of the following algebraic expressions:

   (a) $2 \times P \times Q$ **(b)** $I \times 8$ **(c)** $3 \times x \times y$

   (d) $4 \times q \times w \times z$ **(e)** $b \times b$ **(f)** $k \times 3 \times k$

5. Simplify the following algebraic expressions by collecting like terms:

   (a) $6w - 3w + 12w + 4w$ **(b)** $6x + 5y - 2x - 12y$

   (c) $3a - 2b + 6a - c + 4b - c$ **(d)** $2x^2 + 4x - x^2 - 2x$

   (e) $2cd + 4c - 5dc$ **(f)** $5st + s^2 - 3ts + t^2 + 9$

6. Without using a calculator, find the value of the following:

   (a) $2x - y$ when $x = 7$ and $y = 4$.

   (b) $x^2 - 5x + 12$ when $x = 6$.

   (c) $2m^3$ when $m = 10$.

   (d) $5fg^2 + 2g$ when $f = 2$ and $g = 3$.

   (e) $2v + 4w - (4v - 7w)$ when $v = 20$ and $w = 10$.

7. If $x = 2$ and $y = -3$, evaluate

   (a) $2x + y$ **(b)** $x - y$ **(c)** $3x + 4y$

   (d) xy **(e)** $5xy$ **(f)** $4x - 6xy$

8. **(a)** Without using a calculator, work out the value of $(-4)^2$.

(b) Press the following key sequence on your calculator:

$$\boxed{(-)} \quad \boxed{4} \quad \boxed{x^2}$$

Explain carefully why this does not give the same result as part (a) and give an alternative key sequence that *does* give the correct answer.

9. Without using a calculator, work out

(a) $(5 - 2)^2$ **(b)** $5^2 - 2^2$

Is it true in general that $(a - b)^2 = a^2 - b^2$?

10. Use your calculator to work out the following. Round your answer, if necessary, to two decimal places.

(a) $5.31 \times 8.47 - 1.01^2$ **(b)** $(8.34 + 2.27)/9.41$

(c) $9.53 - 3.21 + 4.02$ **(d)** $2.41 \times 0.09 - 1.67 \times 0.03$

(e) $45.76 - (2.55 + 15.83)$ **(f)** $(3.45 - 5.38)^2$

(g) $4.56(9.02 + 4.73)$ **(h)** $6.85/(2.59 + 0.28)$

11. Multiply out the brackets:

(a) $7(x - y)$ **(b)** $3(5x - 2y)$ **(c)** $4(x + 3)$ **(d)** $7(3x - 1)$

(e) $3(x + y + z)$ **(f)** $x(3x - 4)$ **(g)** $y + 2z - 2(x + 3y - z)$

12. Factorise

(a) $25c + 30$ **(b)** $9x - 18$ **(c)** $x^2 + 2x$

(d) $16x - 12y$ **(e)** $4x^2 - 6xy$ **(f)** $10d - 15e + 50$

13. Multiply out the brackets:

(a) $(x + 2)(x + 5)$ **(b)** $(a + 4)(a - 1)$ **(c)** $(d + 3)(d - 8)$ **(d)** $(2s + 3)(3s + 7)$

(e) $(2y + 3)(y + 1)$ **(f)** $(5t + 2)(2t - 7)$ **(g)** $(3n + 2)(3n - 2)$ **(h)** $(a - b)(a - b)$

14. Simplify the following expressions by collecting together like terms:

(a) $2x + 3y + 4x - y$ **(b)** $2x^2 - 5x + 9x^2 + 2x - 3$

(c) $5xy + 2x + 9yx$ **(d)** $7xyz + 3yx - 2zyx + yzx - xy$

(e) $2(5a + b) - 4b$ **(f)** $5(x - 4y) + 6(2x + 7y)$

(g) $5 - 3(p - 2)$ **(h)** $x(x - y + 7) + xy + 3x$

15. Use the formula for the difference of two squares to factorise

(a) $x^2 - 4$ **(b)** $Q^2 - 49$ **(c)** $x^2 - y^2$ **(d)** $9x^2 - 100y^2$

16. Simplify the following algebraic expressions:

(a) $3x - 4x^2 - 2 + 5x + 8x^2$ **(b)** $x(3x + 2) - 3x(x + 5)$

17. A law firm seeks to recruit top-quality experienced lawyers. The total package offered is the sum of three separate components: a basic salary which is 1.2 times the candidate's current salary together with an additional $3000 for each year worked as a qualified lawyer and an extra $1000 for every year that they are over the age of 21.

Work out a formula that could be used to calculate the total salary, S, offered to someone who is A years of age, has E years of relevant experience and who currently earns $N. Hence work out the salary offered to someone who is 30 years old with five years' experience and who currently earns $150 000.

18. Write down a formula for each situation:

(a) A plumber has a fixed call-out charge of $80 and has an hourly rate of $60. Work out the total charge, C, for a job that takes L hours in which the cost of materials and parts is $K.

(b) An airport currency exchange booth charges a fixed fee of $10 on all transactions and offers an exchange rate of 1 dollar to 0.8 euros. Work out the total charge, C, (in $) for buying x euros.

(c) A firm provides 5 hours of in-house training for each of its semi-skilled workers and 10 hours of training for each of its skilled workers. Work out the total number of hours, H, if the firm employs a semi-skilled and b skilled workers.

(d) A car hire company charges $C a day together with an additional $c per mile. Work out the total charge, X, for hiring a car for d days and travelling m miles during that time.

Exercise 1.1*

1. Without using a calculator, evaluate

(a) $(12 - 8) - (6 - 5)$ **(b)** $12 - (8 - 6) - 5$ **(c)** $12 - 8 - 6 - 5$

2. Put a pair of brackets in the left-hand side of each of the following to give correct statements:

(a) $2 - 7 - 9 + 3 = -17$ **(b)** $8 - 2 + 3 - 4 = -1$ **(c)** $7 - 2 - 6 + 10 = 1$

3. Without using a calculator, work out the value of each of the following expressions in the case when $a = 3$, $b = -4$ and $c = -2$:

(a) $a(b - c)$ **(b)** $3c(a + b)$ **(c)** $a^2 + 2b + 3c$ **(d)** $2abc^2$

(e) $\dfrac{c + b}{2a}$ **(f)** $\sqrt{2(b^2 - c)}$ **(g)** $\dfrac{b}{2c} - \dfrac{a}{3b}$ **(h)** $5a - b^3 - 4c^2$

4. Without using a calculator, evaluate each of the following expressions in the case when $x = -1$, $y = -2$ and $z = 3$:

(a) $x^3 + y^2 + z$ **(b)** $\sqrt{\left(\dfrac{x^2 + y^2 + z}{x^2 + 2xy - z}\right)}$ **(c)** $\dfrac{xyz(x + z)(z - y)}{(x + y)(x - z)}$

5. Multiply out the brackets and simplify

$(x - y)(x + y) - (x + 2)(x - y + 3)$

6. Simplify

(a) $x - y - (y - x)$ (b) $(x - ((y - x) - y))$ (c) $x + y - (x - y) - (x - (y - x))$

7. Multiply out the brackets:

(a) $(x + 4)(x - 6)$ (b) $(2x - 5)(3x - 7)$ (c) $2x(3x + y - 2)$

(d) $(3 + g)(4 - 2g + h)$ (e) $(2x + y)(1 - x - y)$ (f) $(a + b + c)(a - b - c)$

8. Factorise

(a) $9x - 12y$ (b) $x^2 - 6x$ (c) $10xy + 15x^2$

(d) $3xy^2 - 6x^2y + 12xy$ (e) $x^3 - 2x^2$ (f) $60x^4y^6 - 15x^2y^4 + 20xy^3$

9. Use the formula for the difference of two squares to factorise

(a) $p^2 - 25$ (b) $9c^2 - 64$ (c) $32v^2 - 50d^2$ (d) $16x^4 - y^4$

10. Evaluate the following without using a calculator:

(a) $50\,563^2 - 49\,437^2$ (b) $90^2 - 89.99^2$

(c) $759^2 - 541^2$ (d) $123\,456\,789^2 - 123\,456\,788^2$

11. A specialist paint manufacturer receives \$12 for each pot sold. The initial set-up cost for the production run is \$800 and the cost of making each tin of paint is \$3.

(a) Write down a formula for the total profit, π, if the firm manufactures x pots of paint and sells y pots.

(b) Use your formula to calculate the profit when $x = 1000$ and $y = 800$.

(c) State any restrictions on the variables in the mathematical formula in part (a).

(d) Simplify the formula in the case when the firm sells all that it manufactures.

12. Factorise

(a) $2KL^2 + 4KL$ (b) $L^2 - 0.04K^2$ (c) $K^2 + 2LK + L^2$

SECTION 1.2
Further algebra

Objectives

At the end of this section you should be able to:

- Simplify fractions by cancelling common factors.
- Add, subtract, multiply and divide fractions.
- Solve equations by doing the same thing to both sides.
- Recognise the symbols $<$, $>$, $\leq$ and $\geq$.
- Solve linear inequalities.

This section is broken down into three manageable subsections:

- fractions;
- equations;
- inequalities.

The advice offered in Section 1.1 applies equally well here. Please try to study these topics on separate occasions and be prepared to work through the practice problems as they arise in the text.

1.2.1 Fractions

For a numerical fraction such as

$$\frac{7}{8}$$

the number 7, on the top, is called the **numerator** and the number 8, on the bottom, is called the **denominator**. In this text we are also interested in the case when the numerator and denominator involve letters as well as numbers. These are referred to as **algebraic fractions**. For example,

$$\frac{1}{x^2 - 2} \quad \text{and} \quad \frac{2x^2 - 1}{y + z}$$

are both algebraic fractions. The letters x, y and z are used to represent numbers, so the rules for the manipulation of algebraic fractions are the same as those for ordinary numerical fractions. It is therefore essential that you are happy manipulating numerical fractions without a calculator so that you can extend this skill to fractions with letters.

Two fractions are said to be **equivalent** if they represent the same numerical value. We know that 3/4 is equivalent to 6/8 since they are both equal to the decimal number 0.75. It is also intuitively obvious. Imagine breaking a bar of chocolate into four equal pieces and eating three of them. You eat the same amount of chocolate as someone who breaks the bar into eight equal pieces and eats six of them. Each piece is only half the size so you need to compensate by eating twice as many. Formally, we say that when the numerator and denominator are both multiplied by the same number, the value of the fraction remains unchanged. In this example we have

$$\frac{3}{4} = \frac{3 \times 2}{4 \times 2} = \frac{6}{8}$$

This process can be reversed so equivalent fractions are produced when the numerator and denominator are both divided by the same number. For example,

$$\frac{16}{24} = \frac{16/8}{24/8} = \frac{2}{3}$$

so the fractions 16/24 and 2/3 are equivalent. A fraction is said to be in its simplest form or reduced to its lowest terms when there are no factors common to both the numerator and denominator. To express any given fraction in its simplest form, you need to find the highest common factor of the numerator and denominator and then divide the top and bottom of the fraction by this.

Example

Reduce each of the following fractions to its lowest terms:

(a) $\dfrac{14}{21}$ (b) $\dfrac{48}{60}$ (c) $\dfrac{2x}{3xy}$ (d) $\dfrac{3a}{6a + 3b}$ (e) $\dfrac{x - 2}{(x - 2)(x + 1)}$

Solution

(a) The largest number which divides into both 14 and 21 is 7, so we choose to divide top and bottom by 7:

$$\frac{14}{21} = \frac{14/7}{21/7} = \frac{2}{3}$$

An alternative way of writing this (which will be helpful when we tackle algebraic fractions) is:

$$\frac{14}{21} = \frac{2 \times \not7}{3 \times \not7} = \frac{2}{3}$$

(b) The highest common factor of 48 and 60 is 12, so we write:

$$\frac{48}{60} = \frac{4 \times \not{12}}{5 \times \not{12}} = \frac{4}{5}$$

(c) The factor x is common to both $2x$ and $3xy$, so we need to divide top and bottom by x; that is, we cancel the xs:

$$\frac{2x}{3xy} = \frac{2 \times \not{x}}{3 \times \not{x} \times y} = \frac{2}{3y}$$

(d) Factorising the denominator gives

$$6a + 3b = 3(2a + b)$$

which shows that there is a common factor of 3 in the top and bottom which can be cancelled:

$$\frac{3a}{6a + 3b} = \frac{\cancel{3}a}{\cancel{3}(2a + b)} = \frac{a}{2a + b}$$

(e) We see immediately that there is a common factor of $(x - 2)$ in the top and bottom, so this can be cancelled:

$$\frac{\cancel{x - 2}}{(\cancel{x - 2})(x + 1)} = \frac{1}{x + 1}$$

Before we leave this topic, a word of warning is in order. Notice that you can only cancel by dividing by a **factor** of the numerator or denominator. In part (d) of the above example you must not get carried away and attempt to cancel the as, and write something daft like:

$$\frac{a}{2a + b} = \frac{1}{2 + b} \qquad \text{This is NOT true}$$

To see that this is totally wrong, let us try substituting numbers, $a = 3$, $b = 4$, say, into both sides. The left-hand side gives $\dfrac{a}{2a + b} = \dfrac{3}{2 \times 3 + 4} = \dfrac{3}{10}$ whereas the right-hand side gives $\dfrac{1}{2 + b} = \dfrac{1}{2 + 4} = \dfrac{1}{6}$, which is not the same value.

Practice Problem

1. Reduce each of the following fractions to its lowest terms:

(a) $\dfrac{9}{15}$ (b) $\dfrac{24}{30}$ (c) $\dfrac{x}{2xy}$ (d) $\dfrac{3x}{6x + 9x^2}$ (e) $\dfrac{x(x + 1)}{x(x - 4)(x + 1)}$

The rules for multiplication and division are as follows:

> **to multiply fractions you multiply their corresponding numerators and denominators**

In symbols,

$$\frac{a}{b} \times \frac{c}{d} = \frac{a \times c}{b \times d} = \frac{ac}{bd}$$

> **to divide by a fraction you turn it upside down and multiply**

In symbols,

$$\frac{a}{b} \div \frac{c}{d} = \frac{a}{b} \times \frac{d}{c} \qquad \left(\text{turn the divisor upside down} \right)$$

$$= \frac{ad}{bc} \qquad \left(\text{rule of multiplying fractions} \right)$$

Example

Calculate

(a) $\dfrac{2}{3} \times \dfrac{5}{4}$ (b) $2 \times \dfrac{6}{13}$ (c) $\dfrac{6}{7} \div \dfrac{4}{21}$ (d) $\dfrac{1}{2} \div 3$

Solution

(a) The multiplication rule gives

$$\frac{2}{3} \times \frac{5}{4} = \frac{2 \times 5}{3 \times 4} = \frac{10}{12}$$

We could leave the answer like this, although it can be simplified by dividing top and bottom by 2 to get $\tfrac{5}{6}$. It is also valid to 'cancel' by 2 at the very beginning: that is,

$$\frac{{}^{1}\cancel{2}}{3} \times \frac{5}{\cancel{4}_{2}} = \frac{1 \times 5}{3 \times 2} = \frac{5}{6}$$

(b) The whole number 2 is equivalent to the fraction $\tfrac{2}{1}$, so

$$2 \times \frac{6}{13} = \frac{2}{1} \times \frac{6}{13} = \frac{2 \times 6}{1 \times 13} = \frac{12}{13}$$

(c) To calculate

$$\frac{6}{7} \div \frac{4}{21}$$

the divisor is turned upside down to get $\tfrac{21}{4}$ and then multiplied to get

$$\frac{6}{7} \div \frac{4}{21} = \frac{{}^{3}\cancel{6}}{\cancel{7}_{1}} \times \frac{\cancel{21}^{3}}{\cancel{4}_{2}} = \frac{3 \times 3}{1 \times 2} = \frac{9}{2}$$

(d) We write 3 as $\tfrac{3}{1}$, so

$$\frac{1}{2} \div 3 = \frac{1}{2} \div \frac{3}{1} = \frac{1}{2} \times \frac{1}{3} = \frac{1}{6}$$

Practice Problem

2. (1) Without using a calculator, evaluate

    (a) $\dfrac{1}{2} \times \dfrac{3}{4}$ (b) $7 \times \dfrac{1}{4}$ (c) $\dfrac{2}{3} \div \dfrac{8}{9}$ (d) $\dfrac{8}{9} \div 16$

(2) Confirm your answer to part (1) using a calculator.

The rules for addition and subtraction are as follows:

> to add (or subtract) two fractions you write them as equivalent fractions
> with a common denominator and add (or subtract) their numerators

Example

Calculate

(a) $\dfrac{1}{5} + \dfrac{2}{5}$ (b) $\dfrac{1}{4} + \dfrac{2}{3}$ (c) $\dfrac{7}{12} - \dfrac{5}{8}$

Solution

(a) The fractions $\frac{1}{5}$ and $\frac{2}{5}$ already have the same denominator, so to add them we just add their numerators to get

$$\frac{1}{5} + \frac{2}{5} = \frac{1+2}{5} = \frac{3}{5}$$

(b) The fractions $\frac{1}{4}$ and $\frac{2}{3}$ have denominators 4 and 3. One number that is divisible by both 3 and 4 is 12, so we choose this as the common denominator. Now 4 goes into 12 exactly 3 times, so

$$\frac{1}{4} = \frac{1 \times 3}{4 \times 3} = \frac{3}{12} \qquad \text{multiply top and bottom by 3}$$

and 3 goes into 12 exactly 4 times, so

$$\frac{2}{3} = \frac{2 \times 4}{3 \times 4} = \frac{8}{12} \qquad \text{multiply top and bottom by 4}$$

Hence

$$\frac{1}{4} + \frac{2}{3} = \frac{3}{12} + \frac{8}{12} = \frac{3+8}{12} = \frac{11}{12}$$

(c) The fractions $\frac{7}{12}$ and $\frac{5}{8}$ have denominators 12 and 8. One number that is divisible by both 12 and 8 is 24, so we choose this as the common denominator. Now 12 goes into 24 exactly twice, so

$$\frac{7}{12} = \frac{7 \times 2}{24} = \frac{14}{24}$$

and 8 goes into 24 exactly 3 times, so

$$\frac{5}{8} = \frac{5 \times 3}{24} = \frac{15}{24}$$

Hence

$$\frac{7}{12} - \frac{5}{8} = \frac{14}{24} - \frac{15}{24} = \frac{-1}{24}$$

It is not essential that the lowest common denominator is used. Any number will do provided that it is divisible by the two original denominators. If you are stuck, then you could always multiply the original two denominators together. In part (c) the denominators multiply to give 96, so this can be used instead. Now

$$\frac{7}{12} = \frac{7 \times 8}{96} = \frac{56}{96}$$

and

$$\frac{5}{8} = \frac{5 \times 12}{96} = \frac{60}{96}$$

so

$$\frac{7}{12} - \frac{5}{8} = \frac{56}{96} - \frac{60}{96} = \frac{56 - 60}{96} = \frac{-4}{96} = -\frac{1}{24}$$

as before.

Notice how the final answer to part (c) of this example has been written. We have simply used the fact that when a negative number is divided by a positive number, the answer is negative. It is standard practice to write negative fractions like this, so we would write $-\frac{3}{4}$ in preference to either $\frac{3}{-4}$ or $\frac{-3}{4}$ and, of course, $\frac{-3}{-4}$ is written as $\frac{3}{4}$.

Before we leave this topic a word of warning is in order. Notice that you can add or subtract fractions only after you have gone to the trouble of finding a common denominator. In particular, the following short-cut does not give the correct answer:

$$\frac{a}{b} + \frac{c}{d} = \frac{a + c}{b + d} \qquad \text{This is NOT true}$$

As usual you can check for yourself that it is complete rubbish by using actual numbers of your own choosing.

Practice Problem

3. **(1)** Without using a calculator, evaluate

(a) $\dfrac{3}{7} - \dfrac{1}{7}$ (b) $\dfrac{1}{3} + \dfrac{2}{5}$ (c) $\dfrac{7}{18} - \dfrac{1}{4}$

(2) Confirm your answer to part (1) using a calculator.

Provided that you can manipulate ordinary fractions, there is no reason why you should not be able to manipulate algebraic fractions just as easily since the rules are the same.

Example

Find expressions for each of the following:

(a) $\dfrac{x}{x - 1} \times \dfrac{2}{x(x + 4)}$ (b) $\dfrac{2}{x - 1} \div \dfrac{x}{x - 1}$ (c) $\dfrac{x + 1}{x^2 + 2} + \dfrac{x - 6}{x^2 + 2}$ (d) $\dfrac{x}{x + 2} - \dfrac{1}{x + 1}$

Solution

(a) To multiply two fractions we multiply their corresponding numerators and denominators, so

$$\frac{x}{x-1} \times \frac{2}{x(x+4)} = \frac{2x}{(x-1)x(x+4)} = \frac{2}{(x-1)(x+4)}$$

the *x*s cancel top and bottom

(b) To divide by

$$\frac{x}{x-1}$$

we turn it upside down and multiply, so

$$\frac{2}{x-1} \div \frac{x}{x-1} = \frac{2}{x-1} \times \frac{x-1}{x} = \frac{2}{x}$$

the $(x-1)$s cancel top and bottom

(c) The fractions

$$\frac{x+1}{x^2+2} \quad \text{and} \quad \frac{x-6}{x^2+2}$$

already have the same denominator, so to add them we just add their numerators to get

$$\frac{x+1}{x^2+2} + \frac{x-6}{x^2+2} = \frac{x+1+x-6}{x^2+2} = \frac{2x-5}{x^2+2}$$

(d) The fractions

$$\frac{x}{x+2} \quad \text{and} \quad \frac{1}{x+1}$$

have denominators $x+2$ and $x+1$. An obvious common denominator is given by their product, $(x+2)(x+1)$. Now $x+2$ goes into $(x+2)(x+1)$ exactly $x+1$ times, so

$$\frac{x}{x+2} = \frac{x(x+1)}{(x+2)(x+1)}$$

multiply top and bottom by $(x+1)$

Also, $x+1$ goes into $(x+2)(x+1)$ exactly $x+2$ times, so

$$\frac{1}{x+1} = \frac{(x+2)}{(x+2)(x+1)}$$

multiply top and bottom by $(x+2)$

Hence

$$\frac{x}{x+2} - \frac{1}{x+1} = \frac{x(x+1)}{(x+2)(x+1)} - \frac{(x+2)}{(x+2)(x+1)} = \frac{x(x+1)-(x+2)}{(x+2)(x+1)}$$

It is worth multiplying out the brackets on the top to simplify: that is,

$$\frac{x^2+x-x-2}{(x+2)(x+1)} = \frac{x^2-2}{(x+2)(x+1)}$$

Practice Problem

4. Find expressions for the following algebraic fractions, simplifying your answers as far
   as possible.

(a) $\dfrac{5}{x-1} \times \dfrac{x-1}{x+2}$ (b) $\dfrac{x^2}{x+10} \div \dfrac{x}{x+1}$ (c) $\dfrac{4}{x+1} + \dfrac{1}{x+1}$ (d) $\dfrac{2}{x+1} - \dfrac{1}{x+2}$

1.2.2 Equations

In Section 1.1.2 and again in Section 1.2.1, we have seen how to rewrite an algebraic expression in a simpler but equivalent form. For example, when we write things like

$$x^2 + 3x + 3x^2 - 10x = 4x^2 - 7x \qquad \text{(collecting like terms)}$$

or

$$\frac{x}{x+2} - \frac{1}{x+1} = \frac{x^2-2}{(x+2)(x+1)} \qquad \text{(part (d) of the previous worked example)}$$

we have at the back of our minds the knowledge that the left- and right-hand sides are identical so that each statement is true for all possible values of x. For this reason the above relations are called **identities**. Compare these with statements such as:

$$7x - 1 = 13$$

or

$$x^2 - 5x = 1$$

These relations are called **equations** and are only true for particular values of x which need to be found. It turns out that the first equation above has just one solution, whereas the second has two solutions. The latter is called a quadratic equation and will be considered in the next chapter.

One naïve approach to the solution of equations such as $7x - 1 = 13$ might be to use trial and error: that is, we could just keep guessing values of x until we find the one that works. Can you see what x is in this case? However, a more reliable and systematic approach is to actually solve this equation using the rules of mathematics. In fact, the only rule that we need is:

> you can apply whatever mathematical operation you like to an equation,
> *provided that you do the same thing to both sides*

There is only one exception to this rule: you must never divide both sides by zero. This should be obvious because a number such as 11/0 does not exist. (If you do not believe this, try dividing 11 by 0 on your calculator.)

The first obstacle that prevents us from writing down the value of x immediately from the equation $7x - 1 = 13$ is the presence of the -1 on the left-hand side. This can be removed by adding 1. For this to be legal we must also add 1 to the right-hand side to get

$$7x - 1 + 1 = 13 + 1$$
$$7x = 14$$

The second obstacle is the number 7 which is multiplying the x. This can be removed by dividing the left-hand side by 7. Of course, we must also do the same thing to the right-hand side to get

$$\frac{7x}{7} = \frac{14}{7}$$

$$x = 2$$

This is no doubt the solution that you spotted earlier by simple trial and error, and you may be wondering why you need to bother with the formal method. The reason is simple: guesswork will not help to solve more complicated equations in which the solution is non-obvious or even simple equations in which the solution is a fraction. In these circumstances we need to follow the approach of 'balancing the equation'.

Example

Solve

(a) $6x + 1 = 10x - 9$ (b) $3(x - 1) + 2(2x + 1) = 4$

(c) $\dfrac{20}{3x - 1} = 7$ (d) $\dfrac{9}{x + 2} = \dfrac{7}{2x + 1}$ (e) $\sqrt{\dfrac{2x}{x - 6}} = 2$

Solution

(a) To solve

$$6x + 1 = 10x - 9$$

the strategy is to collect terms involving x on one side of the equation, and to collect all of the number terms on to the other side. It does not matter which way round this is done. In this particular case, there are more xs on the right-hand side than there are on the left-hand side. Consequently, to avoid negative numbers, you may prefer to stack the x terms on the right-hand side. The details are as follows:

$1 = 4x - 9$ (subtract $6x$ from both sides)

$10 = 4x$ (add 9 to both sides)

$\dfrac{10}{4} = x$ (divide both sides by 4)

Hence $x = {}^5/_2 = 2^1/_2$.

(b) The novel feature of the equation

$$3(x - 1) + 2(2x + 1) = 4$$

is the presence of brackets. To solve it, we first remove the brackets by multiplying out, and then collect like terms:

$3x - 3 + 4x + 2 = 4$ (multiply out the brackets)

$7x - 1 = 4$ (collect like terms)

Note that this equation is now of the form that we know how to solve:

$7x = 5$ (add 1 to both sides)

$x = \dfrac{5}{7}$ (divide both sides by 7)

(c) The novel feature of the equation

$$\frac{20}{3x - 1} = 7$$

is the fact that it involves an algebraic fraction. This can easily be removed by multiplying both sides by the bottom of the fraction:

$$\frac{20}{3x - 1} \times (3x - 1) = 7(3x - 1)$$

which cancels down to give

$$20 = 7(3x - 1)$$

The remaining steps are similar to those in part (b):

$$20 = 21x - 7 \quad \text{(multiply out the brackets)}$$
$$27 = 21x \quad \text{(add 7 to both sides)}$$
$$\frac{27}{21} = x \quad \text{(divide both sides by 21)}$$

Hence $x = {}^9\!/_7 = 1{}^2\!/_7$.

(d) The next equation,

$$\frac{9}{x + 2} = \frac{7}{2x + 1}$$

looks particularly daunting since there are fractions on both sides. However, these are easily removed by multiplying both sides by the denominators, in turn:

$$9 = \frac{7(x + 2)}{2x + 1} \quad \text{(multiply both sides by } x + 2)$$
$$9(2x + 1) = 7(x + 2) \quad \text{(multiply both sides by } 2x + 1)$$

With practice you can do these two steps simultaneously and write this as the first line of working. The procedure of going straight from

$$\frac{9}{x + 2} = \frac{7}{2x + 1}$$

to

$$9(2x + 1) = 7(x + 2)$$

is called 'cross-multiplication'. In general, if

$$\frac{a}{b} = \frac{c}{d}$$

then

$$ad = bc$$

The remaining steps are similar to those used in the earlier parts of this example:

$$18x + 9 = 7x + 14 \quad \text{(multiply out the brackets)}$$
$$11x + 9 = 14 \quad \text{(subtract } 7x \text{ from both sides)}$$

$$11x = 5 \qquad \text{(subtract 9 from both sides)}$$

$$x = \frac{5}{11} \qquad \text{(divide both sides by 11)}$$

(e) The left-hand side of the final equation

$$\sqrt{\frac{2x}{x - 6}} = 2$$

is surrounded by a square root, which can easily be removed by squaring both sides to get

$$\frac{2x}{x - 6} = 4$$

The remaining steps are 'standard':

$$2x = 4(x - 6) \qquad \text{(multiply both sides by } x - 6\text{)}$$
$$2x = 4x - 24 \qquad \text{(multiply out the brackets)}$$
$$-2x = -24 \qquad \text{(subtract } 4x \text{ from both sides)}$$
$$x = 12 \qquad \text{(divide both sides by } -2\text{)}$$

Looking back over each part of the previous example, notice that there is a common strategy. In each case, the aim is to convert the given equation into one of the form

$$ax + b = c$$

which is the sort of equation that we can easily solve. If the original equation contains brackets, then remove them by multiplying out. If the equation involves fractions, then remove them by cross-multiplying.

Advice

If you have the time, it is always worth checking your answer by substituting your solution back into the original equation. For the last part of the above example, putting $x = 12$ into

$$\sqrt{\frac{2x}{x - 6}} \quad \text{gives} \quad \sqrt{\frac{2 \times 12}{12 - 6}} = \sqrt{\frac{24}{6}} = \sqrt{4} = 2 \quad ✓$$

Practice Problem

5. Solve each of the following equations. Leave your answer as a fraction, if necessary.

(a) $4x + 1 = 25$ **(b)** $4x + 5 = 5x - 7$ **(c)** $3(3 - 2x) + 2(x - 1) = 10$

(d) $\dfrac{4}{x - 1} = 5$ **(e)** $\dfrac{3}{x} = \dfrac{5}{x - 1}$

1.2.3 Inequalities

In Section 1.1.1 we made use of a **number line**:

Although only whole numbers are marked on this diagram, it is implicitly assumed that it can also be used to indicate fractions and decimal numbers. Each point on the line corresponds to a particular number. Conversely, every number can be represented by a particular point on the line. For example, $-2\frac{1}{2}$ lies exactly halfway between -3 and -2. Similarly, $4\frac{7}{8}$ lies $\frac{7}{8}$ of the way between 4 and 5. In theory, we can even find a point on the line corresponding to a number such as $\sqrt{2}$, although it may be difficult to sketch such a point accurately in practice. My calculator gives the value of $\sqrt{2}$ to be $1.414\ 213\ 56$ to eight decimal places. This number therefore lies just less than halfway between 1 and 2.

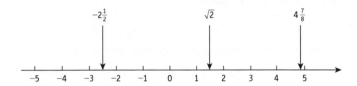

A number line can be used to decide whether or not one number is greater or less than another number. We say that a number a is greater than a number b if a lies to the right of b on the line, and we write this as

$a > b$

Likewise, we say that a is less than b if a lies to the left of b, and we write this as

$a < b$

From the diagram we see that

$-2 > -4$

because -2 lies to the right of -4. This is equivalent to the statement

$-4 < -2$

Similarly,

$0 > -1$ (or equivalently $-1 < 0$)

$2 > -2\frac{1}{2}$ (or equivalently $-2\frac{1}{2} < 2$)

$4\frac{7}{8} > \sqrt{2}$ (or equivalently $\sqrt{2} < 4\frac{7}{8}$)

There are occasions when we would like the letters a and b to stand for mathematical expressions rather than actual numbers. In this situation we sometimes use the symbols $\geq$ and $\leq$ to mean 'greater than or equal to' and 'less than or equal to', respectively.

We have already seen that we can manipulate equations in any way we like, provided that we do the same thing to both sides. An obvious question to ask is whether this rule extends to inequalities.

Consider the true statement

$$1 < 3 \qquad (*)$$

- Adding 4 to both sides gives $5 < 7$, which is true.
- Adding -5 to both sides gives $-4 < -2$, which is true.
- Multiplying both sides by 2 gives $2 < 6$, which is true.

However,

- Multiplying both sides by -6 gives $-6 < -18$, which is false. In fact, quite the reverse is true; -6 is actually greater than -18. This indicates that the rule needs modifying before we can extend it to inequalities and that we must be careful when manipulating inequalities.

Practice Problem

6. Starting with the true statement

$$6 > 3$$

   decide which of the following are valid operations when performed on both sides:

   (a) add 6   (b) multiply by 2   (c) subtract 3

   (d) add -3 (e) divide by 3   (f) multiply by -4

   (g) multiply by -1 (h) divide by -3 (i) add -10

These examples show that the usual rule does apply to inequalities with the important proviso that

> **if both sides are multiplied or divided by a negative number, then the sense of the inequality is reversed**

By this we mean that '$>$' changes to '$<$', '$\le$' changes to '$\ge$' and so on.
   To see how this works out in practice, consider the inequality

$$2x + 3 < 4x + 7$$

If we try to solve this like we did for equations, the first step would be to subtract $4x$ from both sides to get

$$-2x + 3 < 7$$

and then take 3 away from both sides to get

$$-2x < 4$$

Finally, we divide both sides by -2 to get

$$x > -2$$

Notice that the sense has been reversed at this stage because we have divided by a negative number.

Advice

You should check your answer using a couple of test values. Substituting $x = 1$ (which lies to the right of -2 and so should work) into both sides of the original inequality $2x + 3 < 4x + 7$ gives $5 < 11$, which is true. On the other hand, substituting $x = -3$ (which lies to the left of -2 and so should fail) gives $-3 < -5$, which is false. Of course, just checking a couple of numbers like this does not prove that the final inequality is correct, but it should protect you against gross blunders.

Practice Problem

7. Simplify the inequalities

(a) $2x < 3x + 7$ (b) $21x - 19 \geq 4x + 15$

Inequalities arise in business when there is a budgetary restriction on resource allocation. The following example shows how to set up and solve the relevant inequality.

Example

A firm's Human Resources department has a budget of $25 000 to spend on training and laptops. Training courses cost $700 and new laptops are $1200.

(a) If the department trains E employees and buys L laptops, write down an inequality for E and L.

(b) If 12 employees attend courses, how many laptops could be bought?

Solution

(a) The cost of training E employees is $700E$ and the cost of buying L laptops is $1200L$. The total amount spent must not exceed $25 000, so $700E + 1200L \leq 25\,000$.

(b) Substituting $E = 12$ into the inequality gives $8400 + 1200L \leq 25\,000$.

$$1200L \leq 16\,600 \qquad \text{(subtract 8400 from both sides)}$$

$$L \leq 13\frac{5}{6} \qquad \text{(divide both sides by 1200)}$$

so a maximum of 13 laptops could be bought.

Key Terms

Algebraic fraction   Ratio of two expressions; $p(x)/q(x)$ where $p(x)$ and $q(x)$ are algebraic expressions such as $ax^2 + bx + c$ or $dx + e$.

Denominator   The number (or expression) on the bottom of a fraction.

Equation   Equality of two algebraic expressions which is true only for certain values of the variable.

Equivalent fractions   Fractions which may appear different but which have the same numerical value.

Factor   Part of an expression which, when multiplied by all the other factors, gives the complete expression.

Identity   Equality of two algebraic expressions which is true for all values of the variable.

Number line   An infinite line on which the points represent real numbers by their (signed) distance from the origin.

Numerator   The number (or expression) on the top of a fraction.

Exercise 1.2

1. Reduce each of the following numerical fractions to their lowest terms:

    (a) $\dfrac{13}{26}$
    (b) $\dfrac{9}{12}$
    (c) $\dfrac{18}{30}$
    (d) $\dfrac{24}{72}$
    (e) $\dfrac{36}{27}$

2. In 2011 in the United States, 35 out of every 100 adults owned a smartphone. By 2013 this figure increased to 56 out of every 100.

    (a) Express both of these figures as fractions reduced to their lowest terms.

    (b) By what factor did smartphone ownership increase during this period? Give your answer as a mixed fraction in its lowest terms.

3. Reduce each of the following algebraic fractions to their lowest terms:

    (a) $\dfrac{6x}{9}$
    (b) $\dfrac{x}{2x^2}$
    (c) $\dfrac{b}{abc}$
    (d) $\dfrac{4x}{6x^2y}$
    (e) $\dfrac{15a^2b}{20ab^2}$

4. By factorising the numerators and/or denominators of each of the following fractions, reduce each to its lowest terms:

    (a) $\dfrac{2p}{4q + 6r}$
    (b) $\dfrac{x}{x^2 - 4x}$
    (c) $\dfrac{3ab}{6a^2 + 3a}$
    (d) $\dfrac{14d}{21d - 7de}$
    (e) $\dfrac{x + 2}{x^2 - 4}$

5. Which one of the following algebraic fractions can be simplified? Explain why the other two fractions cannot be simplified.

    $$\dfrac{x - 1}{2x - 2}, \quad \dfrac{x - 2}{x + 2}, \quad \dfrac{5t}{10t - s}$$

6. **(1)** Without using a calculator, work out the following, giving your answer in its lowest terms:

(a) $\dfrac{1}{7} + \dfrac{2}{7}$ (b) $\dfrac{2}{9} - \dfrac{5}{9}$ (c) $\dfrac{1}{2} + \dfrac{1}{3}$ (d) $\dfrac{3}{4} - \dfrac{2}{5}$ (e) $\dfrac{1}{6} + \dfrac{2}{9}$ (f) $\dfrac{1}{6} + \dfrac{2}{3}$

(g) $\dfrac{5}{6} \times \dfrac{3}{4}$ (h) $\dfrac{4}{15} \div \dfrac{2}{3}$ (i) $\dfrac{7}{8} \times \dfrac{2}{3}$ (j) $\dfrac{2}{75} \div \dfrac{4}{5}$ (k) $\dfrac{2}{9} \div 3$ (l) $3 \div \dfrac{2}{7}$

(2) Use your calculator to check your answers to part (1).

7. It takes $1^{1}/_{4}$ hours to complete an annual service of a car. If a garage has $47^{1}/_{2}$ hours available, how many cars can it service?

8. Work out each of the following, simplifying your answer as far as possible:

(a) $\dfrac{2}{3x} + \dfrac{1}{3x}$ (b) $\dfrac{2}{x} \times \dfrac{x}{5}$ (c) $\dfrac{3}{x} - \dfrac{2}{x^2}$ (d) $\dfrac{7}{x} + \dfrac{2}{y}$ (e) $\dfrac{a}{2} \div \dfrac{a}{6}$

(f) $\dfrac{5c}{12} + \dfrac{5d}{18}$ (g) $\dfrac{x+2}{y-5} \times \dfrac{y-5}{x+3}$ (h) $\dfrac{4gh}{7} \div \dfrac{2g}{9h}$ (i) $\dfrac{t}{4} \div 5$ (j) $\dfrac{P}{Q} \times \dfrac{Q}{P}$

9. Solve each of the following equations. If necessary give your answer as a mixed fraction reduced to its lowest terms.

(a) $x + 2 = 7$ (b) $3x = 18$ (c) $\dfrac{x}{9} = 2$ (d) $x - 4 = -2$

(e) $2x - 3 = 17$ (f) $3x + 4 = 1$ (g) $\dfrac{x}{6} - 7 = 3$ (h) $3(x - 1) = 2$

(i) $4 - x = 9$ (j) $6x + 2 = 5x - 1$ (k) $5(3x + 8) = 10$ (l) $2(x - 3) = 5(x + 1)$

(m) $\dfrac{4x - 7}{3} = 2$ (n) $\dfrac{4}{x + 1} = 1$ (o) $5 - \dfrac{1}{x} = 1$

10. Which of the following inequalities are true?

(a) $-2 < 1$ (b) $-6 > -4$ (c) $3 < 3$

(d) $3 \leq 3$ (e) $-21 \geq -22$ (f) $4 < 25$

11. Simplify the following inequalities:

(a) $2x > x + 1$ (b) $7x + 3 \leq 9 + 5x$ (c) $x - 5 > 4x + 4$ (d) $x - 1 < 2x - 3$

12. Simplify the following algebraic expression:

$$\dfrac{4}{x^2y} \div \dfrac{2x}{y}$$

13. (a) Solve the equation

$$6(2 + x) = 5(1 - 4x)$$

(b) Solve the inequality

$$3x + 6 \geq 5x - 14$$

Exercise 1.2*

1. Simplify each of the following algebraic fractions:

   (a) $\dfrac{2x - 6}{4}$ (b) $\dfrac{9x}{6x^2 - 3x}$ (c) $\dfrac{4x + 16}{x + 4}$ (d) $\dfrac{x - 1}{1 - x}$

   (e) $\dfrac{x + 6}{x^2 - 36}$ (f) $\dfrac{(x + 3)(2x - 5)}{(2x - 5)(x + 4)}$ (g) $\dfrac{3x}{6x^3 - 15x^2 + 9x}$ (h) $\dfrac{4x^2 - 25y^2}{6x - 15y}$

2. (1) Without using your calculator, evaluate

   (a) $\dfrac{4}{5} \times \dfrac{25}{28}$ (b) $\dfrac{2}{7} \times \dfrac{14}{25} \times \dfrac{5}{8}$ (c) $\dfrac{9}{16} \div \dfrac{3}{8}$ (d) $\dfrac{2}{5} \times \dfrac{1}{12} \div \dfrac{8}{25}$

   (e) $\dfrac{10}{13} - \dfrac{12}{13}$ (f) $\dfrac{5}{9} + \dfrac{2}{3}$ (g) $2\dfrac{3}{5} + 1\dfrac{3}{7}$ (h) $5\dfrac{9}{10} - \dfrac{1}{2} + 1\dfrac{2}{5}$

   (i) $3\dfrac{3}{4} \times 1\dfrac{3}{5}$ (j) $\dfrac{3}{5} \times \left(2\dfrac{1}{3} + \dfrac{1}{2}\right)$ (k) $\dfrac{5}{6} \times \left(2\dfrac{1}{3} - 1\dfrac{2}{5}\right)$ (l) $\left(3\dfrac{1}{3} \div 2\dfrac{1}{6}\right) \div \dfrac{5}{13}$

   (2) Confirm your answer to part (1) using a calculator.

3. Find simplified expressions for the following fractions:

   (a) $\dfrac{x^2 + 6x}{x - 2} \times \dfrac{x - 2}{x}$ (b) $\dfrac{1}{x} \div \dfrac{1}{x + 1}$ (c) $\dfrac{2}{xy} + \dfrac{3}{xy}$ (d) $\dfrac{x}{2} + \dfrac{x + 1}{3}$

   (e) $\dfrac{3}{x} + \dfrac{4}{x + 1}$ (f) $\dfrac{3}{x} + \dfrac{5}{x^2}$ (g) $x - \dfrac{2}{x + 1}$ (h) $\dfrac{5}{x(x + 1)} - \dfrac{2}{x} + \dfrac{3}{x + 1}$

4. Solve the following equations:

   (a) $5(2x + 1) = 3(x - 2)$ (b) $5(x + 2) + 4(2x - 3) = 11$

   (c) $5(1 - x) = 4(10 + x)$ (d) $3(3 - 2x) - 7(1 - x) = 10$

   (e) $9 - 5(2x - 1) = 6$ (f) $\dfrac{3}{2x + 1} = 2$

   (g) $\dfrac{2}{x - 1} = \dfrac{3}{5x + 4}$ (h) $\dfrac{x}{2} + 3 = 7$

   (i) $5 - \dfrac{x}{3} = 2$ (j) $\dfrac{5(x - 3)}{2} = \dfrac{2(x - 1)}{5}$

   (k) $\sqrt{(2x - 5)} = 3$ (l) $(x + 3)(x - 1) = (x + 4)(x - 3)$

   (m) $(x + 2)^2 + (2x - 1)^2 = 5x(x + 1)$ (n) $\dfrac{2x + 7}{3} = \dfrac{x - 4}{6} + \dfrac{1}{2}$

   (o) $\sqrt{\dfrac{45}{2x - 1}} = 3$ (p) $\dfrac{4}{x} - \dfrac{3}{4} = \dfrac{1}{4x}$

5. Two-thirds of Ariadne's money together with five-sevenths of Brian's money is equal to three-fifths of Catriona's money. If Ariadne has \$2.40 and Catriona has \$11.25, write down an equation that you could use to work out how much Brian has. Solve this equation.

6. An amount $P is placed in a savings account. The interest rate is $r\%$ compounded annually so that after n years the savings, S, will be

$$S = P\left(1 + \frac{r}{100}\right)^n$$

(a) Find S when $P = 2000$, $n = 5$ and $r = 10$.

(b) Find P when $S = 65\ 563.62$, $n = 3$ and $r = 3$.

(c) Find r when $S = 7320.50$, $P = 5000$ and $n = 4$.

7. Solve the following inequalities:

(a) $2x - 19 > 7x + 24$ (b) $2(x - 1) < 5(3x + 2)$ (c) $\dfrac{2x - 1}{5} \geq \dfrac{x - 3}{2}$

(d) $3 + \dfrac{x}{3} < 2(x + 4)$ (e) $x < 2x + 1 \leq 7$

8. The design costs of an advertisement in a glossy magazine are $9000 and the cost per cm^2 of print is $50.

(a) Write down an expression for the total cost of publishing an advert which covers x cm^2.

(b) The advertising budget is between $10\ 800 and $12\ 500. Write down and solve an inequality to work out the minimum and maximum area that could be used.

9. List all the whole numbers that satisfy both of the following inequalities simultaneously:

$$-7 \leq 2x < 6 \text{ and } 4x + 1 \leq x + 2$$

10. (a) Simplify

$$\frac{31x - 8}{(2x - 1)(x + 2)} - \frac{14}{x + 2}$$

(b) Solve the equation

$$\frac{x + 1}{8} = \frac{x + 3}{4} - \frac{1}{2}$$

(c) Simplify the inequality

$$(2x + 1)(x - 5) \leq 2(x + 2)(x - 4)$$

11. Simplify

$$\frac{x^2}{x + 1} \div \frac{2x}{x^2 - 1}$$

Graphs of linear equations

Objectives

At the end of this section you should be able to:

● Plot points on graph paper given their coordinates.

● Sketch a line by finding the coordinates of two points on the line.

● Solve simultaneous linear equations graphically.

● Sketch a line by using its slope and intercept.

Consider the two straight lines shown in Figure 1.1. The horizontal line is referred to as the **x axis** and the vertical line is referred to as the **y axis**. The point where these lines intersect is known as the **origin** and is denoted by the letter O. These lines enable us to identify uniquely any point, P, in terms of its **coordinates** (x, y). The first number, x, denotes the horizontal distance along the x axis and the second number, y, denotes the vertical distance along the y axis. The arrows on the axes indicate the positive direction in each case.

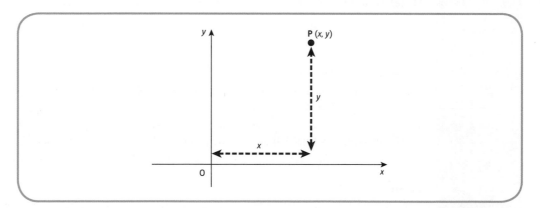

Figure 1.1

Figure 1.2 shows the five points A(2, 3), B(−1, 4), C(−3, −1), D(3, −2) and E(5, 0) plotted on coordinate axes. The point A with coordinates (2, 3) is obtained by starting at the origin, moving 2 units to the right and then moving 3 units vertically upwards. Similarly, the point B with coordinates (−1, 4) is located 1 unit to the left of O (because the x coordinate is negative) and 4 units up.

Note that the point C lies in the bottom left-hand quadrant since its x and y coordinates are both negative. It is also worth noticing that E actually lies on the x axis since its y coordinate is zero. Likewise, a point with coordinates of the form (0, y) for some number y would lie somewhere on the y axis. Of course, the point with coordinates (0, 0) is the origin, O.

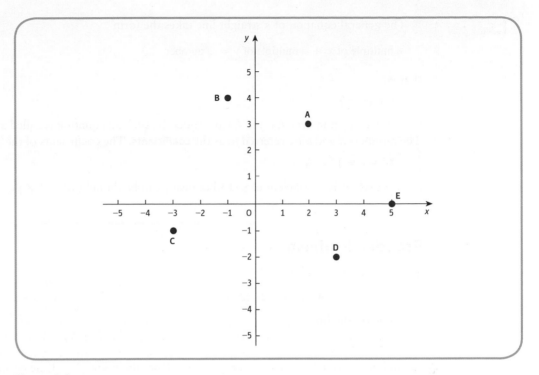

Figure 1.2

Practice Problem

1. Plot the following points on graph paper. What do you observe?

   $(2, 5), (1, 3), (0, 1), (-2, -3), (-3, -5)$

In economics we need to do rather more than just plot individual points on graph paper. We would like to be able to sketch curves represented by equations and to deduce information from such a picture. We restrict our attention in this section to those equations whose graphs are straight lines, deferring consideration of more general curve sketching until Chapter 2.

In Practice Problem 1 you will have noticed that the five points $(2, 5), (1, 3), (0, 1),$ $(-2, -3)$ and $(-3, -5)$ all lie on a straight line. In fact, the equation of this line is

$$-2x + y = 1$$

Any point lies on this line if its x and y coordinates satisfy this equation. For example, $(2, 5)$ lies on the line because when the values $x = 2, y = 5$ are substituted into the left-hand side of the equation, we obtain

$$-2(2) + 5 = -4 + 5 = 1$$

which is the right-hand side of the equation. The other points can be checked similarly (see Table 1.1).

Table 1.1

Point	Check	
$(1, 3)$	$-2(1) + 3 = -2 + 3 = 1$	✓
$(0, 1)$	$-2(0) + 1 = 0 + 1 = 1$	✓
$(-2, -3)$	$-2(-2) - 3 = 4 - 3 = 1$	✓
$(-3, -5)$	$-2(-3) - 5 = 6 - 5 = 1$	✓

The general equation of a straight line takes the form

> a multiple of x + a multiple of y = a number

that is,

$$dx + ey = f$$

for some given numbers d, e and f. Consequently, such an equation is called a **linear equation**. The numbers d and e are referred to as the **coefficients**. The coefficients of the linear equation,

$$-2x + y = 1$$

are -2 and 1 (the coefficient of y is 1 because y can be thought of as $1 \times y$).

Practice Problem

2. Check that the points

$$(-1, 2), (-4, 4), (5, -2), (2, 0)$$

all lie on the line

$$2x + 3y = 4$$

and hence sketch this line on graph paper. Does the point $(3, -1)$ lie on this line?

In general, to sketch a line from its mathematical equation, it is sufficient to calculate the coordinates of any two distinct points lying on it. These two points can be plotted on graph paper and a ruler used to draw the line passing through them. One way of finding the coordinates of a point on a line is simply to choose a numerical value for x and to substitute it into the equation. The equation can then be used to deduce the corresponding value of y. The whole process can be repeated to find the coordinates of the second point by choosing another value for x.

Example

Sketch the line

$$4x + 3y = 11$$

Solution

For the first point, let us choose $x = 5$. Substitution of this number into the equation gives

$$4(5) + 3y = 11$$
$$20 + 3y = 11$$

The problem now is to solve this equation for y:

$$3y = -9 \quad \text{(subtract 20 from both sides)}$$
$$y = -3 \quad \text{(divide both sides by 3)}$$

Consequently, the coordinates of one point on the line are $(5, -3)$.

For the second point, let us choose $x = -1$. Substitution of this number into the equation gives

$$4(-1) + 3y = 11$$
$$-4 + 3y = 11$$

This can be solved for y as follows:

$3y = 15$ (add 4 to both sides)

$y = 5$ (divide both sides by 3)

Hence $(-1, 5)$ lies on the line, which can now be sketched on graph paper as shown in Figure 1.3.

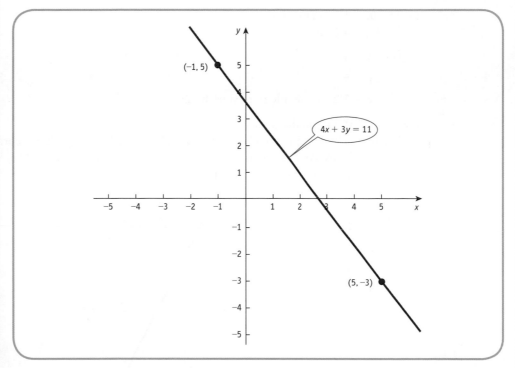

Figure 1.3

Practice Problem

3. Find the coordinates of two points on the line

$$3x - 2y = 4$$

by taking $x = 2$ for the first point and $x = -2$ for the second point. Hence sketch its graph.

In this example we arbitrarily picked two values of x and used the linear equation to work out the corresponding values of y. There is nothing particularly special about the variable x. We could equally well have chosen values for y and solved the resulting equations for x. In fact, the easiest thing to do (in terms of the amount of arithmetic involved) is to put $x = 0$ and find y and then to put $y = 0$ and find x.

Example

Sketch the line

$$2x + y = 5$$

Solution

Setting $x = 0$ gives

$$2(0) + y = 5$$
$$0 + y = 5$$
$$y = 5$$

Hence $(0, 5)$ lies on the line.
    Setting $y = 0$ gives

$$2x + 0 = 5$$
$$2x = 5$$
$$x = 5/2 \qquad \text{(divide both sides by 2)}$$

Hence $(5/2, 0)$ lies on the line.
    The line $2x + y = 5$ is sketched in Figure 1.4. Notice how easy the algebra is using this approach. The two points themselves are also slightly more meaningful. They are the points where the line intersects the coordinate axes.

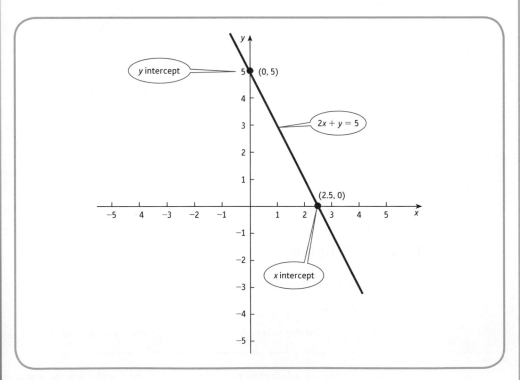

Figure 1.4

Practice Problem

4. Find the coordinates of the points where the line

$$x - 2y = 2$$

intersects the axes. Hence sketch its graph.

In economics it is sometimes necessary to handle more than one equation at the same time. For example, in supply and demand analysis we are interested in two equations, the supply equation and the demand equation. Both involve the same variables Q and P, so it makes sense to sketch them on the same diagram. This enables the market equilibrium quantity and price to be determined by finding the point of intersection of the two lines. We shall return to the analysis of supply and demand in Section 1.5. There are many other occasions in economics and business studies when it is necessary to determine the coordinates of points of intersection. The following is a straightforward example which illustrates the general principle.

Example

Find the point of intersection of the two lines

$$4x + 3y = 11$$
$$2x + y = 5$$

Solution

We have already seen how to sketch these lines in the previous two examples. We discovered that

$$4x + 3y = 11$$

passes through $(5, -3)$ and $(-1, 5)$, and that

$$2x + y = 5$$

passes through $(0, 5)$ and $(5/2, 0)$.

These two lines are sketched on the same diagram in Figure 1.5, from which the point of intersection is seen to be $(2, 1)$.

It is easy to verify that we have not made any mistakes by checking that $(2, 1)$ lies on both lines.

It lies on $4x + 3y = 11$ because $4(2) + 3(1) = 8 + 3 = 11$ ✓
and lies on $2x + y = 5$ because $2(2) + 1 = 4 + 1 = 5$.   ✓

For this reason, we say that $x = 2$, $y = 1$ is the solution of the **simultaneous linear equations**

$$4x + 3y = 11$$
$$2x + y = 5$$

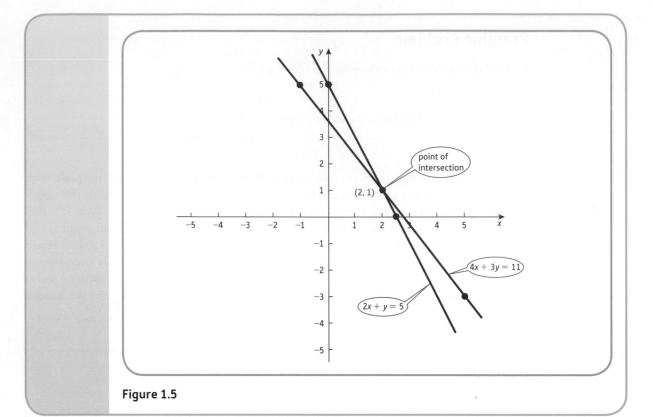

Figure 1.5

Practice Problem

5. Find the point of intersection of

$$3x - 2y = 4$$
$$x - 2y = 2$$

[Hint: you might find your answers to Problems 3 and 4 useful.]

Quite often it is not necessary to produce an accurate plot of an equation. All that may be required is an indication of the general shape together with a few key points or features. It can be shown that, provided e is non-zero, any equation given by

$$dx + ey = f$$

can be rearranged into the special form

$$y = ax + b$$

An example showing you how to perform such a rearrangement will be considered in a moment. The coefficients a and b have particular significance, which we now examine. To be specific, consider

$$y = 2x - 3$$

in which $a = 2$ and $b = -3$.

When x is taken to be zero, the value of y is

$$y = 2(0) - 3 = -3$$

The line passes through $(0, -3)$, so the y intercept is -3. This is just the value of b. In other words, the constant term, b, represents the **intercept** on the y axis.

In the same way it is easy to see that a, the coefficient of x, determines the **slope** of a line. The slope of a straight line is simply the change in the value of y brought about by a 1 unit increase in the value of x. For the equation

$$y = 2x - 3$$

let us choose $x = 5$ and increase this by a single unit to get $x = 6$. The corresponding values of y are then, respectively,

$$y = 2(5) - 3 = 10 - 3 = 7$$
$$y = 2(6) - 3 = 12 - 3 = 9$$

The value of y increases by 2 units when x rises by 1 unit. The slope of the line is therefore 2, which is the value of a. The slope of a line is fixed throughout its length, so it is immaterial which two points are taken. The particular choice of $x = 5$ and $x = 6$ was entirely arbitrary. You might like to convince yourself of this by choosing two other points, such as $x = 20$ and $x = 21$, and repeating the previous calculations.

A graph of the line

$$y = 2x - 3$$

is sketched in Figure 1.6. This is sketched using the information that the intercept is -3 and that for every 1 unit along we go 2 units up. In this example the coefficient of x is positive. This does not have to be the case. If a is negative, then for every increase in x there is a

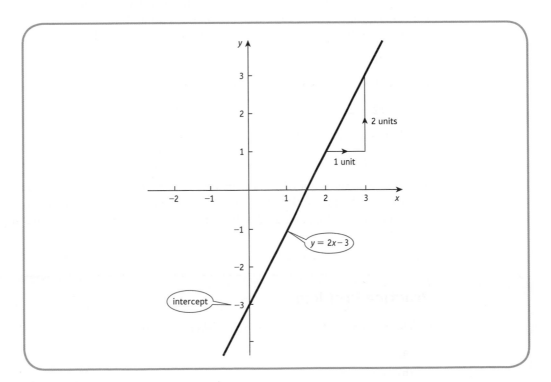

Figure 1.6

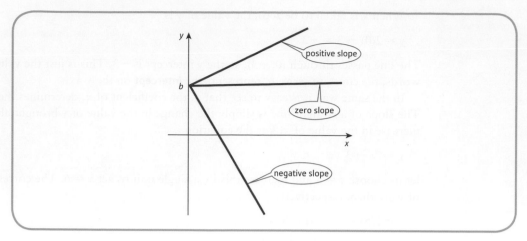

Figure 1.7

corresponding decrease in y, indicating that the line is downhill. If a is zero, then the equation is just

$$y = b$$

indicating that y is fixed at b and the line is horizontal. The three cases are illustrated in Figure 1.7.

It is important to appreciate that in order to use the slope–intercept approach, it is necessary for the equation to be written as

$$y = ax + b$$

If a linear equation does not have this form, it is usually possible to perform a preliminary rearrangement to isolate the variable y on the left-hand side.

For example, to use the slope–intercept approach to sketch the line

$$2x + 3y = 12$$

we begin by removing the x term from the left-hand side. Subtracting $2x$ from both sides gives

$$3y = 12 - 2x$$

and dividing both sides by 3 gives

$$y = 4 - \frac{2}{3}x$$

This is now in the required form with $a = -2/3$ and $b = 4$. The line is sketched in Figure 1.8. A slope of $-2/3$ means that, for every 1 unit along, we go 2/3 units down (or, equivalently, for every 3 units along, we go 2 units down). An intercept of 4 means that it passes through $(0, 4)$.

Practice Problem

6. Use the slope–intercept approach to sketch the lines

   (a) $y = x + 2$

   (b) $4x + 2y = 1$

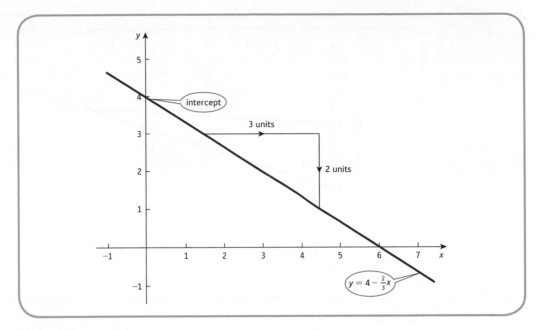

Figure 1.8

We conclude this section with two examples showing how linear graphs can be used in business.

Example

Two new models of a smartphone are launched on 1 January 2018. Predictions of sales are given by:

Model 1: $S_1 = 4 + 0.5n$ Model 2: $S_2 = 8 + 0.1n$

where S_i (in tens of thousands) denotes the monthly sales of model i after n months.

(a) State the values of the slope and intercept of each line and give an interpretation.

(b) Illustrate the sales of both models during the first year by drawing graphs on the same axes.

(c) Use the graph to find the month when sales of Model 1 overtake those of Model 2.

Solution

(a) The intercept for Model 1 is 4. There are 40 000 sales of this phone when the product is launched. The slope is 0.5, so each month, sales increase by 5000. The corresponding figures for Model 2 are 8 and 0.1, respectively.

(b) The intercept for Model 1 is 4, so the line passes through $(0, 4)$. For every one-unit increase in n the value of S_1 increases by 0.5. So, for example, a two-unit increase in n results in a one-unit increase in S_1. The line passes through $(2, 5)$, $(4, 6)$ and so on. The line is sketched in Figure 1.9.

For Model 2, the line passes through $(0, 8)$, and since the slope is 0.1, it passes through $(10, 9)$.

(c) The graphs intersect at $(10, 9)$, so sales of Model 1 overtake sales of Model 2 after 10 months.

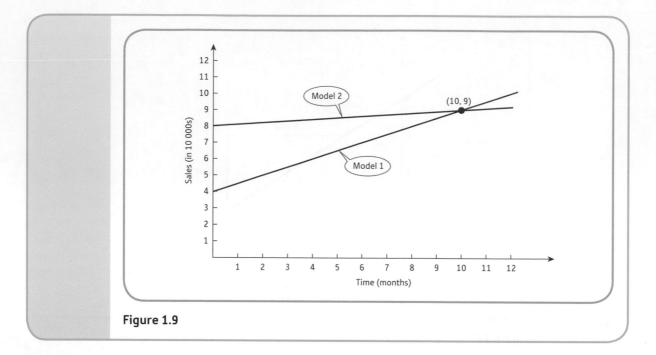

Figure 1.9

Example

Three companies can supply a university with some mathematical software. Each company has a different pricing structure:

Company 1 provides a site licence which costs $130 000 and can be used by anyone at the university;

Company 2 charges $1000 per user;

Company 3 charges a fixed amount of $40 000 for the first 60 users and $500 for each additional user.

(a) Draw a graph of each cost function on the same set of axes.

(b) What advice can you give the university about which company to use?

Solution

(a) If there are n users, then the cost, C, from each supplier is:

Company 1: $C = 130\,000$. The graph is a horizontal line with intercept 130 000

Company 2: $C = 1000n$. The graph is a line passing through the origin with a slope 1000

Company 3: If $n \le 60$ then $C = 40\,000$

If $n > 60$ then $C = 40\,000 + 500(n - 60) = 500n + 10\,000$

The graph for Company 3 is a horizontal line with intercept 40 000 until $n = 60$ after which the line bends upwards with a slope 500.

The graphs are sketched in Figure 1.10.

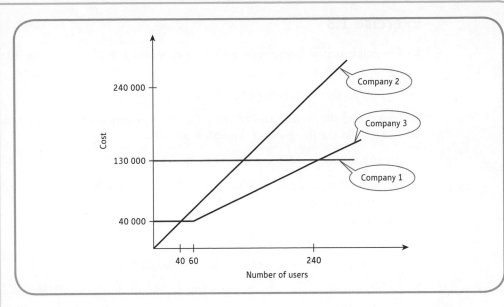

Figure 1.10

(b) The cheapest supplier depends on the number of users:

If $n \leq 40$, Company 2 is the cheapest.

If $40 \leq n \leq 240$, Company 3 is the cheapest.

If $n \geq 240$, Company 1 is the cheapest.

Key Terms

Coefficient   A numerical multiplier of the variables in an algebraic term, such as the numbers 4 and 7 in the expression $4x + 7yz^2$.

Coordinates   A set of numbers that determine the position of a point relative to a set of axes.

Intercept   The point(s) where a graph crosses one of the coordinate axes.

Linear equation   An equation of the form $dx + ey = f$.

Origin   The point where the coordinate axes intersect.

Simultaneous linear equations   A set of linear equations in which there are (usually) the same number of equations and unknowns. The solution consists of values of the unknowns which satisfy all of the equations at the same time.

Slope of a line   Also known as the gradient, it is the change in the value of y when x increases by 1 unit.

x axis   The horizontal coordinate axis pointing from left to right.

y axis   The vertical coordinate axis pointing upwards.

Exercise 1.3

1. On graph paper draw axes with values of x and y between -3 and 10, and plot the following points:

   P(4, 0), Q(-2, 9), R(5, 8), S(-1, -2)

   Hence find the coordinates of the point of intersection of the line passing through P and Q, and the line passing through R and S.

2. An airline charges $300 for a flight of 2000 km and $700 for a flight of 4000 km.

   (a) Plot these points on graph paper with distance on the horizontal axis and cost on the vertical axis.

   (b) Assuming a linear model, estimate

      (i) the cost of a flight of 3200 km;

      (ii) the distance travelled on a flight costing $400.

3. By substituting values into the equation, decide which of the following points lie on the line, $x + 4y = 12$:

   A(12, 0), B(2, 2), C(4, 2), D(-8, 5), E(0, 3)

4. For the line $3x - 5y = 8$,

   (a) find the value of x when $y = 2$;

   (b) find the value of y when $x = 1$.

   Hence write down the coordinates of two points which lie on this line.

5. If $4x + 3y = 24$, complete the following table and hence sketch this line.

x	y
0	
	0
3	

6. Solve the following pairs of simultaneous linear equations graphically:

   (a) $-2x + y = 2$ (b) $3x + 4y = 12$ (c) $2x + y = 4$ (d) $x + y = 1$
        $2x + y = -6$ $x + 4y = 8$ $4x - 3y = 3$ $6x + 5y = 15$

7. State the value of the slope and y intercept for each of the following lines:

   (a) $y = 5x + 9$ (b) $y = 3x - 1$ (c) $y = 13 - x$
   (d) $-x + y = 4$ (e) $4x + 2y = 5$ (f) $5x - y = 6$

8. Use the slope–intercept approach to produce a rough sketch of the following lines:

   (a) $y = -x$ (b) $x - 2y = 6$

9. A taxi firm charges a fixed cost of $4 plus a charge of $2.50 a mile.

   (a) Write down a formula for the cost, C, of a journey of x miles.

   (b) Plot a graph of C against x for $0 \le x \le 20$.

   (c) Hence, or otherwise, work out the distance of a journey which costs $24.

10. The number of people, N, employed in a chain of cafes is related to the number of cafes, n, by the equation:

$$N = 10n + 120$$

(a) Illustrate this relation by plotting a graph of N against n for $0 \leq n \leq 20$.

(b) Hence, or otherwise, calculate the number of

(i) employees when the company has 14 cafes;

(ii) cafes when the company employs 190 people.

(c) State the values of the slope and intercept of the graph and give an interpretation.

11. Monthly sales revenue, S (in $), and monthly advertising expenditure, A (in $), are modelled by the linear relation, $S = 9000 + 12A$.

(a) If the firm does not spend any money on advertising, what is the expected sales revenue that month?

(b) If the firm spends $800 on advertising one month, what is the expected sales revenue?

(c) How much does the firm need to spend on advertising to achieve monthly sales revenue of $15 000?

(d) If the firm increases monthly expenditure on advertising by $1, what is the corresponding increase in sales revenue?

Exercise 1.3*

1. Which of the following points lie on the line $3x - 5y = 25$?

$(5, -2)$, $(10, 1)$, $(-5, 0)$ $(5, 10)$, $(-5, 10)$, $(0, -5)$

2. Solve the following pairs of simultaneous equations graphically:

(a) $y = 3x - 1$ (b) $2x + y = 6$ (c) $2x + 3y = 5$ (d) $3x + 4y = -12$

$y = 2x + 1$ $x - y = -3$ $5x - 2y = -16$ $-2x + 3y = 25$

3. State the value of the slope and y intercept for each of the following lines:

(a) $y = 7x - 34$ (b) $y = 1 - x$ (c) $3x - 2y = 6$ (d) $-4x + 2y = 5$

(e) $x - 5y = 0$ (f) $y = 2$ (g) $x = 4$

4. Identify the two lines in the following list which are parallel:

(a) $3x + 5y = 2$ (b) $5x - 3y = 1$ (c) $5x + 3y = 13$

(d) $10x - 6y = 9$ (e) $y = 0.6x + 2$

5. (a) The Feelgood Gym has a monthly membership fee of $100 and it charges an additional $1 per hour. If I use the gym for x hours in a month, write down an expression for the total cost in terms of x.

(b) Repeat part (a) for the FabulousMe Gym, which charges $35 per month and $3.50 per hour.

(c) By plotting both graphs on the same axes, or otherwise, find the number of hours which gives the same total cost.

6. A bakery discovers that if it decreases the price of its birthday cakes by \$1, it sells 12 more cakes each month.

   (a) Assuming that monthly sales, M, are related to prices, P, by a linear model, $M = aP + b$, state the value of a.

   (b) If the bakery sells 240 cakes in a month when the price of the cake is \$14, work out the value of b.

   (c) Use this model to estimate monthly sales when the price is \$9.

   (d) If the bakery can make only 168 cakes in a month, work out the price that it needs to charge to sell them all.

7. (1) Show that the lines $ax + by = c$ and $dx + ey = f$ are parallel whenever $ae - bd = 0$.

   (2) Use the result of part (1) to comment on the solution of the following simultaneous equations:

   $$2x - 4y = 1$$
   $$-3x + 6y = 7$$

8. Write down the coordinates of the points where the line $ax + by = c$ intercepts the axes.

SECTION 1.4

Algebraic solution of simultaneous linear equations

Objectives

At the end of this section you should be able to:

- Solve a system of two simultaneous linear equations in two unknowns using elimination.
- Detect when a system of equations does not have a solution.
- Detect when a system of equations has infinitely many solutions.
- Solve a system of three simultaneous linear equations in three unknowns using elimination.

In Section 1.3 a graphical method for the solution of simultaneous linear equations was described. Both lines are sketched on the same piece of graph paper and the coordinates of the point of intersection are then simply read off from the diagram. Unfortunately, this approach has several drawbacks. It is not always easy to decide on a suitable scale for the axes. Even if the scale allows all four points (two from each line) to fit on the diagram, there is no guarantee that the point of intersection itself also lies on it. When this happens, you have no alternative but to throw away your graph paper and to start again, choosing a smaller scale in the hope that the solution will now fit. The second drawback concerns the accuracy of the graphical solution. All of the problems in Section 1.3 were deliberately chosen so that the answers had nice numbers in them; whole numbers such as -1, 2 and 5 or, at worst, simple fractions such as $\frac{1}{2}$, $2\frac{1}{2}$ and $-\frac{1}{4}$. In practice, the coefficients of the equations may well involve decimals and we might expect a decimal solution. Indeed, even if the coefficients are whole numbers, the solution itself could involve nasty fractions such as 7/8 or perhaps something like 231/571. A moment's thought should convince you that in these circumstances it is virtually impossible to obtain the solution graphically, even if we use a really large scale and our sharpest HB pencil in the process. The final drawback concerns the nature of the problem itself. Quite frequently in economics, we need to solve three equations in three unknowns or maybe four equations in four unknowns. Unfortunately, the graphical method of solution does not extend to these cases.

In this section an alternative method of solution is described which relies on algebra. It is called the **elimination method**, since each stage of the process eliminates one (or more) of the unknowns. This method always produces the exact solution and can be applied to systems of equations larger than just two equations in two unknowns. In order to illustrate the method, we return to the simple example considered in the previous section:

$$4x + 3y = 11 \tag{1}$$

$$2x + y = 5 \tag{2}$$

The coefficient of x in equation (1) is 4 and the coefficient of x in equation (2) is 2. If these numbers had turned out to be exactly the same, then we could have eliminated the variable x by subtracting one equation from the other. However, we can arrange for this to be the case by multiplying the left-hand side of the second equation by 2. Of course, we must also remember to multiply the right-hand side of the second equation by 2 in order for this operation to be valid. The second equation then becomes

$$4x + 2y = 10 \tag{3}$$

We may now subtract equation (3) from equation (1) to get

$$y = 1$$

You may like to think of this in terms of the usual layout for the subtraction of two ordinary numbers: that is,

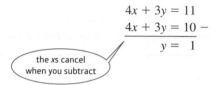

$$
\begin{array}{r}
4x + 3y = 11 \\
4x + 3y = 10 \; - \\
\hline
y = 1
\end{array}
$$

the xs cancel when you subtract

This number can now be substituted into one of the original equations to deduce x. From equation (1)

$$
\begin{aligned}
4x + 3(1) &= 11 \quad \text{(substitute } y = 1\text{)} \\
4x + 3 &= 11 \\
4x &= 8 \quad \text{(subtract 3 from both sides)} \\
x &= 2 \quad \text{(divide both sides by 4)}
\end{aligned}
$$

Hence the solution is $x = 2$, $y = 1$. As a check, substitution of these values into the other original equation (2) gives

$$2(2) + 1 = 5 \quad \checkmark$$

The method of elimination can be summarised as follows.

Step 1

Add/subtract a multiple of one equation to/from a multiple of the other to eliminate x.

Step 2

Solve the resulting equation for y.

Step 3

Substitute the value of y into one of the original equations to deduce x.

Step 4

Check that no mistakes have been made by substituting both x and y into the other original equation.

Example

Solve the system of equations

$$3x + 2y = 1 \tag{1}$$

$$-2x + y = 2 \tag{2}$$

Solution

Step 1

The coefficients of x in equations (1) and (2) are 3 and -2, respectively. We can arrange for these to be the same size (but of opposite sign) by multiplying equation (1) by 2 and multiplying equation (2) by 3. The new equations will then have x coefficients of 6 and -6, so we can eliminate x this time by adding the equations together. The details are as follows.

Doubling the first equation produces

$$6x + 4y = 2 \tag{3}$$

Tripling the second equation produces

$$-6x + 3y = 6 \tag{4}$$

If equation (4) is added to equation (3), then

$$\begin{array}{r} 6x + 4y = 2 \\ -6x + 3y = 6 \ + \\ \hline 7y = 8 \end{array} \tag{5}$$

the xs cancel when you add

Step 2

Equation (5) can be solved by dividing both sides by 7 to get

$$y = 8/7$$

Step 3

If 8/7 is substituted for y in equation (1), then

$$3x + 2\left(\frac{8}{7}\right) = 1$$

$$3x + \frac{16}{7} = 1$$

$$3x = 1 - \frac{16}{7} \qquad \text{(subtract 16/7 from both sides)}$$

$$3x = \frac{7 - 16}{7} \qquad \text{(put over a common denominator)}$$

$$3x = -\frac{9}{7}$$

$$x = \frac{1}{3} \times \left(-\frac{9}{7}\right) \qquad \text{(divide both sides by 3)}$$

$$x - -\frac{3}{7}$$

The solution is therefore $x = -3/7$, $y = 8/7$.

Step 4

As a check, equation (2) gives

$$-2\left(-\frac{3}{7}\right) + \frac{8}{7} = \frac{6}{7} + \frac{8}{7} = \frac{6+8}{7} = \frac{14}{7} = 2 \quad \checkmark$$

Advice

In the general description of the method, we suggested that the variable x is eliminated in step 1. There is nothing special about x. We could equally well eliminate y at this stage and then solve the resulting equation in step 2 for x.

You might like to solve the above example using this alternative strategy. You need to double equation (2) and then subtract from equation (1).

Practice Problem

1. **(a)** Solve the equations

$$3x - 2y = 4$$
$$x - 2y = 2$$

by eliminating one of the variables.

(b) Solve the equations

$$3x + 5y = 19$$
$$-5x + 2y = -11$$

by eliminating one of the variables.

The following examples provide further practice in using the method and illustrate some special cases which may occur.

Example

Solve the system of equations

$$x - 2y = 1$$
$$2x - 4y = -3$$

Solution

The variable x can be eliminated by doubling the first equation and subtracting the second:

both the *x*s and the *y*s cancel!

$$2x - 4y = 2$$
$$\underline{2x - 4y = -3} \; -$$
$$0 = 5$$

The statement '0 = 5' is clearly nonsense and something has gone seriously wrong. To understand what is going on here, let us try to solve this problem graphically.

The line $x - 2y = 1$ passes through the points (0, −1/2) and (1, 0) (check this). The line $2x - 4y = -3$ passes through the points (0, 3/4) and (−3/2, 0) (check this). Figure 1.11 shows that these lines are parallel and so they do not intersect. It is therefore not surprising that we were unable to find a solution using algebra, because this system of equations does not have one. We could have deduced this before when subtracting the equations. The equation that only involves y in step 2 can be written as

$$0y = 5$$

and the problem is to find a value of y for which this equation is true. No such value exists, since

$$\text{zero} \times \text{any number} = \text{zero}$$

and so the original system of equations does not have a solution.

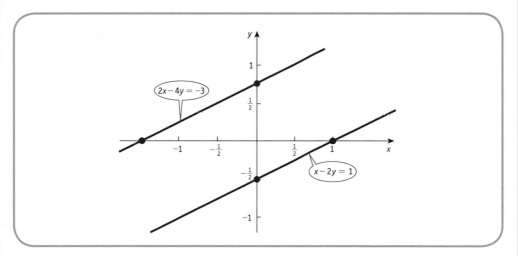

Figure 1.11

Example

Solve the equations

$$2x - 4y = 1$$
$$5x - 10y = 5/2$$

Solution
The variable x can be eliminated by multiplying the first equation by 5, multiplying the second equation by 2 and subtracting

$$10x - 20y = 5$$
$$\underline{10x - 20y = 5} \; -$$
$$0 = 0$$

> everything cancels including the right-hand side!

Again, it is easy to explain this using graphs. The line $2x - 4y = 1$ passes through $(0, -1/4)$ and $(1/2, 0)$. The line $5x - 10y = 5/2$ passes through $(0, -1/4)$ and $(1/2, 0)$. Consequently, both equations represent the same line. From Figure 1.12 the lines intersect along the whole of their length and any point on this line is a solution. This particular system of equations has infinitely many solutions. This can also be deduced algebraically. The equation involving y in step 2 is

$$0y = 0$$

which is true for any value of y.

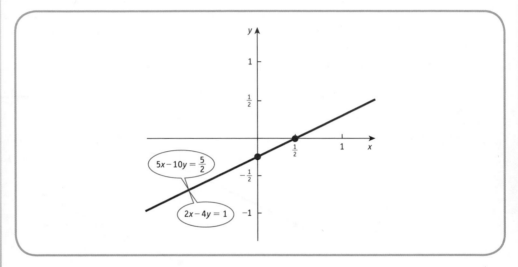

Figure 1.12

Practice Problem

2. Attempt to solve the following systems of equations:

   (a) $3x - 6y = -2$ (b) $-5x + y = 4$
   $\; -4x + 8y = -1$ $\;\;\; 10x - 2y = -8$

   Comment on the nature of the solution in each case.

It is possible to identify when simultaneous equations fail to possess a unique solution by considering the general case:

$$ax + by = c$$
$$dx + ey = f$$

The variable y can be eliminated by multiplying the first equation by e, multiplying the second equation by b and subtracting:

$$aex + bey = ce$$
$$\underline{bdx + bey = bf} \; -$$
$$(ae - bd)x = ce - bf$$

so that

$$x = \frac{ce - bf}{ae - bd}$$

In the same way it is possible to show that

$$y = \frac{af - cd}{ae - bd} \qquad \text{(see Exercise 1.4*, Question 3).}$$

These formulae cannot be used when $ae = bd$ since it is impossible to divide by zero. In this case the system either has no solution or infinitely many solutions. You might like to check that this condition holds for both of the systems in Practice Problem 2.

We now show how the algebraic method can be used to solve three equations in three unknowns. As you might expect, the details are more complicated than for just two equations, but the principle is the same. We begin with a simple example to illustrate the general method. Consider the system

$$x + 3y - z = 4 \tag{1}$$
$$2x + y + 2z = 10 \tag{2}$$
$$3x - y + z = 4 \tag{3}$$

The objective is to find three numbers x, y and z which satisfy these equations simultaneously. Our previous work suggests that we should begin by eliminating x from all but one of the equations.

The variable x can be eliminated from the second equation by multiplying equation (1) by 2 and subtracting equation (2):

$$
\begin{array}{r}
2x + 6y - 2z = 8 \\
2x + y + 2z = 10 - \\
\hline
5y - 4z = -2
\end{array}
\tag{4}
$$

Similarly, we can eliminate x from the third equation by multiplying equation (1) by 3 and subtracting equation (3):

$$
\begin{array}{r}
3x + 9y - 3z = 12 \\
3x - y + z = 4 - \\
\hline
10y - 4z = 8
\end{array}
\tag{5}
$$

At this stage the first equation is unaltered but the second and third equations of the system have changed to equations (4) and (5), respectively, so the current equations are

$$x + 3y - z = 4 \tag{1}$$
$$5y - 4z = -2 \tag{4}$$
$$10y - 4z = 8 \tag{5}$$

Notice that the last two equations constitute a system of just two equations in two unknowns, y and z. This, of course, is precisely the type of problem that we already know how to solve. Once y and z have been calculated, the values can be substituted into equation (1) to deduce x.

We can eliminate y in the last equation by multiplying equation (4) by 2 and subtracting equation (5):

$$
\begin{array}{r}
10y - 8z = -4 \\
10y - 4z = 8 - \\
\hline
-4z = -12
\end{array}
\tag{6}
$$

Collecting together the current equations gives

$$x + 3y - z = \quad 4 \tag{1}$$
$$5y - 4z = \quad -2 \tag{4}$$
$$-4z = -12 \tag{6}$$

From the last equation,

$$z = \frac{-12}{-4} = 3 \qquad \text{(divide both sides by } -4\text{)}$$

If this is substituted into equation (4), then

$$5y - 4(3) = -2$$
$$5y - 12 = -2$$
$$5y = \quad 10 \quad \text{(add 12 to both sides)}$$
$$y = \quad 2 \quad \text{(divide both sides by 5)}$$

Finally, substituting $y = 2$ and $z = 3$ into equation (1) produces

$$x + 3(2) - 3 = 4$$
$$x + 3 = 4$$
$$x = 1 \quad \text{(subtract 3 from sides)}$$

Hence the solution is $x = 1$, $y = 2$, $z = 3$.

As usual, it is possible to check the answer by putting these numbers back into the original equations (1), (2) and (3):

$$1 + 3(2) - 3 = \quad 4 \quad \checkmark$$
$$2(1) + 2 + 2(3) = 10 \quad \checkmark$$
$$3(1) - 2 + 3 = \quad 4 \quad \checkmark$$

The general strategy may be summarised as follows. Consider the system

$$?x + ?y + ?z = ?$$
$$?x + ?y + ?z = ?$$
$$?x + ?y + ?z = ?$$

where ? denotes some numerical coefficient.

Step 1

Add/subtract multiples of the first equation to/from multiples of the second and third equations to eliminate x. This produces a new system of the form

$$?x + ?y + ?z = ?$$
$$?y + ?z = ?$$
$$?y + ?z = ?$$

Step 2

Add/subtract a multiple of the second equation to/from a multiple of the third to eliminate y. This produces a new system of the form

$$?x + ?y + ?z = ?$$
$$?y + ?z = ?$$
$$?z = ?$$

Step 3

Solve the last equation for z. Substitute the value of z into the second equation to deduce y. Finally, substitute the values of both y and z into the first equation to deduce x.

Step 4

Check that no mistakes have been made by substituting the values of x, y and z into the original equations.

It is possible to adopt different strategies from that suggested here. For example, it may be more convenient to eliminate z from the last equation in step 2 rather than y. However, it is important to notice that we use the second equation to do this, not the first. Any attempt to use the first equation in step 2 would reintroduce the variable x into the equations, which is the last thing we want to do at this stage.

Example

Solve the equations

$$4x + y + 3z = 8 \tag{1}$$
$$-2x + 5y + z = 4 \tag{2}$$
$$3x + 2y + 4z = 9 \tag{3}$$

Solution

Step 1

To eliminate x from the second equation we multiply it by 2 and add to equation (1):

$$\begin{array}{r} 4x + y + 3z = 8 \\ -4x + 10y + 2z = 8 \;+ \\ \hline 11y + 5z = 16 \end{array} \tag{4}$$

To eliminate x from the third equation we multiply equation (1) by 3, multiply equation (3) by 4 and subtract:

$$\begin{array}{r} 12x + 3y + 9z = 24 \\ 12x + 8y + 16z = 36 \;- \\ \hline -5y - 7z = -12 \end{array} \tag{5}$$

This produces a new system:

$$4x + y + 3z = 8 \tag{1}$$
$$11y + 5z = 16 \tag{4}$$
$$-5y - 7z = -12 \tag{5}$$

Step 2

To eliminate y from the new third equation (that is, equation (5)) we multiply equation (4) by 5, multiply equation (5) by 11 and add:

$$\begin{array}{r} 55y + 25z = 80 \\ -55y - 77z = -132 \;+ \\ \hline -52z = -52 \end{array} \tag{6}$$

This produces a new system

$$4x + y + 3z = \quad 8 \tag{1}$$
$$11y + 5z = \quad 16 \tag{4}$$
$$-52z = -52 \tag{6}$$

Step 3

The last equation gives

$$z = \frac{-52}{-52} = 1 \quad \text{(divide both sides by } -52)$$

If this is substituted into equation (4), then

$$11y + 5(1) = 16$$
$$11y + 5 = 16$$
$$11y = 11 \quad \text{(subtract 5 from both sides)}$$
$$y = \quad 1 \quad \text{(divide both sides by 11)}$$

Finally, substituting $y = 1$ and $z = 1$ into equation (1) produces

$$4x + 1 + 3(1) = 8$$
$$4x + 4 = 8$$
$$4x = 4 \quad \text{(subtract 4 from both sides)}$$
$$x = 1 \quad \text{(divide both sides by 4)}$$

Hence the solution is $x = 1$, $y = 1$, $z = 1$.

Step 4

As a check the original equations (1), (2) and (3) give, respectively,

$$4(1) + 1 + 3(1) = 8 \quad \checkmark$$
$$-2(1) + 5(1) + 1 = 4 \quad \checkmark$$
$$3(1) + 2(1) + 4(1) = 9 \quad \checkmark$$

Practice Problem

3. Solve the following system of equations:

$$2x + 2y - 5z = -5 \tag{1}$$
$$x - y + z = \quad 3 \tag{2}$$
$$-3x + y + 2z = -2 \tag{3}$$

As you might expect, it is possible for three simultaneous linear equations to have either no solution or infinitely many solutions. An illustration of this is given in Question 5 of Exercise 1.4*. The method described in this section has an obvious extension to larger systems of equations. However, the calculations are extremely tedious to perform by hand. Fortunately, many computer packages are available which can solve large systems accurately and efficiently (a matter of a few seconds to solve 10 000 equations in 10 000 unknowns).

Advice

We shall return to the solution of simultaneous linear equations in Chapter 7 when we describe how matrix theory can be used to solve them. This does not depend on any subsequent chapters in this text, so you might like to read through this material now. Two techniques are suggested. A method based on inverse matrices is covered in Section 7.2 and an alternative using Cramer's rule can be found in Section 7.3.

Key Term

Elimination method   The method in which variables are removed from a system of simultaneous equations by adding (or subtracting) a multiple of one equation to (or from) a multiple of another.

Exercise 1.4

1. Use the elimination method to solve the following pairs of simultaneous linear equations:

    (a) $-2x + y = 2$ **(b)** $3x + 4y = 12$ **(c)** $2x + y = 4$ **(d)** $x + y = 1$

          $2x + y = -6$ $x + 4y = 8$ $4x - 3y = 3$ $6x + 5y = 15$

2. The total annual sales of a book in either paper or electronic form are 3500. Each paper copy of the book costs \$30 and each e-book costs \$25. The total cost is \$97 500.

    (a) If x and y denote the number of copies in paper and electronic form, write down a pair of simultaneous equations.

    (b) Solve the equations to find the number of e-books sold.

3. Sketch the following lines on the same diagram:

    $$2x - 3y = 6, \quad 4x - 6y = 18, \quad x - \frac{3}{2}y = 3$$

    Hence comment on the nature of the solutions of the following systems of equations:

    (a) $2x - 3y = 6$ **(b)** $4x - 6y = 18$

          $x - \dfrac{3}{2}y = 3$ $x - \dfrac{3}{2}y = 3$

4. Use the elimination method to attempt to solve the following systems of equations. Comment on the nature of the solution in each case.

    (a) $-3x + 5y = 4$ **(b)** $6x - 2y = 3$

          $9x - 15y = -12$ $15x - 5y = 4$

5. If the following system of linear equations has infinitely many solutions, find the value of k.

    $$6x - 4y = 2$$
    $$-3x + 2y = k$$

Exercise 1.4*

1. Solve the following pairs of simultaneous equations:

   (a) $y = 3x - 1$ **(b)** $2x + y = 6$ **(c)** $2x + 3y = 5$ **(d)** $3x + 4y = -12$

        $y = 2x + 1$ $x - y = -3$ $5x - 2y = -16$ $-2x + 3y = 25$

2. Write down a possible set of values of the numbers a and b for which the simultaneous equations:

   (a) $2x + 3y = 4$ have infinitely many solutions

        $ax + 6y = b$

   (b) $4x - 6y = 1$ have no solutions

        $2x + ay = b$

3. By eliminating x from the system

   $$ax + by = c$$
   $$dx + ey = f$$

   show that

   $$y = \frac{af - cd}{ae - bd}$$

4. Solve the following systems of equations:

   (a) $x - 3y + 4z = 5$ (1)   **(b)** $3x + 2y - 2z = -5$ (1)

        $2x + y + z = 3$ (2) $4x + 3y + 3z = 17$ (2)

        $4x + 3y + 5z = 1$ (3) $2x - y + z = -1$ (3)

5. Attempt to solve the following systems of equations. Comment on the nature of the solution in each case.

   (a) $x - 2y + z = -2$ (1)   **(b)** $2x + 3y - z = 13$ (1)

        $x + y - 2z = 4$ (2) $x - 2y + 2z = -3$ (2)

        $-2x + y + z = 12$ (3) $3x + y + z = 10$ (3)

6. If the following system of equations has infinitely many solutions, find the value of the constant, k.

   $$x + 2y - 5z = 1$$
   $$2x - y + 3z = 4$$
   $$4x + 3y - 7z = k$$

   What can you say about the nature of the solution for other values of k?

7. A distribution centre sends three different types of parcels. One consignment has 6 small, 8 medium and 9 large parcels which cost \$173.20 to post. Another consignment has 7 small, 13 medium and 17 large parcels with total postage \$291.05. A large parcel costs twice as much to post as a small one. Work out the total cost of posting 3 small parcels, 9 medium parcels and 2 large parcels.

SECTION 1.5
Supply and demand analysis

Objectives

At the end of this section you should be able to:

- Use the function notation, $y = f(x)$.
- Identify the endogenous and exogenous variables in an economic model.
- Identify and sketch a linear demand function.
- Identify and sketch a linear supply function.
- Determine the equilibrium price and quantity for a single-commodity market both graphically and algebraically.
- Determine the equilibrium price and quantity for a multicommodity market by solving simultaneous linear equations.

Microeconomics is concerned with the analysis of the economic theory and policy of individual firms and markets. In this section we focus on one particular aspect known as market equilibrium, in which the supply and demand balance. We describe how the mathematics introduced in the previous two sections can be used to calculate the equilibrium price and quantity. However, before we do this it is useful to explain the concept of a function. This idea is central to nearly all applications of mathematics in economics.

A **function**, f, is a rule which assigns to each incoming number, x, a uniquely defined outgoing number, y. A function may be thought of as a 'black box' that performs a dedicated arithmetic calculation. As an example, consider the rule 'double and add 3'. The effect of this rule on two specific incoming numbers, 5 and -17, is illustrated in Figure 1.13.

Unfortunately, such a representation is rather cumbersome. There are, however, two alternative ways of expressing this rule which are more concise. We can write either

$$y = 2x + 3 \text{ or } f(x) = 2x + 3$$

The first of these is familiar to you from our previous work; corresponding to any incoming number, x, the right-hand side tells you what to do with x to generate the outgoing number, y.

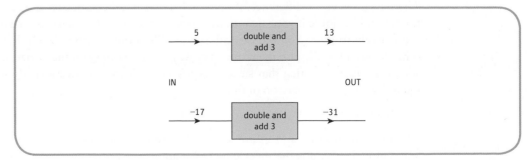

Figure 1.13

The second notation is also useful. It has the advantage that it involves the label f, which is used to name the rule. If, in a piece of economic theory, there are two or more functions, we can use different labels to refer to each one. For example, a second function might be

$$g(x) = -3x + 10$$

and we subsequently identify the respective functions simply by referring to them by name: that is, as either f or g.

The new notation also enables the information conveyed in Figure 1.13 to be written

$f(5) = 13$ (read 'f of 5 equals 13')

$f(-17) = -31$ (read 'f of −17 equals −31')

The number inside the brackets is the incoming value, x, and the right-hand side is the corresponding outgoing value, y.

Practice Problem

1. Evaluate

    (a) $f(25)$ **(b)** $f(1)$ **(c)** $f(17)$ **(d)** $g(0)$ **(e)** $g(48)$ **(f)** $g(16)$

    for the two functions

    $$f(x) = -2x + 50$$
    $$g(x) = -\tfrac{1}{2}x + 25$$

    Do you notice any connection between f and g?

The incoming and outgoing variables are referred to as the **independent** and **dependent** variables, respectively. The value of y clearly 'depends' on the actual value of x that is fed into the function. For example, in microeconomics the quantity demanded, Q, of a good depends on the market price, P. We might express this as

$$Q = f(P)$$

Such a function is called a **demand function**. Given any particular formula for $f(P)$, it is then a simple matter to produce a picture of the corresponding demand curve on graph paper. There is, however, a difference of opinion between mathematicians and economists on how this should be done. If your quantitative methods lecturer is a mathematician, then that person is likely to plot Q on the vertical axis and P on the horizontal axis. Economists, on the other hand, normally plot them the other way round, with Q on the horizontal axis. In doing so, we are merely noting that since Q is related to P, then, conversely, P must be related to Q, and so there is a function of the form

$$P = g(Q)$$

The two functions, f and g, are said to be **inverse functions**: that is, f is the inverse of g and, equivalently, g is the inverse of f. We adopt the economists' approach in this text. In subsequent chapters we shall investigate other microeconomic functions such as total revenue, average cost and profit. It is conventional to plot each of these against Q (that is, with Q on the horizontal axis), so it makes sense to be consistent and to do the same here.

Written in the form $P = g(Q)$, the demand function tells us that P is a function of Q but gives us no information about the precise relationship between these two variables. To find this we need to know the form of the function which can be obtained either from economic theory or from empirical evidence. For the moment we hypothesise that the function is linear, so that

$$P = aQ + b$$

for some appropriate constants (called **parameters**), a and b. Of course, in reality, the relationship between price and quantity is likely to be much more complicated than this. However, the use of linear functions makes the mathematics nice and easy, and the result of any analysis at least provides a first approximation to the truth. The process of identifying the key features of the real world and making appropriate simplifications and assumptions is known as **modelling**. Models are based on economic laws and help to explain and predict the behaviour of real-world situations. Inevitably, there is a conflict between mathematical ease and the model's accuracy. The closer the model comes to reality, the more complicated the mathematics is likely to be.

A graph of a typical linear demand function is shown in Figure 1.14. Elementary theory shows that demand usually falls as the price of a good rises and so the slope of the line is negative. Mathematically, P is then said to be a **decreasing function** of Q.

In symbols we write

$a < 0$ (read '*a* is less than zero')

It is also apparent from the graph that the intercept, b, is positive: that is,

$b > 0$ (read '*b* is greater than zero')

In fact, it is possible in theory for the demand curve to be horizontal with $a = 0$. This corresponds to perfect competition, and we shall return to this special case in Chapter 4.

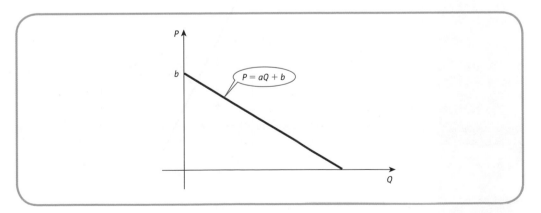

Figure 1.14

Example

Sketch a graph of the demand function

$$P = -2Q + 50$$

Hence, or otherwise, determine the value of

(a) P when $Q = 9$

(b) Q when $P = 10$

Solution

For the demand function

$$P = -2Q + 50$$

$a = -2$, $b = 50$, so the line has a slope of -2 and an intercept of 50. For every 1 unit along, the line goes down by 2 units, so it must cross the horizontal axis when $Q = 25$. (Alternatively, note that when $P = 0$ the equation reads $0 = -2Q + 50$, with solution $Q = 25$.) The graph is sketched in Figure 1.15.

(a) Given any quantity, Q, it is straightforward to use the graph to find the corresponding price, P. A line is drawn vertically upwards until it intersects the demand curve and the value of P is read off from the vertical axis. From Figure 1.15, when $Q = 9$ we see that $P = 32$. This can also be found by substituting $Q = 9$ directly into the demand function to get

$$P = -2(9) + 50 = 32$$

(b) Reversing this process enables us to calculate Q from a given value of P. A line is drawn horizontally until it intersects the demand curve, and the value of Q is read off from the horizontal axis. Figure 1.15 indicates that $Q = 20$ when $P = 10$. Again, this can be found by calculation. If $P = 10$, then the equation reads

$$10 = -2Q + 50$$
$$-40 = -2Q \qquad \text{(subtract 50 from both sides)}$$
$$20 = Q \qquad \text{(divide both sides by } -2\text{)}$$

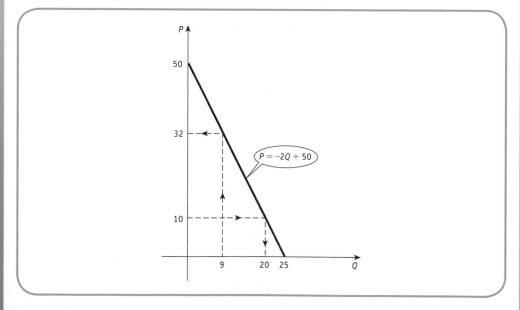

Figure 1.15

Practice Problem

2. Sketch a graph of the demand function

$$P = -3Q + 75$$

Hence, or otherwise, determine the value of

(a) P when $Q = 23$

(b) Q when $P = 18$

Example

A potter makes and sells ceramic bowls. It is observed that when the price is $32, only 9 bowls are sold in a week; but when the price decreases to $10, weekly sales rise to 20. Assuming that demand can be modelled by a linear function,

(a) obtain a formula for P in terms of Q;

(b) sketch a graph of P against Q;

(c) comment on the likely reliability of the model.

Solution

(a) The general formula for a linear demand function is $P = aQ + b$, where a is the slope of the line. The values of the parameters a and b can be worked out in two different ways.

Method 1 – Calculate the slope of the line

Notice that weekly sales have gone up by 11 bowls as a result of a $22 decrease in price. If the relationship is linear, then a 1-unit increase in Q corresponds to a $22/11 = 2$-unit decrease in P, so the graph has a slope of -2. The equation must be given by $P = -2Q + b$. To find b we can use the fact that when $Q = 9$, $P = 32$, so $32 = -2 \times 9 + b$, giving $b = 50$. The demand function is

$$P = -2Q + 50$$

Method 2 – Simultaneous equations

When $Q = 9$, we know that $P = 32$, so $9a + b = 32$

When $Q = 20$, we know that $P = 10$, so $20a + b = 10$

Subtracting the second equation from the first gives $-11a = 22$, so $a = -2$. This value can be substituted into either equation to get $b = 50$ as before.

(b) The graph is sketched in Figure 1.16 using the fact that the intercept is 50 and the slope is -2. Alternatively, it could be sketched using the fact that it passes through $(9, 32)$ and $(20, 10)$.

(c) Although the assumption of a linear relationship may be valid in the middle of the range, it is unlikely to be true at the ends. If the potter were to give away the bowls for free, it is unlikely that the demand would be limited to 25. Similarly, at the other end it would be surprising if no one buys a bowl the moment the price goes above $50. In practice the graph will be curved at each end as shown by the dashed lines in Figure 1.16.

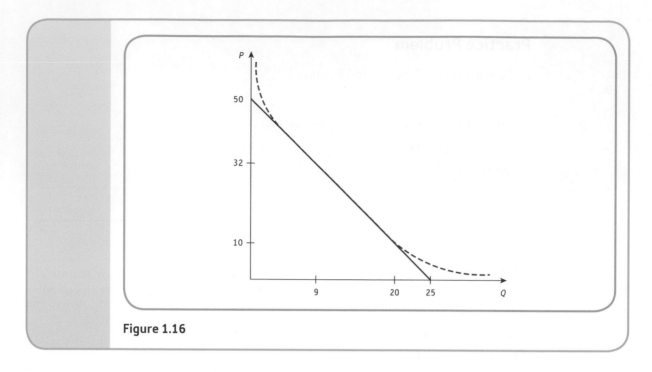

Figure 1.16

The model of consumer demand given so far is fairly crude in that it assumes that quantity depends solely on the price, P, of the good being considered. In practice, Q depends on other factors as well. These include the incomes of consumers, Y, the price of substitutable goods, P_S, the price of complementary goods, P_C, advertising expenditure, A, and consumers' tastes, T. A **substitutable good** is one that could be consumed instead of the good under consideration. For example, in the transport industry, buses and taxis could obviously be substituted for each other in urban areas. A **complementary good** is one that is used in conjunction with other goods. For example, laptops and printers are consumed together. Mathematically, we say that Q is a function of P, Y, P_S, P_C, A and T. This is written as

$$Q = f(P, Y, P_S, P_C, A, T)$$

where the variables inside the brackets are separated by commas. In terms of a 'black box' diagram, this is represented with six incoming lines and one outgoing line as shown in Figure 1.17. In our previous discussion it was implicitly assumed that the variables Y, P_S, P_C, A and T are held fixed. We describe this situation by calling Q and P **endogenous variables**, since they are allowed to vary and are determined within the model. The remaining variables are called **exogenous**, since they are constant and are determined outside the model.

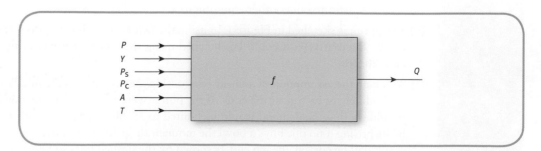

Figure 1.17

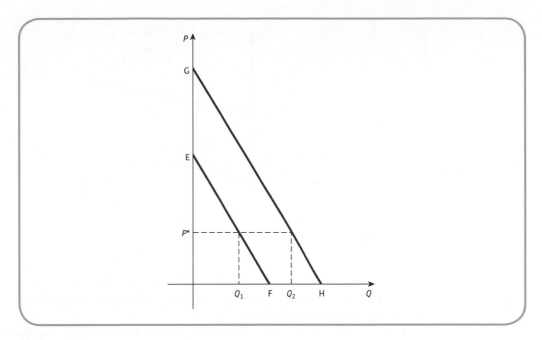

Figure 1.18

Let us return now to the standard demand curve shown in Figure 1.18 as the line EF. This is constructed on the assumption that Y, P_S, P_C, A and T are all constant. Notice that when the price is P^* the quantity demanded is Q_1. Now suppose that income, Y, increases. We would normally expect the demand to rise because the extra income buys more goods at price P^*. The effect is to shift the demand curve to the right because at price P^* consumers can afford the larger number of goods, Q_2. From Figure 1.18 we deduce that if the demand curve is

$$P = aQ + b$$

then a rise in income causes the intercept, b, to increase.

We conclude that if one of the exogenous variables changes, then the whole demand curve moves, whereas if one of the endogenous variables changes, we simply move along the fixed curve.

Incidentally, it is possible that, for some goods, an increase in income actually causes the demand curve to shift to the left. In the 1960s and 1970s, most western economies saw a decline in the domestic consumption of coal as a result of an increase in income. In this case, higher wealth meant that more people were able to install central heating systems which use alternative forms of energy. Under these circumstances the good is referred to as an **inferior good**. On the other hand, a **normal good** is one whose demand rises as income rises. Cars and electrical goods are obvious examples of normal goods. Currently, concern about global warming is also reducing demand for coal. This factor can be incorporated as part of taste, although it is difficult to handle mathematically since it is virtually impossible to quantify taste and so to define T numerically.

The **supply function** is the relation between the quantity, Q, of a good that producers plan to bring to the market and the price, P, of the good. A typical linear supply curve is indicated in Figure 1.19. Economic theory indicates that, as the price rises, so does the supply. Mathematically, P is then said to be an **increasing function** of Q. A price increase encourages existing producers to raise output and entices new firms to enter the market. The line shown in Figure 1.19 has equation

$$P = aQ + b$$

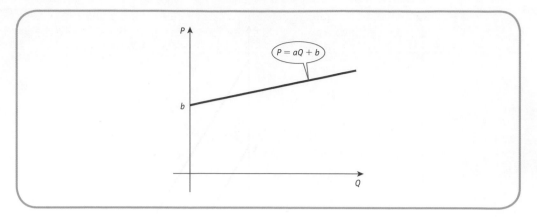

Figure 1.19

with slope $a > 0$ and intercept $b > 0$. Note that when the market price is equal to b, the supply is zero. Only when the price exceeds this threshold level do producers decide that it is worth supplying any good whatsoever.

Again, this is a simplification of what happens in the real world. The supply function does not have to be linear and the quantity supplied, Q, is influenced by things other than price. These exogenous variables include the prices of factors of production (that is, land, capital, labour and enterprise), the profits obtainable on alternative goods, and technology.

In microeconomics we are concerned with the interaction of supply and demand. Figure 1.20 shows typical supply and demand curves sketched on the same diagram. Of particular significance is the point of intersection. At this point the market is in **equilibrium** because the quantity supplied exactly matches the quantity demanded. The corresponding price, P_0, and quantity, Q_0, are called the equilibrium price and quantity.

In practice, it is often the deviation of the market price away from the equilibrium price that is of most interest. Suppose that the market price, P^*, exceeds the equilibrium price, P_0. From Figure 1.20 the quantity supplied, Q_S, is greater than the quantity demanded, Q_D, so there is excess supply. There are stocks of unsold goods, which tend to depress prices and cause firms to cut back production. The effect is for 'market forces' to shift the market back

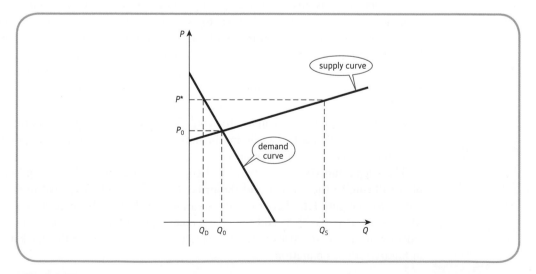

Figure 1.20

down towards equilibrium. Likewise, if the market price falls below equilibrium price, then demand exceeds supply. This shortage pushes prices up and encourages firms to produce more goods, so the market drifts back up towards equilibrium.

Example

The demand and supply functions of a good are given by

$$P = -2Q_D + 50$$
$$P = \tfrac{1}{2}Q_S + 25$$

where P, Q_D and Q_S denote the price, quantity demanded and quantity supplied, respectively.

(a) Determine the equilibrium price and quantity.

(b) Determine the effect on the market equilibrium if the government decides to impose a fixed tax of $5 on each good.

Solution

(a) The demand curve has already been sketched in Figure 1.15. For the supply function

$$P = \tfrac{1}{2}Q_S + 25$$

we have $a = \tfrac{1}{2}$, $b = 25$, so the line has a slope of $\tfrac{1}{2}$ and an intercept of 25. It therefore passes through $(0, 25)$. For a second point, let us choose $Q_S = 20$, say. The corresponding value of P is

$$P = \tfrac{1}{2}(20) + 25 = 35$$

so the line also passes through $(20, 35)$. The points $(0, 25)$ and $(20, 35)$ can now be plotted and the supply curve sketched. Figure 1.21 shows both the demand and supply curves sketched on the same diagram. The point of intersection has coordinates $(10, 30)$, so the equilibrium quantity is 10 and the equilibrium price is 30.

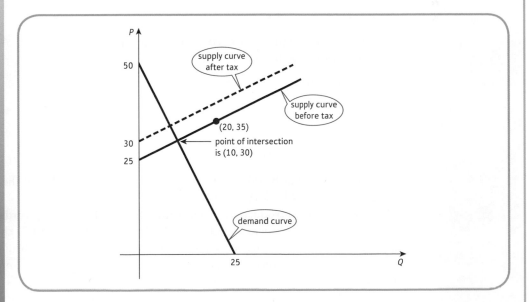

Figure 1.21

It is possible to calculate these values using algebra. In equilibrium, $Q_D = Q_S$. If this common value is denoted by Q, then the demand and supply equations become

$$P = -2Q + 50 \quad \text{and} \quad P = \tfrac{1}{2}Q + 25$$

This represents a pair of simultaneous equations for the two unknowns P and Q and so could be solved using the elimination method described in the previous section. However, this is not strictly necessary because it follows immediately from the above equations that

$$-2Q + 50 = \tfrac{1}{2}Q + 25$$

since both sides are equal to P. This can be rearranged to calculate Q:

$$-2\tfrac{1}{2}Q + 50 = 25 \quad \text{(subtract } \tfrac{1}{2}Q \text{ from both sides)}$$
$$-2\tfrac{1}{2}Q = -25 \quad \text{(subtract 50 from both sides)}$$
$$Q = 10 \quad \text{(divide both sides by } -2\tfrac{1}{2})$$

Finally, P can be found by substituting this value into either of the original equations. The demand equation gives

$$P = -2(10) + 50 = 30$$

As a check, the supply equation gives

$$P = \tfrac{1}{2}(10) + 25 = 30 \quad ✓$$

(b) If the government imposes a fixed tax of $5 per good, then the money that the firm actually receives from the sale of each good is the amount, P, that the consumer pays, less the tax, 5: that is, $P - 5$. Mathematically, this problem can be solved by replacing P with $P - 5$ in the supply equation to get the new supply equation

$$P - 5 = \tfrac{1}{2}Q_S + 25$$

that is,

$$P = \tfrac{1}{2}Q_S + 30$$

The remaining calculations proceed as before. In equilibrium, $Q_D = Q_S$. Again, setting this common value to be Q gives

$$P = -2Q + 50$$
$$P = \tfrac{1}{2}Q + 30$$

Hence

$$-2Q + 50 = \tfrac{1}{2}Q + 30$$

which can be solved as before to give $Q = 8$. Substitution into either of the above equations gives $P = 34$. (Check the details.)

Graphically, the introduction of tax shifts the supply curve upwards by 5 units. Obviously, the demand curve is unaltered. The dashed line in Figure 1.21 shows the new supply curve, from which the new equilibrium quantity is 8 and equilibrium price is 34. Note the effect that government taxation has on the market equilibrium price. This has risen to $34 and so not all of the tax is passed on to the consumer. The consumer pays an additional $4 per good. The remaining $1 of tax must, therefore, be paid by the firm.

Practice Problem

3. The demand and supply functions of a good are given by

$$P = -4Q_D + 120$$
$$P = \tfrac{1}{3}Q_S + 29$$

where P, Q_D and Q_S denote the price, quantity demanded and quantity supplied, respectively.

(a) Calculate the equilibrium price and quantity.

(b) Calculate the new equilibrium price and quantity after the imposition of a fixed tax of \$13 per good. Who pays the tax?

We conclude this section by considering a more realistic model of supply and demand, taking into account substitutable and complementary goods. Let us suppose that there are two goods in related markets, which we call good 1 and good 2. The demand for either good depends on the prices of both good 1 and good 2. If the corresponding demand functions are linear, then

$$Q_{D_1} = a_1 + b_1 P_1 + c_1 P_2$$
$$Q_{D_2} = a_2 + b_2 P_1 + c_2 P_2$$

where P_i and Q_{D_i} denote the price and demand for the ith good and a_i, b_i and c_i are parameters. For the first equation, $a_1 > 0$ because there is a positive demand when the prices of both goods are zero. Also, $b_1 < 0$ because the demand of a good falls as its price rises. The sign of c_1 depends on the nature of the goods. If the goods are substitutable, then an increase in the price of good 2 would mean that consumers would switch from good 2 to good 1, causing Q_{D_1} to increase. Substitutable goods are therefore characterised by a positive value of c_1. On the other hand, if the goods are complementary, then a rise in the price of either good would see the demand fall, so c_1 is negative. Similar results apply to the signs of a_2, b_2 and c_2. The calculation of the equilibrium price and quantity in a two-commodity market model is demonstrated in the following example.

Example

The demand and supply functions for two interdependent commodities are given by

$$Q_{D_1} = 10 - 2P_1 + P_2$$
$$Q_{D_2} = 5 + 2P_1 - 2P_2$$
$$Q_{S_1} = -3 + 2P_1$$
$$Q_{S_2} = -2 + 3P_2$$

where Q_{D_i}, Q_{S_i} and P_i denote the quantity demanded, quantity supplied and price of good i, respectively. Determine the equilibrium price and quantity for this two-commodity model.

Solution

In equilibrium, we know that the quantity supplied is equal to the quantity demanded for each good, so that

$$Q_{D_1} = Q_{S_1} \quad \text{and} \quad Q_{D_2} = Q_{S_2}$$

Let us write these respective common values as Q_1 and Q_2. The demand and supply equations for good 1 then become

$$Q_1 = 10 - 2P_1 + P_2$$
$$Q_1 = -3 + 2P_1$$

Hence

$$10 - 2P_1 + P_2 = -3 + 2P_1$$

since both sides are equal to Q_1. It makes sense to tidy this equation up a bit by collecting all of the unknowns on the left-hand side and putting the constant terms on to the right-hand side:

$$10 - 4P_1 + P_2 = -3 \quad \text{(subtract } 2P_1 \text{ from both sides)}$$
$$-4P_1 + P_2 = -13 \quad \text{(subtract 10 from both sides)}$$

We can perform a similar process for good 2. The demand and supply equations become

$$Q_2 = 5 + 2P_1 - 2P_2$$
$$Q_2 = -2 + 3P_2$$

because $Q_{D_2} = Q_{S_2} = Q_2$ in equilibrium. Hence

$$5 + 2P_1 - 2P_2 = -2 + 3P_2$$
$$5 + 2P_1 - 5P_2 = -2 \quad \text{(subtract } 3P_2 \text{ from both sides)}$$
$$2P_1 - 5P_2 = -7 \quad \text{(subtract 5 from both sides)}$$

We have therefore shown that the equilibrium prices, P_1 and P_2, satisfy the simultaneous linear equations

$$-4P_1 + P_2 = -13 \tag{1}$$

$$2P_1 - 5P_2 = -7 \tag{2}$$

which can be solved by elimination. Following the steps described in Section 1.4, we proceed as follows.

Step 1

Double equation (2) and add to equation (1) to get

$$\begin{array}{r} -4P_1 + P_2 = -13 \\ 4P_1 - 10P_2 = -14 + \\ \hline -9P_2 = -27 \end{array} \tag{3}$$

Step 2

Divide both sides of equation (3) by -9 to get $P_2 = 3$.

Step 3

If this is substituted into equation (1), then

$$-4P_1 + 3 = -13$$
$$-4P_1 = -16 \quad \text{(subtract 3 from both sides)}$$
$$P_1 = 4 \quad \text{(divide both sides by } -4)$$

Step 4

As a check, equation (2) gives

$$2(4) - 5(3) = -7 \quad \checkmark$$

Hence $P_1 = 4$ and $P_2 = 3$.

Finally, the equilibrium quantities can be deduced by substituting these values back into the original supply equations. For good 1,

$$Q_1 = -3 + 2P_1 = -3 + 2(4) = 5$$

For good 2,

$$Q_2 = -2 + 3P_2 = -2 + 3(3) = 7$$

As a check, the demand equations also give

$$Q_1 = 10 - 2P_1 + P_2 = 10 - 2(4) + 3 = 5 \quad \checkmark$$
$$Q_2 = 5 + 2P_1 - 2P_2 = 5 + 2(4) - 2(3) = 7 \quad \checkmark$$

Practice Problem

4. The demand and supply functions for two interdependent commodities are given by

$$Q_{D_1} = 40 - 5P_1 - P_2$$
$$Q_{D_2} = 50 - 2P_1 - 4P_2$$
$$Q_{S_1} = -3 + 4P_1$$
$$Q_{S_2} = -7 + 3P_2$$

where Q_{D_i}, Q_{S_i} and P_i denote the quantity demanded, quantity supplied and price of good i, respectively. Determine the equilibrium price and quantity for this two-commodity model. Are these goods substitutable or complementary?

For a two-commodity market the equilibrium prices and quantities can be found by solving a system of two simultaneous equations. Exactly the same procedure can be applied to a three-commodity market, which requires the solution of a system of three simultaneous equations.

Advice

An example of a three-commodity model can be found in Question 6 of Exercise 1.5*. Alternative methods and further examples are described in Chapter 7. In general, with n goods it is necessary to solve n equations in n unknowns and, as pointed out in Section 1.4, this is best done using a computer package whenever n is large.

Key Terms

Complementary goods   A pair of goods consumed together. As the price of either goes up, the demand for both goods goes down.

Decreasing function   A function, $y = f(x)$, in which y decreases as x increases.

Demand function   A relationship between the quantity demanded and various factors that affect demand, including price.

Dependent variable   A variable whose value is determined by that taken by the independent variables; in $y = f(x)$, the dependent variable is y.

Endogenous variable   A variable whose value is determined within a model.

Equilibrium (market)   This state occurs when quantity supplied and quantity demanded are equal.

Exogenous variable   A variable whose value is determined outside a model.

Function   A rule that assigns to each incoming number, x, a uniquely defined outgoing number, y.

Increasing function   A function, $y = f(x)$, in which y increases as x increases.

Independent variable   A variable whose value determines that of the dependent variable; in $y = f(x)$, the independent variable is x.

Inferior good   A good whose demand decreases as income increases.

Inverse function   A function, written f^{-1}, which reverses the effect of a given function, f, so that $x = f^{-1}(y)$ when $y = f(x)$.

Modelling   The creation of a piece of mathematical theory which represents (a simplification of) some aspect of practical economics.

Normal good   A good whose demand increases as income increases.

Parameter   A constant whose value affects the specific values but not the general form of a mathematical expression, such as the constants a, b and c in $ax^2 + bx + c$.

Substitutable goods   A pair of goods that are alternatives to each other. As the price of one good goes up, the demand for the other rises.

Supply function   A relationship between the quantity supplied and various factors that affect supply, including price.

Exercise 1.5

1. If $f(x) = 3x + 15$ and $g(x) = \frac{1}{3}x - 5$, evaluate

   (a) $f(2)$ (b) $f(10)$ (c) $f(0)$ (d) $g(21)$ (e) $g(45)$ (f) $g(15)$

   What word describes the relationship between f and g?

2. Sketch a graph of the supply function

   $$P = \frac{1}{3}Q + 7$$

   Hence, or otherwise, determine the value of

   (a) P when $Q = 12$
   (b) Q when $P = 10$
   (c) Q when $P = 4$

3. The demand function of a good is

$$Q = 100 - P + 2Y + \tfrac{1}{2}A$$

where Q, P, Y and A denote quantity demanded, price, income and advertising expenditure, respectively.

(a) Calculate the demand when $P = 10$, $Y = 40$ and $A = 6$. Assuming that price and income are fixed, calculate the additional advertising expenditure needed to raise demand to 179 units.

(b) Is this good inferior or normal?

4. The demand, Q, for a certain good depends on its own price, P, and the price of an alternative good, P_A, according to

$$Q = 30 - 3P + P_A$$

(a) Find Q if $P = 4$ and $P_A = 5$.

(b) Is the alternative good substitutable or complementary? Give a reason for your answer.

(c) Determine the value of P if $Q = 23$ and $P_A = 11$.

5. The demand for a good priced at \$50 is 420 units, and when the price is \$80, demand is 240 units. Assuming that the demand function takes the form $Q = aP + b$, find the values of a and b.

6. (a) Copy and complete the following table of values for the supply function

$$P = \tfrac{1}{2}Q + 20$$

Q	0		50
P		25	

Hence, or otherwise, draw an accurate sketch of this function using axes with values of Q and P between 0 and 50.

(b) On the same axes draw the graph of the demand function

$$P = 50 - Q$$

and hence find the equilibrium quantity and price.

(c) The good under consideration is normal. Describe the effect on the equilibrium quantity and price when income rises.

7. The demand and supply functions of a good are given by

$$P = -3Q_D + 48$$
$$P = \tfrac{1}{2}Q_S + 23$$

Find the equilibrium quantity if the government imposes a fixed tax of \$4 on each good.

8. The demand and supply functions for two interdependent commodities are given by

$$Q_{D_1} = 100 - 2P_1 + P_2$$
$$Q_{D_2} = 5 + 2P_1 - 3P_2$$
$$Q_{S_1} = -10 + P_1$$
$$Q_{S_2} = -5 + 6P_2$$

→

where Q_{D_i}, Q_{S_i} and P_i denote the quantity demanded, quantity supplied and price of good i, respectively. Determine the equilibrium price and quantity for this two-commodity model.

9. A demand function of a certain good is given by

$$Q = -20P + 0.04Y + 4T + 3P_r$$

where Q and P denote the quantity and price of the good, Y is income, T is taste and P_r is the price of a related good.

(a) Calculate Q when $P = 8$, $Y = 1000$, $T = 15$ and $P_r = 30$.

(b) Is the related good substitutable or complementary? Give a reason for your answer.

(c) Find the value of P when $Q = 235$, $Y = 8000$, $T = 30$ and $P_r = 25$.

(d) The exogenous variables are now fixed at $Y = 2000$, $T = 10$ and $P_r = 5$. State the values of the slope and vertical intercept when the demand function is sketched with

(i) P on the horizontal axis and Q on the vertical axis;

(ii) Q on the horizontal axis and P on the vertical axis.

Exercise 1.5*

1. Describe the effect on the demand curve due to an increase in

(a) the price of substitutable goods;

(b) the price of complementary goods;

(c) advertising expenditure.

2. If the line, $P = -\frac{2}{3}Q + 6$, is sketched with P on the horizontal axis and Q on the vertical axis, find the gradient, m, and the vertical intercept, c.

3. If the demand function of a good is

$$2P + 3Q_D = 60$$

where P and Q_D denote price and quantity demanded, respectively, find the largest and smallest values of P for which this function is economically meaningful.

4. The demand and supply functions of a good are given by

$$P = -5Q_D + 80$$
$$P = 2Q_S + 10$$

where P, Q_D and Q_S denote price, quantity demanded and quantity supplied, respectively.

(1) Find the equilibrium price and quantity

(a) graphically;

(b) algebraically.

(2) If the government deducts, as tax, 15% of the market price of each good, determine the new equilibrium price and quantity.

5. The supply and demand functions of a good are given by

$$P = Q_S + 8$$
$$P = -3Q_D + 80$$

where P, Q_S and Q_D denote price, quantity supplied and quantity demanded, respectively.

(a) Find the equilibrium price and quantity if the government imposes a fixed tax of $36 on each good.

(b) Find the corresponding value of the government's tax revenue.

6. The demand and supply functions for three interdependent commodities are

$$Q_{D_1} = 15 - P_1 + 2P_2 + P_3$$
$$Q_{D_2} = 9 + P_1 - P_2 - P_3$$
$$Q_{D_3} = 8 + 2P_1 - P_2 - 4P_3$$
$$Q_{S_1} = -7 + P_1$$
$$Q_{S_2} = -4 + 4P_2$$
$$Q_{S_3} = -5 + 2P_3$$

where Q_{D_i}, Q_{S_i} and P_i denote the quantity demanded, quantity supplied and price of good i, respectively. Determine the equilibrium price and quantity for this three-commodity model.

7. The demand and supply functions of a good are given by

$$P = -3Q_D + 60$$
$$P = 2Q_S + 40$$

respectively. If the government decides to impose a tax of t per good, show that the equilibrium quantity is given by

$$Q = 4 - \tfrac{1}{5}t$$

and write down a similar expression for the equilibrium price.

(a) If it is known that the equilibrium quantity is 3, work out the value of t. How much of this tax is paid by the firm?

(b) If, instead of imposing a tax, the government provides a subsidy of $5 per good, find the new equilibrium price and quantity.

8. The linear supply and demand functions for a good are given by

$$P = aQ + b \quad \text{and} \quad P = cQ + d$$

(a) State whether each of the values of the parameters a, b, c and d are positive or negative.

(b) Find expressions, simplified as far as possible, for equilibrium price and quantity.

Transposition of formulae

> ## Objectives
>
> At the end of this section you should be able to:
>
> - Manipulate formulae.
> - Draw a flow chart representing a formula.
> - Use a reverse flow chart to transpose a formula.
> - Change the subject of a formula involving several letters.

Mathematical modelling involves the use of formulae to represent the relationship between economic variables. In microeconomics we have already seen how useful supply and demand formulae are. These provide a precise relationship between price and quantity. For example, the connection between price, P, and quantity, Q, might be modelled by

$$P = -4Q + 100$$

Given any value of Q it is trivial to deduce the corresponding value of P by merely replacing the symbol Q by a number. A value of $Q = 2$, say, gives

$$P = -4 \times 2 + 100$$
$$= -8 + 100$$
$$= 92$$

On the other hand, given P, it is necessary to solve an equation to deduce Q. For example, when $P = 40$, the equation is

$$-4Q + 100 = 40$$

which can be solved as follows:

$$-4Q = -60 \quad \text{(subtract 100 from both sides)}$$
$$Q = 15 \quad \text{(divide both sides by } -4)$$

This approach is reasonable when only one or two values of P are given. However, if we are given many values of P, it is clearly tedious and inefficient for us to solve the equation each time to find Q. The preferred approach is to **transpose** the formula for P. In other words, we rearrange the formula

$$P = \text{an expression involving } Q$$

into

$$Q = \text{an expression involving } P$$

Written this way round, the formula enables us to find Q by replacing P by a number. For the specific formula

$$-4Q + 100 = P$$

the steps are

$$-4Q = P - 100 \qquad \text{(subtract 100 from both sides)}$$

$$Q = \frac{P - 100}{-4} \qquad \text{(divide both sides by } -4\text{)}$$

Notice that

$$\frac{P - 100}{-4} = \frac{P}{-4} - \frac{100}{-4}$$

$$= -\tfrac{1}{4}P + 25$$

so the rearranged formula simplifies to

$$Q = -\tfrac{1}{4}P + 25$$

If we now wish to find Q when $P = 40$, we immediately get

$$Q = -\tfrac{1}{4} \times 40 + 25$$

$$= -10 + 25$$

$$= 15$$

The important thing to notice about the algebra is that the individual steps are identical to those used previously for solving the equation

$$-4Q + 100 = 40$$

i.e. the operations are again

'subtract 100 from both sides'

followed by

'divide both sides by -4'

Practice Problem

1. **(a)** Solve the equation

   $$\tfrac{1}{2}Q + 13 = 17$$

   State clearly exactly what operation you have performed to both sides at each stage of your solution.

   (b) By performing the same operations as part (a), rearrange the formula

   $$\tfrac{1}{2}Q + 13 = P$$

   into the form

   $$Q = \text{an expression involving } P$$

   (c) By substituting $P = 17$ into the formula derived in part (b), check that this agrees with your answer to part (a).

In general, there are two issues concerning formula transposition. First, we need to decide what to do to both sides of the given formula and the order in which they should be performed. Secondly, we need to carry out these steps accurately. The first of these is often the more difficult. However, there is a logical strategy that can be used to help. To illustrate this, consider the task of making Q the subject of

$$P = \tfrac{1}{3}Q + 5$$

that is, of rearranging this formula into the form

$$Q = \text{an expression involving } P$$

Imagine starting with a value of Q and using a calculator to work out P from

$$P = \tfrac{1}{3}Q + 5$$

The diagram that follows shows that two operations are required and indicates the order in which they must be done. This diagram is called a **flow chart**.

To go backwards from P to Q we need to undo these operations. Now the reverse of 'divide by 3' is 'multiply by 3' and the reverse of 'add 5' is 'subtract 5', so the operations needed to transpose the formula are as follows:

This diagram is called a **reverse flow chart**. The process is similar to that of unwrapping a parcel (or peeling an onion); you start by unwrapping the outer layer first and work inwards. If we now actually perform these steps in the order specified by the reverse flow chart, we get

$$\tfrac{1}{3}Q + 5 = P$$
$$\tfrac{1}{3}Q \quad = P - 5 \qquad \text{(subtract 5 from both sides)}$$
$$Q \quad = 3(P - 5) \quad \text{(multiply both sides by 3)}$$

The rearranged formula can be simplified by multiplying out the brackets to give

$$Q = 3P - 15$$

Incidentally, if you prefer, you can actually use the reverse flow chart itself to perform the algebra for you. All you have to do is to pass the letter P through the reverse flow chart. Working from right to left gives

Notice that taking P as the input to the box 'subtract 5' gives the output $P - 5$, and if the whole of this is taken as the input to the box 'multiply by 3', the final output is the answer, $3(P - 5)$. Hence

$$Q = 3(P - 5)$$

Example

Make x the subject of

(a) $y = \sqrt{\dfrac{x}{5}}$ (b) $y = \dfrac{4}{2x + 1}$

Solution

(a) To go from x to y, the operations are

so the steps needed to transpose the formula are

The algebraic details are as follows:

$$\sqrt{\frac{x}{5}} = y$$

$$\frac{x}{5} = y^2 \qquad \text{(square both sides)}$$

$$x = 5y^2 \qquad \text{(multiply both sides by 5)}$$

Hence the transposed formula is

$$x = 5y^2$$

Alternatively, if you prefer, the reverse flow chart can be used directly to obtain

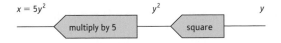

Hence

$$x = 5y^2$$

(b) The forwards flow chart is

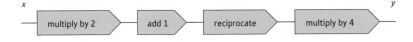

so the reverse flow chart is

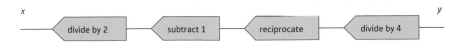

The algebraic details are as follows:

$$\frac{4}{2x+1} = y$$

$$\frac{1}{2x+1} = \frac{y}{4} \qquad \text{(divide both sides by 4)}$$

$$2x + 1 = \frac{4}{y} \qquad \text{(reciprocate both sides)}$$

$$2x = \frac{4}{y} - 1 \qquad \text{(subtract 1 from both sides)}$$

$$= \frac{1}{2}\left(\frac{4}{y} - 1\right) \qquad \text{(divide both sides by 2)}$$

which can be simplified, by multiplying out the brackets, to give

$$x = \frac{2}{y} - \frac{1}{2}$$

Again, the reverse flow chart can be used directly to obtain

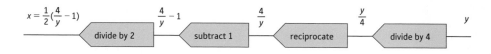

Practice Problem

2. Use flow charts to make x the subject of the following formulae:

(a) $y = 6x^2$ **(b)** $y = \dfrac{1}{7x - 1}$

The following example contains two difficult instances of transposition. In both cases the letter x appears more than once on the right-hand side. If this happens, the technique based on flow charts cannot be used. However, it may still be possible to perform the manipulation even if some of the steps may not be immediately obvious.

Example

Transpose the following formulae to express x in terms of y:

(a) $ax = bx + cy + d$ **(b)** $y = \dfrac{x + 1}{x - 2}$

Solution

(a) In the formula

$$ax = bx + cy + d$$

there are terms involving x on both sides, and since we are hoping to rearrange this into the form

   x = an expression involving y

it makes sense to collect the xs on the left-hand side. To do this we subtract bx from both sides to get

   $ax - bx = cy + d$

Notice that x is a common factor of the left-hand side, so the distributive law can be applied 'in reverse' to take the x outside the brackets: that is,

   $(a - b)x = cy + d$

Finally, both sides are divided by $a - b$ to get

   $$x = \frac{cy + d}{a - b}$$

which is of the desired form.

(b) It is difficult to see where to begin with the formula

   $$y = \frac{x + 1}{x - 2}$$

because there is an x in both the numerator and the denominator. Indeed, the thing that is preventing us getting started is precisely the fact that the expression is a fraction. We can, however, remove the fraction simply by multiplying both sides by the denominator to get

   $(x - 2)y = x + 1$

and if we multiply out the brackets, then

   $xy - 2y = x + 1$

We want to rearrange this into the form

   x = an expression involving y

so we collect the xs on the left-hand side and put everything else on to the right-hand side. To do this we first add $2y$ to both sides to get

   $xy = x + 1 + 2y$

and then subtract x from both sides to get

   $xy - x = 1 + 2y$

The distributive law can now be applied 'in reverse' to take out the common factor of x: that is,

   $(y - 1)x = 1 + 2y$

Finally, dividing through by $y - 1$ gives

   $$x = \frac{1 + 2y}{y - 1}$$

Advice

This example contains some of the hardest algebraic manipulation seen so far in this text. I hope that you managed to follow the individual steps. However, it all might appear as if we have 'pulled rabbits out of hats'. You may feel that, if left on your own, you are never going to be able to decide what to do at each stage. Unfortunately, there is no watertight strategy that always works, although the following five-point plan is worth considering if you get stuck.

To transpose a given formula of the form

$y =$ an expression involving x

into a formula of the form

$x =$ an expression involving y

you proceed as follows:

Step 1   Remove fractions.

Step 2   Multiply out the brackets.

Step 3   Collect all of the xs on to the left-hand side.

Step 4   Take out a factor of x.

Step 5   Divide by the coefficient of x.

You might find it helpful to look back at the previous example in the light of this strategy. In part (b) it is easy to identify each of the five steps. Part (a) also used this strategy, starting with the third step.

Example

Make x the subject of

$$y = \sqrt{\frac{ax + b}{cx + d}}$$

Solution

In this formula there is a square root symbol surrounding the right-hand side. This can be removed by squaring both sides to get

$$y^2 = \frac{ax + b}{cx + d}$$

We now apply the five-step strategy:

Step 1 $(cx + d)y^2 = ax + b$

Step 2 $cxy^2 + dy^2 = ax + b$

Step 3 $cxy^2 - ax = b - dy^2$

Step 4 $(cy^2 - a)x = b - dy^2$

Step 5 $x = \dfrac{b - dy^2}{cy^2 - a}$

Practice Problem

3. Transpose the following formulae to express x in terms of y:

   (a) $x - ay = cx + y$

   (b) $y = \dfrac{x - 2}{x + 4}$

Key Terms

Flow chart   A diagram consisting of boxes of instructions indicating a sequence of operations and their order.

Reverse flow chart   A flow chart indicating the inverse of the original sequence of operations in reverse order.

Transpose a formula   The rearrangement of a formula to make one of the other letters the subject.

Exercise 1.6

1. Make Q the subject of

   $$P = 2Q + 8$$

   Hence find the value of Q when $P = 52$.

2. Write down the formula representing each of the following flow charts

   (a)

   (b)

   (c)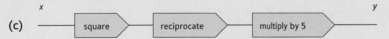

   (d)

3. Draw flow charts for each of the following formulae:

   (a) $y = 5x + 3$ (b) $y = 5(x + 3)$ (c) $y = 6x - 9$ (d) $y = 4x^2 - 6$

   (e) $y = \dfrac{x}{2} + 7$ (f) $y = \dfrac{2}{x}$ (g) $y = \dfrac{1}{x + 3}$

4. Make x the subject of each of the following formulae:

   (a) $y = 9x - 6$ (b) $y = (x + 4)/3$ (c) $y = \dfrac{x}{2}$

   (d) $y = \dfrac{x}{5} + 8$ (e) $y = \dfrac{1}{x + 2}$ (f) $y = \dfrac{4}{3x - 7}$

5. Transpose the formulae:

    (a) $Q = aP + b$ to express P in terms of Q

    (b) $Y = aY + b + I$ to express Y in terms of I

    (c) $Q = \dfrac{1}{aP + b}$ to express P in terms of Q

6. Make x the subject of the formula

$$y = \frac{3}{x} - 2$$

7. In business, the economic order quantity is $Q = \sqrt{\dfrac{2DR}{H}}$.

    (a) Make D the subject of this formula.

    (b) Make H the subject of this formula.

Exercise 1.6*

1. **(1)** Draw flow charts for each of the following formulae:

    (a) $y = 9x + 1$ **(b)** $y = 3 - x$ **(c)** $y = 5x^2 - 8$

    (d) $y = \sqrt{3x + 5}$ **(e)** $y = \dfrac{4}{x^2 + 8}$

    (2) Hence, or otherwise, express x in terms of y in each case.

2. Make x the subject of the following formulae:

    (a) $\dfrac{a}{x} + b = \dfrac{c}{x}$ **(b)** $a - x = \dfrac{b + x}{a}$ **(c)** $e + \sqrt{x + f} = g$

    (d) $a\sqrt{\left(\dfrac{x - n}{m}\right)} = \dfrac{a^2}{b}$ **(e)** $\dfrac{\sqrt{x - m}}{n} = \dfrac{1}{m}$ **(f)** $\dfrac{\sqrt{x} + a}{\sqrt{x} - b} = \dfrac{b}{a}$

3. Transpose the formula

$$V = \frac{5t + 1}{t - 1}$$

    to express t in terms of V.
       Hence, or otherwise, find the value of t when $V = 5.6$.

4. Make r the subject of the formula

$$S = P\left(1 + \frac{r}{100}\right)^n$$

5. Rearrange the formula

$$Y = \frac{-aT + b + I + G}{1 - a + at}$$

    to make each of the following letters the subject:

    (a) G **(b)** T **(c)** t **(d)** a

National income determination

Objectives

At the end of this section you should be able to:

- Identify and sketch linear consumption functions.
- Identify and sketch linear savings functions.
- Set up simple macroeconomic models.
- Calculate equilibrium national income.
- Analyse IS and LM schedules.

Macroeconomics is concerned with the analysis of economic theory and policy at a national level. In this section we focus on one particular aspect known as national income determination. We describe how to set up simple models of the national economy which enable equilibrium levels of income to be calculated. Initially we assume that the economy is divided into two sectors, households and firms. Firms use resources such as land, capital, labour and raw materials to produce goods and services. These resources are known as **factors of production** and are taken to belong to households. **National income** represents the flow of income from firms to households given as payment for these factors. Households can then spend this money in one of two ways. Income can be used for the consumption of goods produced by firms, or it can be put into savings. Consumption, C, and savings, S, are therefore functions of income, Y: that is,

$$C = f(Y)$$
$$S = g(Y)$$

for some appropriate consumption function, f, and savings function, g. Moreover, C and S are normally expected to increase as income rises, so f and g are both increasing functions.

We begin by analysing the **consumption function**. As usual we need to quantify the precise relationship between C and Y. If this relationship is linear, then a graph of a typical consumption function is shown in Figure 1.22. It is clear from this graph that if

$$C = aY + b$$

then $a > 0$ and $b > 0$. The intercept b is the level of consumption when there is no income (that is, when $Y = 0$) and is known as **autonomous consumption**. The slope, a, is the change in C brought about by a 1-unit increase in Y and is known as the **marginal propensity to consume** (MPC). As previously noted, income is used up in consumption and savings, so that

$$Y = C + S$$

It follows that only a proportion of the 1-unit increase in income is consumed; the rest goes into savings. Hence the slope, a, is generally smaller than 1: that is, $a < 1$. It is standard practice in mathematics to collapse the two separate inequalities $a > 0$ and $a < 1$ into the single inequality

$$0 < a < 1$$

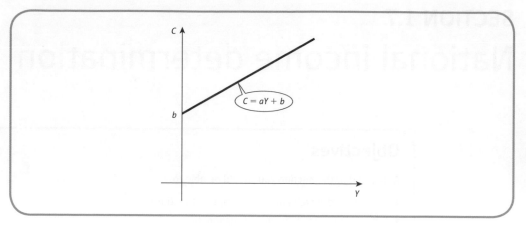

Figure 1.22

The relation

$$Y = C + S$$

enables the precise form of the savings function to be determined from any given consumption function.

To be specific, suppose that the consumption function is given by

$$C = 0.6Y + 10$$

The graph is sketched in Figure 1.23 using the fact that it passes through (0, 10) and (40, 34).

To find the savings function we use the relation

$$Y = C + S$$

which gives

$$
\begin{aligned}
S &= Y - C. &&\text{(subtract } C \text{ from both sides)} \\
&= Y - (0.6Y + 10) &&\text{(substitute } C) \\
&= Y - 0.6Y - 10 &&\text{(multiply out the brackets)} \\
&= 0.4Y - 10 &&\text{(collect terms)}
\end{aligned}
$$

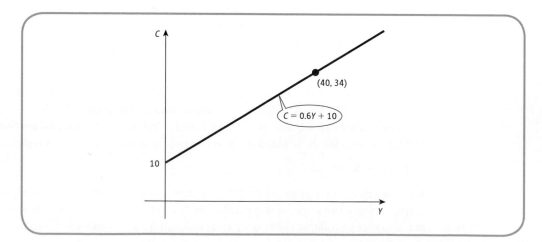

Figure 1.23

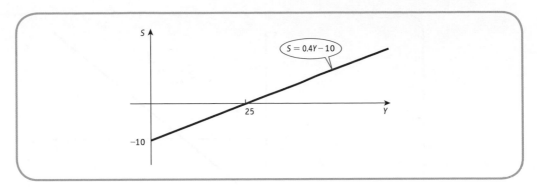

Figure 1.24

The savings function is also linear. Its graph has intercept -10 and slope 0.4. This is sketched in Figure 1.24 using the fact that it passes through $(0, -10)$ and $(25, 0)$.

Practice Problem

1. Determine the savings function that corresponds to the consumption function

    $$C = 0.8Y + 25$$

For the general consumption function

$$C = aY + b$$

we have

$$S = Y - C$$
$$= Y - (aY + b) \quad \text{(substitute } C\text{)}$$
$$= Y - aY - b \quad \text{(multiply out the brackets)}$$
$$= (1 - a)Y - b \quad \text{(take out a common factor of } Y\text{)}$$

The slope of the savings function is called the **marginal propensity to save** (MPS) and is given by $1 - a$: that is,

$$\text{MPS} = 1 - a = 1 - \text{MPC}$$

Moreover, since $a < 1$, we see that the slope, $1 - a$, is positive. Figure 1.25 shows the graph of this savings function. One interesting feature, which contrasts with other economic functions considered so far, is that it is allowed to take negative values. In particular, note that **autonomous savings** (that is, the value of S when $Y = 0$) are equal to $-b$, which is negative because $b > 0$. This is to be expected because whenever consumption exceeds income, households must finance the excess expenditure by withdrawing savings.

Advice

The result, MPC + MPS = 1, is always true, even if the consumption function is non-linear. A proof of this generalisation can be found in Section 4.3.3 in Chapter 4.

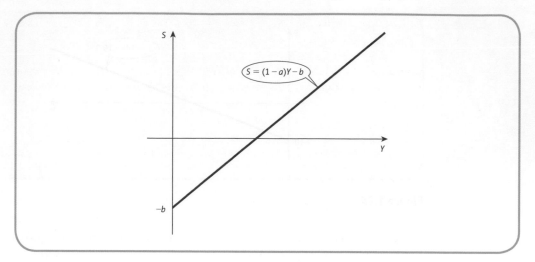

Figure 1.25

The simplest model of the national economy is illustrated in Figure 1.26, which shows the circular flow of income and expenditure. This is fairly crude, since it fails to take into account government activity or foreign trade. In this diagram, **investment**, I, is an injection into the circular flow in the form of spending on capital goods.

Let us examine this more closely and represent the diagrammatic information in symbols. Consider first the box labelled 'Households'. The flow of money entering this box is Y and the flow leaving it is $C + S$. Hence we have the familiar relation

$$Y = C + S$$

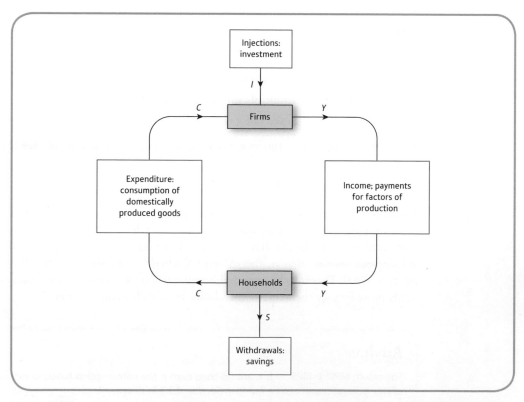

Figure 1.26

For the box labelled 'Firms' the flow entering it is $C + I$ and the flow leaving it is Y, so

$Y = C + I$

Suppose that the level of investment that firms plan to inject into the economy is known to be some fixed value, $I*$. If the economy is in equilibrium, the flow of income and expenditure balance so that

$Y = C + I*$

From the assumption that the consumption function is

$C = aY + b$

for given values of a and b, these two equations represent a pair of simultaneous equations for the two unknowns Y and C. In these circumstances C and Y can be regarded as endogenous variables, since their precise values are determined within the model, whereas $I*$ is fixed outside the model and is exogenous.

Example

Find the equilibrium level of income and consumption if the consumption function is

$C = 0.6Y + 10$

and planned investment $I = 12$.

Solution

We know that

$Y = C + I$ (from theory)

$C = 0.6Y + 10$ (given in problem)

$I = 12$ (given in problem)

If the value of I is substituted into the first equation, then

$Y = C + 12$

The expression for C can also be substituted to give

$Y = 0.6Y + 10 + 12$

$Y = 0.6Y + 22$

$0.4Y = 22$ (subtract $0.6Y$ from both sides)

$Y = 55$ (divide both sides by 0.4)

The corresponding value of C can be deduced by putting this level of income into the consumption function to get

$C = 0.6(55) + 10 = 43$

The equilibrium income can also be found graphically by plotting expenditure against income. In this example the aggregate expenditure, $C + I$, is given by $0.6Y + 22$. This is sketched in Figure 1.27 using the fact that it passes through $(0, 22)$ and $(80, 70)$. Also sketched is the '45° line', so called because it makes an angle of 45° with the horizontal. This line passes through the points $(0, 0)$, $(1, 1)$, . . . , $(50, 50)$ and so on. In other words, at any point on this line expenditure and income are in balance. The equilibrium income can therefore be found by inspecting the point of intersection of this line and the aggregate expenditure line, $C + I$. From Figure 1.27 this occurs when $Y = 55$, which is in agreement with the calculated value.

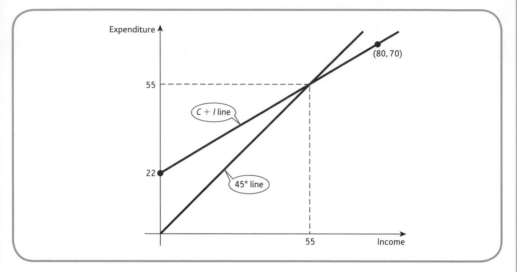

Figure 1.27

Practice Problem

2. Find the equilibrium level of income if the consumption function is

    $$C = 0.8Y + 25$$

    and planned investment $I = 17$. Calculate the new equilibrium income if planned investment rises by 1 unit.

To make the model more realistic, let us now include **government expenditure**, G, and **taxation**, T, in the model. The injections box in Figure 1.26 now includes government expenditure in addition to investment, so

$$Y = C + I + G$$

We assume that planned government expenditure and planned investment are autonomous with fixed values G^* and I^*, respectively, so that in equilibrium

$$Y = C + I^* + G^*$$

The withdrawals box in Figure 1.26 now includes taxation. This means that the income that households have to spend on consumer goods is no longer Y but rather $Y - T$ (income less tax), which is called **disposable income**, Y_d. Hence

$$C = aY_d + b$$

with

$$Y_d = Y - T$$

In practice, the tax will either be autonomous ($T = T^*$ for some lump sum T^*) or be a proportion of national income ($T = tY$ for some proportion t), or a combination of both ($T = tY + T^*$).

Example

Given that

$$G = 20$$
$$I = 35$$
$$C = 0.9Y_d + 70$$
$$T = 0.2Y + 25$$

calculate the equilibrium level of national income.

Solution

At first sight this problem looks rather forbidding, particularly since there are so many variables. However, all we have to do is to write down the relevant equations and to substitute systematically one equation into another until only Y is left.

We know that

$Y = C + I + G$	(from theory)	(1)
$G = 20$	(given in problem)	(2)
$I = 35$	(given in problem)	(3)
$C = 0.9Y_d + 70$	(given in problem)	(4)
$T = 0.2Y + 25$	(given in problem)	(5)
$Y_d = Y - T$	(from theory)	(6)

This represents a system of six equations in six unknowns. The obvious thing to do is to put the fixed values of G and I into equation (1) to get

$$Y = C + 35 + 20 = C + 55 \qquad (7)$$

This has at least removed G and I, so there are only three more variables (C, Y_d and T) left to eliminate. We can remove T by substituting equation (5) into (6) to get

$$Y_d = Y - (0.2Y + 25)$$
$$= Y - 0.2Y - 25$$
$$= 0.8Y - 25 \qquad (8)$$

and then remove Y_d by substituting equation (8) into (4) to get

$$C = 0.9(0.8Y - 25) + 70$$
$$= 0.72Y - 22.5 + 70$$
$$= 0.72Y + 47.5 \qquad (9)$$

We can eliminate C by substituting equation (9) into (7) to get

$Y = C + 55$

$\quad = 0.72Y + 47.5 + 55$

$\quad = 0.72Y + 102.5$

Finally, solving for Y gives

$0.28Y = 102.5$ (subtract 0.72Y from both sides)

$\quad Y = 366$ (divide both sides by 0.28)

Practice Problem

3. Given that

$G = 40$

$I = 55$

$C = 0.8Y_d + 25$

$T = 0.1Y + 10$

calculate the equilibrium level of national income.

To conclude this section we return to the simple two-sector model:

$Y = C + I$

$C = aY + b$

Previously, the investment, I, was taken to be constant. It is more realistic to assume that planned investment depends on the rate of interest, r. As the interest rate rises, so investment falls and we have a relationship

$I = cr + d$

where $c < 0$ and $d > 0$. Unfortunately, this model consists of three equations in the four unknowns Y, C, I and r, so we cannot expect it to determine national income uniquely. The best we can do is to eliminate C and I, say, and to set up an equation relating Y and r. This is most easily understood by an example. Suppose that

$C = 0.8Y + 100$

$I = -20r + 1000$

We know that the commodity market is in equilibrium when

$Y = C + I$

Substitution of the given expressions for C and I into this equation gives

$Y = (0.8Y + 100) + (-20r + 1000)$

$\quad = 0.8Y - 20r + 1100$

which rearranges as

$$0.2Y + 20r = 1100$$

This equation, relating national income, Y, and interest rate, r, is called the **IS schedule**.

We obviously need some additional information before we can pin down the values of Y and r. This can be done by investigating the equilibrium of the money market. The money market is said to be in equilibrium when the supply of money, M_S, matches the demand for money, M_D: that is, when

$$M_S = M_D$$

There are many ways of measuring the **money supply**. In simple terms it can be thought of as consisting of the notes and coins in circulation, together with money held in bank deposits. The level of M_S is assumed to be controlled by the central bank and is taken to be autonomous, so that

$$M_S = M_S^*$$

for some fixed value M_S^*.

The demand for money comes from three sources: transactions, precautions and speculations. The **transactions demand** is used for the daily exchange of goods and services, whereas the **precautionary demand** is used to fund any emergencies requiring unforeseen expenditure. Both are assumed to be proportional to national income. Consequently, we lump these together and write

$$L_1 = k_1 Y$$

where L_1 denotes the aggregate transaction–precautionary demand and k_1 is a positive constant. The **speculative demand** for money is used as a reserve fund in case individuals or firms decide to invest in alternative assets such as government bonds. In Chapter 3 we show that, as interest rates rise, speculative demand falls. We model this by writing

$$L_2 = k_2 r + k_3$$

where L_2 denotes speculative demand, k_2 is a negative constant and k_3 is a positive constant. The total demand, M_D, is the sum of the transaction–precautionary demand and speculative demand: that is,

$$M_D = L_1 + L_2$$
$$= k_1 Y + k_2 r + k_3$$

If the money market is in equilibrium, then

$$M_S = M_D$$

that is,

$$M_S^* = k_1 Y + k_2 r + k_3$$

This equation, relating national income, Y, and interest rate, r, is called the **LM schedule**. If we assume that equilibrium exists in both the commodity and money markets, then the IS and LM schedules provide a system of two equations in two unknowns, Y and r. These can easily be solved either by elimination or by graphical methods.

Example

Determine the equilibrium income and interest rate given the following information about the commodity market:

$$C = 0.8Y + 100$$
$$I = -20r + 1000$$

and the money market:

$$M_S = 2375$$
$$L_1 = 0.1Y$$
$$L_2 = -25r + 2000$$

What effect would a decrease in the money supply have on the equilibrium levels of Y and r?

Solution

The IS schedule for these particular consumption and investment functions has already been obtained in the preceding text. It was shown that the commodity market is in equilibrium when

$$0.2Y + 20r = 1100 \tag{1}$$

For the money market we see that the money supply is

$$M_S = 2375$$

and that the total demand for money (that is, the sum of the transaction–precautionary demand, L_1, and the speculative demand, L_2) is

$$M_D = L_1 + L_2 = 0.1Y - 25r + 2000$$

The money market is in equilibrium when

$$M_S = M_D$$

that is,

$$2375 = 0.1Y - 25r + 2000$$

The LM schedule is therefore given by

$$0.1Y - 25r = 375 \tag{2}$$

Equations (1) and (2) constitute a system of two equations for the two unknowns Y and r. The steps described in Section 1.4 can be used to solve this system:

Step 1

Double equation (2) and subtract from equation (1) to get

$$
\begin{array}{r}
0.2Y + 20r = 1100 \\
0.2Y - 50r = 750 \quad - \\
\hline
70r = 350
\end{array}
\tag{3}
$$

Step 2

Divide both sides of equation (3) by 70 to get

$$r = 5$$

Step 3

Substitute $r = 5$ into equation (1) to get

$$0.2Y + 100 = 1100$$
$$0.2Y = 1000 \qquad \text{(subtract 100 from both sides)}$$
$$Y = 5000 \qquad \text{(divide both sides by 0.2)}$$

Step 4

As a check, equation (2) gives

$$0.1(5000) - 25(5) = 375 \quad \checkmark$$

The equilibrium levels of Y and r are therefore 5000 and 5, respectively.

To investigate what happens to Y and r as the money supply falls, we could just take a smaller value of M_S such as 2300 and repeat the calculations. However, it is more instructive to perform the investigation graphically. Figure 1.28 shows the IS and LM curves plotted on the same diagram with r on the horizontal axis and Y on the vertical axis. These lines intersect at (5, 5000), confirming the equilibrium levels of interest rate and income obtained by calculation. Any change in the money supply will obviously have no effect on the IS curve. On the other hand, a change in the money supply does affect the LM curve. To see this, let us return to the general LM schedule

$$k_1Y + k_2r + k_3 = M_S^*$$

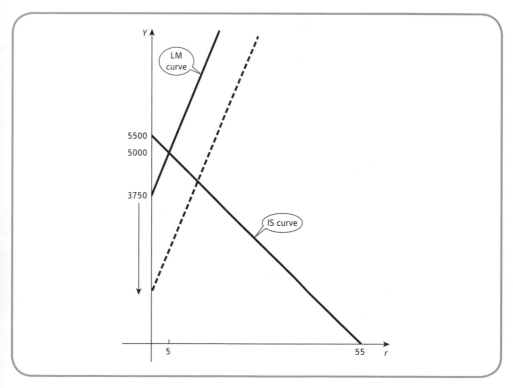

Figure 1.28

and transpose it to express Y in terms of r:

$$k_1 Y = -k_2 r - k_3 + M_S^* \qquad \text{(subtract } k_2 r + k_3 \text{ from both sides)}$$

$$Y = \left(\frac{-k_2}{k_1} \right) r + \frac{-k_3 + M_S^*}{k_1} \qquad \text{(divide both sides by } k_1)$$

Expressed in this form, we see that the LM schedule has slope $-k_2/k_1$ and intercept $(-k_3 + M_S^*)/k_1$.

Any decrease in M_S^* therefore decreases the intercept (but not the slope), and the LM curve shifts downwards. This is indicated by the dashed line in Figure 1.28. The point of intersection shifts both downwards and to the right. We deduce that, as the money supply falls, interest rates rise and national income decreases (assuming that both the commodity and money markets remain in equilibrium).

Advice

It is possible to produce general formulae for the equilibrium level of income in terms of various parameters used to specify the model. As you might expect, the algebra is a little harder, but it does allow for a more general investigation into the effects of varying these parameters. We will return to this in Section 5.3.

Practice Problem

4. Determine the equilibrium income, Y, and interest rate, r, given the following information about the commodity market

    $$C = 0.7Y + 85$$
    $$I = -50r + 1200$$

    and the money market

    $$M_S = 300$$
    $$L_1 = 0.2Y$$
    $$L_2 = -40r + 30$$

    Sketch the IS and LM curves on the same diagram. What effect would an increase in the value of autonomous investment have on the equilibrium values of Y and r?

Key Terms

Autonomous consumption   The level of consumption when there is no income.

Autonomous savings   The withdrawals from savings when there is no income.

Consumption function   The relationship between national income and consumption.

Disposable income   Household income after the deduction of taxes and the addition of benefits.

Factors of production   The inputs to the production of goods and services: land, capital, labour and raw materials.

Government expenditure   The total amount of money spent by government on defence, education, health, police, etc.

Investment   The creation of output not for immediate consumption.

IS schedule   The equation relating national income and interest rate based on the assumption of equilibrium in the goods market.

LM schedule   The equation relating national income and interest rate based on the assumption of equilibrium in the money market.

Marginal propensity to consume   The fraction of a rise in national income which goes into consumption. It is the slope of the consumption function.

Marginal propensity to save   The fraction of a rise in national income which goes into savings. It is the slope of the savings function.

Money supply   The notes and coins in circulation together with money held in bank deposits.

National income   The flow of money from firms to households.

Precautionary demand for money   Money held in reserve by individuals or firms to fund unforeseen future expenditure.

Speculative demand for money   Money held back by firms or individuals for the purpose of investing in alternative assets, such as government bonds, at some future date.

Taxation   Money paid to government based on an individual's income and wealth (direct taxation) together with money paid by suppliers of goods or services based on expenditure (indirect taxation).

Transactions demand for money   Money used for everyday transactions of goods and services.

Exercise 1.7

1. If the consumption function is given by $C = 4200 + 0.75Y$, state the marginal propensity to consume and deduce the marginal propensity to save.

2. If the national income, Y, is 1000 units, then consumption, C, is 800 units. Also whenever income rises by 100, consumption increases by 70. Assuming that the consumption function is linear:

   (a) state the marginal propensity to consume and deduce the marginal propensity to save;

   (b) find an expression for C in terms of Y.

3. If the consumption function is given by

   $$C = 0.7Y + 40$$

   state the values of

(a) autonomous consumption;

(b) marginal propensity to consume.

Transpose this formula to express Y in terms of C and hence find the value of Y when $C = 110$.

4. Write down expressions for the savings function given that the consumption function is

    (a) $C = 0.9Y + 72$ (b) $C = 0.8Y + 100$

5. For a closed economy with no government intervention, the consumption function is

    $$C = 0.6Y + 30$$

    and planned investment is

    $$I = 100$$

    Calculate the equilibrium level of

    (a) national income;

    (b) consumption;

    (c) savings.

6. A consumption function is given by $C = aY + b$.
    It is known that when $Y = 10$, the value of C is 28, and that when $Y = 30$, the value of C is 44.
    By solving a pair of simultaneous equations, find the values of a and b, and deduce that the corresponding savings function is given by

    $$S = 0.2Y - 20$$

    Determine the equilibrium level of income when planned investment $I = 13$.

7. Given that

    $$G = 50$$
    $$I = 40$$
    $$C = 0.75Y_d + 45$$
    $$T = 0.2Y + 80$$

    calculate the equilibrium level of national income.

Exercise 1.7*

1. Write down an expression for the savings function, simplified as far as possible, given that the consumption function is

    (a) $C = 0.7Y + 30$ (b) $C = \dfrac{Y^2 + 500}{Y + 10}$

2. If

$$C = aY + b$$
$$Y = C + I$$
$$I = I^*$$

show that

$$Y = \frac{b + I^*}{1 - a}$$

and obtain a similar expression for C in terms of a, b and I^*.

3. Transpose the formula

$$Y = \frac{b + I^*}{1 - a}$$

to express a in terms of Y, b and I^*.

4. An open economy is in equilibrium when

$$Y = C + I + G + X - M$$

where

Y = national income
C = consumption
I = investment
G = government expenditure
X = exports
M = imports

Determine the equilibrium level of income given that

$C = 0.8Y + 80$
$I = 70$
$G = 130$
$X = 100$
$M = 0.2Y + 50$

5. Given that

consumption,	$C = 0.8Y + 60$
investment,	$I = -30r + 740$
money supply,	$M_S = 4000$
transaction–precautionary demand for money,	$L_1 = 0.15Y$
speculative demand for money,	$L_2 = -20r + 3825$

determine the values of national income, Y, and interest rate, r, on the assumption that both the commodity and the money markets are in equilibrium.

6. Consider the national income model

$$Y = C + I$$
$$C = aY_d + 50$$
$$I = 24$$
$$Y_d = Y - T$$
$$T = 20$$

Show that the equilibrium level of national income is given by

$$Y = \frac{74 - 20a}{1 - a}$$

Transpose this equation to express a in terms of Y.

Hence, or otherwise, find the value of a for which $Y = 155$ and find the value of C.

7. Consider the national income model

$$Y = C + I^* + G^*$$
$$C = a(Y - T), \quad 0 < a < 1$$
$$T = tY, \quad\quad\;\; 0 < t < 1$$

Show that

$$Y = \frac{I^* + G^*}{1 + a(t - 1)}$$

and hence state what happens to Y when

(a) G^* increases   **(b)** t increases

Formal mathematics

The approach adopted in this text is very informal. Emphasis is placed throughout on making both the mathematics and economic applications as accessible as possible. Hopefully this will help you to understand and enjoy the subject. However, it could well be that your lecturers use more formal language and notation. For this reason we conclude each chapter with a brief discussion of more rigorous mathematical language and ideas which provide the framework for more advanced courses which you may take in future years.

In Section 1.2 a number line was used to represent the solutions of linear inequalities. The set of all numbers which lie between two values on the number line is called an **interval** and the notation that we use is summarised in the following table:

Interval	Notation
$a \le x \le b$	[a, b]
$a < x < b$	(a, b)
$a \le x < b$	[a, b)
$a < x \le b$	(a, b]

The first interval, which includes both end points, is called a **closed interval** and the second, which excludes the end points, is called an **open interval**. Using this notation we would write [2, 5] as an abbreviation for $2 \le x \le 5$ and (3, 9] as an abbreviation for $3 < x \le 9$. It is also possible to use this notation to include intervals which are unbounded. For example, the interval $x \ge 6$, which consists of all numbers to the right of 6 on the number line (including 6 itself), can be written as [6, ∞). The symbol ∞ (infinity) is not a number but merely indicates that the interval goes on forever without an upper limit. In this notation we could write the complete set of numbers as $(-\infty, \infty)$.

It is often convenient in mathematics to ignore the sign of a number and deliberately make it positive. This is called the **absolute value** or **modulus** of a number, x, and is written $|x|$. In this notation we have

$$|-5| = 5 \text{ and } |4| = 4$$

If a number is negative, we change the sign to make it positive, whereas if the number is already positive, it is unchanged, so we have

$$|x| = -x \text{ if } x < 0 \quad \text{and} \quad |x| = x \text{ if } x \ge 0$$

Example

Solve the following inequalities giving your answer using interval notation.

(a) $|x| \le 6$ (b) $|2x - 1| < 3$

Solution

(a) If the absolute value of a number x is less than or equal to 6, then the number itself must be between -6 and 6 inclusive, so the solution of the inequality $|x| \leq 6$ can be expressed in interval notation as $[-6, 6]$.

(b) If the absolute value of a number $2x - 1$ is less than 3, then the number itself must be between -3 and 3, so we need to solve

$$-3 < 2x - 1 < 3$$
$$-2 < 2x < 4 \qquad \text{(add 1 to both sides)}$$
$$-1 < x < 2 \qquad \text{(divide both sides by 2)}$$

In interval notation this is written $(-1, 2)$.

In Section 1.5 we introduced the key concept of a function. The **domain** of a function consists of the set of all possible inputs, and the set of corresponding outputs is called the **range** of the function. Sometimes we are forced to restrict the inputs to a function because it is impossible to evaluate the function for certain values of x. For example, it is impossible to evaluate $f(4)$ for the function

$$f(x) = \frac{1}{x - 4}$$

If you try to substitute $x = 4$ into this function, you get '1/0' which is meaningless. On a calculator you get a message 'division by zero' error. For this function the domain consists of all numbers, $x \neq 4$. It is impossible to evaluate $f(x) = \sqrt{x - 3}$ for values of x which are less than 3 because it is impossible to find the square root of negative numbers. For this function the domain consists of all numbers, $x \geq 3$, so in interval notation, the domain is $[3, \infty)$.

Sometimes we choose to restrict the domain of a function so that it makes economic sense. For example, in the demand function, $P = -2Q + 50$, sketched in Figure 1.15, we would choose the domain as $[0, 25]$. We obviously need to exclude negative quantities from the domain and the graph shows that if Q exceeds 25, then P would be negative which is nonsense. From a purely mathematical point of view, there is no problem inputting any number into the function. The line drawn in Figure 1.15 just goes on forever in each direction. However, for the function to be economically meaningful we would choose to restrict the domain to $[0, 25]$. If we do this, then the vertical axis in Figure 1.15 also shows that the corresponding outputs consist of all possible numbers between 0 and 50. In other words, the range of the function is $[0, 50]$.

Mathematical notation exists to make the subject precise and unambiguous. It also provides a convenient shorthand to reduce the amount of writing that we need to do. The following table lists symbols which are often used when presenting mathematical arguments, and you may encounter these when reading higher-level books and journals.

Symbol	Meaning
$\therefore$	therefore
$\exists$	there exists
$\forall$	for all
$\Rightarrow$	implies
$\Leftrightarrow$	is equivalent to

The implies symbol provides a concise way of linking mathematical statements together. We could write the following when solving equations:

$$2x - 8 = 10 \implies 2x = 18 \implies x = 9$$

Use of this symbol has allowed us to fit a string of mathematical steps on a single line of working. The equivalence symbol $\Leftrightarrow$ can be used whenever the implication works both ways. Technically, you could replace $\implies$ by $\Leftrightarrow$ in the algebra above since the steps are reversible. However, it would be pointless to do so, since this piece of mathematics is clearly designed to solve an equation which you do by working from left to right. However, not all implications are reversible, so you must be careful when using the double implication sign. For example, the line

$$x = -5 \implies |x| = 5$$

is true but the reverse is not necessarily true since we have the alternative option of $x = 5$, so it would not be correct to use $\Leftrightarrow$ here. On the other hand, use of $\Leftrightarrow$ in the following line is correct and conveys the important message that two numbers multiply to zero if and only if at least one of them is zero.

$$xy = 0 \iff x = 0 \text{ or } y = 0.$$

Key Terms

Absolute value   The positive value or magnitude of a number.

Closed interval   The set of all real numbers between and including two given numbers: $a \leq x \leq b$.

Domain   The numbers which are used as inputs to a function.

Interval   The set of all real numbers between (and possibly including) two given numbers.

Modulus   The positive value or magnitude of a number.

Open interval   The set of all real numbers between but excluding two given numbers: $a < x < b$.

Range   The numbers which form the set of outputs from a function.

Multiple choice questions

Question 1

A graph of the demand function, $3P + 4Q = 9$ is plotted with Q on the horizontal axis. Find the slope of the line and the intercept on the P-axis.

A. Slope is 9/4 and intercept is -3

B. Slope is 3/4 and intercept is 9/4

C. Slope is 4/3 and intercept is 1/3

D. Slope is $-4/9$ and intercept is 1/3

E. Slope is $-4/3$ and intercept is 3

Question 2

Multiply out the brackets and collect like terms in the expression $5(3x - 4y) - (2x - 3y)$.

A. $13x - 23y$ B. $13x - 17y$ C. $13x - y$ D. $13x - 7y$ E. $13x - 20y$

Question 3

If the supply function is $Q = 4P - 25$, determine the lowest possible price that could be charged.

A. 25   B. 0   C. 25/4   D. 4/25   E. 100

Question 4

Solve the inequality: $2(x + 3) - (5x + 1) \geq 4$

A. $x \geq -1/3$ B. $x \leq -1$ C. $x \geq 1$ D. $x \leq 1/3$ E. $x \geq -3$

Question 5

Solve the simultaneous equations:

$$4x - 2y = 3$$
$$6x - 3y = 4$$

A. No solution

B. Infinitely many solutions

C. $x = 0, y = -1.5$

D. $x = 1, y = 0.5$

E. $x = -0.5, y = -2.5$

Question 6

The demand and supply functions of a good are given by:

$$P = -3Q_D + 75$$
$$P = 2Q_S + 15$$

Determine the equilibrium price.

A. 39   B. 12   C. 60   D. 15   E. 27

Question 7

If the government imposes a fixed tax of $5 on each good sold in Question 6, determine the post-tax equilibrium price.

A. 40   B. 13   C. 41   D. 11   E. 42

Question 8

A demand function is given by $P = aQ + b$. Work out the missing number in the table.

Q	10	14	25
P	6		4.5

A. 5.0   B. 5.6   C. 4.8   D. 5.5   E. 3.6

Question 9

Consider the macroeconomic model:

$$G = 30 \qquad \text{(government expenditure)}$$
$$I = 90 \qquad \text{(planned investment)}$$
$$C = 0.8Y + 20 \qquad \text{(consumption)}$$
$$Y = C + G + I \qquad \text{(equilibrium)}$$

Work out the change in the value of national income Y when government expenditure rises by 1 unit.

A. 13   B. 10   C. 8   D. 5   E. 18

Question 10

Find the value of national income Y when the consumption function is $C = 0.75Y + 4$ and savings are 3.5.

A. 30   B. 2   C. 7   D. 44   E. 54

Question 11

If the supply and demand functions are given by

$$P = aQ_S + b$$
$$P = cQ_D + d$$

what conditions must be imposed on the parameters, a, b, c and d for these equations to be economically meaningful and for the equilibrium to exist?

A. $a > 0, b > 0, c < 0, d < 0, d < b$

B. $a < 0, b < 0, c > 0, d > 0, d < b$

C. $a < 0, b > 0, c > 0, d < 0, d < b$

D. $a > 0, b > 0, c < 0, d > 0, d > b$

E. $a > 0, b < 0, c > 0, d > 0, d > b$

Question 12

Transpose the equation $x = \dfrac{5y + 12}{y + 3}$ to express y in terms of x.

A. $y = \dfrac{3 - 7x}{x - 5}$
B. $y = \dfrac{9}{x - 5}$
C. $y = \dfrac{12}{x - 5}$
D. $y = \dfrac{3(4 - x)}{x - 5}$
E. $y = \dfrac{3x + 8}{x - 5}$

Question 13

Express the following as a single fraction: $\dfrac{4}{x + 2} - \dfrac{1}{x - 1}$

A. $\dfrac{3x + 1}{(x - 1)(x + 2)}$
B. $\dfrac{5x - 2}{(x - 1)(x + 2)}$
C. $\dfrac{3(x - 2)}{(x - 1)(x + 2)}$
D. $\dfrac{5x + 7}{(x - 1)(x + 2)}$
E. $\dfrac{5x - 1}{(x - 1)(x + 2)}$

Question 14

Solve the simultaneous equations

$$ax + by = c$$
$$dx + ey = f$$

A. $x = \dfrac{bf - ce}{ae - bd}, \quad y = \dfrac{cd - bf}{ae - bd}$

B. $x = \dfrac{ce + bf}{bd - ae}, \quad y = \dfrac{af - cd}{bd - ae}$

C. $x = \dfrac{ce - bf}{bd - ae}, \quad y = \dfrac{cd - af}{bd - ae}$

D. $x = \dfrac{bf - ce}{bd - ae}, \quad y = \dfrac{af - cd}{bd - ae}$

E. $x = \dfrac{ce - bf}{ae - bd}, \quad y = \dfrac{af - cd}{ae - bd}$

Question 15

If the following system of equations has infinitely many solutions, find the value of k.

$$x - 2y + 5z = 7$$
$$2x + 3y - 2z = -3$$
$$4x - y + 8z = k$$

A. 11   B. 12   C. 13   D. 14   E. 15

Question 16

Consider the following macroeconomic model:

$$C = 0.7Y + 100$$
$$G = 50$$
$$I = 30$$
$$X = 80$$
$$M = 0.1Y + 50$$

Determine the equilibrium level of national income.

A. 525   B. 675   C. 550   D. 450   E. 400

Question 17

Solve the following system of equations to find z.

$$3x + 5y - z = -12$$
$$2x - 3y + 2z = 22$$
$$x + 4y - 3z = -10$$

A. 4   B. 2   C. 1   D. -3 E. -5

Question 18

Describe what happens to a good when the price of a complementary good decreases.

A. The equilibrium price increases, the equilibrium quantity decreases and the demand curve shifts left.

B. The equilibrium price and quantity both decrease and the demand curve shifts left.

C. The equilibrium price and quantity both increase and the demand curve shifts right.

D. The equilibrium price decreases, the equilibrium quantity increases and the demand curve shifts left.

E. The equilibrium price increases, the equilibrium quantity decreases and the demand curve shifts right.

Examination questions

Question 1

Two take-away delivery services operate in the same town. EatMeNow charges a flat fee of $9 for collection and an additional $0.50 per mile. Deliver4U does not have any flat fee but charges $1.25 per mile.

(a) Draw graphs of the delivery charges against distance for both companies on the same diagram, with 0 to 20 miles plotted on the horizontal axis and 0 to $25 plotted on the vertical axis.

(b) Use your diagram to find the distance when both companies charge the same amount.

(c) If x and y denote distance and charge respectively, write down mathematical expressions for each of the charge functions plotted in part (a) and use algebra to confirm that your answer to part (b) is correct.

Question 2

The market demand and supply functions of a good are given by:

$$Q_D = 400 - 15P$$
$$Q_S = -50 + 10P$$

where Q_D, Q_S and P denote quantity demanded, quantity supplied and price, respectively.

(a) Work out the values of Q_D and Q_S when $P = 5, 10, 15, 20$ and 25, and hence draw accurate graphs of the demand and supply curves on the same diagram with Q plotted on the horizontal axis and P plotted on the vertical axis.

(b) Hence, or otherwise, find the equilibrium price and quantity.

(c) For what values of P is there excess demand?

(d) The government decides to impose a fixed tax of $5 on each good. Describe the effect, if any, on the demand and supply curves on your diagram and calculate the new equilibrium price and quantity.

Question 3

The market equilibrium price and quantity of a good may be found by solving the simultaneous equations:

$$Q + 3P = 48 \quad (1)$$
$$Q - 2P = 30 \quad (2)$$

(a) Explain which of these equations represents the supply curve and which represents the demand curve.

(b) If the demand curve were to be drawn with Q on the horizontal axis and P on the vertical axis, state the values of the slope and vertical intercept.

(c) Determine the equilibrium price and quantity algebraically.

Question 4

In a simple macroeconomic model, the value of national income Y may be found by solving the system:

$$
\begin{array}{ll}
G = 250 & \text{(government expenditure)} \\
T = 50 & \text{(taxation)} \\
I = 100 & \text{(planned investment)} \\
C = 0.75Y_d + 150 & \text{(consumption)}
\end{array}
$$

where disposable income $Y_d = Y - T$.

(a) Calculate the equilibrium level of national income.

(b) Calculate the total increase in government expenditure and investment needed to increase the equilibrium level of national income by 20.

Question 5

The output of a production process, Q, is given by the function

$$Q = \frac{KL}{K + 2L}$$

where K and L denote capital and labour.

(a) Calculate the output when the capital and labour are 40 and 30 units, respectively.

(b) Find the level of labour needed to produce 4 units of output when 10 units of capital are used.

(c) Transpose this formula to express K in terms of Q and L.

Question 6

The equations defining a simple model of the economy are:

$$
\begin{array}{l}
C = 0.75Y + 18 \\
I = 22
\end{array}
$$

where C, Y and I denote consumption, national income and planned investment, respectively.

Use this model to complete the following table of values and hence draw an accurate graph of $C + I$ plotted against Y on the interval $0 \leq Y \leq 200$.

Y	0	100	200
$C + I$			

By drawing a second line on the diagram, calculate the equilibrium level of national income.

Use your graph to explain what happens to the equilibrium level of national income when the marginal propensity to consume decreases with autonomous consumption fixed.

Question 7

The demand and supply functions for two interdependent commodities are given by:

$$Q_{D_1} = 120 - 2P_1 + P_2; \quad Q_{S_1} = -7 + 7P_1$$
$$Q_{D_2} = 168 + 3P_1 - 7P_2; \quad Q_{S_2} = -3 + 20P_2$$

(a) Explain whether these goods are complementary or substitutable.

(b) Determine the equilibrium price and quantity.

(c) The government decides to provide a subsidy of $4 on each unit of good 1 only. What effect does this subsidy have on the equilibrium prices of each good?

Question 8

(a) A baker has $3000 a month to spend on flour and sugar. Flour costs $3 per kilo and sugar costs $4 per kilo. If the baker buys f kg of flour and s kg sugar, write down an inequality for the budget constraint. Hence find the maximum amount of flour that could be bought if the baker orders 270 kg of sugar.

(b) The demand function of a good is given by $P = \dfrac{36}{2Q + 5}$

   (i) Find P when $Q = 3.5$

   (ii) Find Q when $P = 2.4$

   (iii) Rearrange this formula to express Q in terms of P.

(c) Write down a simplified expression for the savings function given that the consumption function is $C = \dfrac{Y^2 + 100}{Y + 2}$.

Question 9

(a) Use the elimination method to solve the following system of equations expressing x and y in terms of parameters m and n.

$$2x + 6y = 1$$
$$3x + my = n$$

For what value of m does this system fail to possess a unique solution?

What can you deduce about the solution when m takes this particular value?

Distinguish between the case when (i) $n = 1.5$ (ii) $n \neq 1.5$.

(b) The equilibrium prices of three related goods satisfy the simultaneous equations

$$5P_1 - 3P_2 = 39$$
$$2P_1 + 4P_2 - 3P_3 = 28$$
$$3P_2 + P_3 = 29$$

Use the elimination method to find P_1, P_2 and P_3.

Question 10

Determine the equilibrium income Y and interest rate r, given the following information about the commodity market:

$$C = 0.6Y + 60$$
$$I = -40r + 1300$$

where C and I denote consumption and planned investment, respectively, and the following information about the money market:

$$M_S = 600$$
$$L_1 = 0.2Y$$
$$L_2 = -30r + 40$$

where M_S, L_1 and L_2 denote money supply, transaction-precautionary demand for money and speculative demand for money, respectively.

The marginal propensity to consume decreases. By producing a rough sketch of the IS and LM curves on the same diagram, explain whether the equilibrium values of Y and r will increase, decrease or stay the same.

CHAPTER 2
Non-linear Equations

The main aim of this chapter is to describe the mathematics of non-linear equations. The approach is similar to that of Chapter 1. There are four sections. Section 2.1 should be read before Section 2.2, and Section 2.3 should be read before Section 2.4.

The first section investigates the simplest non-linear equation, known as a quadratic. A quadratic equation can easily be solved either by factorising it as the product of two linear factors or by using a special formula. You are also shown how to sketch the graphs of quadratic functions. The techniques are illustrated by finding the equilibrium price and quantity for quadratic supply and demand functions.

Section 2.2 introduces additional functions in microeconomics, including revenue and profit. There is very little new material in this section. It mainly consists of applying the ideas of Section 2.1 to sketch graphs of quadratic revenue and profit functions and to find their maximum values.

Finally, the topic of algebra, which we started in Chapter 1, is completed by investigating the rules of indices and logarithms. The basic concepts are covered in Section 2.3. The notation and rules of indices are extremely important and are used frequently in subsequent chapters. Section 2.4 focuses on two specific functions, namely the exponential and natural logarithm functions. If you run into difficulty, or are short of time, then this section could be omitted for the time being, particularly if you do not intend to study the next chapter on the mathematics of finance.

SECTION 2.1
Quadratic functions

Objectives

At the end of this section you should be able to:

- Solve a quadratic equation using 'the formula'.
- Solve a quadratic equation given its factorisation.
- Sketch the graph of a quadratic function using a table of function values.
- Sketch the graph of a quadratic function by finding the coordinates of the intercepts.
- Solve quadratic inequalities using graphs.
- Solve inequalities using sign diagrams.
- Determine equilibrium price and quantity given a pair of quadratic demand and supply functions.

The first chapter considered the topic of linear mathematics. In particular, we described how to sketch the graph of a linear function and how to solve a linear equation (or system of simultaneous linear equations). It was also pointed out that not all economic functions are of this simple form. In assuming that the demand and supply graphs are straight lines, we are certainly making the mathematical analysis easy, but we may well be sacrificing realism. It may be that the demand and supply graphs are curved and, in these circumstances, it is essential to model them using more complicated functions. The simplest non-linear function is known as a **quadratic function** and takes the form

$$f(x) = ax^2 + bx + c$$

for some parameters a, b and c. (In fact, even if the demand function is linear, functions derived from it, such as total revenue and profit, turn out to be quadratic. We investigate these functions in the next section.) For the moment we concentrate on the mathematics of quadratics and show how to sketch graphs of quadratic functions and how to solve quadratic equations.

Consider the elementary equation

$$x^2 - 9 = 0$$

x^2 is an abbreviation for $x \times x$

It is easy to see that the expression on the left-hand side is a special case of the above with $a = 1$, $b = 0$ and $c = -9$. To solve this equation, we add 9 to both sides to get

$$x^2 = 9$$

so we need to find a number, x, which when multiplied by itself produces the value 9. A moment's thought should convince you that there are exactly two numbers that work, namely 3 and -3, because

$$3 \times 3 = 9 \quad \text{and} \quad (-3) \times (-3) = 9$$

These two solutions are called the **square roots** of 9. The symbol $\sqrt{}$ is reserved for the positive square root, so in this notation the solutions are $\sqrt{9}$ and $-\sqrt{9}$. These are usually combined and written as $\pm\sqrt{9}$. The equation

$$x^2 - 9 = 0$$

is trivial to solve because the number 9 has obvious square roots. In general, it is necessary to use a calculator to evaluate square roots. For example, the equation

$$x^2 - 2 = 0$$

can be written as

$$x^2 = 2$$

and so has solutions $x = \pm\sqrt{2}$. My calculator gives 1.414 213 56 (correct to eight decimal places) for the square root of 2, so the above equation has solutions

1.414 213 56   and $-1.414\ 213\ 56$

Example

Solve the following quadratic equations:

(a) $5x^2 - 80 = 0$ **(b)** $x^2 + 64 = 0$ **(c)** $(x + 4)^2 = 81$

Solution

(a) $5x^2 - 80 = 0$

$$5x^2 = 80 \quad \text{(add 80 to both sides)}$$
$$x^2 = 16 \quad \text{(divide both sides by 5)}$$
$$x = \pm 4 \quad \text{(square root both sides)}$$

(b) $x^2 + 64 = 0$

$$x^2 = -64 \quad \text{(subtract 64 from both sides)}$$

This equation does not have a solution because you cannot square a real number and get a negative answer.

(c) $(x + 4)^2 = 81$

$$x + 4 = \pm 9 \quad \text{(square root both sides)}$$

The two solutions are obtained by taking the $+$ and $-$ signs separately. Taking the $+$ sign,

$$x + 4 = 9 \quad \text{so} \quad x = 9 - 4 = 5$$

Taking the $-$ sign,

$$x + 4 = -9 \quad \text{so} \quad x = -9 - 4 = -13$$

The two solutions are 5 and -13.

Practice Problem

1. Solve the following quadratic equations. (Round your solutions to two decimal places if necessary.)

    (a) $x^2 - 100 = 0$ (b) $2x^2 - 8 = 0$ (c) $x^2 - 3 = 0$ (d) $x^2 - 5.72 = 0$

    (e) $x^2 + 1 = 0$ (f) $3x^2 + 6.21 = 0$ (g) $x^2 = 0$

All of the equations considered in Practice Problem 1 are of the special form

$$ax^2 + c = 0$$

in which the coefficient of x is zero. To solve more general quadratic equations, we use a formula that enables the solutions to be calculated in a few lines of working. It can be shown that

$$ax^2 + bx + c = 0$$

has solutions

$$x = \frac{-b \pm \sqrt{(b^2 - 4ac)}}{2a}$$

The following example describes how to use this formula. It also illustrates the fact (which you have already discovered in Practice Problem 1) that a quadratic equation can have two solutions, one solution or no solutions.

Example

Solve the quadratic equations

(a) $2x^2 + 9x + 5 = 0$ (b) $x^2 - 4x + 4 = 0$ (c) $3x^2 - 5x + 6 = 0$

Solution

(a) For the equation

$$2x^2 + 9x + 5 = 0$$

we have $a = 2$, $b = 9$ and $c = 5$. Substituting these values into the formula

$$x = \frac{-b \pm \sqrt{(b^2 - 4ac)}}{2a}$$

gives

$$x = \frac{-9 \pm \sqrt{(9^2 - 4(2)(5))}}{2(2)}$$

$$= \frac{-9 \pm \sqrt{(81 - 40)}}{4}$$

$$= \frac{-9 \pm \sqrt{41}}{4}$$

The two solutions are obtained by taking the $+$ and $-$ signs separately: that is,

$$\frac{-9 + \sqrt{41}}{4} = -0.649 \quad \text{(correct to three decimal places)}$$

$$\frac{-9 - \sqrt{41}}{4} = -3.851 \quad \text{(correct to three decimal places)}$$

It is easy to check that these are solutions by substituting them into the original equation. For example, putting $x = -0.649$ into

$$2x^2 + 9x + 5$$

gives

$$2(-0.649)^2 + 9(-0.649) + 5 = 0.001\ 402$$

which is close to zero, as required. We cannot expect to produce an exact value of zero because we rounded $\sqrt{41}$ to three decimal places. You might like to check for yourself that -3.851 is also a solution.

(b) For the equation

$$x^2 - 4x + 4 = 0$$

we have $a = 1$, $b = -4$ and $c = 4$. Substituting these values into the formula

$$x = \frac{-b \pm \sqrt{(b^2 - 4ac)}}{2a}$$

gives

$$x = \frac{-(-4) \pm \sqrt{((-4)^2 - 4(1)(4))}}{2(1)}$$

$$= \frac{4 \pm \sqrt{(16 - 16)}}{2}$$

$$= \frac{4 \pm \sqrt{0}}{2}$$

$$= \frac{4 \pm 0}{2}$$

Clearly we get the same answer irrespective of whether we take the $+$ or the $-$ sign here. In other words, this equation has only one solution, $x = 2$. As a check, substitution of $x = 2$ into the original equation gives

$$(2)^2 - 4(2) + 4 = 0$$

(c) For the equation

$$3x^2 - 5x + 6 = 0$$

we have $a = 3$, $b = -5$ and $c = 6$. Substituting these values into the formula

$$x = \frac{-b \pm \sqrt{(b^2 - 4ac)}}{2a}$$

gives

$$x = \frac{-(-5) \pm \sqrt{((-5)^2 - 4(3)(6))}}{2(3)}$$

$$= \frac{5 \pm \sqrt{(25 - 72)}}{6}$$

$$= \frac{5 \pm \sqrt{(-47)}}{6}$$

The number under the square root sign is negative and, as you discovered in Practice Problem 1, it is impossible to find the square root of a negative number. We conclude that the quadratic equation

$$3x^2 - 5x + 6 = 0$$

has no solutions.

This example demonstrates the three cases that can occur when solving quadratic equations. The precise number of solutions that an equation can have depends on whether the number under the square root sign is positive, zero or negative. The number $b^2 - 4ac$ is called the **discriminant** because the sign of this number discriminates between the three cases that can occur.

- If $b^2 - 4ac > 0$, then there are two solutions:

$$x = \frac{-b + \sqrt{(b^2 - 4ac)}}{2a} \quad \text{and} \quad x = \frac{-b - \sqrt{(b^2 - 4ac)}}{2a}$$

- If $b^2 - 4ac = 0$, then there is one solution:

$$x = \frac{-b \pm \sqrt{0}}{2a} = \frac{-b}{2a}$$

- If $b^2 - 4ac < 0$, then there are no solutions because $\sqrt{(b^2 - 4ac)}$ does not exist.

Practice Problem

2. Solve the following quadratic equations (where possible):

(a) $2x^2 - 19x - 10 = 0$ (b) $4x^2 + 12x + 9 = 0$

(c) $x^2 + x + 1 = 0$ (d) $x^2 - 3x + 10 = 2x + 4$

The following example demonstrates an interesting application in business.

Example

A company sells packs of printer ink cartridges for \$24. If a customer orders more than 100 packs, the company is prepared to reduce the unit price by 4 cents for each pack bought above 100 up to a maximum of 300 in a single order.

(a) How much does it cost to buy 130 packs?

(b) If the cost is \$5324, how many packs are ordered?

Solution

(a) The first 100 packs cost \$24 each, so total cost for these is $100 \times 24 = \$2400$.

The unit cost of the remaining 30 packs is $24 - 0.04 \times 30 = \$22.80$, so the total cost of the extra 30 packs is $30 \times 22.80 = \$684$. The cost of the complete order is \$3084.

(b) The total cost of the packs bought in excess of 100 is $5324 - 2400 = \$2924$.

If x denotes the number of packs above 100, then the unit price of each of these is $24 - 0.04x$, giving a total cost of $(24 - 0.04x)x = 24x - 0.04x^2$.

Hence

$$24x - 0.04x^2 = 2924$$

which rearranges as $0.04x^2 - 24x + 2924 = 0$.

This quadratic equation can then be solved using the formula:

$$x = \frac{-(-24) \pm \sqrt{(-24)^2 - 4(0.04)(2924)}}{2(0.04)} = \frac{24 \pm \sqrt{576 - 467.84}}{0.08}$$

$$= \frac{24 + \sqrt{108.16}}{0.08} = \frac{24 \pm 10.4}{0.08}$$

giving two solutions, $x = 170$ and $x = 430$. The maximum permissible order is 300, so $x = 170$ giving a total order of $100 + 170 = 270$ packs of cartridges.

You may be familiar with another method for solving quadratic equations. This is based on the factorisation of a quadratic into the product of two linear factors. Section 1.1 described how to multiply out two brackets. One of the examples in that section showed that

$$(x + 1)(x + 2) = x^2 + 3x + 2$$

Consequently, the solutions of the equation

$$x^2 + 3x + 2 = 0$$

are the same as those of

$$(x + 1)(x + 2) = 0$$

Now the only way that two numbers can be multiplied together to produce a value of zero is when (at least) one of the numbers is zero.

> if $ab = 0$, then either $a = 0$ or $b = 0$ (or both)

It follows that either

$$x + 1 = 0 \quad \text{with solution} \quad x = -1$$

or

$$x + 2 = 0 \quad \text{with solution} \quad x = -2$$

The quadratic equation

$$x^2 + 3x + 2 = 0$$

therefore has two solutions, $x = -1$ and $x = -2$.

The difficulty with this approach is that it is impossible, except in very simple cases, to work out the factorisation from any given quadratic, so the preferred method is to use the formula. However, if you are lucky enough to be given the factorisation, or perhaps clever enough to spot the factorisation for yourself, then it does provide a viable alternative.

One important feature of linear functions is that their graphs are always straight lines. Obviously, the intercept and slope vary from function to function, but the shape is always the same. It turns out that a similar property holds for quadratic functions. Now, whenever you are asked to produce a graph of an unfamiliar function, it is often a good idea to tabulate the function, to plot these points on graph paper and to join them up with a smooth curve. The precise number of points to be taken depends on the function but, as a general rule, between 5 and 10 points usually produce a good picture.

A table of values for the simple square function

$$f(x) = x^2$$

is given by

x	-3	-2	-1	0	1	2	3
$f(x)$	9	4	1	0	1	4	9

The first row of the table gives a selection of 'incoming' numbers, x, while the second row shows the corresponding 'outgoing' numbers, y. Points with coordinates (x, y) are then plotted on graph paper to produce the curve shown in Figure 2.1. For convenience, different scales are used on the x and y axes.

Mathematicians call this curve a **parabola**, whereas economists refer to it as **U-shaped**. Notice that the graph is symmetric about the y axis with a minimum point at the origin; if a mirror is placed along the y axis, then the left-hand part is the image of the right-hand part.

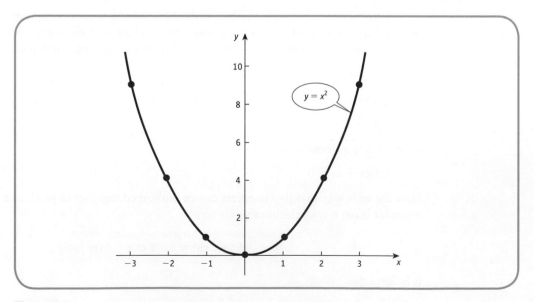

Figure 2.1

Advice

The following problem is designed to give you an opportunity to tabulate and sketch graphs of more general quadratic functions. Please remember that when you substitute numbers into a formula, you must use BIDMAS to decide the order of the operations. For example, in part (a) you need to substitute $x = -1$ into $4x^2 - 12x + 5$. You get

$4(-1)^2 - 12(-1) + 5$

$= 4 + 12 + 5$

$= 21$

Note also that when using a calculator, you must use brackets when squaring negative numbers. In this case a possible sequence of key presses might be

| 4 | (| (−) | 1 |) | x^2 | − | 12 | × | (−) | 1 | + | 5 | = |

Practice Problem

3. Complete the following tables of function values and hence sketch a graph of each quadratic function.

(a) $f(x) = 4x^2 - 12x + 5$

x	−1	0	1	2	3	4
$f(x)$						

(b) $f(x) = -x^2 + 6x - 9$

x	0	1	2	3	4	5	6
$f(x)$							

(c) $f(x) = -2x^2 + 4x - 6$

x	−2	−1	0	1	2	3	4
$f(x)$							

The results of Practice Problem 3 suggest that the graph of a quadratic is always parabolic. Furthermore, whenever the coefficient of x^2 is positive, the graph bends upwards and is a 'happy' parabola (U shape). A selection of U-shaped curves is shown in Figure 2.2. Similarly, when the coefficient of x^2 is negative, the graph bends downwards and is a 'sad' parabola (inverted U shape). A selection of inverted U-shaped curves is shown in Figure 2.3.

The task of sketching graphs from a table of function values is extremely tedious, particularly if only a rough sketch is required. It is usually more convenient just to determine a few key points on the curve. The obvious points to find are the intercepts with the coordinate axes, since these enable us to 'tether' the parabola down in the various positions shown in Figures 2.2 and 2.3. The curve crosses the y axis when $x = 0$. Evaluating the function

$f(x) = ax^2 + bx + c$

at $x = 0$ gives

$f(0) = a(0)^2 + b(0) + c = c$

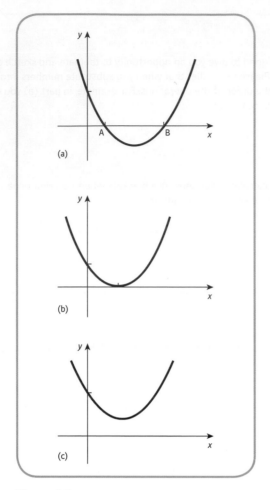

Figure 2.2

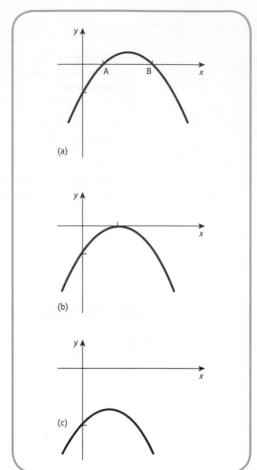

Figure 2.3

so the constant term determines where the curve cuts the vertical axis (as it did for linear functions). The curve crosses the x axis when $y = 0$ or, equivalently, when $f(x) = 0$, so we need to solve the quadratic equation

$$ax^2 + bx + c = 0$$

This can be done using 'the formula' and the solutions are the points where the graph cuts the horizontal axis. In general, a quadratic equation can have two, one or no solutions and these possibilities are illustrated in cases (a), (b) and (c), respectively, in Figures 2.2 and 2.3. In case (a) the curve crosses the x axis at A, turns round and crosses it again at B, so there are two solutions. In case (b) the curve turns round just as it touches the x axis, so there is only one solution. Finally, in case (c) the curve turns round before it has a chance to cross the x axis, so there are no solutions.

The strategy for sketching the graph of a quadratic function

$$f(x) = ax^2 + bx + c$$

may now be stated.

Step 1

Determine the basic shape. The graph has a U shape if $a > 0$, and an inverted U shape if $a < 0$.

Step 2

Determine the y intercept. This is obtained by substituting $x = 0$ into the function, which gives $y = c$.

Step 3

Determine the x intercepts (if any). These are obtained by solving the quadratic equation

$$ax^2 + bx + c = 0$$

This three-step strategy is illustrated in the following example.

Example

Give a rough sketch of the graph of the following quadratic function:

$$f(x) = -x^2 + 8x - 12$$

Solution

For the function

$$f(x) = -x^2 + 8x - 12$$

the strategy is as follows.

Step 1

The coefficient of x^2 is -1, which is negative, so the graph is a 'sad' parabola with an inverted U shape.

Step 2

The constant term is -12, so the graph crosses the vertical axis at $y = -12$.

Step 3

For the quadratic equation

$$-x^2 + 8x - 12 = 0$$

the formula gives

$$x = \frac{-8 \pm \sqrt{(8^2 - 4(-1)(-12))}}{2(-1)} = \frac{-8 \pm \sqrt{(64 - 48)}}{-2}$$

$$= \frac{-8 \pm \sqrt{16}}{-2} = \frac{-8 \pm 4}{-2}$$

so the graph crosses the horizontal axis at

$$x = \frac{-8 + 4}{-2} = 2$$

and

$$x = \frac{-8 - 4}{-2} = 6$$

The information obtained in steps 1–3 is sufficient to produce the sketch shown in Figure 2.4.

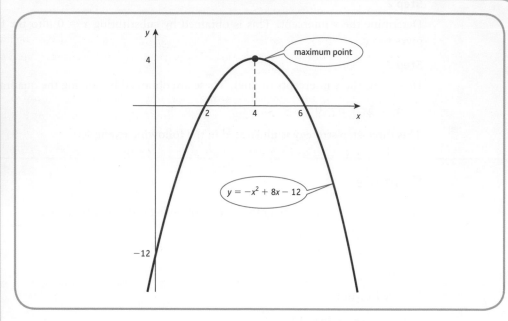

Figure 2.4

In fact, we can go even further in this case and locate the coordinates of the turning point – that is, the maximum point – on the curve. By symmetry, the x coordinate of this point occurs exactly halfway between $x = 2$ and $x = 6$: that is, at

$x = \tfrac{1}{2}(2 + 6) = 4$

The corresponding y coordinate is found by substituting $x = 4$ into the function to get

$f(4) = -(4)^2 + 8(4) - 12 = 4$

The maximum point on the curve therefore has coordinates $(4, 4)$.

Practice Problem

4. Use the three-step strategy to produce rough graphs of the following quadratic functions:

　(a) $f(x) = 2x^2 - 11x - 6$　　(b) $f(x) = x^2 - 6x + 9$

One useful by-product of our work on sketching graphs is that it enables us to solve quadratic inequalities with no extra effort.

Example

Solve the following quadratic inequalities:

(a) $-x^2 + 8x - 12 > 0$　　(b) $-x^2 + 8x - 12 \le 0$

Solution

The graph of the function $f(x) = -x^2 + 8x - 12$ has already been sketched in Figure 2.4.
   The parabola lies above the x axis (that is, the line $y = 0$) between 2 and 6 and is below the x axis outside these values.

(a) The quadratic function takes positive values when the graph is above the x axis, so the inequality has the solution $2 < x < 6$. The values of 2 and 6 must be excluded from the solution since we require the quadratic to be strictly greater than zero.

(b) The graph is on or below the x axis at or to the left of 2, and at or to the right of 6, so the complete solution is $x \leq 2$ and $x \geq 6$.

Practice Problem

5. Use your answers to Practice Problem 4 to write down the solution to each of the following quadratic inequalities:

(a) $2x^2 - 11x - 6 \leq 0$ **(b)** $x^2 - 6x + 9 > 0$

If the quadratic is in factorised form, an alternative method can be used to solve the associated inequality. This is based on a sign diagram. It avoids the need to draw a graph and the method has the added advantage that it can be used to solve other inequalities. We illustrate the technique in the following example.

Example

Use a sign diagram to solve the following inequalities:

(a) $(x - 2)(x + 3) \geq 0$ **(b)** $\dfrac{x}{x + 2} < 0$

Solution

(a) We know that the factor $x - 2$ is zero at $x = 2$. If x is smaller than 2, the factor is negative (for example, when $x = 1$, the factor takes the value $-1 < 0$), and when x is bigger than 2, the factor is positive (for example, when $x = 4$, the factor takes the value $2 > 0$). These results are illustrated on the number line:

The second factor, $x + 3$, takes the value zero at $x = -3$, is negative to the left of -3 and is positive to the right of -3. This is illustrated in the number line diagram:

The expression $(x - 2)(x + 3)$ is the product of the two factors. To the left of -3 the number lines show that both factors are negative, so their product is positive. Between -3 and 2 one factor is negative and the other positive, so their product is negative. Of course, if one factor is zero, the product is automatically zero, irrespective of the sign of the second factor. The complete sign diagram for the product is shown below.

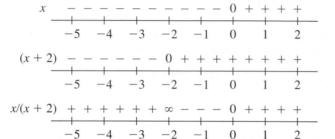

The diagram shows immediately that the inequality $(x - 2)(x + 3) \geq 0$ is satisfied by $x \leq -3, x \geq 2$.

(b) The factor $(x + 2)$ is zero at $x = -2$, negative to the left of $x = -2$, and positive to the right of this. The factor x is obviously zero at $x = 0$, negative to the left of $x = 0$, and positive to the right of this. The complete sign diagram is shown below:

The rules for dividing negative numbers are the same as those for multiplying, so the diagram is completed in the same way as before. The only exception occurs at $x = -2$ because we cannot divide by zero. This is indicated on the diagram by putting the symbol ∞ (infinity) at this position on the line. This diagram shows that the inequality

$$\frac{x}{x + 2} < 0$$ is satisfied by $-2 < x < 0$.

Practice Problem

6. Use a sign diagram to solve the following inequalities:

   (a) $(x - 1)(x - 4) \leq 0$ **(b)** $\dfrac{x - 1}{x + 2} \geq 0$

We conclude this section by solving a particular problem in microeconomics. In Section 1.5 the concept of market equilibrium was introduced, and in each of the problems the supply and demand functions were always given to be linear. The following example shows this to be an unnecessary restriction and indicates that it is almost as easy to manipulate quadratic supply and demand functions.

Example

Given the supply and demand functions

$$P = Q_S^2 + 14Q_S + 22$$
$$P = -Q_D^2 - 10Q_D + 150$$

calculate the equilibrium price and quantity.

Solution

In equilibrium, $Q_S = Q_D$, so if we denote this equilibrium quantity by Q, the supply and demand functions become

$$P = Q^2 + 14Q + 22$$
$$P = -Q^2 - 10Q + 150$$

Hence

$$Q^2 + 14Q + 22 = -Q^2 - 10Q + 150$$

since both sides are equal to P. Collecting like terms gives

$$2Q^2 + 24Q - 128 = 0$$

which is just a quadratic equation in the variable Q. Before using the formula to solve this it is a good idea to divide both sides by 2 to avoid large numbers. This gives

$$Q^2 + 12Q - 64 = 0$$

and so

$$Q = \frac{-12 \pm \sqrt{((12^2) - 4(1)(-64))}}{2(1)}$$
$$= \frac{-12 \pm \sqrt{(400)}}{2}$$
$$= \frac{-12 \pm 20}{2}$$

The quadratic equation has solutions $Q = -16$ and $Q = 4$. Now, the solution $Q = -16$ can obviously be ignored because a negative quantity does not make sense. The equilibrium quantity is therefore 4. The equilibrium price can be calculated by substituting this value into either the original supply or demand equation.

From the supply equation,

$$P = 4^2 + 14(4) + 22 = 94$$

As a check, the demand equation gives

$$P = -(4)^2 - 10(4) + 150 = 94 \quad \checkmark$$

You might be puzzled by the fact that we actually obtain two possible solutions, one of which does not make economic sense. The supply and demand curves are sketched in Figure 2.5. This shows that there are indeed two points of intersection, confirming the mathematical solution. However, in economics the quantity and price are both positive, so the functions are defined only in the top right-hand (that is, positive) quadrant. In this region there is just one point of intersection, at (4, 94).

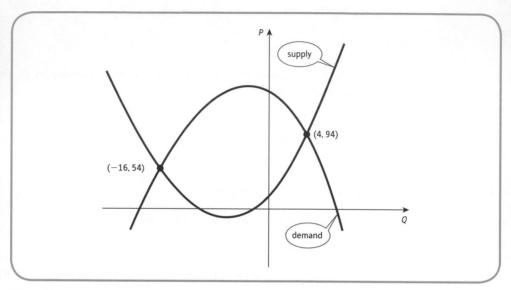

Figure 2.5

Practice Problem

7. Given the supply and demand functions

$$P = 2Q_S^2 + 10Q_S + 10$$
$$P = -Q_D^2 - 5Q_D + 52$$

calculate the equilibrium price and quantity.

Key Terms

Discriminant   The number $b^2 - 4ac$, which is used to indicate the number of solutions of the quadratic equation $ax^2 + bx + c = 0$.

Parabola   The shape of the graph of a quadratic function.

Quadratic function   A function of the form $f(x) = ax^2 + bx + c$ where $a \neq 0$.

Square root   A number that when multiplied by itself equals a given number; the solutions of the equation $x^2 = c$ which are written $\pm\sqrt{c}$.

U-shaped curve   A term used by economists to describe a curve, such as a parabola, which bends upwards, like the letter U.

Exercise 2.1

1. Solve the following quadratic equations:

   (a) $x^2 = 81$ **(b)** $x^2 = 36$ **(c)** $2x^2 = 8$
   (d) $(x - 1)^2 = 9$ **(e)** $(x + 5)^2 = 16$

2. Write down the solutions of the following equations:

   (a) $(x - 1)(x + 3) = 0$ **(b)** $(2x - 1)(x + 10) = 0$ **(c)** $x(x + 5) = 0$
   (d) $(3x + 5)(4x - 9) = 0$ **(e)** $(5 - 4x)(x - 5) = 0$

3. Use 'the formula' to solve the following quadratic equations. (Round your answers to two decimal places.)

   (a) $x^2 - 5x + 2 = 0$ **(b)** $2x^2 + 5x + 1 = 0$ **(c)** $-3x^2 + 7x + 2 = 0$
   (d) $x^2 - 3x - 1 = 0$ **(e)** $2x^2 + 8x + 8 = 0$ **(f)** $x^2 - 6x + 10 = 0$

4. Solve the equation $f(x) = 0$ for each of the following quadratic functions:

   (a) $f(x) = x^2 - 16$ **(b)** $f(x) = x(100 - x)$ **(c)** $f(x) = -x^2 + 22x - 85$
   (d) $f(x) = x^2 - 18x + 81$ **(e)** $f(x) = 2x^2 + 4x + 3$

5. Sketch the graphs of the quadratic functions given in Question 4.

6. Use the results of Question 5 to solve each of the following inequalities:

   (a) $x^2 - 16 \geq 0$ **(b)** $x(100 - x) > 0$ **(c)** $-x^2 + 22x - 85 \geq 0$
   (d) $x^2 - 18x + 81 \leq 0$ **(e)** $2x^2 + 4x + 3 > 0$

7. The production levels of coffee in Mexico, Q (in suitable units) depends on the average summer temperature, T (in °C).
   A statistical model of recent data shows that $Q = -0.046T^2 + 2.3T + 27.6$.

   (a) Complete the table of values and draw a graph of Q against T in the range, $23 \leq T \leq 30$.

T	23	24	25	26	27	28	29	30
Q								

   (b) Average summer temperatures over the last few decades have been about 25°C. However, some climate change models predict that this could rise by several degrees over the next 50 years. Use your graph to comment on the likely impact that this may have on coffee growers in Mexico.

8. Use a sign diagram to solve the following inequalities:

   (a) $x(x - 3) > 0$ **(b)** $(x - 1)(x + 1) \geq 0$ **(c)** $\dfrac{x + 4}{x - 2} < 0$

9. Given the quadratic supply and demand functions

   $$P = Q_S^2 + 2Q_S + 12$$
   $$P = -Q_D^2 - 4Q_D + 68$$

   determine the equilibrium price and quantity.

10. Given the supply and demand functions

$$P = Q_S^2 + 2Q_S + 7$$
$$P = -Q_D + 25$$

determine the equilibrium price and quantity.

11. A clothing supplier sells T-shirts to retailers for \$7 each. If a store agrees to buy more than 30, the supplier is willing to reduce the unit price by 3 cents for each shirt bought above 30, with a maximum single order of 100 shirts.

(a) How much does an order of 40 shirts cost?

(b) If the total cost of an order is \$504.25, how many T-shirts did the store buy altogether?

Exercise 2.1*

1. Solve the following quadratic equations:

(a) $x^2 = 169$ (b) $(x - 5)^2 = 64$ (c) $(2x - 7)^2 = 121$

2. Find the solutions (in terms of d) of the quadratic equation

$$x^2 + 6dx - 7d^2 = 0$$

3. Write down the solutions of the following equations:

(a) $(x - 3)(x + 8) = 0$ (b) $(3x - 2)(2x + 9) = 0$ (c) $x(4x - 3) = 0$

(d) $(6x - 1)^2 = 0$ (e) $(x - 2)(x + 1)(4 - x) = 0$

4. Solve the following quadratic equations, rounding your answers to two decimal places, if necessary:

(a) $x^2 - 15x + 56 = 0$ (b) $2x^2 - 5x + 1 = 0$ (c) $4x^2 - 36 = 0$

(d) $x^2 - 14x + 49 = 0$ (e) $3x^2 + 4x + 7 = 0$ (f) $x^2 - 13x + 200 = 16x + 10$

5. Solve the following inequalities:

(a) $x^2 \geq 64$ (b) $x^2 - 10x + 9 \leq 0$ (c) $2x^2 + 15x + 7 < 0$

(d) $-3x^2 + 2x + 5 \geq 0$ (e) $x^2 + 2x + 1 \leq 0$

6. One solution of the quadratic equation

$$x^2 - 8x + c = 0$$

is known to be $x = 2$. Find the second solution.

7. Find the value of k so that the equation

$$x^2 - 10x + 2k = 8x - k$$

has exactly one root.

8. Use a sign diagram to solve the following inequalities:

    (a) $(x + 3)(x - 4) \geq 0$ **(b)** $(2 - x)(x + 1) > 0$ **(c)** $(x - 1)(x - 2)(x - 3) \leq 0$

    (d) $\dfrac{(x - 2)}{(x - 3)(x - 5)} \geq 0$

9. A firm's monthly cost for paying cleaners' wages is \$47 250. Under a new pay deal each cleaner earns \$375 more each month. If the new pay deal goes through, the firm realises that it will need to reduce the number of cleaners by 3 if it is to cover its costs within the existing budget. What is the monthly salary of a cleaner before the pay rise?

10. Given the supply and demand functions

    $$P = Q_S^2 + 10Q_S + 30$$
    $$P = -Q_D^2 - 8Q_D + 200$$

    calculate the equilibrium price, correct to two decimal places.

11. A pottery can make B bowls and P plates in a week according to the relation

    $$2B^2 + 5B + 25P = 525$$

    (a) If it makes five bowls, how many plates can it make in a week?

    (b) What is the maximum number of bowls that it can produce in a week?

12. A city centre tour guide currently charges \$34 for a full day's tour. The average number of customers is 48. Market research suggests that for every \$1 increase in tour price, the guide can expect to lose two customers per tour.

    (a) Show that if the price increase is \$$x$, then the expected revenue from each tour is

    $$-2x^2 - 20x + 1632$$

    (b) The guide needs to ensure that the expected revenue is at least \$1440. By solving a quadratic inequality, find the range of prices that need to be charged.

    (c) What price should be charged to maximise expected revenue?

13. Given the supply and demand functions

    $$Q_S = (P + 8)\sqrt{P + 20}$$
    $$Q_D = \dfrac{460 - 12P - 3P^2}{\sqrt{P + 20}}$$

    calculate the equilibrium price and quantity.

SECTION 2.2
Revenue, cost and profit

Objectives

At the end of this section you should be able to:

- Sketch the graphs of the total revenue, total cost, average cost and profit functions.
- Find the level of output that maximises total revenue.
- Find the level of output that maximises profit.
- Find the break-even levels of output.

The main aim of this section is to investigate one particular function in economics, namely profit. By making reasonable simplifying assumptions, the profit function is shown to be quadratic and so the methods developed in Section 2.1 can be used to analyse its properties. We describe how to find the levels of output required for a firm to break even and to maximise profit. The **profit** function is denoted by the Greek letter π (pi, pronounced 'pie') and is defined to be the difference between total revenue, TR, and total cost, TC: that is,

$$\pi = \text{TR} - \text{TC}$$

This definition is entirely sensible because TR is the amount of money received by the firm from the sale of its goods, and TC is the amount of money that the firm has to spend to produce these goods. We begin by considering the total revenue and total cost functions in turn.

The **total revenue** received from the sale of Q goods at price P is given by

$$\text{TR} = PQ$$

For example, if the price of each good is $70 and the firm sells 300, then the revenue is

$$\$70 \times 300 = \$21\ 000$$

Given any particular demand function, expressing P in terms of Q, it is a simple matter to obtain a formula for TR solely in terms of Q. A graph of TR against Q can then be sketched.

Example

Given the demand function

$$P = 100 - 2Q$$

express TR as a function of Q and hence sketch its graph.

(a) For what values of Q is TR zero?

(b) What is the maximum value of TR?

Solution

Total revenue is defined by

$$\text{TR} = PQ$$

and, since $P = 100 - 2Q$, we have

$\qquad$ TR $= (100 - 2Q)Q = 100Q - 2Q^2$

This function is quadratic and so its graph can be sketched using the strategy described in Section 2.1.

Step 1

The coefficient of Q^2 is negative, so the graph has an inverted U shape.

Step 2

The constant term is zero, so the graph crosses the TR axis at the origin.

Step 3

To find where the curve crosses the horizontal axis, we could use 'the formula'. However, this is not necessary, since it follows immediately from the factorisation

$\qquad$ TR $= (100 - 2Q)Q$

that TR $= 0$ when either $100 - 2Q = 0$ or $Q = 0$. In other words, the quadratic equation has two solutions, $Q = 0$ and $Q = 50$.

$\qquad$ The total revenue curve is shown in Figure 2.6.

(a) From Figure 2.6, the total revenue is zero when $Q = 0$ and $Q = 50$.

(b) By symmetry, the parabola reaches its maximum halfway between 0 and 50: that is, at $Q = 25$. The corresponding total revenue is given by

$\qquad$ TR $= 100(25) - 2(25)^2 = 1250$

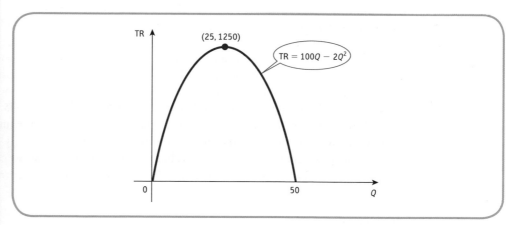

Figure 2.6

Practice Problem

1. Given the demand function

$\qquad$ $P = 1000 - Q$

express TR as a function of Q and hence sketch a graph of TR against Q. What value of Q maximises total revenue, and what is the corresponding price?

In general, given the linear demand function

$$P = aQ + b \ (a < 0, b > 0)$$

the total revenue function is

$$\begin{aligned} TR = PQ &= (aQ + b)Q \\ &= aQ^2 + bQ \end{aligned}$$

This function is quadratic in Q and, since $a < 0$, the TR curve has an inverted U shape. Moreover, since the constant term is zero, the curve always intersects the vertical axis at the origin. This fact should come as no surprise to you; if no goods are sold, the revenue must be zero.

We now turn our attention to the **total cost** function, TC, which relates the production costs to the level of output, Q. As the quantity produced rises, the corresponding cost also rises, so the TC function is increasing. However, in the short run, some of these costs are fixed. **Fixed costs**, FC, include the cost of land, equipment, rent and possibly skilled labour. Obviously, in the long run all costs are variable, but these particular costs take time to vary, so they can be thought of as fixed in the short run. **Variable costs**, on the other hand, vary with output and include the cost of raw materials, components, energy and unskilled labour. If VC denotes the variable cost per unit of output, then the total variable cost, TVC, in producing Q goods is given by

$$TVC = (VC)Q$$

The total cost is the sum of the contributions from the fixed and variable costs, so is given by

$$TC = FC + (VC)Q$$

Now, although this is an important economic function, it does not always convey the information necessary to compare individual firms. For example, suppose that an international car company operates two plants, one in the United States and one in Europe, and suppose that the total annual costs are known to be $200 million and $45 million, respectively. Which of these two plants is regarded as the more efficient? Unfortunately, unless we also know the total number of cars produced, it is impossible to make any judgement. The significant function here is not the total cost, but rather the average cost per car. If the US and European plants manufacture 80 000 and 15 000 cars, respectively, their corresponding average costs are

$$\frac{200\ 000\ 000}{80\ 000} = 2500$$

and

$$\frac{45\ 000\ 000}{15\ 000} = 3000$$

On the basis of these figures, the US plant appears to be the more efficient. In practice, other factors would need to be taken into account before deciding to increase or decrease the scale of operation in either country.

In general, the **average cost** function, AC, is obtained by dividing the total cost by output, so that

$$AC = \frac{TC}{Q} = \frac{FC + (VC)Q}{Q}$$

$$= \frac{FC}{Q} + \frac{(VC)\cancel{Q}}{\cancel{Q}}$$

$$= \frac{FC}{Q} + VC$$

If the fixed costs FC = 1000 and variable costs per unit VC = 4, then the expressions for the total and average costs functions are

$$TC = 1000 + 4Q$$

and

$$AC = \frac{TC}{Q} = \frac{1000 + 4Q}{Q}$$

$$= \frac{1000}{Q} + 4$$

The graph of the total cost function is easily sketched. It is a straight line with intercept 1000 and slope 4. It is sketched in Figure 2.7. The average cost function is of a form that we have not met before, so we have no prior knowledge about its basic shape. Under these circumstances it is useful to tabulate the function. The tabulated values are then plotted on graph paper and a smooth curve obtained by joining the points together. One particular table of function values is

Q	100	250	500	1000	2000
AC	14	8	6	5	4.5

These values are readily checked. For instance, when $Q = 100$,

$$AC = \frac{1000}{100} + 4 = 10 + 4 = 14$$

A graph of the average cost function, based on this table, is sketched in Figure 2.8. This curve is known as a **rectangular hyperbola** and is sometimes referred to by economists as being **L-shaped**.

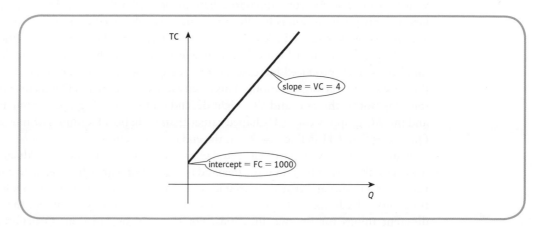

Figure 2.7

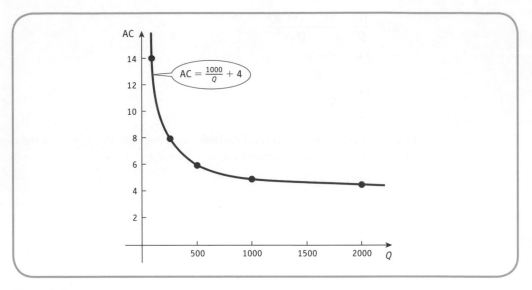

Figure 2.8

Practice Problem

2. Given that fixed costs are 100 and that variable costs are 2 per unit, express TC and AC as functions of Q. Hence sketch their graphs.

In general, whenever the variable cost, VC, is a constant, the total cost function,

$$TC = FC + (VC)Q$$

is linear. The intercept is FC and the slope is VC. For the average cost function

$$AC = \frac{FC}{Q} + VC$$

note that if Q is small, then FC/Q is large, so the graph bends sharply upwards as Q approaches zero. As Q increases, FC/Q decreases and eventually tails off to zero for large values of Q. The AC curve therefore flattens off and approaches VC as Q gets larger and larger. This phenomenon is hardly surprising, since the fixed costs are shared between more and more goods, so have little effect on AC for large Q. The graph of AC therefore has the basic L shape shown in Figure 2.9. This effect, in which the average cost decreases as the number of units produced increases, is one reason for economies of scale, which encourage the growth of large organisations. This discussion assumes that VC is a constant. In practice, this may not be the case, and VC might depend on Q. The TC graph is then no longer linear and the AC graph becomes U-shaped rather than L-shaped. Examples of this can be found in Questions 5 and 11 in Exercise 2.2 at the end of this section.

Figure 2.10 shows typical TR and TC graphs sketched on the same diagram. These are drawn on the assumption that the demand function is linear (which leads to a quadratic total revenue function) and that the variable costs are constant (which leads to a linear total cost function). The horizontal axis represents quantity, Q. Strictly speaking, the label Q means different things for the two functions. For the revenue function, Q denotes the quantity of goods actually sold, whereas for the cost function, it denotes the quantity produced. In

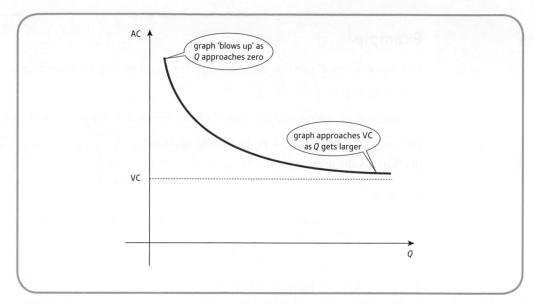

Figure 2.9

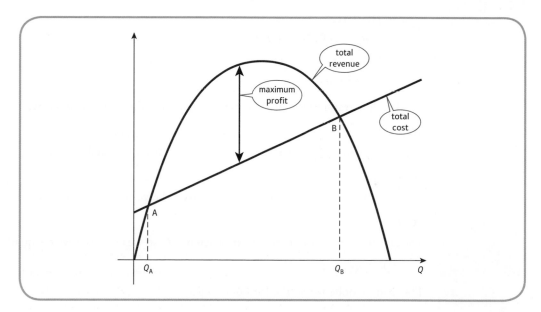

Figure 2.10

sketching both graphs on the same diagram, we are implicitly assuming that these two values are the same and that the firm sells all of the goods that it produces.

The two curves intersect at precisely two points, A and B, corresponding to output levels Q_A and Q_B. At these points the cost and revenue are equal and the firm breaks even. If $Q < Q_A$ or $Q > Q_B$, then the TC curve lies above that of TR, so cost exceeds revenue. For these levels of output the firm makes a loss. If $Q_A < Q < Q_B$, then revenue exceeds cost and the firm makes a profit which is equal to the vertical distance between the revenue and cost curves. The maximum profit occurs where the gap between them is largest. The easiest way of calculating maximum profit is to obtain a formula for profit directly in terms of Q using the defining equation

$$\pi = \text{TR} - \text{TC}$$

Example

If fixed costs are 4, variable costs per unit are 1 and the demand function is

$$P = 10 - 2Q$$

obtain an expression for π in terms of Q and hence sketch a graph of π against Q.

(a) For what values of Q does the firm break even?

(b) What is the maximum profit?

Solution

We begin by obtaining expressions for the total cost and total revenue. For this problem, FC = 4 and VC = 1, so

$$TC = FC + (VC)Q = 4 + Q$$

The given demand function is $P = 10 - 2Q$
so $TR = PQ = (10 - 2Q)Q = 10Q - 2Q^2$
Hence the profit is given by

$$
\begin{aligned}
\pi &= TR - TC \\
&= (10Q - 2Q^2) - (4 + Q) \\
&= 10Q - 2Q^2 - 4 - Q \\
&= -2Q^2 + 9Q - 4
\end{aligned}
$$

To sketch a graph of the profit function we follow the strategy described in Section 2.1.

Step 1

The coefficient of Q^2 is negative, so the graph has an inverted U shape.

Step 2

The constant term is -4, so the graph crosses the vertical axis when $\pi = -4$.

Step 3

The graph crosses the horizontal axis when $\pi = 0$, so we need to solve the quadratic equation

$$-2Q^2 + 9Q - 4 = 0$$

This can be done using 'the formula' to get

$$Q = \frac{-9 \pm \sqrt{81 - 32}}{2(-2)} = \frac{-9 \pm 7}{-4}$$

so $Q = 0.5$ and $Q = 4$.
   The profit curve is sketched in Figure 2.11.

(a) From Figure 2.11 we see that profit is zero when $Q = 0.5$ and $Q = 4$.

(b) By symmetry, the parabola reaches its maximum halfway between 0.5 and 4: that is, at

$$Q = \tfrac{1}{2}(0.5 + 4) = 2.25$$

   The corresponding profit is given by

$$\pi = -2(2.25)^2 + 9(2.25) - 4 = 6.125$$

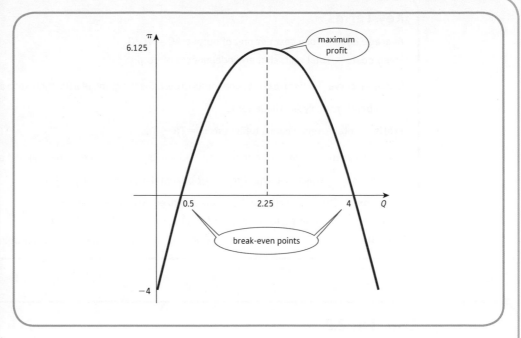

Figure 2.11

Advice

It is important to notice the use of brackets in the previous derivation of π. A common student mistake is to forget to include the brackets and just to write down

$$\pi = TR - TC$$
$$= 10Q - 2Q^2 - 4 + Q$$
$$= -2Q^2 + 11Q - 4$$

This cannot be right, since the whole of the total cost needs to be subtracted from the total revenue, not just the fixed costs. You might be surprised to learn that many economics students make this sort of blunder, particularly under examination conditions.

Practice Problem

3. If fixed costs are 25, variable costs per unit are 2 and the demand function is

$$P = 20 - Q$$

obtain an expression for π in terms of Q and hence sketch its graph.

(a) Find the levels of output which give a profit of 31.

(b) Find the maximum profit and the value of Q at which it is achieved.

Key Terms

Average cost Total cost per unit of output: AC = TC/Q.

Fixed costs Total costs that are independent of output.

L-shaped curve A term used by economists to describe the graph of a function, such as $f(x) = a + \dfrac{b}{x}$, which bends roughly like the letter L.

Profit Total revenue minus total cost: $\pi = $ TR $-$ TC.

Rectangular hyperbola A term used by mathematicians to describe the graph of a function, such as $f(x) = a + \dfrac{b}{x}$, which is a hyperbola with horizontal and vertical asymptotes.

Total cost The sum of the total variable and fixed costs: TC = TVC + FC.

Total revenue A firm's total earnings from the sales of a good: TR = PQ.

Variable costs Total costs that change according to the amount of output produced.

Exercise 2.2

1. **(a)** If the demand function of a good is given by

    $P = 80 - 3Q$

    find the price when $Q = 10$, and deduce the total revenue.

    (b) If fixed costs are 100 and variable costs are 5 per unit, find the total cost when $Q = 10$.

    (c) Use your answers to parts (a) and (b) to work out the corresponding profit.

2. Given the following demand functions, express TR as a function of Q and hence sketch the graphs of TR against Q:

    (a) $P = 4$ **(b)** $P = 7/Q$ **(c)** $P = 10 - 4Q$

3. Given the following total revenue functions, find the corresponding demand functions:

    (a) TR $= 50Q - 4Q^2$ **(b)** TR $= 10$

4. Given that fixed costs are 500 and that variable costs are 10 per unit, express TC and AC as functions of Q. Hence sketch their graphs.

5. Given that fixed costs are 1 and that variable costs are $Q + 1$ per unit, express TC and AC as functions of Q. Hence sketch their graphs.

6. The total cost, TC, of producing 100 units of a good is 600 and the total cost of producing 150 units is 850. Assuming that the total cost function is linear, find an expression for TC in terms of Q, the number of units produced.

7. The total cost of producing 500 items a day in a factory is \$40 000, which includes a fixed cost of \$2000.

    (a) Work out the variable cost per item.

    (b) Work out the total cost of producing 600 items a day.

8. A taxi firm charges a fixed cost of $10 together with a variable cost of $3 per mile.

   (a) Work out the average cost per mile for a journey of 4 miles.

   (b) Work out the minimum distance travelled if the average cost per mile is to be less than $3.25.

9. Find an expression for the profit function given the demand function

   $$2Q + P = 25$$

   and the average cost function

   $$AC = \frac{32}{Q} + 5$$

   Find the values of Q for which the firm

   (a) breaks even;

   (b) makes a loss of 432 units;

   (c) maximises profit.

10. Sketch, on the same diagram, graphs of the total revenue and total cost functions,

    $$TR = -2Q^2 + 14Q$$
    $$TC = 2Q + 10$$

    (1) Use your graphs to estimate the values of Q for which the firm

    (a) breaks even;

    (b) maximises profit.

    (2) Confirm your answers to part (1) using algebra.

11. The demand function for a firm's product is given by $P = 60 - Q$.
    Fixed costs are 100, and the variable costs per good are $Q + 6$.

    (a) Write down an expression for total revenue, TR, in terms of Q and sketch a graph of TR against Q, indicating clearly the intercepts with the coordinate axes.

    (b) Write down an expression for total costs, TC, in terms of Q and deduce that the average cost function is given by

    $$AC = Q + 6 + \frac{100}{Q}$$

    Copy and complete the following table of function values:

Q	2	5	10	15	20
AC	58				

    Draw an accurate graph of AC against Q and state the value of Q that minimises average cost.

    (c) Show that the profit function is given by

    $$\pi = 2(2 - Q)(Q - 25)$$

    State the values of Q for which the firm breaks even, and determine the maximum profit.

Exercise 2.2*

1. If fixed costs are 30, variable costs per unit are $Q + 3$ and the demand function is

   $$P + 2Q = 50$$

   show that the associated profit function is

   $$\pi = -3Q^2 + 47Q - 30.$$

   Find the break-even values of Q and deduce the maximum profit.

2. The profit function of a firm is of the form

   $$\pi = aQ^2 + bQ + c$$

   If it is known that $\pi = 9$, 34 and 19 when $Q = 1$, 2 and 3, respectively, write down a set of three simultaneous equations for the three unknowns, a, b and c. Solve this system to find a, b and c. Hence find the profit when $Q = 4$.

3. A firm's average cost function is given by

   $$AC = \frac{800}{Q} + 2Q + 18$$

   (a) Find, to the nearest whole number, the value of Q at the lowest point on the graph of AC plotted against Q, in the interval, $0 \le Q \le 30$.

   (b) State the value of the fixed costs.

4. If the demand equation is $aP + bQ = c$, fixed costs are d and variable costs are e per unit, find expressions, in terms of Q, for each of the following economic functions:

   (a) total revenue   (b) total cost   (c) average cost   (d) profit

5. The Ennerdale Bank charges its customers for every withdrawal: $0.50 for each online transfer and $0.25 for each cash machine withdrawal. The North Borsetshire Bank charges customers a fixed annual charge of $15 and each debit (online or machine) costs a further $0.30. You may assume that there are no other withdrawals, that the account never goes overdrawn and that any interest due is negligible.

   (a) The proportion of withdrawals that are via online transfers is a and the total number of withdrawals made during the year is N. If the cost of operating the two accounts is the same, show that

   $$a = \frac{1}{5} + \frac{60}{N}$$

   Sketch the graph of this relationship.

   (b) What advice can you offer new customers if at least 60% of the customer's annual withdrawals are from cash machines?

SECTION 2.3
Indices and logarithms

Objectives

At the end of this section you should be able to:

- Evaluate b^n in the case when n is positive, negative, a whole number or a fraction.
- Simplify algebraic expressions using the rules of indices.
- Investigate the returns to scale of a production function.
- Evaluate logarithms in simple cases.
- Use the rules of logarithms to solve equations in which the unknown occurs as a power.

Advice

This section is quite long, with some important ideas. If you are comfortable using the rules of indices and already know what a logarithm is, you should be able to read through the material in one sitting, concentrating on the applications. However, if your current understanding is hazy (or non-existent), you should consider studying this topic on separate occasions. To help with this, the material in this section has been split into the following convenient sub-sections:

- index notation;
- rules of indices;
- logarithms;
- summary.

2.3.1 Index notation

We have already used b^2 as an abbreviation for $b \times b$. In this section we extend the notation to b^n for any value of n, positive, negative, whole number or fraction. In general, if

$$M = b^n$$

we say that b^n is the **exponential form** of M to base b. The number n is then referred to as the **index, power** or **exponent**. An obvious way of extending

$$b^2 = b \times b$$

to other positive whole number powers, n, is to define

$$b^3 = b \times b \times b$$
$$b^4 = b \times b \times b \times b$$

and, in general,

a total of n bs multiplied together

$$b^n = b \times b \times b \times b \times \ldots \times b$$

To include the case of negative powers, consider the following table of values of 2^n:

2^{-3}	2^{-2}	2^{-1}	2^0	2^1	2^2	2^3	2^4
?	?	?	?	2	4	8	16

To work from left to right along the completed part of the table, all you have to do is to multiply each number by 2. Equivalently, if you work from right to left, you simply divide by 2. It makes sense to continue this pattern beyond $2^1 = 2$. Dividing this by 2 gives

$$2^0 = 2 \div 2 = 1$$

and dividing again by 2 gives

$$2^{-1} = 1 \div 2 = {}^1/_2$$

and so on. The completed table is then

2^{-3}	2^{-2}	2^{-1}	2^0	2^1	2^2	2^3	2^4
$\frac{1}{8}$	$\frac{1}{4}$	$\frac{1}{2}$	1	2	4	8	16

Notice that

$$2^{-1} = \frac{1}{2} = \frac{1}{2^1}$$

$$2^{-2} = \frac{1}{4} = \frac{1}{2^2}$$

$$2^{-3} = \frac{1}{8} = \frac{1}{2^3}$$

In other words, negative powers are evaluated by taking the reciprocal of the corresponding positive power. Motivated by this particular example, we define

$$b^0 = 1$$

and

$$b^{-n} = \frac{1}{b^n}$$

where n is any positive whole number.

Example

Evaluate

(a) 3^2　　(b) 4^3　　(c) 7^0　　(d) 5^1　　(e) 5^{-1}

(f) $(-2)^6$　(g) 3^{-4}　(h) $(-2)^{-3}$　(i) $(1.723)^0$

Solution

Using the definitions

$$b^n = b \times b \times b \times \ldots \times b$$

$$b^0 = 1$$

$$b^{-n} = \frac{1}{b^n}$$

we obtain

(a) $3^2 = 3 \times 3 = 9$

(b) $4^3 = 4 \times 4 \times 4 = 64$

(c) $7^0 = 1$

because any number raised to the power of zero equals 1.

(d) $5^1 = 5$

(e) $5^{-1} = \dfrac{1}{5^1} = \dfrac{1}{5}$

(f) $(-2)^6 = (-2) \times (-2) \times (-2) \times (-2) \times (-2) \times (-2) = 64$

where the answer is positive because there are an even number of minus signs.

(g) $3^{-4} = \dfrac{1}{3^4} = \dfrac{1}{3 \times 3 \times 3 \times 3} = \dfrac{1}{81}$

(h) $(-2)^{-3} = \dfrac{1}{(-2)^3} = \dfrac{1}{(-2) \times (-2) \times (-2)} = -\dfrac{1}{8}$

where the answer is negative because there are an odd number of minus signs.

(i) $(1.723)^0 = 1$

Practice Problem

1. **(1)** Without using a calculator, evaluate

    (a) 10^2 **(b)** 10^1 **(c)** 10^0 **(d)** 10^{-1} **(e)** 10^{-2} **(f)** $(-1)^{100}$

    (g) $(-1)^{99}$ **(h)** 7^{-3} **(i)** $(-9)^2$ **(j)** $(72\ 101)^1$ **(k)** $(2.718)^0$

    (2) Confirm your answer to part (1) using a calculator.

We handle fractional powers in two stages. We begin by defining b^m where m is a reciprocal such as $^1/_2$ or $^1/_8$ and then consider more general fractions such as $^3/_4$ or $^3/_8$ later. Assuming that n is a positive whole number, we define

$b^{1/n} = n$th root of b

By this we mean that $b^{1/n}$ is a number which, when raised to the power n, produces b. In symbols, if $c = b^{1/n}$ then $c^n = b$. Using this definition,

$$9^{1/2} = \text{square root of } 9 \quad = 3 \quad (\text{because } 3^2 = 9)$$
$$8^{1/3} = \text{cube root of } 8 \quad = 2 \quad (\text{because } 2^3 = 8)$$
$$625^{1/4} = \text{fourth root of } 625 \ = 5 \quad (\text{because } 5^4 = 625)$$

Of course, the nth root of a number may not exist. There is no number c satisfying $c^2 = -4$, for example, and so $(-4)^{1/2}$ is not defined. It is also possible for some numbers to have more than one nth root. For example, there are two values of c which satisfy $c^4 = 16$, namely $c = 2$ and $c = -2$. In these circumstances it is standard practice to take the positive root, so $16^{1/4} = 2$.

We now turn our attention to the case of b^m, where m is a general fraction of the form p/q for some whole numbers p and q. What interpretation are we going to put on a number such as $16^{3/4}$? To be consistent with our previous definitions, the numerator, 3, can be thought of as an instruction for us to raise 16 to the power of 3, and the denominator tells us to take the fourth root. In fact, it is immaterial in which order these two operations are carried out. If we begin by cubing 16, we get

$$16^3 = 16 \times 16 \times 16 = 4096$$

and taking the fourth root of this gives

$$16^{3/4} = (4096)^{1/4} = 8 \quad \text{(because } 8^4 = 4096\text{)}$$

On the other hand, taking the fourth root first gives

$$16^{1/4} = 2 \quad \text{(because } 2^4 = 16\text{)}$$

and cubing this gives

$$16^{3/4} = 2^3 = 8$$

which is the same answer as before. We therefore see that

$$(16^3)^{1/4} = (16^{1/4})^3$$

This result holds for any base b and fraction p/q (provided that q is positive), so we define

$$b^{p/q} = (b^p)^{1/q} = (b^{1/q})^p$$

To evaluate $25^{-3/2}$ it is easier to find the square root first before raising the number to the power of -3, so

$$25^{-3/2} = (25^{1/2})^{-3} = 5^{-3} = \frac{1}{5^3} = \frac{1}{125}$$

For this particular exponential form we have actually carried out three distinct operations. The minus sign tells us to reciprocate, the fraction, $^1/_2$, tells us to take the square root and the 3 tells us to cube. You might like to check for yourself that you get the same answer irrespective of the order in which these three operations are performed.

Advice

Given that we are allowed to perform these operations in any order, it is usually easier to find the qth root first to avoid having to spot roots of large numbers.

Practice Problem

2. **(1)** Without using your calculator, evaluate

   (a) $16^{1/2}$ **(b)** $27^{1/3}$ **(c)** $4^{5/2}$ **(d)** $8^{-2/3}$ **(e)** $1^{-17/25}$

   (2) Confirm your answer to part (1) using a calculator.

2.3.2 Rules of indices

There are two reasons why the exponential form is useful. First, it is a convenient shorthand for what otherwise might be a very lengthy number. The exponential form

$$9^8$$

is much easier to write down than either of the equivalent forms

$$9 \times 9 \times 9 \times 9 \times 9 \times 9 \times 9 \times 9$$

or

$$43\ 046\ 721$$

Secondly, there are four basic rules of indices which facilitate the manipulation of such numbers. The four rules may be stated as follows:

> **Rule 1** $b^m \times b^n = b^{m+n}$
>
> **Rule 2** $b^m \div b^n = b^{m-n}$
>
> **Rule 3** $(b^m)^n = b^{mn}$
>
> **Rule 4** $(ab)^n = a^n b^n$

It is certainly not our intention to provide mathematical proofs in this text. However, it might help you to remember these rules if we give you a justification based on some simple examples. We consider each rule in turn.

Rule 1

Suppose we want to multiply together 2^2 and 2^5. Now, $2^2 = 2 \times 2$ and $2^5 = 2 \times 2 \times 2 \times 2 \times 2$, so

$$2^2 \times 2^5 = (2 \times 2) \times (2 \times 2 \times 2 \times 2 \times 2)$$

Notice that we are multiplying together a total of seven 2s and so by definition this is just 2^7: that is,

$$2^2 \times 2^5 = 2^7 = 2^{2+5}$$

This confirms rule 1, which tells you that if you multiply two numbers, all you have to do is to add the indices.

Rule 2

Suppose we want to divide 2^2 by 2^5. This gives

$$\frac{\cancel{2} \times \cancel{2}}{2 \times 2 \times 2 \times \cancel{2} \times \cancel{2}} = \frac{1}{2 \times 2 \times 2} = \frac{1}{2^3}$$

Now, by definition, reciprocals are denoted by negative indices, so this is just 2^{-3}; that is,

$$2^2 \div 2^5 = 2^{-3} = 2^{2-5}$$

This confirms rule 2, which tells you that if you divide two numbers, all you have to do is to subtract the indices.

Rule 3

Suppose we want to raise 10^2 to the power 3. By definition, for any number b,

$$b^3 = b \times b \times b$$

so replacing b by 10^2, we have

$$(10^2)^3 = 10^2 \times 10^2 \times 10^2 = (10 \times 10) \times (10 \times 10) \times (10 \times 10) = 10^6$$

because there are six 10s multiplied together: that is,

$$(10^2)^3 = 10^6 = 10^{2 \times 3}$$

This confirms rule 3, which tells you that if you take a 'power of a power', all you have to do is to multiply the indices.

Rule 4

Suppose we want to raise 2×3 to the power 4. By definition,

$$b^4 = b \times b \times b \times b$$

so replacing b by 2×3 gives

$$(2 \times 3)^4 = (2 \times 3) \times (2 \times 3) \times (2 \times 3) \times (2 \times 3)$$

and, because it does not matter in which order numbers are multiplied, this can be written as

$$(2 \times 2 \times 2 \times 2) \times (3 \times 3 \times 3 \times 3)$$

that is,

$$(2 \times 3)^4 = 2^4 \times 3^4$$

This confirms rule 4, which tells you that if you take the power of a product of two numbers, all you have to do is to take the power of each number separately and multiply.

A word of warning is in order regarding these laws. Notice that in rules 1 and 2 the bases of the numbers involved are the same. These rules do not apply if the bases are different. For example, rule 1 gives no information about

$$2^4 \times 3^5$$

Similarly, please notice that in rule 4 the numbers a and b are multiplied together. For some strange reason, some business and economics students seem to think that rule 4 also applies to addition, so that

$$(a + b)^n = a^n + b^n \qquad \text{This statement is NOT true}$$

It would make algebraic manipulation a whole lot easier if it were true, but it is definitely false! If you need convincing of this, note, for example, that

$$(1 + 2)^3 = 3^3 = 27$$

which is not the same as

$$1^3 + 2^3 = 1 + 8 = 9$$

One variation of rule 4 which is true is

$$\left(\frac{a}{b}\right)^n = \frac{a^n}{b^n} \ (b \neq 0)$$

This is all right because division (unlike addition or subtraction) is the same sort of operation as multiplication. In fact,

$$\left(\frac{a}{b}\right)^n$$

can be thought of as

$$\left(a \times \frac{1}{b}\right)^n$$

so applying rule 4 to this product gives

$$a^n \left(\frac{1}{b}\right)^n = \frac{a^n}{b^n}$$

as required.

Advice

There might be occasions (such as in examinations!) when you only half remember a rule or perhaps think that you have discovered a brand new rule for yourself. If you are ever worried about whether some rule is legal or not, you should always check it out by trying numbers, just as we did for $(a + b)^n$. Obviously, one numerical example which actually works does not prove that the rule will always work. However, one example which fails is good enough to tell you that your supposed rule is rubbish.

The following example demonstrates how rules 1–4 are used to simplify algebraic expressions.

Example

Simplify

(a) $x^{1/4} \times x^{3/4}$ **(b)** $\dfrac{x^2 y^3}{x^4 y}$ **(c)** $(x^2 y^{-1/3})^3$

Solution

(a) The expression

$$x^{1/4} \times x^{3/4}$$

represents the product of two numbers in exponential form with the same base. From rule 1, we may add the indices to get

$$x^{1/4} \times x^{3/4} = x^{1/4+3/4} = x^1$$

which is just x.

(b) The expression

$$\frac{x^2 y^3}{x^4 y}$$

is more complicated than that in part (a) since it involves numbers in exponential form with two different bases, x and y. From rule 2,

$$\frac{x^2}{x^4}$$

may be simplified by subtracting indices to get

$$x^2 \div x^4 = x^{2-4} = x^{-2}$$

Similarly,

$$\frac{y^3}{y} = y^3 \div y^1 = y^{3-1} = y^2$$

Hence

$$\frac{x^2 y^3}{x^4 y} = x^{-2} y^2$$

It is not possible to simplify this any further, because x^{-2} and y^2 have different bases. However, if you prefer, this can be written as

$$\frac{y^2}{x^2}$$

because negative powers denote reciprocals.

(c) An obvious first step in the simplification of

$$(x^2 y^{-1/3})^3$$

is to apply rule 4, treating x^2 as the value of a and $y^{-1/3}$ as b to get

$$(x^2 y^{-1/3})^3 = (x^2)^3 (y^{-1/3})^3$$

Rule 3 then allows us to write

$$(x^2)^3 = x^{2 \times 3} = x^6$$
$$(y^{-1/3})^3 = y^{(-1/3) \times 3} = y^{-1}$$

Hence

$$(x^2 y^{-1/3})^3 = x^6 y^{-1}$$

As in part (b), if you think it looks neater, you can write this as

$$\frac{x^6}{y}$$

because negative powers denote reciprocals.

Practice Problem

3. Simplify

    (a) $(x^{3/4})^8$ (b) $\dfrac{x^2}{x^{3/2}}$ (c) $(x^2 y^4)^3$ (d) $\sqrt{x}(x^{5/2} + y^3)$

    [Hint: in part (d) note that $\sqrt{x} = x^{1/2}$ and multiply out the brackets.]

There are occasions throughout this text when we use the rules of indices and definitions of b^n. For the moment, we concentrate on one specific application where we see these ideas in action. The output, Q, of any production process depends on a variety of inputs, known as **factors of production**. These comprise land, capital, labour and enterprise. For simplicity, we restrict our attention to capital and labour. **Capital**, K, denotes all man-made aids to production such as buildings, tools and plant machinery. **Labour**, L, denotes all paid work in the production process. The dependence of Q on K and L may be written as

$$Q = f(K, L)$$

which is called a **production function**. Once this relationship is made explicit, in the form of a formula, it is straightforward to calculate the level of production from any given combination of inputs. For example, if

$$Q = 100K^{1/3}L^{1/2}$$

then the inputs $K = 27$ and $L = 100$ lead to an output

$$Q = 100(27)^{1/3}(100)^{1/2}$$
$$= 100(3)(10)$$
$$= 3000$$

Of particular interest is the effect on output when inputs are scaled in some way. If capital and labour both double, does the production level also double, does it go up by more than double or does it go up by less than double? For the particular production function,

$$Q = 100K^{1/3}L^{1/2}$$

we see that, when K and L are replaced by $2K$ and $2L$, respectively,

$$Q = 100(2K)^{1/3}(2L)^{1/2}$$

Now, by rule 4,

$$(2K)^{1/3} = 2^{1/3}K^{1/3} \text{ and } (2L)^{1/2} = 2^{1/2}L^{1/2}$$

so

$$Q = 100(2^{1/3}K^{1/3})(2^{1/2}L^{1/2})$$
$$= (2^{1/3}2^{1/2})(100K^{1/3}L^{1/2})$$

The second term, $100K^{1/3}L^{1/2}$, is just the original value of Q, so we see that the output is multiplied by

$$2^{1/3}2^{1/2}$$

Using rule 1, this number may be simplified by adding the indices to get

$$2^{1/3}2^{1/2} = 2^{5/6}$$

Moreover, because 5/6 is less than 1, the scale factor is smaller than 2. In fact, my calculator gives

$$2^{5/6} = 1.78 \text{ (to two decimal places)}$$

so output goes up by just less than double.

It is important to notice that the above argument does not depend on the particular value, 2, that is taken as the scale factor. Exactly the same procedure can be applied if the inputs, K and L, are scaled by a general number λ (where λ is a Greek letter pronounced 'lambda'). Replacing K and L by λK and λL, respectively, in the formula

$$Q = 100K^{1/3}L^{1/2}$$

gives

$$Q = 100(\lambda K)^{1/3}(\lambda L)^{1/2}$$
$$= 100\lambda^{1/3}K^{1/3}\lambda^{1/2}L^{1/2} \qquad \text{(rule 4)}$$
$$= (\lambda^{1/3}\lambda^{1/2})(100K^{1/3}L^{1/2})$$
$$= \lambda^{5/6}(100K^{1/3}L^{1/2}) \qquad \text{(rule 1)}$$

We see that the output gets scaled by $\lambda^{5/6}$, which is smaller than λ since the power, 5/6, is less than 1. We describe this by saying that the production function exhibits decreasing returns to scale.

In general, a function

$$Q = f(K, L)$$

is said to be **homogeneous** if

$$f(\lambda K, \lambda L) = \lambda^n f(K, L)$$

for some number, n. This means that when both variables K and L are multiplied by λ, we can pull out all of the λs as a common factor, λ^n. The power, n, is called the **degree of homogeneity**. In the previous example we showed that

$$f(\lambda K, \lambda L) = \lambda^{5/6} f(K, L)$$

and so it is homogeneous of degree 5/6. In general, if the degree of homogeneity, n, satisfies:

- $n < 1$, the function is said to display **decreasing returns to scale**
- $n = 1$, the function is said to display **constant returns to scale**
- $n > 1$, the function is said to display **increasing returns to scale**.

Example

Show that the following production function is homogeneous and find its degree of homogeneity:

$$Q = 2K^{1/2}L^{3/2}$$

Does this function exhibit decreasing returns to scale, constant returns to scale or increasing returns to scale?

Solution

We are given that

$$f(K, L) = 2K^{1/2}L^{3/2}$$

so replacing K by λK and L by λL gives

$$f(\lambda K, \lambda L) = 2(\lambda K)^{1/2}(\lambda L)^{3/2}$$

We can pull out all of the λs by using rule 4 to get

$$2\lambda^{1/2}K^{1/2}\lambda^{3/2}L^{3/2}$$

and then use rule 1 to get

$$\lambda^2(2K^{1/2}L^{3/2})$$

$$\lambda^{1/2}\lambda^{3/2} = \lambda^{1/2+3/2}$$
$$= \lambda^2$$

We have therefore shown that

$$f(\lambda K, \lambda L) = \lambda^2 f(K, L)$$

and so the function is homogeneous of degree 2. Moreover, since $2 > 1$, we deduce that it has increasing returns to scale.

Practice Problem

4. Show that the following production functions are homogeneous and comment on their returns to scale:

   (a) $Q = 7KL^2$ **(b)** $Q = 50K^{1/4}L^{3/4}$

You may well have noticed that all of the production functions considered so far are of the form

$$Q = AK^\alpha L^\beta$$

for some positive constants, A, α and β. (The Greek letters α and β are pronounced 'alpha' and 'beta', respectively.) Such functions are called **Cobb–Douglas production functions**. It is easy to see that they are homogeneous of degree $\alpha + \beta$ because if

$$f(K, L) = AK^\alpha L^\beta$$

then

$$
\begin{aligned}
f(\lambda K, \lambda L) &= A(\lambda K)^\alpha (\lambda L)^\beta \\
&= A\lambda^\alpha K^\alpha \lambda^\beta L^\beta \quad \text{(rule 4)} \\
&= \lambda^{\alpha+\beta}(AK^\alpha L^\beta) \quad \text{(rule 1)} \\
&= \lambda^{\alpha+\beta}f(K, L)
\end{aligned}
$$

Consequently, Cobb–Douglas production functions exhibit

- decreasing returns to scale, if $\alpha + \beta < 1$
- constant returns to scale, if $\alpha + \beta = 1$
- increasing returns to scale, if $\alpha + \beta > 1$.

By the way, not all production functions are of this type. Indeed, it is not even necessary for a production function to be homogeneous. Some examples illustrating these cases are given in Question 5 in Exercise 2.3 at the end of this section. We shall return to the topic of production functions in Chapter 5.

2.3.3 Logarithms

At the beginning of this section we stated that if a number, M, is expressed as

$$M = b^n$$

then b^n is called the exponential form of M to base b. The approach taken so far has simply been to evaluate M from any given values of b and n. In practice, it may be necessary to reverse this process and to find n from known values of M and b. To solve the equation

$$32 = 2^n$$

we need to express 32 as a power of 2. In this case it is easy to work out n by inspection. Simple trial and error easily gives $n = 5$ because

$$2^5 = 32$$

We describe this expression by saying that the logarithm of 32 to base 2 is 5. In symbols we write

$$\log_2 32 = 5$$

Quite generally,

$$\text{if } M = b^n \quad \text{then} \quad \log_b M = n$$

where n is called the logarithm of M to base b.

Advice

Students have been known to regard logarithms as something rather abstract and difficult to understand. There is, however, no need to worry about logarithms, since they simply provide an alternative way of thinking about numbers such as b^n. Read through the following example and then try Practice Problem 5 for yourself. You might discover that they are easier than you expect.

Example

Evaluate

(a) $\log_3 9$ **(b)** $\log_4 2$ **(c)** $\log_7 {}^1/_7$

Solution

(a) To find the value of $\log_3 9$ we convert the problem into one involving powers. From the definition of a logarithm to base 3, we see that the statement

$$\log_3 9 = n$$

is equivalent to

$$9 = 3^n$$

The problem of finding the logarithm of 9 to base 3 is exactly the same as that of writing 9 as a power of 3. The solution of this equation is clearly $n = 2$ since

$$9 = 3^2$$

Hence $\log_3 9 = 2$.

(b) Again, to evaluate $\log_4 2$ we merely rewrite

$$\log_4 2 = n$$

in exponential form as

$$2 = 4^n$$

The problem of finding the logarithm of 2 to base 4 is exactly the same as that of writing 2 as a power of 4. The value of 2 is obtained from 4 by taking the square root, which involves raising 4 to the power of $^1/_2$, so

$$2 = 4^{1/2}$$

Hence $\log_4 2 = {}^1/_2$.

(c) If

$$\log_7 {}^1/_7 = n$$

then

$${}^1/_7 = 7^n$$

The value of $^1/_7$ is found by taking the reciprocal of 7, which involves raising 7 to the power of -1: that is,

$${}^1/_7 = 7^{-1}$$

Hence $\log_7 {}^1/_7 = -1$.

Practice Problem

5. **(1)** Write down the values of n which satisfy

(a) $1000 = 10^n$ **(b)** $100 = 10^n$ **(c)** $10 = 10^n$

(d) $1 = 10^n$ **(e)** $\dfrac{1}{10} = 10^n$ **(f)** $\dfrac{1}{100} = 10^n$

(2) Use your answer to part (1) to write down the values of

(a) $\log_{10} 1000$ **(b)** $\log_{10} 100$ **(c)** $\log_{10} 10$

(d) $\log_{10} 1$ **(e)** $\log_{10} {}^1/_{10}$ **(f)** $\log_{10} {}^1/_{100}$

(3) Confirm your answer to part (2) using a calculator.

Given the intimate relationship between exponentials and logarithms, you should not be too surprised to learn that logarithms satisfy three rules that are comparable with those for indices. The rules of logarithms are as follows:

> **Rule 1** $\log_b(x \times y) = \log_b x + \log_b y$
> **Rule 2** $\log_b(x \div y) = \log_b x - \log_b y$
> **Rule 3** $\log_b x^m = m \log_b x$

The following two examples show how to use these rules to simplify algebraic expressions and how to solve equations in which the unknown appears as a power.

Example

Use the rules of logarithms to express each of the following as a single logarithm:

(a) $\log_b x + \log_b y - \log_b z$ **(b)** $2\log_b x - 3\log_b y$

Solution

(a) The first rule of logs shows that the *sum* of two logs can be written as the log of a *product*, so

$$\log_b x + \log_b y - \log_b z = \log_b(xy) - \log_b z$$

Also, according to rule 2, the *difference* of two logs is the log of a *quotient*, so we can simplify further to get

$$\log_b\left(\frac{xy}{z}\right)$$

(b) Given any combination of logs such as

$$2\log_b x - 3\log_b y$$

the trick is to use the third rule to 'get rid' of the coefficients. Since

$$2\log_b x = \log_b x^2 \quad \text{and} \quad 3\log_b y = \log_b y^3$$

we see that

$$2\log_b x - 3\log_b y = \log_b x^2 - \log_b y^3$$

Only now can we use the second rule of logs, which allows us to write the expression as the single logarithm

$$\log_b\left(\frac{x^2}{y^3}\right)$$

Practice Problem

6. Use the rules of logs to express each of the following as a single logarithm:

(a) $\log_b x - \log_b y + \log_b z$ **(b)** $4\log_b x + 2\log_b y$

Before we continue with this topic, a word of warning is in order. Be careful to learn the rules of logs correctly. A common mistake is to misread rule 1 as

$$\log_b(x + y) = \log_b x + \log_b y \qquad \text{This is NOT true}$$

Remember that logs are just a posh way of thinking about indices and it is when you *multiply* numbers together that you end up adding the indices, so the correct version has to be

$$\log_b(xy) = \log_b x + \log_b y$$

Example

Find the value of x which satisfies

(a) $200(1.1)^x = 20\ 000$ **(b)** $5^x = 2(3)^x$

Solution

(a) An obvious first step in the solution of

$$200(1.1)^x = 20\ 000$$

is to divide both sides by 200 to get

$$(1.1)^x = 100$$

In Chapter 1 it was pointed out that we can do whatever we like to an equation, provided that we do the same thing to both sides. In particular, we may take logarithms of both sides to get

$$\log(1.1)^x = \log(100)$$

Now by rule 3 we have

$$\log(1.1)^x = x \log(1.1)$$

so the equation becomes

$$x \log(1.1) = \log(100)$$

Notice the effect that rule 3 has on the equation. It brings the unknown down to the same level as the rest of the expression. This is the whole point of taking logarithms, since it converts an equation in which the unknown appears as a power into one which can be solved using familiar algebraic methods. Dividing both sides of the equation

$$x \log(1.1) = \log(100)$$

by $\log(1.1)$ gives

$$x = \frac{\log(100)}{\log(1.1)}$$

So far no mention has been made of the base of the logarithm. The above equation for x is true no matter what base is used. It makes sense to use logarithms to base 10 because all scientific calculators have this facility as one of their function keys. Using base 10, my calculator gives

$$x = \frac{\log(100)}{\log(1.1)} = \frac{2}{0.041\ 395\ 685} = 48.32$$

check this using
your own calculator

to two decimal places.

As a check, if this number is substituted back into the original equation, then

$$200(1.1)^x = 200(1.1)^{48.32} = 20\ 004 \quad ✓$$

We cannot expect to obtain the exact answer, because we rounded x to only 2 decimal places.

(b) To solve

$$5^x = 2(3)^x$$

we take logarithms of both sides to get

$$\log(5^x) = \log(2 \times 3^x)$$

The right-hand side is the logarithm of a product and, according to rule 1, can be written as the sum of the logarithms, so the equation becomes

$$\log(5^x) = \log(2) + \log(3^x)$$

As in part (a), the key step is to use rule 3 to 'bring down the powers'. If rule 3 is applied to both $\log(5^x)$ and $\log(3^x)$, then the equation becomes

$$x \log(5) = \log(2) + x \log(3)$$

This is now the type of equation that we know how to solve. We collect xs on the left-hand side to get

$$x \log(5) - x \log(3) = \log(2)$$

and then pull out a common factor of x to get

$$x[\log(5) - \log(3)] = \log(2)$$

Now, by rule 2, the difference of two logarithms is the same as the logarithm of their quotient, so

$$\log(5) - \log(3) = \log(5 \div 3)$$

Hence the equation becomes

$$x \log\left(\frac{5}{3}\right) = \log(2)$$

so

$$x = \frac{\log(2)}{\log(5/3)}$$

Finally, taking logarithms to base 10 using a calculator gives

$$x = \frac{0.301\ 029\ 996}{0.221\ 848\ 750} = 1.36$$

to two decimal places.

As a check, the original equation

$$5^x = 2(3)^x$$

becomes

$$5^{1.36} = 2(3)^{1.36}$$

that is,

$$8.92 = 8.91 \qquad ✓$$

Again, the slight discrepancy is due to rounding errors in the value of x.

Practice Problem

7. Solve the following equations for x:

   (a) $3^x = 7$ **(b)** $5(2)^x = 10^x$

Advice

In this section we have met a large number of definitions and rules concerning indices and logarithms. For convenience, we have collected these together in the form of a summary. The facts relating to indices are particularly important, and you should make every effort to memorise these before proceeding with the rest of this text.

2.3.4 Summary

Indices

If n is a positive whole number, then

$$b^n = b \times b \times \ldots \times b$$
$$b^0 = 1$$
$$b^{-n} - 1/b^n$$
$$b^{1/n} = n\text{th root of } b$$

Also, if p and q are whole numbers with $q > 0$, then

$$b^{p/q} = (b^p)^{1/q} = (b^{1/q})^p$$

The four rules of indices are:

   Rule 1 $b^m \times b^n = b^{m+n}$
   Rule 2 $b^m \div b^n = b^{m-n}$
   Rule 3 $(b^m)^n = b^{mn}$
   Rule 4 $(ab)^n = a^n b^n$

Logarithms

If $M = b^n$, then $n = \log_b M$. The three rules of logarithms are:

   Rule 1 $\log_b(x \times y) = \log_b x + \log_b y$

   Rule 2 $\log_b(x \div y) = \log_b x - \log_b y$

   Rule 3 $\log_b x^m = m \log_b x$

Key Terms

Capital   Man-made assets used in the production of goods and services.

Cobb–Douglas production function   A production function of the form: $Q = AK^{\alpha}L^{\beta}$.

Constant returns to scale   Exhibited by a production function when a given percentage increase in input leads to the same percentage increase in output: $f(\lambda K, \lambda L) = \lambda f(K, L)$.

Decreasing returns to scale   Exhibited by a production function when a given percentage increase in input leads to a smaller percentage increase in output: $f(\lambda K, \lambda L) = \lambda^n f(K, L)$ where $0 < n < 1$.

Degree of homogeneity   The number n in the relation $f(\lambda K, \lambda L) = \lambda^n f(K, L)$.

Exponent   A superscript attached to a variable; the number 5 is the exponent in the expression, $2x^5$.

Exponential form   A representation of a number which is written using powers. For example, 2^5 is the exponential form of the number 32.

Factors of production   The inputs into the production of goods and services: labour, land, capital and raw materials.

Homogeneous function   A function with the property that when all of the inputs are multiplied by a constant, λ, the output is multiplied by λ^n where n is the degree of homogeneity.

Increasing returns to scale   Exhibited by a production function when a given percentage increase in input leads to a larger percentage increase in output: $f(\lambda K, \lambda L) = \lambda^n f(K, L)$ where $n > 1$.

Index   Alternative word for exponent or power.

Labour   All forms of human input to the production process.

Logarithm   The power to which a base must be raised to yield a particular number.

Power   Another word for exponent. If this is a positive integer, then it gives the number of times a number is multiplied by itself.

Production function   The relationship between the output of a good and the inputs used to produce it.

Exercise 2.3

1. **(1)** Without using your calculator, evaluate

   (a) 8^2 **(b)** 2^1 **(c)** 3^{-1} **(d)** 17^0 **(e)** $1^{1/5}$ **(f)** $36^{1/2}$ **(g)** $8^{2/3}$ **(h)** $49^{-3/2}$

   (2) Confirm your answer to part (1) using a calculator.

2. Use the rules of indices to simplify

   (a) $a^3 \times a^8$ **(b)** $\dfrac{b^7}{b^2}$ **(c)** $(c^2)^3$ **(d)** $\dfrac{x^4 y^5}{x^2 y^3}$ **(e)** $(xy^2)^3$

   (f) $y^3 \div y^7$ **(g)** $(x^{1/2})^8$ **(h)** $f^2 \times f^4 \times f$ **(i)** $\sqrt{(y^6)}$ **(j)** $\dfrac{x^3}{x^{-2}}$

3. Write the following expressions using index notation:

   (a) $\sqrt{x}$ **(b)** $\dfrac{1}{x^2}$ **(c)** $\sqrt[3]{x}$ **(d)** $\dfrac{1}{x}$ **(e)** $\dfrac{1}{\sqrt{x}}$ **(f)** $x\sqrt{x}$

4. For the production function, $Q = 200K^{1/4}L^{2/3}$, find the output when

   (a) $K = 16, L = 27$ **(b)** $K = 10\,000, L = 1000$

5. Which of the following production functions are homogeneous? For those functions which are homogeneous, write down their degrees of homogeneity and comment on their returns to scale.

(a) $Q = 500K^{1/3}L^{1/4}$

(b) $Q = 3LK + L^2$

(c) $Q = L + 5L^2K^3$

6. Write down the values of x which satisfy each of the following equations:

   (a) $5^x = 25$ (b) $3^x = \dfrac{1}{3}$ (c) $2^x = \dfrac{1}{8}$

   (d) $2^x = 64$ (e) $100^x = 10$ (f) $8^x = 1$

7. Write down the value of

   (a) $\log_b b^2$ (b) $\log_b b$ (c) $\log_b 1$ (d) $\log_b \sqrt{b}$ (e) $\log_b(1/b)$

8. Use the rules of logs to express each of the following as a single log:

   (a) $\log_b x + \log_b z$

   (b) $3\log_b x - 2\log_b y$

   (c) $\log_b y - 3\log_b z$

9. Express the following in terms of $\log_b x$ and $\log_b y$:

   (a) $\log_b x^2 y$

   (b) $\log_b\left(\dfrac{x}{y^2}\right)$

   (c) $\log_b x^2 y^7$

10. Solve the following equations for x. Give your answers to two decimal places.

    (a) $5^x = 8$ (b) $10^x = 50$ (c) $1.2^x = 3$ (d) $1000 \times 1.05^x = 1500$

11. **(1)** State the values of

    (a) $\log_2 32$ (b) $\log_9\left(\dfrac{1}{3}\right)$

    (2) Use the rules of logs to express

    $$2\log_b x - 4\log_b y$$

    as a single logarithm.

    (3) Use logs to solve the equation

    $$10(1.05)^x = 300$$

    Give your answer correct to one decimal place.

12. **(1)** State the values of x that satisfy the following equations:

    (a) $81 = 3^x$ (b) $\dfrac{1}{25} = 5^x$ (c) $16^{1/2} = 2^x$

    (2) Use the rules of indices to simplify:

    (a) $\dfrac{x^6 y^9}{x^3 y^8}$ (b) $(x^3 y)^5$ (c) $\sqrt{\dfrac{x^9 y^4}{x^5}}$

13. The number of complaints, N, received by a small company each month can be modelled by

$$N = 80\log_{10}(7 + 10t)$$

where t denotes the number of months since the company's launch.

(a) Estimate the number of complaints received by the company each month for the first six months of trading.

(b) Plot a graph of N against t and hence comment on how N varies with t.

14. If two firms A and B use the same labour input, L, their output in the short term is given by $Q_A = 108\sqrt{L}$ and $Q_B = 4L^2$, respectively. Find the non-zero value of L which produces the same level of output for these two firms.

Exercise 2.3*

1. **(1)** Evaluate the following without using a calculator:

(a) $32^{3/5}$ (b) $64^{-5/6}$ (c) $\left(\dfrac{1}{125}\right)^{-4/3}$ (d) $\left(3\dfrac{3}{8}\right)^{2/3}$ (e) $\left(2\dfrac{1}{4}\right)^{-1/2}$

(2) Confirm your answer to part (1) using a calculator.

2. Use the rules of indices to simplify

(a) $y^{3/2} \times y^{1/2}$ (b) $\dfrac{x^2 y}{xy^{-1}}$ (c) $(xy^{1/2})^4$

(d) $(p^2)^{1/3} \div (p^{1/3})^2$ (e) $(24q)^{1/3} \div (3q)^{1/3}$ (f) $(25p^2 q^4)^{1/2}$

3. Write the following expressions using index notation:

(a) $\dfrac{1}{x^7}$ (b) $\sqrt[4]{x}$ (c) $\dfrac{1}{x\sqrt{x}}$ (d) $2x^5\sqrt{x}$ (e) $\dfrac{8}{x(\sqrt[3]{x})}$

4. If $a = \dfrac{2\sqrt{x}}{y^3}$ and $b = 3x^4 y$, simplify $\dfrac{4b}{a^2}$.

5. Show that the production function

$$Q = A[bK^\alpha + (1 - b)L^\alpha]^{1/\alpha}$$

is homogeneous and displays constant returns to scale.

6. Solve the following equations:

(a) $2^{3x} = 4$ (b) $4 \times 2^x = 32$ (c) $8^x = 2 \times \left(\dfrac{1}{2}\right)^x$

7. Use the rules of logs to express each of the following as a single log:

(a) $\log_b(xy) - \log_b x - \log_b y$

(b) $3\log_b x - 2\log_b y$

(c) $\log_b y + 5\log_b x - 2\log_b z$

(d) $2 + 3\log_b x$

8. Express the following in terms of $\log_b x$, $\log_b y$ and $\log_b z$:

(a) $\log_b(x^2 y^3 z^4)$ (b) $\log_b\left(\dfrac{x^4}{y^2 z^5}\right)$ (c) $\log_b\left(\dfrac{x}{\sqrt{yz}}\right)$

9. If $\log_b 2 = p$, $\log_b 3 = q$ and $\log_b 10 = r$, express the following in terms of p, q and r:

(a) $\log_b\left(\dfrac{1}{3}\right)$ (b) $\log_b 12$ (c) $\log_b 0.000\,3$ (d) $\log_b 600$

10. Solve the following equations. Round your answers to two decimal places.

(a) $10(1.07)^x = 2000$ (b) $10^{x-1} = 3$ (c) $5^{x-2} = 5$ (d) $2(7)^{-x} = 3^x$

11. Solve the inequalities giving the bounds to three decimal places:

(a) $3^{2x+1} \le 7$ (b) $0.8^x < 0.04$

12. Solve the equation

$$\log_{10}(x+2) + 1\log_{10}x - 1 = 1\log_{10}\left(\dfrac{3}{2}\right)$$

13. (1) Define the term *homogeneous* when used to describe a production function $f(K, L)$.

(2) If the production function

$$f(K, L) = 4K^m L^{1/3} + 3K$$

is homogeneous, state the value of m.
Does the function display decreasing, constant or increasing returns to scale?

14. (1) State the values of x that satisfy the following equations:

(a) $4 = 8^x$ (b) $5 = \left(\dfrac{1}{25}\right)^x$

(2) Express y in terms of x:

$$2\log_a x = \log_a 7 + \log_a y$$

15. Show that $2\log_{10}x - \dfrac{1}{2}\log_{10}y - \dfrac{1}{3}\log_{10}1000$ can be simplified to

$$\log_{10}\left(\sqrt{\dfrac{x^4}{y}}\right) - 1$$

16. Transpose each of the following production functions for L:

(a) $Q = AK^\alpha L^\beta$ (b) $Q = A[bK^\alpha + (1-b)L^\alpha]^{1/\alpha}$

17. Show that each of these functions is homogeneous and state the degree of homogeneity:

(a) $f(K,L) = \dfrac{K^2 + L^2}{K + L}$

(b) $f(K,L) = KL\log\left(\dfrac{K^2 + L^2}{KL}\right)$

(c) $f(K,L) = A[aK^m + bL^m]^{n/m}$

(d) $f(K,L) = KL^2 g(L/K)$ where g is a general function.

SECTION 2.4

The exponential and natural logarithm functions

Objectives

At the end of this section you should be able to:

- Sketch graphs of general exponential functions.
- Understand how the number e is defined.
- Use the exponential function to model growth and decay.
- Use log graphs to find unknown parameters in simple models.
- Use the natural logarithm function to solve equations.

In the previous section we described how to define numbers of the form b^x, and we discussed the idea of a logarithm, $\log_b x$. It turns out that there is one base (the number e = 2.718 281 . . .) that is particularly important in mathematics. The purpose of this section is to introduce you to this strange number and to consider a few simple applications.

We begin by investigating the graphs of the functions,

$$f(x) = 2^x \quad \text{and} \quad g(x) = 2^{-x}$$

As we pointed out in Section 2.3, a number such as 2^x is said to be in exponential form. The number 2 is called the base and x is called the exponent. Values of this function are easily found either by pressing the power key $\boxed{x^y}$ on a calculator or by using the definition of b^n given in Section 2.3. A selection of these is given in the following table:

x	-3	-2	-1	0	1	2	3	4	5
2^x	0.125	0.25	0.5	1	2	4	8	16	32

A graph of $f(x)$ based on this table is sketched in Figure 2.12. Notice that the graph approaches the x axis for large negative values of x, and it rises rapidly as x increases.

A graph of the negative exponential, $g(x) = 2^{-x}$, shown in Figure 2.13, is based on the following table of values:

x	-5	-4	-3	-2	-1	0	1	2	3
2^{-x}	32	16	8	4	2	1	0.5	0.25	0.125

This function is sketched in Figure 2.13. It is worth noticing that the numbers appearing in the table of 2^{-x} are the same as those of 2^x but arranged in reverse order. Hence the graph of 2^{-x} is obtained by reflecting the graph of 2^x in the y axis.

Figure 2.12 displays the graph of a particular exponential function, 2^x. Quite generally, the graph of any exponential function

$$f(x) = b^x$$

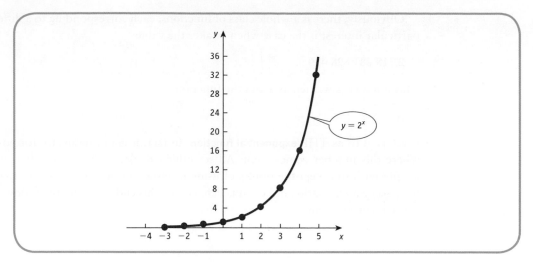

Figure 2.12

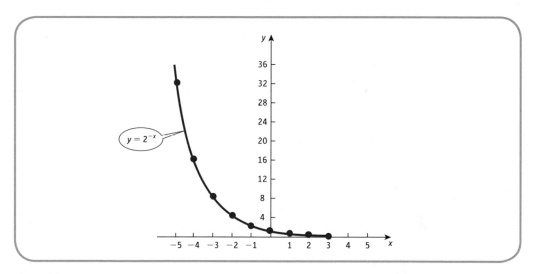

Figure 2.13

has the same basic shape provided $b > 1$. The only difference is that larger values of b produce steeper curves. A similar comment applies to the negative exponential, b^{-x}.

Practice Problem

1. Complete the following table of function values of 3^x and 3^{-x} and hence sketch their graphs.

x	-3	-2	-1	0	1	2	3
3^x							
3^{-x}							

Obviously, there is a whole class of functions, each corresponding to a different base, b. Of particular interest is the case when b takes the value

2.718 281 828 459 . . .

This number is written as e and the function

$$f(x) = e^x$$

is referred to as THE **exponential function**. In fact, it is not necessary for you to understand where this number comes from. All scientific calculators have an e^x button, and you may simply wish to accept the results of using it. However, it might help your confidence if you have some appreciation of how it is defined. To this end, consider the following example and subsequent problem.

Example

Evaluate the expression

$$\left(1 + \frac{1}{m}\right)^m$$

where $m = 1, 10, 100$ and 1000, and comment briefly on the behaviour of this sequence.

Solution

Substituting the values $m = 1, 10, 100$ and 1000 into

$$\left(1 + \frac{1}{m}\right)^m$$

gives

$$\left(1 + \frac{1}{1}\right)^1 = 2^1 = 2$$

$$\left(1 + \frac{1}{10}\right)^{10} = (1.1)^{10} = 2.593\ 742\ 460$$

$$\left(1 + \frac{1}{100}\right)^{100} = (1.01)^{100} = 2.704\ 813\ 829$$

$$\left(1 + \frac{1}{1000}\right)^{1000} = (1.001)^{1000} = 2.716\ 923\ 932$$

The numbers are clearly getting bigger as m increases. However, the rate of increase appears to be slowing down, suggesting that numbers are converging to some fixed value.

The following problem gives you an opportunity to continue the sequence and to discover for yourself the limiting value.

Practice Problem

2. (a) Use the power key x^y on your calculator to evaluate

$$\left(1 + \frac{1}{m}\right)^m$$

where $m = 10\ 000,\ 100\ 000$ and $1\ 000\ 000$.

(b) Use your calculator to evaluate e^1 and compare with your answer to part (a).

Hopefully, the results of Practice Problem 2 should convince you that as m gets larger, the value of

$$\left(1 + \frac{1}{m}\right)^m$$

approaches a limiting value of $2.718\ 281\ 828\ \ldots$, which we choose to denote by the letter e. In symbols we write

$$e = \lim_{m \to \infty}\left(1 + \frac{1}{m}\right)^m$$

The significance of this number can only be fully appreciated in the context of calculus, which we study in Chapter 4. However, it is useful at this stage to consider some preliminary examples. These will give you practice in using the e^x button on your calculator and will give you some idea how this function can be used in modelling.

Advice

The number e has a similar status in mathematics as the number π and is just as useful. It arises in the mathematics of finance, which we discuss in the next chapter. You might like to glance through Section 3.2 now if you need convincing of the usefulness of e.

Example

The percentage, y, of households possessing refrigerators, t years after they have been introduced in a developed country, is modelled by

$$y = 100 - 95e^{-0.15t}$$

(1) Find the percentage of households that have refrigerators

(a) at their launch;

(b) after 1 year;

(c) after 10 years;

(d) after 20 years.

(2) What is the market saturation level?

(3) Sketch a graph of y against t and hence give a qualitative description of the growth of refrigerator ownership over time.

Solution

(1) To calculate the percentage of households possessing refrigerators now and in 1, 10 and 20 years' time, we substitute $t = 0$, 1, 10 and 20 into the formula

$$y = 100 - 95e^{-0.15t}$$

to get

(a) $y(0) = 100 - 95e^{0} = 5\%$

(b) $y(1) = 100 - 95e^{-0.15} = 18\%$

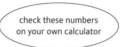
check these numbers on your own calculator

(c) $y(10) = 100 - 95e^{-1.5} = 79\%$

(d) $y(20) = 100 - 95e^{-3.0} = 95\%$

(2) To find the saturation level, we need to investigate what happens to y as t gets ever larger. We know that the graph of a negative exponential function has the basic shape shown in Figure 2.13. Consequently, the value of $e^{-0.15t}$ will eventually approach zero as t increases. The market saturation level is therefore given by

$$y = 100 - 95(0) = 100\%$$

(3) A graph of y against t, based on the information obtained in parts (1) and (2), is sketched in Figure 2.14.

This shows that y grows rapidly to begin with, but slows down as the market approaches saturation level. An economic variable which increases over time but approaches a fixed value like this is said to display **limited growth**. A saturation level of 100% indicates that eventually all households are expected to possess refrigerators, which is not surprising given the nature of the product.

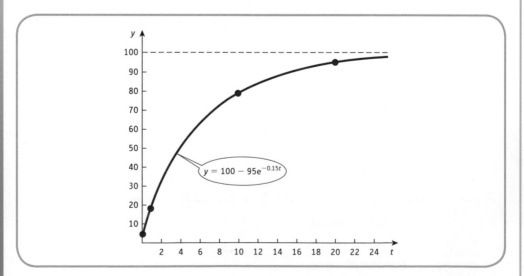

Figure 2.14

Practice Problem

3. The percentage, y, of households possessing microwave ovens t years after they have been launched is modelled by

$$y = \frac{55}{1 + 800e^{-0.3t}}$$

(1) Find the percentage of households that have microwaves

   (a) at their launch;

   (b) after 10 years;

   (c) after 20 years;

   (d) after 30 years.

(2) What is the market saturation level?

(3) Sketch a graph of y against t and hence give a qualitative description of the growth of microwave ownership over time.

In Section 2.3 we noted that if a number M can be expressed as b^n, then n is called the logarithm of M to base b. In particular, for base e,

if $M = e^n$ then $n = \log_e M$

We call logarithms to base e **natural logarithms**. These occur sufficiently frequently to warrant their own notation. Rather than write $\log_e M$, we simply put ln M instead. The three rules of logs can then be stated as

> *Rule 1* $\ln(x \times y) = \ln x + \ln y$
>
> *Rule 2* $\ln(x \div y) = \ln x - \ln y$
>
> *Rule 3* $\ln x^m = m \ln x$

Example

Use the rules of logs to express

(a) $\ln\left(\dfrac{x}{\sqrt{y}}\right)$ in terms of ln x and ln y

(b) $3 \ln p + \ln q - 2 \ln r$ as a single logarithm.

Solution

(a) In this part we need to 'expand', so we read the rules of logs from left to right:

$$\ln\left(\frac{x}{\sqrt{y}}\right) = \ln x - \ln\sqrt{y} \qquad \text{(rule 2)}$$

$$= \ln x - \ln y^{1/2} \qquad \text{(fractional powers denote roots)}$$

$$= \ln x - \frac{1}{2}\ln y \qquad \text{(rule 3)}$$

(b) In this part we need to reverse this process and so read the rules from right to left:

$$3\ln p + \ln q - 2\ln r = \ln p^3 + \ln q - \ln r^2 \qquad \text{(rule 3)}$$

$$= \ln(p^3 q) - \ln r^2 \qquad \text{(rule 1)}$$

$$= \ln\left(\frac{p^3 q}{r^2}\right) \qquad \text{(rule 2)}$$

Practice Problem

4. Use the rules of logs to express

  (a) $\ln(a^2 b^3)$ in terms of $\ln a$ and $\ln b$

  (b) $\frac{1}{2}\ln x - 3\ln y$ as a single logarithm.

As we pointed out in Section 2.3, logs are particularly useful for solving equations in which the unknown occurs as a power. If the base is the number e, then the equation can be solved by using natural logarithms.

Example

An economy is forecast to grow continuously so that the gross national product (GNP), measured in billions of dollars, after t years is given by

  $\text{GNP} = 80e^{0.02t}$

After how many years is GNP forecast to be \$88 billion? What does the model predict about the value of GNP in the long run?

Solution

We need to solve

  $88 = 80e^{0.02t}$

for t. Dividing through by 80 gives

  $1.1 = e^{0.02t}$

Using the definition of natural logarithms we know that

  if $M = e^n$ then $n = \ln M$

If we apply this definition to the equation

$$1.1 = e^{0.02t}$$

we deduce that

$$0.02t = \ln 1.1 = 0.095\ 31 \ldots \quad \text{(check this using your own calculator)}$$

so

$$t = \frac{0.095\ 31}{0.02} = 4.77$$

We therefore deduce that GNP reaches a level of $88 billion after 4.77 years.

A graph of GNP plotted against time would be similar in shape to the graph in Figure 2.14. This shows that GNP just keeps on rising over time (in fact, at an increasing rate). Such a model is said to display **unlimited growth**.

Practice Problem

5. During a recession, a firm's revenue declines continuously so that the revenue, TR (measured in millions of dollars), in t years' time is modelled by

$$TR = 5e^{-0.15t}$$

(a) Calculate the current revenue and also the revenue in two years' time.

(b) After how many years will the revenue decline to $2.7 million?

One important (but rather difficult) problem in modelling is to extract a mathematical formula from a table of numbers. If this relationship is of the form of an exponential, then it is possible to estimate values for some of the parameters involved.

Advice

The following example shows how to find such a formula from data points. This is an important skill. However, it is not crucial to your understanding of subsequent material in this text. You may wish to miss this out on first reading and move straight on to the exercises at the end of this chapter.

Example

The values of GNP, g, measured in billions of dollars, over a period of t years was observed to be

t (years)	2	5	10	20
g (billions of dollars)	12	16	27	74

Model the growth of GNP using a formula of the form

$$g = Be^{At}$$

for appropriate values of A and B. Hence estimate the value of GNP after 15 years.

Solution

Figure 2.15 shows the four points plotted with g on the vertical axis and t on the horizontal axis. The basic shape of the curve joining these points certainly suggests that an exponential function is likely to provide a reasonable model, but it gives no information about what values to use for the parameters A and B. However, since one of the unknown parameters, A, occurs as a power in the relation

$$g = Be^{At}$$

it is a good idea to take natural logs of both sides to get

$$\ln g = \ln(Be^{At})$$

The rules of logs enable us to expand the right-hand side to get

$$\ln(Be^{At}) = \ln B + \ln(e^{At}) \quad \text{(rule 1)}$$
$$= \ln B + At \qquad \text{(definition of a log to base e)}$$

Hence

$$\ln g = At + \ln B$$

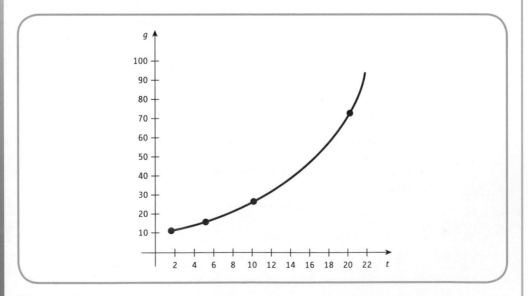

Figure 2.15

Although this does not look like it at first sight, this relation is actually the equation of a straight line! To see this, recall that the usual equation of a line is $y = ax + b$. The log equation is indeed of this form if we put

$$y = \ln g \quad \text{and} \quad x = t$$

The equation then becomes

$$y = Ax + \ln B$$

so a graph of $\ln g$ plotted on the vertical axis with t plotted on the horizontal axis should produce a straight line with slope A and with an intercept on the vertical axis of $\ln B$.

Figure 2.16 shows this graph based on the table of values

$x = t$	2	5	10	20
$y = \ln g$	2.48	2.77	3.30	4.30

As one might expect, the points do not exactly lie on a straight line, since the formula is only a model. However, the line sketched in Figure 2.16 is a remarkably good fit. The slope can be calculated as

$$A = \frac{4 - 3}{18.6 - 7.6} = 0.09$$

and the vertical intercept can be read off the graph as 2.25. This is $\ln B$ and so

$$B = e^{2.25} = 9.49$$

Hence the formula for the approximate relation between g and t is

$$g = 9.49e^{0.09t}$$

An estimate of the GNP after 15 years can be obtained by substituting $t = 15$ into this formula to get

$$g = 36.6 \quad \text{(billion dollars)}$$

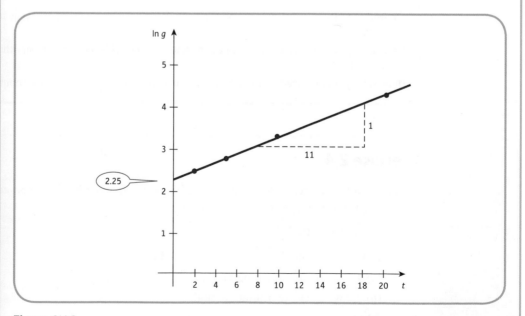

Figure 2.16

Practice Problem

6. Immediately after the launch of a new product, the monthly sales figures (in thousands) are as follows:

t (months)	1	3	6	12
s (sales)	1.8	2.7	5.0	16.5

(1) Complete the following table of values of ln s:

t	1	3	6	12
ln s	0.59		1.61	

(2) Plot these points on graph paper with the values of ln s on the vertical axis and t on the horizontal axis. Draw a straight line passing close to these points. Write down the value of the vertical intercept and calculate the slope.

(3) Use your answers to part (2) to estimate the values of A and B in the relation $s = Be^{At}$.

(4) Use the exponential model derived in part (3) to estimate the sales when

(a) $t = 9$ (b) $t = 60$

Which of these estimates would you expect to be the more reliable? Give a reason for your answer.

Key Terms

Exponential function   The function $f(x) = e^x$; an exponential function in which the base is the number e = 2.718 281....

Limited growth   Used to describe an economic variable which increases over time but which tends to a fixed quantity.

Natural logarithm   A logarithm to base e; if $M = e^n$ then n is the natural logarithm of M and we write, $n = \ln M$.

Unlimited growth   Used to describe an economic variable which increases without bound.

Exercise 2.4

1. The number of items, N, produced each day by an assembly-line worker, t days after an initial training period, is modelled by

$$N = 100 - 100e^{-0.4t}$$

(1) Calculate the number of items produced daily

(a) 1 day after the training period;

(b) 2 days after the training period;

(c) 10 days after the training period.

(2) What is the worker's daily production in the long run?

(3) Sketch a graph of N against t and explain why the general shape might have been expected.

2. Use the rules of logs to expand each of the following:

(a) $\ln xy$ **(b)** $\ln xy^4$ **(c)** $\ln (xy)^2$

(d) $\ln \dfrac{x^5}{y^7}$ **(e)** $\ln \sqrt{\dfrac{x}{y}}$ **(f)** $\ln \sqrt{\dfrac{xy^3}{z}}$

3. Use the rules of logs to express each of the following as a single logarithm:

(a) $\ln x + 2 \ln x$ **(b)** $4 \ln x - 3 \ln y + 5 \ln z$

4. Solve each of the following equations. (Round your answer to two decimal places.)

(a) $e^x = 5.9$ **(b)** $e^x = 0.45$ **(c)** $e^x = -2$

(d) $e^{3x} = 13.68$ **(e)** $e^{-5x} = 0.34$ **(f)** $4e^{2x} = 7.98$

5. The value of a second-hand car reduces exponentially with age, so that its value y after t years can be modelled by the formula

$$y = Ae^{-ax}$$

If the car was worth \$50 000 when new and \$38 000 after two years, find the values of A and a, correct to three decimal places.
    Use this model to predict the value of the car

(a) when the car is five years old;

(b) in the long run.

6. Solve the following equations:

(a) $\ln x = 5$ **(b)** $\ln x = 0$

7. Future sales of two products A and B are given by $S_A = 5e^{0.01t}$ and $S_B = 2e^{0.02t}$. Find the time, t, when sales of the two products are the same.

8. Show that the following production function is homogeneous and state whether it displays decreasing, increasing or constant returns to scale.

$$f(K,L) = (K^2 + L^2)e^{K/L}$$

Exercise 2.4*

1. The value (in cents) of shares, t years after their flotation on the stock market, is modelled by

$$V = 6e^{0.8t}$$

Find the increase in the value of these shares, four years and two months later. Give your answer to the nearest cent.

2. Solve each of the following equations, correct to two decimal places:

(a) $6e^{-2x} = 0.62$ **(b)** $5 \ln(4x) = 9.84$ **(c)** $3 \ln(5x) - 2 \ln(x) = 7$

3. A team of financial advisers guiding the launch of a national newspaper has modelled the future circulation of the newspaper by the equation

$$N = c(1 - e^{-kt})$$

where N is the daily circulation after t days of publication, and c and k are positive constants. Transpose this formula to show that

$$t = \frac{1}{k} \ln\left(\frac{c}{c - N}\right)$$

When the paper is launched, audits show that

$$c = 700\,000 \quad \text{and} \quad k = \frac{1}{30} \ln 2$$

(a) Calculate the daily circulation after 30 days of publication.

(b) After how many days will the daily circulation first reach 525 000?

(c) What advice can you give the newspaper proprietor if it is known that the paper will break even only if the daily circulation exceeds 750 000?

4. A Cobb–Douglas production function is given by

$$Q = 3L^{1/2}K^{1/3}$$

Find an expression for $\ln Q$ in terms of $\ln L$ and $\ln K$.

If a graph were to be sketched of $\ln Q$ against $\ln K$ (for varying values of Q and K but with L fixed), explain briefly why the graph will be a straight line and state its slope and vertical intercept.

5. The following table gives data relating a firm's output, Q, and labour, L:

L	1	2	3	4	5
Q	0.50	0.63	0.72	0.80	0.85

The firm's short-run production function is believed to be of the form

$$Q = AL^n$$

(a) Show that

$$\ln Q = n \ln L + \ln A$$

(b) Using the data supplied, copy and complete the following table:

$\ln L$		0.69		1.39	
$\ln Q$	−0.69		−0.33		−0.16

Plot these points with $\ln L$ on the horizontal axis and $\ln Q$ on the vertical axis. Draw a straight line passing as close as possible to all five points.

(c) By finding the slope and vertical intercept of the line sketched in part (b), estimate the values of the parameters n and A.

6. (a) Multiply out the brackets

$$(3y - 2)(y + 5)$$

(b) Solve the equation

$$3e^{2x} + 13e^x = 10$$

Give your answer correct to three decimal places.

7. **(a)** Make y the subject of the equation

$$x = ae^{by}$$

(b) Make x the subject of the equation

$$y = \ln(3 + e^{2x})$$

8. Solve the following equations for x:

   (a) $\ln(x - 5) = 0$ **(b)** $\ln(x^2 - x - 1) = 0$ **(c)** $x \ln(\sqrt{x} - 4) = 0$

   (d) $e^{5x+1} = 10$ **(e)** $e^{-x^2/2} = 0.25$

9. The demand and supply functions of a good are given by

$$Q_D = Ae^{-k_1 P} \quad \text{and} \quad Q_S = Be^{k_2 P} \text{ respectively}$$

   where A, B, k_1 and k_2 are positive constants.

   Find the equilibrium price and show that the equilibrium quantity is given by

$$(A^{k_2} B^{k_1})^{\frac{1}{k_2 + k_1}}.$$

Formal mathematics

The quadratic functions that we have investigated in this chapter have an obvious extension to cubic functions:

$$f(x) = ax^3 + bx^2 + cx + d$$

Linear, quadratic and cubic functions are all examples of a general class of functions called **polynomials** which are defined by

$$f(x) = a_n x^n + a_{n-1} x^{n-1} + \ldots + a_0$$

The coefficients, a_i, are constants, and the highest power of x is called the **degree** of the polynomial. A quadratic is a polynomial of degree 2, and a cubic has degree 3. Functions such as $f(x) = \dfrac{1}{x} + 4$ and $f(x) = \dfrac{1}{x^2 - 2x + 1}$, however, are not polynomials.

One important property of functions is that of continuity. A simple way of understanding this is to imagine drawing the graph of a function. If this can be done without taking your pen off the page, the function is described as being **continuous** everywhere. An example of such a function is shown in Figure 2.17(a). Polynomials are examples of functions which are continuous at all values of their domain. On the other hand, if the graph has jumps or breaks in it, then the function is **discontinuous** at those points. Figure 2.17(b) shows the graph of a function which is undefined at $x = 2$, and the graph separates into two different branches on either side of $x = 2$. Functions involving reciprocals are examples of functions of this type. Indeed, the graph in Figure 2.17(a) is that of the specific function, $f(x) = \dfrac{1}{x - 2}$. The graph in Figure 2.17(c) also illustrates a function which is discontinuous at $x = 2$ because it has a jump at this point. For values of $x < 2$, the function takes the constant value of 3, whereas when $x \geq 2$, the function takes the constant value of 5. In other words,

$$f(x) = \begin{cases} 3, x < 2 \\ 5, x \geq 2 \end{cases}$$

A function which is defined in separate bits like this is said to be defined piecewise.

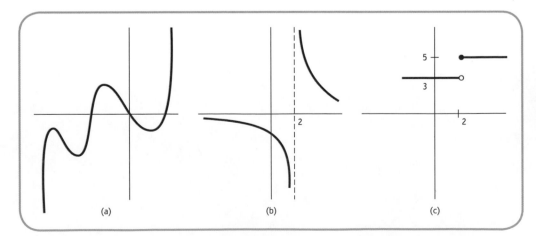

(a)   (b)   (c)

Figure 2.17

The majority of functions in economics are continuous, reflecting the fact that usually there are gradual fluctuations in economic variables without any sudden changes. However, sometimes there are catastrophic events which lead to sudden jumps. For example, the outbreak of war (or rumour of one) can lead to dramatic changes in prices of commodities such as oil or gold.

The above description of continuous functions is easy to visualise but is not very precise. In order to give a formal definition of a continuous function, we need the concept of a limit. We write

$$\lim_{x \to a} f(x)$$ (read 'the limit of f of x, as x tends to a')

for the value that the function gets ever closer to, as x approaches a value a. This is most easily understood via an example.

Example

Find $\lim_{x \to 0} \dfrac{e^x - 1}{x}$

Solution

If we attempt to evaluate the function $f(x) = \dfrac{e^x - 1}{x}$ at $x = 0$, we are faced with $f(0) = \dfrac{0}{0}$ which is undefined. However, if we start with, say, $x = \pm 1$, and allow x to approach 0 from either direction, we can see that the value is in fact 1. This is illustrated in the table of values below, which shows that as x gets closer and closer to 0 (through both positive and negative values), the function approaches 1. In symbols, $\lim_{x \to 0} \dfrac{e^x - 1}{x} = 1$

x	1	0.1	0.01	0.001
$f(x)$	1.71828	1.05171	1.00501	1.00050

x	-1	-0.1	-0.01	-0.001
$f(x)$	0.63212	0.95163	0.99502	0.99950

A graph of $f(x)$ is sketched in Figure 2.18. Although the function is undefined at $x = 0$, the graph shows that it is possible to 'plug the hole' by defining $f(0) = 1$.

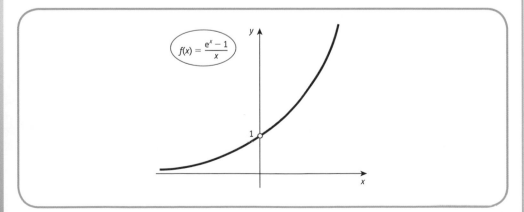

$$f(x) = \frac{e^x - 1}{x}$$

Figure 2.18

Definition A function f is continuous at $x = a$ if $\lim_{x \to a} f(x) = f(a)$

In other words, a function is continuous at $x = a$ provided the function can be evaluated at $x = a$ (so that $f(a)$ exists), and that the limit also exists and equals $f(a)$.

Referring to the functions illustrated in Figure 2.17 and 2.18, we see that:

- The function in Figure 2.17(b) is discontinuous because f is undefined at $x = 2$.
- The function in Figure 2.17(c) is discontinuous because the $\lim_{x \to 2} f(x)$ does not exist (it gives a value 5 as x approaches 2 from the right but a different value of 3 as x approaches 2 from the left).
- The function in Figure 2.18 is discontinuous because f is undefined at $x = 0$.

It is possible to remove the discontinuity for the function, $f(x) = \dfrac{e^x - 1}{x}$. As we saw in the previous example, $\lim_{x \to 0} \dfrac{e^x - 1}{x} = 1$. If we are prepared to define the function piecewise as

$$f(x) = \begin{cases} \dfrac{e^x - 1}{x} & \text{if } x \neq 0 \\ 1 & \text{if } x = 0 \end{cases}$$

then the function is now defined at $x = 0$ and the value of the limit and the function both give the value of 1 at this point.

Continuous functions have many important properties. In particular, it is necessary for a function to be continuous in order even to consider the idea of differentiability which we will investigate in Chapter 4.

Key Terms

Continuous   The name given to a function which can be drawn without taking a pen off the paper. More formally, when $\lim_{x \to a} f(x) = f(a)$ at all points in the domain.

Degree   The highest power in a polynomial.

Discontinuous   The name given to a function which is not continuous everywhere. The graph of the function has jumps or gaps.

Polynomial   A function of the form $a_n x^n + a_{n-1} x^{n-1} + \ldots + a_0$.

Multiple choice questions

Question 1

Simplify $\dfrac{2x^{-3}y^{5/2}}{6x^{-5}y}$

A. $\dfrac{x^{-8}y^{3/2}}{3}$

B $\dfrac{x^{2}y^{3/2}}{3}$

C. $\dfrac{x^{2}y^{5/2}}{3}$

D. $\dfrac{x^{-8}y^{7/2}}{3}$

E. $\dfrac{x^{-8}y^{5/2}}{3}$

Question 2

Use the quadratic formula to solve

$$3x^2 = 7x - 1$$

A. $\dfrac{-7 \pm \sqrt{61}}{6}$

B $\dfrac{-7 \pm \sqrt{37}}{6}$

C $\dfrac{7 \pm \sqrt{61}}{6}$

D. $\dfrac{7 \pm \sqrt{37}}{6}$

E   No real solutions

Question 3

If fixed costs are 20, variable costs per unit are 2 and the demand function is $P + 2Q = 24$, obtain an expression for the profit function in terms of Q.

A. $-2Q^2 + 20Q - 2$

B. $-2Q^2 + 9Q - 10$

C. $-2Q^2 + 22Q - 20$

D. $-2Q^2 + 26Q + 20$

E. $-2Q^2 + 22Q - 10$

Question 4

The graph shows the total revenue function and total cost function plotted on the same diagram. Use the graph to estimate the maximum profit.

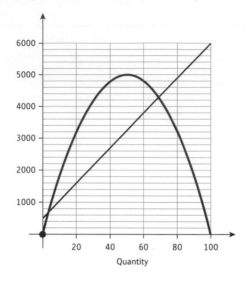

A. 4700

B. 2100

C. 5000

D. 1800

E. 2500

Question 5

If fixed costs are $80 000 and variable costs are $300 per item, how many items can be produced for $123 800?

A. 152

B. 150

C. 146

D. 172

E. 164

Question 6

Which one of the following statements best describes the homogeneity of the production function $f(K, L) = 8\sqrt{L^2K} + 2KL$?

A. It displays decreasing returns to scale

B. It displays increasing returns to scale

C. It displays constant returns to scale

D. It is not homogeneous

E. There is insufficient information

Question 7

A firm's fixed costs are 50 and the variable costs per unit are $3Q$. Draw a sketch graph of the average cost function.

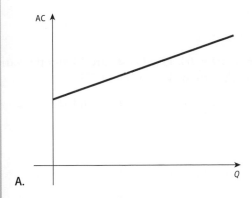

A.

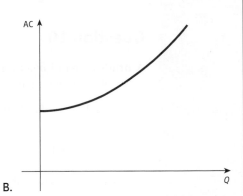

B.

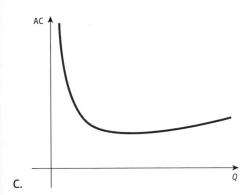

C.

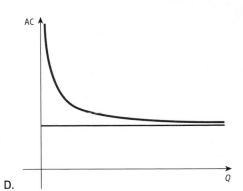

D.

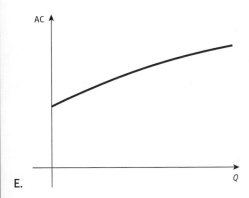

E.

Question 8

Simplify $\log_a 14 - \log_a 7 + 2\log_a x - 3\log_a y - \log_a 1$

A. $\log_a \dfrac{2x^2}{y^3}$
B. $\log_a \dfrac{7x^2}{3y}$
C. $\log_a \dfrac{y^3}{2x^2}$
D. $\log_a \dfrac{7x^2}{y^3}$
E. $\log_a \dfrac{y^2}{7x^3}$

Question 9

If one solution of the quadratic equation, $21x^2 + cx - 10 = 0$ is 2/7, find the second solution.

A. −5/3   **B.** −7/2   **C.** −2/7   **D.** −3/7   **E.** −3/5

Question 10

A firm's demand function is $3P + 2Q = 60$. Fixed costs are 13 and the variable cost per unit is 4. At what quantities does the firm make a profit of 77?

A. 5 and 27   **B.** 9 and 15   **C.** 8 and 20   **D.** 6 and 18   **E.** 4 and 16

Question 11

The demand function of a good is $P = 15 - 2Q - Q^2$. Find the largest possible value of Q.

A. 5   **B.** 15   **C.** 7.5   **D.** 3   **E.** 8

Question 12

The value V (in billions of $) of a non-renewable resource t years from now is given by $V(t) = Ae^{0.05t}$. If it is currently worth $50 billion, after how many years will it be worth $175 billion?

A. $20\ln\left(-\dfrac{7}{2}\right)$ **B.** $-\dfrac{1}{20}\ln\left(\dfrac{2}{7}\right)$ **C.** $20\ln\left(\dfrac{2}{7}\right)$ **D.** $-0.05\ln\left(\dfrac{7}{2}\right)$ **E.** $20\ln\left(\dfrac{7}{2}\right)$

Question 13

Given the supply and demand functions

$$P = Q_S^2 + 8Q_S + 25$$
$$P = -Q_D^2 - 7Q_D + 273$$

determine the equilibrium price.

A. 15.5   **B.** 8   **C.** 105   **D.** 153   **E.** 97

Question 14

Solve the quadratic inequality $-Q^2 + 7Q \geq 10$.

A. $Q \leq 2, Q \geq 5$ **B** $2 \leq Q \leq 5$ **C** $Q \leq -5, Q \geq -2$
D. $-5 \leq Q \leq -2$ **E** No solution

Question 15

Find the exact solution of the equation $18e^{-3x} = 2e^{-5x}$

A. $-\ln 3$ **B.** $2\ln 3$ **C.** $\dfrac{5}{3}\ln 2$ **D.** $\dfrac{3}{5}\ln 2$ **E.** $-\dfrac{3}{5}\ln 2$

Examination questions

Question 1

The output Q of a production process can be modelled by the Cobb-Douglas function, $Q = 100K^{2/3} L^{1/2}$, where K and L denote the inputs of capital and labour, respectively.

(a) Find Q when $K = 8$ and $L = 25$.

(b) Find L when $Q = 9000$ and $K = 27$.

(c) Find K when $Q = 3200$ and $L = 4$.

(d) Show that this function is homogeneous and comment on its return to scale.

Question 2

A firm's fixed costs are 8, variable costs per unit are 2 and the demand function is $P = 8 - Q$ where P and Q denote price and quantity, respectively.

Find an expression for profit, π, in terms of Q and hence sketch a graph of π against Q.

(a) For what values of Q does the firm break-even?

(b) Calculate the maximum profit.

(c) Describe the effect on the graph of the profit function due to a decrease in fixed costs.

Question 3

The supply and demand functions of a good are given by:

$$P = 2Q_S^2 + 3Q_S + 10$$
$$P = -Q_D^2 - 3Q_D + 154$$

where P, Q_S and Q_D denote price, quantity supplied and quantity demanded, respectively.

(a) Determine the equilibrium price and quantity.

(b) If the government imposes a tax of $5 per item, determine the new values of equilibrium price and quantity. Round your answers to two decimal places. Who pays the tax?

Question 4

The demand function of a good is $P = 10 - Q$ and the total cost function is $TC = 12 + 2Q$.

(a) Find an expression for the total revenue function and deduce that the profit function is given by $\pi = -Q^2 + 8Q - 12$.

(b) By solving the quadratic inequality $\pi \geq 3$, determine the range of prices which will ensure that the firm's profit is at least 3 units.

Question 5

(a) Giving FULL details of your working, use the rules of logs to:

    (i) express $5\log_a x - 2\log_a y + \log_a xy$ as a single logarithm

    (ii) evaluate $\log_2 5 + \dfrac{1}{2}\log_2 36 - \log_2 120$

(b) The price of a good over a three-year period is shown in the following table:

Beginning of Year	0	1	2
Price (in $)	1000	1100	1210

Explain why this data can be modelled exactly using an exponential function, $p = Ab^t$ where p denotes the price at the beginning of year t.
State the values of the parameters, A and b.
Assuming that the model continues to be valid in subsequent years, work out the

    (i) price of the good (to the nearest $) at the beginning of year 10;

    (ii) number of complete years for the price of the good to exceed $8000.

Question 6

A firm's fixed costs are 14 and the variable costs are 2 per unit. The corresponding profit function is of the form $\pi = aQ^2 + bQ + c$ where Q denotes quantity.

(a) Write down expressions for the total cost and average cost functions, and sketch their graphs.

(b) Explain why $c = -14$.

(c) The firm makes a loss of 6 when $Q = 1$ and a profit of 4 when $Q = 6$. Write down a pair of simultaneous equations and solve them to find a and b.

(d) Find the break-even points and hence find the maximum profit.

(e) Find an expression for total revenue and deduce the demand function.

Question 7

(a) Simplify

    (i) $\dfrac{3a^2b^4}{6a^{-3}b}$ (ii) $(8x^3 y^6)^{2/3}$ (iii) $\log_b b^6$ (iv) $\log_b xy + \log_b xz - \log_b\left(\dfrac{x}{yz}\right)$

(b) Solve the equation $3^x = 2(5^x)$, giving your answer correct to two decimal places.

(c) The total number of sales, S, made t weeks after the launch of a new model of phone is given by
$$S = 2\,000\,000(1 - e^{-0.2t})$$

    (i) Estimate the number of sales after two weeks.

    (ii) How many weeks does it take for sales to exceed one million? Give your answer correct to one decimal place.

    (iii) Sketch a graph of S against t to show how sales vary over time.

Question 8

The value, V, of a piece of machinery depreciates at a rate which is proportional to V. Two years after purchase, the machinery is worth $45\,125, and four years after purchase, it is worth $40\,725.

(a) If $V = Ab^t$ where t is the number of years after purchase, find A and b, and explain the significance of the number A.

(b) By using your answer to part (a) or otherwise, express V in the form Ae^{rt} where r is given to three significant figures.

(c) If a graph of $\ln V$ is plotted against t, show that the graph will be a straight line, and state the gradient and vertical intercept.

Question 9

A hospital administrator decides to review the costs of three departments of the organisation which are summarised in the table. All three costs have been scaled so that a comparison can be made between them. The variable Q is measured in thousands of patients.

	IT	Retail	Printing
Fixed	1	5	0
Variable	$0.04Q + 0.5$	0.5	1

(a) Derive expressions for the average cost functions for each of these departments.

(b) The diagram shows the graphs of all three average cost functions on the same diagram. Which hospital department corresponds to each graph? Justify your answer.

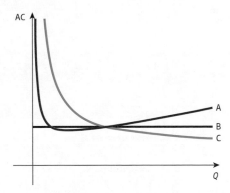

(c) Find the values of Q for which the average cost of IT is less than the average cost of printing.

CHAPTER 3
Mathematics of Finance

This chapter provides an understanding of the way in which financial calculations are worked out. There are four sections, which should be read in the order that they appear.

Section 3.1 revises work on percentages. In particular, a quick method of dealing with percentage increase and decrease calculations is described. This enables an overall percentage change to be deduced easily from a sequence of individual changes. Percentages are used to calculate and interpret index numbers, and to adjust value data for inflation.

Section 3.2 shows how to calculate the future value of a lump sum which is invested to earn interest. This interest can be added to the investment annually, semi-annually, quarterly or even more frequently. The exponential function is used to solve problems in which interest is compounded continuously.

A wide variety of applications are considered in Sections 3.3 and 3.4. In Section 3.3 a mathematical device known as a geometric progression, which is used to calculate the future value of a savings plan and the monthly repayments of a loan, is introduced. Section 3.4 describes the opposite problem of calculating the present value given a future value. The process of working backwards is called discounting. It can be used to decide how much money to invest today in order to achieve a specific target sum in a few years' time. Discounting can be used to appraise different investment projects. On the macroeconomic level, the relationship between interest rates and speculative demand for money is investigated.

The material in this chapter will be of greatest benefit to students on business studies and management courses. This chapter could be omitted without affecting your understanding of the rest of this text.

SECTION 3.1

Percentages

Objectives

At the end of this section you should be able to:

- Understand what a percentage is.
- Solve problems involving a percentage increase or decrease.
- Write down scale factors associated with percentage changes.
- Work out overall percentage changes.
- Calculate and interpret index numbers.
- Adjust value data for inflation.

Advice

The first part of this section provides a leisurely revision of the idea of a percentage as well as a reminder about how to use scale factors to cope with percentage changes. These ideas are crucial to any understanding of financial mathematics. However, if you are already confident in using percentages, you may wish to move straight on to the applications covered in sub-sections 3.1.1 and 3.1.2.

In order to be able to handle financial calculations, it is necessary to use percentages proficiently. The word 'percentage' literally means 'per cent', i.e. per hundredth, so that whenever we speak of $r\%$ of something, we simply mean the fraction $(r/100)$ ths of it.

For example,

$$25\% \text{ is the same as} \quad \frac{25}{100} = \frac{1}{4}$$

$$30\% \text{ is the same as} \quad \frac{30}{100} = \frac{3}{10}$$

$$50\% \text{ is the same as} \quad \frac{50}{100} = \frac{1}{2}$$

Example

Calculate

(a) 15% of 12

(b) 150% of 290

Solution

(a) 15% of 12 is the same as

$$\frac{15}{100} \times 12 = 0.15 \times 12 = 1.8$$

(b) 150% of 290 is the same as

$$\frac{150}{100} \times 290 = 1.5 \times 290 = 435$$

Practice Problem

1. Calculate

(a) 10% of $2.90   (b) 75% of $1250   (c) 24% of $580

Whenever any numerical quantity increases or decreases, it is customary to refer to this change in percentage terms. The following example serves to remind you of how to perform calculations involving percentage changes.

Example

(a) An investment rises from $2500 to $3375. Express the increase as a percentage of the original.
(b) At the beginning of a year, the population of a small village is 8400. If the annual rise in population is 12%, find the population at the end of the year.
(c) In a sale, all prices are reduced by 20%. Find the sale price of a good originally costing $580.

Solution

(a) The rise in the value of the investment is

$$3375 - 2500 = 875$$

As a fraction of the original, this is

$$\frac{875}{2500} = 0.35$$

This is the same as 35 hundredths, so the percentage rise is 35%.

(b) As a fraction,

$$12\% \text{ is the same as } \frac{12}{100} = 0.12$$

so the rise in population is

$$0.12 \times 8400 = 1008$$

Hence the final population is

$$8400 + 1008 = 9408$$

(c) As a fraction,

$$20\% \text{ is the same as } \frac{20}{100} = 0.2$$

so the fall in price is

$$0.2 \times 580 = 116$$

Hence the final price is

$$580 - 116 = \$464$$

Practice Problem

2. **(a)** A firm's annual sales rise from 50 000 to 55 000 from one year to the next. Express the rise as a percentage of the original.

   (b) The government imposes a 15% tax on the price of a good. How much does the consumer pay for a good priced by a firm at $1360?

   (c) Investments fall during the course of a year by 7%. Find the value of an investment at the end of the year if it was worth $9500 at the beginning of the year.

In the previous example and in Practice Problem 2, the calculations were performed in two separate stages. The actual rise or fall was first worked out, and these changes were then applied to the original value to obtain the final answer. It is possible to obtain this answer in a single calculation, and we now describe how this can be done. Not only is this new approach quicker, but it also enables us to tackle more difficult problems. To be specific, let us suppose that the price of a good is set to rise by 9% and that its current price is $78. The new price consists of the original (which can be thought of as 100% of the $78) plus the increase (which is 9% of $78). The final price is therefore

$$100\% + 9\% = 109\% \text{ (of the \$78)}$$

which is the same as

$$\frac{109}{100} = 1.09$$

In other words, in order to calculate the final price, all we have to do is to multiply by the **scale factor**, 1.09. Hence the new price is

$$1.09 \times 78 = \$85.02$$

One advantage of this approach is that it is then just as easy to go backwards and work out the original price from the new price. To go backwards in time we simply *divide* by the scale factor. For example, if the final price of a good is \$1068.20, then before a 9% increase the price would have been

$$1068.20 \div 1.09 = \$980$$

In general, if the percentage rise is $r\%$, then the final value consists of the original (100%) together with the increase ($r\%$), giving a total of

$$\frac{100}{100} + \frac{r}{100} = 1 + \frac{r}{100}$$

To go forwards in time we multiply by this scale factor, whereas to go backwards we divide.

Example

(a) If the annual rate of inflation is 4%, find the price of a good at the end of a year if its price at the beginning of the year is \$25.

(b) The cost of a good is \$750 including a sales tax of 20%. What is the cost excluding the sales tax?

(c) Express the rise from 950 to 1007 as a percentage.

Solution

(a) The scale factor is

$$1 + \frac{4}{100} = 1.04$$

We are trying to find the price *after* the increase, so we *multiply* to get

$$25 \times 1.04 = \$26$$

(b) The scale factor is

$$1 + \frac{20}{100} = 1.2$$

This time we are trying to find the price *before* the increase, so we *divide* by the scale factor to get

$$750 \div 1.2 = \$625$$

(c) The scale factor is

$$\frac{\text{new value}}{\text{old value}} = \frac{1007}{950} = 1.06$$

which can be thought of as

$$1 + \frac{6}{100}$$

so the rise is 6%.

Practice Problem

3. (a) The value of a good rises by 13% in a year. If it was worth $6.5 million at the beginning of the year, find its value at the end of the year.

   (b) The GNP of a country has increased by 63% over the past five years and is now $124 billion. What was the GNP five years ago?

   (c) Sales rise from 115 000 to 123 050 in a year. Find the annual percentage rise.

It is possible to use scale factors to solve problems involving percentage decreases. To be specific, suppose that an investment of $76 falls by 20%. The new value is the original (100%) less the decrease (20%), so it is 80% of the original. The scale factor is therefore 0.8, giving a new value of

$$0.8 \times 76 = \$60.80$$

In general, the scale factor for an $r\%$ decrease is

$$\frac{100}{100} - \frac{r}{100} = 1 - \frac{r}{100}$$

Once again, you multiply by this scale factor when going forwards in time and divide when going backwards.

Example

(a) The value of a car depreciates by 25% in a year. What will a car, currently priced at $43 000, be worth in a year's time?

(b) After a 15% reduction in a sale, the price of a good is $39.95. What was the price before the sale began?

(c) The number of passengers using a rail link fell from 190 205 to 174 989. Find the percentage decrease.

Solution

(a) The scale factor is

$$1 - \frac{25}{100} = 0.75$$

so the new price is

$$43\ 000 \times 0.75 = \$32\ 250 \qquad \text{forwards in time so multiply}$$

(b) The scale factor is

$$1 - \frac{15}{100} = 0.85$$

so the original price was

$$39.95 \div 0.85 = \$47 \qquad \text{backwards in time so divide}$$

(c) The scale factor is

$$\frac{\text{new value}}{\text{old value}} = \frac{174\,989}{190\,205} = 0.92$$

which can be thought of as

$$1 - \frac{8}{100}$$

so the fall is 8%.

Practice Problem

4. (a) Current monthly output from a factory is 25 000. In a recession, this is expected to fall by 65%. Estimate the new level of output.

   (b) As a result of a modernisation programme, a firm is able to reduce the size of its workforce by 24%. If it now employs 570 workers, how many people did it employ before restructuring?

   (c) Shares originally worth $10.50 fall in a stock market crash to $2.10. Find the percentage decrease.

The final application of scale factors that we consider is to the calculation of overall percentage changes. It is often the case that over various periods of time, the price of a good is subject to several individual percentage changes. It is useful to be able to replace these by an equivalent single percentage change spanning the entire period. This can be done by simply multiplying together successive scale factors.

Example

(a) Share prices rise by 32% during the first half of the year and rise by a further 10% during the second half. What is the overall percentage change?

(b) Find the overall percentage change in the price of a good if it rises by 5% in a year but is then reduced by 30% in a sale.

Solution

(a) To find the value of shares at the end of the first 6 months, we would multiply by

$$1 + \frac{32}{100} = 1.32$$

and at the end of the year we would multiply again by the scale factor

$$1 + \frac{10}{100} = 1.1$$

The net effect is to multiply by their product

$$1.32 \times 1.1 = 1.452$$

which can be thought of as

$$1 + \frac{45.2}{100}$$

so the overall change is 45.2%.

Notice that this is not the same as

$$32\% + 10\% = 42\%$$

This is because during the second half of the year, we not only get a 10% rise in the original value, but we also get a 10% rise on the gain accrued during the first 6 months.

(b) The individual scale factors are 1.05 and 0.7, so the overall scale factor is

$$1.05 \times 0.7 = 0.735$$

The fact that this is less than 1 indicates that the overall change is a decrease. Writing

$$0.735 = 1 - 0.265 = 1 - \frac{26.5}{100}$$

we see that this scale factor represents a 26.5% decrease.

Practice Problem

5. Find the single percentage increase or decrease equivalent to

   (a) an increase of 30% followed by an increase of 40%

   (b) a decrease of 30% followed by a decrease of 40%

   (c) an increase of 10% followed by a decrease of 50%.

We conclude this section by describing two applications of percentages in macroeconomics:

- index numbers;
- inflation.

We consider each of these in turn.

3.1.1 Index numbers

Economic data often take the form of a **time series**; values of economic indicators are available on an annual, quarterly or monthly basis, and we are interested in analysing the rise and fall of these numbers over time. **Index numbers** enable us to identify trends and relationships in the data. The following example shows you how to calculate index numbers and how to interpret them.

Example

Table 3.1 shows the values of household spending (in billions of dollars) during a five-year period. Calculate the index numbers when Year 2 is taken as the base year and give a brief interpretation.

Table 3.1

	Year				
	1	2	3	4	5
Household spending	686.9	697.2	723.7	716.6	734.5

Solution

When finding index numbers, a base year is chosen and the value of 100 is allocated to that year. In this example, we are told to take Y2 as the base year, so the index number of Y2 is 100. To find the index number of the year Y3, we work out the scale factor associated with the change in household spending from the base year, Y2 to Y3, and then multiply the answer by 100.

index number = scale factor from base year × 100

In this case, we get

$$\frac{723.7}{697.2} \times 100 = 103.8$$

This shows that the value of household spending in Y3 was 103.8% of its value in Y2. In other words, household spending increased by 3.8% during Y3.

For the year Y4, the value of household spending was 716.6, giving the index number

$$\frac{716.6}{697.2} \times 100 = 102.8$$

This shows that the value of household spending in Y4 was 102.8% of its value in Y2. In other words, household spending increased by 2.8% between Y2 and Y4. Notice that this is less than that calculated for Y3, reflecting the fact that spending actually fell slightly during Y4. The remaining two index numbers are calculated in a similar way and are shown in Table 3.2.

Table 3.2

	Year				
	1	2	3	4	5
Household spending	686.9	697.2	723.7	716.6	734.5
Index number	98.5	100	103.8	102.8	105.3

Practice Problem

6. Calculate the index numbers for the data shown in Table 3.1, this time taking Year 1 as the base year.

Index numbers themselves have no units. They merely express the value of some quantity as a percentage of a base number. This is particularly useful, since it enables us to compare how values of quantities, of varying magnitudes, change in relation to each other. Table 3.3 shows the rise and fall of two share prices during an 8-month period. The prices (in dollars) listed for each share are taken on the last day of each month. Share A is exceptionally cheap. Investors often include this type of share in their portfolio, since they can occasionally make spectacular gains. This was the case with many dot.com shares at the end of the 1990s. The second share is more expensive and corresponds to a larger, more established firm.

Table 3.3

Month	Jan	Feb	Mar	Apr	May	Jun	Jul	Aug
Share A	0.31	0.28	0.31	0.34	0.40	0.39	0.45	0.52
Share B	6.34	6.40	6.45	6.52	6.57	6.43	6.65	7.00

The index numbers have been listed in Table 3.4, taking April as the base month. Notice that both shares are given the same index number of 100 in April. This is despite the fact that the values of the two shares are very different. This creates 'a level playing-field', enabling us to monitor the relative performance of the two shares. The index numbers show quite clearly that share A has outperformed share B during this period. Indeed, if an investor had spent $1000 on shares of type A in January, they could have bought 3225 of them, which would be worth $1677 in August, making a profit of $677. The corresponding profit for share B is only $103.

Table 3.4

Month	Jan	Feb	Mar	Apr	May	Jun	Jul	Aug
Index of share price A (April = 100)	91.2	82.3	91.2	100	117.6	114.7	132.4	152.9
Index of share price B (April = 100)	97.2	98.2	98.9	100	100.8	98.6	102.0	107.4

Incidentally, if the only information you have about the time series is the set of index numbers, then it is possible to work out the percentage changes between any pair of values. Table 3.5 shows the index numbers of the output of a particular firm for two consecutive years.

Table 3.5

	Output							
	Y1Q1	Y1Q2	Y1Q3	Y1Q4	Y2Q1	Y2Q2	Y2Q3	Y2Q4
Index	89.3	98.1	105.0	99.3	100	106.3	110.2	105.7

The table shows that the base quarter is the first quarter of Year 2 because the index number is 100 in Y2Q1. It is, of course, easy to find the percentage change from this quarter to any subsequent quarter. For example, the index number associated with the third quarter of Y2 is 110.2, so we know immediately that the percentage change in output from Y2Q1 to Y2Q3 is 10.2%. However, it is not immediately obvious what the percentage change is from, say, Y1Q2 to Y2Q2. To work this out, note that the scale factor of this change is

$$\frac{106.3}{98.1} = 1.084$$

which corresponds to an 8.4% increase.

Similarly, the scale factor of the change from Y1Q3 to Y2Q1 is

$$\frac{100}{105} = 0.952$$

This is less than 1, reflecting the fact that output has fallen. To find the percentage change, we write the scale factor as

$$1 - 0.048$$

which shows that the percentage decrease is 4.8%.

Practice Problem

7. Use the index numbers listed in Table 3.5 to find the percentage change in output from

(a) Y2Q1 to Y2Q4
(b) Y1Q1 to Y2Q4
(c) Y1Q1 to Y2Q1

It is possible to create sensible index numbers to measure the variation of a bundle of goods over time. To be specific, suppose that a firm buys three products. Table 3.6 shows the number of each type bought in Year 1 together with the unit prices of each item in Year 1 and Year 2.

Table 3.6

Product	Number bought in Year 1	Unit price in Year 1	Unit price in Year 2
A	20	8	10
B	35	18	23
C	10	6	5

The total purchase cost in Year 1 is worked out by multiplying the quantities by the corresponding prices which gives

$$20 \times 8 + 35 \times 18 + 10 \times 6 = 850$$

If we assume that the firm buys the same number of each type in Year 2, the total cost would be

$$20 \times 10 + 35 \times 23 + 10 \times 5 = 1055$$

Taking the base year as Year 1, we see that the index number in Year 1 is 100 and the index number in Year 2 is

$$\frac{1055}{850} \times 100 = 124.1$$

In this calculation we have created a weighted index which assumes that the quantities purchased in Year 2 are the same as the base year. This is referred to as a base-weighted index (or **Laspeyres index**). It provides a good indication to the firm of changing costs, although it becomes unreliable if the firm changes the amount it buys over time. If figures are available for the quantities purchased each year, then it is possible to work out an index based on current values. For example, if the quantities bought in Year 2 are those shown in Table 3.7, then the current weighted index in Year 2 is

$$\frac{17 \times 10 + 38 \times 23 + 12 \times 5}{850} \times 100 = \frac{1104}{850} \times 100 = 129.9$$

Table 3.7

Product	Number bought in Year 2
A	17
B	38
C	12

This is referred to as the **Paasche index**. It has the obvious advantage of reflecting changes in the actual purchases made by the firm. On the downside, it is necessary to know the precise amounts of each item bought every year and, strictly speaking, since the calculations change each year, you are not comparing like quantities.

3.1.2 Inflation

Over a period of time, the prices of many goods and services usually increase. The annual rate of **inflation** is the average percentage change in a given selection of these goods and services, over the previous year. Seasonal variations are taken into account, and the particular basket of goods and services is changed periodically to reflect changing patterns of household expenditure. The presence of inflation is particularly irritating when trying to interpret a time series that involves a monetary value. Inevitably, this will be influenced by inflation during any year, and what is of interest is the fluctuation of a time series 'over and above' inflation. Economists deal with this by distinguishing between nominal and real data. **Nominal data** are the original, raw data such as those listed in tables in the previous sub-section. These are based on the prices that prevailed at the time. **Real data** are the values that have been adjusted to take inflation into account. The standard way of doing this is to pick a year and then convert the values for all other years to the level that they would have had in this base year. This may sound rather complicated, but the idea and calculations involved are really quite simple as the following example demonstrates.

Example

Table 3.8 shows the price (in thousands of dollars) of an average house in a certain town during a five-year period. The price quoted is the value of the house at the end of each year. Use the annual rates of inflation given in Table 3.9 to adjust the prices to those prevailing at the end of Year 2. Compare the rise in both the nominal and real values of house prices during this period.

Table 3.8

	Year				
	1	2	3	4	5
Average house price	72	89	93	100	106

Table 3.9

	Year			
	2	3	4	5
Annual rate of inflation	10.7%	7.1%	3.5%	2.3%

Solution

The raw figures shown in Table 3.8 give the impression that houses increased steadily in value throughout this period, with a quite substantial gain during the first year. However, if inflation had been very high, then the gain in real terms would have been quite small. Indeed, if the rate of inflation were to exceed the percentage rise of these nominal data, then the price of a house would actually fall in real terms. To analyse this situation we will use Table 3.9, which shows the rates of inflation during this period. Notice that since the house prices listed in Table 3.9 are quoted at the end of each year, we are not interested in the rate of inflation during Year 1.

We are told in the question to choose Year 2 as the base year and calculate the value of the house at 'Year 2 prices'. The value of the house at the end of Year 2 is obviously $89 000, since no adjustment needs to be made. At the end of Year 3, the house is worth $93 000. However, during that year, inflation was 7.1%. To adjust this price to 'Year 2 prices' we simply divide by the scale factor 1.071, since we are going backwards in time. We get

$$\frac{93\ 000}{1.071} = 86\ 835$$

In real terms the house has fallen in value by over $2000.

To adjust the price of the house in Year 4 we first need to divide by 1.035 to backtrack to Year 3, and then divide again by 1.071 to reach Year 2. We get

$$\frac{100\ 000}{1.035 \times 1.071} = 90\ 213$$

In real terms there has at least been some gain during Year 4. However, this is less than impressive, and from a purely financial point of view, there would have been more lucrative ways of investing this capital.

For the Year 5 price, the adjusted value is

$$\frac{106\ 000}{1.023 \times 1.035 \times 1.071} = 93\ 476$$

and, for Year 1, the adjusted value is

$$72\ 000 \times 1.107 = 79\ 704$$

going forward in time, so multiply

Table 3.10 lists both the nominal and the 'constant Year 2' values of the house (rounded to the nearest thousand) for comparison. It shows quite clearly that, apart from the gain during Year 2, the increase in value has, in fact, been quite modest.

Table 3.10

	Year				
	1	2	3	4	5
Nominal house price	72	89	94	100	106
Year 2 house price	80	89	87	90	93

Practice Problem

8. Table 3.11 shows the average annual salary (in thousands of dollars) of employees in a small firm, together with the annual rate of inflation for that year. Adjust these salaries to the prices prevailing at the end of Year 2 and so give the real values of the employees' salaries at constant 'Year 2 prices'. Comment on the rise in earnings during this period.

Table 3.11

	Year				
	1	2	3	4	5
Salary	17.3	18.1	19.8	23.5	26.0
Inflation		4.9	4.3	4.0	3.5

Key Terms

Index number   The scale factor of a variable measured from the base year multiplied by 100.

Inflation   The percentage increase in the level of prices over a 12-month period.

Laspeyre index   An index number for groups of data which are weighted by the quantities used in the base year.

Nominal data   Monetary values prevailing at the time that they were measured.

Paasche index   An index number for groups of data which are weighted by the quantities used in the current year.

Real data   Monetary values adjusted to take inflation into account.

Scale factor   The multiplier that gives the final value in percentage problems.

Time series   A sequence of numbers indicating the variation of data over time.

Exercise 3.1

1. Express the following percentages as fractions in their simplest form:

    (a) 35%   (b) 88%   (c) 250%   (d) $17^1/_2$%   (e) 0.2%

2. Calculate each of the following:

    (a) 5% of 24   (b) 8% of 88   (c) 48% of 4563   (d) 112% of 56

3. A firm has 132 female and 88 male employees.

    (a) What percentage of staff are female?

    (b) During the next year 8 additional female staff are employed. If the percentage of female staff is now 56%, how many additional male staff were recruited during the year?

4. Write down the scale factors corresponding to

   (a) an increase of 19%;

   (b) an increase of 250%;

   (c) a decrease of 2%;

   (d) a decrease of 43%.

5. Write down the percentage changes corresponding to the following scale factors:

   (a) 1.04   (b) 1.42   (c) 0.86

   (d) 3.45   (e) 1.0025   (f) 0.04

6. Find the new quantities when

   (a) $16.25 is increased by 12%

   (b) the population of a town, currently at 113 566, rises by 5%

   (c) a good priced by a firm at $87.90 is subject to a sales tax of 15%

   (d) a good priced at $2300 is reduced by 30% in a sale

   (e) a car, valued at $23 000, depreciates by 32%

7. A student discount card reduces a bill in a restaurant from $124 to $80.60. Work out the percentage discount.

8. A shop sells books at '20% below the recommended retail price (r.r.p.)'. If it sells a book for $12.40, find

   (a) the r.r.p.

   (b) the cost of the book after a further reduction of 15% in a sale

   (c) the overall percentage discount obtained by buying the book from the shop in the sale compared with the manufacturer's r.r.p.

9. A TV costs $900 including 20% sales tax. Find the new price if tax is reduced to 15%.

10. An antiques dealer tries to sell a vase at 45% above the $18 000 which the dealer paid at auction.

    (a) What is the new sale price?

    (b) By what percentage can the dealer now reduce the price before making a loss?

11. Find the single percentage increase or decrease equivalent to

    (a) a 10% increase followed by a 25% increase

    (b) a 34% decrease followed by a 65% increase

    (c) a 25% increase followed by a 25% decrease.

    Explain in words why the overall change in part (c) is not 0%.

12. Table 3.12 gives the annual rate of inflation during a five-year period.

Table 3.12

Year	1	2	3	4	5
Annual rate of inflation	1.8%	2.1%	2.9%	2.4%	2.7%

If a nominal house price at the end of Year 1 was $10.8 million, find the real house price adjusted to prices prevailing at the end of Year 4. Round your answer to three significant figures.

13. The price of a good during the last five years is:

    $25 $30 $36 $43 $50

    Calculate the index numbers using the last year as the base year and hence comment on the rise in prices during this period.

14. Table 3.13 shows the monthly index of sales of a good during the first four months of the year.

    Table 3.13

Month	Jan	Feb	Mar	Apr
Index	100	120	145	150

    (a) Which month is chosen as the base year?

    (b) If sales in February are 3840, what are the sales in April?

    (c) What is the index number in May if sales are 4256?

15. Table 3.14 shows the index numbers associated with transport costs during a 20-year period. The public transport costs reflect changes to bus and train fares, whereas private transport costs include purchase, service, petrol, tax and insurance costs of cars.

    Table 3.14

	Year				
	1995	2000	2005	2010	2015
Public transport	100	130	198	224	245
Private transport	100	125	180	199	221

    (1) Which year is chosen as the base year?

    (2) Find the percentage increases in the cost of public transport from

    (a) 1995 to 2000   (b) 2000 to 2005   (c) 2005 to 2010   (d) 2010 to 2015

    (3) Repeat part (2) for private transport.

    (4) Comment briefly on the relative rise in public and private transport costs during this 20-year period.

16. Table 3.15 shows the number of items (in thousands) produced from a factory production line during the course of a year. Taking the second quarter as the base quarter, calculate the associated index numbers. Suggest a possible reason for the fluctuations in output.

    Table 3.15

	Quarter			
	Q1	Q2	Q3	Q4
Output	13.5	1.4	2.5	10.5

17. Table 3.16 shows the prices of a good for each year between Year 1 and Year 6.

Table 3.16

Year	1	2	3	4	5	6
Price ($)	40	48	44	56	60	71

(a) Work out the index numbers, correct to one decimal place, taking Year 2 as the base year.

(b) If the index number for Year 7 is 135, calculate the corresponding price. You may assume that the base year is still Year 2.

(c) If the index number in Year 3 is approximately 73, find the year that is used as the base year.

Exercise 3.1*

1. Total revenue from daily ticket sales to a theme park is $1 352 400. A total of 12 000 tickets were sold and 65% of these were child's tickets with a 30% discount off the adult price. Work out the cost of an adult ticket.

2. The cost of a computer is $6000 including 20% sales tax. In a generous gesture, the government decides to reduce the rate to just 17.5%. Find the cost of the computer after the tax has changed.

3. A coat originally costing $150 is reduced by 25% in a sale and, since nobody bought the coat, a further reduction of 20% of the sale price is applied.

(a) Find the final cost of the coat after both reductions.

(b) Find the overall percentage reduction, and explain why this is not the same as a single reduction of 45%.

4. A furniture store has a sale of 40% off on selected items.
A sales assistant, Carol, reduces the price of a sofa originally costing $1200.

(a) What is the new price?
The manager does not want this sofa to be in the sale and the following day tells another sales assistant, Michael, to restore the sofa back to the original price. He does not know what the original price was and decides to show off his mathematical knowledge by taking the answer to part (a) and multiplying it by 1.4.

(b) Explain carefully why this does not give the correct answer of $1200.

(c) Suggest an alternative calculation that would give the right answer.

5. During 2016 the price of a good increased by 8%. In the sales on 1 January 2017 all items are reduced by 25%.

(a) If the sale price of the good is $688.50, find the original price at the beginning of 2014.

(b) Find the overall percentage change.

(c) What percentage increase would be needed to restore the cost to the original price prevailing on 1 January 2016? Give your answer to one decimal place.

→

6. Table 3.17 shows government expenditure (in billions of dollars) on education for four consecutive years, together with the rate of inflation for each year.

(a) Taking Year 1 as the base year, work out the index numbers of the nominal data given in the third row of the table.

(b) Find the values of expenditure at constant Year 1 prices and hence recalculate the index numbers of real government expenditure.

(c) Give an interpretation of the index numbers calculated in part (b).

Table 3.17

	Year			
	1	2	3	4
Spending	236	240	267	276
Inflation		4.7	4.2	3.4

7. Index numbers associated with the growth of unemployment during an eight-year period are shown in Table 3.18.

(a) What are the base years for the two indices?

(b) If the government had not switched to index 2, what would be the values of index 1 in years 7 and 8?

(c) What values would index 2 have been in years 1, 2, 3, 4 and 5?

(d) If unemployment was 1.2 million in year 4, how many people were unemployed in years 1 and 8?

Table 3.18

	Year							
	1	2	3	4	5	6	7	8
Index 1	100	95	105	110	119	127		
Index 2						100	112	118

8. The prices of a good at the end of each year between Year 1 and Year 6 are listed in Table 3.19, which also shows the annual rate of inflation.

Table 3.19

Year	1	2	3	4	5	6
Price	230	242	251	257	270	284
Inflation		4%	3%	2.5%	2%	2%

(a) Find the values of the prices adjusted to the end of Year 2, correct to two decimal places. Hence, calculate the index numbers of the real data with Year 2 as the base year. Give your answers correct to one decimal place.

(b) If the index number of the real price for Year 7 is 109 and the rate of inflation for that year is 2.5%, work out the nominal value of the price in Year 7. Give your answer rounded to the nearest whole number.

(c) If the index number of the real data in Year 0 is 95.6 and the nominal price is $215, find the rate of inflation for Year 1. Give your answer correct to one decimal place.

9. A firm buys three goods. The number of each type bought in Year 1 is shown in Table 3.20 together with the unit prices for three consecutive years.

Table 3.20

Product	Number bought in Year 1	Unit price in Year 1	Unit price in Year 2	Unit Price in Year 3
A	56	34	36	42
B	40	24	24	23
C	122	13	11	14

(a) Calculate a base-weighted index (Laspeyres) for these data using Year 1 as the base year.

(b) Comment on the values obtained in part (a).

10. The number of goods bought by the firm in Q9 vary over time. Figures for Year 2 and Year 3 are shown in Table 3.21.

Table 3.21

Product	Number bought in Year 2	Number bought in Year 3
A	62	96
B	44	46
C	134	102

(a) Calculate a current-weighted index (Paasche) for these data using Year 1 as the base year.

(b) Compare the values with those obtained in Q9.

Compound interest

Objectives

At the end of this section you should be able to:

- Understand the difference between simple and compound interest.
- Calculate the future value of a principal under annual compounding.
- Calculate the future value of a principal under continuous compounding.
- Determine the annual percentage rate of interest given a nominal rate of interest.

Today, businesses and individuals are faced with a bewildering array of loan facilities and investment opportunities. In this section we explain how these financial calculations are carried out to enable an informed choice to be made between the various possibilities available. We begin by considering what happens when a single lump sum is invested and show how to calculate the amount accumulated over a period of time.

Suppose that someone gives you the option of receiving $500 now or $500 in three years' time. Which of these alternatives would you accept? Most people would take the money now, partly because they may have an immediate need for it, but also because they recognise that $500 is worth more today than in three years' time. Even if we ignore the effects of inflation, it is still better to take the money now, since it can be invested and will increase in value over the three-year period. In order to work out this value, we need to know the rate of interest and the basis on which it is calculated. Let us begin by assuming that the $500 is invested for three years at 10% interest compounded annually. What exactly do we mean by '10% interest compounded annually'? Well, at the end of each year, the interest is calculated and is added on to the amount currently invested. If the original amount is $500, then after one year the interest is 10% of $500, which is

$$\frac{10}{100} \times \$500 = \frac{1}{10} \times \$500 = \$50$$

so the amount rises by $50 to $550.

What happens to this amount at the end of the second year? Is the interest also $50? This would actually be the case with **simple interest**, when the amount of interest received is the same for all years. However, with **compound interest**, we get 'interest on the interest'. Nearly all financial investments use compound rather than simple interest, because investors need to be rewarded for not taking the interest payment out of the fund each year. Under annual compounding the interest obtained at the end of the second year is 10% of the amount invested at the start of that year. This not only consists of the original $500, but also the $50 already received as interest on the first year's investment. Consequently, we get an additional

$$\frac{1}{10} \times \$550 = \$55$$

raising the sum to $605. Finally, at the end of the third year, the interest is

$$\frac{1}{10} \times \$605 = \$60.50$$

so the investment is $665.50. You are therefore $165.50 better off by taking the $500 now and investing it for three years. The calculations are summarised in Table 3.22.

Table 3.22

End of year	Interest ($)	Investment ($)
1	50	550
2	55	605
3	60.50	665.50

The calculations in Table 3.22 were performed by finding the interest earned each year and adding it on to the amount accumulated at the beginning of the year. This approach is rather laborious, particularly if the money is invested over a long period of time. What is really needed is a method of calculating the investment after, say, 10 years without having to determine the amount for the nine intermediate years. This can be done using the scale factor approach discussed in the previous section. To illustrate this, let us return to the problem of investing $500 at 10% interest compounded annually. The original sum of money is called the **principal** and is denoted by P, and the final sum is called the **future value** and is denoted by S. The scale factor associated with an increase of 10% is

$$1 + \frac{10}{100} = 1.1$$

so at the end of one year the total amount invested is $P(1.1)$.

After two years we get

$$P(1.1) \times (1.1) = P(1.1)^2$$

and after three years the future value is

$$S = P(1.1)^2 \times (1.1) = P(1.1)^3$$

Setting $P = 500$, we see that

$$S = 500(1.1)^3 = \$665.50$$

which is, of course, the same as the amount calculated previously.

In general, if the interest rate is $r\%$ compounded annually, then the scale factor is

$$1 + \frac{r}{100}$$

so, after n years,

$$S - P\left(1 + \frac{r}{100}\right)^n$$

Given the values of r, P and n, it is simple to evaluate S using the power key x^y on a calculator.

Example

Find the value, in four years' time, of $10 000 invested at 5% interest compounded annually.

Solution

In this problem, $P = 10\ 000$, $r = 5$ and $n = 4$, so the formula $S = P\left(1 + \dfrac{r}{100}\right)^n$ gives

$$S = 10\ 000\left(1 + \frac{5}{100}\right)^4 = 10\ 000(1.05)^4 = \$12\ 155.06$$

Practice Problem

1. Use the formula

$$S = P\left(1 + \frac{r}{100}\right)^n$$

to find the value, in 10 years' time, of $1000 invested at 8% interest compounded annually.

The compound interest formula derived previously involves four variables, r, n, P and S. Provided that we know any three of these, we can use the formula to determine the remaining variable. This is illustrated in the following example.

Example

A principal of $25 000 is invested at 12% interest compounded annually. After how many years will the investment first exceed $250 000?

Solution

We want to save a total of $250 000 starting with an initial investment of $25 000. The problem is to determine the number of years required for this on the assumption that the interest is fixed at 12% throughout this time. The formula for compound interest is

$$S = P\left(1 + \frac{r}{100}\right)^n$$

We are given that

$$P = 25\ 000, \quad S = 250\ 000, \quad r = 12$$

so we need to solve the equation

$$250\,000 = 25\,000\left(1 + \frac{12}{100}\right)^n$$

for n.

One way of doing this would just be to keep on guessing values of n until we find the one that works. However, a more mathematical approach is to use logarithms, because we are being asked to solve an equation in which the unknown occurs as a power. Following the method described in Section 2.3, we first divide both sides by 25 000 to get

$$10 = (1.12)^n$$

Taking logarithms of both sides gives

$$\log(10) = \log(1.12)^n$$

and if you apply rule 3 of logarithms you get

$$\log(10) = n\log(1.12) \qquad \boxed{\log_b x^m = m\log_b x}$$

Hence

$$n = \frac{\log(10)}{\log(1.12)}$$

$$= \frac{1}{0.49\,218\,023} \quad \text{(taking logarithms to base 10)}$$

$$= 20.3 \qquad\qquad \text{(to one decimal place)}$$

Now we know that n must be a whole number because interest is only added on at the end of each year. We assume that the first interest payment occurs exactly 12 months after the initial investment and every 12 months thereafter. The answer, 20.3, tells us that after only 20 years the amount is less than $250 000, so we need to wait until 21 years have elapsed before it exceeds this amount. In fact, after 20 years

$$S = \$25\,000(1.12)^{20} = \$241\,157.33$$

and after 21 years

$$S = \$25\,000(1.12)^{21} = \$270\,096.21$$

In this example we calculated the time taken for $25 000 to increase by a factor of 10. It can be shown that this time depends only on the interest rate and not on the actual value of the principal. To see this, note that if a general principal, P, increases tenfold, then its future value is $10P$. If the interest rate is 12%, then we need to solve

$$10P = P\left(1 + \frac{12}{100}\right)^n$$

for n. The Ps cancel (indicating that the answer is independent of P) to produce the equation

$$10 = (1.12)^n$$

This is identical to the equation obtained in the previous example and, as we have just seen, has the solution $n = 20.3$.

Practice Problem

2. A firm estimates that its sales will rise by 3% each year and that it needs to sell at least 10 000 goods each year in order to make a profit. Given that its current annual sales are only 9000, how many years will it take before the firm breaks even?

You may have noticed that in all of the previous problems, it is assumed that the interest is compounded annually. It is possible for interest to be added to the investment more frequently than this. For example, suppose that a principal of $500 is invested for three years at 10% interest compounded quarterly. What do we mean by '10% interest compounded quarterly'? Well, it does *not* mean that we get 10% interest every three months. Instead, the 10% is split into four equal portions, one for each quarter. Every three months the interest accrued is

$$\frac{10\%}{4} = 2.5\%$$

so after the first quarter the investment gets multiplied by 1.025 to give

500(1.025)

and after the second quarter it gets multiplied by another 1.025 to give

$500(1.025)^2$

and so on. Moreover, since there are exactly twelve 3-month periods in three years, we deduce that the future value is

$500(1.025)^{12} = \$672.44$

Notice that this is greater than the sum obtained at the start of this section under annual compounding.

This example highlights the fact that the compound interest formula

$$S = P\left(1 + \frac{r}{100}\right)^n$$

derived earlier for annual compounding can also be used for other types of compounding. All that is needed is to reinterpret the symbols r and n. The variable r now represents the rate of interest per time period, and n represents the total number of periods.

Example

A principal of $10 is invested at 12% interest for one year. Determine the future value if the interest is compounded

(a) annually   **(b)** semi-annually   **(c)** quarterly   **(d)** monthly   **(e)** weekly

Solution

The formula for compound interest gives

$$S = P\left(1 + \frac{r}{100}\right)^n$$

(a) If the interest is compounded annually, then $r = 12$, $n = 1$, so

$$S = \$10(1.12)^1 = \$11.20$$

(b) If the interest is compounded semi-annually, then an interest of $12/2 = 6\%$ is added on every six months and, since there are two 6-month periods in a year,

$$S = \$10(1.06)^2 = \$11.24$$

(c) If the interest is compounded quarterly, then an interest of $12/4 = 3\%$ is added on every 3 months and, since there are four 3-month periods in a year,

$$S = \$10(1.03)^4 = \$11.26$$

(d) If the interest is compounded monthly, then an interest of $12/12 = 1\%$ is added on every month and, since there are 12 months in a year,

$$S = \$10(1.01)^{12} = \$11.27$$

(e) If the interest is compounded weekly then an interest of $12/52 = 0.23\%$ is added on every week and, since there are 52 weeks in a year,

$$S = \$10(1.0023)^{52} = \$11.27$$

In the above example we see that the future value rises as the frequency of compounding rises. This is to be expected because the basic feature of compound interest is that we get 'interest on the interest'. However, one important observation that you might not have expected is that, although the future values increase, they appear to be approaching a fixed value. It can be shown that this always occurs. The type of compounding in which the interest is added on with increasing frequency is called **continuous compounding**. In theory, we can find the future value of a principal under continuous compounding using the approach taken in the previous example. We work with smaller and smaller time periods until the numbers settle down to a fixed value. However, it turns out that there is a special formula that can be used to compute this directly. The future value, S, of a principal, P, compounded continuously for t years at an annual rate of $r\%$ is

$$S = Pe^{rt/100}$$

where e is the number

2.718 281 828 459 045 235 36 (to 20 decimal places)

If $r = 12$, $t = 1$ and $P = 10$, then this formula gives

$$S = \$10e^{12 \times 1/100} = \$10e^{0.12} = \$11.27$$

check this using your own calculator

which is in agreement with the limiting value obtained in the previous example.

Advice

The number e and the related natural logarithm function were first introduced in Section 2.4. If you missed this section, you should go back and read through this work now before proceeding. The link between the number e and the above formula for continuous compounding is given in Question 7 in Exercise 3.2* at the end of this section. However, you may prefer to accept it without justification and concentrate on the applications.

Example

A principal of $2000 is invested at 10% interest compounded continuously. After how many days will the investment first exceed $2100?

Solution

We want to save a total of $2100 starting with an initial investment of $2000. The problem is to determine the number of days required for this on the assumption that the interest rate is 10% compounded continuously. The formula for continuous compounding is

$$S = Pe^{rt/100}$$

We are given that

$$S = 2100, P = 2000, r = 10$$

so we need to solve the equation

$$2100 = 2000e^{10t/100}$$

for t. Dividing through by 2000 gives

$$1.05 = e^{0.1t}$$

As explained in Section 2.4, equations such as this can be solved using natural logarithms. Recall that

$$\text{if } M = e^n \quad \text{then} \quad n = \ln M$$

If we apply this definition to the equation

$$1.05 = e^{0.1t}$$

with $M = 1.05$ and $n = 0.1t$, then

$$0.1t = \ln(1.05) = 0.048\ 790\ 2$$

and so $t = 0.488$ to three decimal places.

The variable t which appears in the formula for continuous compounding is measured in years, so to convert it to days we multiply by 365 (assuming that there are 365 days in a year). Hence

$$t = 365 \times 0.488 = 178.1 \text{ days}$$

We deduce that the amount invested first exceeds $2100 some time during the 179th day.

Practice Problems

3. **(1)** A principal, $30, is invested at 6% interest for two years. Determine the future value if the interest is compounded

   (a) annually   **(b)** semi-annually   **(c)** quarterly

   (d) monthly   **(e)** weekly   **(f)** daily

   (2) Use the formula

   $$S = Pe^{rt/100}$$

   to determine the future value of $30 invested at 6% interest compounded continuously for two years. Confirm that it is in agreement with the results of part (1).

4. Determine the rate of interest required for a principal of $1000 to produce a future value of $4000 after 10 years compounded continuously.

Given that there are so many ways of calculating compound interest, people often find it difficult to appraise different investment opportunities. What is needed is a standard 'benchmark' that enables an individual to compare different forms of savings or credit schemes on an equal basis. The one that is commonly used is annual compounding. All firms offering investment or loan facilities are required to provide the effective annual rate. This is often referred to as the **annual percentage rate**, which is abbreviated to APR. The APR is the rate of interest which, when compounded annually, produces the same yield as the nominal (that is, the stated) rate of interest. The phrase 'annual equivalent rate' (AER) is frequently used when applied to savings.

Example

Determine the annual equivalent rate of interest of a deposit account that has a nominal rate of 6.6% compounded monthly.

Solution

The AER is the overall rate of interest, which can be calculated using scale factors. If the account offers a return of 6.6% compounded monthly, then each month the interest is

$$\frac{6.6}{12} = 0.55\%$$

of the amount invested at the beginning of that month. The monthly scale factor is

$$1 + \frac{0.55}{100} = 1.0055$$

so in a whole year the principal gets multiplied by

$$(1.0055)^{12} = 1.068$$

which can be written as

$$1 + \frac{6.8}{100}$$

so the AER is 6.8%.

Practice Problem

5. Determine the annual percentage rate of interest if the nominal rate is 12% compounded quarterly.

Although the aim of this chapter is to investigate the mathematics of finance, the mathematical techniques themselves are more widely applicable. We conclude this section with two examples to illustrate this.

Example

A country's annual GNP (gross national product), currently at $25 000 million, is predicted to grow by 3.5% each year. The population is expected to increase by 2% a year from its current level of 40 million. After how many years will GNP per capita (that is, GNP per head of population) reach $700?

Solution

The per capita value of GNP is worked out by dividing GNP by the size of the population. Initially, this is

$$\frac{25\ 000\ 000\ 000}{40\ 000\ 000} = \$625$$

During the next few years, GNP is forecast to grow at a faster rate than the population, so this value will increase.

The scale factor associated with a 3.5% increase is 1.035, so after n years GNP (in millions of dollars) will be

$$GNP = 25\ 000 \times (1.035)^n$$

Similarly, the population (also in millions) will be

$$population = 40 \times (1.02)^n$$

Hence GNP per capita is

$$\frac{25\ 000 \times (1.035)^n}{40 \times (1.02)^n} = \frac{25\ 000}{40} \times \frac{(1.035)^n}{(1.02)^n} = 625 \times \left(\frac{1.035}{1.02}\right)^n$$

We want to find the number of years required for this to reach 700, so we need to solve the equation

$$625 \times \left(\frac{1.035}{1.02}\right)^n = 700$$

for n. Dividing both sides by 625 gives

$$\left(\frac{1.035}{1.02}\right)^n = 1.12$$

and after taking logs of both sides we get

$$\log\left(\frac{1.035}{1.02}\right)^n = \log(1.12)$$

$$n\log\left(\frac{1.035}{1.02}\right)^n = \log(1.12) \quad \text{(rule 3 of logs)}$$

so that

$$n = \frac{\log(1.12)}{\log(1.035/1.02)} = 7.76$$

We deduce that the target figure of $700 per capita will be achieved after eight years.

Example

A firm decides to increase output at a constant rate from its current level of 50 000 to 60 000 during the next five years. Calculate the annual rate of increase required to achieve this growth.

Solution

If the rate of increase is $r\%$, then the scale factor is $1 + \dfrac{r}{100}$ so, after five years, output will be

$$50\,000\left(1 + \frac{r}{100}\right)^5$$

To achieve a final output of 60 000, the value of r is chosen to satisfy the equation

$$50\,000\left(1 + \frac{r}{100}\right)^5 = 60\,000$$

Dividing both sides by 50 000 gives

$$\left(1 + \frac{r}{100}\right)^5 = 1.2$$

The difficulty in solving this equation is that the unknown, r, is trapped inside the brackets, which are raised to the power of 5. This is analogous to the problem of solving an equation such as

$$x^2 = 5.23$$

which we would solve by taking square roots of both sides to find x. This suggests that we can find r by taking fifth roots of both sides of

$$\left(1 + \frac{r}{100}\right)^5 = 1.2$$

to get

$$1 + \frac{r}{100} = (1.2)^{1/5} = 1.037$$

Hence $r = 3.7\%$.

Practice Problem

6. The turnover of a leading supermarket chain, A, is currently $560 million and is expected to increase at a constant rate of 1.5% a year. Its nearest rival, supermarket B, has a current turnover of $480 million and plans to increase this at a constant rate of 3.4% a year. After how many years will supermarket B overtake supermarket A?

Key Terms

Annual percentage rate   The equivalent annual interest paid for a loan, taking into account the compounding over a variety of time periods.

Compound interest   The interest which is added on to the initial investment, so that this will itself gain interest in subsequent time periods.

Continuous compounding   The limiting value when interest is compounded with ever-increasing frequency.

Future value   The final value of an investment after one or more time periods.

Principal   The value of the original sum invested.

Simple interest   The interest which is paid directly to the investor instead of being added to the original amount.

Exercise 3.2

1. A bank offers a return of 7% interest compounded annually. Find the future value of a principal of $4500 after six years. What is the overall percentage rise over this period?

2. Find the future value of $20 000 in two years' time if compounded quarterly at 8% interest.

3. The value of an asset, currently priced at $100 000, is expected to increase by 20% a year.

   (a) Find its value in 10 years' time.

   (b) After how many years will it be worth $1 million?

4. How long will it take for a sum of money to double if it is invested at 5% interest compounded annually?

5. A piece of machinery depreciates in value by 5% a year. Determine its value in three years' time if its current value is $50 000.

6. A principal, $7000, is invested at 9% interest for eight years. Determine its future value if the interest is compounded

   (a) annually   (b) semi-annually   (c) monthly   (d) continuously

7. Which of the following savings accounts offers the greater return?

   Account A: an annual rate of 8.05% paid semi-annually
   Account B: an annual rate of 7.95% paid monthly

8. Find the future value of $100 compounded continuously at an annual rate of 6% for 12 years.

9. How long will it take for a sum of money to triple in value if invested at an annual rate of 3% compounded continuously?

10. If a piece of machinery depreciates continuously at an annual rate of 4%, how many years will it take for the value of the machinery to halve?

11. A department store has its own credit card facilities, for which it charges interest at a rate of 2% each month. Explain briefly why this is not the same as an annual rate of 24%. What is the annual percentage rate?

12. Determine the APR if the nominal rate is 7% compounded continuously.

13. Current annual consumption of energy is 78 billion units, and this is expected to rise at a fixed rate of 5.8% each year. The capacity of the industry to supply energy is currently 104 billion units.

    (a) Assuming that the supply remains steady, after how many years will demand exceed supply?

    (b) What constant rate of growth of energy production would be needed to satisfy demand for the next 50 years?

14. Find the value, in two years time, of $4000 invested at 5% compounded annually. In the following two years, the interest rate is expected to rise to 8%. Find the final value of the investment at the end of the four-year period, and find the overall percentage increase. Give your answers correct to two decimal places.

15. Find the APR of a loan if the monthly interest rate is 1.65%. Give your answer correct to two decimal places.

16. The future value S of principal P invested for n years with an interest rate r% compounded annually may be calculated using the formula

$$S = P\left(1 + \frac{r}{100}\right)^n$$

    Rearrange this formula to express P in terms of S, r and n.

17. The number of rail passenger journeys made between England and Scotland in 2004 was 5.015 million. In 2011 the figure was 7.419 million. Work out the yearly percentage rate of growth (assumed constant) during this period.

18. Table 3.23 shows the depreciation in the value of two models of car.

    Table 3.23

Year	Year 1	Year 2
Car A	36 000	32 000
Car B	32 000	28 800

    (a) Assuming that the depreciation of Car A is linear, estimate its value in Year 3.
    (b) Assuming that the depreciation of Car B is exponential, estimate its value in Year 3.
    (c) Predict when Car A will be worth less than Car B.

Exercise 3.2*

1. A principal of $7650 is invested at a rate of 3.7% compounded annually. After how many years will the investment first exceed $12 250?

2. A principal of $70 000 is invested at 6% interest for four years. Find the difference in the future value if the interest is compounded quarterly compared to continuous compounding. Round your answer to two decimal places.

3. Midwest Bank offers a return of 5% compounded annually for each and every year. The rival BFB offers a return of 3% for the first year and 7% in the second and subsequent years (both compounded annually). Which bank would you choose to invest in if you decided to invest a principal for (a) two years; (b) three years?

4. A car depreciates by 40% in the first year, 30% in the second year and 20% thereafter. I buy a car for $14 700 when it is two years old.

   (a) How much did it cost when new?

   (b) After how many years will it be worth less than 25% of the amount that I paid for it?

5. The population of a country is currently at 56 million and is forecast to rise by 3.7% each year. It is capable of producing 2500 million units of food each year, and it is estimated that each member of the population requires a minimum of 65 units of food each year. At the moment, the extra food needed to satisfy this requirement is imported, but the government decides to increase food production at a constant rate each year, with the aim of making the country self-sufficient after 10 years. Find the annual rate of growth required to achieve this.

6. Simon decides to buy a new sofa which is available at each of three stores at the same fixed price. He decides to borrow the money using each store's credit facility.

   Store A has an effective rate of interest of 12.6%.
   Store B charges interest at a rate of 10.5% compounded continuously.
   Store C charges interest at a rate of 11.5% compounded quarterly.

   From which store should Simon buy his sofa to minimise the total cost?

7. If a principal, P, is invested at r% interest compounded annually, then its future value, S, after n years is given by

$$S = P\left(1 + \frac{r}{100}\right)^{n}$$

   (a) Use this formula to show that if an interest rate of r% is compounded k times a year, then after t years

$$S = P\left(1 + \frac{r}{100k}\right)^{tk}$$

   (b) Show that if $m = 100k/r$, then the formula in part (a) can be written as

$$S = P\left(\left(1 + \frac{1}{m}\right)^{m}\right)^{rt/100}$$

(c) Use the definition

$$e = \lim_{m \to \infty} \left(1 + \frac{1}{m}\right)^m$$

to deduce that if the interest is compounded with ever-increasing frequency (that is, continuously), then

$$S = Pe^{rt/100}$$

8. World oil reserves are currently estimated to be 600 billion units. If this quantity is reduced by 8% a year, after how many years will oil reserves drop below 100 billion units?

9. The nominal rate of interest of a store card is 18% compounded monthly.

   (a) State the monthly interest rate.

   (b) Find the equivalent annual rate of interest if the compounding is continuous. Round your answer to two decimal places.

10. Write down an expression for the annual percentage growth rate of a country whose GDP increases by a factor of g over a period of n years.

11. (a) A principal, P, is invested at a nominal rate of interest, of $r\%$ compounded n times a year. Show that the AER is given by the formula

$$\text{AER} = 100\left(1 + \frac{r}{100n}\right)^n - 100$$

   (b) Find a formula for AER when the interest is compounded continuously.

SECTION 3.3
Geometric series

Objectives

At the end of this section you should be able to:

- Recognise a geometric progression.
- Evaluate a geometric series.
- Calculate the total investment obtained from a regular savings plan.
- Calculate the instalments needed to repay a loan.

Consider the following sequence of numbers:

2, 6, 18, 54, . . .

One obvious question, often asked in intelligence tests, is, what is the next term in the sequence? All that is required is for you to spot the pattern so that it can be used to generate the next term. In this case, successive numbers are obtained by multiplying by 3, so the fifth term is

$$54 \times 3 = 162$$

the sixth term is

$$162 \times 3 = 486$$

and so on. Any sequence in which terms are calculated by multiplying their predecessor by a fixed number is called a **geometric progression**, and the multiplicative factor itself is called a **geometric ratio**. The sequence above is a geometric progression with geometric ratio 3. The reason for introducing these sequences is not to help you to answer intelligence tests but rather to analyse compound interest problems. You may well have noticed that all of the problems given in the previous section produced such a sequence. For example, if a principal, $500, is invested at 10% interest compounded annually, then the future values in successive years are

$$500(1.1), 500(1.1)^2, 500(1.1)^3, \ldots$$

which we recognise as a geometric progression with geometric ratio 1.1.

Example

Which of the following sequences are geometric progressions? For those sequences that are of this type, write down their geometric ratios.

(a) $1000, -100, 10, -1, \ldots$ (b) $2, 4, 6, 8, \ldots$ (c) $a, ar, ar^2, ar^3, \ldots$

Solution

(a) $1000, -100, 10, -1, \ldots$ is a geometric progression with geometric ratio $-\dfrac{1}{10}$.

(b) $2, 4, 6, 8, \ldots$ is not a geometric progression because to go from one term to the next, you *add* 2. Such a sequence is called an **arithmetic progression** and is of little interest in business and economics.

(c) $a, ar, ar^2, ar^3, \ldots$ is a geometric progression with geometric ratio r.

Practice Problem

1. Decide which of the following sequences are geometric progressions. For those sequences that are of this type, write down their geometric ratios.

   (a) $3, 6, 12, 24, \ldots$ (b) $5, 10, 15, 20, \ldots$ (c) $1, -3, 9, -27, \ldots$

   (d) $8, 4, 2, 1, \, ^1/_2, \ldots$ (e) $500, 500(1.07), 500(1.07)^2, \ldots$

All of the problems considered in Section 3.2 involved a single lump-sum payment into an investment account. The task was simply to determine its future value after a period of time when it is subject to a certain type of compounding. In this section, we extend this to include multiple payments. This situation occurs whenever individuals save regularly or when businesses take out a loan that is paid back using fixed monthly or annual instalments. To tackle these problems we need to be able to sum (that is, to add together) consecutive terms of a geometric progression. Such an expression is called a **geometric series**. Suppose that we want to sum the first six terms of the geometric progression given by the sequence

$$2, 6, 18, 54, \ldots \tag{1}$$

The easiest way of doing this is to write down these six numbers and add them together to get

$$2 + 6 + 18 + 54 + 162 + 486 = 728$$

There is, however, a special formula to sum a geometric series which is particularly useful when there are lots of terms or when the individual terms are more complicated to evaluate. It can be shown that the sum of the first n terms of a geometric progression in which the first term is a, and the geometric ratio is r, is equal to

$$a\left(\frac{r^n - 1}{r - 1}\right) \quad (r \neq 1)$$

Use of the symbol r to denote both the interest rate and the geometric ratio is unfortunate but fairly standard. In practice, it is usually clear from the context what this symbol represents, so no confusion should arise.

A proof of this formula is given in Question 7 in Exercise 3.3* at the end of this section. As a check, let us use it to determine the sum of the first six terms of sequence (1) considered previously. In this case the first term $a = 2$, the geometric ratio $r = 3$ and the number of terms $n = 6$, so the geometric series is equal to

$$2\left(\frac{3^6 - 1}{3 - 1}\right) = 3^6 - 1 = 728$$

which agrees with the previous value found by summing the terms longhand. In this case there is no real benefit in using the formula. However, it would be tedious to evaluate the geometric series

$$500(1.1) + 500(1.1)^2 + 500(1.1)^3 + \cdots + 500(1.1)^{25}$$

longhand, whereas substituting $a = 500(1.1)$, $r = 1.1$ and $n = 25$ into the formula immediately gives

$$500(1.1)\left(\frac{(1.1)^{25} - 1}{1.1 - 1}\right) = 54\ 090.88$$

Practice Problem

2. **(a)** Write down the next term in the sequence

$$1, 2, 4, 8, \ldots$$

and hence find the sum of the first five terms. Check that this agrees with the value obtained using

$$a\left(\frac{r^n - 1}{r - 1}\right)$$

(b) Evaluate the geometric series

$$100(1.07) + 100(1.07)^2 + \cdots + 100(1.07)^{20}$$

There are two particular applications of geometric series that we now consider, involving savings and loans. We begin by analysing savings plans. In the simplest case, an individual decides to invest a regular sum of money into a bank account. This is sometimes referred to as a **sinking fund** and is used to meet some future financial commitment. It is assumed that he or she saves an equal amount and that the money is put into the account at the same time each year (or month). We further assume that the interest rate does not change. The latter may not be an entirely realistic assumption, since it can fluctuate wildly in volatile market conditions. Indeed, banks offer a variety of rates of interest depending on the notice required for withdrawal and on the actual amount of money saved. Question 5 in Exercise 3.3* at the end of this section considers what happens when the interest rate rises as the investment goes above certain threshold levels.

Example

A person saves $100 in a bank account at the beginning of each month. The bank offers a return of 12% compounded monthly.

(a) Determine the total amount saved after 12 months.

(b) After how many months does the amount saved first exceed $2000?

Solution

(a) During the year a total of 12 regular savings of $100 are made. Each $100 is put into an account that gives a return of 12% compounded monthly, or equivalently, a return of 1% each month. However, each payment is invested for a different period of time. For example, the first payment is invested for the full 12 months, whereas the final payment is invested for 1 month only. We need to work out the future value of each payment separately and add them together.

The first payment is invested for 12 months, gaining a monthly interest of 1%, so its future value is

$$100(1.01)^{12}$$

The second payment is invested for 11 months, so its future value is

$$100(1.01)^{11}$$

Likewise, the third payment yields

$$100(1.01)^{10}$$

and so on. The last payment is invested for 1 month, so its future value is

$$100(1.01)^{1}$$

The total value of the savings at the end of 12 months is then

$$100(1.01)^{12} + 100(1.01)^{11} + \cdots + 100(1.01)^{1}$$

If we rewrite this series in the order of ascending powers, we then have the more familiar form

$$100(1.01)^{1} + \cdots + 100(1.01)^{11} + 100(1.01)^{12}$$

This is equal to the sum of the first 12 terms of a geometric progression in which the first term is $100(1.01)$ and the geometric ratio is 1.01. Its value can therefore be found by using

$$a\left(\frac{r^{n} - 1}{r - 1}\right)$$

with $a = 100(1.01)$, $r = 1.01$ and $n = 12$, which gives

$$\$100(1.01)\left(\frac{(1.01)^{12} - 1}{1.01 - 1}\right) = \$1280.93$$

(b) In part (a) we showed that after 12 months the total amount saved is

$$100(1.01) + 100(1.01)^{2} + \cdots + 100(1.01)^{12}$$

Using exactly the same argument, it is easy to see that after n months the account contains

$$100(1.01) + 100(1.01)^{2} + \cdots + 100(1.01)^{n}$$

The formula for the sum of the first n terms of a geometric progression shows that this is the same as

$$100(1.01)\left(\frac{1.01^n - 1}{1.01 - 1}\right) = 10\,100(1.01^n - 1)$$

The problem here is to find the number of months needed for total savings to rise to $2000. Mathematically, this is equivalent to solving the equation

$$10\,100(1.01^n - 1) = 2000$$

for n. Following the strategy described in Section 2.3 gives

$$1.01^n - 1 = 0.198 \qquad \text{(divide both sides by 10 100)}$$
$$1.01^n = 1.198 \qquad \text{(add 1 to both sides)}$$
$$\log(1.01)^n = \log(1.198) \qquad \text{(take logs of both sides)}$$
$$n\log(1.01) = \log(1.198) \qquad \text{(rule 3 of logs)}$$
$$n = \frac{\log(1.198)}{\log(1.01)} \qquad \text{(divide both sides by log(1.01))}$$
$$= 18.2$$

It follows that after 18 months savings are less than $2000, whereas after 19 months savings exceed this amount. The target figure of $2000 is therefore reached at the end of the 19th month.

Practice Problem

3. An individual saves $1000 in a bank account at the beginning of each year. The bank offers a return of 8% compounded annually.

   (a) Determine the amount saved after 10 years.

   (b) After how many years does the amount saved first exceed $20 000?

We now turn our attention to loans. Many businesses finance their expansion by obtaining loans from a bank or other financial institution. Banks are keen to do this provided that they receive interest as a reward for lending money. Businesses pay back loans by monthly or annual repayments. The way in which this repayment is calculated is as follows. Let us suppose that interest is calculated on a monthly basis and that the firm repays the debt by fixed monthly instalments at the end of each month. The bank calculates the interest charged during the first month based on the original loan. At the end of the month, this interest is added on to the original loan, and the repayment is simultaneously deducted to determine the amount owed. The bank then charges interest in the second month based on this new amount, and the process is repeated. Provided that the monthly repayment is greater than the interest charged each month, the amount owed decreases and, eventually, the debt is cleared. In practice, the period during which the loan is repaid is fixed in advance and the monthly repayments are calculated to achieve this end.

Example

Determine the monthly repayments needed to repay a $100 000 loan which is paid back over 25 years when the interest rate is 8% compounded annually.

Solution

In this example the time interval between consecutive repayments is 1 month, whereas the period during which interest is charged is one year. This type of financial calculation typifies the way in which certain types of housing loan are worked out. The interest is compounded annually at 8%, so the amount of interest charged during the first year is 8% of the original loan: that is,

$$\frac{8}{100} \times 100\,000 = 8000$$

This amount is added on to the outstanding debt at the end of the first year. During this time, 12 monthly repayments are made, so if each instalment is x, the outstanding debt must decrease by $12x$. Hence, at the end of the first year, the amount owed is

$$100\,000 + 8000 - 12x = 108\,000 - 12x$$

In order to be able to spot a pattern in the annual debt, let us write this as

$$100\,000(1.08) - 12x$$

where the first part simply reflects the fact that 8% interest is added on to the original sum of $100 000. At the end of the second year, a similar calculation is performed. The amount owed rises by 8% to become

$$[100\,000(1.08) - 12x](1.08) = 100\,000(1.08)^2 - 12x(1.08)$$

and we deduct $12x$ for the repayments to get

$$100\,000(1.08)^2 - 12x(1.08) - 12x$$

This is the amount owed at the end of the second year. Each year we multiply by 1.08 and subtract $12x$, so at the end of the third year we owe

$$[100\,000(1.08)^2 - 12x(1.08) - 12x]\,(1.08) - 12x$$
$$= 100\,000(1.08)^3 - 12x(1.08)^2 - 12x(1.08) - 12x$$

and so on. These results are summarised in Table 3.24. If we continue the pattern, we see that after 25 years the amount owed is

$$100\,000(1.08)^{25} - 12x(1.08)^{24} - 12x(1.08)^{23} - \cdots - 12x$$
$$= 100\,000(1.08)^{25} - 12x[1 + 1.08 + (1.08)^2 + \cdots + (1.08)^{24}]$$

(Taking out a common factor of $12x$ and rewriting powers of 1.08 in ascending order.)

Table 3.24

End of year	Outstanding debt
1	$100\,000(1.08)^1 - 12x$
2	$100\,000(1.08)^2 - 12x(1.08)^1 - 12x$
3	$100\,000(1.08)^3 - 12x(1.08)^2 - 12x(1.08)^1 - 12x$

The first term is easily evaluated using a calculator to get

$$100\,000(1.08)^{25} = 684\,847.520$$

The geometric series inside the square brackets can be worked out from the formula

$$a\left(\frac{r^n - 1}{r - 1}\right)$$

The first term $a = 1$, the geometric ratio $r = 1.08$, and we are summing the first 25 terms, so $n = 25$. (Can you see why there are actually 25 terms in this series rather than 24?) Hence

$$[1 + 1.08 + (1.08)^2 + \cdots + (1.08)^{24}] = \frac{1.08^{25} - 1}{1.08 - 1} = 73.106$$

The amount owed at the end of 25 years is therefore

$$684\,847.520 - 12x(73.106) = 684\,847.520 - 877.272x$$

In this expression, x denotes the monthly repayment, which is chosen so that the debt is completely cleared after 25 years. This will be so if x is the solution of

$$684\,847.520 - 877.272x = 0$$

Hence

$$x = \frac{684\,847.520}{877.272} = \$780.66$$

The monthly repayment on a 25-year loan of \$100 000 is \$780.66, assuming that the interest rate remains fixed at 8% throughout this period.

It is interesting to substitute this value of x into the expressions for the outstanding debt given in Table 3.24. The results are listed in Table 3.25. What is so depressing about these figures is that the debt falls by only about \$1500 to begin with, in spite of the fact that over \$9000 is being repaid each year!

Table 3.25

End of year	Outstanding debt
1	\$98 632.08
2	\$97 154.73
3	\$95 559.18

Practice Problem

4. A person requests an immediate bank overdraft of \$2000. The bank generously agrees to this but insists that it should be repaid by 12 monthly instalments and charges 1% interest every month on the outstanding debt. Determine the monthly repayment.

The mathematics used in this section for problems on savings and loans can be used for other time series. Reserves of non-renewable commodities such as minerals, oil and gas continue to decline, and geometric series can be used to estimate the year in which these stocks are likely to run out.

Example

Total reserves of a non-renewable resource are 250 million tonnes. Annual consumption, currently at 20 million tonnes per year, is expected to rise by 2% a year. After how many years will stocks be exhausted?

Solution

In the first year, consumption will be 20 million tonnes. In the second year, this will rise by 2%, so consumption will be 20(1.02) million tonnes. In the third year, this will again rise by 2% to become $20(1.02)^2$ million tonnes. The total consumption (in millions of tonnes) during the next n years will be

$$20 + 20(1.02) + 20(1.02)^2 + \cdots + 20(1.02)^{n-1}$$

This represents the sum of n terms of a geometric series with first term $a = 20$ and geometric ratio $r = 1.02$, so is equal to

$$20\left(\frac{1.02^n - 1}{1.02 - 1}\right) = 1000(1.02^n - 1)$$

Reserves will run out when this exceeds 250 million, so we need to solve the equation

$$1000(1.02^n - 1) = 250$$

for n. This is easily solved using logarithms:

$$
\begin{aligned}
1.02^n - 1 &= 0.25 && \text{(divide both sides by 1000)} \\
1.02^n &= 1.25 && \text{(add 1 to both sides)} \\
\log(1.02)^n &= \log(1.25) && \text{(take logs of both sides)} \\
n\log(1.02) &= \log(1.25) && \text{(rule 3 of logs)} \\
n &= \frac{\log(1.25)}{\log(1.02)} && \text{(divide both sides by } \log(1.02)) \\
&= 11.27
\end{aligned}
$$

so the reserves will be completely exhausted after 12 years.

Practice Problem

5. It is estimated that world reserves of oil currently stand at 2625 billion units. Oil is currently extracted at an annual rate of 45.5 billion units and this is set to increase by 2.6% a year. After how many years will oil reserves run out?

Example

Current annual extraction of a non-renewable resource is 40 billion units, and this is expected to fall at a rate of 5% each year. Estimate the current minimum level of reserves if this resource is to last in perpetuity (that is, for ever).

Solution

In the first year 40 billion units are extracted. In the second year this falls by 5% to 40(0.95) billion units. In the third year this goes down by a further 5% to $40(0.95)^2$. After n years the total amount extracted will be

$$40 + 40(0.95) + 40(0.95)^2 + \cdots + 40(0.95)^{n-1}$$

Using the formula for the sum of a geometric progression gives

$$40\left(\frac{0.95^n - 1}{0.95 - 1}\right) = 40\left(\frac{0.95^n - 1}{-0.05}\right) = 800(1 - 0.95^n)$$

To see what happens in perpetuity we need to investigate the behaviour 0.95^n as n tends to infinity. Since the magnitude of 0.95 is less than unity, it is easy to see that 0.95^n converges to zero and so the total amount will be 800 billion units.

Key Terms

Arithmetic progression   A sequence of numbers with a constant difference between consecutive terms; the nth term takes the form, $a + bn$.

Geometric progression   A sequence of numbers with a constant ratio between consecutive terms; the nth term takes the form, ar^{n-1}.

Geometric ratio   The constant multiplier in a geometric series.

Geometric series   A sum of the consecutive terms of a geometric progression.

Sinking fund   A fixed sum of money saved at regular intervals which is used to fund some future financial commitment.

Exercise 3.3

1. Find the value of the geometric series

   $$1000 + 1000(1.03) + 1000(1.03)^2 + \cdots + 1000(1.03)^9$$

2. An individual saves $5000 in a bank account at the beginning of each year for 10 years. No further savings or withdrawals are made from the account. Determine the total amount saved if the annual interest rate is 8% compounded:

   (a) annually;

   (b) semi-annually.

3. Determine the monthly repayments needed to repay a $125 000 loan which is paid back over 20 years when the interest rate is 7% compounded annually. Round your answer to two decimal places.

4. A prize fund is set up with a single investment of $5000 to provide an annual prize of $500. The fund is invested to earn interest at a rate of 7% compounded annually. If the first prize is awarded one year after the initial investment, find the number of years for which the prize can be awarded before the fund falls below $500.

5. The current extraction of a certain mineral is 12 million tonnes a year, and this is expected to fall at a constant rate of 6% each year. Estimate the current minimum level of world reserves if the extraction is to last in perpetuity.

6. A person invests $5000 at the beginning of a year in a savings account that offers a return of 4.5% compounded annually. At the beginning of each subsequent year an additional $1000 is invested in the account. How much will there be in the account at the end of 10 years?

7. A person borrows $100 000 at the beginning of a year and agrees to repay the loan in ten equal instalments at the end of each year. Interest is charged at a rate of 6% compounded annually.

   (a) Find the annual repayment.

   (b) Work out the total amount of interest paid and compare this with the total interest paid when repaying the loan in five equal annual instalments instead of ten.

8. A person wishes to save a regular amount at the beginning of each month in order to buy a car in 18 months' time. An account offers a return of 4.8% compounded monthly. Work out the monthly savings if the total amount saved at the end of 18 months is $18 000.

Exercise 3.3*

1. Find the sum of the of the geometric series,

   $$5 - 20 + 80 - 320 + \cdots - 20\ 971\ 520$$

2. A regular saving of $500 is made into a sinking fund at the start of each year for 10 years. Determine the value of the fund at the end of the 10th year on the assumption that the rate of interest is

   (a) 11% compounded annually;

   (b) 10% compounded continuously.

3. Monthly sales figures for January are 5600. This is expected to fall for the following 9 months at a rate of 2% each month. Thereafter sales are predicted to rise at a constant rate of 4% each month. Estimate total sales for the next two years (including the first January).

4. Determine the monthly repayments needed to repay a $50 000 loan that is paid back over 25 years when the interest rate is 9% compounded annually. Calculate the increased monthly repayments needed in the case when

   (a) the interest rate rises to 10%;

   (b) the period of repayment is reduced to 20 years.

5. A bank has three different types of account in which the interest rate depends on the amount invested. The 'ordinary' account offers a return of 6% and is available to every customer. The 'extra' account offers 7% and is available only to customers with $5000 or more to invest. The 'superextra' account offers 8% and is available only to customers with $20 000 or more to invest. In each case, interest is compounded annually and is added to the investment at the end of the year.

   A person saves $4000 at the beginning of each year for 25 years. Calculate the total amount saved at the end of 25 years on the assumption that the money is transferred to a higher-interest account at the earliest opportunity.

6. A business takes out a loan of $500 000 from a bank and agrees to repay the loan by paying a fixed amount of $60 000 at the end of each subsequent year. Once the debt falls below $60 000 the business pays off the outstanding debt as the final payment. Work out the final payment if the interest rate is 7.5% compounded annually.

7. If

$$S_n = a + ar + ar^2 + \cdots + ar^{n-1}$$

write down an expression for rS_n and deduce that

$$rS_n - S_n = ar^n - a$$

Hence show that the sum of the first n terms of a geometric progression with first term a and geometric ratio r is given by

$$a\left(\frac{r^n - 1}{r - 1}\right)$$

provided that $r \neq 1$.

8. At the beginning of a month, a customer owes a credit card company $8480. In the middle of the month, the customer repays A, where $A < 8480, and at the end of the month the company adds interest at a rate of 6% of the outstanding debt. This process is repeated with the customer continuing to pay off the same amount, A, each month.

   (a) Find the value of A for which the customer still owes $8480 at the start of each month.

   (b) If $A = 1000$, calculate the amount owing at the end of the eighth month.

   (c) Show that the value of A for which the whole amount owing is exactly paid off after the nth payment is given by

   $$A = \frac{8480R^{n-1}(R - 1)}{R^n - 1} \quad \text{where} \quad R = 1.06$$

   (d) Find the value of A if the debt is to be paid off exactly after two years.

Investment appraisal

Objectives

At the end of this section you should be able to:

- Calculate present values under discrete and continuous compounding.
- Use net present values to appraise investment projects.
- Calculate the internal rate of return.
- Calculate the present value of an annuity.
- Use discounting to compare investment projects.
- Calculate the present value of government securities.

In Section 3.2 the following two formulas were used to solve compound interest problems

$$S = P\left(1 + \frac{r}{100}\right)^t \tag{1}$$

$$S = Pe^{rt/100} \tag{2}$$

The first of these can be applied to any type of compounding in which the interest is added on to the investment at the end of discrete time intervals. The second formula is used when the interest is added on continuously. Both formulas involve the variables

P = principal

S = future value

r = interest rate

t = time

In the case of discrete compounding, the letter t represents the number of time periods. (In Section 3.2 this was denoted by n.) For continuous compounding, t is measured in years. Given any three of these variables, it is possible to work out the value of the remaining variable. Various examples were considered in Section 3.2. Of particular interest is the case where S, r and t are given, and P is the unknown to be determined. In this situation we know the future value, and we want to work backwards to calculate the original principal. This process is called **discounting** and the principal, P, is called the **present value**. The rate of interest is sometimes referred to as the **discount rate**. Equations (1) and (2) are easily rearranged to produce explicit formulas for the present value under discrete and continuous compounding:

$$P = \frac{S}{(1 + r/100)^t} = S\left(1 + \frac{r}{100}\right)^{-t}$$

reciprocals are denoted by negative powers

$$P = \frac{S}{e^{rt/100}} = Se^{-rt/100}$$

Example

Find the present value of $1000 in four years' time if the discount rate is 10% compounded

(a) semi-annually

(b) continuously

Solution

(a) The discount formula for discrete compounding is

$$P = S\left(1 + \frac{r}{100}\right)^{-t}$$

If compounding occurs semi-annually, then $r = 5$ since the interest rate per six months is $10/2 = 5$, and $t = 8$ since there are eight 6-month periods in four years. We are given that the future value is $1000, so

$$P = \$1000(1.05)^{-8} = \$676.84$$

(b) The discount formula for continuous compounding is

$$P = Se^{-rt/100}$$

In this formula, r is the annual discount rate, which is 10, and t is measured in years, so is 4. Hence the present value is

$$P = \$1000e^{-0.4} = \$670.32$$

Notice that the present value in part (b) is smaller than that in part (a). This is to be expected because continuous compounding always produces a higher yield. Consequently, we need to invest a smaller amount under continuous compounding to produce the future value of $1000 after four years.

Practice Problem

1. Find the present value of $100 000 in 10 years' time if the discount rate is 6% compounded

   (a) annually   **(b)** continuously

Present values are a useful way of appraising investment projects. Suppose that you are invited to invest $600 today in a business venture that is certain to produce a return of $1000 in five years' time. If the discount rate is 10% compounded semi-annually, then part (a) of the previous example shows that the present value of this return is $676.84. This exceeds the initial outlay of $600, so the venture is regarded as profitable. We quantify this profit by calculating the difference between the present value of the revenue and the present value of the costs, which is known as the **net present value** (NPV). In this example, the net present value is

$$\$676.84 - \$600 = \$76.84$$

Quite generally, a project is considered worthwhile when the NPV is positive. Moreover, if a decision is to be made between two different projects, then the one with the higher NPV is the preferred choice.

An alternative way of assessing individual projects is based on the **internal rate of return** (IRR). This is the annual rate which, when applied to the initial outlay, yields the same return as the project after the same number of years. The investment is considered worthwhile provided the IRR exceeds the market rate. Obviously, in practice, other factors such as risk need to be considered before a decision is made.

The following example illustrates both NPV and IRR methods and shows how a value of the IRR itself can be calculated.

Example

A project requiring an initial outlay of $15 000 is guaranteed to produce a return of $20 000 in three years' time. Use the

(a) net present value

(b) internal rate of return

methods to decide whether this investment is worthwhile if the prevailing market rate is 5% compounded annually. Would your decision be affected if the interest rate were 12%?

Solution

(a) The present value of $20 000 in three years' time, based on a discount rate of 5%, is found by setting $S = 20\,000$, $t = 3$ and $r = 5$ in the formula

$$P = S\left(1 + \frac{r}{100}\right)^{-t}$$

This gives

$$P = \$20\,000(1.05)^{-3} = \$17\,276.75$$

The NPV is therefore

$$\$17\,276.75 - \$15\,000 = \$2276.75$$

The project is to be recommended because this value is positive.

(b) To calculate the IRR we use the formula

$$S = P\left(1 + \frac{r}{100}\right)^{t}$$

We are given $S = 20\,000$, $P = 15\,000$ and $t = 3$, so we need to solve

$$20\,000 = 15\,000\left(1 + \frac{r}{100}\right)^{3}$$

for r. An obvious first step is to divide both sides of this equation by 15 000 to get

$$\frac{4}{3} = \left(1 + \frac{r}{100}\right)^{3}$$

→

We can extract r by taking cube roots of both sides of

$$\left(1 + \frac{r}{100}\right)^3 = \frac{4}{3}$$

to get

$$1 + \frac{r}{100} = \left(\frac{4}{3}\right)^{1/3} = 1.1$$

Hence

$$\frac{r}{100} = 1.1 - 1 = 0.1$$

and so the IRR is 10%. The project is therefore to be recommended because this value exceeds the market rate of 5%.

For the last part of the problem we are invited to consider whether our advice would be different if the market rate were 12%. Using the NPV method, we need to repeat the calculations, replacing 5 by 12. The corresponding net present value is then

$$\$20\ 000(1.12)^{-3} - \$15\ 000 = -\$764.40$$

This time the NPV is negative, so the project leads to an effective loss and is not to be recommended. The same conclusion can be reached more easily using the IRR method. We have already seen that the internal rate of return is 10% and can deduce immediately that you would be better off investing the $15 000 at the market rate of 12%, since this gives the higher yield.

Practice Problem

2. An investment project requires an initial outlay of $8000 and will produce a return of $17 000 at the end of five years. Use the

   (a) net present value

   (b) internal rate of return

   methods to decide whether this is worthwhile if the capital could be invested elsewhere at 15% compounded annually.

Advice

This problem illustrates the use of two different methods for investment appraisal. It may appear at first sight that the method based on the IRR is the preferred approach, particularly if you wish to consider more than one interest rate. However, this is not usually the case. The IRR method can give wholly misleading advice when *comparing* two or more projects, and you must be careful when interpreting the results of this method. The following example highlights the difficulty.

Example

Suppose that it is possible to invest in only one of two different projects. Project A requires an initial outlay of $1000 and yields $1200 in four years' time. Project B requires an outlay of $30 000 and yields $35 000 after four years. Which of these projects would you choose to invest in when the market rate is 3% compounded annually?

Solution

Let us first solve this problem using net present values.

For Project A

$$\text{NPV} = \$1200(1.03)^{-4} - \$1000 = \$66.18$$

For Project B

$$\text{NPV} = \$35\ 000(1.03)^{-4} - \$30\ 000 = \$1097.05$$

Both projects are viable as they produce positive net present values. Moreover, the second project is preferred, since it has the higher value. You can see that this recommendation is correct by considering how you might invest $30 000. If you opt for Project A, then the best you can do is to invest $1000 of this amount to give a return of $1200 in four years' time. The remaining $29 000 could be invested at the market rate of 3% to yield

$$\$29\ 000(1.03)^4 = \$32\ 639.76$$

The total return is then

$$\$1200 + \$32\ 639.76 = \$33\ 839.76$$

On the other hand, if you opt for Project B, then the whole of the $30 000 can be invested to yield $35 000. In other words, in four years' time you would be better off by choosing Project B, which confirms the advice given by the NPV method.

However, this is contrary to the advice given by the IRR method. For Project A, the internal rate of return, r_A, satisfies

$$1200 = 1000\left(1 + \frac{r_A}{100}\right)^4$$

Dividing by 1000 gives

$$\left(1 + \frac{r_A}{100}\right)^4 = 1.2$$

and if we take fourth roots, we get

$$1 + \frac{r_A}{100} = (1.2)^{1/4} = 1.047$$

so $r_A = 4.7\%$.

For Project B the internal rate of return, r_B, satisfies

$$35\ 000 = 30\ 000\left(1 + \frac{r_B}{100}\right)^4$$

This can be solved as before to get $r_B = 3.9\%$.

Project A gives the higher internal rate of return even though, as we have seen, Project B is the preferred choice.

The results of this example show that the IRR method is an unreliable way of comparing investment opportunities when there are significant differences between the amounts involved. This is because the IRR method compares percentages, and obviously a large percentage of a small sum could give a smaller profit than a small percentage of a larger sum.

Practice Problem

3. A firm needs to choose between two projects, A and B. Project A involves an initial outlay of $13 500 and yields $18 000 in two years' time. Project B requires an outlay of $9000 and yields $13 000 after two years. Which of these projects would you advise the firm to invest in if the annual market rate of interest is 7%?

So far in this section we have calculated the present value of a single future value. We now consider the case of a sequence of payments over time. The simplest cash flow of this type is an **annuity**, which is a sequence of regular equal payments. It can be thought of as the opposite of a sinking fund. This time a lump sum is invested and, subsequently, equal amounts of money are withdrawn at fixed time intervals. Provided that the payments themselves exceed the amount of interest gained during the time interval between payments, the fund will decrease and eventually become zero. At this point the payments cease. In practice, we are interested in the value of the original lump sum needed to secure a regular income over a known period of time. This can be done by summing the present values of the individual payments.

To be specific, suppose that a person wishes to retire and receive a regular income of $10 000 at the end of each year for the next 10 years. If the interest rate is 7% compounded annually, then the present values can be worked out using the formula

$$P = 10\,000\left(1 + \frac{7}{100}\right)^{-t}$$

The first payment is made at the end of the first year, so its present value is

$$P = \$10\,000(1.07)^{-1} = \$9345.79$$

This means that if we want to take out $10 000 from the fund in one year's time, then we need to invest $9345.79 today. The second payment of $10 000 is made at the end of the second year, so its present value is

$$\$10\,000(1.07)^{-2} = \$8734.39$$

This is the amount of money that needs to be invested now to cover the second payment from the fund. In general, the present value of $10 000 in t years' time is

$$10\,000(1.07)^{-t}$$

so the total present value is

$$10\,000(1.07)^{-1} + 10\,000(1.07)^{-2} + \cdots + 10\,000(1.07)^{-10}$$

This is a geometric series, so we may use the formula

$$a\left(\frac{r^n - 1}{r - 1}\right)$$

In this case, $a = 10\,000(1.07)^{-1}$, $r = 1.07^{-1}$ and $n = 10$, so the present value of the annuity is

$$\$10\,000(1.07)^{-1}\left(\frac{1.07^{-10} - 1}{1.07^{-1} - 1}\right) = \$70\,235.82$$

This represents the amount of money that needs to be invested now so that a regular annual income of $10 000 can be withdrawn from the fund for the next 10 years.

For many people there is a real fear that their pension will not provide an adequate income for the whole of their retirement. If the income stream is to continue for ever, then we need to investigate what happens to the formula

$$a\left(\frac{r^n - 1}{r - 1}\right)$$

as n gets bigger and bigger. In this case $r = 1.07^{-1} < 1$, so as n increases, r^n decreases and tends towards zero. This behaviour can be seen clearly from the table:

n	1	10	100
1.07^{-n}	0.9346	0.5083	0.0012

Setting $r^n = 0$ in the formula for the sum of geometric series shows that if the series goes on for ever, then eventually the sum approaches

$$\frac{a}{1 - r}$$

so that the present value of the annuity in perpetuity is

$$\frac{10\,000(1.07)^{-1}}{1 - 1.07^{-1}} = \$142\,857.14$$

This compares with the figure of $70 235.82 calculated previously to secure the income for 10 years.

Practice Problem

4. Find the present value of an annuity that yields an income of $2000 at the end of each month for 10 years, assuming that the interest rate is 6% compounded monthly.

The argument used in the previous example can be used to calculate the net present value. For instance, suppose that a business requires an initial investment of $60 000, which is guaranteed to return a regular payment of $10 000 at the end of each year for the next 10 years. If the discount rate is 7% compounded annually, then the previous example shows that the present value is $70 235.82. The net present value of the investment is therefore

$$\$70\,235.82 - \$60\,000 = \$10\,235.82$$

A similar procedure can be used when the payments are irregular, although it is no longer possible to use the formula for the sum of a geometric progression. Instead, the present value of each individual payment is calculated and the values are then summed longhand.

Example

A small business has a choice of investing $20 000 in one of two projects. The revenue flows from the two projects during the next four years are listed in Table 3.26. If the interest rate is 11% compounded annually, which of these two projects would you advise the company to invest in?

Table 3.26

| End of year | Revenue ($) | |
	Project A	Project B
1	6 000	10 000
2	3 000	6 000
3	10 000	9 000
4	8 000	1 000
Total	27 000	26 000

Solution

If we simply add together all of the individual receipts, it appears that Project A is to be preferred, since the total revenue generated from Project A is $1000 greater than that from Project B. However, this naïve approach fails to take into account the time distribution.

From Table 3.26 we see that both projects yield a single receipt of $10 000. For Project A this occurs at the end of Year 3, whereas for Project B this occurs at the end of Year 1. This $10 000 is worth more in Project B because it occurs earlier in the revenue stream and, once received, could be invested for longer at the prevailing rate of interest. To compare these projects we need to discount the revenue stream to the present value. The present values obtained depend on the discount rate. Table 3.27 shows the present values based on the given rate of 11% compounded annually. These values are calculated using the formula

$$P = S(1.11)^{-t}$$

For example, the present value of the $10 000 revenue in Project A is given by

$$\$10\,000(1.11)^{-3} = \$7311.91$$

The net present values for Project A and Project B are given by

$$\$20\,422.04 - \$20\,000 = \$422.04$$

and

$$\$21\,109.19 - \$20\,000 = \$1109.19$$

respectively. Consequently, if it is possible to invest in only one of these projects, the preferred choice is Project B.

Table 3.27

| End of year | Discounted revenue ($) | |
	Project A	Project B
1	5405.41	9000.01
2	2434.87	4869.73
3	7311.91	6580.72
4	5269.85	658.73
Total	20 422.04	21 109.19

Practice Problem

5. A firm has a choice of spending $10 000 today on one of two projects. The revenue obtained from these projects is listed in Table 3.28. Assuming that the discount rate is 15% compounded annually, which of these two projects would you advise the company to invest in?

Table 3.28

	Revenue ($)	
End of year	Project A	Project B
1	2000	1000
2	2000	1000
3	3000	2000
4	3000	6000
5	3000	4000

It is sometimes useful to find the internal rate of return of a project yielding a sequence of payments over time. However, as the following example demonstrates, this can be difficult to calculate, particularly when there are more than two payments.

Example

(a) Calculate the IRR of a project which requires an initial outlay of $20 000 and produces a return of $8000 at the end of year 1 and $15 000 at the end of year 2.

(b) Calculate the IRR of a project which requires an initial outlay of $5000 and produces returns of $1000, $2000 and $3000 at the end of years 1, 2 and 3, respectively.

Solution

(a) In the case of a single payment, the IRR is the annual rate of interest, r, which, when applied to the initial outlay, P, yields a known future payment, S. If this payment is made after t years, then

$$S = P\left(1 + \frac{r}{100}\right)^t$$

or, equivalently,

$$P = S\left(1 + \frac{r}{100}\right)^{-t}$$

Note that the right-hand side of this last equation is just the present value of S. Consequently, the IRR can be thought of as the rate of interest at which the present value of S equals the initial outlay P.

The present value of $8000 in one year's time is

$$8000\left(1 + \frac{r}{100}\right)^{-1}$$

where r is the annual rate of interest. Similarly, the present value of \$15 000 in two years' time is

$$15\,000\left(1 + \frac{r}{100}\right)^{-2}$$

If r is to be the IRR, then the sum of these present values must equal the initial investment of \$20 000. In other words, the IRR is the value of r that satisfies the equation

$$20\,000 = 8000\left(1 + \frac{r}{100}\right)^{-1} + 15\,000\left(1 + \frac{r}{100}\right)^{-2}$$

The simplest way of solving this equation is to multiply both sides by $(1 + r/100)^2$ to remove all negative indices. This gives

$$20\,000\left(1 + \frac{r}{100}\right)^{2} = 8000\left(1 + \frac{r}{100}\right) + 15\,000 \qquad \boxed{\begin{array}{c} b^m \times b^n = b^{m+n} \\ b^0 = 1 \end{array}}$$

Now

$$\left(1 + \frac{r}{100}\right)^{2} = \left(1 + \frac{r}{100}\right)\left(1 + \frac{r}{100}\right) = 1 + \frac{r}{50} + \frac{r^2}{10\,000}$$

so if we multiply out the brackets, we obtain

$$20\,000 + 400r + 2r^2 = 8000 + 80r + 15\,000$$

Collecting like terms gives

$$2r^2 + 320r - 3000 = 0$$

This is a quadratic in r, so it can be solved using the formula described in Section 2.1 to get

$$r = \frac{-320 \pm \sqrt{((320)^2 - 4(2)(-3000))}}{2(2)}$$

$$= \frac{-320 \pm 355.5}{4}$$

$$= 8.9\% \text{ or } -168.9\%$$

We can obviously ignore the negative solution, so we can conclude that the IRR is 8.9%.

(b) If an initial outlay of \$5000 yields \$1000, \$2000 and \$3000 at the end of years 1, 2 and 3, respectively, then the internal rate of return, r, satisfies the equation

$$5000 = 1000\left(1 + \frac{r}{100}\right)^{-1} + 2000\left(1 + \frac{r}{100}\right)^{-2} + 3000\left(1 + \frac{r}{100}\right)^{-3}$$

A sensible thing to do here might be to multiply through by $(1 + (r/100))^3$. However, this produces an equation involving r^3 (and lower powers of r), which is no easier to solve than the original. Indeed, a moment's thought should convince you that, in general, when dealing with a sequence of payments over n years, the IRR will satisfy an equation involving r^n (and lower powers of r). Under these circumstances, it is virtually impossible to obtain the exact solution. The best way of proceeding would be to use a non-linear equation-solver routine on a computer, particularly if it is important that an accurate value of r is obtained. However, if all that is needed is a rough approximation, then this can be done by systematic trial and error. We merely substitute likely solutions into the right-hand side of the equation until we find the one that works. For example, putting $r = 5$ gives

$$\frac{1000}{1.05} + \frac{200}{(1.05)^2} + \frac{3000}{(1.05)^3} = 5358$$

Other values of the expression

$$1000\left(1 + \frac{r}{100}\right)^{-1} + 2000\left(1 + \frac{r}{100}\right)^{-2} + 3000\left(1 + \frac{r}{100}\right)^{-3}$$

corresponding to $r = 6, 7, \ldots, 10$ are listed in the following table:

r	6	7	8	9	10
value	5242	5130	5022	4917	4816

Given that we are trying to find r so that this value is 5000, this table indicates that r is somewhere between 8% (which produces a value greater than 5000) and 9% (which produces a value less than 5000).

If a more accurate estimate of IRR is required, then we simply try further values between 8% and 9%. For example, it is easy to check that putting $r = 8.5$ gives 4969, indicating that the exact value of r is between 8% and 8.5%. We conclude that the IRR is 8% to the nearest percentage.

Practice Problem

6. A project requires an initial investment of $12 000. It has a guaranteed return of $8000 at the end of year 1 and a return of $2000 each year at the end of years 2, 3 and 4.

    Estimate the IRR to the nearest percentage. Would you recommend that someone invests in this project if the prevailing market rate is 8% compounded annually?

Practice Problem 6 should have convinced you how tedious it is to calculate the internal rate of return 'by hand' when there are more than two payments in a revenue flow. A computer spreadsheet provides the ideal tool for dealing with this. Excel's Chart Wizard can be used to sketch a graph from which a rough estimate of IRR can be found. A more accurate value can be found using a 'finer' tabulation in the vicinity of this estimate.

We conclude this section by using the theory of discounting to explain the relationship between interest rates and the speculative demand for money. This was first introduced in Section 1.7 in the analysis of LM schedules. Speculative demand consists of money held in reserve to take advantage of changes in the value of alternative financial assets, such as government bonds. As their name suggests, these issues can be bought from the government at a certain price. In return, the government pays out interest on an annual basis for a prescribed number of years. At the end of this period, the bond is redeemed and the purchaser is repaid the original sum. Now, these bonds can be bought and sold at any point in their lifetime. The person who chooses to buy one of these bonds part-way through this period is entitled to all of the future interest payments, together with the final redemption payment. The value of existing securities clearly depends on the number of years remaining before redemption, together with the prevailing rate of interest.

Example

A 10-year bond is originally offered by the government at $5000 with an annual return of 9%. Assuming that the bond has four years left before redemption, calculate its present value assuming that the prevailing interest rate is

(a) 5%   **(b)** 7%   **(c)** 9%   **(d)** 11%   **(e)** 13%

Solution

The government pays annual interest of 9% on the $5000 bond, so agrees to pay the holder $450 every year for 10 years. At the end of the 10 years, the bond is redeemed by the government and $5000 is paid back to the purchaser. If just four years remain between now and the date of redemption, the future cash flow that is paid on the bond is summarised in the second column of Table 3.29. This is similar to that of an annuity except that in the final year an extra payment of $5000 is received when the government pays back the original investment. The present value of this income stream is calculated in Table 3.29 using the given discount rates of 5%, 7%, 9%, 11% and 13% compounded annually. The total present value in each case is given in the last row of this table and varies from $5710 when the interest rate is 5% to $4405 when it is 13%.

Notice that the value of a bond falls as interest rates rise. This is entirely to be expected, since the formula we use to calculate individual present values is

$$P = \frac{S}{(1 + r/100)^t}$$

and larger values of r produce smaller values of P.

Table 3.29

End of year	Cash flow	Present values				
		5%	7%	9%	11%	13%
1	450	429	421	413	405	398
2	450	408	393	379	365	352
3	450	389	367	347	329	312
4	5450	4484	4158	3861	3590	3343
Total present value		5710	5339	5000	4689	4405

The effect of this relationship on financial markets can now be analysed. Let us suppose that the interest rate is high at, say, 13%. As you can see from Table 3.29, the price of the bond is relatively low. Moreover, one might reasonably expect that, in the future, interest rates are likely to fall, thereby increasing the present value of the bond. In this situation an investor would be encouraged to buy this bond in the expectation of not only receiving the cash flow from holding the bond but also receiving a capital gain on its present value. Speculative balances therefore decrease as a result of high interest rates because money is converted into securities. Exactly the opposite happens when interest rates are low. The corresponding present value is relatively high, and, with an expectation of a rise in interest rates and a possible capital loss, investors are reluctant to invest in securities, so speculative balances are high.

Practice Problem

7. A 10-year bond is originally offered by the government at $1000 with an annual return of 7%. Assuming that the bond currently has three years left before redemption and that the prevailing interest rate is 8% compounded annually, calculate its present value.

Key Terms

Annuity   A lump-sum investment designed to produce a sequence of equal regular payments over time.

Discount rate   The interest rate that is used when going backwards in time to calculate the present value from a future value.

Discounting   The process of working backwards in time to find the present values from a future value.

Internal rate of return (IRR)   The interest rate for which the net present value is zero.

Net present value (NPV)   The present value of a revenue flow minus the original cost.

Present value   The amount that is invested initially to produce a specified future value after a given period of time.

Exercise 3.4

1. Determine the present value of $7000 in two years' time if the discount rate is 8% compounded

   (a) quarterly   (b) continuously

2. A small business promises a profit of $8000 on an initial investment of $20 000 after five years.

   (a) Calculate the internal rate of return.

   (b) Would you advise someone to invest in this business if the market rate is 6% compounded annually?

3. An investment company is considering one of two possible business ventures. Project 1 gives a return of $250 000 in four years' time, whereas Project 2 gives a return of $350 000 in eight years' time. Which project should the company invest in when the interest rate is 7% compounded annually?

4. The revenue of a firm (in $100 000s) at the end of each year for the next five years is listed in Table 3.30. Calculate the present value of the revenue stream if the annual discount rate is 8%.

Table 3.30

Year	1	2	3	4	5
Revenue	−20	−14	5	39	64

5. A builder is offered one of two methods of payment:

Option 1: A single sum of $73 000 to be paid now.
Option 2: Five equal payments of $15 000 to be paid quarterly with the first instalment to be paid now.

Advise the builder which offer to accept if the interest rate is 6% compounded quarterly.

6. A financial company invests £250 000 now and receives £300 000 in three years' time. Calculate the internal rate of return.

7. A company has the option of investing in a project and calculates the net present values shown in Table 3.31 at four different discount rates.

Table 3.31

Discount rate	Net present values
3	$5510
4	$630
5	−$3980
6	−$8330

(a) Estimate the internal rate of return of the project.
(b) If the money could be invested elsewhere at 5.5% interest, explain whether you would advise the company to invest in this project.

8. You are given the opportunity of investing in one of three projects. Projects A, B and C require initial outlays of $20 000, $30 000 and $100 000 and are guaranteed to return $25 000, $37 000 and $117 000, respectively, in three years' time. Which of these projects would you invest in if the market rate is 5% compounded annually?

9. Determine the present value of an annuity that pays out $100 at the end of each year

(a) for five years   (b) in perpetuity

if the interest rate is 10% compounded annually.

10. An investor is given the opportunity to invest in one of two projects:

Project A costs $10 000 now and pays back $15 000 at the end of four years.
Project B costs $15 000 now and pays back $25 000 at the end of five years.
The current interest rate is 9%.

By calculating the net present values, decide which, if either, of these projects is to be recommended.

11. A proposed investment costs $130 000 today. The expected revenue flow is $40 000 at the end of year 1, and $140 000 at the end of year 2. Find the internal rate of return, correct to one decimal place.

Exercise 3.4*

1. Find the present value of $450 in six years' time if the discount rate is 9.5% compounded semi-annually. Round your answer to two decimal places.

2. A project requires an initial investment of $7000 and is guaranteed to yield a return of $1500 at the end of the first year, $2500 at the end of the second year and $x at the end of the third year. Find the value of x, correct to the nearest $, given that the net present value is $838.18 when the interest rate is 6% compounded annually.

3. Determine the present value of an annuity, if it pays out $2500 at the end of each year in perpetuity, assuming that the interest rate is 8% compounded annually.

4. A firm decides to invest in a new piece of machinery which is expected to produce an additional revenue of $8000 at the end of every year for 10 years. At the end of this period the firm plans to sell the machinery for scrap, for which it expects to receive $5000. What is the maximum amount that the firm should pay for the machine if it is not to suffer a net loss as a result of this investment? You may assume that the discount rate is 6% compounded annually.

5. During the next three years a business decides to invest $10 000 at the *beginning* of each year. The corresponding revenue that it can expect to receive at the *end* of each year is given in Table 3.32. Calculate the net present value if the discount rate is 4% compounded annually.

Table 3.32

End of year	Revenue ($)
1	5 000
2	20 000
3	50 000

6. A project requires an initial investment of $50 000. It produces a return of $40 000 at the end of year 1 and $30 000 at the end of year 2. Find the exact value of the internal rate of return.

7. A government bond that originally cost $500 with a yield of 6% has five years left before redemption. Determine its present value if the prevailing rate of interest is 15%.

8. An annuity pays out $20 000 per year in perpetuity. If the interest rate is 5% compounded annually, find

   (a) the present value of the whole annuity;

   (b) the present value of the annuity for payments received, starting from the end of the 30th year;

   (c) the present value of the annuity of the first 30 years.

9. An engineering company needs to decide whether or not to build a new factory. The costs of building the factory are $150 million initially, together with a further $100 million at the end of the next two years. Annual operating costs are $5 million commencing at the end of the third year. Annual revenue is predicted to be $50 million commencing at the end of the third year. If the interest rate is 6% compounded annually, find

   (a) the present value of the building costs;

   (b) the present value of the operating costs at the end of n years ($n > 2$);

   (c) the present value of the revenue after n years ($n > 2$);

   (d) the minimum value of n for which the net present value is positive.

10. A project requires an initial outlay of $80 000 and produces a return of $20 000 at the end of year 1, $30 000 at the end of year 2, and $R at the end of year 3. Determine the value of R if the internal rate of return is 10%.

11. An annuity yields an income of $R at the end of each year for the next n years. If the interest rate is r% compounded annually, show that the present value is

$$100R\left(\frac{1 - (1 + r/100)^{-n}}{r}\right)$$

   (a) Find the annual income if the interest rate is 6.5%, the present value is $14 000 and the annuity is paid for 15 years. Give your answer correct to two decimal places.

   (b) Write down a general expression, in terms of r and R, for the present value if the annuity is to be paid in perpetuity.

12. A project requiring an initial outlay of $A produces a return of $a at the end of every year for n years.

   (a) Show that the internal rate of return, r, satisfies the equation

$$A = \frac{100a}{r}\left[1 - \left(1 + \frac{r}{100}\right)^{-n}\right]$$

   (b) Find the internal rate of return of a project which requires an initial outlay of $1 000 000 and gives a return of $10 000 in perpetuity.

Formal mathematics

The Greek letter Σ (sigma) is the equivalent of the letter S (for sum) and is used to express summations in a compact form. Given a sequence of numbers, $x_1, x_2, x_3, \ldots, x_n$ we define

$$\sum_{i=1}^{n} x_i = x_1 + x_2 + x_3 + \cdots + x_n$$

In this case we add together the terms x_i starting with $i = 1$, allowing the subscript to go up in integer steps, and finishing with $i = n$. The values of $i = 1$ and n which appear at the bottom and top of the sigma sign are called the **lower** and **upper limits**, respectively. Using this notation we have:

$$\sum_{i=1}^{5} i^2 = 1^2 + 2^2 + 3^2 + 4^2 + 5^2$$

A typical term is i^2, so we need to add these together starting with $i = 1$ and running through all integer values until we reach $i = 5$.

Likewise:

$$\sum_{i=3}^{7} 2^i = 2^3 + 2^4 + 2^5 + 2^6 + 2^7$$

The lower limit is 3, so we begin by substituting $i = 3$ into the general term 2^i to get 2^3. Subsequent terms are obtained by substituting consecutive integer values, $i = 4, 5, \ldots$ into the general term. The upper limit is 7, so we continue to add together all of the terms up to and including 2^7.

The notation clearly provides a convenient short-hand for what would otherwise be lengthy expressions, and there are other advantages, too. The following properties of sigma notation allow us to manipulate summations algebraically.

Property 1

$$\sum_{i=1}^{n} (x_i + y_i) = \sum_{i=1}^{n} x_i + \sum_{i=1}^{n} y_i$$

Property 2

$$\sum_{i=1}^{n} a x_i = a \sum_{i=1}^{n} x_i \quad \text{where } a \text{ is any constant}$$

These properties are easily checked by writing out the summations longhand. For Property 2 we have

$$\sum_{i=1}^{n} a x_i = a x_1 + a x_2 + \cdots + a x_n = a(x_1 + x_2 + \cdots + x_n) = a \sum_{i=1}^{n} x_i$$

As we have seen in this chapter, financial mathematics often involves the summation of series, and the following example shows how to use it to express the sum of a geometric series using sigma notation.

Example

(a) A person saves $2000 a year in a bank account at the beginning of the year for n years. If the bank offers a return of 4% a year, use sigma notation to write down an expression for the total amount saved.

(b) Use sigma notation to express the sum of the first n terms of a geometric series with first term a and geometric ratio r.

Solution

(a) During a period of n years the total amount saved is

$$2000(1.04) + 2000(1.04)^2 + 2000(1.04)^3 + \cdots + 2000(1.04)^n$$

which can be expressed succinctly as

$$\sum_{i=1}^{n} 2000(1.04)^i = 2000 \sum_{i=1}^{n} 1.04^i \quad \text{(using property 2 to take out the factor of 2000)}$$

(b) Using sigma notation, the sum

$$a + ar + ar^2 + \cdots + ar^{n-1}$$

can be written as

$$\sum_{i=1}^{n} ar^{i-1} = a \sum_{i=1}^{n} r^{i-1} \quad \text{(again using property 2 to take out the factor of } a\text{)}$$

Key Terms

Lower limit   The number which appears at the bottom of the sigma notation to indicate the first term in a summation.

Upper limit   The number which appears at the top of the sigma notation to indicate the last term in a summation.

Multiple choice questions

Question 1

Evaluate the geometric series

$$200 + 200(1.05) + 200(1.05)^2 + \cdots\cdots + 200(1.05)^{20}$$

Round your answer to two decimal places.

A. 7143.85   **B.** 6613.19   **C.** 7701.04   **D.** 6234.18   **E.** 6889.03

Question 2

The price of gold falls by 34% in the first six months of a year and rises by 12% in the last six months. Work out the overall percentage decrease during the year. Round your answer to the nearest unit.

A. 38%   **B.** 18%   **C.** 22%   **D.** 26%   **E.** 15%

Question 3

Average house prices at the start of Year 1 and Year 4 are $200 000 and $230 076. If house prices rose by 10% in Year 1 and 5% in Year 2, work out the percentage change in Year 3.

A. 1.2% increase

B. 1.2% decrease

C. 1.8% increase

D. 2.4% increase

E. 0.4% decrease

Question 4

Work out the missing numbers in the table below which shows the annual spending on health care (to the nearest unit) over a four-year period and the corresponding index number (rounded to one decimal place).

Spending	460	x	512	525
Index number	89.8	95.1	100	y

A. $x = 498$ $y = 103.8$

B. $x = 498$ $y = 102.5$

C. $x = 487$ $y = 103.8$

D. $x = 487$ $y = 102.5$

E. Insufficient information

Question 5

What is the future value of $5000 invested for seven years when the interest rate is 2.8% compounded monthly?

A. $6066.27

B. $6081.25

C. $5082.24

D. $5653.33

E. $5998.34

Question 6

A regular sum of $2500 is invested at the beginning of every year at 3.5% interest compounded annually. Find the total amount invested at the end of 10 years.

A. $29 328.48

B. $26 828.48

C. $30 354.98

D. $34 004.90

E. $25 921.24

Question 7

A sum of $2 million is invested today in a project which is guaranteed to provide a return of $1.5 million at the end of five years and a further $1.25 million at the end of six years. What is the net present value if the discount rate is 4.5% compounded annually?

A. $139 673.45

B. $167 564.09

C. $145 657.62

D. $130 000.09

E. $163 546.24

Question 8

A bank provides a mortgage of $100 000 which is to be repaid by a regular monthly repayment of x for five years. Find the value of x if the bank charges interest at 6% compounded monthly.

A. $6187.57

B. $5998.78

C. $1971.20

D. $1933.28

E. $5308.65

Question 9

If a principal of $3500 is invested at 3.4% interest compounded continuously, what is the future value after six years?

A. $4277.51

B. $4917.13

C. $4292.04

D. $4290.81

E. $4276.98

Question 10

A bond is originally offered by the government for $6000 with an annual return of 6%. If the bond has three years left before maturity, calculate its present value (correct to two decimal places) assuming that the current interest rate is 4%.

A. $6450.98

B. $6269.90

C. $6333.01

D. $6299.07

E. $6447.79

Question 11

Find the APR of a credit card which charges interest at a monthly rate of 3.5%. Give your answer to the nearest whole number.

A. 55%

B. 42%

C. 35%

D. 45%

E. 51%

Question 12

A piece of machinery depreciates in value by 7% a year. After how many years will the machinery be worth half of its original price?

A. 7

B. 8

C. 9

D. 10

E. 11

Question 13

A project requiring an initial outlay of $55 000 is guaranteed to produce a return of $75 000 in three years' time. Calculate the internal rate of return.

A. 11.1% **B.** 10.7% **C.** 10.9% **D.** 11.4% **E.** 11.6%

Question 14

Determine the present value of an annuity which pays out $12 000 at the end of each year in perpetuity if the interest rate is 4% compounded annually.

A. $320 000

B. $312 000

C. $310 000

D. $318 000

E. $300 000

Question 15

The table shows the nominal average annual salary (in thousands of dollars) of employees in the oil industry over a two-year period together with the rate of inflation.

Year	1	2
Salary	96.3	98.7
Inflation	2.8%	−0.5%

Work out the real average annual salary in Year 2 adjusted to prices at the beginning of Year 1.

A. 91.2 **B.** 92.2 **C.** 93.1 **D.** 95.5 **E.** 96.5

Question 16

How much needs to be invested now to secure a regular income of $10 000 at the end of every year for 15 years, if the interest rate is 3.25% compounded annually?

A. $118 456.87

B. $116 683.94

C. $115 432.65

D. $117 248.99

E. $115 765.89

Examination questions

Give all answers to two decimal places unless stated otherwise.

Question 1

A principal of $4000 is invested at an annual rate of 4% interest.

(a) Determine the future value after five years if the interest is compounded quarterly.

(b) Determine the future value after five years if the interest is compounded continuously.

(c) Work out the annual equivalent rate for each method of compounding in parts (a) and (b).

(d) If the interest rate of 4% is compounded continuously, after how many years will the investment increase to $4500?

Question 2

(a) A firm's sales rise by 2.4% in the first six months of the year and fall by 4.9% during the second half. Find the overall percentage change in sales over the whole year.

(b) A student invests a single amount of $P for three years in an account offering a return of 4.8% compounded semi-annually. Find the value of P if the future value is $700. Give your answer to the nearest cent.

(c) A person has a 25-year mortgage at a fixed rate of 6%. If the monthly repayments required to clear the debt are $1500, work out the value of the original loan. Round your answer to the nearest $1000.

Question 3

The number of trees in a forest at the beginning of this year was 4000. Each year 10% of the trees are cut down and 350 new trees are planted.

(a) How many trees are in the forest at the end of (i) this year (ii) next year?

(b) Show that at the end of N years the number of trees will be $3500 + 500(0.9)^N$.

(c) Describe what happens to the number of trees in the long-run.

Question 4

The table shows the prices of two products in two consecutive years. It also shows the quantities bought in Year 1.

Product	Number bought in Year 1	Unit price in Year 1	Unit price in Year 2
A	35	5	6
B	15	12	15

(a) Calculate the Laspeyres index using Year 1 as the base year (weighted according to the numbers bought in Year 1).

(b) The numbers of items bought in Year 2 are shown in the following table. Use this additional information to calculate the Paasche index.

Product	Number bought in Year 2
A	30
B	20

(c) Briefly discuss the relative merits of these two indices.

Question 5

An individual decides to invest in one of two projects, A and B, which both require the same initial outlay of $10 000. Project A yields $11 500 in three years' time whereas Project B yields, $12 100 in four years' time.

Calculate the internal rate of return for each project.

What advice can you give if the prevailing market rate of interest is 4.8%?

Question 6

(a) Country A has twice the GDP of country B. In the future, the annual growth rates of these two countries are expected to be 1% and 4%, respectively. After how many years will the GDP of country B exceed that of country A?

(b) The sum of $4000 is borrowed from a bank at a rate of 4.8% interest compounded monthly. The loan is repaid in monthly instalments of x. Show that at the end of n months, the outstanding debt is given by $4000(1.004)^n - 250x(1.004^n - 1)$.

   (i)   How many months would it take to repay the loan if $x = 100$?
   (ii) What should the monthly repayment be if the debt is to be cleared after 12 months?
   (iii) Describe briefly what happens to the outstanding debt when $x = 16$.

Question 7

(a) A principal, P, is invested in an account with an interest rate, $r\%$, compounded annually. The future value after n years is denoted by S.

   (i)   Find S when $P = \$4000$, $r = 3$ and $n = 6$.
   (ii) Find P when $S = \$3149.28$, $r = 8$ and $n = 3$
   (iii) Find r when $P = \$5000$, $n = 2$ and $S = \$5283.92$
   (iv) Find n when $P = \$75\,000$, $r = 10$ and $S = \$120\,788.25$

(b) Find the present value of an annuity that pays out $5000 at the end of each year

   (i)   for 10 years
   (ii) in perpetuity

if the interest rate is 4% compounded annually.

Question 8

(a) An individual saves $2000 in a bank account at the beginning of each year for 10 years. No further savings or withdrawals are made to the account. Determine the total amount saved if the annual interest is 3.6% compounded semi-annually.

(b) A project requiring an initial outlay of $200\,000 is guaranteed to produce a return of $145\,000 in one year's time and $80\,000 in two years' time. Calculate the net present value of the project if the discount rate is 4.5% compounded semi-annually.

CHAPTER 4
Differentiation

This chapter provides a simple introduction to the general topic of calculus. There are eight sections, which should be read in the order that they appear. It should be possible to omit Sections 4.4 and 4.7 at a first reading, and Section 4.6 can be read any time after Section 4.3.

Section 4.1 provides a leisurely introduction to the basic idea of differentiation. The material is explained using pictures, which will help you to understand the connection between the underlying mathematics and the economic applications in later sections.

There are six rules of differentiation, which are evenly split between Sections 4.2 and 4.4. Section 4.2 considers the easy rules that all students will need to know. However, if you are on a business studies or management course, the more advanced rules in Section 4.4 may not be of relevance and could be ignored. As far as possible, examples given in later sections and chapters are based on the easy rules only so that such students are not disadvantaged. However, the more advanced rules are essential to any proper study of mathematical economics, and their use in deriving general results is unavoidable.

Sections 4.3 and 4.5 describe standard economic applications. Marginal functions associated with revenue, cost, production, consumption and savings functions are all discussed in Section 4.3. The important topic of elasticity is described in Section 4.5. The distinction is made between price elasticity along an arc and price elasticity at a point. Familiar results involving general linear demand functions and the relationship between price elasticity of demand and revenue are derived.

Sections 4.6 and 4.7 are devoted to the topic of optimisation, which is used to find the maximum and minimum values of economic functions. In the first half of Section 4.6 we concentrate on the mathematical technique. The second half contains four examination-type problems, all taken from economics and business, which are solved in detail. In Section 4.7, mathematics is used to derive general results relating to the optimisation of profit and production functions. A simple model of stock control in business is described and a general formula for the economic order quantity derived.

The final section revises two important mathematical functions, namely the exponential and natural logarithm functions. We describe how to differentiate these functions and illustrate their use in economics and business.

Differentiation is probably the most important topic in the whole text, and one that we shall continue in Chapters 5 and 6, since it provides the necessary background theory for much of mathematical economics. You are therefore advised to make every effort to attempt the problems given in each section. The prerequisites include an understanding of the concept of a function together with the ability to manipulate algebraic expressions. These are covered in Chapters 1 and 2, and if you have worked successfully through this material, you should find that you are in good shape to begin calculus.

The derivative of a function

Objectives

At the end of this section you should be able to:

- Find the slope of a straight line given any two points on the line.
- Detect whether a line is uphill, downhill or horizontal using the sign of the slope.
- Recognise the notation $f'(x)$ and dy/dx for the derivative of a function.
- Estimate the derivative of a function by measuring the slope of a tangent.
- Differentiate power functions.

This introductory section is designed to get you started with differential calculus in a fairly painless way. There are really only three things that we are going to do. We discuss the basic idea of something called a derived function, give you two equivalent pieces of notation to describe it, and finally show you how to write down a formula for the derived function in simple cases.

In Chapter 1 the slope of a straight line was defined to be the change in the value of y brought about by a 1-unit increase in x. In fact, it is not necessary to restrict the change in x to a 1-unit increase. More generally, the **slope**, or **gradient**, of a line is taken to be the change in y divided by the corresponding change in x as you move between any two points on the line. It is customary to denote the change in y by Δy, where Δ is the Greek letter 'delta'. Likewise, the change in x is written Δx. In this notation we have

$$\text{slope} = \frac{\Delta y}{\Delta x}$$

Example

Find the slope of the straight line passing through

(a) A (1, 2) and B (3, 4)   **(b)** A (1, 2) and C (4, 1)   **(c)** A (1, 2) and D (5, 2)

Solution

(a) Points A and B are sketched in Figure 4.1. As we move from A to B, the y coordinate changes from 2 to 4, which is an increase of 2 units, and the x coordinate changes from 1 to 3, which is also an increase of 2 units. Hence

$$\text{slope} = \frac{\Delta y}{\Delta x} = \frac{4 - 2}{3 - 1} = \frac{2}{2} = 1$$

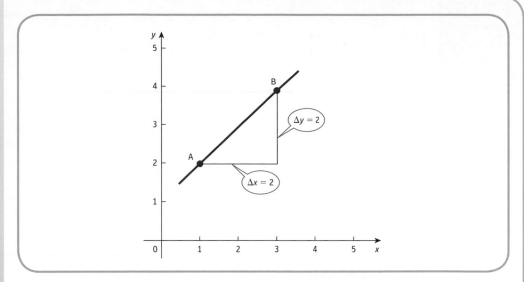

Figure 4.1

(b) Points A and C are sketched in Figure 4.2. As we move from A to C, the y coordinate changes from 2 to 1, which is a decrease of 1 unit, and the x coordinate changes from 1 to 4, which is an increase of 3 units. Hence

$$\text{slope} = \frac{\Delta y}{\Delta x} = \frac{1-2}{4-1} = \frac{-1}{3}$$

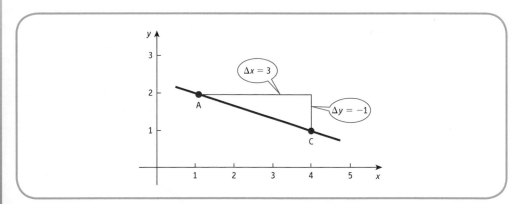

Figure 4.2

(c) Points A and D are sketched in Figure 4.3. As we move from A to D, the y coordinate remains fixed at 2, and the x coordinate changes from 1 to 5, which is an increase of 4 units. Hence

$$\text{slope} = \frac{\Delta y}{\Delta x} = \frac{2-2}{5-1} = \frac{0}{4} = 0$$

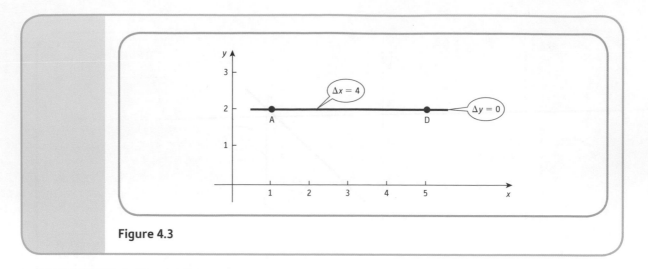

Figure 4.3

Practice Problem

1. Find the slope of the straight line passing through

   (a) E (−1, 3) and F (3, 11)   **(b)** E (−1, 3) and G (4, −2)   **(c)** E (−1, 3) and H (49, 3)

From these examples we see that the gradient is positive if the line is uphill, negative if the line is downhill and zero if the line is horizontal.

Unfortunately, not all functions in economics are linear, so it is necessary to extend the definition of slope to include more general curves. To do this we need the idea of a tangent, which is illustrated in Figure 4.4.

A straight line which passes through a point on a curve and which just touches the curve at this point is called a **tangent**. The slope, or gradient, of a curve at $x = a$ is then defined to be that of the tangent at $x = a$. Since we have already seen how to find the slope of a straight line, this gives us a precise way of measuring the slope of a curve. A simple curve together with a selection of tangents at various points is shown in Figure 4.5. Notice how each tangent passes through exactly one point on the curve and strikes a glancing blow. In this case, the slopes of the tangents increase as we move from left to right along the curve. This reflects the fact that the curve is flat at $x = 0$ but becomes progressively steeper further away.

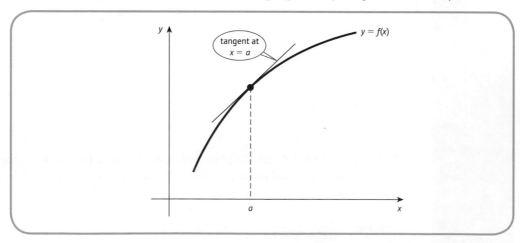

Figure 4.4

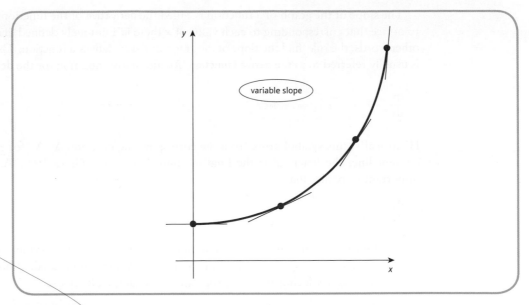

Figure 4.5

This highlights an important difference between the slope of a straight line and the slope of a curve. In the case of a straight line, the gradient is fixed throughout its length and it is immaterial which two points on a line are used to find it. For example, in Figure 4.6 all of the ratios $\Delta y/\Delta x$ have the value $1/2$. However, as we have just seen, the slope of a curve varies as we move along it. In mathematics we use the symbol

$$f'(a) \qquad \text{read 'f dashed of a'}$$

to represent the slope of the graph of a function f at $x = a$. This notation conveys the maximum amount of information with the minimum of fuss. As usual, we need the label f to denote which function we are considering. We certainly need the a to tell us at which point on the curve the gradient is being measured. Finally, the 'prime' symbol $'$ is used to distinguish the gradient from the function value. The notation $f(a)$ gives the height of the curve above the x axis at $x = a$, whereas $f'(a)$ gives the gradient of the curve at this point.

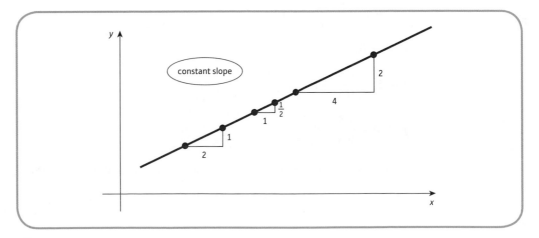

Figure 4.6

The slope of the graph of a function is called the **derivative** of the function. It is interesting to notice that corresponding to each value of x there is a uniquely defined derivative $f'(x)$. In other words, the rule 'find the slope of the graph of f at x' defines a function. This slope function is usually referred to as the **derived function**. An alternative notation for the derived function is

$$\frac{dy}{dx}$$

read 'dee y by dee x'

Historically, this symbol arose from the corresponding notation $\Delta y/\Delta x$ for the gradient of a straight line; the letter 'd' is the English equivalent of the Greek letter Δ. However, it is important to realise that

$$\frac{dy}{dx}$$

does not mean 'dy divided by dx'. It should be thought of as a single symbol representing the derivative of y with respect to x. It is immaterial which notation is used, although the context may well suggest which is more appropriate. For example, if we use

$$y = x^2$$

to identify the square function, then it is natural to use

$$\frac{dy}{dx}$$

for the derived function. On the other hand, if we use

$$f(x) = x^2$$

then $f'(x)$ seems more appropriate.

A graph of the square function based on the table of values

x	−2.0	−1.5	−1.0	−0.5	0.0	0.5	1.0	1.5	2.0
$f(x)$	4	2.25	1	0.25	0	0.25	1	2.25	4

is sketched in Figure 4.7. From this graph we see that the slopes of the tangents are

$$f'(-1.5) = \frac{-1.5}{0.5} = -3$$

$$f'(-0.5) = \frac{-0.5}{0.5} = -1$$

$$f'(0) = 0$$

$$f'(0.5) = \frac{0.5}{0.5} = 1$$

$$f'(1.5) = \frac{1.5}{0.5} = 3$$

The value of $f'(0)$ is zero because the tangent is horizontal at $x = 0$. Notice that

$$f'(-1.5) = -f'(1.5) \quad \text{and} \quad f'(-0.5) = -f'(0.5)$$

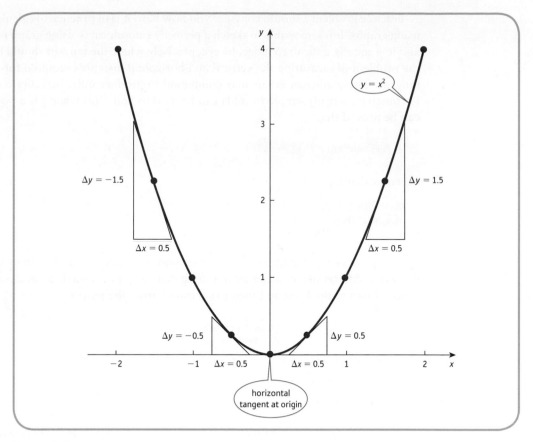

Figure 4.7

This is to be expected because the graph is symmetric about the y axis. The slopes of the tangents to the left of the y axis have the same size as those of the corresponding tangents to the right. However, they have opposite signs since the curve slopes downhill on one side and uphill on the other.

Practice Problem

2. Complete the following table of function values and hence sketch an accurate graph of $f(x) = x^3$.

x	−1.50	−1.25	−1.00	−0.75	−0.50	−0.25	0.00
$f(x)$		−1.95			−0.13		

x	0.25	0.50	0.75	1.00	1.25	1.50
$f(x)$		0.13			1.95	

    Draw the tangents to the graph at $x = -1, 0$ and 1. Hence estimate the values of $f'(-1)$, $f'(0)$ and $f'(1)$.

Practice Problem 2 should convince you how hard it is in practice to calculate $f'(a)$ exactly using graphs. It is impossible to sketch a perfectly smooth curve using graph paper and pencil, and it is equally difficult to judge, by eye, precisely where the tangent should be. There is also the problem of measuring the vertical and horizontal distances required for the slope of the tangent. These inherent errors may compound to produce quite inaccurate values for $f'(a)$. Fortunately, a really simple formula can be used to find $f'(a)$ when f is a power function. It can be proved that

> if $f(x) = x^n$ then $f'(x) = nx^{n-1}$

or, equivalently,

> if $y = x^n$ then $\dfrac{dy}{dx} = nx^{n-1}$

The process of finding the derived function symbolically (rather than using graphs) is known as **differentiation**. In order to differentiate x^n all that needs to be done is to bring the power down to the front and then to subtract 1 from the power:

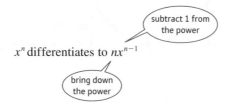

x^n differentiates to nx^{n-1}

To differentiate the square function we set $n = 2$ in this formula to deduce that

$$f(x) = x^2 \text{ differentiates to } f'(x) = 2x^{2-1}$$

that is,

$$f'(x) = 2x^1 = 2x$$

Using this result, we see that

$$f'(-1.5) = 2 \times (-1.5) = -3$$
$$f'(-0.5) = 2 \times (-0.5) = -1$$
$$f'(0) = 2 \times (0) = 0$$
$$f'(0.5) = 2 \times (0.5) = 1$$
$$f'(1.5) = 2 \times (1.5) = 3$$

which are in agreement with the results obtained from the graph in Figure 4.7.

Practice Problem

3. If $f(x) = x^3$, write down a formula for $f'(x)$. Calculate $f'(-1)$, $f'(0)$ and $f'(1)$. Confirm that these are in agreement with your rough estimates obtained in Practice Problem 2.

Example

Differentiate

(a) $y = x^4$ (b) $y = x^{10}$ (c) $y = x$ (d) $y = 1$ (e) $y = 1/x^4$ (f) $y = \sqrt{x}$

Solution

(a) To differentiate $y = x^4$ we bring down the power (that is, 4) to the front and then subtract 1 from the power (that is, $4 - 1 = 3$) to deduce that

$$\frac{dy}{dx} = 4x^3$$

(b) Similarly,

$$\text{if } y = x^{10} \quad \text{then} \quad \frac{dy}{dx} = 10x^9$$

(c) To use the general formula to differentiate x we first need to express $y = x$ in the form $y = x^n$ for some number n. In this case $n = 1$ because $x^1 = x$, so

$$\frac{dy}{dx} = 1x^0 = 1 \quad \text{since} \quad x^0 = 1$$

This result is also obvious from the graph of $y = x$ sketched in Figure 4.8.

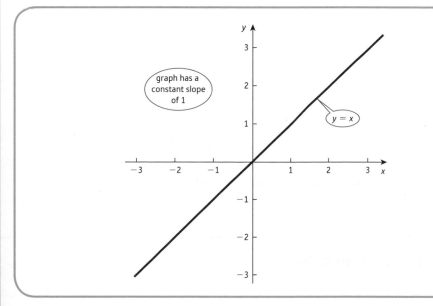

Figure 4.8

(d) Again, to differentiate 1 we need to express $y = 1$ in the form $y = x^n$. In this case $n = 0$ because $x^0 = 1$, so

$$\frac{dy}{dx} = 0x^{-1} = 0$$

This result is also obvious from the graph of $y = 1$ sketched in Figure 4.9.

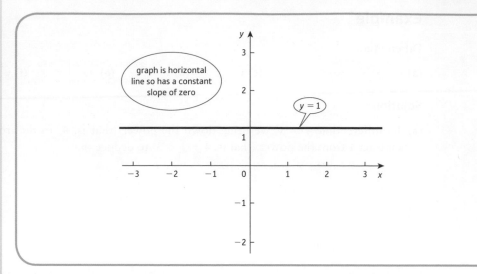

Figure 4.9

(e) Noting that $1/x^4 = x^{-4}$, it follows that

$$\text{if } y = \frac{1}{x^4} \quad \text{then} \quad \frac{dy}{dx} = -4x^{-5} = -\frac{4}{x^5}$$

The power has decreased to -5 because $-4 - 1 = -5$.

(f) Noting that $\sqrt{x} = x^{1/2}$, it follows that if

$$y = \sqrt{x} \quad \text{then} \quad \frac{dy}{dx} = \frac{1}{2}x^{-1/2}$$

$$= \frac{1}{2x^{1/2}} \quad \fbox{negative powers denote reciprocals}$$

$$= \frac{1}{2\sqrt{x}} \quad \fbox{fractional powers denote roots}$$

The power has decreased to $-\frac{1}{2}$ because $\frac{1}{2} - 1 = -\frac{1}{2}$.

Practice Problem

4. Differentiate

  (a) $y = x^5$ **(b)** $y = x^6$ **(c)** $y = x^{100}$ **(d)** $y = 1/x$ **(e)** $y = 1/x^2$

[Hint: in parts (d) and (e) note that $1/x = x^{-1}$ and $1/x^2 = x^{-2}$]

Key Terms

Derivative   The gradient of the tangent to a curve at a point. The derivative at $x = a$ is written $f'(a)$.

Derived function   The rule, f', which gives the gradient of a function, f, at a general point.

Differentiation   The process or operation of determining the first derivative of a function.

Gradient   The gradient of a line measures steepness and is the vertical change divided by the horizontal change between any two points on the line. The gradient of a curve at a point is that of the tangent at that point.

Slope   An alternative word for gradient.

Tangent   A line that just touches a curve at a point.

Exercise 4.1

1. Find the slope of the straight line passing through

   (a) $(2, 5)$ and $(4, 9)$ **(b)** $(3, -1)$ and $(7, -5)$ **(c)** $(7, 19)$ and $(4, 19)$

2. Verify that the points $(0, 2)$ and $(3, 0)$ lie on the line

   $$2x + 3y = 6$$

   Hence find the slope of this line. Is the line uphill, downhill or horizontal?

3. Sketch the graph of the function

   $$f(x) = 5$$

   Explain why it follows from this that

   $$f'(x) = 0$$

4. Differentiate the function

   $$f(x) = x^7$$

   Hence calculate the slope of the graph of

   $$y = x^7$$

   at the point $x = 2$.

5. Differentiate

   (a) $y = x^8$ **(b)** $y = x^{50}$ **(c)** $y = x^{19}$ **(d)** $y = x^{999}$

6. Differentiate the following functions, giving your answer in a similar form, without negative or fractional indices:

   (a) $f(x) = \dfrac{1}{x^3}$ **(b)** $f(x) = \sqrt{x}$ **(c)** $f(x) = \dfrac{1}{\sqrt{x}}$ **(d)** $y = x\sqrt{x}$

7. Complete the following table of function values for the function, $f(x) = x^2 - 2x$:

x	-1	-0.5	0	0.5	1	1.5	2	2.5
$x^2 - 2x$								

   Sketch the graph of this function and, by measuring the slope of the tangents, estimate

   (a) $f'(-0.5)$ **(b)** $f'(1)$ **(c)** $f'(1.5)$

Exercise 4.1*

1. Verify that the points $(0, b)$ and $(1, a + b)$ lie on the line

   $$y = ax + b$$

   Hence show that this line has slope a.

2. Differentiate each of the following functions, expressing your answer in a similar form:

   (a) x^{15} **(b)** $x^4\sqrt{x}$ **(c)** $\sqrt[3]{x}$ **(d)** $\dfrac{1}{\sqrt[4]{x}}$ **(e)** $\dfrac{\sqrt{x}}{x^7}$

3. For each of the graphs

   (a) $y = \sqrt{x}$ **(b)** $y = x\sqrt{x}$ **(c)** $y = \dfrac{1}{\sqrt{x}}$

   A is the point where $x = 4$, and B is the point where $x = 4.1$. In each case find

   (i)   the y coordinates of A and B;

   (ii) the gradient of the chord AB;

   (iii) the value of $\dfrac{dy}{dx}$ at A.

   Compare your answers to parts (ii) and (iii).

4. Find the coordinates of the point(s) at which the curve has the specified gradient.

   (a) $y = x^{2/3}$ gradient $= \dfrac{1}{3}$ **(b)** $y = x^5$, gradient $= 405$

   (c) $y = \dfrac{1}{x^2}$, gradient $= 16$ **(d)** $y = \dfrac{1}{x\sqrt{x}}$, gradient $= -\dfrac{3}{64}$

SECTION 4.2
Rules of differentiation

Objectives

At the end of this section you should be able to:

- Use the constant rule to differentiate a function of the form $cf(x)$.
- Use the sum rule to differentiate a function of the form $f(x) + g(x)$.
- Use the difference rule to differentiate a function of the form $f(x) - g(x)$.
- Evaluate and interpret second-order derivatives.

Advice

In this section we consider three elementary rules of differentiation. Subsequent sections of this chapter describe various applications to economics. However, before you can tackle these successfully, you must have a thorough grasp of the basic techniques involved. The problems in this section are repetitive in nature. This is deliberate. Although the rules themselves are straightforward, it is necessary for you to practise them over and over again before you can become proficient in using them. In fact, mastering the rules of this section is essential for you to proceed further with the rest of the text.

Rule 1 The constant rule

If $h(x) = cf(x)$ then $h'(x) = cf'(x)$

for any constant c.

This rule tells you how to find the derivative of a constant multiple of a function:

> differentiate the function and multiply by the constant

Example

Differentiate

(a) $y = 2x^4$ (b) $y = 10x$

Solution

(a) To differentiate $2x^4$ we first differentiate x^4 to get $4x^3$ and then multiply by 2. Hence

$$\text{if } y = 2x^4 \quad \text{then} \quad \frac{dy}{dx} = 2(4x^3) = 8x^3$$

(b) To differentiate $10x$ we first differentiate x to get 1 and then multiply by 10. Hence

$$\text{if } y = 10x \quad \text{then} \quad \frac{dy}{dx} = 10(1) = 10$$

Practice Problem

1. Differentiate

    (a) $y = 4x^3$ (b) $y = 2/x$

The constant rule can be used to show that

> constants differentiate to zero

To see this, note that the equation

$y = c$

is the same as

$y = cx^0$

because $x^0 = 1$. By the constant rule we first differentiate x^0 to get $0x^{-1}$ and then multiply by c. Hence

if $y = c$ then $\dfrac{dy}{dx} = c(0x^{-1}) = 0$

This result is also apparent from the graph of $y = c$, sketched in Figure 4.10, which is a horizontal line c units away from the x axis. It is an important result and explains why lone constants lurking in mathematical expressions disappear when differentiated.

Rule 2 The sum rule

If $h(x) = f(x) + g(x)$ then $h'(x) = f'(x) + g'(x)$

This rule tells you how to find the derivative of the sum of two functions:

> differentiate each function separately and add

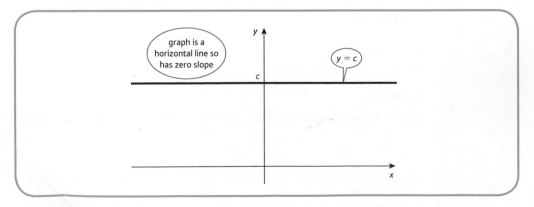

Figure 4.10

Example

Differentiate

(a) $y = x^2 + x^{50}$ **(b)** $y = x^3 + 3$

Solution

(a) To differentiate $x^2 + x^{50}$ we need to differentiate x^2 and x^{50} separately and add. Now

x^2 differentiates to $2x$

and

x^{50} differentiates to $50x^{49}$

so

if $y = x^2 + x^{50}$ then $\dfrac{dy}{dx} = 2x + 50x^{49}$

(b) To differentiate $x^3 + 3$ we need to differentiate x^3 and 3 separately and add. Now

x^3 differentiates to $3x^2$

and

3 differentiates to 0   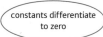 constants differentiate to zero

so

if $y = x^3 + 3$ then $\dfrac{dy}{dx} = 3x^2 + 0 = 3x^2$

Practice Problem

2. Differentiate

(a) $y = x^5 + x$ (b) $y = x^2 + 5$

Rule 3 The difference rule

If $h(x) = f(x) - g(x)$ then $h'(x) = f'(x) - g'(x)$

This rule tells you how to find the derivative of the difference of two functions:

differentiate each function separately and subtract

Example

Differentiate

(a) $y = x^5 - x^2$ **(b)** $y = x - \dfrac{1}{x^2}$

Solution

(a) To differentiate $x^5 - x^2$ we need to differentiate x^5 and x^2 separately and subtract. Now

x^5 differentiates to $5x^4$

and

x^2 differentiates to $2x$

so

if $y = x^5 - x^2$ then $\dfrac{dy}{dx} = 5x^4 - 2x$

(b) To differentiate $x - \dfrac{1}{x^2}$ we need to differentiate x and $\dfrac{1}{x^2}$ separately and subtract. Now

x differentiates to 1

and

$\dfrac{1}{x^2}$ differentiates to $-\dfrac{2}{x^3}$

so

if $y = x - \dfrac{1}{x^2}$ then $\dfrac{dy}{dx} = 1 - \left(-\dfrac{2}{x^3}\right) = 1 + \dfrac{2}{x^3}$

Practice Problem

3. Differentiate

(a) $y = x^2 - x^3$ **(b)** $y = 50 - \dfrac{1}{x^3}$

It is possible to combine these three rules and so to find the derivative of more involved functions, as the following example demonstrates.

Example

Differentiate

(a) $y = 3x^5 + 2x^3$ **(b)** $y = x^3 + 7x^2 - 2x + 10$ **(c)** $y = 2\sqrt{x} + \dfrac{3}{x}$

Solution

(a) The sum rule shows that to differentiate $3x^5 + 2x^3$, we need to differentiate $3x^5$ and $2x^3$ separately and add. By the constant rule

$3x^5$ differentiates to $3(5x^4) = 15x^4$

and

$2x^3$ differentiates to $2(3x^2) = 6x^2$

so

$$\text{if } y = 3x^5 + 2x^3 \quad \text{then} \quad \frac{dy}{dx} = 15x^4 + 6x^2$$

With practice you will soon find that you can just write the derivative down in a single line of working by differentiating term by term. For the function

$$y = 3x^5 + 2x^3$$

we could just write

$$\frac{dy}{dx} = 3(5x^4) + 2(3x^2) = 15x^4 + 6x^2$$

(b) So far we have only considered expressions comprising at most two terms. However, the sum and difference rules still apply to lengthier expressions, so we can differentiate term by term as before. For the function

$$y = x^3 + 7x^2 - 2x + 10$$

we get

$$\frac{dy}{dx} = 3x^2 + 7(2x) - 2(1) + 0 = 3x^2 + 14x - 2$$

(c) To differentiate

$$y = 2\sqrt{x} + \frac{3}{x}$$

we first rewrite it using the notation of indices as

$$y = 2x^{1/2} + 3x^{-1}$$

Differentiating term by term then gives

$$\frac{dy}{dx} = 2\left(\frac{1}{2}\right)x^{-1/2} + 3(-1)x^{-2} = x^{-1/2} - 3x^{-2}$$

which can be written in the more familiar form

$$\frac{1}{\sqrt{x}} - \frac{3}{x^2}$$

Practice Problem

4. Differentiate

(a) $y = 9x^5 + 2x^2$ (b) $y = 5x^8 - \dfrac{3}{x}$

(c) $y = x^2 + 6x + 3$ (d) $y = 2x^4 + 12x^3 - 4x^2 + 7x - 400$

Whenever a function is differentiated, the thing that you end up with is itself a function. This suggests the possibility of differentiating a second time to get the 'slope of the slope function'. This is written as

$f''(x)$ read 'f double dashed of x'

or

$\dfrac{d^2y}{dx^2}$ read 'dee two y by dee x squared'

For example, if

$f(x) = 5x^2 - 7x + 12$

then differentiating once gives

$f'(x) = 10x - 7$

and if we now differentiate $f'(x)$ we get

$f''(x) = 10$

The function $f'(x)$ is called the **first-order derivative** and $f''(x)$ is called the **second-order derivative**.

Example

Evaluate $f''(1)$ where

$f(x) = x^7 + \dfrac{1}{x}$

Solution

To find $f''(1)$ we need to differentiate

$f(x) = x^7 + x^{-1}$

twice and put $x = 1$ into the end result. Differentiating once gives

$f'(x) = 7x^6 + (-1)x^{-2} = 7x^6 - x^{-2}$

and differentiating a second time gives

$f''(x) = 7(6x^5) - (-2)x^{-3} = 42x^5 + 2x^{-3}$

Finally, substituting $x = 1$ into

$f''(x) = 42x^5 + \dfrac{2}{x^3}$

gives

$f''(1) = 42 + 2 = 44$

Practice Problem

5. Evaluate $f''(6)$ where

$$f(x) = 4x^3 - 5x^2$$

It is possible to give a graphical interpretation of the sign of the second-order derivative. Remember that the first-order derivative, $f'(x)$, measures the gradient of a curve. If the derivative of $f'(x)$ is positive (that is, if $f''(x) > 0$) then $f'(x)$ is increasing, so the graph gets steeper as you move from left to right. The curve bends upwards and the function is said to be **convex**. On the other hand, if $f''(x) < 0$, the gradient $f'(x)$ must be decreasing, so the curve bends downwards. The function is said to be **concave**. It is perfectly possible for a curve to be convex for a certain range of values of x and concave for others. This is illustrated in Figure 4.11. For this function, $f''(x) < 0$ to the left of $x = a$, and $f''(x) > 0$ to the right of $x = a$. At $x = a$ itself, the curve changes from bending downwards to bending upwards, and at this point, $f''(a) = 0$.

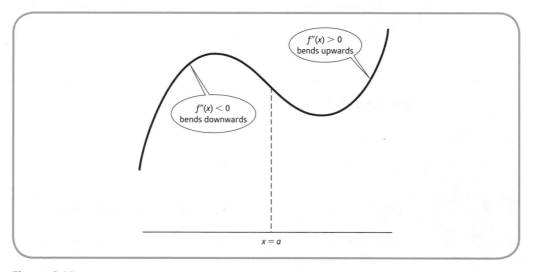

Figure 4.11

The second-order derivative can be used to confirm the convexity of the general quadratic function

$$f(x) = ax^2 + bx + c$$

The first- and second-order derivatives are $f'(x) = 2ax + b$ and $f''(x) = 2a$.

*   If $a > 0$, then $f''(x) > 0$, so the parabola is convex.
*   If $a < 0$, then $f''(x) < 0$, so the parabola is concave.

Of course, if $a = 0$, then $f(x) = bx + c$, which is the equation of a straight line, so the graph bends neither upwards nor downwards.

Throughout this section the functions have all been of the form $y = f(x)$, where the letters x and y denote the variables involved. In economic functions, different symbols are used. It should be obvious, however, that we can still differentiate such functions by applying the rules of this section. For example, if a supply function is given by

$$Q = P^2 + 3P + 1$$

and we need to find the derivative of Q with respect to P, then we can apply the sum and difference rules to obtain

$$\frac{dQ}{dP} = 2P + 3$$

Key Terms

Concave   Graph bends downwards when $f''(x) < 0$.

Convex   Graph bends upwards when $f''(x) > 0$.

First-order derivative   The rate of change of a function with respect to its independent variable. It is the same as the 'derivative' of a function, $y = f(x)$, and is written as $f'(x)$ or dy/dx.

Second-order derivative   The derivative of the first-order derivative. The expression obtained when the original function, $y = f(x)$, is differentiated twice in succession and is written as $f''(x)$ or d^2y/dx^2.

Exercise 4.2

1. Differentiate

   (a) $y = 5x^2$

   (b) $y = \dfrac{3}{x}$

   (c) $y = 2x + 3$

   (d) $y = x^2 + x + 1$

   (e) $y = x^2 - 3x + 2$

   (f) $y = 3x - \dfrac{7}{x}$

   (g) $y = 2x^3 - 6x^2 + 49x - 54$

   (h) $y = ax + b$

   (i) $y = ax^2 + bx + c$

   (j) $y = 4x - \dfrac{3}{x} + \dfrac{7}{x^2}$

2. Evaluate $f'(x)$ for each of the following functions at the given point:

   (a) $f(x) = 3x^9$ at $x = 1$

   (b) $f(x) = x^2 - 2x$ at $x = 3$

   (c) $f(x) = x^3 - 4x^2 + 2x - 8$ at $x = 0$

   (d) $f(x) = 5x^4 - \dfrac{4}{x^4}$ at $x = -1$

   (e) $f(x) = \sqrt{x} - \dfrac{2}{x}$ at $x = 4$

3. By writing $x^2\left(x^2 + 2x - \dfrac{5}{x^2}\right) = x^4 + 2x^3 - 5$, differentiate $x^2\left(x^2 + 2x - \dfrac{5}{x^2}\right)$.

   Use a similar approach to differentiate

   (a) $x^2(3x - 4)$

   (b) $x(3x^3 - 2x^2 + 6x - 7)$

   (c) $(x + 1)(x - 6)$

   (d) $\dfrac{x^2 - 3}{x}$

   (e) $\dfrac{x - 4x^2}{x^3}$

   (f) $\dfrac{x^2 - 3x + 5}{x^2}$

4. Find expressions for d^2y/dx^2 in the case when

   (a) $y = 7x^2 - x$

   (b) $y = \dfrac{1}{x^2}$

   (c) $y = ax + b$

5. Evaluate $f''(2)$ for the function

   $$f(x) = x^3 - 4x^2 + 10x - 7$$

6. If $f(x) = x^2 - 6x + 8$, evaluate $f'(3)$. What information does this provide about the graph of $y = f(x)$ at $x = 3$?

7. By writing $\sqrt{4x} = \sqrt{4} \times \sqrt{x} = 2\sqrt{x}$, differentiate $\sqrt{4x}$.
   Use a similar approach to differentiate

   (a) $\sqrt{25x}$ (b) $\sqrt[3]{27x}$ (c) $\sqrt[4]{16x^3}$ (d) $\sqrt{\dfrac{25}{x}}$

8. Find expressions for

   (a) $\dfrac{dQ}{dP}$ for the supply function $Q = P^2 + P + 1$

   (b) $\dfrac{d(TR)}{dQ}$ for the total revenue function $TR = 50Q - 3Q^2$

   (c) $\dfrac{d(AC)}{dQ}$ for the average cost function $AC = \dfrac{30}{Q} + 10$

   (d) $\dfrac{dC}{dY}$ for the consumption function $C = 3Y + 7$

   (e) $\dfrac{dQ}{dL}$ for the production function $Q = 10\sqrt{L}$

   (f) $\dfrac{d\pi}{dQ}$ for the profit function $\pi = -2Q^3 + 15Q^2 - 24Q - 3$

Exercise 4.2*

1. Find the value of the first-order derivative of the function

$$y = 3\sqrt{x} - \frac{81}{x} + 13$$

when $x = 9$.

2. Find expressions for

(a) $\dfrac{dQ}{dP}$ for the supply function $Q = 2P^2 + P + 1$

(b) $\dfrac{d(TR)}{dQ}$ for the total revenue function $TR = 40Q - 3Q\sqrt{Q}$

(c) $\dfrac{d(AC)}{dQ}$ for the average cost function $AC = \dfrac{20}{Q} + 7Q + 25$

(d) $\dfrac{dC}{dY}$ for the consumption function $C = Y(2Y + 3) + 10$

(e) $\dfrac{dC}{dL}$ for the production function $Q = 200L - 4\sqrt[4]{L}$

(f) $\dfrac{d\pi}{dQ}$ for the profit function $\pi = -Q^3 + 20Q^2 - 7Q - 1$

3. Find the value of the second-order derivative of the following function at the point $x = 4$:

$$f(x) = -2x^3 + 4x^2 + x - 3$$

What information does this provide about the shape of the graph of $f(x)$ at this point?

4. Consider the graph of the function

$$f(x) = 2x^5 - 3x^4 + 2x^2 - 17x + 31$$

at $x = -1$.

Giving reasons for your answers,

(a) state whether the tangent slopes uphill, slopes downhill or is horizontal;

(b) state whether the graph is concave or convex at this point.

5. Use the second-order derivative to show that the graph of the cubic,

$$f(x) = ax^3 + bx^2 + cx + d \ (a > 0)$$

is convex when $x > -b/3a$ and concave when $x < -b/3a$.

6. Find the equation of the tangent to the curve

$$y = 4x^3 - 5x^2 + x - 3$$

at the point where it crosses the y axis.

7. A Pareto income distribution function is given by

$$f(x) = \frac{A}{x^a}, \quad x \geq 1$$

where A and a are positive constants and x is measured in \$100 000s.

(a) Find an expression for $f'(x)$ and hence comment on the slope of this function.

(b) Find an expression for $f''(x)$ and hence comment on the convexity of this function.

(c) Sketch a graph of $f(x)$.

(d) The area under the graph between $x = b$ and $x = c$ measures the proportion of people whose income is in the range, $b \leq x \leq c$. What does this graph indicate about the distributions of income above a threshold of \$100 000?

8. A utility function, $U(x)$, measures the amount of satisfaction gained by an individual who buys x units of a product or service. The Arrow–Pratt coefficient of relative risk aversion is defined by

$$r = -\frac{xU''(x)}{U'(x)}$$

Show that the coefficient of relative risk aversion is constant for the utility function

$$U(x) = \frac{x^{1-\gamma}}{1-\gamma}$$

SECTION 4.3
Marginal functions

Objectives

At the end of this section you should be able to:

- Calculate marginal revenue and marginal cost.
- Derive the relationship between marginal and average revenue for both a monopoly and perfect competition.
- Calculate marginal product of labour.
- State the law of diminishing marginal productivity using the notation of calculus.
- Calculate marginal propensity to consume and marginal propensity to save.

At this stage you may be wondering what on earth differentiation has to do with economics. In fact, we cannot get very far with economic theory without making use of calculus. In this section we concentrate on three main areas that illustrate its applicability:

- revenue and cost;
- production;
- consumption and savings.

We consider each of these in turn.

4.3.1 Revenue and cost

In Chapter 2 we investigated the basic properties of the revenue function, TR. It is defined to be PQ, where P denotes the price of a good and Q denotes the quantity demanded. In practice, we usually know the demand function, which provides a relationship between P and Q. This enables a formula for TR to be written down solely in terms of Q. For example, if

$$P = 100 - 2Q$$

then

$$TR = PQ = (100 - 2Q)Q = 100Q - 2Q^2$$

The formula can be used to calculate the value of TR corresponding to any value of Q. Not content with this, we are also interested in the effect on TR of a change in the value of Q from some existing level. To do this we introduce the concept of marginal revenue. The **marginal revenue**, MR, of a good is defined by

$$MR = \frac{d(TR)}{dQ}$$

> marginal revenue is the derivative of total revenue with respect to demand

For example, the marginal revenue function corresponding to

$$TR = 100Q - 2Q^2$$

is given by

$$\frac{d(TR)}{dQ} = 100 - 4Q$$

If the current demand is 15, say, then

$$MR = 100 - 4(15) = 40$$

You may be familiar with an alternative definition often quoted in elementary economics textbooks. Marginal revenue is sometimes taken to be the change in TR brought about by a 1 unit increase in Q. It is easy to check that this gives an acceptable approximation to MR, although it is not quite the same as the exact value obtained by differentiation. For example, substituting $Q = 15$ into the total revenue function considered previously gives

$$TR = 100(15) - 2(15)^2 = 1050$$

An increase of 1 unit in the value of Q produces a total revenue

$$TR = 100(16) - 2(16)^2 = 1088$$

This is an increase of 38, which, according to the non-calculus definition, is the value of MR when Q is 15. This compares with the exact value of 40 obtained by differentiation.

It is instructive to give a graphical interpretation of these two approaches. In Figure 4.12 the point A lies on the TR curve corresponding to a quantity Q_0. The exact value of MR at this point is equal to the derivative

$$\frac{d(TR)}{dQ}$$

and so is given by the slope of the tangent at A. The point B also lies on the curve but corresponds to a 1-unit increase in Q. The vertical distance from A to B therefore equals the change in TR when Q increases by 1 unit. The slope of the line joining A and B (known as a **chord**) is

$$\frac{\Delta(TR)}{\Delta Q} = \frac{\Delta(TR)}{1} = \Delta(TR)$$

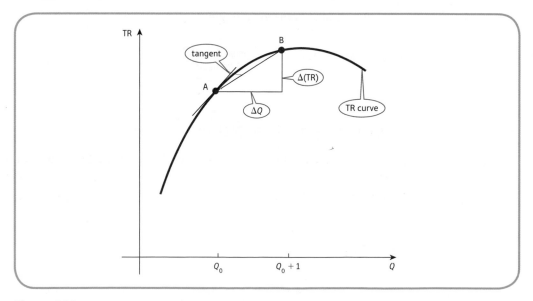

Figure 4.12

In other words, the slope of the chord is equal to the value of MR obtained from the non-calculus definition. Inspection of the diagram reveals that the slope of the tangent is approximately the same as that of the chord joining A and B. In this case the slope of the tangent is slightly the larger of the two, but there is not much in it. We therefore see that the 1-unit-increase approach produces a reasonable approximation to the exact value of MR given by

$$\frac{d(TR)}{dQ}$$

Practice Problem

1. If the demand function is

$$P = 60 - Q$$

find an expression for TR in terms of Q.

(1) Differentiate TR with respect to Q to find a general expression for MR in terms of Q. Hence write down the exact value of MR at $Q = 50$.

(2) Calculate the value of TR when

(a) $Q = 50$ (b) $Q = 51$

and hence confirm that the 1-unit-increase approach gives a reasonable approximation to the exact value of MR obtained in part (1).

The approximation indicated by Figure 4.12 holds for any value of ΔQ. The slope of the tangent at A is the marginal revenue, MR. The slope of the chord joining A and B is $\Delta(TR)/\Delta Q$. It follows that

$$MR \cong \frac{\Delta(TR)}{\Delta Q}$$

This equation can be transposed to give

$$\Delta(TR) \cong MR \times \Delta Q \qquad \text{\small (multiply both sides by } \Delta Q\text{)}$$

that is,

change in total revenue $\cong$ marginal revenue $\times$ change in demand

Moreover, Figure 4.12 shows that the smaller the value of ΔQ, the better the approximation becomes.

Example

If the total revenue function of a good is given by

$$100Q - Q^2$$

write down an expression for the marginal revenue function. If the current demand is 60, estimate the change in the value of TR due to a 2-unit increase in Q.

Solution

If

$$TR = 100Q - Q^2$$

then

$$MR = \frac{d(TR)}{dQ}$$

$$= 100 - 2Q$$

When $Q = 60$

$$MR = 100 - 2(60) = -20$$

If Q increases by 2 units, $\Delta Q = 2$ and the formula

$$\Delta(TR) \cong MR \times \Delta Q$$

shows that the change in total revenue is approximately

$$(-20) \times 2 = -40$$

A 2-unit increase in Q therefore leads to a decrease in TR of about 40.

Practice Problem

2. If the total revenue function of a good is given by

$$1000Q - 4Q^2$$

write down an expression for the marginal revenue function. If the current demand is 30, find the approximate change in the value of TR due to a

(a) 3-unit increase in Q;

(b) 2-unit decrease in Q.

The simple model of demand, originally introduced in Section 1.5, assumed that price, P, and quantity, Q, are linearly related according to an equation,

$$P = aQ + b$$

where the slope, a, is negative and the intercept, b, is positive. A downward-sloping demand curve such as this corresponds to the case of a **monopolist**. A single firm, or possibly a group

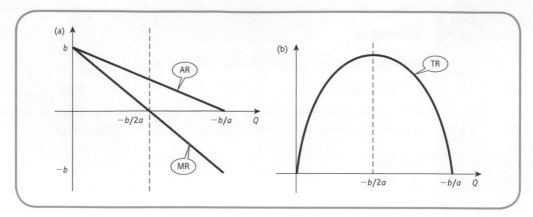

Figure 4.13

of firms forming a cartel, is assumed to be the only supplier of a particular product and so has control over the market price. As the firm raises the price, so demand falls. The associated total revenue function is given by

$$\text{TR} = PQ$$
$$= (aQ + b)Q$$
$$= aQ^2 + bQ$$

An expression for marginal revenue is obtained by differentiating TR with respect to Q to get

$$\text{MR} = 2aQ + b$$

It is interesting to notice that, on the assumption of a linear demand equation, the marginal revenue is also linear with the same intercept, b, but with slope $2a$. The marginal revenue curve slopes downhill exactly twice as fast as the demand curve. This is illustrated in Figure 4.13(a).

The **average revenue**, AR, is defined by

$$\text{AR} = \frac{\text{TR}}{Q}$$

and, since $\text{TR} = PQ$, we have

$$\text{AR} = \frac{PQ}{Q} = P$$

For this reason the demand curve is labelled average revenue in Figure 4.13(a). The above derivation of the result $\text{AR} = P$ is independent of the particular demand function. Consequently, the terms 'average revenue curve' and 'demand curve' are synonymous.

Figure 4.13(a) shows that the marginal revenue takes both positive and negative values. This is to be expected. The total revenue function is a quadratic, and its graph has the familiar parabolic shape indicated in Figure 4.13(b). To the left of $-b/2a$ the graph is uphill, corresponding to a positive value of marginal revenue, whereas to the right of this point it is downhill, giving a negative value of marginal revenue. More significantly, at the maximum point of the TR curve, the tangent is horizontal with zero slope, and so MR is zero.

At the other extreme from a monopolist is the case of **perfect competition**. For this model we assume that there are a large number of firms all selling an identical product and that

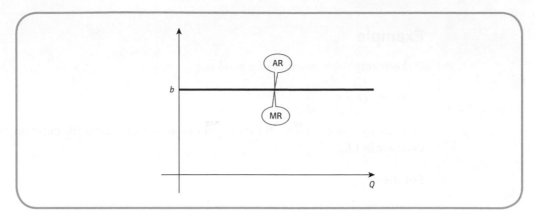

Figure 4.14

there are no barriers to entry into the industry. Since any individual firm produces a tiny proportion of the total output, it has no control over price. The firm can sell only at the prevailing market price and, because the firm is relatively small, it can sell any number of goods at this price. If the fixed price is denoted by b, then the demand function is

$$P = b$$

and the associated total revenue function is

$$\text{TR} = PQ = bQ$$

An expression for marginal revenue is obtained by differentiating TR with respect to Q and, since b is just a constant, we see that

$$\text{MR} = b$$

In the case of perfect competition, the average and marginal revenue curves are the same. They are horizontal straight lines, b units above the Q axis, as shown in Figure 4.14.

So far we have concentrated on the total revenue function. Exactly the same principle can be used for other economic functions. For instance, we define the **marginal cost**, MC, by

$$\text{MC} = \frac{\text{d(TC)}}{\text{d}Q}$$

> marginal cost is the derivative of total cost with respect to output

Again, using a simple geometrical argument, it is easy to see that if Q changes by a small amount ΔQ, then the corresponding change in TC is given by

$$\Delta(\text{TC}) \cong \text{MC} \times \Delta Q$$

change in total cost $\cong$ marginal cost $\times$ change in output

In particular, putting $\Delta Q = 1$ gives

$$\Delta(\text{TC}) \cong \text{MC}$$

so that MC gives the approximate change in TC when Q increases by 1 unit.

Example

If the average cost function of a good is

$$AC = 2Q + 6 + \frac{13}{Q}$$

find an expression for MC. If the current output is 15, estimate the effect on TC of a 3-unit decrease in Q.

Solution

We first need to find an expression for TC using the given formula for AC. Now we know that the average cost is just the total cost divided by Q: that is,

$$AC = \frac{TC}{Q}$$

Hence

$$TC = (AC)Q$$

$$= \left(2Q + 6 + \frac{13}{Q}\right)Q$$

and, after multiplying out the brackets, we get

$$TC = 2Q^2 + 6Q + 13$$

In this formula the last term, 13, is independent of Q and so must denote the fixed costs. The remaining part, $2Q^2 + 6Q$, depends on Q and so represents the total variable costs. Differentiating gives

$$MC = \frac{d(TC)}{dQ}$$

$$= 4Q + 6$$

Notice that because the fixed costs are constant, they differentiate to zero and so have no effect on the marginal cost. When $Q = 15$,

$$MC = 4(15) + 6 = 66$$

Also, if Q decreases by 2 units, then $\Delta Q = -2$. Hence the change in TC is given by

$$\Delta(TC) \cong MC \times \Delta Q = 66 \times (-2) = -132$$

so TC decreases by 132 units approximately.

Practice Problem

3. Find the marginal cost given the average cost function

$$AC = \frac{100}{Q} + 2$$

Deduce that a 1-unit increase in Q will always result in a 2-unit increase in TC, irrespective of the current level of output.

4.3.2 Production

Production functions were introduced in Section 2.3. In the simplest case output, Q, is assumed to be a function of labour, L, and capital, K. Moreover, in the short run the input K can be assumed to be fixed, so Q is then only a function of one input L. (This is not a valid assumption in the long run, and in general, Q must be regarded as a function of at least two inputs. Methods for handling this situation are considered in the next chapter.) The variable L is usually measured in terms of the number of workers or possibly in terms of the number of worker hours. Motivated by our previous work, we define the **marginal product of labour**, MP_L, by

$$MP_L = \frac{dQ}{dL}$$

marginal product of labour is the derivative of output with respect to labour

As before, this gives the approximate change in Q that results from using 1 more unit of L.

It is instructive to work out numerical values of MP_L for the particular production function

$$Q = 300L^{1/2} - 4L$$

where L denotes the actual size of the workforce.

Differentiating Q with respect to L gives

$$
\begin{aligned}
MP_L &= \frac{dQ}{dL} \\
&= 300(\tfrac{1}{2} L^{-1/2}) - 4 \\
&= 150L^{-1/2} - 4 \\
&= \frac{150}{\sqrt{L}} - 4
\end{aligned}
$$

Substituting $L = 1, 9, 100$ and 2500 in turn into the formula for MP_L gives:

(a) When $L = 1$

$$MP_L = \frac{150}{\sqrt{9}} - 4 = 146$$

(b) When $L = 9$

$$MP_L = \frac{150}{\sqrt{1}} - 4 = 46$$

(c) When $L = 100$

$$MP_L = \frac{150}{\sqrt{100}} - 4 = 11$$

(d) When $L = 2500$

$$MP_L = \frac{150}{\sqrt{2500}} - 4 = -1$$

Notice that the values of MP_L decline with increasing L. Part (a) shows that if the workforce consists of only one person then to employ two people would increase output by approximately 146. In part (b) we see that to increase the number of workers from 9 to 10 would result in about 46 additional units of output. In part (c) we see that a 1-unit increase in labour from a level of 100 increases output by only 11. In part (d) the situation is even worse. This indicates that to increase staff actually reduces output! The latter is a rather surprising result, but it is borne out by what occurs in real production processes. This may be due to problems of overcrowding on the shopfloor or to the need to create an elaborate administration to organise the larger workforce.

This production function illustrates the **law of diminishing marginal productivity** (sometimes called the **law of diminishing returns**). It states that the increase in output due to a 1-unit increase in labour will eventually decline. In other words, once the size of the workforce has reached a certain threshold level, the marginal product of labour will get smaller. For the production function

$$Q = 300L^{1/2} - 4L$$

the value of MP_L continually goes down with rising L. This is not always so. It is possible for the marginal product of labour to remain constant or to go up to begin with for small values of L. However, if it is to satisfy the law of diminishing marginal productivity, then there must be some value of L above which MP_L decreases.

A typical product curve is sketched in Figure 4.15, which has slope

$$\frac{dQ}{dL} = MP_L$$

Between 0 and L_0 the curve bends upwards, becoming progressively steeper, and so the slope function, MP_L, increases. Mathematically, this means that the slope of MP_L is positive: that is,

$$\frac{d(MP_L)}{dQ} > 0$$

Now MP_L is itself the derivative of Q with respect to L, so we can use the notation for the second-order derivative and write this as

$$\frac{d^2Q}{dL^2} > 0$$

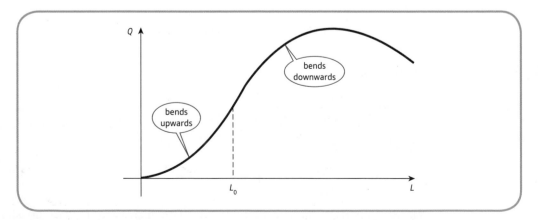

Figure 4.15

Similarly, if L exceeds the threshold value of L_0, then Figure 4.15 shows that the product curve bends downwards and the slope decreases. In this region, the slope of the slope function is negative, so that

$$\frac{d^2Q}{dL^2} < 0$$

The law of diminishing returns states that this must happen eventually: that is,

$$\frac{d^2Q}{dL^2} < 0$$

for sufficiently large L.

Practice Problem

4. A Cobb–Douglas production function is given by

$$Q = 5L^{1/2}K^{1/2}$$

Assuming that capital, K, is fixed at 100, write down a formula for Q in terms of L only. Calculate the marginal product of labour when

(a) $L = 1$ **(b)** $L = 9$ **(c)** $L = 10\ 000$

Verify that the law of diminishing marginal productivity holds in this case.

4.3.3 Consumption and savings

In Chapter 1 the relationship between consumption, C, savings, S, and national income, Y, was investigated. If we assume that national income is only used up in consumption and savings then

$$Y = C + S$$

Of particular interest is the effect on C and S due to variations in Y. Expressed simply, if national income rises by a certain amount, are people more likely to go out and spend their extra income on consumer goods, or will they save it? To analyse this behaviour we use the concepts **marginal propensity to consume**, MPC, and **marginal propensity to save**, MPS, which are defined by

$$\text{MPC} = \frac{dC}{dY} \quad \text{and} \quad \text{MPS} = \frac{dS}{dY}$$

> marginal propensity to consume is the derivative of consumption with respect to income

> marginal propensity to save is the derivative of savings with respect to income

These definitions are consistent with those given in Section 1.7, where MPC and MPS were taken to be the slopes of the linear consumption and savings curves, respectively. At first sight it appears that, in general, we need to work out two derivatives in order to evaluate MPC and

MPS. However, this is not strictly necessary. Recall that we can do whatever we like to an equation provided we do the same thing to both sides. Consequently, we can differentiate both sides of the equation

$$Y = C + S$$

with respect to Y to deduce that

$$\frac{dY}{dY} = \frac{dC}{dY} + \frac{dS}{dY} = \text{MPC} + \text{MPS}$$

Now we are already familiar with the result that when we differentiate x with respect to x, the answer is 1. In this case Y plays the role of x, so

$$\frac{dY}{dY} = 1$$

Hence

$$1 = \text{MPC} + \text{MPS}$$

This formula is identical to the result given in Section 1.7 for simple linear functions. In practice, it means that we need only work out one of the derivatives. The remaining derivative can then be calculated directly from this equation.

Example

If the consumption function is

$$C = 0.01Y^2 + 0.2Y + 50$$

calculate MPC and MPS when $Y = 30$.

Solution

In this example the consumption function is given, so we begin by finding MPC. To do this we differentiate C with respect to Y. If

$$C = 0.01Y^2 + 0.2Y + 50$$

then

$$\frac{dC}{dY} = 0.02Y + 0.2$$

so, when $Y = 30$,

$$\text{MPC} = 0.02(30) + 0.2 = 0.8$$

To find the corresponding value of MPS we use the formula

$$\text{MPC} + \text{MPS} = 1$$

which gives

$$\text{MPS} = 1 - \text{MPC} = 1 - 0.8 = 0.2$$

This indicates that when national income increases by 1 unit (from its current level of 30), consumption rises by approximately 0.8 units, whereas savings rise by only about 0.2 units. At this level of income the nation has a greater propensity to consume than it has to save.

Practice Problem

5. If the savings function is given by

$$S = 0.02Y^2 - Y + 100$$

calculate the values of MPS and MPC when $Y = 40$. Give a brief interpretation of these results.

Key Terms

Average revenue   Total revenue per unit of output: $AR = TR/Q = P$.

Chord   A straight line joining two points on a curve.

Law of diminishing marginal productivity (law of diminishing returns)   Once the size of the workforce exceeds a particular value, the increase in output due to a 1-unit increase in labour will decline: $d^2Q/dL^2 < 0$ for sufficiently large L.

Marginal cost   The cost of producing 1 more unit of output: $MC = d(TC)/dQ$.

Marginal product of labour   The extra output produced by 1 more unit of labour: $MP_L = dQ/dL$.

Marginal propensity to consume   The fraction of a rise in national income which goes into consumption: $MPC = dC/dY$.

Marginal propensity to save   The fraction of a rise in national income which goes into savings: $MPS = dS/dY$.

Marginal revenue   The extra revenue gained by selling 1 more unit of a good: $MR = d(TR)/dQ$.

Monopolist   The only firm in the industry.

Perfect competition   A situation in which there are no barriers to entry in an industry where there are many firms selling an identical product at the market price.

Exercise 4.3

1. If the demand function is

   $$P = 100 - 4Q$$

   find expressions for TR and MR in terms of Q. Hence estimate the change in TR brought about by a 0.3-unit increase in output from a current level of 12 units.

2. If the demand function is

   $$P = 80 - 3Q$$

   show that

   $$MR = 2P - 80$$

3. A monopolist's demand function is given by

   $$P + Q = 100$$

   Write down expressions for TR and MR in terms of Q and sketch their graphs. Find the value of Q which gives a marginal revenue of zero and comment on the significance of this value.

4. If the average cost function of a good is

$$AC = \frac{15}{Q} + 2Q + 9$$

find an expression for TC. What are the fixed costs in this case? Write down an expression for the marginal cost function.

5. A firm's production function is

$$Q = 50L - 0.01L^2$$

where L denotes the size of the workforce. Find the value of MP_L in the case when

(a) $L = 1$ (b) $L = 10$ (c) $L = 100$ (d) $L = 1000$

Does the law of diminishing marginal productivity apply to this particular function?

6. If the consumption function is

$$C = 50 + 2\sqrt{Y}$$

calculate MPC and MPS when $Y = 36$ and give an interpretation of these results.

7. If the consumption function is

$$C = 0.02Y^2 + 0.1Y + 25$$

find the value of Y when MPS = 0.38.

8. The price of a company's shares, P, recorded in dollars at midday is a function of time, t, measured in days since the beginning of the year. Give an interpretation of the statement:

$$\frac{dP}{dt} = 0.25$$

when $t = 6$.

9. If the demand function is

$$P = 3000 - 2\sqrt{Q}$$

find expressions for TR and MR. Calculate the marginal revenue when $Q = 9$ and give an interpretation of this result.

Exercise 4.3*

1. A firm's demand function is given by

$$P = 100 - 4\sqrt{Q} - 3Q$$

(a) Write down an expression for total revenue, TR, in terms of Q.

(b) Find an expression for the marginal revenue, MR, and find the value of MR when $Q = 9$.

(c) Use the result of part (b) to *estimate* the change in TR when Q increases by 0.25 units from its current level of 9 units and compare this with the exact change in TR.

2. The consumption function is

$$C = 0.01Y^2 + 0.8Y + 100$$

   (a) Calculate the values of MPC and MPS when $Y = 8$.

   (b) Use the fact that $C + S = Y$ to obtain a formula for S in terms of Y. By differentiating this expression, find the value of MPS at $Y = 8$ and verify that this agrees with your answer to part (a).

3. The fixed costs of producing a good are 100 and the variable costs are $2 + Q/10$ per unit.

   (a) Find expressions for TC and MC.

   (b) Evaluate MC at $Q = 30$ and hence estimate the change in TC brought about by a 2-unit increase in output from a current level of 30 units.

   (c) At what level of output does MC = 22?

4. Show that the law of diminishing marginal productivity holds for the production function

$$Q = 6L^2 - 0.2L^3$$

5. A firm's production function is given by

$$Q = 5\sqrt{L} - 0.1L$$

   (a) Find an expression for the marginal product of labour, MP_L.

   (b) Solve the equation $\text{MP}_L = 0$ and briefly explain the significance of this value of L.

   (c) Show that the law of diminishing marginal productivity holds for this function.

6. A firm's average cost function takes the form

$$AC = 4Q + a + \frac{6}{Q}$$

   and it is known that MC = 35 when $Q = 3$. Find the value of AC when $Q = 6$.

7. The total cost of producing a good is given by

$$TC = 250 + 20Q$$

   The marginal revenue is 18 at $Q = 219$. If production is increased from its current level of 219, would you expect profit to increase, decrease or stay the same? Give reasons for your answer.

8. Given the demand and total cost functions

$$P = 150 - 2Q \quad \text{and} \quad TC = 40 + 0.5Q^2$$

   find the marginal profit when $Q = 25$ and give an interpretation of this result.

9. If the total cost function is given by $TC = aQ^2 + bQ + c$, show that

$$\frac{d(AC)}{dQ} = \frac{MC - AC}{Q}$$

SECTION 4.4

Further rules of differentiation

Objectives

At the end of this section you should be able to:

- Use the chain rule to differentiate a function of a function.
- Use the product rule to differentiate the product of two functions.
- Use the quotient rule to differentiate the quotient of two functions.
- Differentiate complicated functions using a combination of rules.

Section 4.2 introduced you to the basic rules of differentiation. Unfortunately, not all functions can be differentiated using these rules alone. For example, we are unable to differentiate the functions

$$x\sqrt{(2x - 3)} \quad \text{and} \quad \frac{x}{x^2 + 1}$$

using just the constant, sum or difference rules. The aim of the present section is to describe three further rules which allow you to find the derivative of more complicated expressions. Indeed, the totality of all six rules will enable you to differentiate any mathematical function. Although you may find that the rules described in this section take you slightly longer to grasp than before, they are vital to any understanding of economic theory.

The first rule that we investigate is called the chain rule, and it can be used to differentiate functions such as

$$y = (2x + 3)^{10} \quad \text{and} \quad y = \sqrt{(1 + x^2)}$$

The distinguishing feature of these expressions is that they represent a 'function of a function'. To understand what we mean by this, consider how you might evaluate

$$y = (2x + 3)^{10}$$

on a calculator. You would first work out an intermediate number u, say, given by

$$u = 2x + 3$$

and then raise it to the power of 10 to get

$$y = u^{10}$$

This process is illustrated using the flow chart in Figure 4.16. Note how the incoming number x is first processed by the inner function, 'double and add 3'. The output u from this is then passed on to the outer function, 'raise to the power of 10', to produce the final outgoing number y.

The function

$$y = \sqrt{(1 + x^2)}$$

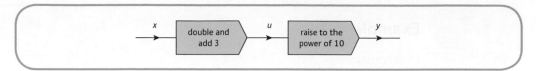

Figure 4.16

can be viewed in the same way. To calculate y you perform the inner function, 'square and add 1', followed by the outer function, 'take square roots'.

The chain rule for differentiating a function of a function may now be stated.

Rule 4 The chain rule

If y is a function of u, which is itself a function of x, then

$$\frac{dy}{dx} = \frac{dy}{du} \times \frac{du}{dx}$$

> differentiate the outer function and multiply by the derivative of the inner function

To illustrate this rule, let us return to the function

$$y = (2x + 3)^{10}$$

in which

$$y = u^{10} \quad \text{and} \quad u = 2x + 3$$

Now

$$\frac{dy}{du} = 10u^9 = 10(2x + 3)^9$$

$$\frac{du}{dx} = 2$$

The chain rule then gives

$$\frac{dy}{dx} = \frac{dy}{du} \times \frac{du}{dx} = 10(2x + 3)^9(2) = 20(2x + 3)^9$$

With practice it is possible to perform the differentiation without explicitly introducing the variable u. To differentiate

$$y = (2x + 3)^{10}$$

we first differentiate the outer power function to get

$$10(2x + 3)^9$$

and then multiply by the derivative of the inner function, $2x + 3$, which is 2, so

$$\frac{dy}{dx} = 20(2x + 3)^9$$

Example

Differentiate

(a) $y = (3x^2 - 5x + 2)^4$

(b) $y = \dfrac{1}{3x + 7}$

(c) $y = \sqrt{(1 + x^2)}$

Solution

(a) The chain rule shows that to differentiate $(3x^2 - 5x + 2)^4$ we first differentiate the outer power function to get

$$4(3x^2 - 5x + 2)^3$$

and then multiply by the derivative of the inner function, $3x^2 - 5x + 2$, which is $6x - 5$. Hence if

$$y = (3x^2 - 5x + 2)^4 \quad \text{then} \quad \frac{dy}{dx} = 4(3x^2 - 5x + 2)^3(6x - 5)$$

(b) To use the chain rule to differentiate

$$y = \frac{1}{3x + 7}$$

recall that reciprocals are denoted by negative powers, so that

$$y = (3x + 7)^{-1}$$

The outer power function differentiates to get

$$-(3x + 7)^{-2}$$

and the inner function, $3x + 7$, differentiates to get 3. By the chain rule we just multiply these together to deduce that

$$\text{if } y = \frac{1}{3x + 7} \quad \text{then} \quad \frac{dy}{dx} = -(3x + 7)^{-2}(3) = \frac{-3}{(3x + 7)^2}$$

(c) To use the chain rule to differentiate

$$y = \sqrt{(1 + x^2)}$$

recall that roots are denoted by fractional powers, so that

$$y = (1 + x^2)^{1/2}$$

The outer power function differentiates to get

$$\frac{1}{2}(1 + x^2)^{-1/2}$$

and the inner function, $1 + x^2$, differentiates to get $2x$. By the chain rule we just multiply these together to deduce that

$$\text{if } y = \sqrt{(1 + x^2)} \quad \text{then} \quad \frac{dy}{dx} = \frac{1}{2}(1 + x^2)^{-1/2}(2x) = \frac{x}{\sqrt{(1 + x^2)}}$$

Practice Problem

1. Differentiate

   (a) $y = (3x - 4)^5$ **(b)** $y = (x^2 + 3x + 5)^3$ **(c)** $y = \dfrac{1}{2x - 3}$ **(d)** $y = \sqrt{(4x - 3)}$

The next rule is used to differentiate the product of two functions, $f(x)g(x)$. In order to give a clear statement of this rule, we write

$$u = f(x) \quad \text{and} \quad v = g(x)$$

Rule 5 The product rule

If $y = uv$ then $\dfrac{dy}{dx} = u\dfrac{dv}{dx} + v\dfrac{du}{dx}$

This rule tells you how to differentiate the product of two functions:

> multiply each function by the derivative of the other and add

Example

Differentiate

(a) $y = x^2(2x + 1)^3$ **(b)** $x\sqrt{(6x + 1)}$ **(c)** $y = \dfrac{x}{1 + x}$

Solution

(a) The function $x^2(2x + 1)^3$ involves the product of two simpler functions, namely x^2 and $(2x + 1)^3$, which we denote by u and v, respectively. (It does not matter which function we label u and which we label v. The same answer is obtained if u is $(2x + 1)^3$ and v is x^2. You might like to check this for yourself later.) Now if

$$u = x^2 \quad \text{and} \quad v = (2x + 1)^3$$

then

$$\frac{du}{dx} = 2x \quad \text{and} \quad \frac{dv}{dx} = 6(2x + 1)^2$$

where we have used the chain rule to find dv/dx. By the product rule,

$$\frac{dy}{dx} = u\frac{dv}{dx} + v\frac{du}{dx}$$
$$= x^2[6(2x + 1)^2] + (2x + 1)^3(2x)$$

The first term is obtained by leaving u alone and multiplying it by the derivative of v. Similarly, the second term is obtained by leaving v alone and multiplying it by the derivative of u.

If desired, the final answer may be simplified by taking out a common factor of $2x(2x + 1)^2$. This factor goes into the first term $3x$ times and into the second $2x + 1$ times. Hence

$$\frac{dy}{dx} = 2x(2x + 1)^2[3x + (2x + 1)] = 2x(2x + 1)^2(5x + 1)$$

(b) The function $x\sqrt{(6x + 1)}$ involves the product of the simpler functions

$$u = x \quad \text{and} \quad v = \sqrt{6x + 1} = (6x + 1)^{1/2}$$

for which

$$\frac{du}{dx} = 1 \quad \text{and} \quad \frac{dv}{dx} = \frac{1}{2}(6x + 1)^{-1/2} \times 6 = 3(6x + 1)^{-1/2}$$

where we have used the chain rule to find dv/dx. By the product rule,

$$\frac{dy}{dx} = u\frac{dv}{dx} + v\frac{du}{dx}$$

$$= x[3(6x + 1)^{-1/2}] + (6x + 1)^{1/2}(1)$$

$$= \frac{3x}{\sqrt{(6x + 1)}} + \sqrt{(6x + 1)}$$

If desired, this can be simplified by putting the second term over a common denominator

$$\sqrt{(6x + 1)}$$

To do this we multiply the top and bottom of the second term by $\sqrt{6x + 1}$ to get

$$\frac{(6x + 1)}{\sqrt{(6x + 1)}} \qquad \boxed{\begin{array}{l} \sqrt{(6x + 1)} \times \sqrt{(6x + 1)} \\ = 6x + 1 \end{array}}$$

Hence

$$\frac{dy}{dx} = \frac{3x + (6x + 1)}{\sqrt{(6x + 1)}} = \frac{9x + 1}{\sqrt{(6x + 1)}}$$

(c) At first sight it is hard to see how we can use the product rule to differentiate

$$\frac{x}{1 + x}$$

since it appears to be the quotient and not the product of two functions. However, if we recall that reciprocals are equivalent to negative powers, we may rewrite it as

$$x(1 + x)^{-1}$$

It follows that we can put

$$u = x \quad \text{and} \quad v = (1 + x)^{-1}$$

which gives

$$\frac{du}{dx} = 1 \quad \text{and} \quad \frac{dv}{dx} = -(1 + x)^{-2}$$

where we have used the chain rule to find dv/dx. By the product rule

$$\frac{dy}{dx} = u\frac{dv}{dx} + v\frac{du}{dx}$$

$$\frac{dy}{dx} = x[-(1 + x)^{-2}] + (1 + x)^{-1}(1)$$

$$= \frac{-x}{(1 + x)^2} + \frac{1}{1 + x}$$

If desired, this can be simplified by putting the second term over a common denominator

$$(1 + x)^2$$

To do this we multiply the top and bottom of the second term by $1 + x$ to get

$$\frac{1 + x}{(1 + x)^2}$$

Hence

$$\frac{dy}{dx} = \frac{-x}{(1 + x)^2} + \frac{1 + x}{(1 + x)^2} = \frac{-x + (1 + x)}{(1 + x)^2} = \frac{1}{(1 + x)^2}$$

Practice Problem

2. Differentiate

(a) $y = x(3x - 1)^6$ **(b)** $y = x^3\sqrt{(2x + 3)}$ **(c)** $y = \dfrac{x}{x - 2}$

Advice

You may have found the product rule the hardest of the rules so far. This may have been due to the algebraic manipulation that is required to simplify the final expression. If this is the case, do not worry about it at this stage. The important thing is that you can use the product rule to obtain some sort of an answer even if you cannot tidy it up at the end. This is not to say that the simplification of an expression is pointless. If the result of differentiation is to be used in a subsequent piece of theory, it may well save time in the long run if it is simplified first.

One of the most difficult parts of Practice Problem 2 is part (c), since this involves algebraic fractions. For this function, it is necessary to manipulate negative indices and to put two individual fractions over a common denominator. You may feel that you are unable to do either of these processes with confidence. For this reason we conclude this section with a rule that is specifically designed to differentiate this type of function. The rule itself is quite complicated. However, as will become apparent, it does the algebra for you, so you may prefer to use it rather than the product rule when differentiating algebraic fractions.

Rule 6 The quotient rule

$$\text{If } y = \frac{u}{v} \quad \text{then} \quad \frac{dy}{dx} = \frac{v\,du/dx = v\,dv/dx}{v^2}$$

This rule tells you how to differentiate the quotient of two functions:

> bottom times derivative of top, minus top times derivative of bottom, all over bottom squared

Example

Differentiate

(a) $y = \dfrac{x}{1 + x}$ **(b)** $y = \dfrac{1 + x^2}{2 - x^3}$

Solution

(a) In the quotient rule, u is used as the label for the numerator and v is used for the denominator, so to differentiate

$$\frac{x}{1 + x}$$

we must take

$$u = x \quad \text{and} \quad v = 1 + x$$

for which

$$\frac{du}{dx} = 1 \quad \text{and} \quad \frac{dv}{dx} = 1$$

By the quotient rule

$$\frac{dy}{dx} = \frac{v\,du/dx - u\,du/dx}{v^2}$$

$$= \frac{(1 + x)(1) - x(1)}{(1 + x^2)}$$

$$= \frac{1 + x - x}{(1 + x^2)}$$

$$= \frac{1}{(1 + x^2)}$$

Notice how the quotient rule automatically puts the final expression over a common denominator. Compare this with the algebra required to obtain the same answer using the product rule in part (c) of the previous example.

(b) The numerator of the algebraic fraction

$$\frac{1 + x^2}{2 - x^3}$$

is $1 + x^2$ and the denominator is $2 - x^3$, so we take

$$u = 1 + x^2 \quad \text{and} \quad v = 2 - x^3$$

for which

$$\frac{du}{dx} = 2x \quad \text{and} \quad \frac{dv}{dx} = -3x^2$$

By the quotient rule

$$\frac{dy}{dx} = \frac{v\,du/dx - u\,dv/dx}{v^2}$$

$$= \frac{(2 - x^3)(2x) - (1 + x^2)(-3x^2)}{(2 - x^3)^3}$$

$$= \frac{4x - 2x^4 + 3x^2 + 3x^4}{(2 - x^3)^3}$$

$$= \frac{x^4 + 3x^2 + 4x}{(2 - x^3)^3}$$

Practice Problem

3. Differentiate

   (a) $y = \dfrac{x}{x - 2}$ (b) $y = \dfrac{x - 1}{x + 1}$

   [You might like to check that your answer to part (a) is the same as that obtained in Practice Problem 2(c).]

Advice

The product and quotient rules give alternative methods for the differentiation of algebraic fractions. It does not matter which rule you go for; use whichever rule is easiest for you.

Exercise 4.4

1. Use the chain rule to differentiate

   (a) $y = (5x + 1)^3$ (b) $y = (2x - 7)^8$ (c) $y = (x + 9)^5$

   (d) $y = (4x^2 - 7)^3$ (e) $y = (x^2 + 4x - 3)^4$ (f) $y = \sqrt{(2x + 1)}$

   (g) $y = \dfrac{1}{3x + 1}$ (h) $y = \dfrac{1}{(4x - 3)^2}$ (i) $y = \dfrac{1}{\sqrt{(2x + 5)}}$

2. Use the product rule to differentiate

   (a) $y = x(3x + 4)^2$ (b) $y = x^2(x - 2)^3$ (c) $y = x\sqrt{(x + 2)}$

   (d) $y = (x - 1)(x + 6)^3$ (e) $y = (2x + 1)(x + 5)^3$ (f) $y = x^3(2x - 5)^4$

3. Use the quotient rule to differentiate

   (a) $y = \dfrac{x}{x - 5}$ (b) $y = \dfrac{x}{(x + 7)}$ (c) $y = \dfrac{x + 3}{x - 2}$

   (d) $y = \dfrac{2x + 9}{3x + 1}$ (e) $y = \dfrac{x}{(5x + 6)}$ (f) $y = \dfrac{x + 4}{3x - 7}$

4. Differentiate

   $$y = (5x + 7)^2$$

   (a) by using the chain rule;

   (b) by first multiplying out the brackets and then differentiating term by term.

5. Differentiate

   $$y = x^5(x + 2)^2$$

   (a) by using the product rule;

   (b) by first multiplying out the brackets and then differentiating term by term.

6. Find expressions for marginal revenue in the case when the demand function is given by

   (a) $P = (100 - Q)^3$ (b) $P = \dfrac{1000}{Q + 4}$

7. If the consumption function is

   $$C = \frac{300 + 2Y^2}{1 + Y}$$

   calculate MPC and MPS when $Y = 36$ and give an interpretation of these results.

Exercise 4.4*

1. Use the chain rule to differentiate

   (a) $y = (2x + 1)^{10}$ **(b)** $y = (x^2 + 3x - 5)^3$ **(c)** $y = \dfrac{1}{7x - 3}$

   (d) $y = \dfrac{1}{x^2 + 1}$ **(e)** $y = \sqrt{(8x - 1)}$ **(f)** $y = \dfrac{1}{\sqrt[3]{(6x - 5)}}$

2. Use the product rule to differentiate

   (a) $y = x^2(x + 5)^3$ **(b)** $y = x^5(4x + 5)^2$ **(c)** $y = x^4(x + 1)^{1/2}$

3. Use the quotient rule to differentiate

   (a) $y = \dfrac{x^2}{x + 4}$ **(b)** $y = \dfrac{2x - 1}{x + 1}$ **(c)** $y = \dfrac{x^3}{\sqrt{(x - 1)}}$

4. Differentiate

   (a) $y = x(x - 3)^4$ **(b)** $y = x\sqrt{(2x - 3)}$ **(c)** $y = \dfrac{x^3}{(3x + 5)^2}$ **(d)** $y = \dfrac{x}{x^2 + 1}$

   (e) $y = \dfrac{ax + b}{cx + d}$ **(f)** $y = (ax + b)^m(cx + d)^n$ **(g)** $y = x(x + 2)^2(x + 3)^3$

5. Find an expression, simplified as far as possible, for the second-order derivative of the function, $y = \dfrac{x}{2x + 1}$.

6. Find expressions for marginal revenue in the case when the demand function is given by

   (a) $P = \sqrt{(100 - 2Q)}$ **(b)** $P = \dfrac{100}{\sqrt{2 + Q}}$

7. Determine the marginal propensity to consume for the consumption function

   $$C = \frac{650 + 2Y^2}{9 + Y}$$

   when $Y = 21$, correct to three decimal places.

   Deduce the corresponding value of the marginal propensity to save and comment on the implications of these results.

8. If the total cost function is given by

   $$TC = \frac{2Q^2 + 10Q}{Q + 3}$$

   show that the marginal cost function is

   $$MC = 2 + \frac{12}{(Q + 3)^2}$$

   Hence comment on the behaviour of MC as Q increases.

9. If the demand function of a good is $P = a - \sqrt{bQ + c}$ show that the marginal revenue function is

   $$MR = a - \frac{3bQ + 2c}{2\sqrt{bQ + c}}$$

SECTION 4.5
Elasticity

Objectives

At the end of this section you should be able to:

- Calculate price elasticity averaged along an arc.
- Calculate price elasticity evaluated at a point.
- Decide whether supply and demand are inelastic, unit elastic or elastic.
- Understand the relationship between price elasticity of demand and revenue.
- Determine the price elasticity for general linear demand functions.

One important problem in business is to determine the effect on revenue of a change in the price of a good. Let us suppose that a firm's demand curve is downward-sloping. If the firm lowers the price, then it will receive less for each item, but the number of items sold increases. The formula for total revenue, TR, is

$$TR = PQ$$

and it is not immediately obvious what the net effect on TR will be as P decreases and Q increases. The crucial factor here is not the absolute changes in P and Q but rather the proportional or percentage changes. Intuitively, we expect that if the percentage rise in Q is greater than the percentage fall in P, then the firm experiences an increase in revenue. Under these circumstances we say that demand is **elastic**, since the demand is relatively sensitive to changes in price. Similarly, demand is said to be **inelastic** if demand is relatively insensitive to price changes. In this case, the percentage change in quantity is less than the percentage change in price. A firm can then increase revenue by raising the price of the good. Although demand falls as a result, the increase in price more than compensates for the reduced volume of sales and revenue rises. Of course, it could happen that the percentage changes in price and quantity are equal, leaving revenue unchanged. We use the term **unit elastic** to describe this situation.

We quantify the responsiveness of demand to price change by defining the **price elasticity of demand** to be

$$E = \frac{\text{percentage change in demand}}{\text{percentage change in price}}$$

Notice that because the demand curve slopes downwards, a positive change in price leads to a negative change in quantity and vice versa. Consequently, the value of E is always negative. It is usual for economists to ignore the negative sign and consider just the magnitude of elasticity. If this positive value is denoted by $|E|$, then the previous classification of demand functions can be restated more succinctly as:

Demand is said to be

- inelastic if $|E| < 1$
- unit elastic if $|E| = 1$
- elastic if $|E| > 1$

As usual, we denote the changes in P and Q by ΔP and ΔQ respectively, and seek a formula for E in terms of these symbols. To motivate this, suppose that the price of a good is \$12 and that it rises to \$18. A moment's thought should convince you that the percentage change in price is then 50%. You can probably work this out in your head without thinking too hard. However, it is worthwhile identifying the mathematical process involved. To obtain this figure we first express the change

$$18 - 12 = 6$$

as a fraction of the original to get

$$\frac{6}{12} = 0.5$$

and then multiply by 100 to express it as a percentage. This simple example gives us a clue as to how we might find a formula for E. In general, the percentage change in price is

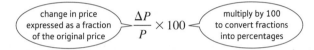

Similarly, the percentage change in quantity is

$$\frac{\Delta Q}{Q} \times 100$$

Hence

$$E = \left(\frac{\Delta Q}{Q} \times 100 \right) \div \left(\frac{\Delta P}{P} \times 100 \right)$$

Now, when we divide two fractions, we turn the denominator upside down and multiply, so

$$E = \left(\frac{\Delta Q}{Q} \times \cancel{100} \right) \times \left(\frac{P}{\cancel{100} \times \Delta P} \right)$$

$$= \frac{P}{Q} \times \frac{\Delta Q}{\Delta P}$$

A typical demand curve is illustrated in Figure 4.17, in which a price fall from P_1 to P_2 causes an increase in demand from Q_1 to Q_2.

To be specific, let us suppose that the demand function is given by

$$P = 200 - Q^2$$

with $P_1 = 136$ and $P_2 = 119$.

The corresponding values of Q_1 and Q_2 are obtained from the demand equation

$$P = 200 - Q^2$$

by substituting $P = 136$ and 119, respectively, and solving for Q. For example, if $P = 136$, then

$$136 = 200 - Q^2$$

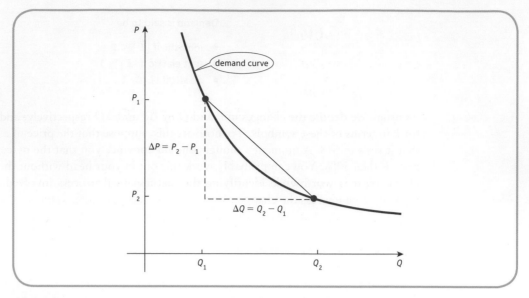

Figure 4.17

which rearranges to give

$$Q^2 = 200 - 136 = 64$$

This has solution $Q = \pm 8$ and, since we can obviously ignore the negative quantity, we have $Q_1 = 8$. Similarly, setting $P = 119$ gives $Q_2 = 9$. The elasticity formula is

$$E = \frac{P}{Q} \times \frac{\Delta Q}{\Delta P}$$

and the values of ΔP and ΔQ are easily worked out to be

$$\Delta P = 119 - 136 = -17$$

$$\Delta Q = 9 - 8 = 1$$

However, it is not at all clear what to take for P and Q. Do we take P to be 136 or 119? Clearly we are going to get two different answers depending on our choice. A sensible compromise is to use their average and take

$$P = \frac{1}{2}(136 + 119) = 127.5$$

Similarly, averaging the Q values gives

$$Q = \frac{1}{2}(8 + 9) = 8.5$$

Hence

$$E = \frac{127.5}{8.5} \times \left(\frac{1}{-17} \right) = -0.88$$

This value is an estimate of elasticity averaged over a section of the demand curve between (Q_1, P_1) and (Q_2, P_2). For this reason, it is called **arc elasticity** and is obtained by replacing P by $\frac{1}{2}(P_1 + P_2)$ and Q by $\frac{1}{2}(Q_1 + Q_2)$ in the general formula.

Practice Problem

1. Given the demand function

    $P = 1000 - 2Q$

   calculate the arc elasticity as P falls from 210 to 200.

A disappointing feature of this approach is the need to compromise and calculate the elasticity averaged along an arc rather than calculate the exact value at a point. A formula for the latter can easily be deduced from

$$E = \frac{P}{Q} \times \frac{\Delta Q}{\Delta P}$$

by considering the limit as ΔQ and ΔP tend to zero in Figure 4.17. All that happens is that the arc shrinks to a point and the ratio $\Delta Q/\Delta P$ tends to dQ/dP. The price elasticity at a point (**point elasticity**) may therefore be found from

$$E = \frac{P}{Q} \times \frac{dQ}{dP}$$

Example

Given the demand function

   $P = 50 - 2Q$

find the elasticity when the price is 30. Is demand inelastic, unit elastic or elastic at this price?

Solution

To find dQ/dP we need to differentiate Q with respect to P. However, we are actually given a formula for P in terms of Q, so we need to transpose

   $P = 50 - 2Q$

for Q. Adding $2Q$ to both sides gives

   $P + 2Q = 50$

and if we subtract P, then

   $2Q = 50 - P$

Finally, dividing through by 2 gives

   $Q = 25 - \frac{1}{2}P$

Hence

$$\frac{dQ}{dP} = -\frac{1}{2}$$

→

We are given that $P = 30$, so at this price, demand is

$$Q = 25 - \frac{1}{2}(30) = 10$$

These values can now be substituted into

$$E = \frac{P}{Q} \times \frac{dQ}{dP}$$

to get

$$E = \frac{30}{10} \times \left(-\frac{1}{2}\right) = -1.5$$

Moreover, since $|1.5| > 1$, demand is elastic at this price.

Practice Problem

2. Given the demand function

$$P = 100 - Q$$

calculate the magnitude of the price elasticity of demand when the price is

(a) 10   (b) 50   (c) 90

Is the demand inelastic, unit elastic or elastic at these prices?

It is quite common in economics to be given the demand function in the form

$$P = f(Q)$$

where P is a function of Q. In order to evaluate elasticity, it is necessary to find

$$\frac{dQ}{dP}$$

which assumes that Q is actually given as a function of P. Consequently, we may have to transpose the demand equation and find an expression for Q in terms of P before we perform the differentiation. This was the approach taken in the previous example. Unfortunately, if $f(Q)$ is a complicated expression, it may be difficult, if not impossible, to carry out the initial rearrangement to extract Q. An alternative approach is based on the fact that

$$\frac{dQ}{dP} = \frac{1}{dP/dQ}$$

A proof of this can be obtained via the chain rule, although we omit the details. This result shows that we can find dQ/dP by just differentiating the original demand function to get dP/dQ and reciprocating.

Example

Given the demand function

$$P = -Q^2 - 4Q + 96$$

find the price elasticity of demand when $P = 51$. If this price rises by 2%, calculate the corresponding percentage change in demand.

Solution

We are given that $P = 51$, so to find the corresponding demand we need to solve the quadratic equation

$$-Q^2 - 4Q + 96 = 51$$

that is,

$$-Q^2 - 4Q + 45 = 0$$

To do this we use the standard formula

$$\frac{-b \pm \sqrt{b^2 - 4ac}}{2a}$$

discussed in Section 2.1, which gives

$$Q = \frac{-(-4) \pm \sqrt{((-4)^2 - 4(-1)(45))}}{2(-1)}$$

$$= \frac{4 \pm \sqrt{196}}{-2}$$

$$= \frac{4 \pm 14}{-2}$$

The two solutions are −9 and 5. As usual, the negative value can be ignored, since it does not make sense to have a negative quantity, so $Q = 5$.

To find the value of E we also need to calculate

$$\frac{\mathrm{d}Q}{\mathrm{d}P}$$

from the demand equation, $P = -Q^2 - 4Q + 96$. It is not at all easy to transpose this for Q. Indeed, we would have to use the formula for solving a quadratic, as before, replacing the number 51 with the letter P. Unfortunately, this expression involves square roots and the subsequent differentiation is quite messy. (You might like to have a go at this yourself!) However, it is easy to differentiate the given expression with respect to Q to get

$$\frac{\mathrm{d}P}{\mathrm{d}Q} = -2Q - 4$$

and so

$$\frac{\mathrm{d}Q}{\mathrm{d}P} = \frac{1}{\mathrm{d}P/\mathrm{d}Q} = \frac{1}{-2Q - 4}$$

Finally, putting $Q = 5$ gives

$$\frac{dQ}{dP} = -\frac{1}{14}$$

The price elasticity of demand is given by

$$E = \frac{P}{Q} \times \frac{dQ}{dP}$$

and if we substitute $P = 51$, $Q = 5$ and $dQ/dP = -1/14$, we get

$$E = \frac{51}{5} \times \left(-\frac{1}{14} \right) = -0.73$$

To discover the effect on Q due to a 2% rise in P, we return to the original definition

$$E = \frac{\text{percentage change in demand}}{\text{percentage change in price}}$$

We know that $E = -0.73$ and that the percentage change in price is 2%, so

$$-0.73 = \frac{\text{percentage change in demand}}{2\%}$$

which shows that demand changes by

$$-0.73 \times 2\% = -1.46\%$$

A 2% rise in price therefore leads to a fall in demand of 1.46%.

Practice Problem

3. Given the demand equation

$$P = -Q^2 - 10Q + 150$$

find the price elasticity of demand when $Q = 4$. Estimate the percentage change in price needed to increase demand by 10%.

The **price elasticity of supply** is defined in an analogous way to that of demand. We define

$$E = \frac{\text{percentage change in supply}}{\text{percentage change in price}}$$

An increase in price leads to an increase in supply, so E is positive.

Example

Given the supply function

$$P = 10 + \sqrt{Q}$$

find the price elasticity of supply

(a) averaged along an arc between $Q = 100$ and $Q = 105$;

(b) at the point $Q = 100$.

Solution

(a) We are given that

$$Q_1 = 100, Q_2 = 105$$

so that

$$P_1 = 10 + \sqrt{100} = 20 \text{ and } P_2 = 10 + \sqrt{105} = 20.247$$

Hence

$$\Delta P = 20.247 - 20 = 0.247, \qquad \Delta Q = 105 - 100 = 5$$

$$P = \frac{1}{2}(20 + 20.247) = 20.123, \qquad Q = \frac{1}{2}(100 + 105) = 102.5$$

The formula for arc elasticity gives

$$E = \frac{P}{Q} \times \frac{\Delta Q}{\Delta P} = \frac{20.123}{102.5} \times \frac{5}{0.247} = 3.97$$

(b) To evaluate the elasticity at the point $Q = 100$, we need to find the derivative, $\dfrac{dQ}{dP}$. The supply equation

$$P = 10 + Q^{1/2}$$

differentiates to give

$$\frac{dP}{dQ} = \frac{1}{2}Q^{-1/2} = \frac{1}{2\sqrt{Q}}$$

so that

$$\frac{dQ}{dP} = 2\sqrt{Q}$$

At the point $Q = 100$, we get

$$\frac{dQ}{dP} = 2\sqrt{100} = 20$$

The formula for point elasticity gives

$$E = \frac{P}{Q} \times \frac{dQ}{dP} = \frac{20}{100} \times 20 = 4$$

Notice that, as expected, the answers to parts (a) and (b) are nearly the same.

Practice Problem

4. If the supply equation is

$$Q = 150 + 5P + 0.1P^2$$

calculate the price elasticity of supply

(a) averaged along an arc between $P = 9$ and $P = 11$;

(b) at the point $P = 10$.

Advice

The concept of elasticity can be applied to more general functions, and we consider some of these in the next chapter. For the moment we investigate the theoretical properties of demand elasticity. The following material is more difficult to understand than the foregoing, so you may prefer just to concentrate on the conclusions and skip the intermediate derivations.

We begin by analysing the relationship between elasticity and marginal revenue. Marginal revenue, MR, is given by

$$MR = \frac{d(TR)}{dQ}$$

Now, TR is equal to the product PQ, so we can apply the product rule to differentiate it. If

$$u = P \quad \text{and} \quad v = Q$$

then

$$\frac{du}{dQ} = \frac{dP}{dQ} \quad \text{and} \quad \frac{dv}{dQ} = \frac{dQ}{dQ} = 1$$

By the product rule

$$MR = u\frac{dv}{dQ} + v\frac{du}{dQ}$$

$$= P + Q \times \frac{dP}{dQ}$$

$$= P\left(1 + \frac{Q}{P} \times \frac{dP}{dQ}\right)$$

check this by multiplying out the brackets

Now

$$\frac{P}{Q} \times \frac{dQ}{dP} = E$$

so

$$\frac{Q}{P} \times \frac{dP}{dQ} = \frac{1}{E}$$

turn both sides upside down

This can be substituted into the expression for MR to get

$$\text{MR} = P\left(1 + \frac{1}{E}\right)$$

The connection between marginal revenue and demand elasticity is now complete, and this formula can be used to justify the intuitive argument that we gave at the beginning of this section concerning revenue and elasticity. Observe that if $-1 < E < 0$ then $1/E < -1$, so MR is negative for any value of P. It follows that the revenue function is decreasing in regions where demand is inelastic, because MR determines the slope of the revenue curve. Similarly, if $E < -1$, then $1/E > -1$, so MR is positive for any price, P, and the revenue curve is upwards. In other words, the revenue function is increasing in regions where demand is elastic. Finally, if $E = -1$, then MR is 0, and so the slope of the revenue curve is horizontal at points where demand is unit elastic.

Throughout this section we have taken specific functions and evaluated the elasticity at particular points. It is more instructive to consider general functions and to deduce general expressions for elasticity. Consider the standard linear downward-sloping demand function

$$P = aQ + b$$

when $a < 0$ and $b > 0$. As noted in Section 4.3, this typifies the demand function faced by a monopolist. To transpose this equation for Q, we subtract b from both sides to get

$$aQ = P - b$$

and then divide through by a to get

$$Q = \frac{1}{a}(P - b)$$

Hence

$$\frac{dQ}{dP} = \frac{1}{a}$$

The formula for elasticity of demand is

$$E = \frac{P}{Q} \times \frac{dQ}{dP}$$

so replacing Q by $(1/a)(P - b)$ and dQ/dP by $1/a$ gives

$$E = \frac{P}{(1/a)(P - b)} \times \frac{1}{a}$$

$$= \frac{P}{P - b}$$

Notice that this formula involves P and b but not a. Elasticity is therefore independent of the slope of linear demand curves. In particular, this shows that, corresponding to any price P, the elasticities of the two demand functions sketched in Figure 4.18 are identical. This is perhaps a rather surprising result. We might have expected demand to be more elastic at point A than at point B, since A is on the steeper curve. However, the mathematics shows that this is not the case. (Can you explain, in economic terms, why this is so?)

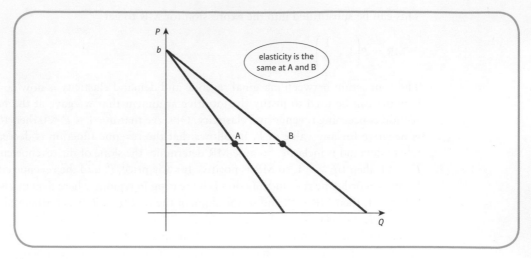

Figure 4.18

Another interesting feature of the result

$$E = \frac{P}{P - b}$$

is the fact that b occurs in the denominator of this fraction, so that corresponding to any price, P, the larger the value of the intercept, b, the smaller the magnitude of the elasticity. In Figure 4.19, the magnitude of the elasticity at C is smaller than that at D because C lies on the curve with the larger intercept.

The dependence of E on P is also worthy of note. It shows that elasticity varies along a linear demand curve. This is illustrated in Figure 4.20. At the left-hand end, $P = b$, so

$$E = \frac{b}{b - b} = \frac{b}{0} = \infty \quad \text{(read 'infinity')}$$

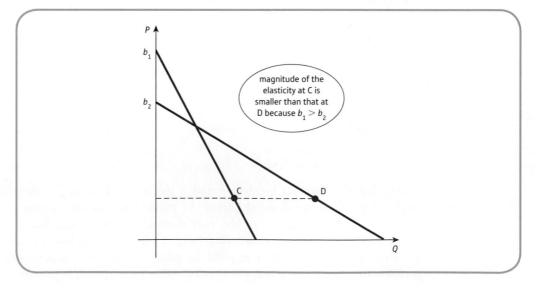

Figure 4.19

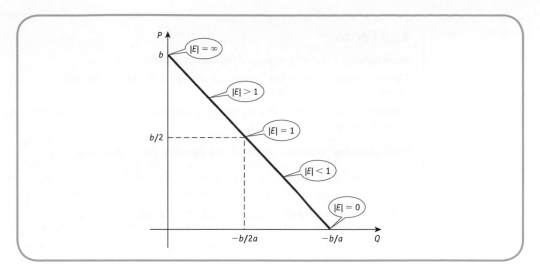

Figure 4.20

At the right-hand end, $P = 0$, so

$$E = \frac{0}{0 - b} = \frac{0}{-b} = 0$$

As you move down the demand curve, the magnitude of elasticity decreases from ∞ to 0, taking all possible values. Demand is unit elastic when $E = -1$ and the price at which this occurs can be found by solving

$$\frac{P}{P - b} = -1 \quad \text{for} \quad P$$

$$P = b - P \quad \text{(multiply both sides by } P - b)$$

$$2P = b \quad \quad \text{(add } P \text{ to both sides)}$$

$$P = \frac{b}{2} \quad \quad \text{(divide both sides by 2)}$$

The corresponding quantity can be found by substituting $P = b/2$ into the transposed demand equation to get

$$Q = \frac{1}{a}\left(\frac{b}{2} - b\right) = -\frac{b}{2a}$$

Demand is unit elastic exactly halfway along the demand curve. To the left of this point, $|E| > 1$ and demand is elastic, whereas to the right, $|E| < 1$ and demand is inelastic.

In our discussion of general demand functions, we have concentrated on those which are represented by straight lines since these are commonly used in simple economic models. There are other possibilities, and Question 4 in Exercise 4.5* investigates a class of functions that have constant elasticity.

Key Terms

Arc elasticity   Elasticity measured between two points on a curve.

Elastic demand   Where the percentage change in demand is more than the corresponding percentage change in price: $|E| > 1$.

Inelastic demand   Where the percentage change in demand is less than the corresponding percentage change in price: $|E| < 1$.

Point elasticity   Elasticity measured at a particular point on a curve: $E = \dfrac{P}{Q} \times \dfrac{dQ}{dP}$.

Price elasticity of demand   A measure of the responsiveness of the change in demand due to a change in price: (percentage change in demand) ÷ (percentage change in price).

Price elasticity of supply   A measure of the responsiveness of the change in supply due to a change in price: (percentage change in supply) ÷ (percentage change in price).

Unit elasticity of demand   Where the percentage change in demand is the same as the percentage change in price: $|E| = 1$.

Exercise 4.5

1. Given the demand function

    $$P = 500 - 4Q^2$$

    calculate the price elasticity of demand averaged along an arc joining $Q = 8$ and $Q = 10$.

2. Find the price elasticity of demand at the point $Q = 9$ for the demand function

    $$P = 500 - 4Q^2$$

    and compare your answer with that of Question 1.

3. Find the price elasticity of demand at $P = 6$ for each of the following demand functions:

    (a) $P = 30 - 2Q$

    (b) $P = 30 - 12Q$

    (c) $P = \sqrt{(100 - 2Q)}$

4. (a) If an airline increases prices for business class flights by 8%, demand falls by about 2.5%. Estimate the elasticity of demand. Is demand elastic, inelastic or unit elastic?

    (b) Explain whether you would expect a similar result to hold for economy class flights.

5. The demand function of a good is given by

    $$Q = \frac{1000}{P^2}$$

    (a) Calculate the price elasticity of demand at $P = 5$ and hence estimate the percentage change in demand when P increases by 2%.

    (b) Comment on the accuracy of your estimate in part (a) by calculating the exact percentage change in demand when P increases from 5 to 5.1.

6. (a) Find the elasticity of demand in terms of Q for the demand function, $P = 20 - 0.05Q$.

   (b) For what value of Q is demand unit elastic?

   (c) Find an expression for MR and verify that MR = 0 when demand is unit elastic.

7. Consider the supply equation

   $$Q = 4 + 0.1P^2$$

   (a) Write down an expression for dQ/dP.

   (b) Show that the supply equation can be rearranged as

   $$P = \sqrt{(10Q - 40)}$$

   Differentiate this to find an expression for dP/dQ.

   (c) Use your answers to parts (a) and (b) to verify that

   $$\frac{dQ}{dP} = \frac{1}{dP/dQ}$$

   (d) Calculate the elasticity of supply at the point $Q = 14$.

8. If the supply equation is

   $$Q = 7 + 0.1P + 0.004P^2$$

   find the price elasticity of supply if the current price is 80.

   (a) Is supply elastic, inelastic or unit elastic at this price?

   (b) Estimate the percentage change in supply if the price rises by 5%.

Exercise 4.5*

1. Find the elasticity for the demand function

   $$Q = 80 - 2P - 0.5P^2$$

   averaged along an arc joining $Q = 32$ to $Q = 50$. Give your answer to 2 decimal places.

2. Consider the supply equation

   $$P = 7 + 2Q^2$$

   By evaluating the price elasticity of supply at the point $P = 105$, estimate the percentage increase in supply when the price rises by 7%.

3. If the demand equation is

   $$Q + 4P = 60$$

   find a general expression for the price elasticity of demand in terms of P. For what value of P is demand unit elastic?

4. Show that the price elasticity of demand is constant for the demand functions

   $$P = \frac{A}{Q^n}$$

   where A and n are positive constants.

5. Find a general expression for the point elasticity of supply for the function

$$Q = aP + b \ (a > 0)$$

Deduce that the supply function is

(a) unit elastic when $b = 0$;

(b) elastic when $b < 0$.

Give a brief geometrical interpretation of these results.

6. A supply function is given by

$$Q = 40 + 0.1P^2$$

(1) Find the price elasticity of supply averaged along an arc between $P = 11$ and $P = 13$. Give your answer correct to three decimal places.

(2) Find an expression for price elasticity of supply at a general point, P.

Hence:

(a) Estimate the percentage change in supply when the price increases by 5% from its current level of 17. Give your answer correct to one decimal place.

(b) Find the price at which supply is unit elastic.

7. **(a)** Show that the elasticity of the supply function

$$P = aQ + b$$

is given by

$$E = \frac{P}{P - b}$$

(b) Consider the two supply functions

$$P = 2Q + 5 \text{ and } P = aQ + b$$

The quantity supplied is the same for both functions when $P = 10$, and at this point, the price elasticity of supply for the second function is five times larger than that for the first function. Find the values of a and b.

8. **(a)** If E denotes the elasticity of a general supply function, $Q = f(P)$, show that the elasticity of:

(i) $Q = [f(P)]^n$ is nE **(ii)** $Q = \lambda f(P)$ is E **(iii)** $Q = \lambda + f(P)$ is $\dfrac{f(P)E}{\lambda + f(P)}$

where n and λ are positive constants.

(b) Show that the elasticity of the supply function $Q = P$ is 1 and use the results of part (a) to write down the elasticity of

(i) $Q = P^3$ **(ii)** $Q = 10P\sqrt{P}$ **(iii)** $Q = 5\sqrt{P} - 2$

SECTION 4.6
Optimisation of economic functions

Objectives

At the end of this section you should be able to:

- Use the first-order derivative to find the stationary points of a function.
- Use the second-order derivative to classify the stationary points of a function.
- Find the maximum and minimum points of an economic function.
- Use stationary points to sketch graphs of economic functions.

In Section 2.1 a simple three-step strategy was described for sketching graphs of quadratic functions of the form

$$f(x) = ax^2 + bx + c$$

The basic idea is to solve the corresponding equation

$$ax^2 + bx + c = 0$$

to find where the graph crosses the x axis. Provided that the quadratic equation has at least one solution, it is then possible to deduce the coordinates of the maximum or minimum point of the parabola. For example, if there are two solutions, then by symmetry the graph turns round at the point exactly halfway between these solutions. Unfortunately, if the quadratic equation has no solution, then only a limited sketch can be obtained using this approach.

In this section we show how the techniques of calculus can be used to find the coordinates of the turning point of a parabola. The beauty of this approach is that it can be used to locate the maximum and minimum points of any economic function, not just those represented by quadratics. Look at the graph in Figure 4.21. Points B, C, D, E, F and G are referred to as the **stationary points** (sometimes called **critical points**, **turning points** or **extrema**) of the function. At a stationary point the tangent to the graph is horizontal, and so has zero slope.

Consequently, at a stationary point of a function $f(x)$,

$$f'(x) = 0$$

The reason for using the word 'stationary' is historical. Calculus was originally used by astronomers to predict planetary motion. If a graph of the distance travelled by an object is sketched against time, then the speed of the object is given by the slope, since this represents the rate of change of distance with respect to time. It follows that if the graph is horizontal at some point, then the speed is zero and the object is instantaneously at rest: that is, stationary.

Stationary points are classified into one of three types: local maxima, local minima and stationary points of inflection.

At a **local maximum** (sometimes called a relative maximum), the graph falls away on both sides. Points B and E are the local maxima for the function sketched in Figure 4.21.

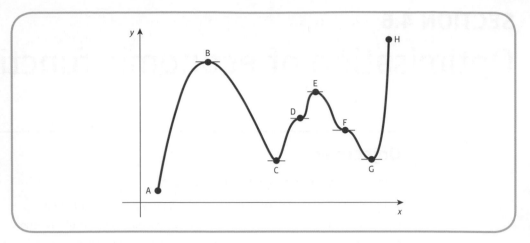

Figure 4.21

The word 'local' is used to highlight the fact that, although these are the maximum points relative to their locality or neighbourhood, they may not be the overall or global maximum. In Figure 4.21 the highest point on the graph actually occurs at the right-hand end, H, which is not a stationary point, since the slope is not zero at H.

At a **local minimum** (sometimes called a relative minimum), the graph rises on both sides. Points C and G are the local minima in Figure 4.21. Again, it is not necessary for the global minimum to be one of the local minima. In Figure 4.21 the lowest point on the graph occurs at the left-hand end, A, which is not a stationary point.

At a **stationary point of inflection**, the graph rises on one side and falls on the other. The stationary points of inflection in Figure 4.21 are labelled D and F. These points are of little value in economics, although they do sometimes assist in sketching graphs of economic functions. Maxima and minima, on the other hand, are important. The calculation of the maximum points of the revenue and profit functions is clearly worthwhile. Likewise, it is useful to be able to find the minimum points of average cost functions.

For most examples in economics, the local maximum and minimum points coincide with the global maximum and minimum. For this reason we shall drop the word 'local' when describing stationary points. However, always bear in mind that the global maximum and minimum could actually be attained at an end point and this possibility may need to be checked. This can be done by comparing the function values at the end points with those of the stationary points and then deciding which of them gives rise to the largest or smallest values.

Two obvious questions remain. How do we find the stationary points of any given function, and how do we classify them? The first question is easily answered. As we mentioned earlier, stationary points satisfy the equation

$$f'(x) = 0$$

so all we need is to differentiate the function, to equate to zero and to solve the resulting algebraic equation. The classification is equally straightforward. It can be shown that if a function has a stationary point at $x = a$, then

- if $f''(a) > 0$, then $f(x)$ has a minimum at $x = a$;
- if $f''(a) < 0$, then $f(x)$ has a maximum at $x = a$.

Therefore, we need only to differentiate the function a second time and to evaluate this second-order derivative at each point. A point is a minimum if this value is positive and a maximum if this value is negative. These facts are consistent with our interpretation of the second-order derivative in Section 4.2. If $f''(a) > 0$, the graph bends upwards at $x = a$ (points C and G in Figure 4.21). If $f''(a) < 0$, the graph bends downwards at $x = a$ (points B and E in Figure 4.21). There is, of course, a third possibility, namely $f''(a) = 0$. Sadly, when this happens, it provides no information whatsoever about the stationary point. The point $x = a$ could be a maximum, minimum or inflection. This situation is illustrated in Question 2 in Exercise 4.6* at the end of this section.

Advice

If you are unlucky enough to encounter this case, you can always classify the point by tabulating the function values in the vicinity and use these to produce a local sketch.

To summarise, the method for finding and classifying stationary points of a function, $f(x)$, is as follows:

Step 1

Solve the equation $f'(x) = 0$ to find the stationary points, $x = a$.

Step 2

If

- $f''(a) > 0$, then the function has a minimum at $x = a$.
- $f''(a) < 0$, then the function has a maximum at $x = a$.
- $f''(a) = 0$, then the point cannot be classified using the available information.

Example

Find and classify the stationary points of the following functions. Hence sketch their graphs.

(a) $f(x) = x^2 - 4x + 5$ (b) $f(x) = 2x^3 + 3x^2 - 12x + 4$

Solution

(a) In order to use steps 1 and 2 we need to find the first- and second-order derivatives of the function

$$f(x) = x^2 - 4x + 5$$

Differentiating once gives

$$f'(x) = 2x - 4$$

and differentiating a second time gives

$$f''(x) = 2$$

Step 1

The stationary points are the solutions of the equation

$$f'(x) = 0$$

so we need to solve

$$2x - 4 = 0$$

This is a linear equation so has just one solution. Adding 4 to both sides gives

$$2x = 4$$

and dividing through by 2 shows that the stationary point occurs at

$$x = 2$$

Step 2

To classify this point we need to evaluate

$$f''(2)$$

In this case

$$f''(x) = 2$$

for all values of x, so in particular

$$f''(2) = 2$$

This number is positive, so the function has a minimum at $x = 2$.

We have shown that the minimum point occurs at $x = 2$. The corresponding value of y is easily found by substituting this number into the function to get

$$y = (2)^2 - 4(2) + 5 = 1$$

so the minimum point has coordinates $(2, 1)$. A graph of $f(x)$ is shown in Figure 4.22.

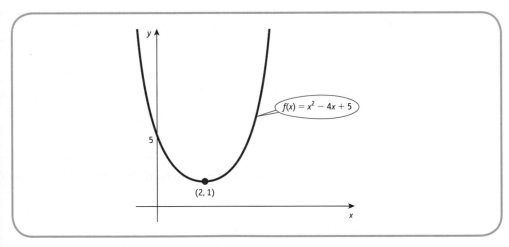

Figure 4.22

(b) In order to use steps 1 and 2 we need to find the first- and second-order derivatives of the function

$$f(x) = 2x^3 + 3x^2 - 12x + 4$$

Differentiating once gives

$$f'(x) = 6x^2 + 6x - 12$$

and differentiating a second time gives

$$f''(x) = 12x + 6$$

Step 1

The stationary points are the solutions of the equation

$$f'(x) = 0$$

so we need to solve

$$6x^2 + 6x - 12 = 0$$

This is a quadratic equation and so can be solved using 'the formula'. However, before doing so, it is a good idea to divide both sides by 6 to avoid large numbers. The resulting equation

$$x^2 + x - 2 = 0$$

has solution

$$x = \frac{-1 \pm \sqrt{(1^2 - 4(1)(-2))}}{2(1)} = \frac{-1 \pm \sqrt{9}}{2} = \frac{-1 \pm 3}{2} = -2, 1$$

In general, whenever $f(x)$ is a cubic function, the stationary points are the solutions of a quadratic equation, $f'(x) = 0$. Moreover, we know from Section 2.1 that such an equation can have two, one or no solutions. It follows that a cubic equation can have two, one or no stationary points. In this particular example we have seen that there are two stationary points, at $x = -2$ and $x = 1$.

Step 2

To classify these points we need to evaluate $f''(-2)$ and $f''(1)$. Now,

$$f''(-2) = 12(-2) + 6 - -18$$

This is negative, so there is a maximum at $x = -2$. When $x = -2$,

$$y = 2(-2)^3 + 3(-2)^2 - 12(-2) + 4 = 24$$

so the maximum point has coordinates $(-2, 24)$. Now

$$f''(1) = 12(1) + 6 = 18$$

This is positive, so there is a minimum at $x = 1$. When $x = 1$,

$$y = 2(1)^3 + 3(1)^2 - 12(1) + 4 = -3$$

so the minimum point has coordinates $(1, -3)$.

This information enables a partial sketch to be drawn as shown in Figure 4.23. Before we can be confident about the complete picture, it is useful to plot a few more points such as those below:

x	−10	0	10
y	−1816	4	2184

This table indicates that when x is positive, the graph falls steeply downwards from a great height. Similarly, when x is negative, the graph quickly disappears off the bottom of the page. The curve cannot wiggle and turn round except at the two stationary points already plotted (otherwise it would have more stationary points, which we know is not the case). We now have enough information to join up the pieces and so sketch a complete picture as shown in Figure 4.24.

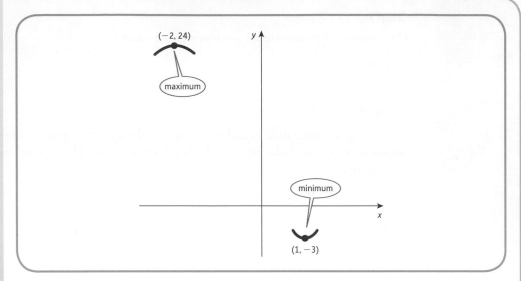

Figure 4.23

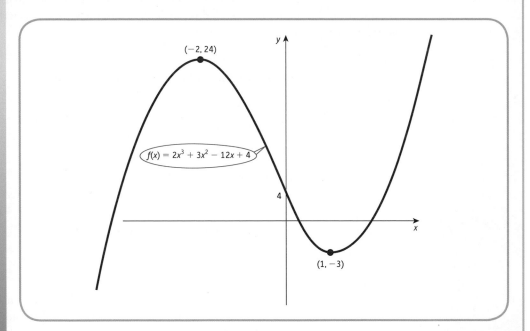

Figure 4.24

In an ideal world it would be nice to calculate the three points at which the graph crosses the x axis. These are the solutions of

$$2x^3 + 3x^2 - 12x + 4 = 0$$

There is a formula for solving cubic equations, just as there is for quadratic equations, but it is extremely complicated and is beyond the scope of this text.

Practice Problem

1. Find and classify the stationary points of the following functions. Hence sketch their graphs.

   (a) $y = 3x^2 + 12x - 35$ (b) $y = -2x^3 + 15x^2 - 36x + 27$

The task of finding the maximum and minimum values of a function is referred to as **optimisation**. This is an important topic in mathematical economics. It provides a rich source of examination questions, and we devote the remaining part of this section and the whole of the next to applications of it. In this section we demonstrate the use of stationary points by working through four 'examination-type' problems in detail. These problems involve the optimisation of specific revenue, cost, profit and production functions. They are not intended to exhaust all possibilities, although they are fairly typical. The next section describes how the mathematics of optimisation can be used to derive general theoretical results.

Example

A firm's short-run production function is given by

$$Q = 6L^2 - 0.2L^3$$

where L denotes the number of workers.

(a) Find the size of the workforce that maximises output and hence sketch a graph of this production function.

(b) Find the size of the workforce that maximises the average product of labour. Calculate MP_L and AP_L at this value of L. What do you observe?

Solution

(a) In the first part of this example we want to find the value of L, which maximises

$$Q = 6L^2 - 0.2L^3$$

Step 1

At a stationary point

$$\frac{dQ}{dL} = 12L - 0.6L^2 = 0$$

This is a quadratic equation and so we could use 'the formula' to find L. However, this is not really necessary in this case because both terms have a common factor of L, and the equation may be written as

$$L(12 - 0.6L) = 0$$

It follows that either

$$L = 0 \text{ or } 12 - 0.6L = 0$$

that is, the equation has solutions

$$L = 0 \text{ and } L = 12/0.6 = 20$$

Step 2

It is obvious on economic grounds that $L = 0$ is a minimum and presumably $L = 20$ is the maximum. We can, of course, check this by differentiating a second time to get

$$\frac{d^2Q}{dL^2} = 12 - 1.2L$$

When $L = 0$,

$$\frac{d^2Q}{dL^2} = 12 > 0$$

which confirms that $L = 0$ is a minimum. The corresponding output is given by

$$Q = 6(0)^2 - 0.2(0)^3 = 0$$

as expected. When $L = 20$,

$$\frac{d^2Q}{dL^2} = -12 < 0$$

which confirms that $L = 20$ is a maximum.

The firm should therefore employ 20 workers to achieve a maximum output

$$Q = 6(20)^2 - 0.2(20)^3 = 800$$

We have shown that the minimum point on the graph has coordinates $(0, 0)$ and the maximum point has coordinates $(20, 800)$. There are no further turning points, so the graph of the production function has the shape sketched in Figure 4.25.

It is possible to find the precise values of L at which the graph crosses the horizontal axis. The production function is given by

$$Q = 6L^2 - 0.2L^3$$

so we need to solve

$$6L^2 - 0.2L^3 = 0$$

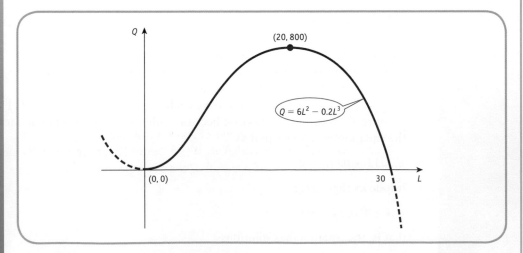

Figure 4.25

We can take out a factor of L^2 to get

$$L^2(6 - 0.2L) = 0$$

Hence, either

$$L^2 = 0 \text{ or } 6 - 0.2L = 0$$

The first of these merely confirms the fact that the curve passes through the origin, whereas the second shows that the curve intersects the L axis at $L = 6/0.2 = 30$.

(b) In the second part of this example we want to find the value of L which maximises the average product of labour. This is a concept that we have not met before in this text, although it is not difficult to guess how it might be defined.

The **average product of labour**, AP_L, is taken to be total output divided by labour, so that in symbols

$$AP_L = \frac{Q}{L}$$

This is sometimes called **labour productivity**, since it measures the average output per worker.

In this example,

$$AP_L = \frac{6L^2 - 0.2L^3}{L} = 6L - 0.2L^2$$

Step 1

At a stationary point

$$\frac{d(AP_L)}{dL} = 0$$

so

$$6 - 0.4L = 0$$

which has solution $L = 6/0.4 = 15$.

Step 2

To classify this stationary point we differentiate a second time to get

$$\frac{d(AP_L)}{dL} = -0.4 < 0$$

which shows that it is a maximum.

The labour productivity is therefore greatest when the firm employs 15 workers. In fact, the corresponding labour productivity, AP_L, is

$$6(15) - 0.2(15)^2 = 45$$

In other words, the largest number of goods produced per worker is 45.

Finally, we are invited to calculate the value of MP_L at this point. To find an expression for MP_L we need to differentiate Q with respect to L to get

$$MP_L = 12L - 0.6L^2$$

When $L = 15$,

$$MP_L = 12(15) - 0.6(15)^2 = 45$$

We observe that at $L = 15$ the values of MP_L and AP_L are equal.

In this particular example we discovered that at the point of maximum average product of labour

marginal product of labour $=$ average product of labour

There is nothing special about this example, and in the next section we show that this result holds for any production function.

Practice Problem

2. A firm's short-run production function is given by

$$Q = 300L^2 - L^4$$

where L denotes the number of workers. Find the size of the workforce that maximises the average product of labour and verify that at this value of L

$$MP_L = AP_L$$

Example

The demand equation of a good is

$$P + Q = 30$$

and the total cost function is

$$TC = \tfrac{1}{2}Q^2 + 6Q + 7$$

(a) Find the level of output that maximises total revenue.

(b) Find the level of output that maximises profit. Calculate MR and MC at this value of Q. What do you observe?

Solution

(a) In the first part of this example we want to find the value of Q which maximises total revenue. To do this we use the given demand equation to find an expression for TR and then apply the theory of stationary points in the usual way.

The total revenue is defined by

$$TR = PQ$$

We seek the value of Q which maximises TR, so we express TR in terms of the variable Q only. The demand equation

$$P + Q = 30$$

can be rearranged to get

$$P = 30 - Q$$

Hence

$$
\begin{aligned}
TR &= (30 - Q)Q \\
&= 30Q - Q^2
\end{aligned}
$$

Step 1

At a stationary point

$$\frac{d(TR)}{dQ} = 0$$

so

$$30 - 2Q = 0$$

which has the solution $Q = 30/2 = 15$.

Step 2

To classify this point we differentiate a second time to get

$$\frac{d^2(TR)}{dQ^2} = -2$$

This is negative, so TR has a maximum at $Q = 15$.

(b) In the second part of this example we want to find the value of Q which maximises profit. To do this we begin by determining an expression for profit in terms of Q. Once this has been done, it is then a simple matter to work out the first- and second-order derivatives and so to find and classify the stationary points of the profit function.

The profit function is defined by

$$\pi = TR - TC$$

From part (a)

$$TR = 30Q - Q^2$$

We are given the total cost function

$$TC = \tfrac{1}{2}Q^2 + 6Q + 7$$

Hence

$$\begin{aligned}
\pi &= (30Q - Q^2) - (\tfrac{1}{2}Q^2 + 6Q + 7) \\
&= 30Q - Q^2 - \tfrac{1}{2}Q^2 - 6Q - 7 \\
&= -\tfrac{3}{2}Q^2 + 24Q - 7
\end{aligned}$$

Step 1

At a stationary point

$$\frac{d\pi}{dQ} = 0$$

so

$$-3Q + 24 = 0$$

which has solution $Q = 24/3 = 8$.

Step 2

To classify this point we differentiate a second time to get

$$\frac{d^2\pi}{dQ^2} = -3$$

This is negative, so π has a maximum at $Q = 8$. In fact, the corresponding maximum profit is

$$\pi = -{}^3/_2(8)^2 + 24(8) - 7 = 89$$

Finally, we are invited to calculate the marginal revenue and marginal cost at this particular value of Q. To find expressions for MR and MC we need only differentiate TR and TC, respectively. If

$$TR = 30Q - Q^2$$

then

$$MR = \frac{d(TR)}{dQ}$$
$$= 30 - 2Q$$

so when $Q = 8$

$$MR = 30 - 2(8) = 14$$

If

$$TC = {}^1/_2Q^2 + 6Q + 7$$

then

$$MC = \frac{d(TC)}{dQ}$$
$$= Q + 6$$

so when $Q = 8$

$$MC = 8 + 6 = 14$$

We observe that at $Q = 8$, the values of MR and MC are equal.

In this particular example we discovered that at the point of maximum profit,

marginal revenue = marginal cost

There is nothing special about this example, and in the next section we show that this result holds for any profit function.

Practice Problem

3. The demand equation of a good is given by

$$P + 2Q = 20$$

and the total cost function is

$$Q^3 - 8Q^2 + 20Q + 2$$

(a) Find the level of output that maximises total revenue.

(b) Find the maximum profit and the value of Q at which it is achieved. Verify that, at this value of Q, MR = MC.

Example

The cost of building an office block, x floors high, is made up of three components:

(1) $10 million for the land;

(2) $$^{1}/_{4}$ million per floor;

(3) specialised costs of $10 000$x$ per floor.

How many floors should the block contain if the average cost per floor is to be minimised?

Solution

The $10 million for the land is a fixed cost because it is independent of the number of floors. Each floor costs $$^{1}/_{4}$ million, so if the building has x floors altogether, then the cost will be 250 000x.

In addition there are specialised costs of 10 000x per floor, so if there are x floors, this will be

$$(10\ 000x)x = 10\ 000x^2$$

Notice the square term here, which means that the specialised costs rise dramatically with increasing x. This is to be expected, since a tall building requires a more complicated design. It may also be necessary to use more expensive materials.

The total cost, TC, is the sum of the three components: that is,

$$TC = 10\ 000\ 000 + 250\ 000x + 10\ 000x^2$$

The average cost per floor, AC, is found by dividing the total cost by the number of floors: that is,

$$AC = \frac{TC}{x} = \frac{10\ 000\ 000 + 250\ 000x + 10\ 000x^2}{x}$$

$$= \frac{10\ 000\ 000}{x} + 250\ 000 + 10\ 000x$$

$$= 10\ 000\ 000x^{-1} + 250\ 000 + 10\ 000x$$

Step 1

At a stationary point

$$\frac{d(AC)}{dx} = 0$$

In this case

$$\frac{d(AC)}{dx} = -10\ 000\ 000x^{-2} + 10\ 000 = \frac{-10\ 000\ 000}{x^2} + 10\ 000$$

so we need to solve

$$10\ 000 = \frac{10\ 000\ 000}{x^2} \quad \text{or equivalently,} \quad 10\ 000x^2 = 10\ 000\ 000$$

Hence

$$x^2 = \frac{10\ 000\ 000}{10\ 000} = 1000$$

This has the solution

$$x = \pm\sqrt{1000} = \pm 31.6$$

We can obviously ignore the negative value because it does not make sense to build an office block with a negative number of floors, so we can deduce that $x = 31.6$.

Step 2

To confirm that this is a minimum we need to differentiate a second time. Now

$$\frac{d(AC)}{dx} = -10\,000\,000x^{-2} + 10\,000$$

so

$$\frac{d^2(AC)}{dx^2} = -2(-10\,000\,000)x^{-3} = \frac{20\,000\,000}{x^3}$$

When $x = 31.6$, we see that

$$\frac{d^2(AC)}{dx^2} = \frac{20\,000\,000}{(31.6)^3} = 633.8$$

It follows that $x = 31.6$ is indeed a minimum because the second-order derivative is a positive number.

At this stage it is tempting to state that the answer is 31.6. This is mathematically correct but is a physical impossibility since x must be a whole number. To decide whether to take x to be 31 or 32, we simply evaluate AC for these two values of x and choose the one that produces the lower average cost.

When $x = 31$,

$$AC = \frac{10\,000\,000}{31} + 250\,000 + 10\,000(31) = \$882\,581$$

When $x = 32$,

$$AC = \frac{10\,000\,000}{32} + 250\,000 + 10\,000(32) = \$882\,500$$

Therefore, an office block 32 floors high produces the lowest average cost per floor.

Practice Problem

4. The total cost function of a good is given by

    $$TC = Q^2 + 3Q + 36$$

    Calculate the level of output that minimises average cost. Find AC and MC at this value of Q. What do you observe?

Example

The supply and demand equations of a good are given by

$$P = Q_S + 8$$

and

$$P = -3Q_D + 80$$

respectively.

The government decides to impose a tax, t, per unit. Find the value of t which maximises the government's total tax revenue on the assumption that equilibrium conditions prevail in the market.

Solution

The idea of taxation was first introduced in Chapter 1. In Section 1.5 the equilibrium price and quantity were calculated from a given value of t. In this example t is unknown, but the analysis is exactly the same. All we need to do is to carry the letter t through the usual calculations and then to choose t at the end so as to maximise the total tax revenue.

To take account of the tax we replace P by $P - t$ in the supply equation. This is because the price that the supplier actually receives is the price, P, that the consumer pays less the tax, t, deducted by the government. The new supply equation is then

$$P - t = Q_S + 8$$

so that

$$P = Q_S + 8 + t$$

In equilibrium

$$Q_S = Q_D$$

If this common value is denoted by Q, then the supply and demand equations become

$$P = Q + 8 + t$$
$$P = -3Q + 80$$

Hence

$$Q + 8 + t = -3Q + 80$$

since both sides are equal to P. This can be rearranged to give

$$Q = -3Q + 72 - t \quad \text{(subtract } 8 + t \text{ from both sides)}$$
$$4Q = 72 - t \qquad \text{(add } 3Q \text{ to both sides)}$$
$$Q = 18 - \tfrac{1}{4}t \qquad \text{(divide both sides by 4)}$$

Now, if the number of goods sold is Q and the government tax revenue, T, is given by

$$T = tQ$$
$$= t(18 - \tfrac{1}{4}t)$$
$$= 18t - \tfrac{1}{4}t^2$$

This, then, is the expression that we wish to maximise.

Step 1

At a stationary point

$$\frac{dT}{dt} = 0$$

so

$$18 - \frac{1}{2}t = 0$$

which has solution

$$t = 36$$

Step 2

To classify this point we differentiate a second time to get

$$\frac{d^2T}{dt^2} = -\frac{1}{2} < 0$$

which confirms that it is a maximum.

Hence the government should impose a tax of $36 on each good.

Practice Problem

5. The supply and demand equations of a good are given by

$$P = \tfrac{1}{2}Q_S + 25$$

and

$$P = -2Q_D + 50$$

respectively.

The government decides to impose a tax, t, per unit. Find the value of t which maximises the government's total tax revenue on the assumption that equilibrium conditions prevail in the market.

In theory a spreadsheet such as Excel could be used to solve optimisation problems, although it cannot handle the associated mathematics. The preferred method is to use a symbolic computation system such as Maple, Matlab, Mathcad or Derive which can not only sketch the graphs of functions but also differentiate and solve equations. Consequently, it is possible to obtain the exact solution using one of these packages.

Key Terms

Average product of labour (labour productivity)   Output per worker: $AP_L = Q/L$.

Maximum (local) point   A point on a curve which has the highest function value in comparison with other values in its neighbourhood; at such a point the first-order derivative is zero and the second-order derivative is either zero or negative.

Minimum (local) point   A point on a curve which has the lowest function value in comparison with other values in its neighbourhood; at such a point the first-order derivative is zero and the second-order derivative is either zero or positive.

Optimisation   The determination of the optimal (usually stationary) points of a function.

Stationary point of inflection   A stationary point that is neither a maximum nor a minimum; at such a point both the first- and second-order derivatives are zero.

Stationary points (critical points, turning points, extrema)   Points on a graph at which the tangent is horizontal; at a stationary point the first-order derivative is zero.

Exercise 4.6

1. Find and classify the stationary points of the following functions. Hence give a rough sketch of their graphs.

    (a) $y = -x^2 + x + 1$ (b) $y = x^2 - 4x + 4$ (c) $y = x^2 - 20x + 105$ (d) $y = -x^3 + 3x$

2. If the demand equation of a good is

    $$P = 40 - 2Q$$

    find the level of output that maximises total revenue.

3. A firm's short-run production function is given by

    $$Q = 30L^2 - 0.5L^3$$

    Find the value of L which maximises AP_L and verify that $MP_L = AP_L$ at this point.

4. If the fixed costs are 13 and the variable costs are $Q + 2$ per unit, show that the average cost function is

    $$AC = \frac{13}{Q} + Q + 2$$

    (a) Calculate the values of AC when $Q = 1, 2, 3, \dots, 6$. Plot these points on graph paper and hence produce an accurate graph of AC against Q.

    (b) Use your graph to estimate the minimum average cost.

    (c) Use differentiation to confirm your estimate obtained in part (b).

5. The demand and total cost functions of a good are

    $$4P + Q - 16 = 0$$

    and

    $$TC = 4 + 2Q - \frac{3Q^2}{10} + \frac{Q^3}{20}$$

    respectively.

(a) Find expressions for TR, π, MR and MC in terms of Q.

(b) Solve the equation

$$\frac{d\pi}{dQ} = 0$$

and hence determine the value of Q which maximises profit.

(c) Verify that, at the point of maximum profit, MR = MC.

6. The supply and demand equations of a good are given by

$$3P - Q_S = 3$$

and

$$2P + Q_D = 14$$

respectively.

The government decides to impose a tax, t, per unit. Find the value of t which maximises the government's total tax revenue on the assumption that equilibrium conditions prevail in the market.

7. A manufacturer has fixed costs of \$200 each week, and the variable costs per unit can be expressed by the function, VC = $2Q - 36$.

(a) Find an expression for the total cost function and deduce that the average cost function is given by

$$AC = \frac{200}{Q} + 2Q - 36$$

(b) Find the stationary point of this function and show that this is a minimum.

(c) Verify that, at this stationary point, average cost is the same as marginal cost.

8. A firm's short-run production function is given by

$$Q = 3\sqrt{L}$$

where L is the number of units of labour.

If the price per unit sold is \$50 and the price per unit of labour is \$10, find the value of L needed to maximise profits. You may assume that the firm sells all that it produces, and you can ignore all other costs.

9. The average cost per person of hiring a tour guide on a week's river cruise for a maximum party size of 30 people is given by

$$AC = 3Q^2 - 192Q + 3500 \qquad (0 < Q \le 30)$$

Find the minimum average cost for the trip.

10. An electronic components firm launches a new product on 1 January. During the following year a rough estimate of the number of orders, S, received t days after the launch is given by

$$S = t^2 - 0.002t^3$$

What is the maximum number of orders received on any one day of the year?

Exercise 4.6*

1. A firm's demand function is

    $P = 60 - 0.5Q$

    If fixed costs are 10 and variable costs are $Q + 3$ per unit, find the maximum profit.

2. Show that all of the following functions have a stationary point at $x = 0$. Verify in each case that $f''(0) = 0$. Classify these points by producing a rough sketch of each function.

    (a) $f(x) = x^3$ **(b)** $f(x) = x^4$ **(c)** $f(x) = -x^6$

3. If fixed costs are 15 and the variable costs are $2Q$ per unit, write down expressions for TC, AC and MC. Find the value of Q which minimises AC and verify that AC = MC at this point.

4. Daily sales, S, of a new product for the first two weeks after the launch is modelled by

    $S = t^3 - 24t^2 + 180t + 60$ $(0 \le t \le 13)$

    where t is the number of days.

    (a) Find and classify the stationary points of this function.

    (b) Sketch a graph of S against t on the interval $0 \le t \le 13$.

    (c) Find the maximum and minimum daily sales during the period between $t = 5$ and $t = 9$.

5. If the demand function of a good is

    $P = \sqrt{(1000 - 4Q)}$

    find the value of Q which maximises total revenue.

6. A firm's total cost and demand functions are given by

    $TC = Q^2 + 50Q + 10$ and $P = 200 - 4Q$

    respectively.

    (a) Find the level of output needed to maximise the firm's profit.

    (b) The government imposes a tax of $\$t$ per good. If the firm adds this tax to its costs and continues to maximise profit, show that the price of the good increases by two-fifths of the tax, irrespective of the value of t.

7. Given that the cubic function $f(x) = x^3 + ax^2 + bx + c$ has a stationary point at $(2, 5)$ and that it passes through $(1, 3)$, find the values of a, b and c.

8. The total revenue function of a good is given by:

    $TR = 0.2Q^3$ on $0 \le Q \le 5$

    $TR = -4Q^2 + 55Q - 150$ on $5 \le Q \le 10$

    (a) Sketch a graph of TR against Q on the interval $0 \le Q \le 10$.

    (b) Find the maximum revenue and the value of Q at which it is achieved.

    (c) For what value of Q is the marginal revenue a maximum?

SECTION 4.7

Further optimisation of economic functions

Objectives

At the end of this section you should be able to:

- Show that, at the point of maximum profit, marginal revenue equals marginal cost.
- Show that, at the point of maximum profit, the slope of the marginal revenue curve is less than that of marginal cost.
- Maximise profits of a firm with and without price discrimination in different markets.
- Show that, at the point of maximum average product of labour, average product of labour equals marginal product of labour.
- Derive a formula for the economic order quantity in stock control.

The previous section demonstrated how mathematics can be used to optimise particular economic functions. Those examples suggested two important results:

1. If a firm maximises profit, then MR = MC.
2. If a firm maximises average product of labour, then $AP_L = MP_L$.

Although these results were found to hold for all of the examples considered in Section 4.6, it does not necessarily follow that the results are always true. The aim of this section is to prove these assertions without reference to specific functions and hence to demonstrate their generality.

Advice

You may prefer to skip these proofs at a first reading and just concentrate on the worked example (as well as Practice Problem 2 and Question 3 in Exercise 4.7*) on price discrimination.

Justification of the first result turns out to be really quite easy. Profit, π, is defined to be the difference between total revenue, TR, and total cost, TC: that is,

$$\pi = TR - TC$$

To find the stationary points of π we differentiate with respect to Q and equate to zero: that is,

$$\frac{d\pi}{dQ} = \frac{d(TR)}{dQ} - \frac{d(TC)}{dQ} = 0$$

where we have used the difference rule to differentiate the right-hand side. In Section 4.3 we defined

$$MR = \frac{d(TR)}{dQ} \text{ and } MC = \frac{d(TC)}{dQ}$$

so the previous equation is equivalent to

$$MR - MC = 0$$

and so MR = MC as required.

The stationary points of the profit function can therefore be found by sketching the MR and MC curves on the same diagram and inspecting the points of intersection. Figure 4.26 shows typical marginal revenue and marginal cost curves. The result

$$MR = MC$$

holds for any stationary point. Consequently, if this equation has more than one solution, then we need some further information before we can decide on the profit-maximising level of output. In Figure 4.26 there are two points of intersection, Q_1 and Q_2, and it turns out (as you discovered in Practice Problem 3 and Question 5 of Exercise 4.6 in the previous section) that one of these is a maximum while the other is a minimum. Obviously, in any actual example, we can classify these points by evaluating second-order derivatives. However, it would be nice to make this decision just by inspecting the graphs of marginal revenue and marginal cost. To see how this can be done, let us return to the equation

$$\frac{d\pi}{dQ} = MR - MC$$

and differentiate again with respect to Q to get

$$\frac{d^2\pi}{dQ^2} = \frac{d(MR)}{dQ} - \frac{d(MC)}{dQ}$$

Now, if $d^2\pi/dQ^2 < 0$, then the profit is a maximum. This will be so when

$$\frac{d(MR)}{dQ} < \frac{d(MC)}{dQ}$$

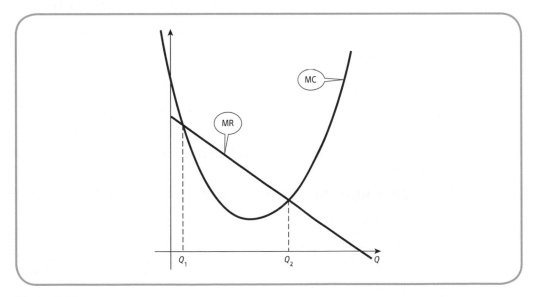

Figure 4.26

that is, when the slope of the marginal revenue curve is less than the slope of the marginal cost curve.

Looking at Figure 4.26, we deduce that this criterion is true at Q_2, so this must be the desired level of output needed to maximise profit. Note also from Figure 4.26 that the statement 'the slope of the marginal revenue curve is less than the slope of the marginal cost curve' is equivalent to saying that 'the marginal cost curve cuts the marginal revenue curve from below'. It is this latter form that is often quoted in economics textbooks. A similar argument shows that, at a minimum point, the marginal cost curve cuts the marginal revenue curve from above, and so we can deduce that profit is a minimum at Q_1 in Figure 4.26. In practice, the task of sketching the graphs of MR and MC and reading off the coordinates of the points of intersection is not an attractive one, particularly if MR and MC are complicated functions. However, it might turn out that MR and MC are both linear, in which case a graphical approach is feasible.

Practice Problem

1. A monopolist's demand function is

    $$P = 25 - 0.5Q$$

    The fixed costs of production are 7 and the variable costs are $Q + 1$ per unit.

    (a) Show that

    $$TR = 25Q - 0.5Q^2 \text{ and } TC = Q^2 + Q + 7$$

    and deduce the corresponding expressions for MR and MC.

    (b) Sketch the graphs of MR and MC on the same diagram and hence find the value of Q which maximises profit.

Quite often a firm identifies more than one market in which it wishes to sell its goods. For example, a firm might decide to export goods to several countries and demand conditions are likely to be different in each one. The firm may be able to take advantage of this and increase overall profit by charging different prices in each country. The theoretical result 'marginal revenue equals marginal cost' can be applied in each market separately to find the optimal pricing policy.

Example

A firm is allowed to charge different prices for its domestic and industrial customers. If P_1 and Q_1 denote the price and demand for the domestic market, then the demand equation is

$$P_1 + Q_1 = 500$$

If P_2 and Q_2 denote the price and demand for the industrial market, then the demand equation is

$$2P_2 + 3Q_2 = 720$$

The total cost function is

$$TC = 50\,000 + 20Q$$

where $Q = Q_1 + Q_2$. Determine the prices (in dollars) that the firm should charge to maximise profits:

(a) with price discrimination;

(b) without price discrimination.

Compare the profits obtained in parts (a) and (b).

Solution

(a) The important thing to notice is that the total cost function is independent of the market and so marginal costs are the same in each case. In fact, since

$$TC = 50\ 000 + 20Q$$

we have MC = 20. All we have to do to maximise profits is to find an expression for the marginal revenue for each market and to equate this to the constant value of marginal cost.

Domestic market

The demand equation

$$P_1 + Q_1 = 500$$

rearranges to give

$$P_1 = 500 - Q_1$$

so the total revenue function for this market is

$$TR_1 = (500 - Q_1)Q_1 = 500Q_1 - Q_1^2$$

Hence

$$MR_1 = \frac{d(TR_1)}{dQ_1} = 500 - 2Q_1$$

For maximum profit

$$MR_1 = MC$$

so

$$500 - 2Q_1 = 20$$

which has solution $Q_1 = 240$. The corresponding price is found by substituting this value into the demand equation to get

$$P_1 = 500 - 240 = \$260$$

To maximise profit the firm should charge its domestic customers \$260 per good.

Industrial market

The demand equation

$$2P_2 + 3Q_2 = 720$$

rearranges to give

$$P_2 = 360 - {}^3/_2Q_2$$

so the total revenue function for this market is

$$TR_2 = (360 - {}^3/_2Q_2)Q_2 = 360Q - {}^3/_2Q_2^2$$

→

Hence

$$MR_2 = \frac{d(TR_2)}{dQ_2} = 360 - 3Q_2$$

For maximum profit

$$MR_2 = MC$$

so

$$360 - 3Q_2 = 20$$

which has solution $Q_2 = 340/3$. The corresponding price is obtained by substituting this value into the demand equation to get

$$P_2 = 360 - \frac{3}{2}\left(\frac{340}{3}\right) = \$190$$

To maximise profits the firm should charge its industrial customers \$190 per good, which is lower than the price charged to its domestic customers.

(b) If there is no price discrimination, then $P_1 = P_2 = P$, say, and the demand functions for the domestic and industrial markets become

$$P + Q_1 = 500$$

and

$$2P + 3Q_2 = 720$$

respectively. We can use these to deduce a single demand equation for the combined market. We need to relate the price, P, of each good to the total demand, $Q = Q_1 + Q_2$.

This can be done by rearranging the given demand equations for Q_1 and Q_2 and then adding. For the domestic market

$$Q_1 = 500 - P$$

and for the industrial market

$$Q_2 = 240 - \tfrac{2}{3}P$$

Hence

$$Q = Q_1 + Q_2 = 740 - \tfrac{5}{3}P$$

The demand equation for the combined market is therefore

$$Q + \tfrac{5}{3}P = 740$$

The usual procedure for profit maximisation can now be applied. This demand equation rearranges to give

$$P = 444 - \tfrac{3}{5}Q$$

enabling the total revenue function to be written as

$$TR = \left(444 - \frac{3}{5}Q\right)Q = 444Q - \frac{3Q^2}{5}$$

Hence

$$MR = \frac{d(TR)}{dQ} = 444 - \frac{6}{5}Q$$

For maximum profit

$$MR = MC$$

so

$$444 - \frac{6}{5}Q = 20$$

which has solution $Q = 1060/3$. The corresponding price is found by substituting this value into the demand equation to get

$$P = 444 - \frac{3}{5}\left(\frac{1060}{3}\right) = \$232$$

To maximise profit without discrimination, the firm needs to charge a uniform price of \$232 for each good. Notice that this price lies between the prices charged to its domestic and industrial customers with discrimination.

To evaluate the profit under each policy we need to work out the total revenue and subtract the total cost. In part (a) the firm sells 240 goods at \$260 each in the domestic market and sells 340/3 goods at \$190 each in the industrial market, so the total revenue received is

$$240 \times 260 + \frac{340}{3} \times 190 = \$83\ 933.33$$

The total number of goods produced is

$$240 + \frac{340}{3} = \frac{1060}{3}$$

so the total cost is

$$50\ 000 + 20 \times \frac{1060}{3} = \$57\ 066.67$$

Therefore, the profit with price discrimination is

$$83\ 933.33 - 57\ 066.67 = \$26\ 866.67$$

In part (b) the firm sells 1060/3 goods at \$232 each, so total revenue is

$$\frac{1060}{3} \times 232 = \$81\ 973.33$$

Now the total number of goods produced under both pricing policies is the same: that is, 1060/3. Consequently, the total cost of production in part (b) must be the same as part (a): that is,

$$TC = \$57\ 066.67$$

The profit without price discrimination is

$$81\ 973.33 - 57\ 066.67 = \$24\ 906.66$$

As expected, the profits are higher with discrimination than without.

Practice Problem

2. A firm has the possibility of charging different prices in its domestic and foreign markets. The corresponding demand equations are given by

$$Q_1 = 300 - P_1$$
$$Q_2 = 400 - 2P_2$$

The total cost function is

$$TC = 5000 + 100Q$$

where $Q = Q_1 + Q_2$.

Determine the prices (in dollars) that the firm should charge to maximise profits

(a) with price discrimination;

(b) without price discrimination.

Compare the profits obtained in parts (a) and (b).

In the previous example and in Practice Problem 2 we assumed that the marginal costs were the same in each market. The level of output that maximises profit with price discrimination was found by equating marginal revenue to this common value of marginal cost. It follows that the marginal revenue must be the same in each market. In symbols,

$$MR_1 = MC \text{ and } MR_2 = MC$$

so

$$MR_1 = MR_2$$

This fact is obvious on economic grounds. If it were not true, then the firm's policy would be to increase sales in the market where marginal revenue is higher and to decrease sales by the same amount in the market where the marginal revenue is lower. The effect would be to increase revenue while keeping costs fixed, thereby raising profit. This property leads to an interesting result connecting price, P, with elasticity of demand, E. In Section 4.5 we derived the formula

$$MR = P\left(1 + \frac{1}{E}\right)$$

If we let the price elasticity of demand in two markets be denoted by E_1 and E_2 corresponding to prices P_1 and P_2, then the equation

$$MR_1 = MR_2$$

becomes

$$P_1\left(1 + \frac{1}{E_1}\right) = P_2\left(1 + \frac{1}{E_2}\right)$$

This equation holds whenever a firm chooses its prices P_1 and P_2 to maximise profits in each market. Note that if $|E_1| < |E_2|$, then this equation can be true only if $P_1 > P_2$. In other words, the firm charges the higher price in the market where the magnitude of the elasticity of demand is lower.

Practice Problem

3. Calculate the price elasticity of demand at the point of maximum profit for each of the demand functions given in Practice Problem 2 with price discrimination. Verify that the firm charges the higher price in the market with the lower value of $|E|$.

The previous discussion concentrated on profit. We now turn our attention to average product of labour and prove result (2) stated at the beginning of this section. This concept is defined by

$$\text{AP}_L = \frac{Q}{L}$$

where Q is output and L is labour. The maximisation of AP_L is a little more complicated than before, since it is necessary to use the quotient rule to differentiate this function. In the notation of Section 4.4 we write

$$u = Q \quad \text{and} \quad v = L$$

so

$$\frac{\mathrm{d}u}{\mathrm{d}L} = \frac{\mathrm{d}Q}{\mathrm{d}L} = \text{MP}_L \quad \text{and} \quad \frac{\mathrm{d}v}{\mathrm{d}L} = \frac{\mathrm{d}L}{\mathrm{d}L} = 1$$

where we have used the fact that the derivative of output with respect to labour is the marginal product of labour.

The quotient rule gives

$$\frac{\mathrm{d}(\text{AP}_L)}{\mathrm{d}L} = \frac{v\,\mathrm{d}u\,/\,\mathrm{d}L - u\,\mathrm{d}v\,/\,\mathrm{d}L}{v^2}$$

$$= \frac{L(\text{MP}_L) - Q(1)}{L^2}$$

$$= \frac{\text{MP}_L - Q\,/\,L}{L} \qquad \text{\small divide top and bottom by } L$$

$$= \frac{\text{MP}_L - \text{AP}_L}{L} \qquad \text{\small by definition, } AP_L = \frac{Q}{L}$$

At a stationary point

$$\frac{\mathrm{d}(\text{AP}_L)}{\mathrm{d}L} = 0$$

Hence

$$\text{MP}_L = \text{AP}_L$$

as required.

This analysis shows that, at a stationary point of the average product of labour function, the marginal product of labour equals the average product of labour. The above argument provides a formal proof that this result is true for any average product of labour function. Figure 4.27

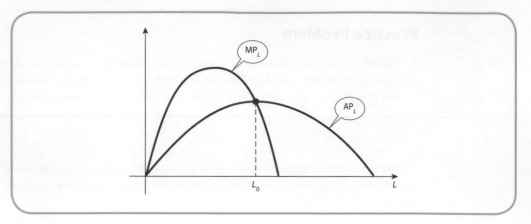

Figure 4.27

shows typical average and marginal product functions. Note that the two curves intersect at the peak of the AP_L curve. To the left of this point the AP_L function is increasing, so that

$$\frac{d(AP_L)}{dL} > 0$$

Now, we have just seen that

$$\frac{d(AP_L)}{dL} = \frac{MP_L - AP_L}{L}$$

so we deduce that, to the left of the maximum, $MP_L > AP_L$. In other words, in this region the graph of marginal product of labour lies above that of average product of labour. Similarly, to the right of the maximum, AP_L is decreasing, so that

$$\frac{d(AP_L)}{dL} < 0$$

and hence $MP_L < AP_L$. The graph of marginal product of labour therefore lies below that of average product of labour in this region.

We deduce that if the stationary point is a maximum, then the MP_L curve cuts the AP_L curve from above. A similar argument can be used for any average function. The particular case of the average cost function is investigated in Question 8 in Exercise 4.7*.

We conclude this section by investigating a simple model of inventory control in business. Most firms need to buy and store goods during the year. A furniture manufacturer has to obtain wood and other raw materials to make its goods, and a grocery store needs to have a regular supply of frozen food to store in its freezers. Management needs to make decisions about when to order more stock and the size of each order. Let us suppose that the annual demand is D items and that the firm orders Q of these at regular intervals during the year. For example, if the demand is 12 000, the firm might place an order for 1000 items each month. Alternatively, the firm could increase the order size to 3000 items and thereby reduce the number of orders to just 12 000/3000 = 4 times a year. In general, orders are made D/Q times a year.

There are many costs incurred in inventory control (including opportunity costs), but we shall consider just two: ordering costs and holding costs. We consider each of these in turn.

There will always be a cost of raising an order which includes a fixed administrative charge, delivery charge and the cost of setting up a production run. If the cost of placing each order is R, then the total cost is found by multiplying R by the number of orders, D/Q, so

$$\text{total annual order cost} = \frac{DR}{Q}$$

The other major cost incurred is the stockholding cost. This includes the cost of storage, insurance and interest lost on the capital used to buy these goods waiting to be sold. In the simplest model we will assume that the level of stock falls at a constant rate throughout the year and that the firm waits until the stock levels are zero before reordering. If we further assume that the stock is replenished instantly, then the variation of stock levels during the course of a year would be modelled by the pattern shown in Figure 4.28. In practice this may not occur. There are likely to be seasonal variations in demand, so the gradients of each section of the graph may vary from one cycle to the next, and demand may not even be linear. Also, it is not good practice to wait until shelves are empty before reordering stock and, since goods do not arrive instantly, firms build in a lead time to allow for this. However, as a first model of the real situation, we will assume that stock levels follow the pattern shown in Figure 4.28.

In each period the average number of items stored is $Q/2$, and, since this pattern is replicated throughout the year, the average number of items held in store each year is $Q/2$. If it costs $H to store one item for one year, then the total annual holding cost is

$$H \times \frac{Q}{2} = \frac{HQ}{2}$$

If C denotes the total cost per annum, then we can add the order and holding costs to deduce that

$$C = \frac{DR}{Q} + \frac{HQ}{2}$$

Figure 4.29 shows a graph of order cost, holding cost and total cost plotted against Q. As expected, to cut down on the order costs it is best to make Q as large as possible so that you don't have to incur the overheads for ordering the goods. On the other hand, to minimise holding costs you want to make Q as small as possible. These conflicting interests lead to an overall single minimum as shown by the graph of C in Figure 4.29.

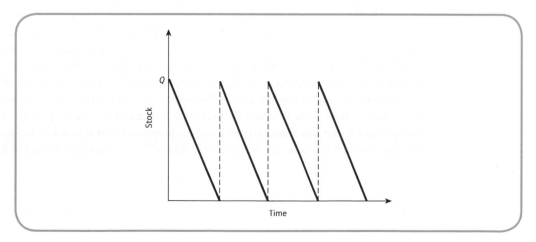

Figure 4.28

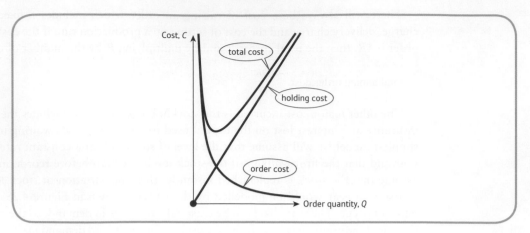

Figure 4.29

At a stationary point, $\dfrac{dC}{dQ} = 0$, so we need to differentiate

$$C = (DR)Q^{-1} + \frac{HQ}{2}$$

with respect to Q. The remaining letters, D, R and H, are all constants so

$$\frac{dC}{dQ} = -(DR)Q^{-2} + \frac{H}{2} = \frac{-DR}{Q^2} + \frac{H}{2}$$

The stationary point can be found by solving

$$\frac{H}{2} = \frac{DR}{Q^2}$$

for Q:

$$Q^2 = \frac{2DR}{H}$$

so

$$Q = \sqrt{\frac{2DR}{H}}$$

This value of Q is called the **economic order quantity** (EOQ). It provides a formula for the optimal order size in terms of annual demand, D, cost of placing each order, R, and annual cost of holding an item in stock, H. If the order exceeds EOQ, then you order less frequently and, although the ordering costs decrease, the holding costs rise more than this. On the other hand, if the order is below the EOQ, then you order more frequently and, although the holding costs decrease, this is offset by higher ordering costs. The graph shown in Figure 4.29 shows clearly that this stationary point is a minimum, but it is possible to show this by investigating the sign of the second-order derivative, d^2C/dQ^2 (see Question 5 in Exercise 4.7*).

> **Key Term**
>
> **Economic order quantity**   The quantity of a product that should be ordered so as to minimise the total cost that includes ordering costs and holding costs.

Exercise 4.7*

1. A firm's demand function is

   $$P = aQ + b \ (a < 0, b > 0)$$

   Fixed costs are c and variable costs per unit are d.

   (a) Write down general expressions for TR and TC.

   (b) By differentiating the expressions in part (a), deduce MR and MC.

   (c) Use your answers to (b) to show that profit, π, is maximised when

   $$Q = \frac{d - b}{2a}$$

2. (a) In Section 4.5 the following relationship between marginal revenue, MR, and price elasticity of demand, E, was derived:

   $$\text{MR} = P\left(1 + \frac{1}{E}\right)$$

   Use this result to show that at the point of maximum total revenue, $E = -1$.

   (b) Verify the result of part (a) for the demand function

   $$2P + 3Q = 60$$

3. The demand functions for a firm's domestic and foreign markets are

   $$P_1 = 50 - 5Q_1$$
   $$P_2 = 30 - 4Q_2$$

   and the total cost function is

   $$\text{TC} = 10 + 10Q$$

   where $Q = Q_1 + Q_2$. Determine the prices needed to maximise profit

   (a) with price discrimination;

   (b) without price discrimination.

   Compare the profits obtained in parts (a) and (b).

4. Show that if the marginal cost curve cuts the marginal revenue curve from above, then profit is a minimum.

5. (a) Find an expression for the second-order derivative, $\mathrm{d}^2C/\mathrm{d}Q^2$, of the cost function

   $$C = \frac{DR}{Q} + \frac{HQ}{2}$$

   and hence show that the economic order quantity, $Q = \sqrt{\dfrac{2DR}{H}}$, is a minimum point.

   (b) Obtain a simplified expression for the minimum cost.

6. (a) The annual demand of a good is 2000 units, the fixed cost of placing an order is $40 and the annual cost of storing an item is $100. Assuming that the same order is placed at regular intervals throughout the year, and that the firm waits for stock levels to reduce to zero before ordering new stock, work out how many items should be ordered each time to minimise total costs. What is the minimum total cost?

(b) Repeat part (a) if the annual cost of storage costs falls to $64.

(c) Repeat part (a) if the fixed cost of placing an order rises to $160.

(d) What effect do changes in order costs and holding costs have on the minimum total cost?

7. If the total cost function $TC = aQ^2 + bQ + c$, write down an expression for the average cost function, AC. Show that AC is a minimum when $Q = \sqrt{\dfrac{c}{a}}$ and find the corresponding value of AC.

8. (a) Show that, at a stationary point of an average cost function, average cost equals marginal cost.

(b) Show that if the marginal cost curve cuts the average cost curve from below, then average cost is a minimum.

9. In a competitive market the equilibrium price, P, and quantity, Q, are found by setting $Q_S = Q_D = Q$ in the supply and demand equations

$$P = aQ_S + b \ (a > 0, b > 0)$$
$$P = -cQ_D + d \ (c > 0, d > 0)$$

If the government levies an excise tax, t, per unit, show that

$$Q = \frac{d - b - t}{a + c}$$

Deduce that the government's tax revenue, $T = tQ$, is maximised by taking

$$t = \frac{d - b}{2}$$

SECTION 4.8

The derivative of the exponential and natural logarithm functions

Objectives

At the end of this section you should be able to:

- Differentiate the exponential function.
- Differentiate the natural logarithm function.
- Use the chain, product and quotient rules to differentiate combinations of these functions.
- Appreciate the use of the exponential function in economic modelling.

In this section we investigate the derived functions associated with the exponential and natural logarithm functions, e^x and $\ln x$. The approach that we adopt is similar to that used in Section 4.1. The derivative of a function determines the slope of the graph of a function. Consequently, to discover how to differentiate an unfamiliar function, we first produce an accurate sketch and then measure the slopes of the tangents at selected points.

Advice

The functions e^x and $\ln x$ were first introduced in Section 2.4. You might find it useful to remind yourself how these functions are defined before working through the rest of the current section.

Figure 4.30 shows a sketch of the exponential function, e^x, based on the table of values:

x	−2.0	−1.5	−1.0	−0.5	0.0	0.5	1.0	1.5
$f(x)$	0.14	0.22	0.37	0.61	1.00	1.65	2.72	4.48

From the graph we see that the slopes of the tangents at $x = -1$, $x = 0$ and $x = 1$ are

$$f'(-1) = \frac{0.20}{0.50} = 0.4$$

$$f'(0) = \frac{0.50}{0.50} = 1.0$$

$$f'(1) = \frac{1.35}{0.50} = 2.7$$

These results are obtained by measurement and so are quoted to only one decimal place. We cannot really expect to achieve any greater accuracy using this approach.

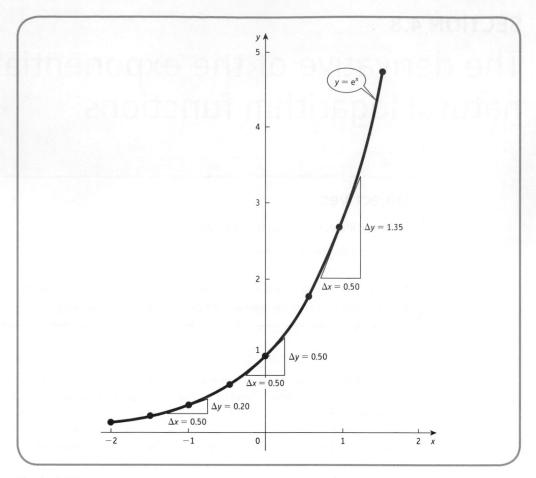

Figure 4.30

The values of x, $f(x)$ and $f'(x)$ are summarised in the following table. The values of $f(x)$ are rounded to one decimal place in order to compare with the graphical estimates of $f'(x)$.

x	−1	0	1
$f(x)$	0.4	1.0	2.7
$f'(x)$	0.4	1.0	2.7

Notice that the values of $f(x)$ and $f'(x)$ are identical to within the accuracy quoted.

These results suggest that the slope of the graph at each point is the same as the function value at that point: that is, e^x differentiates to itself. Symbolically,

if $f(x) = e^x$ then $f'(x) = e^x$

or, equivalently,

if $y = e^x$ then $\dfrac{dy}{dx} = e^x$

Practice Problem

1. Use your calculator to complete the following table of function values and hence sketch an accurate graph of $f(x) = \ln x$:

x	0.50	1.00	1.50	2.00	2.50	3.00	3.50	4.00
$f(x)$			0.41				1.25	

Draw the tangents to the graph at $x = 1$, 2 and 3. Hence estimate the values of $f'(1)$, $f'(2)$ and $f'(3)$. Suggest a general formula for the derived function $f'(x)$.

[Hint: for the last part you may find it helpful to rewrite your estimates of $f'(x)$ as simple fractions.]

In fact, it is possible to prove that, for any value of the constant m,

$$\text{if} \quad y = e^{mx} \quad \text{then} \quad \frac{dy}{dx} = me^{mx}$$

and

$$\text{if} \quad y = \ln mx \quad \text{then} \quad \frac{dy}{dx} = \frac{1}{x}$$

In particular, we see by setting $m = 1$ that

e^x differentiates to e^x

and that

$\ln x$ differentiates to $\dfrac{1}{x}$

which agree with our practical investigations.

Example

Differentiate

(a) $y = e^{2x}$

(b) $y = e^{-7x}$

(c) $y = \ln 5x \ (x > 0)$

(d) $y = \ln 559x \ (x > 0)$

Solution

(a) Setting $m = 2$ in the general formula shows that

$$\text{if} \quad y = e^{2x} \quad \text{then} \quad \frac{dy}{dx} = 2e^{2x}$$

Notice that when exponential functions are differentiated, the power itself does not change. All that happens is that the coefficient of x comes down to the front.

(b) Setting $m = -7$ in the general formula shows that

$$\text{if} \quad y = e^{-7x} \quad \text{then} \quad \frac{dy}{dx} = -7e^{-7x}$$

(c) Setting $m = 5$ in the general formula shows that

$$\text{if} \quad y = \ln 5x \quad \text{then} \quad \frac{dy}{dx} = \frac{1}{x}$$

Notice the restriction $x > 0$ stated in the question. This is needed to ensure that we do not attempt to take the logarithm of a negative number, which is impossible.

(d) Setting $m = 559$ in the general formula shows that

$$\text{if} \quad y = \ln 559x \quad \text{then} \quad \frac{dy}{dx} = \frac{1}{x}$$

Notice that we get the same answer as part (c). The derivative of the natural logarithm function does not depend on the coefficient of x. This fact may seem rather strange, but it is easily accounted for. The first rule of logarithms shows that $\ln 559x$ is the same as

$$\ln 559 + \ln x$$

The first term is merely a constant and so differentiates to zero, and the second term differentiates to $1/x$.

Practice Problem

2. Differentiate

(a) $y = e^{3x}$ **(b)** $y = e^{-x}$ **(c)** $y = \ln 3x \ (x > 0)$ **(d)** $y = \ln 51\ 234x \ (x > 0)$

The chain rule can be used to explain what happens to the m when differentiating e^{mx}. The outer function is the exponential, which differentiates to itself, and the inner function is mx, which differentiates to m. Hence, by the chain rule,

$$\text{if} \quad y = e^{mx} \quad \text{then} \quad \frac{dy}{dx} = e^{mx} \times m = me^{mx}$$

Similarly, noting that the natural logarithm function differentiates to the reciprocal function,

$$\text{if} \quad y = \ln mx \quad \text{then} \quad \frac{dy}{dx} = \frac{1}{mx} \times m = \frac{1}{x}$$

The chain, product and quotient rules can be used to differentiate more complicated functions involving e^x and $\ln x$.

Example

Differentiate

(a) $y = x^3 e^{2x}$ **(b)** $y = \ln(x^2 + 2x + 1)$ **(c)** $y = \dfrac{e^{3x}}{x^2 + 2}$

Solution

(a) The function $x^3 e^{2x}$ involves the product of two simpler functions, x^3 and e^{2x}, so we need to use the product rule to differentiate it. Putting

$$u = x^3 \quad \text{and} \quad v = e^{2x}$$

gives

$$\frac{du}{dx} = 3x^2 \quad \text{and} \quad \frac{dv}{dx} = 2e^{2x}$$

By the product rule,

$$\frac{dy}{dx} = u\frac{dv}{dx} + v\frac{du}{dx} = x^3\left[2e^{2x}\right] + e^{2x}\left[3x^2\right] = 2x^3 e^{2x} + 3x^2 e^{2x}$$

There is a common factor of $x^2 e^{2x}$, which goes into the first term $2x$ times and into the second term 3 times. Hence

$$\frac{dy}{dx} = x^2 e^{2x}(2x + 3)$$

(b) The expression $\ln(x^2 + 2x + 1)$ can be regarded as a function of a function, so we can use the chain rule to differentiate it. We first differentiate the outer log function to get

$$\frac{1}{x^2 + 2x + 1}$$

and then multiply by the derivative of the inner function, $x^2 + 2x + 1$, which is $2x + 2$. Hence

$$\frac{dy}{dx} = \frac{2x + 2}{x^2 + 2x + 1}$$

(c) The function

$$\frac{e^{3x}}{x^2 + 2}$$

is the quotient of the simpler functions

$$u = e^{3x} \quad \text{and} \quad v = x^2 + 2$$

for which

$$\frac{du}{dx} = 3e^{3x} \quad \text{and} \quad \frac{dv}{dx} = 2x$$

By the quotient rule,

$$\frac{dy}{dx} = \frac{v\dfrac{du}{dx} - u\dfrac{dv}{dx}}{v^2} = \frac{(x^2 + 2)(3e^{3x}) - e^{3x}(2x)}{(x^2 + 2)^2} = \frac{e^{3x}[3(x^2 + 2) - 2x]}{(x^2 + 2)^2} = \frac{e^{3x}(3x^2 - 2x + 6)}{(x^2 + 2)^2}$$

Practice Problem

3. Differentiate

(a) $y = x^4 \ln x$ (b) $y = e^{x^2}$ (c) $y = \dfrac{\ln x}{x + 2}$

Notice the effect that the chain rule has on the derivative of an exponential function such as $y = e^{x^2}$ which you differentiated in part (b) of Practice Problem 3. In general:

If $y = e^{u(x)}$ then $\dfrac{dy}{dx} = e^{u(x)} \times u'(x)$

All you have to do is to write down the original function and then multiply by the derivative of the exponent. To differentiate $y = e^{x^2}$, first write down e^{x^2} and then multiply it by

$\dfrac{d}{dx}(x^2) = 2x$ to get $2xe^{x^2}$.

Advice

If you ever need to differentiate a function of the form:

ln (an inner function involving products, quotients or powers of x)

then it is usually quicker to use the rules of logs to expand the expression before you begin. The three rules are

    Rule 1 $\ln(x \times y) = \ln x + \ln y$

    Rule 2 $\ln(x \div y) = \ln x - \ln y$

    Rule 3 $\ln x^m = m \ln x$

The following example shows how to apply this 'trick' in practice.

Example

Differentiate

(a) $y = \ln(x(x + 1)^4)$ (b) $y = \ln\left(\dfrac{x}{\sqrt{(x + 5)}}\right)$

Solution

(a) From rule 1

    $\ln(x(x + 1)^4) = \ln x + \ln(x + 1)^4$

which can be simplified further using rule 3 to give

    $y = \ln x + 4 \ln(x + 1)$

Differentiation of this new expression is simple. We see immediately that

    $\dfrac{dy}{dx} = \dfrac{1}{x} + \dfrac{4}{x + 1}$

If desired, the final answer can be put over a common denominator

$$\frac{1}{x} + \frac{4}{x+1} = \frac{(x+1)+4x}{x(x+1)} = \frac{5x+1}{x(x+1)}$$

(b) The quickest way to differentiate

$$y = \ln\left(\frac{x}{\sqrt{(x+5)}}\right)$$

is to expand first to get

$$y = \ln x - \ln(x+5)^{1/2} \quad \text{(rule 2)}$$

$$= \ln x - \frac{1}{2}\ln(x+5) \quad \text{(rule 3)}$$

Again this expression is easy to differentiate:

$$\frac{dy}{dx} = \frac{1}{x} - \frac{1}{2(x+5)}$$

If desired, this can be written as a single fraction:

$$\frac{1}{x} - \frac{1}{2(x+5)} = \frac{2(x+5)-x}{2x(x+5)} = \frac{x+10}{2x(x+5)}$$

Practice Problem

4. Differentiate the following functions by first expanding each expression using the rules of logs:

(a) $y = \ln(x^3(x+2)^4)$ **(b)** $y = \ln\left(\frac{x^2}{2x+3}\right)$

Exponential and natural logarithm functions provide good mathematical models in many areas of economics, and we conclude this chapter with some illustrative examples.

Example

A firm's short-run production function is given by

$$Q = L^2 e^{-0.01L}$$

Find the value of L that maximises the average product of labour.

Solution

The average product of labour is given by

$$AP_L = \frac{Q}{L} = \frac{L^2 e^{-0.01L}}{L} = Le^{-0.01L}$$

To maximise this function we adopt the strategy described in Section 4.6.

Step 1

At a stationary point

$$\frac{d(AP_L)}{dL} = 0$$

To differentiate $Le^{-0.01L}$, we use the product rule. If

$$u = L \quad \text{and} \quad v = e^{-0.01L}$$

then

$$\frac{du}{dL} = 1 \quad \text{and} \quad \frac{dv}{dL} = -0.01e^{-0.01L}$$

e^{mx} differentiates to me^{mx}

By the product rule,

$$\frac{d(AP_L)}{dL} = u\frac{dv}{dL} + v\frac{du}{dL} = L(-0.01e^{-0.01L}) + e^{-0.01L} = (1 - 0.01L)e^{-0.01L}$$

We know that a negative exponential is never equal to zero. (Although $e^{-0.01L}$ gets ever closer to zero as L increases, it never actually reaches it for finite values of L.) Hence the only way that

$$(1 - 0.01L)e^{-0.01L}$$

can equal zero is when

$$1 - 0.01L = 0$$

which has the solution $L = 100$.

Step 2

To show that this is a maximum we need to differentiate a second time. To do this we apply the product rule to

$$(1 - 0.01L)e^{-0.01L}$$

taking

$$u = 1 - 0.01L \quad \text{and} \quad v = e^{-0.01L}$$

for which

$$\frac{du}{dL} = -0.01 \quad \text{and} \quad \frac{dv}{dL} = -0.01e^{-0.01L}$$

Hence

$$\frac{d^2(AP_L)}{dL^2} = u\frac{dv}{dL} + v\frac{du}{dL} = (1 - 0.01L)(-0.01e^{-0.01L}) + e^{-0.01L}(-0.01) = (-0.02 + 0.0001L)e^{-0.01L}$$

Finally, putting $L = 100$ into this gives

$$\frac{d^2(AP_L)}{dL^2} = -0.0037$$

The fact that this is negative shows that the stationary point, $L = 100$, is indeed a maximum.

Practice Problem

5. The demand function of a good is given by

$$Q = 1000e^{-0.2P}$$

If fixed costs are 100 and the variable costs are 2 per unit, show that the profit function is given by

$$\pi = 1000Pe^{-0.2P} - 2000e^{-0.2P} - 100$$

Find the price needed to maximise profit.

Example

A firm estimates that the total revenue received from the sale of Q goods is given by

$$TR = \ln(1 + 1000Q^2)$$

Calculate the marginal revenue when $Q = 10$.

Solution

The marginal revenue function is obtained by differentiating the total revenue function. To differentiate $\ln(1 + 1000Q^2)$, we use the chain rule. We first differentiate the outer log function to get

$$\frac{1}{1 + 1000Q^2}$$

natural logs differentiate to reciprocals

and then multiply by the derivative of the inner function, $1 + 1000Q^2$, to get $2000Q$. Hence

$$MR = \frac{d(TR)}{dQ} = \frac{2000Q}{1 + 1000Q^2}$$

At $Q = 10$,

$$MR = \frac{2000(10)}{1 + 1000(10)^2} = 0.2$$

Practice Problem

6. If the demand equation is

$$P = 200 - 40 \ln(Q + 1)$$

calculate the price elasticity of demand when $Q = 20$.

Exercise 4.8

1. Write down the derivative of

    (a) $y = e^{6x}$ (b) $y = e^{-342x}$ (c) $y = 2e^{-x} + 4e^{x}$ (d) $y = 10e^{4x} - 2x^2 + 7$

2. If \$4000 is saved in an account offering a return of 4% compounded continuously, the future value, S, after t years is given by

    $$S = 4000e^{0.04t}$$

    (1) Calculate the value of S when

    (a) $t = 5$ (b) $t = 5.01$

    and hence estimate the rate of growth at $t = 5$. Round your answers to two decimal places.

    (2) Write down an expression for $\dfrac{dS}{dt}$ and hence find the exact value of the rate of growth after five years.

3. Write down the derivative of

    (a) $y = \ln(3x)\ (x > 0)$ (b) $y = \ln(-13x)\ (x < 0)$

4. Use the chain rule to differentiate

    (a) $y = e^{x^3}$ (b) $y = \ln(x^4 + 3x^2)$

5. Use the product rule to differentiate

    (a) $y = x^4 e^{2x}$ (b) $y = x \ln x$

6. Use the quotient rule to differentiate

    (a) $y = \dfrac{e^{4x}}{x^2 + 2}$ (b) $y = \dfrac{e^x}{\ln x}$

7. Find and classify the stationary points of

    (a) $y = xe^{-x}$ (b) $y = \ln x - x$

    Hence sketch their graphs.

8. Since the beginning of the year, weekly sales of a luxury good are found to have decreased exponentially. After t weeks, sales can be modelled by $3000e^{-0.02t}$.

    (a) Work out the weekly sales when $t = 12$ and $t = 13$ and hence find the decrease in sales during this time.

    (b) Use differentiation to work out the rate of decrease in sales after 12 weeks and compare this with your answer to part (a).

9. Find the output needed to maximise profit given that the total cost and total revenue functions are

    $$\text{TC} = 2Q \text{ and } \text{TR} = 100 \ln(Q + 1)$$

    respectively.

10. If a firm's production function is given by

    $$Q = 700Le^{-0.02L}$$

    find the value of L that maximises output.

11. The demand function of a good is given by

$$P = 100e^{-0.1Q}$$

Show that demand is unit elastic when $Q = 10$.

Exercise 4.8*

1. Differentiate:

(a) $y = e^{2x} - 3e^{-4x}$ (b) xe^{4x} (c) $\dfrac{e^{-x}}{x^2}$ (d) $x^m \ln x$ (e) $x(\ln x - 1)$

(f) $\dfrac{x^n}{\ln x}$ (g) $\dfrac{e^{mx}}{(ax + b)^n}$ (h) $\dfrac{e^{ax}}{(\ln bx)^n}$ (i) $\dfrac{e^x - 1}{e^x + 1}$

2. Use the rules of logarithms to expand each of the following functions. Hence find their derivatives.

(a) $y = \ln\left(\dfrac{x}{x + 1}\right)$ (b) $y = \ln(x\sqrt{(3x - 1)})$ (c) $y = \ln\sqrt{\dfrac{x + 1}{x - 1}}$

3. The growth rate of an economic variable, y, is defined to be $\dfrac{dy}{dt} \div y$.

(a) Use this definition to find the growth rate of the variable, $y = Ae^{kt}$.

(b) The gross domestic product, GDP, and the size of the population, N, of a country grow exponentially, so that after t years, GDP $= Ae^{at}$ and $N = Be^{bt}$.

(i) State the growth rates for GDP and N.

(ii) Show that the GDP per capita also grows exponentially and write down its growth rate.

4. Differentiate the following functions with respect to x, simplifying your answers as far as possible:

(a) $y = x^4 e^{-2x^2}$ (b) $y = \ln\left(\dfrac{x}{(x + 1)^2}\right)$

5. Find and classify the stationary points of

(a) $y = xe^{ax}$ (b) $y = \ln(ax^2 + bx)$

where $a < 0$.

6. (a) Use the quotient rule to show that the derivative of the function

$$y = \frac{2x + 1}{\sqrt{4x + 3}}$$

is given by

$$\frac{4(x + 1)}{(4x + 3)\sqrt{4x + 3}}$$

$\longrightarrow$

(b) Use the chain rule to differentiate the function

$$y = \ln\left(\frac{2x + 1}{\sqrt{4x + 3}}\right)$$

(c) Confirm that your answer to part (b) is correct by first expanding

$$\ln\left(\frac{2x + 1}{\sqrt{4x + 3}}\right)$$

using the rules of logs and then differentiating.

7. A firm's short-run production function is given by

$$Q = L^3 e^{-0.02L}$$

Find the value of L that maximises the average product of labour.

8. Find an expression for the price elasticity of demand for the demand curve

$$P = 500 - 75 \ln(2Q + 1)$$

9. Find an expression for the marginal revenue for each of the following demand curves:

(a) $P = \dfrac{e^{Q^2}}{Q^2}$ **(b)** $P = \ln\left(\dfrac{2Q}{3Q + 1}\right)$

10. The demand function of a good is given by $Q = 4000e^{-0.01P}$

(a) Find an expression, in terms of P, for the elasticity of demand and hence determine the range of values of P when the demand is inelastic.

(b) Find the price which maximises total revenue.

11. If the total cost function is given by $TC = 20\sqrt{Q}e^{Q/4}$, find the value of Q which minimises average cost.

12. The logistic model of growth takes the general form,

$$y = \frac{k}{1 + be^{-at}}$$

where k, a and b are positive constants.

(a) Find an expression for dy/dt and deduce that the gradient is positive.

(b) Find an expression for d^2y/dt^2 and deduce that the graph is convex when $t < (\ln b)/a$ and concave when $t > (\ln b)/a$.

(c) State the coordinates of the point where the graph intercepts the y axis, and describe the behaviour of the graph as $t \to \infty$.

(d) Sketch a graph of this logistic function.

13. An art collector owns a painting which is currently valued at \$2 million. After t years it is expected that the painting will be worth V million dollars where $V = 2e^{\sqrt{t}}$.

(a) If the interest rate is 10% compounded continuously, show that after t years the present value of the painting is given by $PV = 2e^{\sqrt{t}-0.1t}$.

(b) The collector decides to sell the painting after T years where T is chosen to maximise PV. Work out the value of T.

Formal mathematics

In more advanced books on mathematics, the derivative is defined via the concept of a limit and is usually written in symbols as

$$\frac{dy}{dx} = \lim_{\Delta x \to \infty} \frac{\Delta y}{\Delta x}$$

Look at Figure 4.31. Points A and B both lie on the curve $y = f(x)$ and their x and y coordinates differ by Δx and Δy, respectively. A line AB which joins two points on the curve is known as a chord, and it has slope $\Delta y / \Delta x$.

Now look at Figure 4.32, which shows a variety of chords, AB_1, AB_2, AB_3, ..., corresponding to smaller and smaller 'widths' Δx. As the right-hand end points, B_1, B_2, B_3, ..., get closer to A, the 'width', Δx, tends to zero. More significantly, the slope of the chord gets closer to that of the tangent at A. We describe this by saying that in the limit, as Δx tends to zero, the slope of the chord, $\Delta y / \Delta x$, is equal to that of the tangent. This limit is written

$$\lim_{\Delta x \to 0} \frac{\Delta y}{\Delta x}$$

We deduce that the formal definition

$$\frac{dy}{dx} = \lim_{\Delta x \to \infty} \frac{\Delta y}{\Delta x}$$

coincides with the idea that dy/dx represents the slope of the tangent, which is the approach adopted in this text.

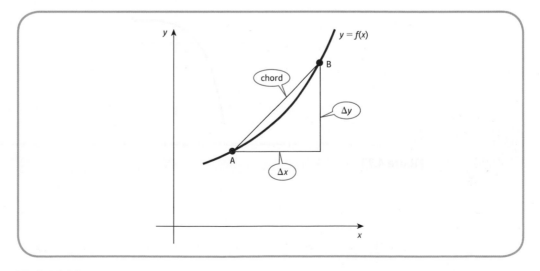

Figure 4.31

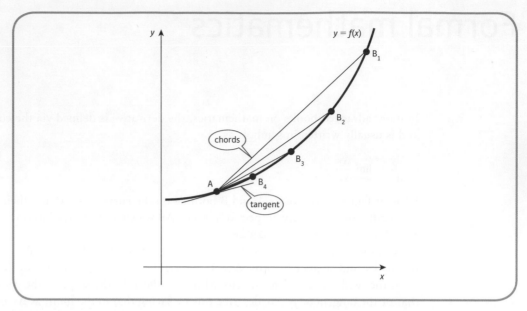

Figure 4.32

Throughout this chapter we have assumed that all functions can be differentiated. The function must at least be continuous at a point before we can even think about trying to draw a tangent at any point. For the function sketched in Figure 4.33, tangents could be drawn at every point on the graph except at $x = 2$, where the graph is discontinuous. We say that this function is not differentiable at $x = 2$.

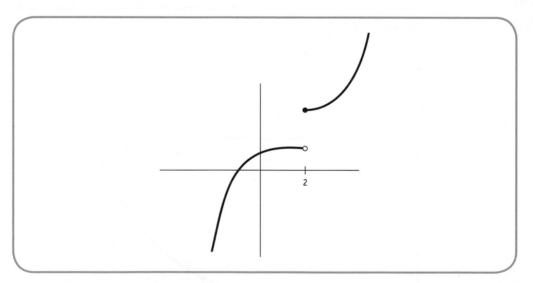

Figure 4.33

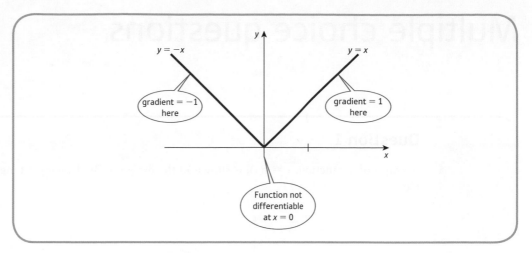

Figure 4.34

Even if a function is continuous everywhere, it still might not be possible to draw a tangent unless the curve is smooth. A classic example of such a function is the modulus function, $f(x) = |x|$ which is defined as

$$|x| = \begin{cases} -x, & \text{if } x < 0 \\ x, & \text{if } x \geq 0 \end{cases}$$

The graph of the modulus function is sketched in Figure 4.34 and has a sharp corner at $x = 0$, making it impossible to draw a tangent there.

To the left of the origin the graph has a constant slope of -1, and to the right of the origin the graph has a constant slope of $+1$. However, at $x = 0$ we cannot draw a tangent, so the modulus function is differentiable at all values of x except for $x = 0$. This can also be seen from the definition,

$$f'(x) = \lim_{\Delta x \to 0} \frac{\Delta y}{\Delta x}$$

As $\Delta x \to 0$ through positive values (i.e. from the right) the limit is $+1$, whereas as $\Delta x \to 0$ through negative values (i.e. from the left) the limit is -1. The limits can both be found, but the fact that they are different values prevents us from finding the derivative at $x = 0$.

Multiple choice questions

Question 1

A graph of a function, $y = f(x)$, is shown in the diagram. By drawing a tangent, estimate $f'(6)$.

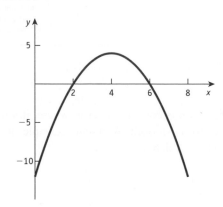

A. 0 **B.** -2 **C.** 2 **D.** 4 **E.** -4

Question 2

Work out the gradient of the curve $y = x^2 - 2x + 4\sqrt{x} - \dfrac{16}{x}$ at $x = 4$.

A. 8 **B.** 7 **C.** 6 **D.** 5 **E.** 4

Question 3

If the total revenue and total cost functions are $TR = 36Q - Q^2$ and $TC = 10 + 3Q$, find the maximum profit.

A. 272.25

B. 262.25

C. 282.25

D. 292.25

E. 302.25

Question 4

The total revenue function is $TR = 120Q - 5Q^2$ and $Q = 5$. Use differentiation to estimate the change in TR brought about by a 0.25 increase in Q.

A. 17.50 **B.** 17.81 **C.** 23.75 **D.** 26.24 **E.** 14.75

Question 5

A cubic function is given by $y = 2x^3 - 5x^2 + 13x - 40$. Is this function increasing or decreasing, and is it convex or concave, at $x = 0.5$?

A. Increasing and concave

B. Decreasing and concave

C. Increasing and convex

D. Decreasing and convex

E. Indeterminate

Question 6

Graphs of marginal revenue and marginal cost functions based on linear models for the demand and total cost functions of a good are shown in the diagram. The quantity is currently 20 units. Describe the qualitative effect on total revenue, total cost and profit if the quantity increases to 21 units.

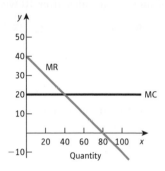

A. TR decreases, TC decreases, π decreases

B. TR increases, TC increases, π decreases

C. TR decreases, TC decreases, π increases

D. TR decreases, TC increases, π decreases

E. TR increases, TC increases, π increases

Question 7

Find the y-coordinate of the (local) maximum point on the graph of the cubic function $f(x) = -x^3 + 21x^2 - 135x + 300$.

A. 25   **B.** 39   **C.** 57   **D.** 5   **E.** 9

Question 8

If the supply function $Q - 10 + 0.1P + aP^2$ is unit elastic at $P = 10$, find the value of a.

A. 0.1   **B.** 0.2   **C.** 0.3   **D.** 0.4   **E.** 0.5

Question 9

If the demand function is $P = (40 - 2Q)^2$ on $0 \le Q \le 20$, find the marginal revenue at $Q = 5$.

A. 120   B. −120   C. −60   D. −1140   E. 300

Question 10

Calculate the MPC at $Y = 8$, if the consumption function is $C = \dfrac{10 + Y^2}{2 + Y}$.

A. 0.92   B. 0.14   C. 0.42   D. 0.86   E. 0.74

Question 11

The weekly sales $S(t)$ of a new product follow the logistic model: $S(t) = \dfrac{10\,000}{1 + 5e^{-0.02t}}$
Find the rate of increase in sales after 10 weeks.

A. 31.6   B. 29.7   C. 38.5   D. 42.3   E. 45.9

Question 12

Find an expression for the marginal revenue function in terms of Q when the demand function is $Q = \dfrac{100 - P}{2P}$

A. $\dfrac{100}{(2Q + 1)^2}$ B. $-\dfrac{200}{(2Q + 1)^2}$ C. $\dfrac{200}{(2Q + 1)^2}$ D. $\dfrac{100 + Q}{(2Q + 1)^2}$ E. $\dfrac{100 - Q}{(2Q + 1)^2}$

Question 13

Find the gradient of the curve $y = x(3x + 2)^3$ at $x = 2$.

A. 896   B. 1664   C. 1152   D. 384   E. 128

Question 14

If $f''(x) = 0$ and $f'(x) \ne 0$ for all x, what type of function is $f(x)$?

A. Zero

B. Constant

C. Linear

D. Quadratic

E. Cubic

Question 15

In the simplest model of inventory control, which of the graphs shown in the diagram represent total cost, holding cost and order cost?

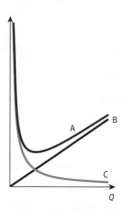

A. A is total cost, B is order cost and C is holding cost

B. A is total cost, B is holding cost and C is order cost

C. A is holding cost, B is total cost and C is order cost

D. A is holding cost, B is order cost and C is total cost

E. A is order cost, B is holding cost and C is total cost

Question 16

If the demand function is $P = 40 - 5Q$, find the values of P for which demand is inelastic.

A. $P > 8$ B. $P > 20$ C. $P < 8$ D. $P < 20$ E. $P > 4$

Question 17

The supply function of a good is given by $P = 4 + 2Q + 0.1Q^2$. Calculate the arc elasticity of supply as Q increases from 10 to 12.

A. 1.04   B. 0.07   C. 1.21   D. 0.34   E. 0.83

Question 18

If the total cost of producing Q goods is given by TC $= Q^2 + 10Q + 9$, find the level of output which minimises average cost.

A. 2   B. 3   C. 4   D. 5   E. 6

Question 19

What type of economic problem is solved by equating marginal product of labour and average product of labour?

A. Maximise output

B. Maximise labour productivity

C. Maximise profit

D. Minimise marginal product of labour

E. Minimise average product of labour

Question 20

Weekly sales of a good have decreased exponentially. After t weeks, sales can be modelled by $4500e^{-0.05t}$. Use differentiation to find the rate of decrease after 20 weeks.

A. 225   B. 166   C. 4500   D. 450   E. 83

Question 21

Find $\dfrac{dy}{dx}$ when $y = \ln\left(\dfrac{\sqrt{x}}{x+4}\right)$, expressing your answer as a single fraction.

A. $\dfrac{x+8}{2x(x+4)}$

B. $\dfrac{3x+4}{2x(x+4)}$

C. $\dfrac{4-x}{2x(x+4)}$

D. $\dfrac{2-x}{2x(x+4)}$

E. $\dfrac{3x+8}{2x(x+4)}$

Question 22

The price and demand of a good are currently \$100 and 400, respectively. After a price increase of \$20, the demand falls by 50. Calculate the arc elasticity of demand.

A. $-\dfrac{3}{4}$

B. $-\dfrac{5}{8}$

C. $-\dfrac{6}{7}$

D. $-\dfrac{11}{15}$

E. $-\dfrac{2}{3}$

Question 23

The demand function of a good is $P = -Q^2 - 4Q + 120$. Calculate the price elasticity of demand when $P = 75$.

A. $-\dfrac{15}{14}$ B. $-\dfrac{9}{7}$ C. $-\dfrac{9}{8}$ D. $-\dfrac{11}{15}$ E. $-\dfrac{15}{11}$

Question 24

The graph of a derived function, $f'(x)$ is given by:

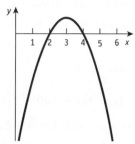

Which one of the graphs below shows the original function, $f(x)$?

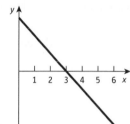

A.

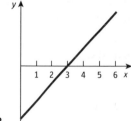

B.

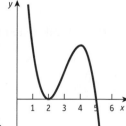

C.

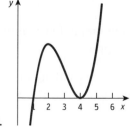

D.

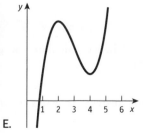

E.

Examination questions

Question 1

Find an expression, in terms of Q, for the marginal revenue when the demand function is $Q + 4P = 70$. Hence

(a) estimate the change in total revenue when Q decreases from 40 to 39.75;

(b) find the value of Q at which the total revenue is a maximum.

Question 2

A cubic function is given by $f(x) = (x + 3)(x - 1)(9 - 2x)$.

(a) By multiplying out the brackets, show that $f(x) = -2x^3 + 5x^2 + 24x - 27$.

(b) Find an expression for the first-order derivative and hence find the coordinates of the stationary points.

(c) Find an expression for the second-order derivative and hence classify the stationary points found in part (b).

(d) Sketch a graph of $f(x)$ showing clearly on your sketch where the curve crosses the coordinate axes.

Question 3

(a) Find the gradient of each of the following curves at $x = 9$:

   (i) $y = 5x^2$ (ii) $y = \dfrac{27}{x}$ (iii) $y = 6\sqrt{x}$

(b) If the supply function of a good is $Q = 0.01P^2 + P + 30$, calculate the price elasticity of supply

   (i) averaged along an arc between $P = 20$ and $P = 30$;

   (ii) at the point $P = 25$.

Question 4

(a) Consider the function $f(x) = 2x^3 + 7x + 1$.

   (i) Work out the values of $f(2)$ and $f(2.1)$, and hence calculate the gradient of the straight line joining $(2, f(2))$ and $(2.1, f(2.1))$.

   (ii) Work out the value of $f'(2)$.

   (iii) By using a sketch graph, explain why your answers to parts (i) and (ii) are very similar but are not equal.

(b) The average cost function of a good is given by $AC = 3Q + 8 + \dfrac{15}{Q}$

    (i) Find an expression for the marginal cost function.

    (ii) If the current output is 30, use your answer to part (i) to estimate the effect on TC of a 0.5-unit increase in Q, and compare this with the actual change in TC.

Question 5

The demand and supply functions of a good are given by $P + 2Q_\mathrm{D} = 13$ and $P - Q_\mathrm{S} = 4$, respectively.

(a) Determine the market equilibrium price.

(b) Find the elasticity of supply at this price.

(c) Estimate the percentage increase in price needed to increase supply by 2% of its equilibrium value. Is supply elastic, inelastic or unit elastic at market equilibrium?

Question 6

(a) Differentiate

    (i) $y = 6e^{2x}$ **(ii)** $y = \ln(x^2 + 1)$

(b) Evaluate the first- and second-order derivatives of the cubic $y = x^3 + 2x^2 - 6x + 7$ at $x = 2$, and hence state whether the graph is

    (i) increasing or decreasing at this point;

    (ii) convex or concave at this point.

Question 7

(a) Find the gradient of each of the following curves at $x = 1$:

    (i) $y = x(1 + x)^4$

    (ii) $y = (x^2 + 6)^3$

    (iii) $y = \dfrac{2x}{x + 1}$

    (iv) $y = \ln\left(\dfrac{x + 1}{\sqrt{x + 3}}\right)$

(b) A firm's short-run production function is given by $Q = Le^{-0.02L}$. Find the marginal product of labour at $L = 50$, and give a brief interpretation of this value.

Question 8

A company monitors its daily profit during the first five years of trading. The variation of profit over time can be modelled approximately by the cubic

$$\pi = t^3 - 9t^2 + 24t - 16 \quad (0 \le t \le 5)$$

where t denotes the time in years since the launch of the company.

(a) Verify that the firm makes a loss initially and that it breaks even after the first year.

(b) Solve the equation, $d\pi/dt = 0$ to find the coordinates of the stationary points on the curve.

(c) By examining the sign of the second-order derivative $d^2\pi/dt^2$ at each stationary point, determine their nature.

(d) Sketch a graph of π against t.

(e) Identify the times at which the profit function is increasing and decreasing.

(f) Identify the times at which the graph is concave and convex.

(g) Summarise, in non-mathematical terms, how the firm's profit has changed during the first five years of trading.

Question 9

A firm's short-run production function is given by $Q = 10L + 6L^2 - 0.1L^3$.

(a) Write down expressions for the marginal product of labour and average product of labour.

(b) Determine the value of L which maximises the average product of labour.

(c) Use calculus to show that the law of diminishing returns holds.

Question 10

(a) Find an expression, simplified as far as possible, for marginal revenue for the demand function
$$P = \sqrt{400 - 6Q}$$

(b) Find an expression for the marginal propensity to consume for the consumption function $C = \dfrac{200 + Y^2}{10 + Y}$ and deduce that the marginal propensity to save is given by

$$\text{MPS} = \frac{300}{(10 + Y)^2}.$$

Question 11

The supply and demand functions of a good are given by

$$P = aQ_S + b$$
$$P = -cQ_D + d$$

where P, Q_S and Q_D denote the price, quantity supplied and quantity demanded, respectively, and where a, b, c and d are positive constants.

The government imposes a fixed tax, t, per unit.

(a) By drawing sketch graphs on the same diagram, explain why the condition $d - b > 0$ is required for the pre-tax market equilibrium to exist.

(b) Find expressions for the equilibrium price and quantity both before and after the tax is imposed.

(c) Write down the ratio of the tax that is paid by the supplier and consumer, respectively.

(d) Find the value of t which optimises government tax revenue and show mathematically that this is a maximum.

Question 12

A monopolistic firm produces goods in a market where the demand function is $P = 43 - 0.3Q$ and the corresponding total cost function is $TC = 0.01Q^3 - 0.4Q^2 + 3Q$.

(a) What can you say about the fixed costs of this firm?

(b) Find the (non-zero) output for which average cost is equal to marginal cost, and explain the significance of this value.

(c) Find the output which maximises profit and calculate the price elasticity of demand at this point.

Question 13

A firm's demand function is given by $P = a + b\sqrt{Q}$ where P and Q denote the price and quantity demanded, respectively, and a and b are parameters $(a > 0, b < 0)$.

(a) Obtain a general expression for the price elasticity of demand in terms of P and deduce that demand is unit elastic when $P = a/3$.

(b) Write down an expression for total revenue, TR, and hence find the value of Q at the stationary point of this function. By considering the second-order derivative of TR, show that your stationary point is a maximum.

Question 14

(a) By applying the product rule to the expression $TR = PQ$, prove that marginal revenue, MR, satisfies

$$MR = P\left(1 + \frac{1}{E}\right)$$

where E is the price elasticity of demand.

Hence explain why the total revenue is a decreasing function in regions where the demand is inelastic.

(b) A building supplier is allowed to charge different prices to its trade and individual customers. The corresponding demand equations are given by

$$Q_1 = 200 - 2P_1$$
$$Q_2 = 250 - P_2$$

respectively. The total cost function is $TC = 100 + 20Q$ where $Q = Q_1 + Q_2$.

Find the prices that the firm should charge its trade and individual customers to maximise total profit.

Calculate the elasticities at these prices and verify that the firm charges the higher price in the market where the magnitude of the elasticity of demand is lower. Use the result of part (a) to explain why this is always true.

Question 15

The diagram provides a model for the variation of stock levels of a good during the course of a year where:

D = annual demand

Q = size of each order made at regular intervals during the year

R = cost of raising each order

H = cost of storing an item for a year.

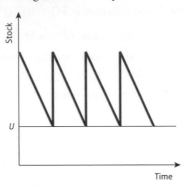

The diagram shows that stock levels fall at a constant rate and that these are instantly replenished when the level falls to U units.

(a) Explain why the annual holding cost is given by $\text{AHC} = \left(\dfrac{1}{2}Q + U \right)H$.

(b) Explain why the annual order cost is $\text{AOC} = \dfrac{DR}{Q}$.

(c) Assuming that the total cost, $C = \text{AHC} + \text{AOC}$, show that C is minimised when $Q = \sqrt{\dfrac{2DR}{H}}$. Use second-order derivatives to show that your stationary point is a minimum.

Question 16

(a) The supply function of a good is given by $P = Q^2 + 2Q + 8$. Find the price elasticity of supply when $P = 128$ and hence estimate the percentage change in supply due to a 5% increase in price. Is supply elastic, inelastic or unit elastic at this price?

(b) The demand function of the same good is $P = aQ + b$. Find the values of a and b if it is known that the market equilibrium price is 56 and that demand is unit elastic at $P = 40$.

CHAPTER 5
Partial Differentiation

This chapter continues the topic of calculus by describing how to differentiate functions of more than one variable. In many ways this chapter can be regarded as the climax of the whole text. It is the summit of the mathematical mountain that we have been merrily climbing. Not only are the associated mathematical ideas and techniques quite sophisticated, but also partial differentiation provides a rich source of applications. In one sense there is no new material presented here. If you know how to differentiate a function of one variable, then you also know how to partially differentiate a function of several variables because the rules are the same. Similarly, if you can optimise a function of one variable, then you need have no fear of unconstrained and constrained optimisation. Of course, if you cannot use the elementary rules of differentiation or cannot find the maximum and minimum values of a function as described in Chapter 4, then you really are fighting a lost cause. Under these circumstances, you are best advised to omit this chapter entirely. There is no harm in doing this, because it does not form the prerequisite for any of the later topics. However, you will miss out on one of the most elegant and useful branches of mathematics.

It is important that Sections 5.1 and 5.2 are read first, but the remaining four sections can be studied in any order. Sections 5.1 and 5.2 follow the familiar pattern. We begin by looking at the mathematical techniques and then use them to determine marginal functions and elasticities. Section 5.3 describes the multiplier concept and completes the topic of national income determination which you studied in Chapter 1.

The final three sections are devoted to optimisation. For functions of several variables, optimisation problems are split into two groups, unconstrained and constrained. Unconstrained problems, tackled in Section 5.4, involve the maximisation and minimisation of functions in which the variables are free to take any values whatsoever. In a constrained problem only certain combinations of the variables are examined. For example, a firm might wish to minimise costs but is constrained by the need to satisfy production quotas, or an individual might want to maximise utility but is subject to a budgetary constraint, and so on. There are two ways of solving constrained problems: the method of substitution and the method of Lagrange multipliers, described in Sections 5.5 and 5.6, respectively.

SECTION 5.1

Functions of several variables

Objectives

At the end of this section you should be able to:

- Use the function notation, $z = f(x, y)$.
- Determine the first-order partial derivatives, f_x and f_y.
- Determine the second-order partial derivatives, f_{xx}, f_{xy}, f_{yx} and f_{yy}.
- Appreciate that, for most functions, $f_{xy} = f_{yx}$.
- Use the small increments formula.
- Perform implicit differentiation.

Most relationships in economics involve more than two variables. The demand for a good depends not only on its own price but also on the price of substitutable and complementary goods, incomes of consumers, advertising expenditure and so on. Likewise, the output from a production process depends on a variety of inputs, including land, capital and labour. To analyse general economic behaviour, we must extend the concept of a function, and particularly the differential calculus, to functions of several variables.

A **function, f, of two variables** is a rule that assigns to each incoming pair of numbers, (x, y), a uniquely defined outgoing number, z. This is illustrated in Figure 5.1. The 'black box' f performs some arithmetic operation on x and y to produce z. For example, the rule might be 'multiply the two numbers together and add twice the second number'. In symbols we write this either as

$$f(x, y) = xy + 2y$$

or as

$$z = xy + 2y$$

In order to be able to evaluate the function, we have to specify the numerical values of both x and y.

For example, substituting $x = 3$ and $y = 4$ gives

$$f(3,4) = 3 \times 4 + 2 \times 4 = 20$$

Figure 5.1

and substituting $x = 4$ and $y = 3$ gives

$$f(4,3) = 4 \times 3 + 2 \times 3 = 18$$

Notice that, for this function, $f(3,4)$ is not the same as $f(4,3)$, so in general we must be careful to write down the correct ordering of the variables.

We have used the labels x and y for the two incoming numbers (called the **independent variables**) and z for the outgoing number (called the **dependent variable**). We could equally well have written the above function as

$$y = x_1 x_2 + 2x_2$$

say, using x_1 and x_2 to denote the independent variables and using y this time to denote the dependent variable. The use of subscripts may seem rather cumbersome, but it provides an obvious extension to functions of more than two variables. In general, a function of n variables can be written

$$y = f(x_1, x_2, \ldots, x_n)$$

Practice Problem

1. If

$$f(x, y) = 5x + xy^2 - 10$$

and

$$g(x_1, x_2, x_3) = x_1 \mid x_2 \mid x_3$$

evaluate

(a) $f(0, 0)$ (b) $f(1, 2)$ (c) $f(2, 1)$ (d) $g(5, 6, 10)$ (e) $g(0, 0, 0)$ (f) $g(10, 5, 6)$

A function of one variable can be given a pictorial description using graphs, which help to give an intuitive feel for its behaviour. Figure 5.2 shows the graph of a typical function

$$y = f(x)$$

in which the horizontal axis determines the incoming number, x, and the vertical axis determines the corresponding outgoing number, y. The height of the curve directly above any point on the x axis represents the value of the function at this point.

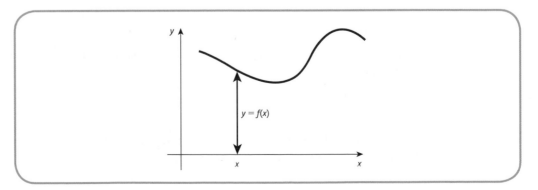

Figure 5.2

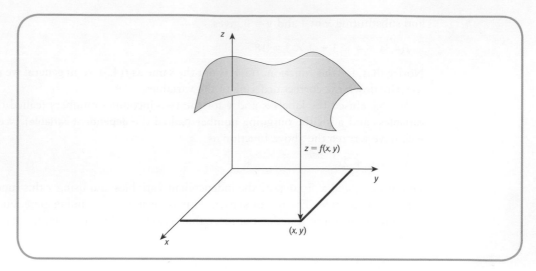

Figure 5.3

An obvious question to ask is whether there is a pictorial representation of functions of several variables. The answer is yes in the case of functions of two variables, although it is not particularly easy to construct. A function

$$z = f(x, y)$$

can be thought of as a surface, rather like a mountain range, in three-dimensional space as shown in Figure 5.3. If you visualise the incoming point with coordinates (x, y) as lying in a horizontal plane, then the height of the surface, z, directly above it represents the value of the function at this point. As you can probably imagine, it is not an easy task to sketch the surface by hand from an equation such as

$$f(x, y) = xy^3 + 4x$$

although three-dimensional graphics packages are available for most computers which can produce such a plot.

It is impossible to provide any sort of graphical interpretation for functions of more than two variables. For example, a function of, say, four variables would require five dimensions, one for each of the incoming variables and a further one for the outgoing variable! In spite of this setback we can still perform the task of differentiating functions of several variables and, as we shall see in the remaining sections of this chapter, such derivatives play a vital role in analysing economic behaviour.

Given a function of two variables,

$$z = f(x, y)$$

we can determine two first-order derivatives. The **partial derivative** of f with respect to x is written as

$$\frac{\partial z}{\partial x} \quad \text{or} \quad \frac{\partial f}{\partial x} \quad \text{or} \quad f_x$$

and is found by differentiating f with respect to x, with y held constant. Similarly, the **partial derivative** of f with respect to y is written as

$$\frac{\partial z}{\partial y} \quad \text{or} \quad \frac{\partial f}{\partial y} \quad \text{or} \quad f_y$$

and is found by differentiating f with respect to y, with x held constant. We use curly ds in the notation

$$\frac{\partial f}{\partial x}$$

read 'partial dee f
by dee x'

to distinguish partial differentiation of functions of several variables from ordinary differentiation of functions of one variable. The alternative notation, f_x, is analogous to the f' notation for ordinary differentiation.

Example

Find the first-order partial derivatives of the functions

(a) $f(x, y) = x^2 + y^3$ **(b)** $f(x, y) = x^2 y$

Solution

(a) To differentiate the function

$$f(x, y) = x^2 + y^3$$

with respect to x, we work as follows. By the sum rule we know that we can differentiate each part separately and add. Now, when we differentiate x^2 with respect to x, we get $2x$. However, when we differentiate y^3 with respect to x, we get 0. To see this, note from the definition of partial differentiation with respect to x, that the variable y is held constant. Of course, if y is a constant, then so is y^3 and, as we discovered in Chapter 4, constants differentiate to zero. Hence

$$\frac{\partial f}{\partial x} = 2x + 0 = 2x$$

In the same way

$$\frac{\partial f}{\partial y} = 0 + 3y^2 = 3y^2$$

This time x is held constant, so x^2 goes to zero, and when we differentiate y^3 with respect to y, we get $3y^2$.

(b) To differentiate the function

$$f(x, y) = x^2 y$$

with respect to x, we differentiate in the normal way, taking x as the variable while pretending that y is a constant. Now, when we differentiate a constant multiple of x^2, we differentiate x^2 to get $2x$ and then multiply by the constant. For example,

$$7x^2 \quad \text{differentiates to} \quad 7(2x) = 14x$$
$$-100x^2 \quad \text{differentiates to} \quad -100(2x) = -200x$$

and

$$cx^2 \quad \text{differentiates to} \quad c(2x) = 2cx$$

for any constant c. In our case, y, plays the role of a constant, so

x^2y differentiates to $(2x)y = 2xy$

Hence

$f_x = 2xy$

Similarly, to find f_y we treat y as the variable and x as a constant in the expression

$f(x, y) = x^2y$

Now, when we differentiate a constant multiple of y we just get the constant, so cy differentiates to c. In our case, x^2 plays the role of c, so x^2y differentiates to x^2. Hence

$f_y = x^2$

Practice Problem

2. Find expressions for the first-order partial derivatives for the functions

   (a) $f(x, y) = 5x^4 - y^2$ (b) $f(x, y) = x^2y^3 - 10x$

In general, when we differentiate a function of two variables, the thing we end up with is itself a function of two variables. This suggests the possibility of differentiating a second time. In fact there are four **second-order partial derivatives**. We write

$$\frac{\partial^2 z}{\partial x^2} \quad \text{or} \quad \frac{\partial^2 f}{\partial x^2} \quad \text{or} \quad f_{xx}$$

for the function obtained by differentiating twice with respect to x,

$$\frac{\partial^2 z}{\partial y^2} \quad \text{or} \quad \frac{\partial^2 f}{\partial y^2} \quad \text{or} \quad f_{yy}$$

for the function obtained by differentiating twice with respect to y,

$$\frac{\partial^2 z}{\partial y \partial x} \quad \text{or} \quad \frac{\partial^2 f}{\partial y \partial x} \quad \text{or} \quad f_{yx}$$

for the function obtained by differentiating first with respect to x and then with respect to y, and

$$\frac{\partial^2 z}{\partial x \partial y} \quad \text{or} \quad \frac{\partial^2 f}{\partial x \partial y} \quad \text{or} \quad f_{xy}$$

for the function obtained by differentiating first with respect to y and then with respect to x.

Example

Find expressions for the second-order partial derivatives f_{xx}, f_{yy}, f_{yx} and f_{xy} for the functions

(a) $f(x, y) = x^2 + y^3$ **(b)** $f(x, y) = x^2 y$

Solution

(a) The first-order partial derivatives of the function

$$f(x, y) = x^2 + y^3$$

have already been found and are given by

$$f_x = 2x, \quad f_y = 3y^2$$

To find f_{xx} we differentiate f_x with respect to x to get

$$f_{xx} = 2$$

To find f_{yy} we differentiate f_y with respect to y to get

$$f_{yy} = 6y$$

To find f_{yx} we differentiate f_x with respect to y to get

$$f_{yx} = 0$$

Note how f_{yx} is obtained. Starting with the original function

$$f(x, y) = x^2 + y^3$$

we first differentiate with respect to x to get $2x$, and when we differentiate this with respect to y we keep x constant, so it goes to zero. Finally, to find f_{xy} we differentiate f_y with respect to x to get

$$f_{xy} = 0$$

Note how f_{xy} is obtained. Starting with the original function

$$f(x, y) = x^2 + y^3$$

we first differentiate with respect to y to get $3y^2$, and when we differentiate this with respect to x we keep y constant, so it goes to zero.

(b) The first-order partial derivatives of the function

$$f(x, y) = x^2 y$$

have already been found and are given by

$$f_x = 2xy, \quad f_y = x^2$$

Hence

$$f_{xx} = 2y, \quad f_{yy} = 0 \quad f_{yx} = 2x, \quad f_{xy} = 2x$$

Practice Problem

3. Find expressions for the second-order partial derivatives of the functions

   (a) $f(x, y) = 5x^4 - y^2$ 　　　(b) $f(x, y) = x^2y^3 - 10x$

   [Hint: you might find your answer to Practice Problem 2 useful.]

Looking back at the expressions obtained in the previous example and Practice Problem 3, notice that in all cases

$$\frac{\partial^2 f}{\partial y \partial x} = \frac{\partial^2 f}{\partial x \partial y} \qquad \boxed{f_{yx} = f_{xy}}$$

It can be shown that this result (known as Young's theorem) holds for all functions that arise in economics. It is immaterial in which order the partial differentiation is performed. Differentiating with respect to x then y gives the same expression as differentiating with respect to y then x. (In fact, there are some weird mathematical functions for which this result is not true, although they need not concern us.)

Although we have concentrated exclusively on functions of two variables, it should be obvious how to work out partial derivatives of functions of more than two variables. For the general function

$$y = f(x_1, x_2, \ldots, x_n)$$

there are n first-order partial derivatives, written as

$$\frac{\partial f}{\partial x_i} \quad \text{or} \quad f_i \quad (i = 1, 2, \ldots, n)$$

which are found by differentiating with respect to one variable at a time, keeping the remaining $n - 1$ variables fixed. The second-order partial derivatives are determined in an analogous way.

For the function

$$f(x_1, x_2, x_3) = x_1^3 + x_1x_3^2 + 5x_2^4$$

we could differentiate first with respect to x_1 to get

$$f_1 = \frac{\partial f}{\partial x_1} = 3x_1^2 + x_3^2$$

and if we further differentiate this with respect to x_3, we get

$$f_{31} = \frac{\partial^2 f}{\partial x_3 \partial x_1} = 2x_3$$

In fact, as we have just noted for functions of two variables, we get the same answer if we differentiate in reverse order. You might like to check this for yourself.

Practice Problem

4. Find expressions for the partial derivatives f_1, f_{11} and f_{21} in the case when

   $$f(x_1, x_2, x_3) = x_1x_2 + x_1^5 - x_2^2x_3$$

We have seen how to work out partial derivatives but have yet to give any meaning to them. To provide an interpretation of a partial derivative, let us recall the corresponding situation for functions of one variable of the form

$$y = f(x)$$

The derivative, dy/dx, gives the rate of change of y with respect to x. In other words, if x changes by a small amount Δx, then the corresponding change in y satisfies

$$\Delta y \cong \frac{dy}{dx} \times \Delta x$$

Moreover, the accuracy of the approximation improves as Δx becomes smaller and smaller.

Advice

You might like to remind yourself of the reasoning behind this approximation, which was explained graphically in Section 4.3.1.

Given the way in which a partial derivative is found, we can deduce that for a function of two variables

$$z = f(x, y)$$

if x changes by a small amount Δx and y is held fixed, then the corresponding change in z satisfies

$$\Delta z \cong \frac{\partial z}{\partial x} \times \Delta x$$

Similarly, if y changes by Δy and x is fixed, then z changes by

$$\Delta z \cong \frac{\partial z}{\partial y} \times \Delta y$$

In practice, of course, x and y may both change simultaneously. If this is the case, then the net change in z will be the sum of the individual changes brought about by changes in x and y separately, so that

$$\Delta z \cong \frac{\partial z}{\partial x} \Delta x + \frac{\partial z}{\partial y} \Delta y$$

This is referred to as the **small increments formula**. Although this is only an approximation, it can be shown that for most functions the corresponding error tends to zero as Δx and Δy both tend to zero. For this reason the formula is sometimes quoted with an equality sign and written as

$$dz = \frac{\partial z}{\partial x} dx + \frac{\partial z}{\partial y} dy$$

where the symbols dx, dy and dz are called **differentials** and represent limiting values of Δx, Δy and Δz, respectively.

Example

If

$$z = x^3y - y^3x$$

evaluate

$$\frac{\partial z}{\partial x} \text{ and } \frac{\partial z}{\partial y}$$

at the point (1, 3). Hence estimate the change in z when x increases from 1 to 1.1 and y decreases from 3 to 2.8 simultaneously.

Solution

If

$$z = x^3y - y^3x$$

then

$$\partial z/\partial x = 3x^2y - y^3 \quad \text{and} \quad \partial z/\partial y = x^3 - 3y^2x$$

so at the point (1, 3)

$$\frac{\partial z}{\partial x} = 3(1)^2(3) - 3^3 = -18$$

$$\frac{\partial z}{\partial y} = 1^3 - 3(3)^2(1) = -26$$

Now, since x increases from 1 to 1.1, the change in x is

$$\Delta x = 0.1 \qquad \text{positive numbers denote increases}$$

and, since y decreases from 3 to 2.8, the change in y is

$$\Delta y = -0.2 \qquad \text{negative numbers denote decreases}$$

The small increments formula states that

$$\Delta z \cong \frac{\partial z}{\partial x}\Delta x + \frac{\partial z}{\partial y}\Delta y$$

The change in z is therefore

$$\Delta z \cong (-18)(0.1) + (-26)(-0.2) = 3.4$$

so z increases by approximately 3.4.

Practice Problem

5. If

$$z = xy - 5x + 2y$$

evaluate

$$\frac{\partial z}{\partial x} \text{ and } \frac{\partial z}{\partial y}$$

at the point $(2, 6)$.

(a) Use the small increments formula to estimate the change in z as x decreases from 2 to 1.9 and y increases from 6 to 6.1.

(b) Confirm your estimate of part (a) by evaluating z at $(2, 6)$ and $(1.9, 6.1)$.

One important application of the small increments formula is to implicit differentiation. We hope by now that you are entirely happy differentiating functions of one variable such as

$$y = x^3 + 2x^2 + 5 \qquad \boxed{\frac{dy}{dx} = 3x^2 + 4x}$$

Suppose, however, that you are asked to find dy/dx given the equation

$$y^3 + 2xy^2 - x = 5$$

This is much more difficult. The reason for the difference is that in the first case, y is given explicitly in terms of x, whereas in the second case, the functional dependence of y on x is only given implicitly. You would need to somehow rearrange this equation and to write y in terms of x before you could differentiate it. Unfortunately, this is impossible because of the presence of the y^3 term. The trick here is to regard the expression on the left-hand side of the equation as a function of the two variables x and y, so that

$$f(x, y) = y^3 + 2xy^2 - x$$

or, equivalently,

$$z = y^3 + 2xy^2 - x$$

The equation

$$y^3 + 2xy^2 - x = 5$$

then reads

$$z = 5$$

In general, the differential form of the small increments formula states that

$$dz = \frac{\partial z}{\partial x} dx + \frac{\partial z}{\partial y} dy$$

In our particular case, z takes the constant value of 5, so it does not change. Hence $dz = 0$ and the formula reduces to

$$0 = \frac{\partial z}{\partial x} dx + \frac{\partial z}{\partial y} dy$$

which rearranges as

$$\frac{\partial z}{\partial y}dy = -\frac{\partial z}{\partial x}dx$$

that is,

$$\frac{dy}{dx} = \frac{-\partial z/\partial x}{\partial z/\partial y}$$

This formula can be used to find dy/dx given any implicit function

$$f(x, y) = \text{constant}$$

that is,

$$\text{if} \quad f(x, y) = \text{constant} \quad \text{then} \quad \frac{dy}{dx} = -\frac{f_x}{f_y}$$

The technique of finding dy/dx from $-f_x/f_y$ is called **implicit differentiation** and can be used whenever it is difficult or impossible to obtain an explicit representation for y in terms of x.

For the function

$$f(x, y) = y^3 + 2xy^2 - x$$

we have

$$f_x = 2y^2 - 1 \quad \text{and} \quad f_y = 3y^2 + 4xy$$

so that

$$\frac{dy}{dx} = -\frac{f_x}{f_y} = -\left(\frac{2y^2 - 1}{3y^2 + 4xy}\right) = \frac{-2y^2 + 1}{3y^2 + 4xy}$$

Practice Problem

6. Use implicit differentiation to find expressions for dy/dx given that

   (a) $xy - y^3 + y = 0$ **(b)** $y^5 - xy^2 = 10$

Key Terms

Dependent variable   A variable whose value is determined by that taken by the independent variables; in $z = f(x, y)$, the dependent variable is z.

Differentials   Limiting values of incremental changes. In the limit, the approximation $\Delta z \cong \frac{\partial z}{\partial x} \times \Delta x$ becomes d$z = \frac{\partial z}{\partial x} \times$ dx where dz and dx are the differentials.

Function of two variables   A rule which assigns to each pair of incoming numbers, x and y, a uniquely defined outgoing number, z.

Implicit differentiation   The process of obtaining dy/dx where the function is not given explicitly as an expression for y in terms of x.

Independent variable   Variables whose values determine that of the dependent variable; in $z = f(x, y)$, the independent variables are x and y.

Partial derivative   The derivative of a function of two or more variables with respect to one of these variables, the others being regarded as constant.

Second-order partial derivative   The partial derivative of a first-order partial derivative. For example, f_{xy} is the second-order partial derivative when f is differentiated first with respect to y and then with respect to x.

Small increments formula   The result $\Delta z \cong \dfrac{\partial z}{\partial x}\Delta x + \dfrac{\partial z}{\partial y}\Delta y$

Exercise 5.1

1. If

   $$f(x, y) = 3x^2y^3$$

   evaluate $f(2, 3), f(5, 1)$ and $f(0, 7)$.

2. If

   $$f(x, y) = 2x^2 + xy$$

   write down an expression for

   (a) $f(a, a)$ **(b)** $f(b, -b)$

3. If

   $$f(x, y) = xy^2 + 4x^3$$

   show that

   $$f(2x, 2y) = 8f(x, y)$$

4. Write down expressions for the first-order partial derivatives, $\dfrac{\partial z}{\partial x}$ and $\dfrac{\partial z}{\partial y}$, for

   (a) $z = x^2 + 4y^5$ **(b)** $z = 3x^3 - 2e^y$ **(c)** $z = xy + 6y$ **(d)** $z = x^6y^2 + 5y^3$

5. If

   $$f(x, y) = x^4y^5 - x^2 + y^2$$

   write down expressions for the first-order partial derivatives, f_x and f_y. Hence evaluate $f_x(1, 0)$ and $f_y(1, 1)$.

6. Use the small increments formula to estimate the change in

   $$z = x^2y^4 - x^6 + 4y$$

   when

   (a) x increases from 1 to 1.1 and y remains fixed at 0;

   (b) x remains fixed at 1 and y decreases from 0 to -0.5;

   (c) x increases from 1 to 1.1 and y decreases from 0 to -0.5.

7. **(a)** If

$$f(x, y) = y - x^3 + 2x$$

write down expressions for f_x and f_y. Hence use implicit differentiation to find dy/dx given that

$$y - x^3 + 2x = 1$$

(b) Confirm your answer to part (a) by rearranging the equation

$$y - x^3 + 2x = 1$$

to give y explicitly in terms of x and using ordinary differentiation.

8. Find the first-order partial derivatives, $\dfrac{\partial z}{\partial u}, \dfrac{\partial z}{\partial v}, \dfrac{\partial z}{\partial w}$, for each of the following functions:

(a) $z = u + v^2 - 5w^3 + 2uv$ **(b)** $z = 6u^{1/2}v^{1/3}w^{1/6}$

9. **(a)** Use the small increments formula to estimate the change in

$$z = x^3 - 2xy$$

when x increases from 5 to 5.5 and y increases from 8 to 8.8.

(b) By evaluating z at $(5, 8)$ and $(5.5, 8.8)$, work out the exact change in z, and hence calculate the percentage error in using the small increments formula.

Exercise 5.1*

1. If

$$f(x, y) = 2xy + 3x$$

verify that $f(5, 7) \neq f(7, 5)$. Find all pairs of numbers, (x, y) for which $f(x, y) = f(y, x)$.

2. If

$$f(w, x, y) = 5w^{0.34}x^{0.25}y^{0.41}$$

show that $f(kw, kx, ky) = kf(w, x, y)$.

3. Find expressions for all first- and second-order partial derivatives of the following functions. In each case verify that

$$\frac{\partial^2 z}{\partial y \partial x} = \frac{\partial^2 z}{\partial x \partial y}$$

(a) $z = xy$ **(b)** $z = e^x y$ **(c)** $z = x^2 + 2x + y$ **(d)** $z = 16x^{1/4}y^{3/4}$ **(e)** $z = \dfrac{y}{x^2} + \dfrac{x}{y}$

4. If

$$z = x^2y^3 - 10xy + y^2$$

evaluate $\partial z/\partial x$ and $\partial z/\partial y$ at the point $(2, 3)$. Hence estimate the change in z as x increases by 0.2 and y decreases by 0.1.

5. Find the first-order derivatives, $\dfrac{\partial z}{\partial u}, \dfrac{\partial z}{\partial v}, \dfrac{\partial z}{\partial w}$, for each of the following functions

   (a) $z = (6u + vw^3)^4$ **(b)** $z = u\sqrt{w}e^{-vw}$

6. If $f(x,y) = x^3 e^{-2y}$ evaluate all first- and second-order derivatives at $(e, 1)$.

7. Verify that $x = 1$, $y = -1$ satisfy the equation $x^2 - 2y^3 = 3$. Use implicit differentiation to find the value of dy/dx at this point.

8. A function of three variables is given by

   $$f(x_1, x_2, x_3) = \frac{x_1 x_3^2}{x_2} + \ln(x_2 x_3)$$

   Find all of the first- and second-order derivatives of this function and verify that

   $$f_{12} = f_{21}, \quad f_{13} = f_{31} \quad \text{and} \quad f_{23} = f_{32}$$

9. Write down an expression for a function, $f(x, y)$, with first-order partial derivatives,

   $$\frac{\partial f}{\partial x} = 3xy(xy + 2) \quad \frac{\partial f}{\partial y} = x^2(2xy + 3)$$

10. Evaluate the second-order partial derivative, f_{23}, of the function

    $$f(x_1, x_2, x_3) = \frac{x_3 x_2^3}{x_1} + x_2 e^{x_3}$$

    at the point, $(3, 2, 0)$.

11. Find the value of $\dfrac{dy}{dx}$ at the point $(-2, 1)$ for the function which is defined implicitly by

    $$x^2 y - \frac{x}{y} = 6$$

12. Use implicit differentiation to find expressions, in terms of x and y, for $\dfrac{dy}{dx}$ for each of the following:

    (a) $x^3 y + 4xy^2 = 6$ **(b)** $12x^{1/3}y^{1/4} + x = 8$ **(c)** $ye^{xy} = 10$ **(d)** $\dfrac{x^2 + y^2}{x + y} = 5$

SECTION 5.2

Partial elasticity and marginal functions

Objectives

At the end of this section you should be able to:

- Calculate partial elasticities.

- Calculate marginal utilities.

- Calculate the marginal rate of commodity substitution along an indifference curve.

- Calculate marginal products.

- Calculate the marginal rate of technical substitution along an isoquant.

- State Euler's theorem for homogeneous production functions.

The first section of this chapter described the technique of partial differentiation. Hopefully, you have discovered that partial differentiation is no more difficult than ordinary differentiation. The only difference is that for functions of several variables you have to be clear at the outset which letter in a mathematical expression is to be the variable, and to bear in mind that all remaining letters are then just constants in disguise! Once you have done this, the actual differentiation itself obeys the usual rules. In Sections 4.3 and 4.5 we considered various microeconomic applications. Given the intimate relationship between ordinary and partial differentiation, you should not be too surprised to learn that we can extend these applications to functions of several variables. We concentrate on three main areas:

- elasticity of demand;

- utility;

- production.

We consider each of these in turn.

5.2.1 Elasticity of demand

Suppose that the demand, Q, for a certain good depends on its price, P, the price of an alternative good, P_A, and the income of consumers, Y, so that

$$Q = f(P, P_A, Y)$$

for some demand function, f.

Of particular interest is the responsiveness of demand to changes in any one of these three variables. This can be measured quantitatively using elasticity. The (own) **price elasticity of demand** is defined to be

$$E_P = \frac{\text{percentage change in } Q}{\text{percentage change in } P}$$

with P_A and Y held constant. This definition is identical to the one given in Section 4.5, so following the same mathematical argument presented there, we deduce that

$$E_P = \frac{P}{Q} \times \frac{\partial Q}{\partial P}$$

The partial derivative notation is used here because Q is now a function of several variables, and P_A and Y are held constant.

In an analogous way we can measure the responsiveness of demand to changes in the price of the alternative good. The **cross-price elasticity of demand** is defined to be

$$E_{P_A} = \frac{\text{percentage change in } Q}{\text{percentage change in } P_A}$$

with P and Y held constant. Again, the usual mathematical argument shows that

$$E_{P_A} = \frac{P_A}{Q} \times \frac{\partial Q}{\partial P_A}$$

The sign of E_{P_A} could turn out to be positive or negative depending on the nature of the alternative good. If the alternative good is substitutable, then Q increases as P_A rises, because consumers buy more of the given good as it becomes relatively less expensive. Consequently,

$$\frac{\partial Q}{\partial P_A} > 0$$

and so $E_{P_A} > 0$. If the alternative good is complementary, then Q decreases as P_A rises, because the bundle of goods as a whole becomes more expensive. Consequently,

$$\frac{\partial Q}{\partial P_A} < 0$$

and so $E_{P_A} < 0$.

Finally, the **income elasticity of demand** is defined to be

$$E_Y = \frac{\text{percentage change in } Q}{\text{percentage change in } Y}$$

and can be found from

$$E_Y = \frac{Y}{Q} \times \frac{\partial Q}{\partial Y}$$

Again, E_Y can be positive or negative. If a good is inferior, then demand falls as income rises and E_Y is negative. Canned vegetables, a supermarket's own-brand white bread and bus transportation are examples of inferior goods. If a good is normal, then demand rises as income rises and E_Y is positive. Sometimes the value of E_Y of a normal good might even exceed 1. These goods are called **superior**. For these goods the percentage rise in consumption is greater than the percentage increase in income. If income elasticity of demand is 1.25, a rise of 40% in income leads to a 50% increase in consumption. Examples of superior goods include sports cars, caviar and quality wine.

Example

Given the demand function

$$Q = 100 - 2P + P_A + 0.1Y$$

where $P = 10$, $P_A = 12$ and $Y = 1000$, find the

(a) price elasticity of demand;

(b) cross-price elasticity of demand;

(c) income elasticity of demand.

Is the alternative good substitutable or complementary?

Solution

We begin by calculating the value of Q when $P = 10$, $P_A = 12$ and $Y = 1000$. The demand function gives

$$Q = 100 - 2(10) + 12 + 0.1(1000) = 192$$

(a) To find the price elasticity of demand we partially differentiate

$$Q = 100 - 2P + P_A + 0.1Y$$

with respect to P to get

$$\frac{\partial Q}{\partial P} = -2$$

Hence

$$E_P = \frac{P}{Q} \times \frac{\partial Q}{\partial P} = \frac{10}{192} \times (-2) = -0.10$$

(b) To find the cross-price elasticity of demand we partially differentiate

$$Q = 100 - 2P + P_A + 0.1Y$$

with respect to P_A to get

$$\frac{\partial Q}{\partial P_A} = 1$$

Hence

$$E_{P_A} = \frac{P_A}{Q} \times \frac{\partial Q}{\partial P_A} = \frac{12}{192} \times 1 = 0.06$$

The fact that this is positive shows that the two goods are substitutable.

(c) To find the income elasticity of demand we partially differentiate

$$Q = 100 - 2P + P_A + 0.1Y$$

with respect to Y to get

$$\frac{\partial Q}{\partial Y} = 0.1$$

Hence

$$E_Y = \frac{Y}{Q} \times \frac{\partial Q}{\partial Y} = \frac{1000}{192} \times 0.1 = 0.52$$

Practice Problem

1. Given the demand function

$$Q = 500 - 3P - 2P_A + 0.01Y$$

where $P = 20$, $P_A = 30$ and $Y = 5000$, find

(a) the price elasticity of demand;

(b) the cross-price elasticity of demand;

(c) the income elasticity of demand.

If income rises by 5%, calculate the corresponding percentage change in demand. Would this good be classified as inferior, normal or superior?

5.2.2 Utility

So far in this text we have concentrated almost exclusively on the behaviour of producers. In this case it is straightforward to identify the primary objective, which is to maximise profit. We now turn our attention to consumers. Unfortunately, it is not so easy to identify the motivation for their behaviour. One tentative suggestion is that consumers try to maximise earned income. However, if this were the case, then individuals would try to work 24 hours a day for seven days a week, which is not so. In practice, people like to allocate a reasonable proportion of time to leisure activities.

Consumers are faced with a choice of how many hours each week to spend working and how many to devote to leisure. In the same way, a consumer needs to decide how many items of various goods to buy and has a preference between the options available. To analyse the behaviour of consumers quantitatively, we associate with each set of options a number, U, called **utility**, which indicates the level of satisfaction. Suppose that there are two goods, G1 and G2, and that the consumer buys x_1 items of G1 and x_2 items of G2. The variable U is then a function of x_1 and x_2, which we write as

$$U = U(x_1, x_2)$$

If

$$U(3, 7) = 20 \quad \text{and} \quad U(4, 5) = 25$$

for example, then the consumer derives greater satisfaction from buying four items of G1 and five items of G2 than from buying three items of G1 and seven items of G2.

Utility is a function of two variables, so we can work out two first-order partial derivatives,

$$\frac{\partial U}{\partial x_1} \quad \text{and} \quad \frac{\partial U}{\partial x_2}$$

The derivative

$$\frac{\partial U}{\partial x_i}$$

gives the rate of change of U with respect to x_i and is called the **marginal utility of x_i**. If x_i changes by a small amount Δx_i and the other variable is held fixed, then the change in U satisfies

$$\Delta U \cong \frac{\partial U}{\partial x_i} \Delta x_i$$

If x_1 and x_2 both change, then the net change in U can be found from the small increments formula

$$\Delta U \cong \frac{\partial U}{\partial x_1} \Delta x_1 + \frac{\partial U}{\partial x_2} \Delta x_2$$

Example

Given the utility function

$$U = x_1^{1/4} x_2^{3/4}$$

determine the value of the marginal utilities

$$\frac{\partial U}{\partial x_1} \quad \text{and} \quad \frac{\partial U}{\partial x_2}$$

when $x_1 = 100$ and $x_2 = 200$. Hence estimate the change in utility when x_1 decreases from 100 to 99 and x_2 increases from 200 to 201.

Solution

If

$$U = x_1^{1/4} x_2^{3/4}$$

then

$$\frac{\partial U}{\partial x_1} = \frac{1}{4} x_1^{-3/4} x_2^{3/4} \quad \text{and} \quad \frac{\partial U}{\partial x_2} = \frac{3}{4} x_1^{1/4} x_2^{-1/4}$$

so when $x_1 = 100$ and $x_2 = 200$

$$\frac{\partial U}{\partial x_1} = \frac{1}{4}(100)^{-3/4}(200)^{3/4} = 0.42$$

$$\frac{\partial U}{\partial x_2} = \frac{3}{4}(100)^{1/4}(200)^{-1/4} = 0.63$$

Now, x_1 decreases by 1 unit, so

$$\Delta x_1 = -1$$

and x_2 increases by 1 unit, so

$$\Delta x_2 = 1$$

The small increments formula states that

$$\Delta U \cong \frac{\partial U}{\partial x_1} \Delta x_1 + \frac{\partial U}{\partial x_2} \Delta x_2$$

The change in utility is therefore

$$\Delta U \cong (0.42)(-1) + (0.63)(1) = 0.21$$

Note that for the particular utility function

$$U = x_1^{1/4} x_2^{3/4}$$

given in the previous example, the second-order derivatives

$$\frac{\partial^2 U}{\partial x_1^2} = \frac{-3}{16} x_1^{-7/4} x_2^{3/4} \quad \text{and} \quad \frac{\partial^2 U}{\partial x_2^2} = \frac{-3}{16} x_1^{1/4} x_2^{-5/4}$$

are both negative. Now $\partial^2 U/\partial x_1^2$ is the partial derivative of marginal utility $\partial U/\partial x_1$ with respect to x_1. The fact that this is negative means that marginal utility of x_1 decreases as x_1 rises. In other words, as the consumption of good G1 increases, each additional item of G1 bought confers less utility than the previous item. A similar property holds for G2. This is known as the **law of diminishing marginal utility**.

Advice

You might like to compare this with the law of diminishing marginal productivity discussed in Section 4.3.2.

Practice Problem

2. An individual's utility function is given by

    $$U = 1000x_1 + 450x_2 + 5x_1 x_2 - 2x_1^2 - x_2^2$$

    where x_1 is the amount of leisure measured in hours per week, and x_2 is earned income measured in dollars per week.
    Determine the value of the marginal utilities

    $$\frac{\partial U}{\partial x_1} \quad \text{and} \quad \frac{\partial U}{\partial x_2}$$

    when $x_1 = 138$ and $x_2 = 500$.
    Hence estimate the change in U if the individual works for an extra hour, which increases earned income by $15 per week.
    Does the law of diminishing marginal utility hold for this function?

It was pointed out in Section 5.1 that functions of two variables could be represented by surfaces in three dimensions. This is all very well in theory, but in practice the task of sketching such a surface by hand is virtually impossible. This difficulty has been faced by geographers for years, and the way they circumvent the problem is to produce a two-dimensional contour map. A contour is a curve joining all points at the same height above sea level. Exactly the same device can be used for utility functions. Rather than attempt to sketch the surface, we draw an **indifference map**. This consists of **indifference curves** joining points (x_1, x_2) which give the same value of utility. Mathematically, an indifference curve is defined by an equation

$$U(x_1, x_2) = U_0$$

for some fixed value of U_0. A typical indifference map is sketched in Figure 5.4.
Points A and B both lie on the lower indifference curve, $U_0 = 20$. Point A corresponds to the case when the consumer buys a_1 units of G1 and a_2 units of G2. Likewise, point B corresponds

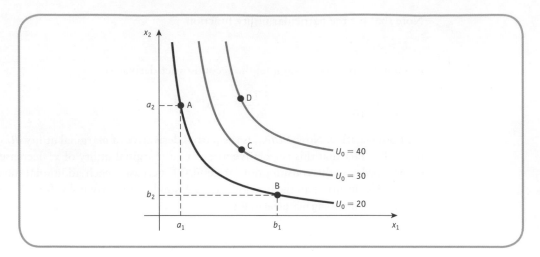

Figure 5.4

to the case when the consumer buys b_1 units of G1 and b_2 units of G2. Both of these combinations yield the same level of satisfaction and the consumer is indifferent to choosing between them. In symbols we have

$U(a_1, a_2) = 20$ and $U(b_1, b_2) = 20$

Points C and D lie on indifference curves that are further away from the origin. The combinations of goods that these points represent yield higher levels of utility and so are ranked above those of A and B.

Indifference curves are usually downward-sloping. If fewer purchases are made of G1, then the consumer has to compensate for this by buying more of type G2 to maintain the same level of satisfaction. Note also from Figure 5.4 that the slope of an indifference curve varies along its length, taking large negative values close to the vertical axis and becoming almost zero as the curve approaches the horizontal axis. Again, this is to be expected for any function that obeys the law of diminishing marginal utility. A consumer who currently owns a large number of items of G2 and relatively few of G1 is likely to value G1 more highly. Consequently, he or she might be satisfied in sacrificing a large number of items of G2 to gain just one or two extra items of G1. In this region the marginal utility of x_1 is much greater than that of x_2, which accounts for the steepness of the curve close to the vertical axis. Similarly, as the curve approaches the horizontal axis, the situation is reversed and the curve flattens off. We quantify this exchange of goods by introducing the **marginal rate of commodity substitution**, MRCS. This is defined to be the increase in x_2 necessary to maintain a constant value of utility when x_1 decreases by 1 unit. This is illustrated in Figure 5.5.

Starting at point E, we move 1 unit to the left. The value of MRCS is then the vertical distance that we need to travel if we are to remain on the indifference curve passing through E. Now this sort of '1-unit change' definition is precisely the approach that we took in Section 4.3 when discussing marginal functions. In that section we actually defined the marginal function to be the derived function and we showed that the '1-unit change' definition gave a good approximation to it. If we do the same here, then we can define

$$\text{MRCS} = -\frac{dx_2}{dx_1}$$

The derivative, dx_2/dx_1, determines the slope of an indifference curve when x_1 is plotted on the horizontal axis and x_2 is plotted on the vertical axis. This is negative, so we deliberately

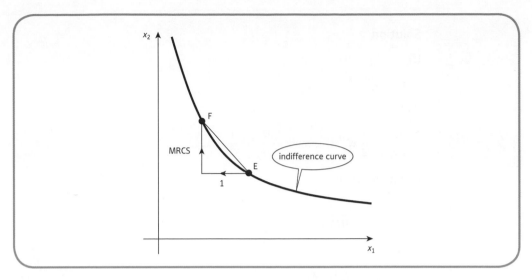

Figure 5.5

put a minus sign in front to make MRCS positive. This definition is useful only if we can find the equation of an indifference curve with x_2 given explicitly in terms of x_1. However, we may only know the utility function

$U(x_1, x_2)$

so that the indifference curve is determined implicitly from an equation

$U(x_1, x_2) = U_0$

This is precisely the situation that we discussed at the end of Section 5.1. The formula for implicit differentiation gives

$$\frac{dx_2}{dx_1} = -\frac{\partial U/\partial x_1}{\partial U/\partial x_2}$$

Hence

$$\text{MRCS} = -\frac{dx_2}{dx_1} = \frac{\partial U/\partial x_1}{\partial U/\partial x_2}$$

marginal rate of commodity substitution is the marginal utility of x_1 divided by the marginal utility of x_2

Example

Given the utility function

$$U = x_1^{1/2} x_2^{1/2}$$

find a general expression for MRCS in terms of x_1 and x_2.

Calculate the particular value of MRCS for the indifference curve that passes through (300, 500). Hence estimate the increase in x_2 required to maintain the current level of utility when x_1 decreases by 3 units.

Solution

If

$$U = x_1^{1/2} x_2^{1/2}$$

then

$$\frac{\partial U}{\partial x_1} = \frac{1}{2} x_1^{-1/2} x_2^{1/2} \quad \text{and} \quad \frac{\partial U}{\partial x_2} = \frac{1}{2} x_1^{1/2} x_2^{-1/2}$$

Using the result

$$\text{MRCS} = \frac{\partial U/\partial x_1}{\partial U/\partial x_2}$$

we see that

$$\text{MRCS} = \frac{\frac{1}{2} x_1^{-1/2} x_2^{1/2}}{\frac{1}{2} x_1^{1/2} x_2^{-1/2}}$$

$$= x_1^{-1} x_2^1$$

rule 2 of indices;
$b^m \div b^n = b^{m-n}$

$b^1 = b,$
$b^{-1} = \dfrac{1}{b}$

$$= \frac{x_2}{x_1}$$

At the point (300, 500)

$$\text{MRCS} = \frac{500}{300} = \frac{5}{3}$$

Now MRCS approximates the increase in x_2 required to maintain a constant level of utility when x_1 decreases by 1 unit. In this example x_1 decreases by 3 units, so we multiply MRCS by 3. The approximate increase in x_2 is

$$\frac{5}{3} \times 3 = 5$$

We can check the accuracy of this approximation by evaluating U at the old point (300, 500) and the new point (297, 505). We get

$$U(300, 500) = (300)^{1/2} (500)^{1/2} = 387.30$$
$$U(297, 505) = (297)^{1/2} (505)^{1/2} = 387.28$$

This shows that, to all intents and purposes, the two points do indeed lie on the same indifference curve.

Practice Problem

3. Calculate the value of MRCS for the utility function given in Practice Problem 2 at the point (138, 500). Hence estimate the increase in earned income required to maintain the current level of utility if leisure time falls by two hours per week.

5.2.3 Production

Production functions were first introduced in Section 2.3. We assume that output, Q, depends on capital, K, and labour, L, so we can write

$$Q = f(K, L)$$

Such functions can be analysed in a similar way to utility functions. The partial derivative

$$\frac{\partial Q}{\partial K}$$

gives the rate of change of output with respect to capital and is called the **marginal product of capital**, MP_K. If capital changes by a small amount ΔK, with labour held constant, then the corresponding change in Q is given by

$$\Delta Q \cong \frac{\partial Q}{\partial K} \Delta K$$

Similarly,

$$\frac{\partial Q}{\partial L}$$

gives the rate of change of output with respect to labour and is called the **marginal product of labour**, MP_L. If labour changes by a small amount ΔL, with capital held constant, then the corresponding change in Q is given by

$$\Delta Q \cong \frac{\partial Q}{\partial L} \Delta L$$

If K and L both change simultaneously, then the net change in Q can be found from the small increments formula

$$\Delta Q \cong \frac{\partial Q}{\partial K} \Delta K + \frac{\partial Q}{\partial L} \Delta L$$

The contours of a production function are called **isoquants**. In Greek 'iso' means 'equal', so the word 'isoquant' literally translates as 'equal quantity'. Points on an isoquant represent all possible combinations of inputs (K, L) which produce a constant level of output, Q_0. A typical isoquant map is sketched in Figure 5.6. Notice that we have adopted the standard convention of plotting labour on the horizontal axis and capital on the vertical axis.

The lower curve determines the input pairs needed to output 100 units. Higher levels of output correspond to isoquants further away from the origin. Again, the general shape of the curves is to be expected. For example, as capital is reduced, it is necessary to increase labour to compensate and so maintain production levels. Moreover, if capital continues to decrease, the rate of substitution of labour for capital goes up. We quantify this exchange of inputs by defining the **marginal rate of technical substitution**, MRTS, to be

$$-\frac{dK}{dL}$$

so that MRTS is the positive value of the slope of an isoquant. As in the case of a utility function, the formula for implicit differentiation shows that

$$\text{MRTS} = \frac{\partial Q/\partial L}{\partial Q/\partial K} = \frac{MP_L}{MP_K}$$

> marginal rate of technical substitution is the marginal product of labour divided by the marginal product of capital

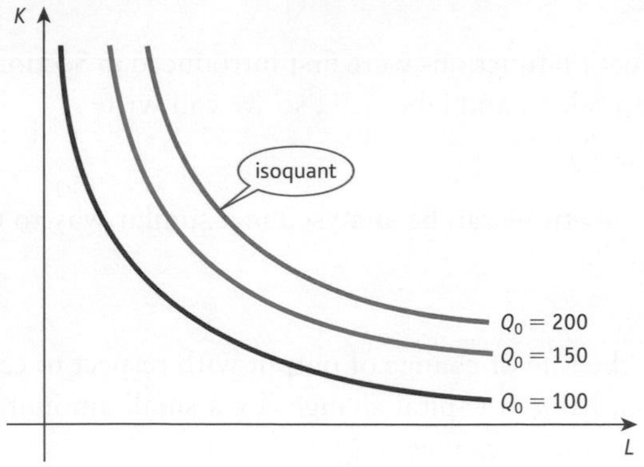

Figure 5.6

As an example, consider the Cobb–Douglas production function given by

$$Q = AK^\alpha L^\beta$$

where A, α and β are positive constants. Partial differentiation of

$$Q = AK^\alpha L^\beta$$

with respect to K and L gives

$$\text{MP}_K = \alpha A K^{\alpha-1} L^\beta \quad \text{and} \quad \text{MP}_L = \beta A K^\alpha L^{\beta-1}$$

Hence

$$\text{MRTS} = \frac{\text{MP}_L}{\text{MP}_K} = \frac{\beta A K^\alpha L^{\beta-1}}{\alpha A K^{\alpha-1} L^\beta} = \frac{\beta K}{\alpha L}$$

Practice Problem

4. Given the production function

$$Q = K^2 + 2L^2$$

write down expressions for the marginal products

$$\frac{\partial Q}{\partial K} \quad \text{and} \quad \frac{\partial Q}{\partial L}$$

Hence show that

(a) $\text{MRTS} = \dfrac{2L}{K}$

(b) $K\dfrac{\partial Q}{\partial K} + L\dfrac{\partial Q}{\partial L} = 2Q$

Advice

Production functions and the concept of homogeneity were covered in Section 2.3. You might find it useful to revise this before reading the next paragraph.

Recall that a production function is described as being homogeneous of degree n if, for any number λ,

$$f(\lambda K, \lambda L) = \lambda^n f(K, L)$$

A production function is then said to display decreasing returns to scale, constant returns to scale or increasing returns to scale, depending on whether $n < 1$, $n = 1$ or $n > 1$, respectively. One useful result concerning homogeneous functions is known as **Euler's theorem**, which states that

$$K\frac{\partial f}{\partial K} + L\frac{\partial f}{\partial L} = nf(K, L)$$

In fact, you have already verified this in Practice Problem 4(b) for the particular production function

$$Q = K^2 + 2L^2$$

which is easily shown to be homogeneous of degree 2. We have no intention of proving this theorem, although you are invited to confirm its validity for general Cobb–Douglas production functions in Question 4 in Exercise 5.2* at the end of this section.

The special case $n = 1$ is worthy of note because the right-hand side is then simply $f(K, L)$, which is equal to the output, Q. Euler's theorem for homogeneous production functions of degree 1 states that

$$\boxed{\text{Capital times marginal product of capital}} + \boxed{\text{labour times marginal product of labour}} = \boxed{\text{total output}}$$

If each input factor is paid an amount equal to its marginal product, then each term on the left-hand side gives the total bill for that factor. For example, if each unit of labour is paid MP_L, then the cost of L units of labour is $L(MP_L)$. Provided that the production function displays constant returns to scale, Euler's theorem shows that the sum of the factor payments is equal to the total output.

Key Terms

Cross-price elasticity of demand   The responsiveness of demand for one good due to a change in the price of another: (percentage change in quantity) ÷ (percentage change in the price of the alternative good).

Euler's theorem   If each input is paid the value of its marginal product, the total cost of these inputs is equal to total output, provided there are constant returns to scale.

Income elasticity of demand   The responsiveness of demand for one good due to a change in income: (percentage change in quantity) ÷ (percentage change in income).

Indifference curve   A curve indicating all combinations of two goods which give the same level of utility.

Indifference map   A diagram showing the graphs of a set of indifference curves. The further the curve is from the origin, the greater the level of utility.

Isoquant   A curve indicating all combinations of two factors which give the same level of output.

Law of diminishing marginal utility   The law which states that the increase in utility due to the consumption of an additional good will eventually decline: $\partial^2 U/\partial x_i^2 < 0$ for sufficiently large x_i.

Marginal product of capital   The additional output produced by a 1 unit increase in capital: $MP_K = \partial Q/\partial K$.

Marginal product of labour   The additional output produced by a 1-unit increase in labour: $MP_L = \partial Q / \partial L$.

Marginal rate of commodity substitution (MRCS)   The amount by which one input needs to increase to maintain a constant value of utility when the other input decreases by 1 unit: $MRCS = \partial U / \partial x_1 \div \partial U / \partial x_2$.

Marginal rate of technical substitution (MRTS)   The amount by which capital needs to rise to maintain a constant level of output when labour decreases by 1 unit: $MRTS = MP_L / MP_K$.

Marginal utility   The extra satisfaction gained by consuming 1 extra unit of a good: $\partial U / \partial x_i$.

Price elasticity of demand   A measure of the responsiveness of the change in demand due to a change in price: (percentage change in demand) $\div$ (percentage change in price).

Superior good   A normal good for which the percentage rise in consumption exceeds the percentage increase in income.

Utility   The satisfaction gained from the consumption of a good.

Exercise 5.2

1. Given the demand function

    $$Q = 1000 - 5P - P_A^2 + 0.005Y^3$$

    where $P = 15$, $P_A = 20$ and $Y = 100$, find the income elasticity of demand and explain why this is a superior good.

    Give your answer correct to two decimal places.

2. Given the demand function

    $$Q = 200 - 2P - P_A + 0.1Y^2$$

    where $P = 10$, $P_A = 15$ and $Y = 100$, find

    (a) the price elasticity of demand;

    (b) the cross-price elasticity of demand;

    (c) the income elasticity of demand.

    Estimate the percentage change in demand if P_A rises by 3%. Is the alternative good substitutable or complementary?

3. A utility function is given by $U = 2x^2 + y^2$.

    (a) State the equation of the indifference curve which passes through (4, 2).

    (b) Calculate the marginal utilities at (4, 2) and hence work out the gradient of the curve at this point.

4. The satisfaction gained by consuming x units of good 1 and y units of good 2 is measured by the utility function

    $$U = 2x^2 + 5y^3$$

    Currently an individual consumes 20 units of good 1 and 8 units of good 2.

    (a) Find the marginal utility of good 1 and hence estimate the increase in satisfaction gained from consuming one more unit of good 1.

    (b) Find the marginal utility of good 2 and hence estimate the increase in satisfaction gained from consuming one more unit of good 2.

5. Given the demand function

$$Q = \frac{P_A Y}{P^2}$$

find the income elasticity of demand.

6. Given the utility function

$$U = x_1^{1/2} x_2^{1/3}$$

determine the value of the marginal utilities

$$\frac{\partial U}{\partial x_1} \quad \text{and} \quad \frac{\partial U}{\partial x_2}$$

at the point $(25, 8)$. Hence

(a) estimate the change in utility when x_1 and x_2 both increase by 1 unit;

(b) find the marginal rate of commodity substitution at this point.

7. Evaluate MP_K and MP_L for the production function

$$Q = 2LK + \sqrt{L}$$

given that the current levels of K and L are 7 and 4, respectively. Hence

(a) write down the value of MRTS;

(b) estimate the increase in capital needed to maintain the current level of output given a 1-unit decrease in labour.

8. If $Q = 2K^3 + 3L^2K$, show that $K(MP_K) + L(MP_L) = 3Q$.

9. The demand functions for two commodities, A and B, are given by

$$Q_A = AP^{-0.5}Y^{0.5} \text{ and } Q_B = BP^{-1.5}Y^{1.5} \quad \text{where } A \text{ and } B \text{ are positive constants}$$

(a) Find the price elasticity of demand for each good and hence comment on the relative sensitivity of demand due to changes in price.

(b) Find the income elasticity of demand for each good. Which good is normal and which is superior? Give a reason for your answer.

10. A firm's production function is given by $Q = 18K^{1/6}L^{5/6}$.

(a) Show that this function displays constant returns to scale.

(b) Find expressions for the marginal products of capital and labour.

(c) State what happens to the marginal product of labour when

(i) labour increases with capital held constant;

(ii) capital increases with labour held constant.

Exercise 5.2*

1. The demand function of a good is given by

$$Q = 500 - 4P + 0.02Y$$

Price and income are known to be $P = 20$ and $Y = 14\,000$, respectively.

(a) Find the income elasticity of demand.

(b) Estimate the percentage change in demand when income rises by 8%, and comment on the growth potential of this good in an expanding economy.

2. Find the value of the marginal rate of technical substitution for the production function,

$$Q = 300K^{2/3}L^{1/2}$$

when $K = 40$, $L = 60$.

3. A utility function is given by

$$U = x_1^{2/3}x_2^{1/2}$$

Find the value of x_2 if the points $(64, 256)$ and $(512, x_2)$ lie on the same indifference curve.

4. Show that the Cobb–Douglas production function $Q = AK^\alpha L^\beta$ is homogeneous of degree $\alpha + \beta$ and that

(a) $K\dfrac{\partial Q}{\partial K} + L\dfrac{\partial Q}{\partial L} = (\alpha + \beta)Q$

(b) $K^2\dfrac{\partial^2 Q}{\partial K^2} + 2KL\dfrac{\partial^2 Q}{\partial K\partial L} + L^2\dfrac{\partial^2 Q}{\partial L^2} = (\alpha + \beta)(\alpha + \beta - 1)Q$

5. An individual's utility function is given by

$$U = Ax_1^{0.7}x_2^{0.5}$$

where x_1 and x_2 denote the number of units consumed of goods 1 and 2.

(a) Show that the marginal utility of x_1 is positive and give an interpretation of this result.

(b) Show that the second-order derivative $\dfrac{\partial^2 U}{\partial x_1 \partial x_2}$ is positive and give an interpretation of this result.

(c) Show that the second-order derivative $\dfrac{\partial^2 U}{\partial x_1^2}$ is negative and give an interpretation of this result.

6. If a firm's production function is given by

$$Q = 5L + 7K$$

sketch the isoquant corresponding to an output level, $Q = 700$. Use your graph to find the value of MRTS and confirm this using partial differentiation.

7. A firm's production function is given by

$$Q = 10\sqrt{(KL)} + 3L$$

with $K = 90$ and $L = 40$.

(a) Find the values of the marginal products, MP_K and MP_L.

(b) Use the results of part (a) to estimate the overall effect on Q when K increases by 3 units and L decreases by 2 units.

(c) State the value of the marginal rate of technical substitution and give an interpretation of this value.

8. A firm's production function is

$$Q = A[bK^\alpha + (1 - b)L^\alpha]^{1/\alpha}$$

(a) Show that the marginal rate of technical substitution is given by

$$\text{MRTS} = \frac{1 - b}{b}\left(\frac{K}{L}\right)^{1-\alpha}$$

(b) Show that the marginal products satisfy the relation

$$K\frac{\partial Q}{\partial K} + L\frac{\partial Q}{\partial L} = Q$$

9. The demand function of a good is given by

$$Q = a - bP - cP_A + dY$$

where P is the price of the good, P_A is the price of an alternative good, Y is income and the coefficients a, b, c and d are all positive. It is known that $P = 50$, $P_A = 30$, $Y = 1000$ and $Q = 5000$.

(a) Is the alternative good substitutable or complementary? Give a reason for your answer.

(b) Find expressions, in terms of b, c and d, for the

(i) price elasticity of demand;

(ii) cross-price elasticity of demand;

(iii) income elasticity of demand.

(c) The cross-price elasticity is -0.012. The income elasticity is four times the magnitude of the price elasticity. When income increases by 10%, the demand increases by 2%. Determine the values of a, b, c and d.

10. The demand function of a good is given by

$$Q = kP^{-a}P_A^b Y^c$$

where P is the own price, P_A is the price of an alternative good and Y is income. The letters k, a, b and c are positive constants.

(a) Explain why the alternative good is substitutable.

(b) Show that own price elasticity, cross-price elasticity and income elasticity are $-a$, b and c, respectively.

(c) Explain briefly why the proportion of income spent on this good is given by PQ/Y and deduce that for this demand function, this proportion is

$$kP^{1-a}P_A^b Y^{c-1}$$

Hence show that when $c > 1$, the proportion of income spent on this good rises with income.

11. Find the marginal rate of commodity substitution for each of these utility functions and hence state whether the indifference map consists of convex curves, concave curves or straight lines.

(a) $U = (2x_1 + 3x_2)^3$ (b) $U = 5x_1^3 x_2$ (c) $U = 2\sqrt{x_1} + 6\sqrt{x_2}$

SECTION 5.3
Comparative statics

Objectives

At the end of this section you should be able to:

- Use structural equations to derive the reduced form of macroeconomic models.
- Calculate national income multipliers.
- Use multipliers to give a qualitative description of economic models.
- Use multipliers to give a quantitative description of economic models.
- Calculate multipliers for the linear one-commodity market model.

Advice

The content of this section is quite difficult since it depends on ideas covered earlier in this text. You might find it helpful to read quickly through Section 1.7 now before tackling the new material.

The simplest macroeconomic model, discussed in Section 1.7, assumes that there are two sectors, households and firms, and that household consumption, C, is modelled by a linear relationship of the form

$$C = aY + b \tag{1}$$

In this equation Y denotes national income and a and b are parameters. The parameter a is the marginal propensity to consume and lies in the range $0 < a < 1$. The parameter b is the autonomous consumption and satisfies $b > 0$. In equilibrium

$$Y = C + I \tag{2}$$

where I denotes investment, which is assumed to be given by

$$I = I^* \tag{3}$$

for some constant I^*. Equations (1), (2) and (3) describe the structure of the model and as such are called **structural equations**. Substituting equations (1) and (3) into equation (2) gives

$$Y = aY + b + I^*$$

$$Y - aY = b + I^* \qquad \text{(subtract } aY \text{ from both sides)}$$

$$(1 - a)Y = b + I^* \qquad \text{(take out a common factor of } Y\text{)}$$

$$Y = \frac{b + I^*}{1 - a} \qquad \text{(divide both sides by } 1 - a\text{)}$$

This is known as the **reduced form** because it compresses the model into a single equation in which the endogenous variable, Y, is expressed in terms of the exogenous variable, I^*, and parameters, a and b. The process of analysing the equilibrium level of income in this way is referred to as **statics** because it assumes that the equilibrium state is attained instantaneously. The branch of mathematical economics which investigates time dependence is known as **dynamics** and is considered in Chapter 9.

We should like to do rather more than just to calculate the equilibrium values here. In particular, we are interested in the effect on the endogenous variables in a model brought about by changes in the exogenous variables and parameters. This is known as **comparative statics**, since we seek to compare the effects obtained by varying each variable and parameter in turn. The actual mechanism for change will be ignored, and it will be assumed that the system returns to equilibrium instantaneously. The equation

$$Y = \frac{b + I^*}{1 - a}$$

shows that Y is a function of three variables, a, b and I^*, so we can write down three partial derivatives

$$\frac{\partial Y}{\partial a}, \frac{\partial Y}{\partial b}, \frac{\partial Y}{\partial I^*}$$

The only hard one to work out is the first, and this is found using the chain rule by writing

$$Y = (b + I^*)(1 - a)^{-1}$$

which gives

$$\frac{\partial Y}{\partial a} = (b + I^*)(-1)(1 - a)^{-2}(-1) = \frac{b + I^*}{(1 - a)^2}$$

To interpret this derivative let us suppose that the marginal propensity to consume, a, changes by Δa with b and I^* held constant. The corresponding change in Y is given by

$$\Delta Y = \frac{\partial Y}{\partial a} \Delta a$$

Strictly speaking, the '=' sign should really be '≅'. However, as we have seen in the previous two sections, provided that Δa is small, the approximation is reasonably accurate. In any case, we could argue that the model itself is only a first approximation to what is really happening in the economy and so any further small inaccuracies that are introduced are unlikely to have any significant effect on our conclusions. The above equation shows that the change in national income is found by multiplying the change in the marginal propensity to consume by the partial derivative $\partial Y/\partial a$. For this reason, the partial derivative is called the **marginal propensity to consume multiplier** for Y. In the same way, $\partial Y/\partial b$ and $\partial Y/\partial I^*$ are called the **autonomous consumption multiplier** and the **investment multiplier**, respectively.

Multipliers enable us to explain the behaviour of the model both qualitatively and quantitatively. The qualitative behaviour can be described simply by inspecting the multipliers as they stand, before any numerical values are assigned to the variables and parameters. It is usually possible to state whether the multipliers are positive or negative and hence whether an increase in an exogenous variable or parameter leads to an increase or decrease in the corresponding endogenous variable. In the present model it is apparent that the marginal propensity to consume multiplier for Y is positive because it is known that b and I^* are both positive, and the denominator $(1 - a)^2$ is clearly positive. Therefore, national income rises whenever a rises.

Once the exogenous variables and parameters have been assigned specific numerical values, the behaviour of the model can be explained quantitatively. For example, if $b = 10$, $I^* = 30$ and $a = 0.5$, then the marginal propensity to consume multiplier is

$$\frac{b + I^*}{(1-a)^2} = \frac{10 + 30}{(1 - 0.5)^2} = 160$$

This means that when the marginal propensity to consume rises by, say, 0.02 units, the change in national income is

$$160 \times 0.02 = 3.2$$

Of course, if a, b and I^* change by amounts Δa, Δb and ΔI^* simultaneously, then the small increments formula shows that the change in Y can be found from

$$\Delta Y = \frac{\partial Y}{\partial a}\Delta a + \frac{\partial Y}{\partial b}\Delta b + \frac{\partial Y}{\partial I^*}\Delta I^*$$

The investment multiplier in this model can be found by first writing

$$Y = \frac{b}{1-a} + \frac{I^*}{1-a}$$

so that

$$\frac{\partial Y}{\partial I^*} = \frac{1}{1-a}$$

which is positive because $a < 1$. To analyse this multiplier quantitatively let us suppose that the marginal propensity to consume, $a = 0.6$, and consider what happens to national income when investment rises by 4 units. In this case the investment multiplier is

$$\frac{1}{1-a} = \frac{1}{1 - 0.6} = \frac{1}{0.4} = 2.5$$

so if investment were to rise by 4 units, the change in national income would be $2.5 \times 4 = 10$.

Practice Problem

1. By substituting

$$Y = \frac{b + I^*}{1 - a}$$

into

$$C = aY + b$$

write down the reduced equation for C in terms of a, b and I^*. Hence show that the investment multiplier for C is

$$\frac{a}{1-a}$$

Deduce that an increase in investment always leads to an increase in consumption. Calculate the change in consumption when investment rises by 2 units if the marginal propensity to consume is $^1/_2$.

The following example is more difficult because it involves three sectors: households, firms and government. However, the basic strategy for analysing the model is the same. We first obtain the reduced form, which is differentiated to determine the relevant multipliers. These can then be used to discuss the behaviour of national income both qualitatively and quantitatively.

Example

Consider the three-sector model

$$Y = C + I + G \tag{1}$$

$$C = aY_d + b \qquad (0 < a < 1, b > 0) \tag{2}$$

$$Y_d = Y - T \tag{3}$$

$$T = tY + T^* \qquad (0 < t < 1, T^* > 0) \tag{4}$$

$$I = I^* \qquad (I^* > 0) \tag{5}$$

$$G = G^* \qquad (G^* > 0) \tag{6}$$

where G denotes government expenditure and T denotes taxation.

(a) Show that

$$Y = \frac{-aT^* + b + I^* + G^*}{1 - a + at}$$

(b) Write down the government expenditure multiplier and autonomous taxation multiplier. Deduce the direction of change in Y due to increases in G^* and T^*.

(c) If it is government policy to finance any increase in expenditure, ΔG^*, by an increase in autonomous taxation, ΔT^*, so that

$$\Delta G^* = \Delta T^*$$

show that national income rises by an amount that is less than the rise in expenditure.

(d) If $a = 0.7$, $b = 50$, $T^* = 200$, $t = 0.2$, $I^* = 100$ and $G^* = 300$, calculate the equilibrium level of national income, Y, and the change in Y due to a 10-unit increase in government expenditure.

Solution

(a) We need to 'solve' equations (1)–(6) for Y. An obvious first move is to substitute equations (2), (5) and (6) into equation (1) to get

$$Y = aY_d + b + I^* + G^* \tag{7}$$

Now, from equations (3) and (4),

$$Y_d = Y - T$$
$$= Y - (tY + T^*)$$
$$= Y - tY - T^*$$

so this can be put into equation (7) to get

$$Y = a(Y - tY - T^*) + b + I^* + G^*$$
$$= aY - atY - aT^* + b + I^* + G^*$$

Collecting terms in Y on the left-hand side gives

$$(1 - a + at)Y = -aT^* + b + I^* + G^*$$

which produces the desired equation

$$Y = \frac{-aT^* + b + I^* + G^*}{1 - a + at}$$

(b) The government expenditure multiplier is

$$\frac{\partial Y}{\partial G^*} = \frac{1}{1 - a + at}$$

and the autonomous taxation multiplier is

$$\frac{\partial Y}{\partial T^*} = \frac{-a}{1 - a + at}$$

We are given that $a < 1$, so $1 - a > 0$. Also, we know that a and t are both positive, so their product, at, must be positive. The expression $(1 - a) + at$ is therefore positive, being the sum of two positive terms. The government expenditure multiplier is therefore positive, which shows that any increase in G^* leads to an increase in Y. The autonomous taxation multiplier is negative because its numerator is negative and its denominator is positive. This shows that any increase in T^* leads to a decrease in Y.

(c) Government policy is to finance a rise in expenditure out of autonomous taxation, so that

$$\Delta G^* = \Delta T^*$$

From the small increments formula

$$\Delta Y = \frac{\partial Y}{\partial G^*}\Delta G^* + \frac{\partial Y}{\partial T^*}\Delta T^*$$

we deduce that

$$\Delta Y = \left(\frac{\partial Y}{\partial G^*} + \frac{\partial Y}{\partial T^*}\right)\Delta G^* = \left(\frac{1}{1 - a + at} + \frac{a}{1 - a + at}\right)\Delta G^* = \left(\frac{1 - a}{1 - a + at}\right)\Delta G^*$$

The multiplier

$$\frac{1 - a}{1 - a + at}$$

is called the **balanced budget multiplier** and is positive because the numerator and denominator are both positive. An increase in government expenditure leads to an increase in national income. However, the denominator is greater than the numerator by an amount at, so that

$$\frac{1 - a}{1 - a + at} < 1$$

and $\Delta Y < \Delta G^*$, showing that the rise in national income is less than the rise in expenditure.

(d) To solve this part of the problem we simply substitute the numerical values $a = 0.7$, $b = 50$, $T^* = 200$, $t = 0.2$, $I^* = 100$ and $G^* = 300$ into the results of parts (a) and (b). From part (a)

$$Y = \frac{-aT^* + b + I^* + G^*}{1 - a + at} = \frac{-0.7(200) + 50 + 100 + 300}{1 - 0.7 + 0.7(0.2)} = 704.5$$

From part (b) the government expenditure multiplier is

$$\frac{1}{1 - a + at} = \frac{1}{0.44} = 2.27$$

and we are given that $\Delta G^* = 10$, so the change in national income is

$$2.27 \times 10 = 22.7$$

Practice Problem

2. Consider the four-sector model

   $$Y = C + I + G + X - M$$
   $$C = aY + b \qquad (0 < a < 1, b > 0)$$
   $$I = I^* \qquad (I^* > 0)$$
   $$G = G^* \qquad (G^* > 0)$$
   $$X = X^* \qquad (X^* > 0)$$
   $$M = mY + M^* \qquad (0 < m < 1, M^* > 0)$$

   where X and M denote exports and imports, respectively, and m is the marginal propensity to import.

   (a) Show that

   $$Y = \frac{b + I^* + G^* + X^* - M^*}{1 - a + m}$$

   (b) Write down the autonomous export multiplier

   $$\frac{\partial Y}{\partial X^*}$$

   and the marginal propensity to import multiplier

   $$\frac{\partial Y}{\partial m}$$

   Deduce the direction of change in Y due to increases in X^* and m.

   (c) If $a = 0.8$, $b = 120$, $I^* = 100$, $G^* = 300$, $X^* = 150$, $m = 0.1$ and $M^* = 40$, calculate the equilibrium level of national income, Y, and the change in Y due to a 10-unit increase in autonomous exports.

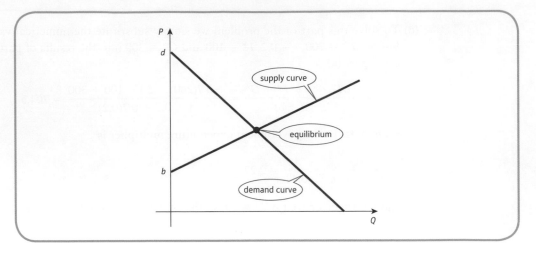

Figure 5.7

So far, all of the examples of comparative statics that we have considered have been taken from macroeconomics. The same approach can be used in microeconomics. For example, let us analyse the equilibrium price and quantity in supply and demand theory.

Figure 5.7 illustrates the simple linear one-commodity market model described in Section 1.5. The equilibrium values of price and quantity are determined from the point of intersection of the supply and demand curves. The supply curve is a straight line with a positive slope and intercept, so its equation may be written as

$$P = aQ_S + b \quad (a > 0, b > 0)$$

The demand equation is also linear but has a negative slope and a positive intercept, so its equation may be written as

$$P = -cQ_D + d \quad (c > 0, d > 0)$$

It is apparent from Figure 5.7 that in order for these two lines to intersect in the positive quadrant, it is necessary for the intercept on the demand curve to lie above that on the supply curve, so we require

$$d > b$$

or equivalently

$$d - b > 0$$

In equilibrium Q_S and Q_D are equal. If we let their common value be denoted by Q, then the supply and demand equations become

$$P = aQ + b$$

$$P = -cQ + d$$

and so

$$aQ + b = -cQ + d$$

since both sides are equal to P.

To solve for Q we first collect like terms together, which gives

$$(a + c)Q = d - b$$

and then divide by the coefficient of Q to get

$$Q = \frac{d - b}{a + c}$$

(Incidentally, this confirms the restriction $d - b > 0$. If this were not true, then Q would be either zero or negative, which does not make economic sense.)

Equilibrium quantity is a function of the four parameters a, b, c and d, so there are four multipliers

$$\frac{\partial Q}{\partial a} = -\frac{d - b}{(a + c)^2}$$

$$\frac{\partial Q}{\partial b} = -\frac{1}{a + c}$$

$$\frac{\partial Q}{\partial c} = -\frac{d - b}{(a + c)^2}$$

$$\frac{\partial Q}{\partial d} = \frac{1}{a + c}$$

where the chain rule is used to find $\partial Q/\partial a$ and $\partial Q/\partial c$.

We noted previously that all of the parameters are positive and that $d - b > 0$, so

$$\frac{\partial Q}{\partial a} < 0, \quad \frac{\partial Q}{\partial b} < 0, \quad \frac{\partial Q}{\partial c} < 0 \quad \text{and} \quad \frac{\partial Q}{\partial d} > 0$$

This shows that an increase in a, b or c causes a decrease in Q, whereas an increase in d causes an increase in Q.

It is possible to confirm the signs of these multipliers graphically. For example, from the supply equation

$$P = aQ_S + b$$

we see that a small increase in the value of the parameter a causes the supply curve to become slightly steeper, as indicated by the dashed line in Figure 5.8. The effect is to shift the point of intersection to the left, and so the equilibrium quantity decreases from Q_1 to Q_2 which is consistent with a negative value of the multiplier, $\partial Q/\partial a$.

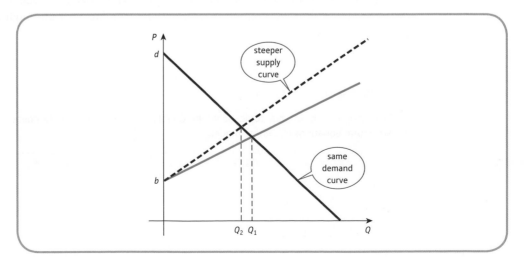

Figure 5.8

Given any pair of supply and demand equations, we can easily calculate the effect on the equilibrium quantity. For example, consider the equations

$$P = Q_S + 1$$
$$P = -2Q_D + 5$$

and let us suppose that we need to calculate the change in equilibrium quantity when the coefficient of Q_S increases from 1 to 1.1. In this case we have

$$a = 1, \quad b = 1, \quad c = 2, \quad d = 5$$

To find ΔQ we first evaluate the multiplier

$$\frac{\partial Q}{\partial a} = -\frac{d - b}{(a + c)^2} = -\frac{5 - 1}{(1 + 2)^2} = -0.44$$

and then multiply by 0.1 to get

$$\Delta Q = (-0.44) \times 0.1 = -0.044$$

An increase of 0.1 in the slope of the supply curve therefore produces a decrease of 0.044 in the equilibrium quantity.

Practice Problem

3. Give a graphical confirmation of the sign of the multiplier

    $$\frac{\partial Q}{\partial d}$$

    for the linear one-commodity market model

    $$P = aQ_S + b \qquad (a > 0, b > 0)$$
    $$P = -cQ_D + d \quad (c > 0, d > 0)$$

Throughout this section all of the relations in each model have been assumed to be linear. It is possible to analyse non-linear relations in a similar way, although this is beyond the scope of this text.

Advice

We shall return to this topic again in Chapter 7 when we use Cramer's rule to solve the structural equations of a linear model.

Key Terms

Autonomous consumption multiplier   The number by which you multiply the change in autonomous consumption to deduce the corresponding change in, say, national income: $\partial Y/\partial b$.

Balanced budget multiplier   The number by which you multiply the change in government expenditure to deduce the corresponding change in, say, national income, $\partial Y/\partial G^*$, assuming that this change is financed entirely by a change in taxation.

Comparative statics   Examination of the effect on equilibrium values due to changes in the parameters of an economic model.

Dynamics   Analysis of how equilibrium values vary over time.

Investment multiplier   The number by which you multiply the change in investment to deduce the corresponding change in, say, national income: $\partial Y/\partial I^*$.

Marginal propensity to consume multiplier   The number by which you multiply the change in MPC to deduce the corresponding change in, say, national income: $\partial Y/\partial a$.

Reduced form   The final equation obtained when endogenous variables are eliminated in the course of solving a set of structural equations in a macroeconomic model.

Statics   The determination of the equilibrium values of variables in an economic model which do not change over time.

Structural equations   A collection of equations that describe the equilibrium conditions of a macroeconomic model.

Exercise 5.3*

1. Consider the three-sector model

$$Y = C + I + G \tag{1}$$
$$C = aY_d + b \qquad (0 < a < 1, b > 0) \tag{2}$$
$$Y_d = Y - T \tag{3}$$
$$T = T^* \qquad (T^* > 0) \tag{4}$$
$$I = I^* \qquad (I^* > 0) \tag{5}$$
$$G = G^* \qquad (G^* > 0) \tag{6}$$

(a) Show that

$$C = \frac{aI^* + aG^* - aT^* + b}{1 - a}$$

(b) Write down the investment multiplier for C. Decide the direction of change in C due to an increase in I^*.

(c) If $a = 0.9$, $b = 80$, $I^* = 60$, $G^* = 40$ and $T^* = 20$, calculate the equilibrium level of consumption, C, and also the change in C due to a 2-unit change in investment.

2. The reduced form of a macroeconomic model is

$$Y = \frac{b + I^* + G^* - aT^*}{1 - a - at}$$

where t is the marginal rate of taxation.

Find an expression for the marginal rate of taxation multiplier.

3. Consider the four-sector macroeconomic model

$$Y = C + I + G + X - M$$

$$C = aY_d + b \qquad (0 < a < 1, b > 0)$$

$$Y_d = Y - T$$

$$T = tY + T^* \qquad (0 < t < 1, T^* > 0)$$

$$I = I^* \qquad (I^* > 0)$$

$$G = G^* \qquad (G^* > 0)$$

$$X = X^* \qquad (X^* > 0)$$

$$M = mY_d + M^* \qquad (0 < m < 1, M^* > 0)$$

(1) Show that

$$Y = \frac{b + (m - a)T^* + I^* + G^* + X^* - M^*}{1 - a + at + m - mt}$$

(2) (a) Write down the autonomous taxation multiplier. Deduce that an increase in T^* causes a decrease in Y on the assumption that a country's marginal propensity to import, m, is less than its marginal propensity to consume, a.

(b) Write down the government expenditure multiplier. Deduce that an increase in G^* causes an increase in Y.

(3) Let $a = 0.7$, $b = 150$, $t = 0.25$, $m = 0.1$, $T^* = 100$, $I^* = 100$, $G^* = 500$, $M^* = 300$ and $X^* = 160$.

(a) Calculate the equilibrium level of national income.

(b) Calculate the change in Y due to an 11-unit increase in G^*.

(c) Find the increase in autonomous taxation required to restore Y to its level calculated in part (a).

4. Show that the equilibrium price for a linear one-commodity market model

$$P = aQ_S + b \qquad (a > 0, b > 0)$$

$$P = -cQ_D + d \qquad (c > 0, d > 0)$$

where $d - b > 0$, is given by

$$P = \frac{ad + bc}{a + c}$$

Find expressions for the multipliers

$$\frac{\partial P}{\partial a}, \frac{\partial P}{\partial b}, \frac{\partial P}{\partial c}, \frac{\partial P}{\partial d}$$

and deduce the direction of change in P due to an increase in a, b, c or d.

5. Consider the three-sector macroeconomic model

$$Y = C + I + G$$
$$C = aY_d + b \quad (0 < a < 1, b > 0)$$
$$Y_d = Y - T$$
$$T = T^* \qquad (T^* > 0)$$
$$I = I^* \qquad (I^* > 0)$$
$$G = G^* \qquad (G^* > 0)$$

(a) Show that

$$Y = \frac{1}{1-a}(b - aT^* + I^* + G^*)$$

(b) Write down expressions for the government expenditure multiplier, $\partial Y/\partial G^*$, and the taxation multiplier, $\partial Y/\partial T^*$, and deduce that if both government expenditure and taxation increase by 1 unit, then the equilibrium value of income also rises by 1 unit, irrespective of the value of a.

(c) State the value of the balanced budget multiplier.

6. (1) For the commodity market

$$Y = C + I$$
$$C = aY + b \qquad (0 < a < 1, b > 0)$$
$$I = cr + d \qquad (c < 0, d > 0)$$

where r is the interest rate, show that when the commodity market is in equilibrium,

$$(1 - a)Y - cr = b + d$$

(2) For the money market

(money supply)	$M_S = M_S^*$	$(M_S^* > 0)$
(total demand for money)	$M_D = k_1 Y + k_2 r + k_3$	$(k_1 > 0, k_2 < 0, k_3 > 0)$
(equilibrium)	$M_D = M_S$	

show that when the money market is in equilibrium

$$k_1 Y + k_2 r = M_S^* - k_3$$

(3) (a) By solving the simultaneous equations derived in parts (1) and (2), show that when the commodity and money markets are both in equilibrium

$$Y = \frac{k_2(b + d) + c(M_S^* - k_3)}{(1 - a)k_2 + ck_1}$$

(b) Write down the money supply multiplier, $\partial Y/\partial M_S^*$, and deduce that an increase in M_S^* causes an increase in Y.

7. Consider the three-sector model

$$Y = C + I$$

$$C = aY_d + b \quad (0 < a < 1, b > 0)$$

$$Y_d = Y - T$$

$$T = tY + T^* \quad (0 < t < 1, T^* > 0)$$

$$I = cr + d \quad (c < 0, d > 0)$$

(a) Show that

$$Y = \frac{b + d - aT^* + cr}{1 - a(1 - t)}$$

(b) Find expressions for the multipliers $\partial Y/\partial c$ and $\partial Y/\partial a$.

(c) State whether the value of Y increases or decreases as a result of an increase in the value of c. Give a reason for your answer.

(d) If $a = 0.8$, $b = 100$, $t = 0.25$, $T^* = 250$, $c = -60$, $d = 1700$ and $r = 8$, calculate the equilibrium level of income, Y, and use the multiplier obtained in part (b) to estimate the change in Y due to a 0.01 increase in the marginal propensity to consume.

8. The demand and total cost functions of a good are $P = a - bQ$ and $TC = f + vQ$, respectively, where a, b, f and v are positive constants.

(a) Show that the maximum profit is given by $\pi = \dfrac{(a - v)^2}{4b} - f$.

(b) Find expressions for the multipliers, $\dfrac{\partial \pi}{\partial a}, \dfrac{\partial \pi}{\partial b}, \dfrac{\partial \pi}{\partial f}$ and $\dfrac{\partial \pi}{\partial v}$.

(c) Use your answers to part (b) to comment on the direction of change in the maximum profit due to an increase in a, b, f or v.

SECTION 5.4
Unconstrained optimisation

Objectives

At the end of this section you should be able to:

- Use the first-order partial derivatives to find the stationary points of a function of two variables.

- Use the second-order partial derivatives to classify the stationary points of a function of two variables.

- Find the maximum profit of a firm that produces two goods.

- Find the maximum profit of a firm that sells a single good in different markets with price discrimination.

As you might expect, methods for finding the maximum and minimum points of a function of two variables are similar to those used for functions of one variable. However, the nature of economic functions of several variables forces us to subdivide optimisation problems into two types, unconstrained and constrained. To understand the distinction, consider the utility function

$$U(x_1, x_2) = x_1^{1/4} x_2^{3/4}$$

The value of U measures the satisfaction gained from buying x_1 items of a good G1 and x_2 items of a good G2. The natural thing to do here is to try to pick x_1 and x_2 to make U as large as possible, thereby maximising utility. However, a moment's thought should convince you that, as it stands, this problem does not have a finite solution. The factor $x_1^{1/4}$ can be made as large as we please by taking ever-increasing values of x_1 and likewise for the factor $x_2^{3/4}$. In other words, utility increases without bound as more and more items of goods G1 and G2 are bought. In practice, of course, this does not occur, since there is a limit to the amount of money that an individual has to spend on these goods. For example, suppose that the cost of each item of G1 and G2 is $2 and $3, respectively, and that we allocate $100 for the purchase of these goods. The total cost of buying x_1 items of G1 and x_2 items of G2 is

$$2x_1 + 3x_2$$

so we require

$$2x_1 + 3x_2 = 100$$

The problem now is to maximise the utility function

$$U = x_1^{1/4} x_2^{3/4}$$

subject to the budgetary constraint

$$2x_1 + 3x_2 = 100$$

The constraint prevents us from taking ever-increasing values of x_1 and x_2 and leads to a finite solution.

We describe how to solve constrained optimisation problems in the following two sections. For the moment, we concentrate on the simple case of optimising functions

$$z = f(x, y)$$

without any constraints. This is typified by the problem of profit maximisation, which usually has a finite solution without the need to impose constraints. In a sense the constraints are built into the profit function, which is defined by

$$\pi = TR - TC$$

because there is a conflict between trying to make total revenue, TR, as large as possible and trying to make total cost, TC, as small as possible.

Let us begin by recalling how to find and classify stationary points of functions of one variable

$$y = f(x)$$

In Section 4.6 we used the following strategy:

Step 1

Solve the equation

$$f'(x) = 0$$

to find the stationary points, $x = a$.

Step 2

If

- $f''(a) > 0$, then the function has a minimum at $x = a$
- $f''(a) < 0$, then the function has a maximum at $x = a$
- $f''(a) = 0$, then the point cannot be classified using the available information.

For functions of two variables

$$z = f(x, y)$$

the stationary points are found by solving the simultaneous equations

$$\frac{\partial z}{\partial x} = 0$$

$$\frac{\partial z}{\partial y} = 0$$

that is,

$$f_x(x, y) = 0$$

$$f_y(x, y) = 0$$

This is a natural extension of the one-variable case. We first write down expressions for the first-order partial derivatives and then equate to zero. This represents a system of two equations for the two unknowns x and y, which we hope can be solved. Stationary points obtained in this way can be classified into one of three types: **minimum point**, **maximum point** and **saddle point**.

Figure 5.9(a) shows the shape of a surface in the neighbourhood of a minimum. It can be thought of as the bottom of a bowl-shaped valley. If you stand at the minimum point and walk in any direction, then you are certain to start moving upwards. Mathematically, we can classify a stationary point (a, b) as a minimum provided that all three of the following conditions hold:

$$\frac{\partial^2 z}{\partial x^2} > 0, \ \frac{\partial^2 z}{\partial y^2} > 0, \ \left(\frac{\partial^2 z}{\partial x^2}\right)\left(\frac{\partial^2 z}{\partial y^2}\right) - \left(\frac{\partial^2 z}{\partial x \partial y}\right)^2 > 0$$

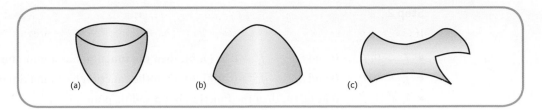

Figure 5.9

when $x = a$ and $y = b$: that is,

$$f_{xx}(a, b) > 0, \qquad f_{yy}(a, b) > 0, \qquad f_{xx}(a, b) f_{yy}(a, b) - [f_{xy}(a, b)]^2 > 0$$

This triple requirement is obviously more complicated than the single condition needed in the case of a function of one variable. However, once the second-order partial derivatives have been evaluated at the stationary point, the three conditions are easily checked.

Figure 5.9(b) shows the shape of a surface in the neighbourhood of a maximum. It can be thought of as the summit of a mountain. If you stand at the maximum point and walk in any direction, then you are certain to start moving downwards. Mathematically, we can classify a stationary point (a, b) as a maximum provided that all three of the following conditions hold:

$$\frac{\partial^2 z}{\partial x^2} < 0, \; \frac{\partial^2 z}{\partial y^2} < 0, \; \left(\frac{\partial^2 z}{\partial x^2}\right)\left(\frac{\partial^2 z}{\partial y^2}\right) - \left(\frac{\partial^2 z}{\partial x \partial y}\right)^2 > 0$$

when $x = a$ and $y = b$: that is,

$$f_{xx}(a, b) < 0, \qquad f_{yy}(a, b) < 0, \qquad f_{xx}(a, b) f_{yy}(a, b) - [f_{xy}(a, b)]^2 > 0$$

Of course, any particular mountain range may well have lots of valleys and summits. Likewise, a function of two variables can have more than one minimum or maximum.

Figure 5.9(c) shows the shape of a surface in the neighbourhood of a saddle point. As its name suggests, it can be thought of as the middle of a horse's saddle. If you sit at this point and edge towards the head or tail, then you start moving upwards. On the other hand, if you edge sideways, then you start moving downwards (and will probably fall off!). Mathematically, we can classify a stationary point (a, b) as a saddle point provided that the following single condition holds:

$$\left(\frac{\partial^2 z}{\partial x^2}\right)\left(\frac{\partial^2 z}{\partial y^2}\right) - \left(\frac{\partial^2 z}{\partial x \partial y}\right)^2 < 0$$

when $x = a$ and $y = b$: that is,

$$f_{xx}(a, b) f_{yy}(a, b) - [f_{xy}(a, b)]^2 < 0$$

To summarise, the method for finding and classifying stationary points of a function $f(x, y)$ is as follows:

Step 1

Solve the simultaneous equations

$$f_x(x, y) = 0$$
$$f_y(x, y) = 0$$

to find the stationary points, (a, b).

Step 2

If

- $f_{xx} > 0, f_{yy} > 0$ and $f_{xx}f_{yy} - f_{xy}^2 > 0$ at (a, b), then the function has a minimum at (a, b)
- $f_{xx} < 0, f_{yy} < 0$ and $f_{xx}f_{yy} - f_{xy}^2 > 0$ at (a, b), then the function has a maximum at (a, b)
- $f_{xx}f_{yy} - f_{xy}^2 < 0$ at (a, b), then the function has a saddle point at (a, b).

Before we consider examples from economics, we will illustrate the method by finding and classifying the stationary points of the function

$$f(x, y) = x^3 - 3x + xy^2$$

In order to use steps 1 and 2 we need to find all first- and second-order partial derivatives of the function

$$f(x, y) = x^3 - 3x + xy^2$$

These are easily worked out as

$$f_x = 3x^2 - 3 + y^2$$
$$f_y = 2xy$$
$$f_{xx} = 6x$$
$$f_{xy} = 2y$$
$$f_{yy} = 2x$$

Step 1

The stationary points are the solutions of the simultaneous equations

$$f_x(x, y) = 0$$
$$f_y(x, y) = 0$$

so we need to solve

$$3x^2 - 3 + y^2 = 0$$
$$2xy = 0$$

We have solved simultaneous equations on many occasions throughout this text. So far these have been linear. This time, however, we need to solve a pair of non-linear equations. Unfortunately, there is no standard method for solving such systems. We have to rely on our wits in any particular instance. The trick here is to begin with the second equation

$$2xy = 0$$

The only way that the product of three numbers can be equal to zero is when one or more of the individual numbers forming the product are zero. We know that $2 \neq 0$, so either $x = 0$ or $y = 0$. We investigate these two possibilities separately:

- Case 1: $x = 0$. Substituting $x = 0$ into the first equation

$$3x^2 - 3 + y^2 = 0$$

gives

$$-3 + y^2 = 0$$

that is,

$$y^2 = 3$$

There are therefore two possibilities for y to go with $x = 0$, namely $y = -\sqrt{3}$ and $y = \sqrt{3}$. Hence $(0, -\sqrt{3})$ and $(0, \sqrt{3})$ are stationary points.

- Case 2: $y = 0$. Substituting $y = 0$ into the first equation

$$3x^2 - 3 + y^2 = 0$$

gives

$$3x^2 - 3 = 0$$

that is,

$$x^2 = 1$$

There are therefore two possibilities for x to go with $y = 0$, namely $x = -1$ and $x = 1$. Hence $(-1, 0)$ and $(1, 0)$ are stationary points.

These two cases indicate that there are precisely four stationary points, $(0, -\sqrt{3})$, $(0, \sqrt{3})$, $(-1, 0)$ and $(1, 0)$.

Step 2

To classify these points we need to evaluate the second-order partial derivatives

$$f_{xx} = 6x, \qquad f_{yy} = 2x, \qquad f_{xy} = 2y$$

at each point and check the signs of

$$f_{xx}, f_{yy} \text{ and } f_{xx}f_{yy} - f_{xy}^2$$

- Point $(0, -\sqrt{3})$

$$f_{xx} = 6(0) = 0, \qquad f_{yy} = 2(0) = 0, \qquad f_{xy} = -2\sqrt{3}$$

Hence

$$f_{xx}f_{yy} - f_{xy}^2 = 0(0) - (-2\sqrt{3})^2 = -12 < 0$$

and so $(0, -\sqrt{3})$ is a saddle point.

- Point $(0, \sqrt{3})$

$$f_{xx} = 6(0) = 0, \quad f_{yy} = 2(0) = 0, \quad f_{xy} = 2\sqrt{3}$$

Hence

$$f_{xx}f_{yy} - f_{xy}^2 = 0(0) - (2\sqrt{3})^2 = -12 < 0$$

and so $(0, \sqrt{3})$ is a saddle point.

- Point $(-1, 0)$

$$f_{xx} = 6(-1) = -6, \qquad f_{yy} = 2(-1) = -2, \qquad f_{xy} = 2(0) = 0$$

Hence

$$f_{xx}f_{yy} - f_{xy}^2 = (-6)(-2) - 0^2 = 12 > 0$$

and so $(-1, 0)$ is not a saddle point. Moreover, since

$$f_{xx} < 0 \text{ and } f_{yy} < 0$$

we deduce that $(-1, 0)$ is a maximum.

- Point $(1, 0)$

$$f_{xx} = 6(1) = 6, \qquad f_{yy} = 2(1) = 2, \qquad f_{xy} = 2(0) = 0$$

Hence

$$f_{xx}f_{yy} - f_{xy}^2 = 6(2) - 0^2 = 12 > 0$$

and so $(1, 0)$ is not a saddle point. Moreover, since

$$f_{xx} > 0 \text{ and } f_{yy} > 0$$

we deduce that $(1, 0)$ is a minimum.

Practice Problem

1. Find and classify the stationary points of the function

$$f(x, y) = x^2 + 6y - 3y^2 + 10$$

We now consider two examples from economics, both involving the maximisation of profit. The first considers the case of a firm producing two different goods, whereas the second involves a single good sold in two different markets.

Example

A firm is a perfectly competitive producer and sells two goods G1 and G2 at $1000 and $800, respectively. The total cost of producing these goods is given by

$$\text{TC} = 2Q_1^2 + 2Q_1Q_2 + Q_2^2$$

where Q_1 and Q_2 denote the output levels of G1 and G2, respectively. Find the maximum profit and the values of Q_1 and Q_2 at which this is achieved.

Solution

The fact that the firm is perfectly competitive tells us that the price of each good is fixed by the market and does not depend on Q_1 and Q_2. The actual prices are stated in the question as $1000 and $800. If the firm sells Q_1 items of G1 priced at $1000, then the revenue is

$$\text{TR}_1 = 1000Q_1$$

Similarly, if the firm sells Q_2 items of G2 priced at $800, then the revenue is

$$\text{TR}_2 = 800Q_2$$

The total revenue from the sale of both goods is then

$$\text{TR} = \text{TR}_1 + \text{TR}_2 = 1000Q_1 + 800Q_2$$

We are given that the total cost is

$$\text{TC} = 2Q_1^2 + 2Q_1Q_2 + Q_2^2$$

so the profit function is

$$\pi = \text{TR} - \text{TC}$$
$$= (1000Q_1 + 800Q_2) - (2Q_1^2 + 2Q_1Q_2 + Q_2^2)$$
$$= 1000Q_1 + 800Q_2 - 2Q_1^2 - 2Q_1Q_2 - Q_2^2$$

This is a function of the two variables, Q_1 and Q_2, that we wish to optimise. The first- and second-order partial derivatives are

$$\frac{\partial \pi}{\partial Q_1} = 1000 - 4Q_1 - 2Q_2$$

$$\frac{\partial \pi}{\partial Q_2} = 800 - 2Q_1 - 2Q_2$$

$$\frac{\partial^2 \pi}{\partial Q_1^2} = -4$$

$$\frac{\partial^2 \pi}{\partial Q_1 \partial Q_2} = -2$$

$$\frac{\partial^2 \pi}{\partial Q_2^2} = -2$$

The two-step strategy then gives the following:

Step 1

At a stationary point

$$\frac{\partial \pi}{\partial Q_1} = 0$$

$$\frac{\partial \pi}{\partial Q_2} = 0$$

so we need to solve the simultaneous equations

$$1000 - 4Q_1 - 2Q_2 = 0$$
$$800 - 2Q_1 - 2Q_2 = 0$$

that is,

$$4Q_1 + 2Q_2 = 1000 \tag{1}$$

$$2Q_1 + 2Q_2 = 800 \tag{2}$$

The variable Q_2 can be eliminated by subtracting equation (2) from (1) to get

$$2Q_1 = 200$$

and so $Q_1 = 100$. Substituting this into either equation (1) or (2) gives $Q_2 = 300$. The profit function therefore has one stationary point at (100, 300).

Step 2

To show that the point really is a maximum, we need to check that

$$\frac{\partial^2 \pi}{\partial Q_1^2} < 0, \ \frac{\partial^2 \pi}{\partial Q_2^2} < 0, \ \left(\frac{\partial^2 \pi}{\partial Q_1^2}\right)\left(\frac{\partial^2 \pi}{\partial Q_2^2}\right) - \left(\frac{\partial^2 \pi}{\partial Q_1 \partial Q_2}\right) > 0$$

at this point. In this example the second-order partial derivatives are all constant. We have

$$\frac{\partial^2 \pi}{\partial Q_1^2} = -4 < 0 \quad ✓$$

$$\frac{\partial^2 \pi}{\partial Q_2^2} = -2 < 0 \quad ✓$$

$$\left(\frac{\partial^2 \pi}{\partial Q_1^2}\right)\left(\frac{\partial^2 \pi}{\partial Q_2^2}\right) - \left(\frac{\partial^2 \pi}{\partial Q_1 \partial Q_2}\right) = (-4)(-2) - (-2)^2 = 4 > 0 \quad ✓$$

confirming that the firm's profit is maximised by producing 100 items of G1 and 300 items of G2.

The actual value of this profit is obtained by substituting $Q_1 = 100$ and $Q_2 = 300$ into the expression

$$\pi = 1000Q_1 + 800Q_2 - 2Q_1^2 - 2Q_1Q_2 - Q_2^2$$

to get

$$\pi = 1000(100) + 800(300) - 2(100)^2 - 2(100)(300) - (300)^2 = \$170\,000$$

Practice Problem

2. A firm is a monopolistic producer of two goods G1 and G2. The prices are related to quantities Q_1 and Q_2 according to the demand functions

$$P_1 = 50 - Q_1$$
$$P_2 = 95 - 3Q_2$$

If the total cost function is

$$TC = Q_1^2 + 3Q_1Q_2 + Q_2^2$$

show that the firm's profit function is

$$\pi = 50Q_1 - 2Q_1^2 - 95Q_2 - 4Q_2^2 - 3Q_1Q_2$$

Hence find the values of Q_1 and Q_2 which maximise π and deduce the corresponding prices.

Example

A firm is allowed to charge different prices for its domestic and industrial customers. If P_1 and Q_1 denote the price and demand for the domestic market, then the demand equation is

$$P_1 + Q_1 = 500$$

If P_2 and Q_2 denote the price and demand for the industrial market, then the demand equation is

$$2P_2 + 3Q_2 = 720$$

The total cost function is

$$TC = 50\,000 + 20Q$$

where $Q = Q_1 + Q_2$. Determine the firm's pricing policy that maximises profit with price discrimination and calculate the value of the maximum profit.

Solution

The topic of price discrimination has already been discussed in Section 4.7. This particular problem is identical to the worked example solved in that section using ordinary differentiation. You might like to compare the details of the two approaches.

Our current aim is to find an expression for profit in terms of Q_1 and Q_2 which can then be optimised using partial differentiation. For the domestic market the demand equation is

$$P_1 + Q_1 = 500$$

which rearranges as

$$P_1 = 500 - Q_1$$

The total revenue function for this market is then

$$TR_1 = P_1Q_1 = (500 - Q_1)Q_1 = 500Q_1 - Q_1^2$$

For the industrial market the demand equation is

$$2P_2 + 3Q_2 = 720$$

which rearranges as

$$P_2 = 360 - \tfrac{3}{2}Q_2$$

The total revenue function for this market is then

$$TR_2 = P_2Q_2 = (360 - \tfrac{3}{2}Q_2)Q_2 = 360Q_2 - \tfrac{3}{2}Q_2^2$$

The total revenue received from sales in both markets is

$$TR = TR_1 + TR_2 = 500Q_1 - Q_1^2 + 360Q_2 - \tfrac{3}{2}Q_2^2$$

The total cost of producing these goods is given by

$$TC = 50\,000 + 20Q$$

$\rightarrow$

and, since $Q = Q_1 + Q_2$, we can write this as

$$TC = 50\ 000 + 20(Q_1 + Q_2)$$
$$= 50\ 000 + 20Q_1 + 20Q_2$$

The firm's profit function is therefore

$$\pi = TR - TC$$
$$= (500Q_1 - Q_1^2 + 360Q_2 - {}^3/_2Q_2^2) - (50\ 000 + 20Q_1 + 20Q_2)$$
$$480Q_1 - Q_1^2 + 340Q_2 - {}^3/_2Q_2^2 - 50\ 000$$

This is a function of the two variables, Q_1 and Q_2, that we wish to optimise. The first- and second-order partial derivatives are

$$\frac{\partial \pi}{\partial Q_1} = 480 - 2Q_1$$

$$\frac{\partial \pi}{\partial Q_2} = 340 - 3Q_2$$

$$\frac{\partial^2 \pi}{\partial Q_1^2} = -2$$

$$\frac{\partial^2 \pi}{\partial Q_1 \partial Q_2} = 0$$

$$\frac{\partial^2 \pi}{\partial Q_2^2} = -3$$

The two-step strategy gives the following:

Step 1

At a stationary point

$$\frac{\partial \pi}{\partial Q_1} = 0$$

$$\frac{\partial \pi}{\partial Q_2} = 0$$

so we need to solve the simultaneous equations

$$480 - 2Q_1 = 0$$
$$340 - 3Q_2 = 0$$

These are easily solved because they are 'uncoupled'. The first equation immediately gives

$$Q_1 = \frac{480}{2} = 240$$

while the second gives

$$Q_2 = \frac{340}{3}$$

Step 2

It is easy to check that the conditions for a maximum are satisfied:

$$\frac{\partial^2 \pi}{\partial Q_1^2} = -2 < 0$$

$$\frac{\partial^2 \pi}{\partial Q_2^2} = -3 < 0$$

$$\left(\frac{\partial^2 \pi}{\partial Q_1^2}\right)\left(\frac{\partial^2 \pi}{\partial Q_2^2}\right) - \left(\frac{\partial^2 \pi}{\partial Q_1 \partial Q_2}\right)^2 = (-2)(-3) - 0^2 = 6 > 0$$

The question actually asks for the optimum prices rather than the quantities. These are found by substituting

$$Q_1 = 240 \text{ and } Q_2 = \frac{340}{3}$$

into the corresponding demand equations. For the domestic market

$$P_1 = 500 - Q_1 = 500 - 240 = \$260$$

For the industrial market

$$P_2 = 360 - \frac{3}{2}Q_1 = 360 - \frac{3}{2}\left(\frac{340}{3}\right) = \$190$$

Finally, we substitute the values of Q_1 and Q_2 into the profit function

$$\pi = 480Q_1 - Q_1^2 + 340Q_2 - \frac{3}{2}Q_2^2 - 50\,000$$

to deduce that the maximum profit is \$26 866.67.

Practice Problem

3. A firm has the possibility of charging different prices in its domestic and foreign markets. The corresponding demand equations are given by

    $$Q_1 = 300 - P_1$$

    $$Q_2 = 400 - 2P_2$$

    The total cost function is

    $$TC = 5000 + 100Q$$

    where $Q = Q_1 + Q_2$. Determine the prices that the firm should charge to maximise profit with price discrimination and calculate the value of this profit.

    [You have already solved this particular example in Practice Problem 2(a) of Section 4.7.]

> ## Key Terms
>
> **Maximum point (of a function of two variables)**   A point on a surface which has the highest function value in comparison with other values in its neighbourhood; at such a point the surface looks like the top of a mountain.
>
> **Minimum point (of a function of two variables)**   A point on a surface which has the lowest function value in comparison with other values in its neighbourhood; at such a point the surface looks like the bottom of a valley or bowl.
>
> **Saddle point**   A stationary point which is neither a maximum or minimum and at which the surface looks like the middle of a horse's saddle.

Exercise 5.4

1. **(a)** Find the first-order partial derivatives, $\dfrac{\partial z}{\partial x}$, $\dfrac{\partial z}{\partial y}$, of the function

    $$z = 2x^2 + y^2 - 12x - 8y + 50$$

    and hence find the stationary point.

    (b) Find the second-order partial derivatives, $\dfrac{\partial^2 z}{\partial x^2}$, $\dfrac{\partial^2 z}{\partial y^2}$ and $\dfrac{\partial^2 z}{\partial x \partial y}$, and hence show that the stationary point is a minimum.

2. Find and classify the stationary points of the following functions:

    (a) $f(x, y) = x^3 + y^3 - 3x - 3y$ **(b)** $f(x, y) = x^3 + 3xy^2 - 3x^2 - 3y^2 + 10$

3. A firm's profit function for the production of two goods is given by

    $$\pi = 24Q_1 - Q_1^2 - Q_1Q_2 - 2Q_2^2 + 33Q_2 - 43$$

    Find the output levels needed to maximise profit. Use second-order derivatives to confirm that the stationary point is a maximum.

4. A perfectly competitive producer sells two goods, G1 and G2, at $70 and $50, respectively. The total cost of producing these goods is given by

    $$TC = Q_1^2 + Q_1Q_2 + Q_2^2$$

    where Q_1 and Q_2 denote the output levels of G1 and G2. Find the maximum profit and the values of Q_1 and Q_2 at which this is achieved.

5. An individual's utility function is given by

    $$U = 260x_1 + 310x_2 + 5x_1x_2 - 10x_1^2 - x_2^2$$

    where x_1 is the amount of leisure measured in hours per week and x_2 is earned income measured in dollars per week. Find the values of x_1 and x_2 which maximise U. What is the corresponding hourly rate of pay?

6. A monopolist produces the same product at two factories. The cost functions for each factory are as follows:

    $$TC_1 = 8Q_1 \quad \text{and} \quad TC_2 = Q_2^2$$

    The demand function for the good is

    $$P = 100 - 2Q$$

    where $Q = Q_1 + Q_2$. Find the values of Q_1 and Q_2 which maximise profit.

7. A monopolist sells its product in two isolated markets with demand functions

$$P_1 = 32 - Q_1 \quad \text{and} \quad P_2 = 40 - 2Q_2$$

The total cost function is $\text{TC} = 4(Q_1 + Q_2)$.

(a) Show that the profit function is given by

$$\pi = 28Q_1 + 36Q_2 - Q_1^2 - 2Q_2^2$$

(b) Find the values of Q_1 and Q_2 which maximise profit and calculate the value of the maximum profit. Verify that the second-order conditions for a maximum are satisfied.

8. (a) If the monopolist in Question 7 is no longer allowed to discriminate between the two markets and must charge the same price, P, show that the total demand, $Q = Q_1 + Q_2$, is given by

$$Q = 52 - \frac{3}{2}P$$

and deduce that the profit function is $\pi = \dfrac{1}{3}(92Q - 2Q^2)$.

(b) Find the maximum profit in part (a) and hence work out how much profit is lost by the firm when it can no longer discriminate between the two markets.

Exercise 5.4*

1. Find and classify the stationary points of the each of the following functions:

(a) $f(x, y) = x^3 + x^2 - xy + y^2 + 10$

(b) $f(x, y) = (2xy + y^2)e^x$

(c) $f(x, y) = x^2 - y^2 - 4xy - y^3$

2. A firm's production function is given by

$$Q = 2L^{1/2} + 3K^{1/2}$$

where Q, L and K denote the number of units of output, labour and capital. Labour costs are \$2 per unit, capital costs are \$1 per unit and output sells at \$8 per unit. Show that the profit function is

$$\pi = 16L^{1/2} + 24K^{1/2} - 2L - K$$

and hence find the maximum profit and the values of L and K at which it is achieved.

3. A firm sells a good to both UK and EU customers. The demand function is the same for both markets and is given by

$$20P_i + Q_i = 5000$$

where the subscript, i, takes the values 1 and 2 corresponding to the UK and EU, respectively.

Although the variable and fixed costs are the same for each market, the EU now charges a fixed tariff of \$50 per unit, so the joint total cost function is

$$TC = 40Q_1 + 90Q_2 + 2000$$

Find the maximum total profit.

4. The demand functions for a firm's domestic and foreign markets are

$$P_1 = 50 - 5Q_1$$

$$P_2 = 30 - 4Q_2$$

and the total cost function is

$$TC = 10 + 10Q$$

where $Q = Q_1 + Q_2$. Determine the prices needed to maximise profit with price discrimination and calculate the value of the maximum profit.

[You have already solved this particular example in Question 3(a) in Exercise 4.7*.]

5. A firm is able to sell its product in two different markets. The corresponding demand functions are

$$P_1 + 2Q_1 = 100$$

$$2P_2 + Q_2 = 2a$$

and the total cost function is

$$TC = 500 + 10Q$$

where $Q = Q_1 + Q_2$ and a is a positive constant.

Determine, in terms of a, the prices needed to maximise profit

(a) with price discrimination;

(b) without price discrimination.

Show that the profit with price discrimination is always greater than the profit without discrimination, irrespective of the value of a.

6. (a) A firm's production function is given by $Q = f(K, L)$. The fixed prices of each unit of output, capital and labour are p, r and w, respectively. Explain briefly why the profit function is given by

$$\pi(K, L) = pf(K, L) - rK - wL$$

Show that at a stationary point

$$\frac{\partial f}{\partial K} = \frac{r}{p} \quad \text{and} \quad \frac{\partial f}{\partial L} = \frac{w}{p}$$

Give an economic interpretation of these results.

(b) Use the result of part (a), or otherwise, to find the values of K and L which maximise profit when the production function is $Q = K^{1/2}L^{1/3}$, $p = 24$, $r = 1.5$ and $w = 8$. Verify that the second-order conditions for a maximum are satisfied in this case.

7. A firm manufactures two goods labelled 1 and 2. It sells Q_i items of good i for a fixed price per unit of p_i. The total cost of producing good i is $c_iQ_i^2$.

Explain briefly why the profit function is given by

$$\pi(Q_1, Q_2) = p_1Q_1 + p_2Q_2 - c_1Q_1^2 - c_2Q_2^2$$

Find the values of Q_1 and Q_2 which maximise π and verify that the second-order conditions for a maximum are satisfied. Find an expression for the maximum profit.

8. The unit prices of two goods A and B are p and q. The total cost of producing x items of type A and y items of type B is

$$TC = 4x^2 + 2y^2 + 2xy + 100$$

Find the values of x and y that maximise profit.

SECTION 5.5
Constrained optimisation

Objectives

At the end of this section you should be able to:

- Give a graphical interpretation of constrained optimisation.
- Show that when a firm maximises output subject to a cost constraint, the ratio of marginal product to price is the same for all inputs.
- Show that when a consumer maximises utility subject to a budgetary constraint, the ratio of marginal utility to price is the same for all goods.
- Use the method of substitution to solve constrained optimisation problems in economics.

Advice

In this section we begin by proving some theoretical results before describing the method of substitution. You might prefer to skip the theory at a first reading and begin with the examples.

In Section 5.4 we described how to find the optimum (that is, maximum or minimum) of a function of two variables

$$z = f(x, y)$$

where the variables x and y are free to take any values. As we pointed out at the beginning of that section, this assumption is unrealistic in many economic situations. An individual wishing to maximise utility is subject to an income constraint, and a firm wishing to maximise output is subject to a cost constraint.

In general, we want to optimise a function,

$$z = f(x, y)$$

called the **objective function** subject to a constraint

$$\varphi(x, y) = M$$

Here φ, the Greek letter phi, is a known function of two variables and M is a known constant. The problem is to pick the pair of numbers (x, y) which maximises or minimises $f(x, y)$ as before. This time, however, we limit the choice of pairs to those which satisfy

$$\varphi(x, y) = M$$

A graphical interpretation should make this clear. To be specific, let us suppose that a firm wants to maximise output and that the production function is of the form

$$Q = f(K, L)$$

Let the costs of each unit of capital and labour be P_K and P_L, respectively. The cost to the firm of using as input K units of capital and L units of labour is

$$P_K K + P_L L$$

so if the firm has a fixed amount, M, to spend on these inputs, then

$$P_K K + P_L L = M$$

The problem is one of trying to maximise the objective function

$$Q = f(K, L)$$

subject to the cost constraint

$$P_K K + P_L L = M$$

Sketched in Figure 5.10 is a typical isoquant map. As usual, points on any one isoquant yield the same level of output, and as output rises, the isoquants themselves move further away from the origin. Also sketched in Figure 5.10 is the cost constraint. This is called an **isocost curve** because it gives all combinations of K and L which can be bought for a fixed cost, M.

The fact that

$$P_K K + P_L L = M$$

is represented by a straight line should come as no surprise to you by now. We can even rewrite it in the more familiar '$y = ax + b$' form and so identify its slope and intercept. In Figure 5.10, L is plotted on the horizontal axis and K is plotted on the vertical axis, so we need to rearrange

$$P_K K + P_L L = M$$

to express K in terms of L. Subtracting $P_L L$ from both sides and dividing through by P_K gives

$$K = \left(-\frac{P_L}{P_K} \right) L + \frac{M}{P_K}$$

The isocost curve is therefore a straight line with slope $-P_L/P_K$ and intercept M/P_K. Graphically, our constrained problem is to choose that point on the isocost line which maximises output. This is given by the point labelled A in Figure 5.10. Point A certainly lies on the isocost line

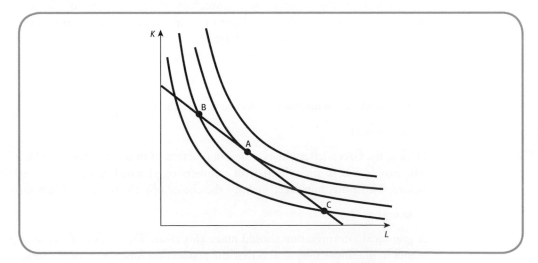

Figure 5.10

and it maximises output because it also lies on the highest isoquant. Other points, such as B and C, also satisfy the constraint, but they lie on lower isoquants and so yield smaller levels of output than A. Point A is characterised by the fact that the isocost line is tangential to an isoquant. In other words, the slope of the isocost line is the same as that of the isoquant at A.

Now we have already shown that the isocost line has slope $-P_L/P_K$. In Section 5.2 we defined the marginal rate of technical substitution, MRTS, to be minus the slope of an isoquant, so at point A we must have

$$\frac{P_L}{P_K} = \text{MRTS}$$

We also showed that

$$\text{MRTS} = \frac{\text{MP}_L}{\text{MP}_K}$$

so

$$\frac{P_L}{P_K} = \frac{\text{MP}_L}{\text{MP}_K}$$

> the ratio of the input prices is equal to the ratio of their marginal products

This relationship can be rearranged as

$$\frac{\text{MP}_L}{P_L} = \frac{\text{MP}_K}{P_K}$$

so when output is maximised subject to a cost constraint

> the ratio of marginal product to price is the same for all inputs

The marginal product determines the change in output due to a 1-unit increase in input. This optimisation condition therefore states that the last dollar spent on labour yields the same addition to output as the last dollar spent on capital.

The above discussion has concentrated on production functions. An analogous situation arises when we maximise utility functions

$$U = U(x_1, x_2)$$

where x_1, x_2 denote the number of items of goods G1, G2 that an individual buys. If the prices of these goods are denoted by P_1 and P_2 and the individual has a fixed budget, M, to spend on these goods then, the corresponding constraint is

$$P_1 x_1 + P_2 x_2 = M$$

This budgetary constraint plays the role of the cost constraint, and indifference curves are analogous to isoquants. Consequently, we analyse the problem by superimposing the budget line on an indifference map. The corresponding diagram is virtually indistinguishable from that of Figure 5.10. The only change is that the axes would be labelled x_1 and x_2 rather than L and K. Once again, the maximum point of the constrained problem occurs at the point of tangency, so that at this point the slope of the budget line is that of an indifference curve. Hence

$$\frac{P_1}{P_2} = \text{MRCS}$$

In Section 5.2 we derived the result

$$\text{MRCS} = \frac{\partial U/\partial x_1}{\partial U/\partial x_2}$$

Writing the partial derivatives $\partial U/\partial x_i$ more concisely as U_i we can deduce that

$$\frac{P_1}{P_2} = \frac{U_1}{U_2}$$

that is,

> the ratio of the prices of the goods is equal to the ratio of their marginal utilities

Again, this relationship can be rearranged into the more familiar form

$$\frac{U_1}{P_1} = \frac{U_2}{P_2}$$

so when utility is maximised subject to a budgetary constraint,

> the ratio of marginal utility to price is the same for all goods consumed

If individuals allocate their budgets between goods in this way, then utility is maximised when the last dollar spent on each good yields the same addition to total utility. Under these circumstances, the consumer has achieved maximum satisfaction within the constraint of a fixed budget, so there is no tendency to reallocate income between these goods. Obviously, the consumer's equilibrium will be affected if there is a change in external conditions such as income or the price of any good. For example, suppose that P_1 suddenly increases, while P_2 and M remain fixed. If this happens, then the equation

$$\frac{U_1}{P_1} = \frac{U_2}{P_2}$$

turns into an inequality

$$\frac{U_1}{P_1} < \frac{U_2}{P_2}$$

so equilibrium no longer holds. Given that P_1 has increased, consumers find that the last dollar spent no longer buys as many items of G1, so utility can be increased by purchasing more of G2 and less of G1. By the law of diminishing marginal utility, the effect is to increase U_1 and to decrease U_2. The process of reallocation continues until the ratio of marginal utilities to prices is again equal and equilibrium is again established.

The graphical approach provides a useful interpretation of constrained optimisation. It has also enabled us to justify some familiar results in microeconomics. However, it does not give us a practical way of actually solving such problems. It is very difficult to produce an accurate isoquant or indifference map from any given production or utility function. We now describe an alternative approach, known as the **method of substitution**.

To illustrate the method we will show how to find the minimum value of the objective function

$$z = -2x^2 + y^2$$

subject to the constraint $y = 2x - 1$.

The obvious thing to do is to substitute the expression for y given by the constraint directly into the function that we are trying to optimise to get

$$z = -2x^2 + (2x - 1)^2$$
$$= -2x^2 + 4x^2 - 4x + 1$$
$$= 2x^2 - 4x + 1$$

Note the wonderful effect that this has on z. Instead of z being a function of two variables, x and y, it is now just a function of the one variable, x. Consequently, the minimum value of z can be found using the theory of stationary points discussed in Chapter 4.

At a stationary point

$$\frac{dz}{dx} = 0$$

that is,

$$4x - 4 = 0$$

which has solution $x = 1$. Differentiating a second time, we see that

$$\frac{d^2z}{dx} = 4 > 0$$

confirming that the stationary point is a minimum. The value of z can be found by substituting $x = 1$ into

$$z = 2x^2 - 4x + 1$$

to get

$$z = 2(1)^2 - 4(1) + 1 = -1$$

It is also possible to find the value of y at the minimum. To do this we substitute $x = 1$ into the constraint

$$y = 2x - 1$$

to get

$$y = 2(1) - 1 = 1$$

The constrained function therefore has a minimum value of −1 at the point (1, 1).

The method of substitution for optimising

$$z = f(x, y)$$

subject to

$$\varphi(x, y) = M$$

may be summarised as follows:

Step 1

Use the constraint

$$\varphi(x, y) = M$$

to express y in terms of x.

Step 2

Substitute this expression for y into the objective function

$z = f(x, y)$

to write z as a function of x only.

Step 3

Use the theory of stationary points of functions of one variable to optimise z.

Practice Problem

1. Find the maximum value of the objective function

$z = 2x^2 - 3xy + 2y + 10$

subject to the constraint $y = x$.

Advice

The most difficult part of the three-step strategy is step 1, where we rearrange the given constraint to write y in terms of x. In Practice Problem 1 this step was exceptionally easy because the constraint was linear. The constraint was even presented in the appropriate form to begin with, so no extra work was required. In general, if the constraint is non-linear, it may be difficult or impossible to perform the initial rearrangement. If this happens, then you could try working the other way round and expressing x in terms of y, although there is no guarantee that this will be possible, either. However, when step 1 can be tackled successfully, the method does provide a really quick way of solving constrained optimisation problems.

To illustrate this we now use the method of substitution to solve two economic problems that both involve production functions. In the first example, output is maximised subject to cost constraint, and in the second example, cost is minimised subject to an output constraint.

Example

A firm's unit capital and labour costs are $1 and $2, respectively. If the production function is given by

$Q = 4LK + L^2$

find the maximum output and the levels of K and L at which it is achieved when the total input costs are fixed at $105. Verify that the ratio of marginal product to price is the same for both inputs at the optimum.

Solution

We are told that 1 unit of capital costs $1 and that 1 unit of labour costs $2. If the firm uses K units of capital and L units of labour, then the total input costs are

$K + 2L$

This is fixed at $105, so

$K + 2L = 105$

The mathematical problem is to maximise the objective function

$Q = 4LK + L^2$

subject to the constraint

$K + 2L = 105$

The three-step strategy is as follows:

Step 1

Rearranging the constraint to express K in terms of L gives

$K = 105 - 2L$

Step 2

Substituting this into the objective function

$Q = 4LK + L^2$

gives

$Q = 4L(105 - 2L) + L^2 = 420L - 7L^2$

and so output is now a function of the one variable, L.

Step 3

At a stationary point

$$\frac{dQ}{dL} = 0$$

that is,

$420 - 14L = 0$

which has solution $L = 30$. Differentiating a second time gives

$$\frac{d^2Q}{dL^2} = -14 < 0$$

confirming that the stationary point is a maximum.

The maximum output is found by substituting $L = 30$ into the objective function

$Q = 420L - 7L^2$

to get

$Q = 420(30) - 7(30)^2 = 6300$

The corresponding level of capital is found by substituting $L = 30$ into the constraint

$K = 105 - 2L$

to get

$K = 105 - 2(30) = 45$

The firm should therefore use 30 units of labour and 45 units of capital to produce a maximum output of 6300.

Finally, we are asked to check that the ratio of marginal product to price is the same for both inputs. From the formula

$$Q = 4LK + L^2$$

we see that the marginal products are given by

$$\text{MP}_L = \frac{\partial Q}{\partial L} = 4K + 2L \quad \text{and} \quad \text{MP}_K = \frac{\partial Q}{\partial K} = 4L$$

so at the optimum

$$\text{MP}_L = 4(45) + 2(30) = 240$$

and

$$\text{MP}_K = 4(30) = 120$$

The ratios of marginal products to prices are then

$$\frac{\text{MP}_L}{P_L} = \frac{240}{2} = 120$$

and

$$\frac{\text{MP}_K}{P_K} = \frac{120}{1} = 120$$

which are seen to be the same.

Practice Problem

2. An individual's utility function is given by

    $$U = x_1 x_2$$

    where x_1 and x_2 denote the number of items of two goods, G1 and G2. The prices of the goods are $2 and $10, respectively. Assuming that the individual has $400 available to spend on these goods, find the utility-maximising values of x_1 and x_2. Verify that the ratio of marginal utility to price is the same for both goods at the optimum.

Example

A firm's production function is given by

$$Q = 2K^{1/2}L^{1/2}$$

Unit capital and labour costs are $4 and $3, respectively. Find the values of K and L which minimise total input costs if the firm is contracted to provide 160 units of output.

Solution

Given that capital and labour costs are $4 and $3 per unit, the total cost of using K units of capital and L units of labour is

TC $= 4K + 3L$

The firm's production quota is 160, so

$2K^{1/2}L^{1/2} = 160$

The mathematical problem is to minimise the objective function

TC $= 4K + 3L$

subject to the constraint

$2K^{1/2}L^{1/2} = 160$

Step 1

Rearranging the constraint to express L in terms of K gives

$L^{1/2} = \dfrac{80}{K^{1/2}}$ (divide both sides by $2K^{1/2}$)

$L = \dfrac{6400}{K}$ (square both sides)

Step 2

Substituting this into the objective function

TC $= 4K + 3L$

gives

TC $= 4K + \dfrac{19\,200}{K}$

and so total cost is now a function of the one variable, K.

Step 3

At a stationary point

$\dfrac{d(TC)}{dK} = 0$

that is,

$4 - \dfrac{19\,200}{K^2} = 0$

This can be written as

$4 = \dfrac{19\,200}{K^2}$

so that

$$K^2 = \frac{19\,200}{4} = 4800$$

Hence

$$K = \sqrt{4800} = 69.28$$

Differentiating a second time gives

$$\frac{d^2(TC)}{dK^2} = \frac{38\,400}{K^3} > 0 \quad \text{because} \quad K > 0$$

confirming that the stationary point is a minimum.

Finally, the value of L can be found by substituting $K = 69.28$ into the constraint

$$L = \frac{6400}{K}$$

to get

$$L = \frac{6400}{69.28} = 92.38$$

We are not asked for the minimum cost, although this could easily be found by substituting the values of K and L into the objective function.

Practice Problem

3. A firm's total cost function is given by

$$TC = 3x_1^2 + 2x_1x_2 + 7x_2^2$$

where x_1 and x_2 denote the number of items of goods G1 and G2, respectively, that are produced. Find the values of x_1 and x_2 which minimise costs if the firm is committed to providing 40 goods of either type in total.

Key Terms

Isocost curve A line showing all combinations of two factors which can be bought for a fixed cost.

Method of substitution The method of solving constrained optimisation problems whereby the constraint is used to eliminate one of the variables in the objective function.

Objective function A function that one seeks to optimise (usually) subject to constraints.

Exercise 5.5

1. **(a)** Make y the subject of the formula $9x + 3y = 2$.

    (b) The function,

    $$z = 3xy$$

    is subject to the constraint

    $$9x + 3y = 2$$

    Use your answer to part (a) to show that

    $$z = 2x - 9x^2$$

    Hence find the maximum value of z and the corresponding values of x and y.

2. Find the maximum value of

    $$z = 6x - 3x^2 + 2y$$

    subject to the constraint

    $$y - x^2 = 2$$

3. Find the maximum value of

    $$z = 80x - 0.1x^2 + 100y - 0.2y^2$$

    subject to the constraint

    $$x + y = 500$$

4. A firm's production function is given by

    $$Q = 50KL$$

    Unit capital and labour costs are \$2 and \$3, respectively. Find the values of K and L which minimise total input costs if the production quota is 1200.

5. The total cost of producing x items of product A and y items of product B is

    $$TC = 22x^2 + 8y^2 - 5xy$$

    If the firm is committed to producing 20 items in total, write down the constraint connecting x and y. Hence find the number of each type that should be produced to minimise costs.

6. Find the maximum value of the utility function, $U = x_1 x_2$, subject to the budgetary constraint, $x_1 + 4x_2 = 360$.

7. A firm produces two goods A and B. The weekly cost of producing x items of A and y items of B is

    $$TC = 0.2x^2 + 0.05y^2 + 0.1xy + 2x + 5y + 1000$$

    (a) State the minimum value of TC in the case when there are no constraints.

    (b) Find the minimum value of TC when the firm is committed to producing 500 goods of either type in total.

8. A firm's production function is given by $Q = AKL$ where A is a positive constant.

Unit costs of capital and labour are \$2 and \$1, respectively. The firm spends a total of \$1000 on these inputs.

(a) Write down the cost constraint.

(b) Write down expressions for the marginal products of capital and labour.

(c) Use the fact that at the maximum output, the ratio of the input prices is equal to the ratio of their marginal products to show that $L = 2K$.

(d) Use your answers to parts (a) and (c) to find the values of K and L which maximise output.

Exercise 5.5*

1. (a) Find the minimum value of the objective function

$$z = 9x^2 + 2y^2 - 3xy$$

subject to the constraint

$$x + y = 40.$$

(b) Find the maximum value of the objective function

$$-16x^2 - 2y^2 + 4x + 9y + 2xy$$

subject to the constraint

$$y = 4x$$

2. A firm's production function is given by

$$Q = 10K^{1/2}L^{1/4}$$

Unit capital and labour costs are \$4 and \$5, respectively, and the firm spends a total of \$60 on these inputs. Find the values of K and L which maximise output.

3. A firm's production function is given by

$$Q = 2L^{1/2} + 3K^{1/2}$$

where Q, L and K denote the number of units of output, labour and capital, respectively. Labour costs are \$2 per unit, capital costs are \$1 per unit and output sells at \$8 per unit. If the firm is prepared to spend \$99 on input costs, find the maximum profit and the values of K and L at which it is achieved.

[You might like to compare your answer with the corresponding unconstrained problem that you solved in Question 2 of Exercise 5.4*.]

4. A consumer's utility function is

$$U = \ln x_1 + 2 \ln x_2$$

Find the values of x_1 and x_2 which maximise U subject to the budgetary constraint

$$2x_1 + 3x_2 = 18$$

5. An individual's utility function is given by

$$U = x_1\sqrt{x_2}$$

where x_1 and x_2 denote the monthly consumption of two goods. Unit prices of these goods are $2 and $4, respectively, and the total monthly expenditure on these goods is $300.

(a) Write down the budgetary constraint.

(b) Show that if the budgetary constraint is satisfied, the maximum value of U is 500, and write down the corresponding values of x_1 and x_2. Verify that the stationary point is a maximum.

(c) Draw the three indifference curves, $x_1\sqrt{x_2} = 400$, $x_1\sqrt{x_2} = 500$ and $x_1\sqrt{x_2} = 600$, on the same diagram. Hence show that the maximum point of the constrained problem occurs at a point where the budgetary constraint is a tangent to an indifference curve.

6. A firm wishes to maximise output, $Q = K^2L$, subject to a budgetary constraint

$$3K + 2L = 900$$

(a) Find the values of K and L which maximise output.

(b) Draw a graph to illustrate the fact that at this maximum output the budget line is a tangent to a particular isoquant.

7. A utility function, $U(x_1, x_2) = \sqrt{x_1} + x_2$, is subject to a budgetary constraint, $x_2 = b - ax_1$ where a and b are positive constants.

(a) Show that the maximum value of U is $U^* = \dfrac{4ab + 1}{4a}$.

(b) By considering the signs of $\dfrac{\partial U^*}{\partial a}$ and $\dfrac{\partial U^*}{\partial b}$, state what happens to the value of the optimal utility due to changes in a or b.

SECTION 5.6

Lagrange multipliers

Objectives

At the end of this section you should be able to:

- Use the method of Lagrange multipliers to solve constrained optimisation problems.
- Give an economic interpretation of Lagrange multipliers.
- Use Lagrange multipliers to maximise a Cobb–Douglas production function subject to a cost constraint.
- Use Lagrange multipliers to show that when a firm maximises output subject to a cost constraint, the ratio of marginal product to price is the same for all inputs.

We now describe the method of Lagrange multipliers for solving constrained optimisation problems. This is the preferred method, since it handles non-linear constraints and problems involving more than two variables with ease. It also provides some additional information that is useful when solving economic problems.

To optimise an objective function

$$f(x, y)$$

subject to a constraint

$$\varphi(x, y) = M$$

we work as follows.

Step 1

Define a new function

$$g(x, y, \lambda) = f(x, y) + \lambda[M - \varphi(x, y)]$$

Step 2

Solve the simultaneous equations

$$\frac{\partial g}{\partial x} = 0$$

$$\frac{\partial g}{\partial y} = 0$$

$$\frac{\partial g}{\partial \lambda} = 0$$

for the three unknowns, x, y and λ.

The basic steps of the method are straightforward. In step 1 we combine the objective function and constraint into a single function. To do this we first consider

$$M - \varphi(x, y)$$

and multiply by the scalar (i.e. number) λ (the Greek letter 'lambda'). This scalar is called the **Lagrange multiplier**. Finally, we add on the objective function to produce the new function

$$g(x, y, \lambda) = f(x, y) + \lambda[M - \varphi(x, y)]$$

This is called the **Lagrangian** function. The right-hand side involves the three letters x, y and λ, so g is a function of three variables.

In step 2 we work out the three first-order partial derivatives

$$\frac{\partial g}{\partial x}, \frac{\partial g}{\partial y}, \frac{\partial g}{\partial \lambda}$$

and equate these to zero to produce a system of three simultaneous equations for the three unknowns x, y and λ. The point (x, y) is then the optimal solution of the constrained problem. The number λ can also be given a meaning, and we consider this later.

To illustrate the new method consider trying to optimise the value of

$$x^2 - 3xy + 12x$$

subject to the constraint

$$2x + 3y = 6$$

Step 1

In this case

$$f(x, y) = x^2 - 3xy + 12x$$

$$\varphi(x, y) = 2x + 3y$$

$$M = 6$$

so the Lagrangian function is given by

$$g(x, y, \lambda) = x^2 - 3xy + 12x + \lambda(6 - 2x - 3y)$$

Step 2

Working out the three partial derivatives of g gives

$$\frac{\partial g}{\partial x} = 2x - 3y + 12 - 2\lambda$$

$$\frac{\partial g}{\partial y} = -3x - 3\lambda$$

$$\frac{\partial g}{\partial \lambda} = 6 - 2x - 3y$$

so we need to solve the simultaneous equations

$$2x - 3y + 12 - 2\lambda = 0$$

$$-3x - 3\lambda = 0$$

$$6 - 2x - 3y = 0$$

that is,

$$2x - 3y - 2\lambda = -12 \tag{1}$$

$$-3x - 3\lambda = 0 \tag{2}$$

$$2x + 3y = 6 \tag{3}$$

We can eliminate x from equation (2) by multiplying equation (1) by 3, multiplying equation (2) by 2 and adding. Similarly, x can be eliminated from equation (3) by subtracting equation (3) from (1). These operations give

$$-9y - 12\lambda = -36 \tag{4}$$

$$-6y - 2\lambda = -18 \tag{5}$$

The variable y can be eliminated by multiplying equation (4) by 6 and equation (5) by 9, and subtracting to get

$$-54\lambda = -54 \tag{6}$$

so $\lambda = 1$. Substituting this into equations (5) and (2) gives $y = 8/3$ and $x = -1$, respectively.

The optimal solution is therefore $(-1, 8/3)$, and the corresponding value of the objective function

$$x^2 - 3xy + 12x$$

is

$$(-1)^2 - 3(-1)(^8/_3) + 12(-1) = -3$$

Practice Problem

1. Use Lagrange multipliers to optimise

    $$2x^2 - xy$$

    subject to

    $$x + y = 12$$

Looking back at your own solution to Practice Problem 1, notice that the third equation in step 2 is just a restatement of the original constraint. It is easy to see that this is always the case because if

$$g(x, y, \lambda) = f(x, y) + \lambda[M - \varphi(x, y)]$$

then

$$\frac{\partial g}{\partial \lambda} = M - \varphi(x, y)$$

The equation

$$\frac{\partial g}{\partial \lambda} = 0$$

then implies the constraint

$$\varphi(x, y) = M$$

Example

A monopolistic producer of two goods, G1 and G2, has a joint total cost function

$$TC = 10Q_1 + Q_1Q_2 + 10Q_2$$

where Q_1 and Q_2 denote the quantities of G1 and G2 respectively. If P_1 and P_2 denote the corresponding prices then the demand equations are

$$P_1 = 50 - Q_1 + Q_2$$

$$P_2 = 30 + 2Q_1 - Q_2$$

Find the maximum profit if the firm is contracted to produce a total of 15 goods of either type. Estimate the new optimal profit if the production quota rises by 1 unit.

Solution

The first thing that we need to do is to write down expressions for the objective function and constraint. The objective function is profit and is given by

$$\pi = TR - TC$$

The total cost function is given to be

$$TC = 10Q_1 + Q_1Q_2 + 10Q_2$$

However, we need to use the demand equations to obtain an expression for TR. Total revenue from the sale of G1 is

$$TR_1 = P_1Q_1 = (50 - Q_1 + Q_2)Q_1 = 50Q_1 - Q_1^2 + Q_2Q_1$$

and total revenue from the sale of G2 is

$$TR_2 = P_2Q_2 = (30 + 2Q_1 - Q_2)Q_2 = 30Q_2 + 2Q_1Q_2 - Q_2^2$$

so

$$
\begin{aligned}
TR &= TR_1 + TR_2 \\
&= 50Q_1 - Q_1^2 + Q_2Q_1 + 30Q_2 + 2Q_1Q_2 - Q_2^2 \\
&= 50Q_1 - Q_1^2 + 3Q_1Q_2 + 30Q_2 - Q_2^2
\end{aligned}
$$

Hence

$$
\begin{aligned}
\pi &= TR - TC \\
&= (50Q_1 - Q_1^2 + 3Q_1Q_2 + 30Q_2 - Q_2^2) - (10Q_1 + Q_1Q_2 + 10Q_2) \\
&= 40Q_1 - Q_1^2 + 2Q_1Q_2 + 20Q_2 - Q_2^2
\end{aligned}
$$

The constraint is more easily determined. We are told that the firm produces 15 goods in total, so

$$Q_1 + Q_2 = 15$$

The mathematical problem is to maximise the objective function

$$\pi = 40Q_1 - Q_1^2 + 2Q_1Q_2 + 20Q_2 - Q_2^2$$

subject to the constraint

$$Q_1 + Q_2 = 15$$

Step 1

The Lagrangian function is

$$g(Q_1, Q_2, \lambda) = 40Q_1 - Q_1^2 + 2Q_1Q_2 + 20Q_2 - Q_2^2 + \lambda(15 - Q_1 - Q_2)$$

Step 2

The simultaneous equations

$$\frac{\partial g}{\partial Q_1} = 0, \ \frac{\partial g}{\partial Q_2} = 0, \ \frac{\partial g}{\partial \lambda} = 0$$

are

$$40 - 2Q_1 + 2Q_2 - \lambda = 0$$

$$2Q_1 + 20 - 2Q_2 - \lambda = 0$$

$$15 - Q_1 - Q_2 = 0$$

that is,

$$-2Q_1 + 2Q_2 - \lambda = -40 \tag{1}$$

$$2Q_1 - 2Q_2 - \lambda = -20 \tag{2}$$

$$Q_1 + Q_2 = 15 \tag{3}$$

The obvious way of solving this system is to add equations (1) and (2) to get

$$-2\lambda = -60$$

so $\lambda = 30$. Putting this into equation (1) gives

$$-2Q_1 + 2Q_2 = -10 \tag{4}$$

Equations (3) and (4) constitute a system of two equations for the two unknowns Q_1 and Q_2. We can eliminate Q_1 by multiplying equation (3) by 2 and adding equation (4) to get

$$4Q_2 = 20$$

so $Q_2 = 5$. Substituting this into equation (3) gives

$$Q_1 = 15 - 5 = 10$$

The maximum profit is found by substituting $Q_1 = 10$ and $Q_2 = 5$ into the formula for π to get

$$\pi = 40(10) - (10)^2 + 2(10)(5) + 20(5) - 5^2 = 475$$

The final part of this example wants us to find the new optimal profit when the production quota rises by 1 unit. One way of doing this is just to repeat the calculations replacing the previous quota of 15 by 16, although this is extremely tedious and not strictly necessary. There is a convenient shortcut based on the value of the Lagrange multiplier λ. To understand this, let us replace the production quota, 15, by the variable M, so that the Lagrangian function is

$$g(Q_1, Q_2, \lambda, M) = 40Q_1 - Q_1^2 + 2Q_1Q_2 + 20Q_2 - Q_2^2 + \lambda(M - Q_1 - Q_2)$$

The expression on the right-hand side involves Q_1, Q_2, λ and M, so g is now a function of four variables. If we partially differentiate with respect to M, then

$$\frac{\partial g}{\partial M} = \lambda$$

We see that λ is a multiplier not only in the mathematical sense but also in the economic sense. It represents the (approximate) change in g due to a 1-unit increase in M. Moreover, if the constraint is satisfied, then

$$Q_1 + Q_2 = M$$

and the expression for g reduces to

$$40Q_1 - Q_1^2 + 2Q_1Q_2 + 20Q_2 - Q_2^2$$

which is equal to the profit. The value of the Lagrange multiplier represents the change in optimal profit brought about by a 1-unit increase in the production quota. In this case, $\lambda = 30$, so the profit rises by 30 to become 505.

The interpretation placed on the value of λ in this example applies quite generally. Given an objective function

$$f(x, y)$$

and constraint

$$\varphi(x, y) = M$$

the value of λ gives the approximate change in the optimal value of f due to a 1-unit increase in M.

Practice Problem

2. A consumer's utility function is given by

$$U(x_1, x_2) = 2x_1x_2 + 3x_1$$

where x_1 and x_2 denote the number of items of two goods G1 and G2 that are bought. Each item costs \$1 for G1 and \$2 for G2. Use Lagrange multipliers to find the maximum value of U if the consumer's income is \$83. Estimate the new optimal utility if the consumer's income rises by \$1.

The Lagrange multiplier method can be used to solve the problem of maximising the general Cobb–Douglas production function

$$Q = AK^\alpha L^\beta \qquad (A, \alpha \text{ and } \beta \text{ are positive constants})$$

when it is subject to a cost constraint

$$P_K K + P_L L = M$$

This problem appears very hard at first sight because it does not involve specific numbers. However, it is easy to handle such generalised problems provided that we do not panic.

Step 1

The Lagrangian function is

$$g(K, L, \lambda) = AK^{\alpha}L^{\beta} + \lambda(M - P_K K - P_L L)$$

Step 2

The simultaneous equations

$$\frac{\partial g}{\partial K} = 0, \ \frac{\partial g}{\partial L} = 0, \ \frac{\partial g}{\partial \lambda} = 0$$

are

$$A\alpha K^{\alpha-1}L^{\beta} - \lambda P_K = 0 \tag{1}$$

$$A\beta K^{\alpha}L^{\beta-1} - \lambda P_L = 0 \tag{2}$$

$$M - P_K K - P_L L = 0 \tag{3}$$

These equations look rather forbidding. Before we begin to solve them, it pays to simplify equations (1) and (2) slightly by introducing $Q = AK^{\alpha}L^{\beta}$. Notice that

$$A\alpha K^{\alpha-1}L^{\beta} = \frac{\alpha(AK^{\alpha}L^{\beta})}{K} = \frac{\alpha Q}{K}$$

$$A\beta K^{\alpha}L^{\beta-1} = \frac{\beta(AK^{\alpha}L^{\beta})}{L} = \frac{\beta Q}{L}$$

so equations (1), (2) and (3) can be written

$$\frac{\alpha Q}{K} - \lambda P_K = 0 \tag{4}$$

$$\frac{\beta Q}{L} - \lambda P_L = 0 \tag{5}$$

$$P_K K + P_L L = M \tag{6}$$

Equations (4) and (5) can be rearranged to give

$$\lambda = \frac{\alpha Q}{P_K K} \quad \text{and} \quad \lambda = \frac{\beta Q}{P_L L}$$

so that

$$\frac{\alpha Q}{P_K K} = \frac{\beta Q}{P_L L}$$

and hence

$$\frac{P_K K}{\alpha} = \frac{P_L L}{\beta} \qquad \text{(divide both sides by } Q \text{ and turn both sides upside down)}$$

that is,

$$P_K K = \frac{\alpha}{\beta} P_L L \qquad \text{(multiply through by } \alpha\text{)} \tag{7}$$

Substituting this into equation (6) gives

$$\frac{\alpha}{\beta} P_L L + P_L L = M$$

$$\alpha L + \beta L = \frac{\beta M}{P_L} \qquad \text{(multiply through by } \beta/P_L)$$

$$(a + \beta)L = \frac{\beta M}{P_L} \qquad \text{(factorise)}$$

$$L = \frac{\beta M}{(\alpha + \beta)P_L} \qquad \text{(divide through by } \alpha + \beta)$$

Finally, we can put this into equation (7) to get

$$P_K K = \frac{\alpha M}{\alpha + \beta}$$

so

$$K = \frac{\alpha M}{(\alpha + \beta)P_K}$$

The values of K and L which optimise Q are therefore

$$\frac{\alpha M}{(\alpha + \beta)P_K} \quad \text{and} \quad \frac{\beta M}{(\alpha + \beta)P_L}$$

Practice Problem

3. Use Lagrange multipliers to find expressions for x_1 and x_2 which maximise the utility function

    $$U = x_1^{1/2} + x_2^{1/2}$$

    subject to the general budgetary constraint

    $$P_1 x_1 + P_2 x_2 = M$$

The previous work illustrates the power of mathematics when solving economics problems. The main advantage of using algebra and calculus rather than just graphs and tables of numbers is their generality. In future, if we need to maximise any particular Cobb–Douglas production function subject to any particular cost constraint, all we have to do is to quote the previous result. By substituting specific values of M, α, β, P_K and P_L into the general formulas for K and L, we can write down the solution in a matter of seconds. In fact, we can use mathematics to generalise still further. Rather than work with production functions of a prescribed form such as

$$Q = A K^\alpha L^\beta$$

we can obtain results pertaining to any production function

$$Q = f(K, L)$$

For instance, we can use Lagrange multipliers to justify a result that we derived graphically in Section 5.5. At the beginning of that section we showed that when output is maximised, subject to a cost constraint, the ratio of marginal product to price is the same for all inputs. To obtain this result using Lagrange multipliers we simply write down the Lagrangian function

$$g(K, L, \lambda) = f(K, L) + \lambda(M - P_K K - P_L L)$$

which corresponds to a production function

$$f(K, L)$$

and cost constraint

$$P_K K + P_L L = M$$

The simultaneous equations

$$\frac{\partial g}{\partial K} = 0, \frac{\partial g}{\partial L} = 0, \frac{\partial g}{\partial \lambda} = 0$$

are

$$\text{MP}_K - \lambda P_K = 0 \tag{1}$$

$$\text{MP}_L - \lambda P_L = 0 \tag{2}$$

$$M - P_K K - P_L L = 0 \tag{3}$$

because

$$\frac{\partial f}{\partial K} = \text{MP}_K \quad \text{and} \quad \frac{\partial f}{\partial K} = \text{MP}_L$$

Equations (1) and (2) can be rearranged to give

$$\lambda = \frac{\text{MP}_K}{P_K} \quad \text{and} \quad \lambda = \frac{\text{MP}_L}{P_L}$$

so

$$\frac{\text{MP}_K}{P_K} = \frac{\text{MP}_L}{P_L}$$

as required.

Key Terms

Lagrange multiplier   The number λ which is used in the Lagrangian function. In economics this gives the approximate change in the optimal value of the objective function when the value of the constraint is increased by 1 unit.

Lagrangian   The function $f(x, y) + \lambda[M - \varphi(x, y)]$, where $f(x, y)$ is the objective function and $\varphi(x, y) = M$ is the constraint. The stationary point of this function is the solution of the associated constrained optimisation problem.

Advice

There now follow some additional problems for you to try. If you feel that you need even more practice, then you are advised to rework the questions in Section 5.5 using Lagrange multipliers.

Exercise 5.6

1. Use Lagrange multipliers to find the maximum value of

    $$z = x + 2xy$$

    subject to the constraint

    $$x + 2y = 5$$

2. **(a)** Use Lagrange multipliers to find the maximum value of

    $$z = 4xy$$

    subject to the constraint

    $$x + 2y = 40$$

    State the associated values of x, y and λ.

    (b) Repeat part (a) when the constraint is changed to

    $$x + 2y = 41$$

    (c) Verify that the value of the Lagrange multiplier in part (a) is approximately the same as the change in the optimal value of z when the right-hand side of the constraint is increased by 1 unit.

3. A firm's production function is given by

    $$Q = KL$$

    Unit capital and labour costs are \$2 and \$1, respectively. Find the maximum level of output if the total cost of capital and labour is \$6.

4. A firm's production function is given by $Q = 80KL$. Unit capital and labour costs are \$2 and \$1, respectively. The firm is contracted to provide 4000 units of output and wants to fulfil this contract at minimal cost.

    (a) Explain briefly why the Lagrangian function is

    $$g(K, L, \lambda) = 2K + L + \lambda[50 - KL]$$

    (b) Write down expressions for $\dfrac{\partial g}{\partial K}$, $\dfrac{\partial g}{\partial L}$ and $\dfrac{\partial g}{\partial \lambda}$.

    (c) Find values of K and L which fulfil the quota with minimal cost to the firm.

5. A firm's production function is given by

    $$Q = 80KL$$

    which is subject to a budgetary constraint, $3K + 5L = 1500$.

(a) Work out the first-order partial derivatives of the Lagrangian function

$$g(K, L, \lambda) = 80KL + \lambda[1500 - 3K - 5L]$$

(b) Find values of K and L which maximise output and satisfy the budgetary constraint.

(c) Estimate the increase in optimal output which results when the total budget of 1500 is increased to 1501.

6. A monopolistic producer of two goods, G1 and G2, has a total cost function

$$TC = 5Q_1 + 10Q_2$$

where Q_1 and Q_2 denote the quantities of G1 and G2, respectively. If P_1 and P_2 denote the corresponding prices, then the demand equations are

$$P_1 = 50 - Q_1 - Q_2$$

$$P_2 = 100 - Q_1 - 4Q_2$$

Find the maximum profit if the firm's total costs are fixed at $100. Estimate the new optimal profit if total costs rise to $101.

Exercise 5.6*

1. (a) Use Lagrange multipliers to find the optimal value of

$$z = x + 2y$$

subject to the constraint

$$x + y^2 = M$$

(b) Show that in this case the value of λ gives the exact change in the optimal value of z when M increases by 1 unit.

2. A production function is given by $Q = 200K^{0.8}L^{0.6}$.

(a) Find the optimal value of Q when the inputs are subject to a budgetary constraint of $5K + 2L = 2000$.

(b) Find the optimal value of input costs, $C = 5K + 2L$, when the inputs are constrained by an output quota of $Q = 8000$.

3. (a) Find the maximum value of $Q = K^{0.4}L^{0.6}$ if the budgetary constraint is $3K + 5L = 3000$.

(b) What happens to the optimal output if the available budget doubles?

4. A firm that manufactures speciality bicycles has a profit function

$$\pi = 5x^2 - 10xy + 3y^2 + 240x$$

where x denotes the number of frames and y denotes the number of wheels. Find the maximum profit assuming that the firm does not want any spare frames or wheels left over at the end of the production run.

5. Find the maximum value of

$$Q = 10\sqrt{(KL)}$$

subject to the cost constraint

$$K + 4L = 16$$

Estimate the change in the optimal value of Q if the cost constraint is changed to

$$K + 4L = 17$$

6. A consumer's utility function is given by

$$U = \alpha \ln x_1 + \beta \ln x_2$$

Find the values of x_1 and x_2 which maximise U subject to the budgetary constraint

$$P_1 x_1 + P_2 x_2 = M$$

7. An advertising agency spends $\$x$ on a newspaper campaign and a further $\$y$ promoting its client's products on local radio. It receives 15% commission on all sales that the client receives. The agency has $\$10\,000$ to spend in total, and the client earns $\$M$ from its sales, where

$$M = \frac{100\,000x}{50 + x} + \frac{40\,000y}{30 + y}$$

Use the method of Lagrange multipliers to determine how much should be spent on advertising in newspapers and on radio to maximise the agency's net income. Give your answers correct to two decimal places.

8. A firm produces three goods, A, B and C. The number of items of each are x, y and z, respectively. The firm is committed to producing a total number of 30 items of types A and B. The firm's associated profit function is

$$\pi = 8x + 12y + 4z - 0.5x^2 - 0.5y^2 - z^2$$

How many goods of each type must be produced to maximise profit subject to the constraint?

9. A firm decides to invest x units of capital in project A and y units in project B. The expected return for 1 unit of investment is $\$400$ in project A and $\$800$ in project B. However, in order to meet the expectations of the firm's ethical and environmental policy, the values of x and y must satisfy the constraint

$$x^2 + y^2 - 4x - 6y = 67$$

How many units of each type should the firm buy in order to maximise total return?

10. Use the method of Lagrange multipliers to show that when a utility function, $U = U(x_1, x_2)$, is optimised subject to a budgetary constraint, $P_1 x_1 + P_2 x_2 = M$, the ratio of marginal utility to price is the same for both goods.

11. A function, $z = ax + by$, is to be optimised subject to the constraint, $x^2 + y^2 = 1$ where a and b are positive constants. Use Lagrange multipliers to show that this problem has only one solution in the positive quadrant (i.e. in the region $x > 0$, $y > 0$) and that the optimal value of z is $\sqrt{a^2 + b^2}$.

Formal mathematics

In Section 5.1 we stated that the partial derivative, $\partial f/\partial x$, is found by 'differentiating f with respect to x with y held constant'. Whilst this tells you exactly what to do to work it out, it is very imprecise and gives no real geometrical insight into what it represents.

Look carefully at the surface, $z = f(x, y)$ shown in Figure 5.11. Underneath the surface in the (x, y)-plane is the line, $y = b$, and the point (a, b) which lies on this line. Vertically above this line, etched on the surface itself, is a curve. As you move along this curve from F to G to H, the y coordinate remains fixed at $y = b$ and the height z varies, in accordance with any changes in x. The gradient of the tangent to this curve at the point (a, b) measures the rate of change of the function as x varies with y fixed. This is the value of the partial derivative $\partial f/\partial x$ evaluated at (a, b). If you imagine yourself walking on the surface along the line FH, the gradient measures how steep the path is. In Figure 5.11 the curve is uphill at the point G so $f_x(a, b) > 0$. Also, the curve is concave, so the second-order partial derivative, $f_{xx}(a, b) < 0$. A similar interpretation can be given for the partial derivative with respect to y. It is the gradient of the curve RS running parallel to the y axis in Figure 5.11.

We can use this geometrical interpretation to give a formal definition of a partial derivative. In Figure 5.12 the point V is directly above (a, b) so is at a height, $f(a, b)$. The point W is a short distance away along the curve directly above $(a + \Delta x, b)$, so it is at a height $f(a + \Delta x, b)$. The gradient of the chord VW is given by

$$\frac{f(a + \Delta x, b) - f(a, b)}{\Delta x}$$

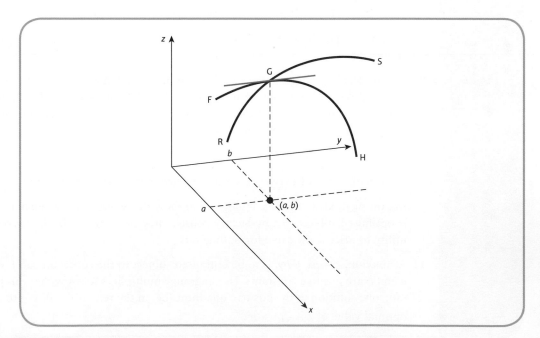

Figure 5.11

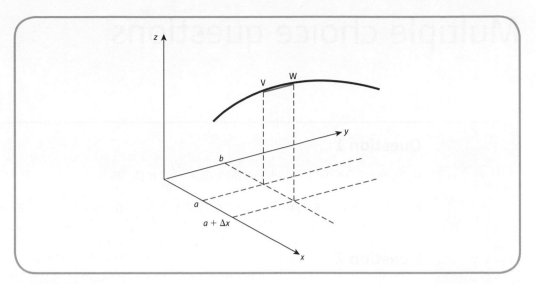

Figure 5.12

As Δx gets smaller and smaller, the gradient of the chord approaches that of the tangent so we can define

$$f_x(a, b) = \lim_{\Delta x \to 0} \frac{f(a + \Delta x, b) - f(a, b)}{\Delta x}$$

A similar argument gives

$$f_y(a, b) = \lim_{\Delta y \to 0} \frac{f(a, b + \Delta y) - f(a, b)}{\Delta y}$$

Multiple choice questions

Question 1

If $f(x, y) = 2x^7 + 3x^2 y^3$, work out the value $\dfrac{\partial^2 f}{\partial x \partial y}$ at $(2, 3)$.

A. 780   **B.** 340   **C.** 126   **D.** 544   **E.** 324

Question 2

If the function $f(x, y) = 4xy + x^2 y^3$ satisfies the equation $2x^2 \dfrac{\partial^2 f}{\partial x^2} + y^2 \dfrac{\partial^2 f}{\partial y^2} + nxy = 10f$, determine the value of n.

A. 2   **B.** 10   **C.** 6   **D.** 8   **E.** 40

Question 3

Find the marginal rate of technical substitution for the Cobb–Douglas production function $Q = AK^\alpha L^\beta$.

A. $\dfrac{\beta K}{\alpha L}$

B. $\dfrac{\beta L}{\alpha K}$

C. $\dfrac{\alpha K}{\beta L}$

D. $\dfrac{\alpha L}{\beta K}$

E. None of the above

Question 4

If the method of Lagrange multipliers is used to find the maximum value of $10xy$ subject to the constraint $7x + 3y = 15$, work out the value of the Lagrange multiplier.

A. $\dfrac{42}{25}$ **B.** $\dfrac{25}{7}$ **C.** $\dfrac{7}{5}$ **D.** $\dfrac{3}{7}$ **E.** $\dfrac{2}{3}$

Question 5

Find the value of z at the minimum point of the function $z = x^3 + y^3 - 24xy + 1000$.

A. 978   **B.** 1000   **C.** 488   **D.** 1022   **E.** 968

Question 6

The demand function of a good is given by $Q = 100 - 6P + 0.1Y^2$. Find the income elasticity of demand when $P = 10$ and $Y = 20$.

A. 2   **B.** 0.8   **C.** 0.5   **D.** 1   **E.** 0.75

Question 7

A consumer's utility function is given by $U = 4\ln x_1 + \ln x_2$. Find the values of x_1 and x_2 which maximise U subject to the budgetary constraint $x_1 + 2x_2 = 100$.

A. $x_1 = 80, x_2 = 10$

B. $x_1 = 20, x_2 = 40$

C. $x_1 = 60, x_2 = 20$

D. $x_1 = 40, x_2 = 30$

E. $x_1 = 30, x_2 = 70$

Question 8

The supply and demand functions are given by

$$P = aQ_S + b$$
$$P = cQ_D + d$$

where a, b and d are positive constants, and c is a negative constant. Find the multiplier, $\dfrac{\partial Q}{\partial c}$, for the equilibrium quantity.

A. $\dfrac{-1}{a + c}$ **B.** $\dfrac{b - d}{(a - c)^2}$ **C.** $\dfrac{1}{a + c}$ **D.** $\dfrac{1}{(a + c)^2}$ **E.** $\dfrac{d - b}{(a - c)^2}$

Question 9

The demand function of a good is given by $Q = 100 - 3P + 2P_A + 0.1Y$ where Q, P, P_A and Y denote quantity demanded, price of the good, price of an alternative good and income, respectively. Find the cross-price elasticity of demand when $P = 20$, $P_A = 15$ and $Y = 300$.

A. 0.1   **B.** 0.2   **C.** 0.3   **D.** 0.4   **E.** 0.5

Question 10

The production function of a firm is given by $Q = K^{0.2}L^{0.7}$ where Q, K and L denote output, capital and labour, respectively. The firm currently uses 300 units of capital and 500 units of labour. If the firm decreases labour by 2.8, estimate the increase in capital needed to maintain current output levels.

A. 5.4   **B.** 4.8   **C.** 6.4   **D.** 6.2   **E.** 5.9

Question 11

On an isoquant diagram, capital is plotted on the vertical axis and labour is plotted on the horizontal axis. Unit prices of capital and labour are \$24 and \$18, respectively, and the firm has a fixed amount to spend on these inputs. Work out the gradient of the associated isocost line.

A. $-3/4$

B. $-4/3$

C. $-2/3$

D. $-3/2$

E. Insufficient information

Question 12

An individual's utility function for the consumption of two goods, 1 and 2, is given by $U = a\sqrt{x_1} + b\sqrt{x_2}$. Find an expression for the marginal rate of commodity substitution at the point $(4, 9)$.

A. $\dfrac{3a}{4b}$ B. $\dfrac{a}{2b}$ C. $\dfrac{5a}{2b}$ D. $\dfrac{3a}{2b}$ E. $\dfrac{5a}{3b}$

Question 13

The price of the goods 1 and 2 in Question 12 are \$1 and \$2, respectively. If the individual has a budget of \$100 to spend on these goods, determine the optimal consumption of good 1.

A. $\dfrac{200a^2}{2a^2 + b^2}$

B. $\dfrac{100a^2}{a^2 + 2b^2}$

C. $\dfrac{200a^2}{a^2 + 2b^2}$

D. $\dfrac{100a^2}{4a^2 + b^2}$

E. $\dfrac{200a^2}{4a^2 + b^2}$

Question 14

An increase in the price of a good by 5% leads to an increase of 2% in the demand for an alternative good. Calculate the cross-price elasticity of demand and state whether these goods are complementary or substitutable.

A. 2.5 and substitutable

B. -0.4 and complementary

C. 0.4 and substitutable

D. -2.5 and complementary

E. -0.4 and substitutable

Examination questions

Question 1

A function of two variables is given by $f(x, y) = 2x + 3x^2y - y^2$.

(a) Find expressions for the first-order and second-order partial derivatives of f.

(b) Evaluate $f_x(1, 2)$ and $f_y(1, 2)$, and use the small increments formula to estimate the change in f as x increases by 0.2 and y decreases by 0.1 at the point $(1, 2)$.

(c) A curve is defined implicitly by $2x + 3x^2y - y^2 = 4$. Verify that $(1, 2)$ lies on this curve and find the gradient at this point.

Question 2

The demand function of a good is given by

$$Q = 1000 - 2P - 0.5P_A^2 + 0.01Y$$

where Q, P, P_A and Y denote the quantity demanded, the price of the good, the price of an alternative good and income, respectively.

Find the cross-price elasticity of demand and income elasticity of demand when $P = 15$, $P_A = 20$ and $Y = 3000$.

(a) Explain whether the good is inferior, normal or superior.

(b) Use the small increments formula to estimate the change in demand if P increases by 0.5, P_A decreases by 0.25 and Y is unchanged.

Question 3

Sophie has $50 to spend on goods 1 and 2. The unit prices of these goods are $1 and $2, respectively. Her utility function is given by $U = x_1x_2 + 2x_1 + 2x_2$

(a) Write down Sophie's budgetary constraint and deduce that $U = 48x_2 - 2x_2^2 + 100$.

(b) Hence work out Sophie's optimal consumption of these goods.

Question 4

A firm's production function is given by $Q = \sqrt{KL} + \dfrac{1}{4}\ln(KL^3)$.

(a) Write down expressions for the marginal product of labour and marginal product of capital.

(b) The firm currently uses 18 units of capital and 50 units of labour, and decides to reduce the level of labour to 49 units. Estimate the corresponding increase in capital if output is to remain unchanged.

Question 5

A firm is the sole producer of two goods labelled 1 and 2. The demand functions are given by

$$Q_1 = 495 - P_1 - P_2$$
$$Q_2 = 695 - P_1 - 2P_2$$

where Q_i and P_i denote the quantity demanded and price of good i, respectively. The total cost function is

$$TC = Q_1^2 + Q_1Q_2 + Q_2^2$$

(a) Are these goods substitutable or complementary?

(b) Show that the profit function is given by

$$\pi = 259Q_1 + 200Q_2 + Q_1Q_2 - 3Q_1^2 - 2Q_2^2$$

(c) Find the values of Q_1 and Q_2 which maximise the profit and verify that the second-order conditions for a maximum are satisfied.

(d) Find the prices that the producer should charge to maximise profit.

Question 6

A firm's unit capital and labour costs are \$4 and \$1, respectively. If the production function is given by $Q = \sqrt{LK}$ and total input costs are \$120, use the method of Lagrange multipliers to find the levels of K and L which maximise output.

Verify that the ratio of marginal products to price is the same for both inputs at the optimum.

Question 7

A firm's production function is given by $Q = 16\sqrt{K} + 6\sqrt{L}$ where Q, K and L denote output, capital and labour, respectively. The cost of providing each unit of capital and labour is \$80 and \$27, respectively.

Find the number of units of capital and labour if the firm wishes to minimise total costs whilst satisfying a production quota of 102 units of output.

Question 8

Find and classify the stationary points of the function $C(x, y) = (2xy - x^2)e^{-y} + 100$.

Question 9

A firm's production function is given by $Q = \dfrac{K^2L}{K + 4L}$ where K and L denote capital and labour, respectively.

(a) Show that this production function is homogeneous of degree 2.

(b) Calculate the marginal products, MP_K and MP_L and hence verify that Euler's theorem holds for this function.

The firm currently uses 40 units of capital and 15 units of labour.

(c) Calculate the marginal rate of technical substitution and give a brief interpretation of this number.

(d) The firm decides to reduce capital by 0.5 units. Use the small increments formula to estimate the increase in labour needed to increase the total output by 1 unit.

Question 10

An individual needs to allocate the 168 hours available each week to work, W, hours and free time, F, hours. He earns \$20 an hour (after deductions), and his utility function is given by $U = 6E^{1/3} F^{2/3}$ where E denotes his weekly earnings.

Explain briefly why the Lagrangian for this problem may be written as

$$L(E, F, \lambda) = 6E^{1/3} F^{2/3} + \lambda(3360 - E - 20F)$$

Hence find the optimal number of hours worked in a week.

If the hourly rate of pay increases, does the optimal number of hours worked in a week increase, decrease or stay the same?

Question 11

A firm intends to maximise the output Q which satisfies a production function of the form, $Q = f(K, L)$, subject to a budgetary constraint, $16K + 25L = 220$ where K and L denote capital and labour, respectively.

Work out the value of capital if $L = 4$ and the constraint is satisfied.

Calculate the slope of the constraint when K is plotted on the vertical axis and L is plotted on the horizontal axis.

Write down the marginal rate of technical substitution at the maximum and justify your answer using a general diagram showing isoquants of the production function.

Question 12

(a) A function is defined implicitly by

$$x^3 + 2xy + y^4 = 61$$

Verify that the point $(-2, 3)$ lies on this curve and find the gradient at this point.

(b) Find and classify the stationary point on the surface defined by

$$z = 4x^2 - xy + 3y^2 - 8x + y + 3$$

Question 13

An individual's utility function is given by $U = \dfrac{x_1 x_2}{2x_1 + x_2}$ where x_1 and x_2 denote the number of good 1 and the number of good 2 that she wishes to buy.

(a) Write down expressions for the marginal utilities, $\dfrac{\partial U}{\partial x_1}$ and $\dfrac{\partial U}{\partial x_2}$, and show that the law of diminishing marginal utilities holds for each of these goods.

(b) Calculate the marginal rate of commodity substitution for the indifference curve which passes through $(1, 3)$ and hence estimate the increase in x_2 required to maintain the current level of utility when x_1 decreases by 0.02 units.

(c) Use Lagrange multipliers to find the optimal values of x_1 and x_2 if the individual maximises utility subject to a budgetary constraint, $x_1 + 8x_2 = 100$.

Question 14

A firm's unit capital and labour costs are \$1 and \$2, respectively, and the total input costs are fixed at \$$M$. If the production function is given by $Q = 8KL$, use the method of Lagrange multipliers to show that the optimum output is M^2, and find the levels of K and L at which it is achieved.

(a) Verify that the ratio of marginal product to price is the same for both inputs at the optimum, and give an interpretation of this result.

(b) Verify that the Lagrange multiplier gives the approximate change in optimal output when the input costs increase by one unit.

(c) Write down the equation of the isoquant that passes through the optimum point and hence show that the cost constraint is a tangent to the isoquant at this point. Explain why this was to be expected.

Question 15

(a) The equations for the IS model are given by:

$$Y = C + I$$
$$C = aY + b \ (0 < a < 1, b > 0)$$
$$I = cr + d \ (c < 0, d > 0)$$

where Y, C, I and r denote national income, consumption, investment and interest rate, and a, b, c and d are parameters.

Show that when the commodity market is in equilibrium,

$$(1 - a)Y - cr = b + d$$

(b) The equations for the LM model are given by:

$$M_S = M_D$$
$$M_S = M^*_S \qquad \qquad (M^*_S > 0)$$
$$M_D = k_1Y + k_2r + k_3 \qquad (k_1 > 0, k_2 < 0, k_3 > 0)$$

where M_S and M_D denote the money supply and total demand for money.

Show that when the money market is in equilibrium,

$$k_1Y + k_2r = M^*_S - k_3$$

(c) Use the results of parts (a) and (b) to show that when the commodity and money markets are both in equilibrium, national income is given by

$$Y = \frac{k_2(b + d) + c(M^*_S - k_3)}{(1 - a)k_2 + ck_1}$$

Write down an expression for the multiplier, $\dfrac{\partial Y}{\partial b}$. Giving reasons for your answer, state whether national income increases or decreases as a result of an increase in autonomous consumption.

6.00	104.37	2.95	0
5.00	105.08	3.34	0
4.03	104.07	2.05	0
2.00	103.34	3.24	0
6.05	105.25	3.51	0
3.00	105.25	2.44	0

$\sqrt{x}$

7.00	103.37	3.34
5.00	105.01	2.95
3.03	102.07	2.34
1.00	103.34	4.54
7.06	104.45	3.44
6.00	102.03	0.21

CHAPTER 6
Integration

This chapter concludes the topic of calculus by considering the integration of functions of one variable. It is in two sections, which should be read in the order that they appear.

Section 6.1 introduces the idea of integration as the opposite process to that of differentiation. It enables you to recover an expression for the total revenue function from any given marginal revenue function, to recover the total cost function from any marginal cost function and so on. You will no doubt be pleased to discover that no new mathematical techniques are needed for this. All that is required is for you to put your brain into reverse gear. Of course, driving backwards is a little harder to master than going forwards. However, with practice you should find integration almost as easy as differentiation.

Section 6.2 shows how integration can be used to find the area under the graph of a function. This process is called definite integration. We can apply the technique to supply and demand curves and so calculate producer's and consumer's surpluses. Definite integration can also be used to determine capital stock and to discount a continuous revenue stream.

SECTION 6.1
Indefinite integration

Objectives

At the end of this section you should be able to:

- Recognise the notation for indefinite integration.
- Write down the integrals of simple power and exponential functions.
- Integrate functions of the form $af(x) + bg(x)$.
- Find the total cost function given any marginal cost function.
- Find the total revenue function given any marginal revenue function.
- Find the consumption and savings functions given either the marginal propensity to consume or the marginal propensity to save.
- Use the method of inspection to integrate more complicated functions.

Throughout mathematics there are many pairs of operations which cancel each other out and take you back to where you started. Perhaps the most obvious pair is multiplication and division. If you multiply a number by a non-zero constant, k, and then divide by k, you end up with the number you first thought of. This situation is described by saying that the two operations are **inverses** of each other. In calculus, the inverse of differentiation is called **integration**.

Suppose that you are required to find a function, $F(x)$, which differentiates to

$$f(x) = 3x^2$$

Can you guess what $F(x)$ is in this case? Given such a simple function, it is straightforward to write down the answer by inspection. It is

$$F(x) = x^3$$

because

$$F'(x) = 3x^2 = f(x) \quad \checkmark$$

as required.

As a second example, consider

$$f(x) = x^7$$

Can you think of a function, $F(x)$, which differentiates to this? Recall that when power functions are differentiated, the power decreases by 1, so it makes sense to do the opposite here and to try

$$F(x) = x^8$$

Unfortunately, this does not quite work out, because it differentiates to

$$8x^7$$

which is eight times too big. This suggests that we try

$$F(x) = \tfrac{1}{8}x^8$$

which does work because

$$F'(x) = {}^8/_8 x^7 = x^7 = f(x) \quad \checkmark$$

In general, if $F'(x) = f(x)$, then $F(x)$, is said to be the **integral** (sometimes called the **anti-derivative** or **primitive**) of $f(x)$ and is written

$$F(x) = \int f(x)dx$$

read 'integral of f of x dee x'

In this notation

$$\int 3x^2 dx = x^3$$

and

$$\int x^7 dx = {}^1/_8 x^8$$

Here is a problem for you to try. Do not let the notation

$$\int dx$$

put you off. It is merely an instruction for you to think of a function that differentiates to whatever is squashed between the integral sign '$\int$' and dx. If you get stuck, try adding 1 on to the power. Differentiate your guess, and if it does not quite work out, then go back and try again, adjusting the coefficient accordingly.

Practice Problem

1. Find

(a) $\int 2x\, dx$ (b) $\int 4x^3 dx$ (c) $\int 100x^{99} dx$ (d) $\int x^3 dx$ (e) $\int x^{18} dx$

In Practice Problem 1(a) you probably wrote

$$\int 2x\, dx = x^2$$

However, there are other possibilities. For example, both of the functions

$$x^2 + 6 \text{ and } x^2 - 59$$

differentiate to $2x$, because constants differentiate to zero. In fact, we can add any constant, c, to x^2 to obtain a function that differentiates to $2x$. Hence

$$\int 2x\, dx = x^2 + c$$

The arbitrary constant, c, is called the **constant of integration**. In general, if $F(x)$ is any function that differentiates to $f(x)$, then so does

$F(x) + c$

Hence

$$\int f(x)dx = F(x) + c$$

In Practice Problem 1 you used guesswork to find various integrals. In theory most integrals can be worked out in this way. However, considerable ingenuity (and luck!) may be required when integrating complicated functions. It is possible to develop various rules similar to those of differentiation, which we discussed in Chapter 4, although even then we sometimes have to resort to sheer trickery. It is not our intention to plod through each rule as we did in Chapter 4, for the simple reason that they are rarely needed in economics. However, it is worthwhile showing you a direct way of integrating simple functions such as

$2x - 3x^2 + 10x^3$ and $x - e^{2x} + 5$

We begin by finding general formulae for

$$\int x^n dx \quad \text{and} \quad \int e^{mx} dx$$

To integrate $f(x) = x^n$ an obvious first guess is

$F(x) = x^{n+1}$

This gives

$F'(x) = (n + 1)x^n$

which is $n + 1$ times too big. This suggests that we try again with

$$F(x) = \frac{1}{n + 1}x^{n+1}$$

which checks out because

$$F'(x) = \frac{n + 1}{n + 1}x^n = x^n = f(x) \qquad ✓$$

Hence

$$\int x^n dx = \frac{1}{n + 1}x^{n+1} + c$$

To integrate a power function you simply add 1 to the power and divide by the number you get. This formula holds whenever n is positive, negative, a whole number or a fraction. There is just one exception to the rule, when $n = -1$. The formula cannot be used to integrate

$$\frac{1}{x}$$

because it is impossible to divide by zero. An alternative result is therefore required in this case. We know from Chapter 4 that the natural logarithm function

$\ln x$

differentiates to give

$$\frac{1}{x}$$

and so

$$\int \frac{1}{x} dx = \ln x + c$$

The last basic integral that we wish to determine is

$$\int e^{mx} dx$$

In Section 4.8 we showed that to differentiate an exponential function all we need to do is to multiply by the coefficient of x. To integrate we do exactly the opposite and divide by the coefficient of x, so

$$\int e^{mx} dx = \frac{1}{m} e^{mx} + c$$

It is easy to check that this is correct, because if

$$F(x) = \frac{1}{m} e^{mx}$$

then

$$F'(x) = \frac{m}{m} e^{mx} = e^{mx} \quad ✓$$

Example

Find

(a) $\int x^6 dx$ (b) $\int \frac{1}{x^2} dx$ (c) $\int \sqrt{x} dx$ (d) $\int e^{2x} dx$

Solution

The formula

$$\int x^n dx = \frac{1}{n+1} x^{n+1} + c$$

can be used to find the first three integrals by substituting particular values for n.

(a) Putting $n = 6$ gives

$$\int x^6 dx = \frac{1}{7} x^7 + c$$

(b) Putting $n = -2$ gives

$$\int \frac{1}{x^2} dx = \int x^{-2} dx = \frac{1}{-1} x^{-1} + c = -\frac{1}{x} + c$$

(c) Putting $n = \frac{1}{2}$ gives

$$\int \sqrt{x} dx = \int x^{1/2} dx = \frac{1}{3/2} x^{3/2} + c = \frac{2}{3} x^{3/2} + c$$

(d) To find

$$\int e^{2x} dx$$

we put $m = 2$ into the formula

$$\int e^{mx} dx = \frac{1}{m} e^{mx} + c$$

to get

$$\int e^{2x} dx = \frac{1}{2} e^{2x} + c$$

Practice Problem

2. Find

(a) $\int x^4 dx$ **(b)** $\int \frac{1}{x^3} dx$ **(c)** $\int x^{1/3} dx$ **(d)** $\int e^{3x} dx$

(e) $\int 1 dx$ **(f)** $\int x dx$ **(g)** $\int \frac{1}{x} dx$

[Hint: in parts (b), (e) and (f) note that $1/x^3 = x^{-3}$, $1 = x^0$ and $x = x^1$, respectively.]

In Section 4.2 we described three rules of differentiation known as the constant, sum and difference rules. Given that integration is the inverse operation, these three rules also apply whenever we integrate a function. The integral of a constant multiple of a function is obtained by integrating the function and multiplying by the constant. The integral of the sum (or difference) of two functions is obtained by integrating the functions separately and adding (or subtracting). These three rules can be combined into the single rule:

$$\int [af(x) + bg(x)] dx = a \int f(x) dx + b \int g(x) dx$$

This enables us to integrate an expression 'term by term', as the following example demonstrates.

Example

Find

(a) $\displaystyle\int (2x^2 - 4x^6)\mathrm{d}x$ 　　(b) $\displaystyle\int \left(7e^{-x} + \frac{2}{x}\right)\mathrm{d}x$ 　　(c) $\displaystyle\int (5x^2 + 3x + 2)\mathrm{d}x$

Solution

(a) $\displaystyle\int (2x^2 - 4x^6)\mathrm{d}x = 2\int x^2\mathrm{d}x - 4\int x^6\mathrm{d}x$

Putting $n = 2$ and $n = 6$ into

$$\int x^n\mathrm{d}x = \frac{1}{n+1}x^{n+1}$$

gives $\displaystyle\int x^2\mathrm{d}x = \frac{1}{3}x^3$ and $\displaystyle\int x^6\mathrm{d}x = \frac{1}{7}x^7$

Hence

$$\int (2x^2 - 4x^6)\mathrm{d}x = \frac{2}{3}x^3 - \frac{4}{7}x^7$$

Finally, we add an arbitrary constant to get

$$\int (2x^2 - 4x^6)\mathrm{d}x = \frac{2}{3}x^3 - \frac{4}{7}x^7 + c$$

As a check:

$$\text{if } F(x) = \frac{2}{3}x^3 - \frac{4}{7}x^7 + c \quad \text{then} \quad F'(x) = 2x^2 - 4x^6 \quad ✓$$

(b) $\displaystyle\int \left(7e^{-x} + \frac{2}{x}\right)\mathrm{d}x = 7\int e^{-x}\mathrm{d}x + 2\int \frac{1}{x}\mathrm{d}x$

Now

$$\int e^{mx}\mathrm{d}x = \frac{1}{m}e^{mx}$$

so putting $m = -1$ gives

$$\int e^{-x}\mathrm{d}x = \frac{1}{-1}e^{-x} = -e^{-x}$$

Also, we know that the reciprocal function integrates to the natural logarithm function, so

$$\int \frac{1}{x}\mathrm{d}x = \ln x$$

Hence

$$\int \left(7e^{-x} + \frac{2}{x}\right)\mathrm{d}x = -7e^{-x} + 2\ln x$$

Finally, we add an arbitrary constant to get

$$\int \left(7e^{-x} + \frac{2}{x}\right)dx = -7e^{-x} + 2\ln x + c$$

As a check:

if $F(x) = -7e^{-x} + 2\ln x + c$ then $F'(x) = 7e^{-x} + \dfrac{2}{x}$ ✓

(c) $\displaystyle\int (5x^2 + 3x + 2)dx = 5\int x^2 dx + 3\int x dx + 2\int 1 dx$

Putting $n = 2$, 1 and 0 into

$$\int x^n dx = \frac{1}{n+1}x^{n+1}$$

gives

$$\int x^2 dx = \frac{1}{3}x^3, \quad \int x dx = \frac{1}{2}x^2, \quad \int 1 dx = x$$

Hence

$$\int (5x^2 + 3x + 2)dx = \frac{5}{3}x^3 + \frac{3}{2}x^2 + 2x$$

Finally, we add an arbitrary constant to get

$$\int (5x^2 + 3x + 2)dx = \frac{5}{3}x^3 + \frac{3}{2}x^2 + 2x + c$$

As a check:

if $F(x) = \dfrac{5}{3}x^3 + \dfrac{3}{2}x^2 + 2x + c$ then $F'(x) = 5x^2 + 3x + 2$ ✓

Advice

We have written out the solution to this example in detail to show you exactly how integration is performed. With practice you will probably find that you can just write the answer down in a single line of working, although it is always a good idea to check (at least in your head, if not on paper), by differentiating your answer, that you have not made any mistakes.

The technique of integration that we have investigated produces a function of x. In the next section a different type of integration is discussed which produces a single number as the end result. For this reason we use the word **indefinite** to describe the type of integration considered here to distinguish it from the **definite** integration in Section 6.2.

Practice Problem

3. Find the indefinite integrals

(a) $\int (2x - 4x^3)dx$ (b) $\int \left(10x^4 + \dfrac{5}{x^2}\right)dx$ (c) $\int (7x^2 - 3x + 2)dx$

In Section 4.3 we described several applications of differentiation to economics. Starting with any basic economic function, we can differentiate to obtain the corresponding marginal function. Integration allows us to work backwards and to recover the original function from any marginal function. For example, by integrating a marginal cost function, the total cost function is found. Likewise, given a marginal revenue function, integration enables us to determine the total revenue function, which in turn can be used to find the demand function. These ideas are illustrated in the following example, which also shows how the constant of integration can be given a specific numerical value in economic problems.

Example

(a) A firm's marginal cost function is

$$MC = Q^2 + 2Q + 4$$

Find the total cost function if the fixed costs are 100.

(b) The marginal revenue function of a monopolistic producer is

$$MR = 10 - 4Q$$

Find the total revenue function and deduce the corresponding demand function.

(c) Find an expression for the consumption function if the marginal propensity to consume is given by

$$MPC = 0.5 + \frac{0.1}{\sqrt{Y}}$$

and consumption is 85 when income is 100.

Solution

(a) We need to find the total cost from the marginal cost function

$$MC = Q^2 + 2Q + 4$$

Now

$$MC = \frac{d(TC)}{dQ}$$

so

$$TC = \int MC dQ = \int (Q^2 + 2Q + 4)dQ = \frac{Q^3}{3} + Q^2 + 4Q + c$$

The fixed costs are given to be 100. These are independent of the number of goods produced and represent the costs incurred when the firm does not produce any goods whatsoever. Putting $Q = 0$ into the TC function gives

$$\text{TC} = \frac{0^3}{3} + 0^2 + 4(0) + c = c$$

The constant of integration is therefore equal to the fixed costs of production, so $c = 100$. Hence

$$\text{TC} = \frac{Q^3}{3} + Q^2 + 4Q + 100$$

(b) We need to find the total revenue from the marginal revenue function

$$\text{MR} = 10 - 4Q$$

Now

$$\text{MR} = \frac{d(\text{TR})}{dQ}$$

so

$$\text{TR} = \int \text{MR}dQ = \int (10 - 4Q)dQ = 10Q - 2Q^2 + c$$

Unlike in part (a) of this example, we have not been given any additional information to help us to pin down the value of c. We do know, however, that when the firm produces no goods, the revenue is zero, so that $\text{TR} = 0$ when $Q = 0$. Putting this condition into

$$\text{TR} = 10Q - 2Q^2 + c$$

gives

$$0 = 10(0) - 2(0)^2 + c = c$$

The constant of integration is therefore equal to zero. Hence

$$\text{TR} = 10Q - 2Q^2$$

Finally, we can deduce the demand equation from this. To find an expression for total revenue from any given demand equation, we normally multiply by Q, because $\text{TR} = PQ$. This time we work backwards, so we divide by Q to get

$$P = \frac{\text{TR}}{Q} = \frac{10Q - 2Q^2}{Q} = 10 - 2Q$$

so the demand function is

$$P = 10 - 2Q$$

(c) We need to find consumption given that the marginal propensity to consume is

$$\text{MPC} = 0.5 + \frac{0.1}{\sqrt{Y}}$$

Now

$$\text{MPC} = \frac{dC}{dY}$$

so

$$C = \int \text{MPC}dY = \int \left(0.5 + \frac{0.1}{\sqrt{Y}} \right) dY = 0.5Y + 0.2\sqrt{Y} + c$$

where the second term is found from

$$\int \frac{0.1}{\sqrt{Y}} dY = 0.1 \int Y^{-1/2} dY = 0.1 \left(\frac{1}{1/2} Y^{1/2} \right) = 0.2\sqrt{Y}$$

The constant of integration can be calculated from the additional information that $C = 85$ when $Y = 100$. Putting $Y = 100$ into the expression for C gives

$$85 = 0.5(100) + 0.2\sqrt{100} + c = 52 + c$$

and so

$$c = 85 - 52 = 33$$

Hence

$$C = 0.5Y + 0.2\sqrt{Y} + 33$$

Practice Problem

4. **(a)** A firm's marginal cost function is

$$MC = 2$$

Find an expression for the total cost function if the fixed costs are 500. Hence find the total cost of producing 40 goods.

(b) The marginal revenue function of a monopolistic producer is

$$MR = 100 - 6Q$$

Find the total revenue function and deduce the corresponding demand function.

(c) Find an expression for the savings function if the marginal propensity to save is given by

$$MPS = 0.4 - 0.1Y^{-1/2}$$

and savings are zero when income is 100.

So far, we have seen how easy it is to integrate a function written as a linear combination of power functions. We began the chapter by using 'guesswork' to integrate the simple power function x^7. We did this by trying x^8 and then fiddled around with the numerical coefficient to make it work. The same approach can be used to integrate a wide variety of more complicated functions. To find

$$\int (2x + 7)^5 \, dx$$

we would increase the power by 1 and so try $(2x + 7)^6$ in the first instance. This differentiates to

$$6(2x + 7)^5 \times 2 = 12(2x + 7)^5 \text{ (by the chain rule)}$$

This is 12 times too big, so we go back to the original guess and divide it by 12 to get

$$\int (2x + 7)^5 \, dx = \frac{1}{12} (2x + 7)^6 + c$$

This approach is variously known as the method of 'guesswork', 'inspection' and 'recognition'. As a second example, consider the task of trying to think of a function which differentiates to

$$x^2(1 + x^3)^4$$

At first glance this appears to be fiendishly difficult, but help is at hand from the chain rule. Notice that the term outside the brackets is more or less the same as the derivative of the term inside the brackets. The inside, $1 + x^3$, actually differentiates to $3x^2$ which, apart from the 3, agrees with the factor in front of the brackets. We are now in a position to make a guess for the integral of $x^2(1 + x^3)^4$. We can mentally ignore the x^2 (knowing that when we get round to differentiating our guess, it will be automatically generated from the chain rule) and concentrate on integrating the brackets. This is a power of 4, so it makes sense to try differentiating the same bracket raised to a power of 5. Our first guess for the integral is therefore

$$F(x) = (1 + x^3)^5$$

and when we use the chain rule to differentiate this, we get

$$F'(x) = 5(1 + x^3)^4 \times 3x^2 = 15x^2 (1 + x^3)^4$$

This is nearly right but is 15 times too big, so it suggests that we try

$$F(x) = \frac{1}{15}\left(1 + x^3\right)^5$$

which does work because

$$F'(x) = \frac{1}{15} \times 5\left(1 + x^3\right)^4 \times 3x^2 = x^2\left(1 + x^3\right)^4$$

Hence

$$\int x^2(1 + x^3)^4 \, dx = \frac{1}{15}\left(1 + x^3\right)^5 + c$$

Most of what we have written down above can be ticked off in your head and the answer just written straight down.

Example

Find

(a) $\displaystyle\int x^2 e^{-x^3} dx$ (b) $\displaystyle\int \frac{x}{\left(1+4x^2\right)^3} dx$ (c) $\displaystyle\int \frac{x^9}{1+x^{10}} dx$

Solution

(a) The exponent $-x^3$ basically differentiates to x^2 (apart from an extra numerical factor, -3, which can be sorted out later). The chain rule will generate this term so can just concentrate on the exponential function which integrates to itself. Our first guess is

$$F(x) = e^{-x^3}$$

which differentiates to give

$$F'(x) = -3x^2 e^{-x^3}$$

This is -3 times too big, so

$$\int x^2 e^{-x^3} dx = -\frac{1}{3} e^{-x^3} + c$$

(b) The inside of the brackets, $1 + 4x^2$, differentiates to $8x$ which (apart from the numerical coefficient) coincides with the top of the fraction. We can therefore just concentrate on the rest of the function which is $(1 + 4x^2)^{-3}$. An obvious guess is obtained by increasing the power by 1, so we try

$$F(x) = (1 + 4x^2)^{-2}$$

which differentiates to give

$$F'(x) = -2(1 + 4x^2)^{-3} \times 8x = \frac{-16x}{(1 + 4x^2)^3}$$

This is -16 times too big, so

$$\int \frac{x}{(1 + 4x^2)^3} dx = \frac{-1}{16(1 + 4x^2)^2} + c$$

(c) For the integral,

$$\int \frac{x^9}{1 + x^{10}} dx$$

we notice that the top of the fraction is basically the derivative of the bottom. Reciprocal functions like this integrate to natural logarithms, so our first guess at the answer is

$$F(x) = \ln(1 + x^{10})$$

The chain rule automatically gives us the extra x^9 that we need. Differentiating our guess gives

$$F'(x) = \frac{1}{1 + x^{10}} \times 10x^9 = \frac{10x^9}{1 + x^{10}}$$

This is 10 times too big, so

$$\int \frac{x^9}{1 + x^{10}} dx = \frac{1}{10} \ln(1 + x^{10}) + c$$

Practice Problem

5. Find

(a) $\int (5x + 1)^3 dx$ (b) $\int x(1 + x^2)^7 dx$ (c) $\int \frac{4x^3}{2 + x^4} dx$ (d) $\int e^x(1 + e^x)^3 dx$

Key Terms

Anti-derivative   A function whose derivative is a given function.

Constant of integration   The arbitrary constant that appears in an expression when finding an indefinite integral.

Definite integration   The process of finding the area under a graph by subtracting the values obtained when the limits are substituted into the anti-derivative.

Indefinite integration   The process of obtaining an anti-derivative.

Integral   The number $\int_a^b f(x)dx$ (definite integral) or the function $\int f(x)dx$ (indefinite integral).

Integration   The generic name for the evaluation of definite or indefinite integrals.

Inverse (operation)   The operation that reverses the effect of a given operation and takes you back to the original. For example, the inverse of halving is doubling.

Primitive   An alternative word for an anti-derivative.

Exercise 6.1

1. Find

   (a) $\int 6x^5 dx$ (b) $\int x^4 dx$ (c) $\int 10e^{10x} dx$

   (d) $\int \dfrac{1}{x} dx$ (e) $\int x^{3/2} dx$ (f) $\int (2x^3 - 6x) dx$

   (g) $\int (x^2 - 8x + 3) dx$ (h) $\int (ax + b) dx$ (i) $\int \left(7x^3 + 4e^{-2x} - \dfrac{3}{x^2} \right) dx$

2. (a) Find the total cost if the marginal cost is

   $$MC = Q + 5$$

   and fixed costs are 20.

   (b) Find the total cost if the marginal cost is

   $$MC = 3e^{0.5Q}$$

   and fixed costs are 10.

3. The marginal cost function is given by

   $$MC = 2Q + 6$$

   If the total cost is 212 when $Q = 8$, find the total cost when $Q = 14$.

4. Find the total revenue and demand functions corresponding to each of the following marginal revenue functions:

   (a) $MR = 20 - 2Q$ (b) $MR = \dfrac{6}{\sqrt{Q}}$

5. Find the consumption function if the marginal propensity to consume is 0.6 and consumption is 10 when income is 5. Deduce the corresponding savings function.

6. Find the short-run production functions corresponding to each of the following marginal product of labour functions:

   (a) $1000 - 3L^2$ (b) $\dfrac{6}{\sqrt{L}} - 0.01$

7. A firm's marginal revenue and marginal cost functions are given by

   $$MR = 10 - 4Q \text{ and } MC = 1$$

   If fixed costs are 4, find the profit when $Q = 2$.

8. (1) Differentiate

   $$F(x) = (2x + 1)^5$$

   Hence find

   $$\int (2x + 1)^4 dx$$

(2) Use the approach suggested in part (1) to find

(a) $\int (3x - 2)^7 dx$ (b) $\int (2 - 4x)^9 dx$ (c) $\int \sqrt{2x + 1}\, dx$ (d) $\int \dfrac{1}{7x + 3} dx$

Exercise 6.1*

1. Find

(a) $\int x(x^5 - 2) dx$ (b) $\int x^{10} - 3\sqrt{x} + e^{-x} dx$ (c) $\int x^3 - \dfrac{5}{x^6} + \dfrac{2}{x} - 4e^{-4x} dx$

2. **(a)** Find the consumption function given that

$$MPC = 20 + \frac{10}{Y^{3/4}}$$

and that consumption is 420 when $Y = 16$.

(b) If the marginal cost is

$$MC = 15 + 3Q^2$$

find an expression for the variable cost per unit.

3. Find the total cost function, TC, when the fixed costs are C and the marginal cost is

(a) $aQ + b$ (b) ae^{bQ}

4. Use integration by inspection to write down the indefinite integral of:

(a) $(4x - 7)^5$ (b) $\dfrac{1}{3x + 1}$ (c) $\dfrac{1}{\sqrt{2x + 3}}$ (d) $x(1 + x^2)^4$

(e) $\dfrac{x^3}{(1 + x^4)^2}$ (f) xe^{-x^2} (g) $\dfrac{(1 + \ln x)^2}{x}$ (h) $\dfrac{x^2}{\sqrt{x^3 + 5}}$

5. **(a)** Show that

$$\sqrt{x}(\sqrt{x} + x^2) = x + x^{5/2}$$

Hence find

$$\int \sqrt{x}(\sqrt{x} + x^2) dx$$

(b) Use the approach suggested in part (a) to integrate each of the following functions:

$$x^4\left(x^6 + \frac{1}{x^2}\right), \quad e^{2x}(e^{3x} + e^{-x} + 3), \quad x^{3/2}\left(\sqrt{x} - \frac{1}{\sqrt{x}}\right)$$

6. **(a)** Show that

$$\frac{x^4 - x^2 + \sqrt{x}}{x} = x^3 - x + x^{-1/2}$$

Hence find

$$\int \frac{x^4 - x^2 + \sqrt{x}}{x} \, dx$$

(b) Use the approach suggested in part (a) to integrate each of the following functions:

$$\frac{x^2 - x}{x^3}, \quad \frac{e^x - e^{-x}}{e^{2x}}, \quad \frac{\sqrt{x} - x\sqrt{x} + x^2}{x\sqrt{x}}$$

7. Find an expression for the savings function when

$$\text{MPC} = 0.4 + \frac{0.4}{\sqrt{Y}} \quad \text{and} \quad C = 50 \quad \text{when} \quad Y = 100$$

8. Find $f(x)$ when $f''(x) = 6x$, $f(0) = 2$ and $f'(0) = -4$.

9. **(a)** Differentiate the function, $x \ln x$.

(b) Use the result of part (a) to find $\int \ln x \, dx$.

10. The number of units, N, produced each hour by a new employee after t hours on the job satisfies

$$\frac{dN}{dt} = 10e^{-0.1t}$$

Assuming that she is unable to produce any goods at the beginning of her shift, calculate how many she can produce per hour after eight hours. How many units per hour will she be able to produce in the long run?

11. The rate of growth in the number of shops, n, in a chain of local grocery stores after t months satisfies

$$\frac{dn}{dt} = \frac{3}{\sqrt{t}}$$

Initially there are two stores.
    Estimate the number of shops in the chain after 9 months.

12. A firm's marginal revenue and marginal cost functions are given by

$$\text{MR} = 240 - 0.6Q^2 \quad \text{and} \quad \text{MC} = 150 + 0.3Q^2$$

If fixed costs are 50, determine the maximum profit.

13. Use integration by inspection to find:

(a) $\displaystyle \int (ax + b)^n \, dx \quad (n \neq -1)$ **(b)** $\displaystyle \int e^{ax + b} \, dx$ **(c)** $\displaystyle \int \frac{1}{ax + b} \, dx$

14. Use differentiation to show that

(a) $\displaystyle \int \frac{4x}{(2x + 3)^2} \, dx = \ln(2x + 3) + \frac{3}{2x + 3} + c$

(b) $\displaystyle \int x^2 e^x \, dx = e^x(x^2 - 2x + 2) + c$

SECTION 6.2
Definite integration

Objectives

At the end of this section you should be able to:

- Recognise the notation for definite integration.
- Evaluate definite integrals in simple cases.
- Calculate the consumer's surplus.
- Calculate the producer's surplus.
- Calculate the capital stock formation.
- Calculate the present value of a continuous revenue stream.

One rather tedious task that you may remember from school is that of finding areas. Sketched in Figure 6.1 is a region bounded by the curve $y = x^2$, the lines $x = 1$ and $x = 2$, and the x axis. At school you may well have been asked to find the area of this region by 'counting' squares on graph paper. A much quicker and more accurate way of calculating this area is to use integration. We begin by integrating the function

$$f(x) = x^2$$

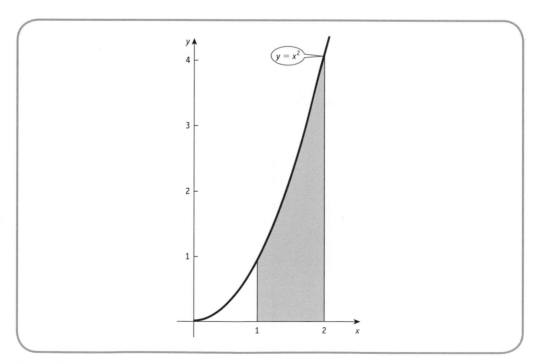

Figure 6.1

to get

$$F(x) = \frac{1}{3}x^3$$

In our case we want to find the area under the curve between $x = 1$ and $x = 2$, so we evaluate

$$F(1) = \frac{1}{3}(1)^3 = \frac{1}{3}$$

$$F(2) = \frac{1}{3}(2)^3 = \frac{8}{3}$$

Finally, we subtract $F(1)$ from $F(2)$ to get

$$F(2) - F(1) = \frac{8}{3} - \frac{1}{3} = \frac{7}{3}$$

This number is the exact value of the area of the region sketched in Figure 6.1. Given the connection with integration, we write this area as

$$\int_1^2 x^2 dx$$

In general, the **definite integral**

$$\int_a^b f(x)dx$$

denotes the area under the graph of $f(x)$ between $x = a$ and $x = b$ as shown in Figure 6.2. The numbers a and b are called the **limits of integration**, and it is assumed throughout this section that $a < b$ and that $f(x) \geq 0$ as indicated in Figure 6.2.

The technique of evaluating definite integrals is as follows. A function $F(x)$ is found which differentiates to $f(x)$. Methods of obtaining $F(x)$ have already been described in Section 6.1. The new function, $F(x)$, is then evaluated at the limits $x = a$ and $x = b$ to get $F(a)$ and $F(b)$. Finally, the second number is subtracted from the first to get the answer

$$F(b) - F(a)$$

In symbols,

$$\int_a^b f(x)dx = F(b) - F(a)$$

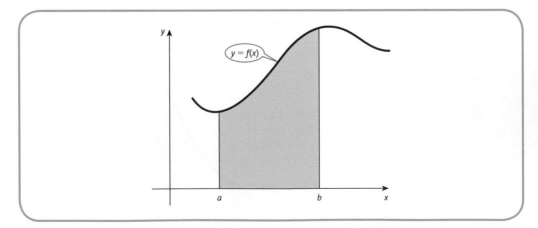

Figure 6.2

The process of evaluating a function at two distinct values of x and subtracting one from the other occurs sufficiently frequently in mathematics to warrant a special notation. We write

$$[F(x)]_a^b$$

as an abbreviation for $F(b) - F(a)$, so that definite integrals are evaluated as

$$\int_a^b f(x)dx = [F(x)]_a^b = F(b) - F(a)$$

where $F(x)$ is the indefinite integral of $f(x)$. Using this notation, the evaluation of

$$\int_1^2 x^2 dx$$

would be written as

$$\int_1^2 x^2 dx = \left[\frac{1}{3}x^3\right]_1^2 = \frac{1}{3}(2)^3 - \frac{1}{3}(1)^3 = \frac{7}{3}$$

Note that it is not necessary to include the constant of integration, because it cancels out when we subtract $F(a)$ from $F(b)$.

Example

Evaluate the definite integrals

(a) $\displaystyle\int_2^6 3dx$ **(b)** $\displaystyle\int_0^2 (x + 1)dx$

Solution

(a) $\displaystyle\int_2^6 3dx = [3x]_2^6 = 3(6) - 3(2) = 12$

This value can be confirmed graphically. Figure 6.3 shows the region under the graph of $y = 3$ between $x = 2$ and $x = 6$. This is a rectangle, so its area can be found from the formula

    area $=$ base $\times$ height

which gives

    area $= 4 \times 3 = 12$ ✓

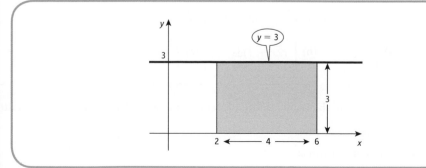

Figure 6.3

(b) $\int_{0}^{2} (x + 1)dx = \left[\frac{x^2}{2} + x \right]_{0}^{2} = \left(\frac{2^2}{2} + 2 \right) - \left(\frac{0^2}{2} + 0 \right) = 4$

Again, this value can be confirmed graphically. Figure 6.4(a) shows the region under the graph of $y = x + 1$ between $x = 0$ and $x = 2$. This can also be regarded as one-half of the rectangle illustrated in Figure 6.4(b). This rectangle has a base of 2 units and a height of 4 units, so it has area

$2 \times 4 = 8$

The area of the region shown in Figure 6.4(a) is therefore

$\frac{1}{2} \times 8 = 4$ ✓

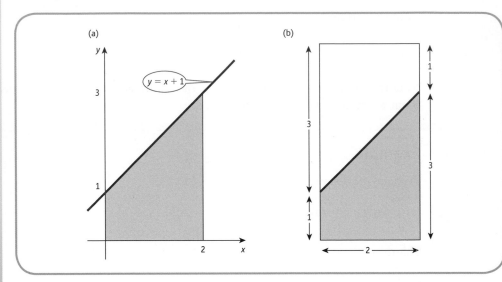

Figure 6.4

In this example we deliberately chose two very simple functions so that we could demonstrate the fact that definite integrals really do give the areas under graphs. The beauty of the integration technique, however, is that it can be used to calculate areas under quite complicated functions for which alternative methods would fail to produce the exact value.

Practice Problem

1. Evaluate the following definite integrals:

(a) $\int_{0}^{1} x^3 dx$ (b) $\int_{2}^{5} (2x + 1)dx$ (c) $\int_{1}^{4} (x^2 - x + 1)dx$ (d) $\int_{0}^{1} e^x dx$

To illustrate the applicability of definite integration, we concentrate on four topics:

- consumer's surplus;
- producer's surplus;
- investment flow;
- discounting.

We consider each of these in turn.

6.2.1 Consumer's surplus

The demand function, $P = f(Q)$, sketched in Figure 6.5, gives the different prices that consumers are prepared to pay for various quantities of a good. At $Q = Q_0$ the price $P = P_0$. The total amount of money spent on Q_0 goods is then $Q_0 P_0$, which is given by the area of the rectangle OABC. Now, P_0 is the price that consumers are prepared to pay for the last unit that they buy, which is the Q_0th good. For quantities up to Q_0 they would actually be willing to pay the higher price given by the demand curve. The shaded area BCD therefore represents the benefit to the consumer of paying the fixed price of P_0 and is called the **consumer's surplus**, CS. The value of CS can be found by observing that

area BCD = area OABD − area OABC

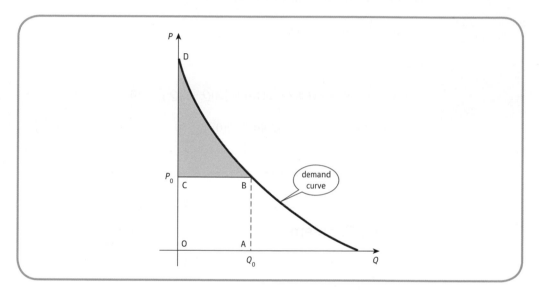

Figure 6.5

The area OABD is the area under the demand curve $P = f(Q)$, between $Q = 0$ and $Q = Q_0$, and so is equal to

$$\int_0^{Q_0} f(Q)\mathrm{d}Q$$

The region OABC is a rectangle with base Q_0 and height P_0 so

area OABC $= Q_0 P_0$

Hence

$$\text{CS} = \int_0^{Q_0} f(Q)\mathrm{d}Q - Q_0 P_0$$

Example

Find the consumer's surplus at $Q = 5$ for the demand function

$P = 30 - 4Q$

Solution

In this case

$$f(Q) = 30 - 4Q$$

and $Q_0 = 5$. The price is easily found by substituting $Q = 5$ into

$$P = 30 - 4Q$$

to get

$$P_0 = 30 - 4(5) = 10$$

The formula for consumer's surplus

$$CS = \int_0^{Q_0} f(Q)dQ - Q_0 P_0$$

gives

$$CS = \int_0^5 (30 - 4Q)dQ - 5(10) = [30Q - 2Q^2]_0^5 - 50$$

$$= [30(5) - 2(5)^2] - [30(0) - 2(0)^2] - 50$$

$$= 50$$

Practice Problem

2. Find the consumer's surplus at $Q = 8$ for the demand function

$$P = 100 - Q^2$$

6.2.2 Producer's surplus

The supply function, $P = g(Q)$, sketched in Figure 6.6 gives the different prices at which producers are prepared to supply various quantities of a good. At $Q = Q_0$ the price $P = P_0$. Assuming that all goods are sold, the total amount of money received is then $Q_0 P_0$, which is given by the area of the rectangle OABC.

Now, P_0 is the price at which the producer is prepared to supply the last unit, which is the Q_0th good. For quantities up to Q_0 they would actually be willing to accept the lower price given by the supply curve. The shaded area BCD therefore represents the benefit to the producer of selling at the fixed price of P_0 and is called the **producer's surplus**, PS. The value of PS is found by observing that

area BCD = area OABC − area OABD

The region OABC is a rectangle with base Q_0 and height P_0, so

area OABC = $Q_0 P_0$

The area OABD is the area under the supply curve $P = g(Q)$, between $Q = 0$ and $Q = Q_0$, and so is equal to

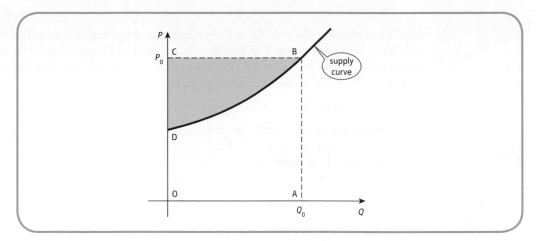

Figure 6.6

$$\int_0^{Q_0} g(Q)\,\mathrm{d}Q$$

Hence

$$\mathrm{PS} = Q_0 P_0 - \int_0^{Q_0} g(Q)\,\mathrm{d}Q$$

Example

Given the demand function

$$P = 35 - Q_\mathrm{D}^2$$

and supply function

$$P = 3 + Q_\mathrm{S}^2$$

find the producer's surplus assuming pure competition.

Solution

On the assumption of pure competition, the price is determined by the market. Therefore, before we can calculate the producer's surplus, we need to find the market equilibrium price and quantity. Denoting the common value of Q_D and Q_S by Q, the demand and supply functions are

$$P = 35 - Q^2$$

and

$$P = 3 + Q^2$$

so that

$$
\begin{aligned}
35 - Q^2 &= 3 + Q^2 && \text{(both sides are equal to } P\text{)} \\
35 - 2Q^2 &= 3 && \text{(subtract } Q^2 \text{ from both sides)} \\
-2Q^2 &= -32 && \text{(subtract 35 from both sides)} \\
Q^2 &= 16 && \text{(divide both sides by } -2\text{)}
\end{aligned}
$$

which has solution $Q = \pm 4$. We can obviously ignore the negative solution because it does not make economic sense. The equilibrium quantity is therefore equal to 4. The corresponding price can be found by substituting this into either the demand or the supply equation. From the demand equation we have

$$P_0 = 35 - (4)^2 = 19$$

The formula for the producer's surplus,

$$PS = Q_0 P_0 - \int_0^{Q_0} g(Q)dQ$$

gives

$$PS = 4(19) - \int_0^4 (3 + Q^2)dQ$$

$$= 76 - \left[3Q + \frac{Q^3}{3} \right]_0^4$$

$$= 76 - \{[3(4) + \tfrac{1}{3}(4)^3] - [3(0) - \tfrac{1}{3}(0)^3]\}$$

$$= 42\tfrac{2}{3}$$

Practice Problem

3. Given the demand equation

   $$P = 50 - 2Q_D$$

   and supply equation

   $$P = 10 + 2Q_S$$

   calculate

   (a) the consumer's surplus   **(b)** the producer's surplus

   assuming pure competition.

6.2.3 Investment flow

Net investment, I, is defined to be the rate of change of capital stock, K, so that

$$I = \frac{dK}{dt}$$

Here, $I(t)$ denotes the flow of money, measured in dollars per year, and $K(t)$ is the amount of capital accumulated at time t as a result of this investment flow and is measured in dollars.

Given a formula for capital stock in terms of time, we simply differentiate to find net investment. Conversely, if we know the net investment function, then we integrate to find the capital stock. In particular, to calculate the capital formation during the time period from $t = t_1$ to $t = t_2$, we evaluate the definite integral

$$\int_{t_1}^{t_2} I(t)dt$$

Example

If the investment flow is

$$I(t) = 9000\sqrt{t}$$

calculate

(a) the capital formation from the end of the first year to the end of the fourth year;

(b) the number of years required before the capital stock exceeds $100 000.

Solution

(a) In this part we need to calculate the capital formation from $t = 1$ to $t = 4$, so we evaluate the definite integral

$$\int_1^4 9000\sqrt{t}\,dt = 9000\int_1^4 t^{1/2}dt = 9000\left[\frac{2}{3}t^{3/2}\right]_1^4 = 9000\left(\frac{16}{3} - \frac{2}{3}\right) = \$42\,000$$

(b) In this part we need to calculate the number of years required to accumulate a total of $100 000. After T years the capital stock is

$$\int_0^T 9000\sqrt{t}\,dt = 9000\int_0^T t^{1/2}dt$$

We want to find the value of T so that

$$9000\int_0^T t^{1/2}dt = 100\,000$$

The integral is easily evaluated as

$$9000\left[\frac{2}{3}t^{3/2}\right]_0^T = 9000\left(\frac{2}{3}T^{3/2} - \frac{2}{3}(0)^{3/2}\right) = 6000T^{3/2}$$

so T satisfies

$$6000T^{3/2} = 100\,000$$

This non-linear equation can be solved by dividing both sides by 6000 to get

$$T^{3/2} = 16.67$$

and then raising both sides to the power of $^2/_3$, which gives

$$T = 6.5$$

The capital stock reaches the $100 000 level about halfway through the seventh year.

Practice Problem

4. If the net investment function is given by

$$I(t) = 800t^{1/3}$$

calculate

(a) the capital formation from the end of the first year to the end of the eighth year;

(b) the number of years required before the capital stock exceeds $48 600.

6.2.4 Discounting

In Chapter 3 the formula

$$P = Se^{-rt/100}$$

was used to calculate the present value, P, when a single future value, S, is discounted at $r\%$ interest continuously for t years. We also discussed the idea of an annuity. This is a fund that provides a series of discrete regular payments, and we showed how to calculate the original lump sum needed to secure these payments for a prescribed number of years. This amount is called the present value of the annuity. If the fund is to provide a continuous revenue stream for n years at an annual rate of S dollars per year, then the present value can be found by evaluating the definite integral

$$P = \int_0^n Se^{-rt/100} dt$$

For example, if the discount rate is 9%, the present value of a continuous revenue stream of a $1000 a year for five years is

$$P = \int_0^5 1000e^{-0.09t} dt$$

$$= 1000 \int_0^5 e^{-0.09t} dt$$

$$= 1000 \left[\frac{-1}{0.09} e^{-0.09t} \right]_0^5$$

$$= -\frac{1000}{0.09} [e^{-0.09t}]_0^5$$

$$= -\frac{1000}{0.09} (e^{-0.45} - 1) \quad \boxed{e^0 = 1}$$

$$= \$4026.35$$

Practice Problem

5. Calculate the present value of a continuous revenue stream for 10 years at a constant rate of $5000 per year if the discount rate is 6%.

Key Terms

Consumer's surplus   The excess cost that a person would have been prepared to pay for goods over and above what is actually paid.

Definite integral   The number $\int_a^b f(x)dx$ which represents the area under the graph of $f(x)$ between $x = a$ and $x = b$.

Limits of integration   The numbers a and b which appear in the definite integral, $\int_a^b f(x)dx$.

Net investment   Rate of change of capital stock over time: $I = dK/dt$.

Producer's surplus   The excess revenue that a producer has actually received over and above the lower revenue that it was prepared to accept for the supply of its goods.

Exercise 6.2

1. Evaluate each of the following integrals:

    (a) $\displaystyle\int_1^3 4x^2 dx$ (b) $\displaystyle\int_2^3 \frac{2}{x^3} dx$ (c) $\displaystyle\int_1^4 \frac{6}{\sqrt{x}} dx$ (d) $\displaystyle\int_1^2 4x^3 - 3x^2 + 4x + 2\, dx$

2. Find the exact areas under each of the following curves:

    (a) $y = 2x^2 + x + 3$ between $x = 1$ and $x = 5$
    (b) $y = (x - 2)^2$ between $x = 2$ and $x = 3$
    (c) $y = 3\sqrt{x}$ between $x = 4$ and $x = 25$
    (d) $y = e^x$ between $x = 0$ and $x = 1$
    (e) $y = \dfrac{1}{x}$ between $x = 1$ and $x = e$

3. Evaluate each of the following definite integrals:

    (a) $\displaystyle\int_0^2 x^3 dx$ (b) $\displaystyle\int_{-2}^2 x^3 dx$

    By sketching a rough graph of the cube function between and $x = -2$ and 2, suggest a reason for your answer to part (b). What is the actual area between the x axis and the graph of $y = x^3$, over this range?

4. Find the consumer's surplus at $P = 5$ for the following demand functions:

    (a) $P = 25 - 2Q$ (b) $P = \dfrac{10}{\sqrt{Q}}$

5. Find the producer's surplus at $Q = 9$ for the following supply functions:

    (a) $P = 12 + 2Q$ (b) $P = 20\sqrt{Q} + 15$

6. Find the consumer's surplus for the demand function

    $$P = 50 - 2Q - 0.01Q^2$$

    when

    (a) $Q = 10$ (b) $Q = 11$

7. Given the demand function

$$P = -Q_D^2 - 4Q_D + 68$$

and the supply function

$$P = Q_S^2 + 2Q_S + 12$$

Find

(a) the consumer's surplus

(b) the producer's surplus

assuming pure competition.

8. If the investment flow is

$$I(t) = 5000t^{1/4}$$

calculate the capital formation from the end of the second year to halfway through the fifth year. Give your answer to the nearest whole number.

9. Given the investment flow

$$I(t) = 2400\sqrt{t}$$

(a) Calculate the total capital formation during the first four years.

(b) Find an expression for the annual capital formation during the Nth year and hence find the first year in which the annual capital formation exceeds $4000.

10. Calculate the present value of a revenue stream for eight years at a constant rate of $12 000 per year if the discount rate is 7.5%.

11. A company begins its extraction of oil from a newly discovered oil field at $t = 0$. The rate of extraction, measured in thousands of barrels per year, is given by

$$\frac{dN}{dt} = 30t^2 - 4t^3$$

Calculate the number of barrels extracted during the first four years of operation.

Exercise 6.2*

1. Evaluate

(a) $\displaystyle\int_{-1}^{2} 5x^2 - 4x + 6\,dx$ (b) $\displaystyle\int_{2}^{10} \frac{1}{(2x + 5)\sqrt{(2x + 5)}}\,dx$

2. (a) Find the consumer's surplus at $Q = 8$ for the demand function

$$P = 50 - 4Q$$

(b) The producer's surplus at $Q = a$ for the supply function

$$P = 6 + 8Q$$

is known to be 400. Find the value of a.

3. The demand function is given by

   $$P = 74 - Q_D^2$$

   and the supply function is

   $$P = (Q_S + 2)^2$$

   Calculate the consumer's and producer's surplus under pure competition.

4. If the supply and demand functions are given by $P = Q + 50$ and $P = \dfrac{4000}{Q + 20}$, respectively, find the equilibrium price and quantity, and calculate the consumer's and producer's surplus.

5. If the supply and demand functions are given by $P = 20e^{0.4Q}$ and $P = 100e^{-0.2Q}$, respectively, find the equilibrium price and quantity, and calculate the consumer's and producer's surplus.

6. If the net investment function is given by

   $$I(t) = 100e^{0.1t}$$

   calculate

   (a) the capital formation from the end of the second year to the end of the fifth year;

   (b) the number of years required before the capital stock exceeds \$100 000.

7. Find the expression for capital formation between $t = 0$ and $t = T$ for the following net investment functions:

   (a) $I(t) = At^\alpha$ **(b)** $I(t) = Ae^{\alpha t}$

   where A and α are positive constants.

8. Calculate the present value of a continuous revenue stream of \$1000 per year if the discount rate is 5% and the money is paid

   (a) for 3 years   **(b)** for 10 years   **(c)** for 100 years   **(d)** in perpetuity

9. The present value of a continuous revenue stream of \$5000 per year with a discount rate of 10% over n years is \$25 000. Find the value of n correct to one decimal place.

10. Write down an expression for $g'(x)$ when

    $$g(x) = \int_2^x (5t^2 - 2t)\,dt$$

11. Write down an expression for the present value of a continuous revenue stream for n years at a constant rate of \$S per year if the discount rate is $r\%$.

12. If a firm's profit function is $\pi = f(Q)$ and the level of output, Q, varies between a and b units, then the firm's average profit is given by

    $$\frac{1}{b - a}\int_a^b f(Q)\,dQ$$

    Calculate a firm's average profit when TR $= 100(1 - e^{-0.1Q})$, TC $= 0.1Q^2 + 2Q + 1$ and output varies from 3 to 8 units.

13. A newly elected government decides to reduce pollution in major cities by investing in a green spaces project. The subsequent investment flow is given by

$$I(t) = 0.6t^2 + 10$$

where t is measured in years from the start of the government term and I is measured in millions of dollars per year. Five years later, as a result of a change of administration, planned investment is dramatically reduced so that for the following five years, investment flow $J(t)$ is given by

$$J(t) = 25e^{0.4(5-t)} \text{ for } 5 \le t \le 10$$

(a) Verify that $I(5) = J(5)$ and sketch a graph of the investment flow for the complete 10-year period.

(b) After how many years does the total capital spent on this project first exceed $110 million? Give your answer to one decimal place.

14. The demand function of a good is given by $P = 80 - 6\sqrt{Q}$

(a) Find the change in consumer's surplus due to a decrease in price from $P = 62$ to $P = 56$.

(b) Sketch a graph of the demand function and shade the area which corresponds to the change in consumer's surplus calculated in part (a).

Formal mathematics

In Section 6.2 integration was used to find the area between the x axis, the curve $y = f(x)$ and the vertical lines $x = a$ and $x = b$. In all cases the region was bounded on all sides leading to a finite area. It is sometimes possible to find the area of unbounded regions such as that shown in Figure 6.7. Integrals representing such areas are referred to as **improper integrals**. It may seem surprising that a region which 'goes on forever' can actually have a finite area at all. However, provided the graph approaches the x axis fast enough, the area itself is finite and has a value which we can find using integration. Formally we define:

$$\int_a^\infty f(x)\mathrm{d}x = \lim_{N \to \infty} \int_a^N f(x)\mathrm{d}x \quad \text{(assuming the limit exists)}$$

We first work out an expression, in terms of N, for the area under the curve between $x = a$ and $x = N$, and then see whether or not it converges as N tends to ∞.

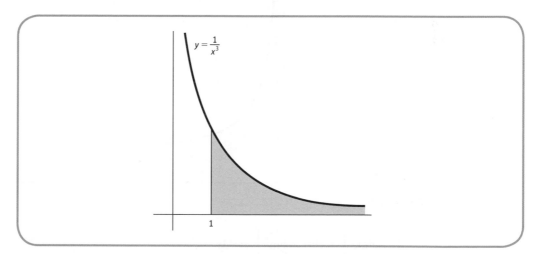

Figure 6.7

Example

Evaluate the following integrals (where possible):

(a) $\displaystyle\int_1^\infty \frac{1}{x^3}\mathrm{d}x$ **(b)** $\displaystyle\int_1^\infty \frac{1}{\sqrt{x}}\mathrm{d}x$

Solution

(a) We begin by finding the finite area under the graph of $y = x^{-3}$ from $x = 1$ to $x = N$:

$$\int_1^N x^{-3}\mathrm{d}x = \left[-\frac{1}{2}x^{-2}\right]_1^N = -\frac{1}{2}N^{-2} + \frac{1}{2} = \frac{1}{2} - \frac{1}{2N^2}$$

From the definition of an infinite integral we now consider what happens to this expression as N increases without bound.

$$\int_1^\infty \frac{1}{x^3}dx = \lim_{N\to\infty}\left(\frac{1}{2} - \frac{1}{2N^2}\right) = \frac{1}{2} \quad \text{because } \frac{1}{2N^2} \to 0 \text{ as } N \to \infty$$

In this case the unbounded region, shown in Figure 6.7, has a finite area of $^1/_2$.

(b) We begin by finding the finite area under the graph of $y = x^{-1/2}$ from $x = 1$ to $x = N$:

$$\int_1^N x^{-1/2}dx = \left[2x^{1/2}\right]_1^N = 2N^{1/2} - 2 = 2\sqrt{N} - 2$$

In this case the term $\sqrt{N}$ is not finite as $N \to \infty$, so the integral does not exist.

A similar situation arises when there is 'leakage' along the y axis as shown in Figure 6.8.

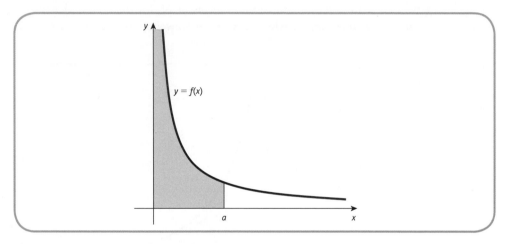

Figure 6.8

We define $\displaystyle\int_0^a f(x)dx = \lim_{N\to 0}\int_N^a f(x)dx$

which may or may not exist, depending on how quickly the curve approaches the y axis.

Example

Evaluate the following integrals (where possible):

(a) $\displaystyle\int_0^1 \frac{1}{x^3}dx$ **(b)** $\displaystyle\int_0^1 \frac{1}{\sqrt{x}}dx$

Solution

(a) $\displaystyle\int_N^1 x^{-3}dx = \left[-\frac{1}{2}x^{-2}\right]_N^1 = -\frac{1}{2} + \frac{1}{2N^2}$ which is not finite as $N \to 0$, so the integral does not exist.

(b) $\displaystyle\int_N^1 x^{-\frac{1}{2}}dx = \left[2x^{\frac{1}{2}}\right]_N^1 = 2 - 2\sqrt{N}$ which converges to 2 as $N \to 0$, so $\displaystyle\int_0^1 \frac{1}{\sqrt{x}}dx = 2$.

Multiple choice questions

Question 1

Find the indefinite integral $\int 4x^3 - 5x + 5 - \dfrac{1}{x} + \dfrac{3}{x^2}\,dx$

A. $x^4 - 2.5x^2 + 5x - \ln x + \dfrac{3}{x} + c$

B. $x^4 - 2.5x^2 + 5x - \ln x - \dfrac{3}{x} + c$

C. $x^4 - 2.5x^2 + 5x + \dfrac{2}{x} - \dfrac{3}{x^2} + c$

D. $x^4 - 2.5x^2 + 5x - \dfrac{1}{x^2} - \dfrac{3}{x} + c$

E. $x^4 - 2.5x^2 + 5x - \ln x - \dfrac{3}{x^2} + c$

Question 2

Evaluate the definite integral $\int_2^3 3x^2 - 4x + 8\,dx$

A. 31   B. 15   C. 12   D. 27   E. 17

Question 3

If the marginal revenue function is given by $\mathrm{MR} = 100 - 6Q^2$, find the corresponding demand function.

A. $P = 100Q^2 - 2Q^3$ B. $P = 100 - 2Q^2$ C. $P = 100 - 2Q^3$

D. $P = 100Q - 2Q^2$ E. $P = 100Q - 2Q^3$

Question 4

The supply function of a good is $P = 40 + 0.002Q^2$. Which of the following could be used to work out the producer's surplus at (Q_0, P_0)?

A. $\displaystyle\int_0^{Q_0} 40 + 0.002Q^2\,dQ + P_0Q_0$

B. $Q_0P_0 + \displaystyle\int_0^{P_0} 40 + 0.002Q^2\,dQ$

C. $\displaystyle\int_0^{Q_0} 40 + 0.002Q^2\,dQ - P_0Q_0$

D. $Q_0P_0 - \displaystyle\int_0^{Q_0} 40 + 0.002Q^2\,dQ$

E. $\displaystyle\int_0^{P_0} 40 + 0.002Q^2\,dQ$

Question 5

If the investment flow of a company is $I(t) = 8000t^{1/3}$, calculate the capital formation during the first eight years.

A. 96 000   **B.** 128 000   **C.** 76 800   **D.** 256 000   **E.** 84 000

Question 6

Calculate the present value of a continuous revenue stream for five years at a constant rate of $7500 per year if the discount rate is 3.4%.

A. $34 485.70

B. $36 678.54

C. $36 798.45

D. $38 775.00

E. $38 993.63

Question 7

The marginal propensity to consume is given by $\text{MPC} = 0.5 + \dfrac{2}{\sqrt{Y}}$ where Y is national income. If consumption is 20 when $Y = 0$, find the consumption when $Y = 16$.

A. 28   **B.** 24   **C.** 36   **D.** 44   **E.** 34

Question 8

The diagram shows the graphs of $y = 4$ and $y = 0.5x^2 + 2$. Find the shaded area.

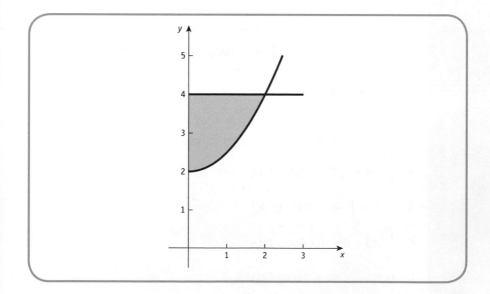

A. 5/3

B. 8/3

C. 4/3

D. 16/3

E. 20/3

Question 9

If $\displaystyle\int_{a}^{2a} 8x - 6 \ dx = 18$ where $a > 0$, find a.

A. 1.5

B. 2.0

C. 2.5

D. 3

E. 3.5

Question 10

What is the consumer's surplus at $P = 75$ when the demand function is $P = 100 - Q^2$?

A. 75/3

B. 125/3

C. 225/3

D. 250/3

E. 100/3

Question 11

Find the value of $\displaystyle\int_{2}^{6} \frac{1}{\sqrt{2x - 3}}\, dx$

A. 3/2

B. 1

C. 4

D. 1/2

E. 2

Examination questions

Question 1

A monopolist has a marginal cost function, $6Q^2 + 5Q$, and the fixed costs are 25. The demand function is $2P + Q = 510$.

(a) Find an expression for the profit function in terms of Q.

(b) Hence find the production level that maximises profit and explain why this is a maximum.

Question 2

(a) Find the area under the curve $y = x^2 + 2x + 3$ between $x = 1$ and $x = 2$.

(b) Integrate each of the following functions with respect to x:

    (i) $x^5 - 2x^2 + 9$ (ii) $e^x + \dfrac{3}{x}$ (iii) $x + \dfrac{2}{x^3} - 9\sqrt{x}$

(c) Show that $\dfrac{1}{x - 1} + \dfrac{2}{x + 3} = \dfrac{3x + 1}{(x - 1)(x + 3)}$

    Deduce that $\displaystyle\int_{2}^{5} \dfrac{3x + 1}{(x - 1)(x + 3)}\, dx = 2\ln\dfrac{16}{5}$

Question 3

An investment flow is $I(t) = 900\sqrt{t}$ where t is measured in years.

(a) Calculate the total capital formation during the first four years.

(b) Calculate the total capital formation from the end of the second year to the beginning of the sixth year. Round your answer to two decimal places.

(c) Find an expression for the total capital formation during the first N years and hence find the year in which the total capital formation reaches 16 200.

Question 4

A firm's marginal revenue and marginal cost functions are given by

    $MR = 140 - 6Q$ and $MC = Q^2 + Q + 20$

Fixed costs are 10.

(a) Write down an expression for total revenue and deduce the corresponding demand function.

(b) Write down an expression for the total cost function.

(c) Find the value of Q which maximises profit, π, and state the corresponding value of π.

Question 5

The supply and demand functions of a good are given by

$$P = 32 + Q_S^2$$

$$P = 140 - \frac{Q_D^2}{3}$$

where P, Q_S and Q_D denote the price, quantity supplied and quantity demanded, respectively.

(a) Draw sketch graphs of these functions on the same diagram with quantity on the horizontal axis and price on the vertical axis.

(b) Calculate the producer's and consumer's surpluses at the equilibrium point.

(c) If the government imposes a fixed tax on this good explain the effect, if any, on

  (i) equilibrium price and quantity;

  (ii) consumer's surplus.

Question 6

A fund is established to provide a continuous revenue stream at a constant rate for a pre-scribed number of years when the discount rate is 4%.

(a) Calculate the present value if the fund provides $4000 per year for eight years. Give your answer to the nearest cent.

(b) Determine the number of years that will fund an annual pay-out of $4000 if the present value is $45 000. Give your answer to the nearest year.

Question 7

(a) Find the following indefinite integrals:

  (i) $\int \dfrac{2}{1 + 6x} \, dx$

  (ii) $\int x\sqrt{1 + 3x^2} \, dx$

(b) The supply of a good can be modelled by a linear function, $aP + bQ = 1$ where a and b are constants. It is known that when the price, P is 12, the quantity supplied, Q is 6 and the producer's surplus is 18. Find the values of a and b.

Question 8

(a) Find the total cost function given that the marginal cost function $MC = 2Q + 3\sqrt{Q}$ and that total costs are 40 when $Q = 4$.

(b) The inverse demand function for a good is $Q - \dfrac{10 - P}{2P}$. Find the consumer's surplus when the price $P = 2$. Round your answer to two decimal places.

Question 9

The price elasticity of demand is given by $E = \dfrac{-P}{2Q^2}$, where P and Q denote price and quantity demanded, respectively. It is known that quantity demanded is 5 when the price is 10. Find an expression for the demand function.

Question 10

(a) Sketch a graph of the supply curve $P = 4 + Q^2$ on the interval $0 \le Q \le 3$.

(b) On the same diagram, sketch the line, $P = 13$.

(c) Work out the exact area bounded between the curve $P = 4 + Q^2$, the line $P = 13$ and the P axis. Explain what this area represents.

Question 11

A hospital trust decides to install a new rooftop solar power system which will save money on its energy bills. It estimates that t years after installation the savings flow (in \$1000s per year) will steadily increase according to

$$S(t) = 0.3t + 45.6$$

The flow of money needed to repair and maintain the system in subsequent years is modelled by

$$C(t) = 0.5t^2 + 2t$$

(a) Draw a sketch graph of the savings and cost functions on the same diagram.

(b) Solve the equation $S(t) = C(t)$ to determine the period during which the savings exceed the maintenance costs, and shade the area which determines the net savings during this time.

(c) Use integration to find the exact value of net savings in part (b).

Question 12

The demand function of a good is given by $P = \dfrac{80}{\sqrt[3]{Q}}$

(a) Show that the price elasticity of demand is a constant.

(b) Sketch a graph of the demand curve.

(c) Shade the area which gives the consumer's surplus at $Q = 64$ and use integration to calculate its value.

CHAPTER 7
Matrices

The impression that you may have gained from reading this text is that mathematics consists of one main topic, calculus, and that every other topic is just a variation on this theme. This is far from the truth. In this chapter and the next, we look at two refreshingly different branches of mathematics. It would be useful for you to have studied Chapter 1, although even this is not essential. There are three sections which need to be read in order.

Section 7.1 introduces the concept of a matrix, which is a convenient mathematical way of representing information displayed in a table. By defining the matrix operations of addition, subtraction and multiplication, it is possible to develop an algebra of matrices. Simple economic examples are used to illustrate these definitions, and it is shown that the rules of matrix manipulation are almost identical to those of ordinary arithmetic. In Section 7.2 you are shown how to calculate the inverse of a matrix. This is analogous to the reciprocal of a number and enables matrix equations to be solved. In particular, inverses provide an alternative way of solving systems of simultaneous linear equations and so can be used to solve problems in statics. Section 7.3 describes Cramer's rule for solving systems of linear equations. This method is a particularly useful way of solving economic models where only a selection of endogenous variables need to be determined.

SECTION 7.1

Basic matrix operations

Objectives

At the end of this section you should be able to:

- Understand the notation and terminology of matrix algebra.
- Find the transpose of a matrix.
- Add and subtract matrices.
- Multiply a matrix by a scalar.
- Multiply matrices together.
- Represent a system of linear equations in matrix notation.

Suppose that a firm produces three types of good, G1, G2 and G3, which it sells to two customers, C1 and C2. The monthly sales for these goods are given in Table 7.1.

During the month the firm sells 3 items of G2 to customer C1, 6 items of G3 to customer C2, and so on. It may well be obvious from the context exactly what these numbers represent. Under these circumstances it makes sense to ignore the table headings and to write this information more concisely as

$$\mathbf{A} = \begin{bmatrix} 7 & 3 & 4 \\ 1 & 5 & 6 \end{bmatrix}$$

which is an example of a matrix. Quite generally, any rectangular array of numbers surrounded by a pair of brackets is called a **matrix** (plural **matrices**), and the individual numbers constituting the array are called **entries** or **elements**. In this text we use square brackets, although it is equally correct to use parentheses (that is, round brackets) instead. It helps to think of a matrix as being made up of rows and columns. The matrix **A** has two rows and three columns and is said to have order 2×3. In general, a matrix of **order** $m \times n$ has m rows and n columns.

We denote matrices by capital letters in bold type (that is, **A, B, C, . . .**) and their elements by the corresponding lower-case letter in ordinary type. In fact, we use a rather clever double subscript notation so that a_{ij} stands for the element of **A** which occurs in row i and column j. Referring to the matrix **A** above, we see that

$a_{12} = 3$ (row 1 and column 2 of **A**)

and $a_{23} = 6$ (row 2 and column 3 of **A**)

Table 7.1

		Monthly sales for goods		
		G1	G2	G3
Sold to	C1	7	3	4
customer	C2	1	5	6

A general matrix **D** of order 3×2 would be written

$$\begin{bmatrix} d_{11} & d_{12} \\ d_{21} & d_{22} \\ d_{31} & d_{32} \end{bmatrix}$$

Similarly, a 3×3 matrix labelled **E** would be written

$$\begin{bmatrix} e_{11} & e_{12} & e_{13} \\ e_{21} & e_{22} & e_{23} \\ e_{31} & e_{32} & e_{33} \end{bmatrix}$$

Practice Problem

1. Let

$$\mathbf{A} = \begin{bmatrix} 1 & 2 \\ 3 & 4 \end{bmatrix} \quad \mathbf{B} = [1 \quad -1 \quad 0 \quad 6 \quad 2] \quad \mathbf{C} = \begin{bmatrix} 1 & 0 & 2 & 3 & 1 \\ 5 & 7 & 9 & 0 & 2 \\ 3 & 4 & 6 & 7 & 8 \end{bmatrix} \quad \mathbf{D} = [6]$$

(a) State the orders of the matrices **A**, **B**, **C** and **D**.

(b) Write down (if possible) the values of

$$a_{11}, \ a_{22}, \ b_{14}, \ c_{25}, \ c_{33}, \ c_{43}, \ d_{11}$$

All we have done so far is to explain what matrices are and to provide some notation for handling them. A matrix certainly gives us a convenient shorthand to describe information presented in a table. However, we would like to go further than this and to use matrices to solve problems in economics. To do this we describe several mathematical operations that can be performed on matrices, namely:

- transposition;
- addition and subtraction;
- scalar multiplication;
- matrix multiplication.

One obvious omission from the list is matrix division. Strictly speaking, it is impossible to divide one matrix by another, although we can get fairly close to the idea of division by defining something called an inverse, which we consider in Section 7.2.

Advice

If you have not met matrices before, you might like to split this section into two separate parts. You are advised to work through the material as far as 7.1.4 now, leaving matrix multiplication for another session.

7.1.1 Transposition

In Table 7.1 the rows correspond to the two customers and the columns correspond to the three goods. The matrix representation of the table is then

$$\mathbf{A} = \begin{bmatrix} 7 & 3 & 4 \\ 1 & 5 & 6 \end{bmatrix}$$

The same information about monthly sales could easily have been presented the other way round, as shown in Table 7.2. The matrix representation would then be

$$\mathbf{B} = \begin{bmatrix} 7 & 1 \\ 3 & 5 \\ 4 & 6 \end{bmatrix}$$

We describe this situation by saying that **A** and **B** are transposes of each other and write

$$\mathbf{A}^{\mathrm{T}} = \mathbf{B} \qquad \boxed{\text{read 'A transpose equals B'}}$$

or equivalently

$$\mathbf{B}^{\mathrm{T}} = \mathbf{A} \qquad \boxed{\text{read 'B transpose equals A'}}$$

The **transpose** of a matrix is found by replacing rows by columns, so that the first row becomes the first column, the second row becomes the second column, and so on. The number of rows of **A** is then the same as the number of columns of $\mathbf{A}^{\mathrm{T}}$ and vice versa. Consequently, if **A** has order $m \times n$, then $\mathbf{A}^{\mathrm{T}}$ has order $n \times m$.

Example

Write down the transpose of the matrices

$$\mathbf{D} = \begin{bmatrix} 1 & 7 & 0 & 3 \\ 2 & 4 & 6 & 0 \\ 5 & 1 & 9 & 2 \end{bmatrix} \quad \mathbf{E} = \begin{bmatrix} -6 \\ 3 \end{bmatrix}$$

Solution

The transpose of the 3×4 matrix **D** is the 4×3 matrix

$$\mathbf{D}^{\mathrm{T}} = \begin{bmatrix} 1 & 2 & 5 \\ 7 & 4 & 1 \\ 0 & 6 & 9 \\ 3 & 0 & 2 \end{bmatrix}$$

The transpose of the 2×1 matrix **E** is the 1×2 matrix

$$\mathbf{E}^{\mathrm{T}} = [-6 \quad 3]$$

Table 7.2

		Sold to customer	
		C1	C2
Monthly	G1	7	1
sales for	G2	3	5
goods	G3	4	6

Practice Problem

2. Write down the transpose of the following matrices:

$$A = \begin{bmatrix} 1 & 4 & 0 & 1 & 2 \\ 3 & 7 & 6 & 1 & 4 \\ 2 & 1 & 3 & 5 & -1 \\ 2 & -5 & 1 & 8 & 0 \end{bmatrix}$$

$$B = \begin{bmatrix} 1 & 5 & 7 & 9 \end{bmatrix}$$

$$C = \begin{bmatrix} 1 & 2 & 3 \\ 2 & 4 & 5 \\ 3 & 5 & 6 \end{bmatrix}$$

There are two particular shapes of matrices which are given special names. A matrix that has only one row, such as

$$c = \begin{bmatrix} 5 & 2 & 1 & -4 \end{bmatrix}$$

is called a **row vector**, and a matrix that has only one column, such as

$$d = \begin{bmatrix} -3 \\ 10 \\ 6 \\ -7 \\ 1 \\ 9 \\ 2 \end{bmatrix}$$

is called a **column vector**. It is standard practice to identify vectors using lower-case rather than upper-case letters. In books they are set in bold type. If you are writing them down by hand, then you should underline the letters and put

$$\underline{c} \text{ (or possibly } \underline{c}) \quad \text{and} \quad \underline{d} \text{ (or possibly } \underline{d})$$

This is a useful convention since it helps to distinguish scalar quantities such as x, y, a, b, which denote single numbers, from vector quantities such as x, y, a, b, which denote matrices with one row or column. Incidentally, it is actually quite expensive to print column vectors in books and journals since it is wasteful on space, particularly if the number of elements is large. It is then more convenient to use the transpose notation and write the vector horizontally. For example, the 7×1 matrix d given previously would be printed as

$$d = \begin{bmatrix} -3 & 10 & 6 & -7 & 1 & 9 & 2 \end{bmatrix}^T$$

where the superscript T tells us that it is the column vector that is intended.

7.1.2 Addition and subtraction

Let us suppose that, for the two-customer three-product example, the matrix

$$A = \begin{bmatrix} 7 & 3 & 4 \\ 1 & 5 & 6 \end{bmatrix}$$

gives the sales for the month of January. Similarly, the monthly sales for February might be given by

$$B = \begin{bmatrix} 6 & 2 & 1 \\ 0 & 4 & 4 \end{bmatrix}$$

This means, for example, that customer C1 buys 7 items of G1 in January and 6 items of G1 in February. Customer C1 therefore buys a total of

$$7 + 6 = 13$$

items of G1 during the two months. A similar process can be applied to the remaining goods and customers, so that the matrix giving the sales for the two months is

$$C = \begin{bmatrix} 7+6 & 3+2 & 4+1 \\ 1+0 & 5+4 & 6+4 \end{bmatrix}$$
$$= \begin{bmatrix} 13 & 5 & 5 \\ 1 & 9 & 10 \end{bmatrix}$$

We describe this by saying that **C** is the **sum** of the two matrices **A** and **B** and writing

$$C = A + B$$

In general, to add (or subtract) two matrices of the same size, we simply add (or subtract) their corresponding elements. It is obvious from this definition that, for any two $m \times n$ matrices, **A** and **B**,

$$A + B = B + A$$

because it is immaterial which way round two numbers are added. Note that in order to combine matrices in this way, it is necessary for them to have the same order. For example, it is impossible to add the matrices

$$D = \begin{bmatrix} 1 & -7 \\ 1 & 3 \end{bmatrix} \quad \text{and} \quad E = \begin{bmatrix} 1 & 2 \\ 1 & 1 \\ 3 & 5 \end{bmatrix}$$

because **D** has order 2×2 and **E** has order 3×2.

Example

Let

$$A = \begin{bmatrix} 9 & -3 \\ 4 & 1 \\ 2 & 0 \end{bmatrix} \quad \text{and} \quad B = \begin{bmatrix} 5 & 2 \\ -1 & 6 \\ 3 & 4 \end{bmatrix}$$

Find

(a) $A + B$ **(b)** $A - B$ **(c)** $A - A$

Solution

(a) $A + B = \begin{bmatrix} 9 & -3 \\ 4 & 1 \\ 2 & 0 \end{bmatrix} + \begin{bmatrix} 5 & 2 \\ -1 & 6 \\ 3 & 4 \end{bmatrix} = \begin{bmatrix} 14 & -1 \\ 3 & 7 \\ 5 & 4 \end{bmatrix}$

(b) $A - B = \begin{bmatrix} 9 & -3 \\ 4 & 1 \\ 2 & 0 \end{bmatrix} - \begin{bmatrix} 5 & 2 \\ -1 & 6 \\ 3 & 4 \end{bmatrix} = \begin{bmatrix} 4 & -5 \\ 5 & -5 \\ -1 & -4 \end{bmatrix}$

(c) $A - A = \begin{bmatrix} 9 & -3 \\ 4 & 1 \\ 2 & 0 \end{bmatrix} - \begin{bmatrix} 9 & -3 \\ 4 & 1 \\ 2 & 0 \end{bmatrix} = \begin{bmatrix} 0 & 0 \\ 0 & 0 \\ 0 & 0 \end{bmatrix}$

The result of part (c) of this example is a 3×2 matrix in which every entry is zero. Such a matrix is called a **zero matrix** and is written **0**. In fact, there are lots of zero matrices, each corresponding to a particular order. For example,

$$[0] \quad \begin{bmatrix} 0 & 0 \\ 0 & 0 \end{bmatrix} \quad \begin{bmatrix} 0 \\ 0 \\ 0 \\ 0 \end{bmatrix} \quad \begin{bmatrix} 0 & 0 & 0 & 0 & 0 & 0 \\ 0 & 0 & 0 & 0 & 0 & 0 \\ 0 & 0 & 0 & 0 & 0 & 0 \\ 0 & 0 & 0 & 0 & 0 & 0 \end{bmatrix}$$

are the 1×1, 2×2, 4×1 and 4×6 zero matrices, respectively. However, despite this, we shall use the single symbol **0** for all of these since it is usually clear in any actual example what the order is and hence which particular zero matrix is being used. It follows from the definition of addition and subtraction that, for any matrix **A**,

$A - A = 0$

$A + 0 = A$

The role played by the matrix **0** in matrix algebra is therefore similar to that of the number **0** in ordinary arithmetic.

Practice Problem

3. Let

$$A = \begin{bmatrix} 7 & 5 \\ 2 & 1 \end{bmatrix} \quad B = \begin{bmatrix} 5 \\ 4 \end{bmatrix} \quad C = \begin{bmatrix} 2 \\ 2 \end{bmatrix} \quad D = \begin{bmatrix} -6 & 2 \\ 1 & -9 \end{bmatrix} \quad 0 = \begin{bmatrix} 0 \\ 0 \end{bmatrix}$$

Find (where possible)

(a) $A + D$ (b) $A + C$ (c) $B - C$ (d) $C - 0$ (e) $D - D$

7.1.3 Scalar multiplication

Returning to the two-customer three-product example, let us suppose that the sales are the same each month and are given by

$$A = \begin{bmatrix} 7 & 3 & 4 \\ 1 & 5 & 6 \end{bmatrix}$$

This means, for example, that customer C1 buys 7 items of G1 every month, so in a whole year C1 buys

$$12 \times 7 = 84$$

items of G1. A similar process applies to the remaining goods and customers, and the matrix giving the annual sales is

$$B = \begin{bmatrix} 12 \times 7 & 12 \times 3 & 12 \times 4 \\ 12 \times 1 & 12 \times 5 & 12 \times 6 \end{bmatrix} = \begin{bmatrix} 84 & 36 & 48 \\ 12 & 60 & 72 \end{bmatrix}$$

Matrix **B** is found by scaling each element in **A** by 12, and we write

$$B = 12A$$

In general, to multiply a matrix **A** by a scalar k, we simply multiply each element of **A** by k. If

$$A = \begin{bmatrix} 1 & 2 & 3 \\ 4 & 5 & 6 \\ 7 & 8 & 9 \end{bmatrix}$$

then

$$2A = \begin{bmatrix} 2 & 4 & 6 \\ 8 & 10 & 12 \\ 14 & 16 & 18 \end{bmatrix}$$

$$-A = (-1)A = \begin{bmatrix} -1 & -2 & -3 \\ -4 & -5 & -6 \\ -7 & -8 & -9 \end{bmatrix}$$

$$0A = \begin{bmatrix} 0 & 0 & 0 \\ 0 & 0 & 0 \\ 0 & 0 & 0 \end{bmatrix} = 0$$

In ordinary arithmetic we know that

$$a(b + c) = ab + ac$$

for any three numbers a, b and c. It follows from our definitions of matrix addition and scalar multiplication that

$$k(A + B) = kA + kB$$

for any $m \times n$ matrices **A** and **B**, and scalar k.

Another property of matrices is

$$k(lA) = (kl)A$$

for scalars k and l. Again, this follows from the comparable property

$$a(bc) = (ab)c$$

for ordinary numbers.

You are invited to check these two matrix properties for yourself in the following problem.

Practice Problem

4. Let

$$A = \begin{bmatrix} 1 & -2 \\ 3 & 5 \\ 0 & 4 \end{bmatrix} \quad \text{and} \quad B = \begin{bmatrix} 0 & -1 \\ 2 & 7 \\ 1 & 6 \end{bmatrix}$$

(1) Find

(a) $2A$ (b) $2B$ (c) $A + B$ (d) $2(A + B)$

Hence verify that

$$2(A + B) = 2A + 2B$$

(2) Find

(a) $3A$ (b) $-6A$

Hence verify that

$$-2(3A) = -6A$$

7.1.4 Matrix multiplication

Advice

Hopefully, you have found the matrix operations considered so far in this section easy to understand. We now turn our attention to matrix multiplication. If you have never multiplied matrices before, you may find that it requires a bit more effort to grasp, and you should allow yourself extra time to work through the problems. There is no need to worry. Once you have performed a dozen or so matrix multiplications, you will find that the technique becomes second nature, although the process may appear rather strange and complicated at first sight.

We begin by showing you how to multiply a row vector by a column vector. To illustrate this let us suppose that goods G1, G2 and G3 sell at \$50, \$30 and \$20, respectively, and let us introduce the row vector

$$\mathbf{p} = [50 \quad 30 \quad 20]$$

If the firm sells a total of 100, 200 and 175 goods of type G1, G2 and G3, respectively, then we can write this information as the column vector

$$\mathbf{q} = \begin{bmatrix} 100 \\ 200 \\ 175 \end{bmatrix}$$

The total revenue received from the sale of G1 is found by multiplying the price, $50, by the quantity, 100, to get

$50 \times 100 = \$5000$

Similarly, the revenue from G2 and G3 is

$30 \times 200 = \$6000$

and

$20 \times 175 = \$3500$

respectively. The total revenue of the firm is therefore

TR = $5000 + $6000 + $3500 = $14 500

The value of TR is a single number and can be regarded as a 1×1 matrix: that is,

[14 500]

This 1×1 matrix is obtained by multiplying together the price vector, **p**, and the quantity vector, **q**, to get

$$[50 \quad 30 \quad 20] \begin{bmatrix} 100 \\ 200 \\ 175 \end{bmatrix} = [14\ 500]$$

The value 14 500 is found by multiplying the corresponding elements of **p** and **q** and then adding together: that is,

$$[50 \quad 30 \quad 20] \begin{bmatrix} 100 \\ 200 \\ 175 \end{bmatrix} = [5000 + 6000 + 3500] = [14\ 500]$$

In general, if **a** is the row vector

$[a_{11} \quad a_{12} \quad a_{13} \quad \ldots \quad a_{1s}]$

and **b** is the column vector

$$\begin{bmatrix} b_{11} \\ b_{21} \\ b_{31} \\ \\ b_{s1} \end{bmatrix}$$

then we define the matrix product

$$\mathbf{ab} = [a_{11} \quad a_{12} \quad a_{13} \quad \ldots \quad a_{1s}] \begin{bmatrix} b_{11} \\ b_{21} \\ b_{31} \\ \\ b_{s1} \end{bmatrix}$$

to be the 1×1 matrix

$$[a_{11}b_{11} + a_{12}b_{21} + a_{13}b_{31} + \ldots + a_{1s}b_{s1}]$$

It is important to notice that the single element in the 1×1 matrix **ab** is found by multiplying each element of **a** by the corresponding element of **b**. Consequently, it is essential that both vectors have the same number of elements. In other words, if **a** has order $1 \times s$ and **b** has order $t \times 1$, then it is only possible to form the product **ab** when $s = t$.

Example

If

$$\mathbf{a} = [1 \quad 2 \quad 3 \quad 4], \quad \mathbf{b} = \begin{bmatrix} 2 \\ 5 \\ -1 \\ 0 \end{bmatrix} \quad \text{and} \quad \mathbf{c} = \begin{bmatrix} 6 \\ 9 \\ 2 \end{bmatrix}$$

find **ab** and **ac**.

Solution

Using the definition of the multiplication of a row vector by a column vector we have

$$\mathbf{ab} = [1 \quad 2 \quad 3 \quad 4] \begin{bmatrix} 2 \\ 5 \\ -1 \\ 0 \end{bmatrix} = [1(2) + 2(5) + 3(-1) + 4(0)] = [9]$$

We have set out the calculations in this way so that you can see how the value, 9, is obtained. There is no need for you to indicate this in your own answers and you may simply write

$$[1 \quad 2 \quad 3 \quad 4] \begin{bmatrix} 2 \\ 5 \\ -1 \\ 0 \end{bmatrix} = [9]$$

without bothering to insert any intermediate steps.

It is impossible to multiply **a** and **c** because **a** has four elements and **c** has only three elements. You can see the problem if you actually try to perform the calculations, since there is no entry in **c** with which to multiply the 4 in **a**.

$$[1 \quad 2 \quad 3 \quad 4] \begin{bmatrix} 6 \\ 9 \\ 2 \end{bmatrix} = [1(6) + 2(9) + 3(2) + 4(?)]$$

Practice Problem

5. Let

$$\mathbf{a} = [1 \quad -1 \quad 0 \quad 3 \quad 2], \quad \mathbf{b} = [1 \quad 2 \quad 9], \quad \mathbf{c} = \begin{bmatrix} 0 \\ -1 \\ 1 \\ 1 \\ 2 \end{bmatrix} \quad \text{and} \quad \mathbf{d} = \begin{bmatrix} -2 \\ 1 \\ 0 \end{bmatrix}$$

Find (where possible)

(a) ac   (b) bd   (c) ad

We now turn our attention to general matrix multiplication, which is defined as follows. If $\mathbf{A}$ is an $m \times s$ matrix and $\mathbf{B}$ is an $s \times n$ matrix, then

$$\mathbf{C} = \mathbf{AB}$$

is an $m \times n$ matrix and c_{ij} is found by multiplying the ith row of $\mathbf{A}$ into the jth column of $\mathbf{B}$.

There are three things to notice about this definition. First, the number of columns of $\mathbf{A}$ is the same as the number of rows of $\mathbf{B}$. Unless this condition is satisfied, it is impossible to form the product $\mathbf{AB}$. Secondly, the matrix $\mathbf{C}$ has order $m \times n$, where m is the number of rows of $\mathbf{A}$ and n is the number of columns of $\mathbf{B}$. Finally, the elements of $\mathbf{C}$ are found by multiplying row vectors by column vectors.

To illustrate the technique consider what happens when we find the product of the two matrices

$$\mathbf{A} = \begin{bmatrix} 2 & 1 & 0 \\ 1 & 0 & 4 \end{bmatrix} \quad \text{and} \quad \mathbf{B} = \begin{bmatrix} 3 & 1 & 2 & 1 \\ 1 & 0 & 1 & 2 \\ 5 & 4 & 1 & 1 \end{bmatrix}$$

It is a good idea to check before you begin any detailed calculations that it is possible to multiply these matrices and also to identify the order of the resulting matrix. In this case

$\mathbf{A}$ is a 2×3 matrix   and $\mathbf{B}$ is a 3×4 matrix

Matrix $\mathbf{A}$ has three columns and $\mathbf{B}$ has the same number of rows, so it *is* possible to find $\mathbf{AB}$. Moreover, $\mathbf{AB}$ must have order 2×4 because $\mathbf{A}$ has two rows and $\mathbf{B}$ has four columns. Hence

$$\begin{bmatrix} 2 & 1 & 0 \\ 1 & 0 & 4 \end{bmatrix} \begin{bmatrix} 3 & 1 & 2 & 1 \\ 1 & 0 & 1 & 2 \\ 5 & 4 & 1 & 1 \end{bmatrix} = \begin{bmatrix} c_{11} & c_{12} & c_{13} & c_{14} \\ c_{21} & c_{22} & c_{23} & c_{24} \end{bmatrix}$$

All that remains for us to do is to calculate the eight numbers c_{ij}.

The number c_{11} in the top left-hand corner lies in the first row and first column, so to find its value we multiply the first row of $\mathbf{A}$ into the first column of $\mathbf{B}$ to get

$$\begin{bmatrix} 2 & 1 & 0 \\ 1 & 0 & 4 \end{bmatrix} \begin{bmatrix} 3 & 1 & 2 & 1 \\ 1 & 0 & 1 & 2 \\ 5 & 4 & 1 & 1 \end{bmatrix} \begin{bmatrix} 7 & c_{12} & c_{13} & c_{14} \\ c_{21} & c_{22} & c_{23} & c_{24} \end{bmatrix}$$

because $2(3) + 1(1) + 0(5) = 7$.

The number c_{12} lies in the first row and second column, so to find its value we multiply the first row of **A** into the second column of **B** to get

$$\begin{bmatrix} 2 & 1 & 0 \\ 1 & 0 & 4 \end{bmatrix} \begin{bmatrix} 3 & 1 & 2 & 1 \\ 1 & 0 & 1 & 2 \\ 5 & 4 & 1 & 1 \end{bmatrix} \begin{bmatrix} 7 & 2 & c_{13} & c_{14} \\ c_{21} & c_{22} & c_{23} & c_{24} \end{bmatrix}$$

because $2(1) + 1(0) + 0(4) = 2$.

The values of c_{13} and c_{14} are then found in a similar way by multiplying the first row of **A** into the third and fourth columns of **B**, respectively, to get

$$\begin{bmatrix} 2 & 1 & 0 \\ 1 & 0 & 4 \end{bmatrix} \begin{bmatrix} 3 & 1 & 2 & 1 \\ 1 & 0 & 1 & 2 \\ 5 & 4 & 1 & 1 \end{bmatrix} \begin{bmatrix} 7 & 2 & 5 & 4 \\ c_{21} & c_{22} & c_{23} & c_{24} \end{bmatrix}$$

because $2(2) + 1(1) + 0(1) = 5$ and $2(1) + 1(2) + 0(1) = 4$.

Finally, we repeat the whole procedure along the second row of **C**. The elements c_{21}, c_{22}, c_{23} and c_{24} are calculated by multiplying the second row of **A** into the four columns of **B** in succession to get

$$\begin{bmatrix} 2 & 1 & 0 \\ 1 & 0 & 4 \end{bmatrix} \begin{bmatrix} 3 & 1 & 2 & 1 \\ 1 & 0 & 1 & 2 \\ 5 & 4 & 1 & 1 \end{bmatrix} \begin{bmatrix} 7 & 2 & 5 & 4 \\ 23 & 17 & 6 & 5 \end{bmatrix}$$

because

$$1(3) + 0(1) + 4(5) = 23$$
$$1(1) + 0(0) + 4(4) = 17$$
$$1(2) + 0(1) + 4(1) = 6$$
$$1(1) + 0(2) + 4(1) = 5$$

In this example we have indicated how to build up the matrix **C** in a step-by-step manner and have used highlights to show you how the calculations are performed. This approach has been adopted merely as a teaching device. There is no need for you to set your calculations out in this way, and you are encouraged to write down your answer in a single line of working.

Advice

Take the trouble to check before you begin that it is possible to form the matrix product and to anticipate the order of the end result. This can be done by jotting down the orders of the original matrices side by side. The product exists if the inner numbers are the same and the order of the answer is given by the outer numbers: that is,

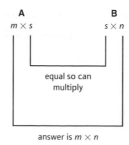

For example, if **A**, **B** and **C** have orders 3×5, 5×2 and 3×4 respectively, then **AB** exists and has order 3×2 because

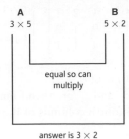

but it is impossible to form **AC** because

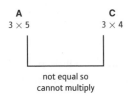

Practice Problem

6. Write down the order of the matrices

$$\mathbf{A} = \begin{bmatrix} 1 & 2 \\ 0 & 1 \\ 3 & 1 \end{bmatrix} \quad \text{and} \quad \mathbf{B} = \begin{bmatrix} 1 & 2 \\ 3 & 4 \end{bmatrix}$$

Hence verify that it is possible to form the matrix product

$$\mathbf{C} = \mathbf{AB}$$

and write down the order of **C**. Calculate all of the elements of **C**.

We have already noted that matrix operations have similar properties to those of ordinary arithmetic. Some particular rules of arithmetic are:

$$a(b + c) = ab + ac \quad \text{(distributive law)}$$
$$(a + b)c = ac + bc \quad \text{(distributive law)}$$
$$a(bc) = (ab)c \quad \text{(associative law)}$$
$$ab = ba \quad \text{(commutative law)}$$

An obvious question to ask is whether they have a counterpart in matrix algebra. It turns out that provided the matrices **A**, **B** and **C** have the correct orders for the appropriate sums and products to exist, then

$$\mathbf{A}(\mathbf{B} + \mathbf{C}) = \mathbf{AB} + \mathbf{AC}$$
$$(\mathbf{A} + \mathbf{B})\mathbf{C} = \mathbf{AC} + \mathbf{BC}$$
$$\mathbf{A}(\mathbf{BC}) = (\mathbf{AB})\mathbf{C}$$

However, although it is true that

$$ab = ba$$

for numbers, this result does **not** extend to matrices. Even if **AB** and **BA** both exist, it is not necessarily true that

AB = BA

This is illustrated in the following example.

Example

If

$$\mathbf{A} = \begin{bmatrix} 1 & -1 \\ 2 & 1 \end{bmatrix} \quad \text{and} \quad \mathbf{B} = \begin{bmatrix} 1 & 3 \\ 1 & 2 \end{bmatrix}$$

evaluate **AB** and **BA**.

Solution

It is easy to check that it is possible to form both products **AB** and **BA** and that they both have order 2 × 2. In fact

$$\mathbf{AB} = \begin{bmatrix} 1 & -1 \\ 2 & 1 \end{bmatrix}\begin{bmatrix} 1 & 3 \\ 1 & 2 \end{bmatrix} = \begin{bmatrix} 0 & 1 \\ 3 & 8 \end{bmatrix}$$

$$\mathbf{BA} = \begin{bmatrix} 1 & 3 \\ 1 & 2 \end{bmatrix}\begin{bmatrix} 1 & -1 \\ 2 & 1 \end{bmatrix} = \begin{bmatrix} 7 & 2 \\ 5 & 1 \end{bmatrix}$$

so **AB ≠ BA**.

There are certain pairs of matrices which do commute (that is, for which **AB = BA**) and we shall investigate some of these in the next section. However, these are very much the exception. We therefore have the 'non-property' that, in general,

AB ≠ BA

Practice Problems

7. Let

$$\mathbf{A} = \begin{bmatrix} 2 & 1 & 1 \\ 5 & 1 & 0 \\ -1 & 1 & 4 \end{bmatrix}, \quad \mathbf{B} = \begin{bmatrix} 1 \\ 2 \\ 1 \end{bmatrix}, \quad \mathbf{C} = \begin{bmatrix} 1 & 2 \\ 3 & 1 \end{bmatrix}, \quad \mathbf{D} = \begin{bmatrix} 1 & 1 \\ -1 & 1 \\ 2 & 1 \end{bmatrix} \quad \text{and} \quad \mathbf{E} = \begin{bmatrix} 1 & 2 & 3 \\ 4 & 5 & 6 \end{bmatrix}$$

Find (where possible)

(a) AB   (b) BA   (c) CD   (d) DC

(e) AE   (f) EA   (g) DE   (h) ED

→

8. Evaluate the matrix product **Ax**, where

$$\mathbf{A} = \begin{bmatrix} 1 & 4 & 7 \\ 2 & 6 & 5 \\ 8 & 9 & 5 \end{bmatrix} \quad \text{and} \quad \mathbf{x} = \begin{bmatrix} x \\ y \\ z \end{bmatrix}$$

Hence show that the system of linear equations

$$x + 4y + 7z = -3$$
$$2x + 6y + 5z = 10$$
$$8x + 9y + 5z = 1$$

can be written as **Ax = b** where

$$\mathbf{b} = \begin{bmatrix} -3 \\ 10 \\ 1 \end{bmatrix}$$

We conclude this section by showing you how to express a familiar problem in matrix notation. Section 1.4 described the method of elimination for solving systems of simultaneous linear equations. For example, we might want to find values of x and y which satisfy

$$2x - 5y = 6$$
$$7x + 8y = -1$$

Motivated by the result of Practice Problem 8, we write this as

$$\mathbf{Ax = b}$$

where

$$\mathbf{A} = \begin{bmatrix} 2 & -5 \\ 7 & 8 \end{bmatrix} \quad \mathbf{x} = \begin{bmatrix} x \\ y \end{bmatrix} \quad \mathbf{b} = \begin{bmatrix} 6 \\ -1 \end{bmatrix}$$

It is easy to check that this is correct simply by multiplying out **Ax** to get

$$\begin{bmatrix} 2 & -5 \\ 7 & 8 \end{bmatrix} \begin{bmatrix} x \\ y \end{bmatrix} = \begin{bmatrix} 2x - 5y \\ 7x + 8y \end{bmatrix}$$

and so the matrix equation **Ax = b** reads

$$\begin{bmatrix} 2x - 5y \\ 7x + 8y \end{bmatrix} = \begin{bmatrix} 6 \\ -1 \end{bmatrix}$$

that is,

$$2x - 5y = 6$$
$$7x + 8y = -1$$

Quite generally, any system of n linear equations in n unknowns can be written as

$$\mathbf{Ax = b}$$

where $\mathbf{A}$, $\mathbf{x}$ and $\mathbf{b}$ are $n \times n$, $n \times 1$ and $n \times 1$ matrices, respectively. The matrix $\mathbf{A}$ consists of the coefficients, the vector $\mathbf{x}$ consists of the unknowns and the vector $\mathbf{b}$ consists of the right-hand sides. The definition of matrix multiplication allows us to write a linear system in terms of matrices, although it is not immediately obvious that there is any advantage in doing so. In the next section we introduce the concept of a matrix inverse and show you how to use this to solve systems of equations expressed in matrix form.

Throughout this section we have noted various properties that matrices satisfy. For convenience these are summarised in the next sub-section.

7.1.5 Summary

Provided that the indicated sums and products make sense,

$$\mathbf{A} + \mathbf{B} = \mathbf{B} + \mathbf{A}$$
$$\mathbf{A} - \mathbf{A} = \mathbf{0}$$
$$\mathbf{A} + \mathbf{0} = \mathbf{A}$$
$$k(\mathbf{A} + \mathbf{B}) = k\mathbf{A} + k\mathbf{B}$$
$$k(l\mathbf{A}) = (kl)\mathbf{A}$$
$$\mathbf{A}(\mathbf{B} + \mathbf{C}) = \mathbf{A}\mathbf{B} + \mathbf{A}\mathbf{C}$$
$$(\mathbf{A} + \mathbf{B})\mathbf{C} = \mathbf{A}\mathbf{C} + \mathbf{B}\mathbf{C}$$
$$\mathbf{A}(\mathbf{B}\mathbf{C}) = (\mathbf{A}\mathbf{B})\mathbf{C}$$

We also have the non-property that, in general,

$$\mathbf{A}\mathbf{B} \neq \mathbf{B}\mathbf{A}$$

Key Terms

Column vector   A matrix with one column.

Elements   The individual numbers inside a matrix. (Also called **entries**.)

Matrix   A rectangular array of numbers, set out in rows and columns, surrounded by a pair of brackets. (Plural **matrices**.)

Order (of a matrix)   The dimensions of a matrix. A matrix with m rows and n columns has order $m \times n$.

Row vector   A matrix with one row.

Transpose (of a matrix)   The matrix obtained from a given matrix by interchanging rows and columns. The transpose of a matrix $\mathbf{A}$ is written $\mathbf{A}^\mathsf{T}$.

Zero matrix   A matrix in which every element is zero.

Exercise 7.1

1. The monthly sales (in thousands) of burgers (B1) and bites (B2) in three fast-food restaurants (R1, R2, R3) are as follows:

	R1	R2	R3
B1	35	27	13
B2	42	39	24

   January

	R1	R2	R3
B1	31	17	3
B2	25	29	16

   February

   (a) Write down two 2×3 matrices **J** and **F**, representing sales in January and February, respectively.

   (b) By finding $\mathbf{J} + \mathbf{F}$, write down the matrix for the total sales over the two months.

   (c) By finding $\mathbf{J} - \mathbf{F}$, write down the matrix for the difference in sales for the two months.

2. If

   $$\mathbf{A} = \begin{bmatrix} 2 & 3 & 1 & 9 \\ 1 & 0 & 5 & 0 \\ 6 & 7 & 8 & 4 \end{bmatrix} \quad \mathbf{B} = \begin{bmatrix} 1 & 7 & 9 & 6 \\ 2 & 1 & 0 & 5 \\ 6 & 4 & 5 & 3 \end{bmatrix}$$

   work out

   (a) $2\mathbf{A}$ (b) $2\mathbf{B}$ (c) $2\mathbf{A} + 2\mathbf{B}$ (d) $2(\mathbf{A} + \mathbf{B})$

   Do you notice any connection between your answers to parts (c) and (d)?

3. If **A**, **B** and **C** are matrices with orders, 3×3, 2×3 and 4×2, respectively, which of the following matrix calculations are possible? If the calculation *is* possible, state the order of the resulting matrix

   $$4\mathbf{B}, \quad \mathbf{A} + \mathbf{B}, \quad 3\mathbf{B}^\mathrm{T} + \mathbf{C}, \quad \mathbf{AB}, \quad \mathbf{B}^\mathrm{T}\mathbf{A}, \quad (\mathbf{CB})^\mathrm{T}, \quad \mathbf{CBA}$$

4. A firm manufactures three products, P1, P2 and P3, which it sells to two customers, C1 and C2. The number of items of each product that are sold to these customers is given by

   $$\mathbf{A} = \begin{array}{c} \text{C1} \\ \text{C2} \end{array} \begin{bmatrix} 6 & 7 & 9 \\ 2 & 1 & 2 \end{bmatrix} \begin{array}{l} \text{P1 P2 P3} \end{array}$$

   The firm charges both customers the same price for each product according to

   $$\mathbf{B} = [100 \quad 500 \quad 200]^\mathrm{T} \quad \text{P1 P2 P3}$$

   To make each item of type P1, P2 and P3, the firm uses four raw materials, R1, R2, R3 and R4. The number of tonnes required per item is given by

   $$\mathbf{C} = \begin{array}{c} \text{P1} \\ \text{P2} \\ \text{P3} \end{array} \begin{bmatrix} 1 & 0 & 0 & 1 \\ 1 & 1 & 2 & 1 \\ 0 & 0 & 1 & 1 \end{bmatrix} \begin{array}{l} \text{R1 R2 R3 R4} \end{array}$$

The cost per tonne of raw materials is

$$\begin{array}{cccc} \text{R1} & \text{R2} & \text{R3} & \text{R4} \end{array}$$
$$\mathbf{D} = [20 \quad 10 \quad 15 \quad 15]^{\mathrm{T}}$$

In addition, let

$$\mathbf{E} = [1 \quad 1]$$

Find the following matrix products and give an interpretation of each one.

(a) **AB**   (b) **AC**   (c) **CD**   (d) **ACD**   (e) **EAB**

(f) **EACD**   (g) **EAB – EACD**

5. A firm orders 12, 30 and 25 items of goods G1, G2 and G3. The cost of each item of G1, G2 and G3 is \$8, \$30 and \$15, respectively.

(a) Write down suitable price and quantity vectors, and use matrix multiplication to work out the total cost of the order.

(b) Write down the new price vector when the cost of G1 rises by 20%, the cost of G2 falls by 10% and the cost of G3 is unaltered. Use matrix multiplication to work out the new cost of the order and hence find the overall percentage change in total cost.

6. (1) Let

$$\mathbf{A} = \begin{bmatrix} 1 & 2 \\ 3 & 4 \\ 5 & 6 \end{bmatrix} \quad \text{and} \quad \mathbf{B} = \begin{bmatrix} 1 & -1 \\ 2 & 1 \\ -3 & 4 \end{bmatrix}$$

Find

(a) $\mathbf{A}^{\mathrm{T}}$ (b) $\mathbf{B}^{\mathrm{T}}$ (c) $\mathbf{A} + \mathbf{B}$ (d) $(\mathbf{A} + \mathbf{B})^{\mathrm{T}}$

Do you notice any connection between $(\mathbf{A} + \mathbf{B})^{\mathrm{T}}$, $\mathbf{A}^{\mathrm{T}}$ and $\mathbf{B}^{\mathrm{T}}$?

(2) Let

$$\mathbf{C} = \begin{bmatrix} 1 & 4 \\ 5 & 9 \end{bmatrix} \quad \text{and} \quad \mathbf{D} = \begin{bmatrix} 2 & 1 & 0 \\ -1 & 0 & 1 \end{bmatrix}$$

Find

(a) $\mathbf{C}^{\mathrm{T}}$ (b) $\mathbf{D}^{\mathrm{T}}$ (c) $\mathbf{CD}$ (d) $(\mathbf{CD})^{\mathrm{T}}$

Do you notice any connection between $(\mathbf{CD})^{\mathrm{T}}$, $\mathbf{C}^{\mathrm{T}}$ and $\mathbf{D}^{\mathrm{T}}$?

7. Verify the equations

(a) $\mathbf{A}(\mathbf{B} + \mathbf{C}) = \mathbf{AB} + \mathbf{AC}$ (b) $(\mathbf{AB})\mathbf{C} = \mathbf{A}(\mathbf{BC})$

in the case when

$$\mathbf{A} = \begin{bmatrix} 5 & -3 \\ 2 & 1 \end{bmatrix}, \quad \mathbf{B} = \begin{bmatrix} 1 & 5 \\ 4 & 0 \end{bmatrix} \quad \text{and} \quad \mathbf{C} = \begin{bmatrix} -1 & 1 \\ 1 & 2 \end{bmatrix}$$

8. If

$$\mathbf{A} = [1 \quad 2 \quad -4 \quad 3] \quad \text{and} \quad \mathbf{B} = \begin{bmatrix} 1 \\ 7 \\ 3 \\ 2 \end{bmatrix}$$

find **AB** and **BA**.

9. **(a)** Evaluate the matrix product $\mathbf{Ax}$, where

$$\mathbf{A} = \begin{bmatrix} 7 & 5 \\ 1 & 3 \end{bmatrix} \quad \text{and} \quad \mathbf{x} = \begin{bmatrix} x \\ y \end{bmatrix}$$

Hence show that the system of linear equations

$$7x + 5y = 3$$
$$x + 3y = 2$$

can be written as $\mathbf{Ax} = \mathbf{b}$ where $\mathbf{b} = \begin{bmatrix} 3 \\ 2 \end{bmatrix}$.

(b) The system of equations

$$2x + 3y - 2z = 6$$
$$x - y + 2z = 3$$
$$4x + 2y + 5z = 1$$

can be expressed in the form $\mathbf{Ax} = \mathbf{b}$. Write down the matrices $\mathbf{A}$, $\mathbf{x}$ and $\mathbf{b}$.

Exercise 7.1*

1. Matrices $\mathbf{A}$, $\mathbf{B}$, $\mathbf{C}$ and $\mathbf{D}$ have orders 3×5, 5×2, 5×5 and 3×5, respectively. State whether it is possible to perform the following matrix operations.

If it *is* possible, state the order of the resulting matrix.

(a) $7\mathbf{B}$ **(b)** $(\mathbf{A} + \mathbf{C})^{\mathrm{T}}$ **(c)** $\mathbf{A} - 2\mathbf{D}$ **(d)** $\mathbf{BC}$

(e) $\mathbf{CB}^{\mathrm{T}}$ **(f)** $\mathbf{D}^{\mathrm{T}}\mathbf{A}$ **(g)** $\mathbf{A}^{\mathrm{T}} + \mathbf{B}^{\mathrm{T}}$

2. Two matrices $\mathbf{A}$ and $\mathbf{B}$ are given by

$$\mathbf{A} = \begin{bmatrix} a - 1 & b \\ a + b & 3c - b \end{bmatrix} \quad \text{and} \quad \mathbf{B} = \begin{bmatrix} 1 & 3a \\ 2c & d + 1 \end{bmatrix}$$

If $\mathbf{A} = \mathbf{B}$, find the values of a, b, c and d.

3. Consider the matrices

$$\mathbf{A} = \begin{bmatrix} a & b & c \\ d & e & f \end{bmatrix} \quad \text{and} \quad \mathbf{B} = \begin{bmatrix} g & h \\ i & j \\ k & l \end{bmatrix}$$

(a) Write down the matrices $\mathbf{A}^{\mathrm{T}}$ and $\mathbf{B}^{\mathrm{T}}$.

(b) Work out the matrix products $\mathbf{AB}$ and $\mathbf{B}^{\mathrm{T}}\mathbf{A}^{\mathrm{T}}$.

(c) State the relationship between $\mathbf{AB}$ and $\mathbf{B}^{\mathrm{T}}\mathbf{A}^{\mathrm{T}}$, and use this result to simplify $(\mathbf{A}^{\mathrm{T}}\mathbf{B}^{\mathrm{T}}\mathbf{C}^{\mathrm{T}})^{\mathrm{T}}$.

4. A chain of sports shops, A, B and C, sells T-shirts, trainers and tennis racquets. The weekly sales and profit per item are shown in the tables below:

Sales per week	Shop A	Shop B	Shop C
T-shirts	60	40	25
Trainers	80	123	90
Tennis racquets	10	0	25

Profit per item	Shop A ($)	Shop B ($)	Shop C ($)
T-shirts	1	1	1.50
Trainers	5	8	6
Tennis racquets	20	25	30

The 3×3 matrices formed from the sales and profit tables are denoted by $\mathbf{S}$ and $\mathbf{P}$, respectively.

(a) If $\mathbf{SP}^{\mathrm{T}}$ is denoted by $\mathbf{A}$, find the element a_{11} and give a brief interpretation of this number.

(b) If $\mathbf{S}^{\mathrm{T}}\mathbf{P}$ is denoted by $\mathbf{B}$, find the element b_{33} and give a brief interpretation of this number.

5. On a small island there are supermarkets A, L, S and W. In the current year, 30% of customers buy groceries from A, 20% from L, 40% from S and 10% from W. However, each year,

  A retains 80% of its customers but loses 10% to L, 5% to S and 5% to W.
  L retains 90% of its customers but loses 5% to A and 5% to S.
  S retains 75% of its customers but loses 10% to A, 10% to L and 5% to W.
  W retains 85% of its customers losing 5% to A, 5% to L and 5% to S.

(a) If the original market share is represented by the column vector

$$\mathbf{x} = \begin{bmatrix} 0.3 \\ 0.2 \\ 0.4 \\ 0.1 \end{bmatrix}$$

and the matrix representing the transition in supermarket loyalty is

$$\mathbf{T} = \begin{bmatrix} 0.8 & 0.05 & 0.1 & 0.05 \\ 0.1 & 0.9 & 0.1 & 0.05 \\ 0.05 & 0.05 & 0.75 & 0.05 \\ 0.05 & 0 & 0.05 & 0.85 \end{bmatrix}$$

work out the matrix product, $\mathbf{Tx}$, and give an interpretation of the elements of the resulting vector.

(b) Assuming that the same transition matrix applies in subsequent years, work out the percentage of customers who buy groceries in supermarket L after

   (i) two years   (ii) three years

6. If $\mathbf{A} = \begin{bmatrix} 3 & -1 & 4 \\ 0 & 2 & 1 \end{bmatrix}$ and $\mathbf{B} = \begin{bmatrix} 4 & 0 & 7 \\ 2 & 5 & 1 \end{bmatrix}$ find the matrix $\mathbf{X}$ which satisfies the matrix equation: $2\mathbf{A} + \mathbf{X}^{\mathrm{T}} = 3\mathbf{B}$.

→

7. Matrices, **A**, **B** and **C** are given by

$$\mathbf{A} = \begin{bmatrix} 3 & -2 & 4 \\ 6 & 1 & 0 \\ -5 & 9 & 5 \end{bmatrix}, \quad \mathbf{B} = \begin{bmatrix} 1 & 5 & 0 \\ 4 & 4 & 7 \\ 2 & 3 & -9 \end{bmatrix} \quad \text{and} \quad \mathbf{C} = \begin{bmatrix} 3 & -2 & -7 \\ -4 & 5 & 1 \\ 3 & 0 & 6 \end{bmatrix}$$

If $\mathbf{D} = \mathbf{A}(2\mathbf{B} + 3\mathbf{C})$, find d_{23}.

8. Let

$$\mathbf{A} = \begin{bmatrix} a & b \\ c & d \end{bmatrix}, \quad \mathbf{A}^{-1} = \frac{1}{ad - bc}\begin{bmatrix} d & -b \\ -c & a \end{bmatrix} \qquad (ad - bc \neq 0)$$

$$\mathbf{I} = \begin{bmatrix} 1 & 0 \\ 0 & 1 \end{bmatrix} \quad \text{and} \quad \mathbf{x} = \begin{bmatrix} x \\ y \end{bmatrix}$$

Show that

(a) $\mathbf{AI} = \mathbf{A}$ and $\mathbf{IA} = \mathbf{A}$ **(b)** $\mathbf{A}^{-1}\mathbf{A} = \mathbf{I}$ and $\mathbf{AA}^{-1} = \mathbf{I}$ **(c)** $\mathbf{Ix} = \mathbf{x}$

9. For the commodity market:

$$C = aY + b \quad \text{and} \quad I = cr + d$$

For the money market:

$$M_S = M_S^* \quad \text{and} \quad M_D = k_1 Y + k_2 r + k_3$$

If both markets are in equilibrium, find the matrix, **A**, such that $\mathbf{Ax} = \mathbf{b}$, where $\mathbf{x} = \begin{bmatrix} r \\ Y \end{bmatrix}$ and $\mathbf{b} = \begin{bmatrix} M_s^* - k_3 \\ b + d \end{bmatrix}$.

SECTION 7.2
Matrix inversion

Objectives

At the end of this section you should be able to:

- Write down the 2 × 2 and 3 × 3 identity matrices.

- Detect whether a matrix is singular or non-singular.

- Calculate the determinant and inverse of a 2 × 2 matrix.

- Calculate the cofactors of a 3 × 3 matrix.

- Use cofactors to find the determinant and inverse of a 3 × 3 matrix.

- Use matrix inverses to solve systems of linear equations arising in economics.

In this and the following section we consider **square** matrices, in which the number of rows and columns are equal. For simplicity we concentrate on 2 × 2 and 3 × 3 matrices, although the ideas and techniques apply more generally to $n \times n$ matrices of any size. We have already seen that, with one notable exception, the algebra of matrices is virtually the same as the algebra of numbers. There are, however, two important properties of numbers which we have yet to consider. The first is the existence of a number, 1, which satisfies

$$a1 = a \quad \text{and} \quad 1a = a$$

for any number, a. The second is the fact that corresponding to any non-zero number, a, we can find another number, a^{-1}, with the property that

$$a^{-1}a = 1 \quad \text{and} \quad aa^{-1} = 1 \qquad \boxed{a^{-1} = \dfrac{1}{a}}$$

If you have worked through Question 8 of Exercise 7.1* you will know how to extend these to 2 × 2 matrices. In part (a) you showed that, for any 2 × 2 matrix, **A**,

$$\mathbf{AI} = \mathbf{A} \quad \text{and} \quad \mathbf{IA} = \mathbf{A}$$

where

$$\mathbf{I} = \begin{bmatrix} 1 & 0 \\ 0 & 1 \end{bmatrix}$$

The matrix **I** is called the **identity** matrix and is analogous to the number 1 in ordinary arithmetic. You also showed in part (b) of Question 8 that corresponding to the 2 × 2 matrix

$$\mathbf{A} = \begin{bmatrix} a & b \\ c & d \end{bmatrix}$$

there is another matrix

$$\mathbf{A}^{-1} = \frac{1}{ad - bc} \begin{bmatrix} d & -b \\ -c & a \end{bmatrix}$$

with the property that

$$\mathbf{A}^{-1}\mathbf{A} = \mathbf{I} \quad \text{and} \quad \mathbf{A}\mathbf{A}^{-1} = \mathbf{I}$$

The matrix $\mathbf{A}^{-1}$ is said to be the **inverse** of $\mathbf{A}$ and is analogous to the reciprocal of a number. The formula for $\mathbf{A}^{-1}$ looks rather complicated, but the construction of $\mathbf{A}^{-1}$ is in fact very easy. Starting with some matrix

$$\mathbf{A} = \begin{bmatrix} a & b \\ c & d \end{bmatrix}$$

we first swap the two numbers on the leading diagonal (that is, the elements along the line joining the top left-hand corner to the bottom right-hand corner of $\mathbf{A}$) to get

$$\begin{bmatrix} d & b \\ c & a \end{bmatrix} \qquad \text{swap } a \text{ and } d$$

Secondly, we change the sign of the 'off-diagonal' elements to get

$$\begin{bmatrix} d & -b \\ -c & a \end{bmatrix} \qquad \text{change signs of } b \text{ and } c$$

Finally, we multiply the matrix by the scalar

$$\frac{1}{ad - bc}$$

to get

$$\frac{1}{ad - bc}\begin{bmatrix} d & -b \\ -c & a \end{bmatrix} \qquad \text{divide each element by } ad - bc$$

The number $ad - bc$ is called the **determinant** of $\mathbf{A}$ and is written as

$$\det(\mathbf{A}) \quad \text{or} \quad \left| \mathbf{A} \right| \quad \text{or} \quad \begin{vmatrix} a & b \\ c & d \end{vmatrix}$$

Notice that the last step in the calculation is impossible if

$$\left| \mathbf{A} \right| = 0$$

because we cannot divide by zero. We deduce that the inverse of a matrix exists only if the matrix has a non-zero determinant. This is comparable to the situation in arithmetic where a reciprocal of a number exists provided the number is non-zero. If the matrix has a non-zero determinant, it is said to be **non-singular**; otherwise it is said to be **singular**.

As an example, consider the matrices

$$\mathbf{A} = \begin{bmatrix} 1 & 2 \\ 3 & 4 \end{bmatrix} \quad \text{and} \quad \mathbf{B} = \begin{bmatrix} 2 & 5 \\ 4 & 10 \end{bmatrix}$$

The determinant of the first matrix is

$$\det(\mathbf{A}) = \begin{vmatrix} 1 & 2 \\ 3 & 4 \end{vmatrix} = 1(4) - 2(3) = 4 - 6 = -2$$

We see that $\det(\mathbf{A}) \neq 0$, so the matrix is non-singular and the inverse exists. To find $\mathbf{A}^{-1}$ we swap the diagonal elements, 1 and 4, change the sign of the off-diagonal elements, 2 and 3, and divide by the determinant, -2. Hence

$$\mathbf{A}^{-1} = -\frac{1}{2}\begin{bmatrix} 4 & -2 \\ -3 & 1 \end{bmatrix} = \begin{bmatrix} -2 & 1 \\ 3/2 & -1/2 \end{bmatrix}$$

Of course, if $\mathbf{A}^{-1}$ really is the inverse of $\mathbf{A}$, then $\mathbf{A}^{-1}\mathbf{A}$ and $\mathbf{A}\mathbf{A}^{-1}$ should multiply out to give $\mathbf{I}$. As a check:

$$\mathbf{A}^{-1}\mathbf{A} = \begin{bmatrix} -2 & 1 \\ 3/2 & -1/2 \end{bmatrix}\begin{bmatrix} 1 & 2 \\ 3 & 4 \end{bmatrix} = \begin{bmatrix} 1 & 0 \\ 0 & 1 \end{bmatrix} \quad \checkmark$$

$$\mathbf{A}\mathbf{A}^{-1} = \begin{bmatrix} 1 & 2 \\ 3 & 4 \end{bmatrix}\begin{bmatrix} -2 & 1 \\ 3/2 & -1/2 \end{bmatrix} = \begin{bmatrix} 1 & 0 \\ 0 & 1 \end{bmatrix} \quad \checkmark$$

To discover whether or not the second matrix

$$\mathbf{B} = \begin{bmatrix} 2 & 5 \\ 4 & 10 \end{bmatrix}$$

has an inverse, we need to find its determinant.

$$\det(\mathbf{B}) = \begin{vmatrix} 2 & 5 \\ 4 & 10 \end{vmatrix} = 2(10) - 5(4) = 20 - 20 = 0$$

We see that $\det(\mathbf{B}) = 0$, so this matrix is singular and the inverse does not exist.

Practice Problem

1. Find (where possible) the inverse of the following matrices. Are these matrices singular or non-singular?

$$\mathbf{A} = \begin{bmatrix} 6 & 4 \\ 1 & 2 \end{bmatrix} \quad \mathbf{B} = \begin{bmatrix} 6 & 4 \\ 3 & 2 \end{bmatrix}$$

One reason for calculating the inverse of a matrix is that it helps us to solve matrix equations in the same way that the reciprocal of a number is used to solve algebraic equations. We have already seen in Section 7.1 how to express a system of linear equations in matrix form. Any 2×2 system

$$ax + by = e$$
$$cx + dy = f$$

can be written as

$$\mathbf{A}\mathbf{x} = \mathbf{b}$$

where

$$\mathbf{A} = \begin{bmatrix} a & b \\ c & d \end{bmatrix} \quad \mathbf{x} = \begin{bmatrix} x \\ y \end{bmatrix} \quad \mathbf{b} = \begin{bmatrix} e \\ f \end{bmatrix}$$

The coefficient matrix, **A**, and right-hand-side vector, **b**, are assumed to be given and the problem is to determine the vector of unknowns, **x**. Multiplying both sides of

Ax = b

by $\mathbf{A}^{-1}$ gives

$$\mathbf{A}^{-1}(\mathbf{Ax}) = \mathbf{A}^{-1}\mathbf{b}$$
$$(\mathbf{A}^{-1}\mathbf{A})\mathbf{x} = \mathbf{A}^{-1}\mathbf{b} \quad \text{(associative property)}$$
$$\mathbf{Ix} = \mathbf{A}^{-1}\mathbf{b} \quad \text{(definition of an inverse)}$$
$$\mathbf{x} = \mathbf{A}^{-1}\mathbf{b} \quad \text{(Question 8(c) in Exercise 7.1*)}$$

The solution vector **x** can therefore be found simply by multiplying $\mathbf{A}^{-1}$ by **b**. We are assuming here that $\mathbf{A}^{-1}$ exists. If the coefficient matrix is singular, then the inverse cannot be found and the system of linear equations does not possess a unique solution; there are either infinitely many solutions or no solution.

Advice

These special cases are dealt with using the elimination method described in Section 1.4. You might find it instructive to revise both Sections 1.4 and 1.5.

The following example illustrates the use of inverses to find equilibrium prices in supply and demand models.

Example

The equilibrium prices P_1 and P_2 for two goods satisfy the equations

$$-4P_1 + P_2 = -13$$
$$2P_1 - 5P_2 = -7$$

Express this system in matrix form and hence find the values of P_1 and P_2.

Solution
Using the notation of matrices, the simultaneous equations

$$-4P_1 + P_2 = -13$$
$$2P_1 - 5P_2 = -7$$

can be written as

$$\begin{bmatrix} -4 & 1 \\ 2 & -5 \end{bmatrix}\begin{bmatrix} P_1 \\ P_2 \end{bmatrix} = \begin{bmatrix} -13 \\ -7 \end{bmatrix}$$

that is, as

Ax = b

where

$$\mathbf{A} = \begin{bmatrix} -4 & 1 \\ 2 & -5 \end{bmatrix} \quad \mathbf{x} = \begin{bmatrix} P_1 \\ P_2 \end{bmatrix} \quad \mathbf{b} = \begin{bmatrix} -13 \\ -7 \end{bmatrix}$$

The matrix $\mathbf{A}$ has determinant

$$\begin{vmatrix} -4 & 1 \\ 2 & -5 \end{vmatrix} = (-4)(-5) - (1)(2) = 20 - 2 = 18$$

To find $\mathbf{A}^{-1}$ we swap the diagonal elements, -4 and -5, change the sign of the off-diagonal elements, 1 and 2, and divide by the determinant, 18, to get

$$\mathbf{A}^{-1} = \frac{1}{18}\begin{bmatrix} -5 & -1 \\ -2 & -4 \end{bmatrix}$$

Finally, to calculate $\mathbf{x}$ we multiply $\mathbf{A}^{-1}$ by $\mathbf{b}$ to get

$$\mathbf{x} = \mathbf{A}^{-1}\mathbf{b} = \frac{1}{18}\begin{bmatrix} -5 & -1 \\ -2 & -4 \end{bmatrix}\begin{bmatrix} -13 \\ -7 \end{bmatrix} = \frac{1}{18}\begin{bmatrix} 72 \\ 54 \end{bmatrix} = \begin{bmatrix} 4 \\ 3 \end{bmatrix}$$

Hence $P_1 = 4$ and $P_2 = 3$.

Practice Problem

2. The equilibrium prices P_1 and P_2 for two goods satisfy the equations

    $$9P_1 + P_2 = 43$$
    $$2P_1 + 7P_2 = 57$$

    Express this system in matrix form and hence find the values of P_1 and P_2.

    [You have already solved this particular system in Practice Problem 4 of Section 1.5. You might like to compare the work involved in solving this system using the method of elimination described in Chapter 1 and the method based on matrix inverses considered here.]

Simultaneous equations also arise in macroeconomics.

The equilibrium levels of consumption, C, and income, Y, for the simple two-sector macroeconomic model satisfy the structural equations

$$Y = C + I*$$

$$C = aY + b$$

where a and b are parameters in the range $0 < a < 1$ and $b > 0$, and $I*$ denotes investment.

The reduced form of the structural equations for this simple model has already been found in Section 5.3. It is instructive to reconsider this problem using matrices. The objective is to express the endogenous variables, Y and C, in terms of the exogenous variable $I*$ and parameters a and b. The 'unknowns' of this problem are therefore Y and C, and we begin by rearranging the structural equations so that these variables appear on the left-hand sides. Subtracting C from both sides of

$$Y = C + I*$$

gives

$$Y - C = I* \tag{1}$$

and if we subtract aY from both sides of

$$C = aY + b$$

we get

$$-aY + C = b \tag{2}$$

(It is convenient to put the term involving Y first so that the variables align with those of equation (1).)

In matrix form, equations (1) and (2) become

$$\begin{bmatrix} 1 & -1 \\ -a & 1 \end{bmatrix} \begin{bmatrix} Y \\ C \end{bmatrix} = \begin{bmatrix} I^* \\ b \end{bmatrix}$$

that is,

$$\mathbf{Ax} = \mathbf{b}$$

where

$$\mathbf{A} = \begin{bmatrix} 1 & -1 \\ -a & 1 \end{bmatrix} \quad \mathbf{x} = \begin{bmatrix} Y \\ C \end{bmatrix} \quad \mathbf{b} = \begin{bmatrix} I^* \\ b \end{bmatrix}$$

The matrix $\mathbf{A}$ has determinant

$$\begin{vmatrix} 1 & -1 \\ -a & 1 \end{vmatrix} = 1(1) - (-1)(-a) = 1 - a$$

which is non-zero because $a < 1$.

To find $\mathbf{A}^{-1}$, we swap the diagonal elements, 1 and 1, change the sign of the off-diagonal elements, -1 and $-a$, and divide by the determinant, $1 - a$, to get

$$\mathbf{A}^{-1} = \frac{1}{1-a} \begin{bmatrix} 1 & 1 \\ a & 1 \end{bmatrix}$$

Finally, to determine $\mathbf{x}$ we multiply $\mathbf{A}^{-1}$ by $\mathbf{b}$ to get

$$\mathbf{x} = \mathbf{A}^{-1}\mathbf{b} = \frac{1}{1-a} \begin{bmatrix} 1 & 1 \\ a & 1 \end{bmatrix} \begin{bmatrix} I^* \\ b \end{bmatrix} = \frac{1}{1-a} \begin{bmatrix} I^* + b \\ aI^* + b \end{bmatrix}$$

Hence

$$Y = \frac{I^* + b}{1-a} \quad \text{and} \quad C = \frac{aI^* + b}{1-a}$$

The inverse matrix obviously provides a useful way of solving the structural equations of a macroeconomic model. In addition, the elements of the inverse matrix can be given an important economic interpretation. To see this, let us suppose that the investment I^* changes by an amount ΔI^* to become $I^* + \Delta I^*$, with the parameter b held fixed. The new values of Y and C are obtained by replacing I^* by $I^* + \Delta I^*$ in the expressions for Y and C, and are given by

$$\frac{I^* + \Delta I^* + b}{1-a} \quad \text{and} \quad \frac{a(I^* + \Delta I^*) + b}{1-a}$$

respectively. The change in the value of Y is therefore

$$\Delta Y = \frac{I^* + \Delta I^* + b}{1-a} - \frac{I^* + b}{1-a} = \left(\frac{1}{1-a} \right) \Delta I^*$$

and the change in the value of C is

$$\Delta C = \frac{a(I^* + \Delta I^*) + b}{1 - a} - \frac{aI^* + b}{1 - a} = \left(\frac{a}{1 - a}\right)\Delta I^*$$

In other words, the changes to Y and C are found by multiplying the change in I^* by

$$\frac{1}{1 - a} \quad \text{and} \quad \frac{a}{1 - a}$$

respectively. For this reason we call

$$\frac{1}{1 - a}$$

the investment multiplier for Y and

$$\frac{a}{1 - a}$$

the investment multiplier for C.

Now the inverse matrix is

$$\mathbf{A}^{-1} = \begin{bmatrix} \dfrac{1}{1 - a} & \dfrac{1}{1 - a} \\ \dfrac{a}{1 - a} & \dfrac{1}{1 - a} \end{bmatrix}$$

and we see that these multipliers are precisely the elements that appear in the first column. It is easy to show, using a similar argument, that the second column contains the multipliers for Y and C due to changes in the autonomous consumption, b. The four elements in the inverse matrix can thus be interpreted as follows:

$$\begin{matrix} & I^* & b \\ Y & \begin{bmatrix} \text{investment multiplier } Y & \text{autonomous consumption multiplier for } Y \\ \text{investment multiplier } C & \text{autonomous consumption multiplier for } C \end{bmatrix} \\ C & \end{matrix}$$

Practice Problem

3. The general linear supply and demand equations for a one-commodity market model are given by

$$P = aQ_S + b \qquad (a > 0, b > 0)$$
$$P = -cQ_D + d \qquad (c > 0, d > 0)$$

Show that in matrix notation the equilibrium price, P, and quantity, Q, satisfy

$$\begin{bmatrix} 1 & -a \\ 1 & c \end{bmatrix}\begin{bmatrix} P \\ Q \end{bmatrix} = \begin{bmatrix} b \\ d \end{bmatrix}$$

Solve this system to express P and Q in terms of a, b, c and d. Write down the multiplier for Q due to changes in b and deduce that an increase in b leads to a decrease in Q.

The concepts of determinant, inverse and identity matrices apply equally well to 3×3 matrices. The identity matrix is easily dealt with. It can be shown that the 3×3 identity matrix is

$$\mathbf{I} = \begin{bmatrix} 1 & 0 & 0 \\ 0 & 1 & 0 \\ 0 & 0 & 1 \end{bmatrix}$$

You are invited to check that, for any 3×3 matrix $\mathbf{A}$,

$$\mathbf{AI} = \mathbf{A} \quad \text{and} \quad \mathbf{IA} = \mathbf{A}$$

Before we can discuss the determinant and inverse of a 3×3 matrix, we need to introduce an additional concept known as a **cofactor**. Corresponding to each element a_{ij} of a matrix $\mathbf{A}$, there is a cofactor, A_{ij}. A 3×3 matrix has nine elements, so there are nine cofactors to be computed. The cofactor, A_{ij}, is defined to be the determinant of the 2×2 matrix obtained by deleting row i and column j of $\mathbf{A}$ (known as a **minor**), prefixed by a '+' or '−' sign according to the following pattern:

$$\begin{bmatrix} + & - & + \\ - & + & - \\ + & - & + \end{bmatrix}$$

For example, suppose we wish to calculate A_{23}, which is the cofactor associated with a_{23} in the matrix

$$\mathbf{A} = \begin{bmatrix} a_{11} & a_{12} & a_{13} \\ a_{21} & a_{22} & a_{23} \\ a_{31} & a_{32} & a_{33} \end{bmatrix}$$

The element a_{23} lies in the second row and third column. Consequently, we delete the second row and third column to produce the 2×2 matrix

$$\begin{bmatrix} a_{11} & a_{12} \\ a_{31} & a_{32} \end{bmatrix}$$

The cofactor, A_{23}, is the determinant of this 2×2 matrix prefixed by a '−' sign because from the pattern

$$\begin{bmatrix} + & - & + \\ - & + & - \\ + & - & + \end{bmatrix}$$

we see that a_{23} is in a minus position. In other words,

$$A_{3} = - \begin{vmatrix} a_{11} & a_{12} \\ a_{31} & a_{32} \end{vmatrix}$$
$$= -(a_{11}a_{32} - a_{12}a_{31})$$
$$= -a_{11}a_{32} + a_{12}a_{31}$$

The '±' pattern can also be worked out using $(-1)^{i+j}$ since when $i + j$ is even, $(-1)^{i+j} = +1$, and when $i + j$ is odd, $(-1)^{i+j} = -1$. For the cofactor A_{23} worked out previously, $(-1)^{2+3} = (-1)^{5} = -1$, confirming that the element a_{23} is in the minus position.

Example

Find all the cofactors of the matrix

$$\mathbf{A} = \begin{bmatrix} 2 & 4 & 1 \\ 4 & 3 & 7 \\ 2 & 1 & 3 \end{bmatrix}$$

Solution

Let us start in the top left-hand corner and work row by row. For cofactor A_{11}, the element $a_{11} = 2$ lies in the first row and first column, so we delete this row and column to produce the 2×2 matrix

$$\begin{bmatrix} 3 & 7 \\ 1 & 3 \end{bmatrix}$$

Cofactor A_{11} is the determinant of this 2×2 matrix, prefixed by a '+' sign because from the pattern

$$\begin{bmatrix} + & - & + \\ - & + & - \\ + & - & + \end{bmatrix}$$

we see that a_{11} is in a plus position. Hence

$$
\begin{aligned}
A_{11} &= + \begin{vmatrix} 3 & 7 \\ 1 & 3 \end{vmatrix} \\
&= +(3(3) - 7(1)) \\
&= 9 - 7 \\
&= 2
\end{aligned}
$$

For cofactor A_{12}, the element $a_{12} = 4$ lies in the first row and second column, so we delete this row and column to produce the 2×2 matrix

$$\begin{bmatrix} 4 & 7 \\ 2 & 3 \end{bmatrix}$$

Cofactor A_{12} is the determinant of this 2×2 matrix, prefixed by a '−' sign because from the pattern

$$\begin{bmatrix} + & - & + \\ - & + & - \\ + & - & + \end{bmatrix}$$

we see that a_{12} is in a minus position. Hence

$$
\begin{aligned}
A_{12} &= - \begin{vmatrix} 4 & 7 \\ 2 & 3 \end{vmatrix} \\
&= -(4(3) - 7(2)) \\
&= -(12 - 14) \\
&= 2
\end{aligned}
$$

→

We can continue in this way to find the remaining cofactors:

$$A_{13} = + \begin{vmatrix} 4 & 3 \\ 2 & 1 \end{vmatrix} = -2$$

$$A_{21} = - \begin{vmatrix} 4 & 1 \\ 1 & 3 \end{vmatrix} = -11$$

$$A_{22} = + \begin{vmatrix} 2 & 1 \\ 2 & 3 \end{vmatrix} = 4$$

$$A_{23} = - \begin{vmatrix} 2 & 4 \\ 2 & 1 \end{vmatrix} = 6$$

$$A_{31} = + \begin{vmatrix} 4 & 1 \\ 3 & 7 \end{vmatrix} = 25$$

$$A_{32} = - \begin{vmatrix} 2 & 1 \\ 4 & 7 \end{vmatrix} = -10$$

$$A_{33} = + \begin{vmatrix} 2 & 4 \\ 4 & 3 \end{vmatrix} = -10$$

Practice Problem

4. Find all the cofactors of the matrix

$$\mathbf{A} = \begin{bmatrix} 1 & 3 & 3 \\ 1 & 4 & 3 \\ 1 & 3 & 4 \end{bmatrix}$$

We are now in a position to describe how to calculate the determinant and inverse of a 3×3 matrix. The determinant is found by multiplying the elements in any one row or column by their corresponding cofactors and adding together. It does not matter which row or column is chosen; exactly the same answer is obtained in each case. If we expand along the first row of the matrix

$$\mathbf{A} = \begin{bmatrix} a_{11} & a_{12} & a_{13} \\ a_{21} & a_{22} & a_{23} \\ a_{31} & a_{32} & a_{33} \end{bmatrix}$$

we get

$$\det(\mathbf{A}) = a_{11}A_{11} + a_{12}A_{12} + a_{13}A_{13}$$

Similarly, if we expand down the second column, we get

$$\det(\mathbf{A}) = a_{12}A_{12} + a_{22}A_{22} + a_{32}A_{32}$$

The fact that we get the same answer irrespective of the row and column that we use for expansion is an extremely useful property. It provides us with an obvious check on our calculations. Also, there are occasions when it is more convenient to expand along certain rows or columns than others.

Example

Find the determinants of the following matrices:

$$\mathbf{A} = \begin{bmatrix} 2 & 4 & 1 \\ 4 & 3 & 7 \\ 2 & 1 & 3 \end{bmatrix} \quad \text{and} \quad \mathbf{B} = \begin{bmatrix} 10 & 7 & 5 \\ 0 & 2 & 0 \\ 2 & 7 & 3 \end{bmatrix}$$

Solution

We have already calculated all nine cofactors of the matrix

$$\mathbf{A} = \begin{bmatrix} 2 & 4 & 1 \\ 4 & 3 & 7 \\ 2 & 1 & 3 \end{bmatrix}$$

in the previous example. It is immaterial which row or column we use. Let us choose the second row. The cofactors corresponding to the three elements 4, 3, 7 in the second row were found to be $-11, 4, 6$, respectively. Consequently, if we expand along this row, we get

$$\begin{vmatrix} 2 & 4 & 1 \\ 4 & 3 & 7 \\ 2 & 1 & 3 \end{vmatrix} = 4(-11) + 3(4) + 7(6) = 10$$

As a check, let us also expand down the third column. The elements in this column are 1, 7, 3 with cofactors $-2, 6, -10$, respectively. Hence, if we multiply each element by its cofactor and add, we get

$$1(-2) + 7(6) + 3(-10) = 10$$

which is the same as before. If you are interested, you might like to confirm for yourself that the value of 10 is also obtained when expanding along rows 1 and 3, and down columns 1 and 2.

The matrix

$$\mathbf{B} = \begin{bmatrix} 10 & 7 & 5 \\ 0 & 2 & 0 \\ 2 & 7 & 3 \end{bmatrix}$$

is entirely new to us, so we have no prior knowledge about its cofactors. In general, we need to evaluate all three cofactors in any one row or column to find the determinant of a 3×3 matrix. In this case, however, we can be much lazier. Observe that all but one of the elements in the second row are zero, so when we expand along this row, we get

$$\begin{aligned} \det(\mathbf{B}) &= b_{21}B_{21} + b_{22}B_{22} + b_{23}B_{23} \\ &= 0B_{21} + 2B_{22} + 0B_{23} \\ &= 2B_{22} \end{aligned}$$

Hence B_{22} is the only cofactor that we need to find. This corresponds to the element in the second row and second column, so we delete this row and column to produce the 2×2 matrix

$$\begin{bmatrix} 10 & 5 \\ 2 & 3 \end{bmatrix}$$

The element b_{22} is in a plus position, so

$$B_{22} = + \begin{vmatrix} 10 & 5 \\ 2 & 3 \end{vmatrix} = 20$$

Hence,

$$\det(\mathbf{B}) = 2B_{22} = 2 \times 20 = 40$$

Practice Problem

5. Find the determinants of

$$\mathbf{A} = \begin{bmatrix} 1 & 3 & 3 \\ 1 & 4 & 3 \\ 1 & 3 & 4 \end{bmatrix} \quad \text{and} \quad \mathbf{B} = \begin{bmatrix} 270 & -372 & 0 \\ 552 & 201 & 0 \\ 999 & 413 & 0 \end{bmatrix}$$

[Hint: you might find your answer to Practice Problem 4 useful when calculating the determinant of **A**.]

The inverse of the 3 × 3 matrix

$$\mathbf{A} = \begin{bmatrix} a_{11} & a_{12} & a_{13} \\ a_{21} & a_{22} & a_{23} \\ a_{31} & a_{32} & a_{33} \end{bmatrix}$$

is given by

$$\mathbf{A}^{-1} = \frac{1}{|\mathbf{A}|} \begin{bmatrix} A_{11} & A_{21} & A_{31} \\ A_{12} & A_{22} & A_{32} \\ A_{13} & A_{23} & A_{33} \end{bmatrix}$$

Once the cofactors of **A** have been found, it is easy to construct $\mathbf{A}^{-1}$. We first stack the cofactors in their natural positions

$$\begin{bmatrix} A_{11} & A_{12} & A_{13} \\ A_{21} & A_{22} & A_{23} \\ A_{31} & A_{32} & A_{33} \end{bmatrix}$$

called the adjugate matrix

Secondly, we take the transpose to get

$$\begin{bmatrix} A_{11} & A_{21} & A_{31} \\ A_{12} & A_{22} & A_{32} \\ A_{13} & A_{23} & A_{33} \end{bmatrix}$$

called the adjoint matrix

Finally, we multiply by the scalar

$$\frac{1}{|\mathbf{A}|}$$

to get

$$\mathbf{A}^{-1} = \frac{1}{|\mathbf{A}|} \begin{bmatrix} A_{11} & A_{21} & A_{31} \\ A_{12} & A_{22} & A_{32} \\ A_{13} & A_{23} & A_{33} \end{bmatrix}$$

divide each element by the determinant

The last step is impossible if

$$|\mathbf{A}| = 0$$

because we cannot divide by zero. Under these circumstances, the inverse does not exist and the matrix is singular.

Advice

It is a good idea to check that no mistakes have been made by verifying that

$$\mathbf{A}^{-1}\mathbf{A} = \mathbf{I} \quad \text{and} \quad \mathbf{A}\mathbf{A}^{-1} = \mathbf{I}$$

Example

Find the inverse of

$$\mathbf{A} = \begin{bmatrix} 2 & 4 & 1 \\ 4 & 3 & 7 \\ 2 & 1 & 3 \end{bmatrix}$$

Solution

The cofactors of this particular matrix have already been calculated as

$$A_{11} = 2, \qquad A_{12} = 2, \qquad A_{13} = -2$$
$$A_{21} = -11, \quad A_{22} = 4, \qquad A_{23} = 6$$
$$A_{31} = 25, \qquad A_{32} = -10, \quad A_{33} = -10$$

Stacking these numbers in their natural positions gives the adjugate matrix

$$\begin{bmatrix} 2 & 2 & -2 \\ -11 & 4 & 6 \\ 25 & -10 & -10 \end{bmatrix}$$

The adjoint matrix is found by transposing this to get

$$\begin{bmatrix} 2 & -11 & -25 \\ 2 & 4 & -10 \\ -2 & 6 & -10 \end{bmatrix}$$

In the previous example the determinant was found to be 10, so

$$\mathbf{A}^{-1} = \frac{1}{10} \begin{bmatrix} 2 & -11 & 25 \\ 2 & 4 & -10 \\ -2 & 6 & -10 \end{bmatrix} = \begin{bmatrix} 1/5 & -11/10 & 5/2 \\ 1/5 & 2/5 & -1 \\ -1/5 & 3/5 & -1 \end{bmatrix}$$

As a check:

$$\mathbf{A}^{-1}\mathbf{A} = \begin{bmatrix} 1/5 & -11/10 & 5/2 \\ 1/5 & 2/5 & -1 \\ -1/5 & 3/5 & -1 \end{bmatrix}\begin{bmatrix} 2 & 4 & 1 \\ 4 & 3 & 7 \\ 2 & 1 & 3 \end{bmatrix} = \begin{bmatrix} 1 & 0 & 0 \\ 0 & 1 & 0 \\ 0 & 0 & 1 \end{bmatrix} = \mathbf{I} \checkmark$$

$$\mathbf{A}\mathbf{A}^{-1} = \begin{bmatrix} 2 & 4 & 1 \\ 4 & 3 & 7 \\ 2 & 1 & 3 \end{bmatrix}\begin{bmatrix} 1/5 & -11/10 & 5/2 \\ 1/5 & 2/5 & -1 \\ -1/5 & 3/5 & -1 \end{bmatrix} = \begin{bmatrix} 1 & 0 & 0 \\ 0 & 1 & 0 \\ 0 & 0 & 1 \end{bmatrix} = \mathbf{I} \checkmark$$

Practice Problem

6. Find (where possible) the inverses of

$$\mathbf{A} = \begin{bmatrix} 1 & 3 & 3 \\ 1 & 4 & 3 \\ 1 & 3 & 4 \end{bmatrix} \quad \text{and} \quad \mathbf{B} = \begin{bmatrix} 270 & -372 & 0 \\ 552 & 201 & 0 \\ 999 & 413 & 0 \end{bmatrix}$$

[Hint: you might find your answers to Practice Problems 4 and 5 useful.]

Inverses of 3×3 matrices can be used to solve systems of three linear equations in three unknowns. The general system

$$a_{11}x + a_{12}y + a_{13}z = b_1$$
$$a_{21}x + a_{22}y + a_{23}z = b_2$$
$$a_{31}x + a_{32}y + a_{33}z = b_3$$

can be written as

$$\mathbf{Ax} = \mathbf{b}$$

where

$$\mathbf{A} = \begin{bmatrix} a_{11} & a_{12} & a_{13} \\ a_{21} & a_{22} & a_{23} \\ a_{31} & a_{32} & a_{33} \end{bmatrix} \quad \mathbf{x} = \begin{bmatrix} x \\ y \\ z \end{bmatrix} \quad \mathbf{b} = \begin{bmatrix} b_1 \\ b_2 \\ b_3 \end{bmatrix}$$

The vector of unknowns, $\mathbf{x}$, can be found by inverting the coefficient matrix, $\mathbf{A}$, and multiplying by the right-hand-side vector, $\mathbf{b}$, to get

$$\mathbf{x} = \mathbf{A}^{-1}\mathbf{b}$$

Example

Determine the equilibrium prices of three interdependent commodities that satisfy

$$2P_1 + 4P_2 + P_3 = 77$$
$$4P_1 + 3P_2 + 7P_3 = 114$$
$$2P_1 + P_2 + 3P_3 = 48$$

Solution

In matrix notation this system of equations can be written as

$$\mathbf{Ax} = \mathbf{b}$$

where

$$\mathbf{A} = \begin{bmatrix} 2 & 4 & 1 \\ 4 & 3 & 7 \\ 2 & 1 & 3 \end{bmatrix} \quad \mathbf{x} = \begin{bmatrix} P_1 \\ P_2 \\ P_3 \end{bmatrix} \quad \mathbf{b} = \begin{bmatrix} 77 \\ 114 \\ 48 \end{bmatrix}$$

The inverse of the coefficient matrix has already been found in the previous example and is

$$\mathbf{A}^{-1} = \begin{bmatrix} 1/5 & -11/10 & 5/2 \\ 1/5 & 2/5 & -1 \\ -1/5 & 3/5 & -1 \end{bmatrix}$$

so

$$\begin{bmatrix} P_1 \\ P_2 \\ P_3 \end{bmatrix} = \begin{bmatrix} 1/5 & -11/10 & 5/2 \\ 1/5 & 2/5 & -1 \\ -1/5 & 3/5 & -1 \end{bmatrix} \begin{bmatrix} 77 \\ 114 \\ 48 \end{bmatrix} = \begin{bmatrix} 10 \\ 13 \\ 5 \end{bmatrix}$$

The equilibrium prices are therefore given by

$$P_1 = 10, \quad P_2 = 13, \quad P_3 = 5$$

Practice Problem

7. Determine the equilibrium prices of three interdependent commodities that satisfy

$$P_1 + 3P_2 + 3P_3 = 32$$
$$P_1 + 4P_2 + 3P_3 = 37$$
$$P_1 + 3P_2 + 4P_3 = 35$$

[Hint: you might find your answer to Practice Problem 6 useful.]

Throughout this section, we have concentrated on 2×2 and 3×3 matrices. The method described can be extended to larger matrices of order $n \times n$. The cofactor A_{ij} would be the determinant of the $(n - 1) \times (n - 1)$ matrix left when row i and column j are deleted prefixed by $(-1)^{i+j}$. However, the cofactor approach is very inefficient. The amount of working rises dramatically as n increases, making this method inappropriate for large matrices. The preferred method for solving simultaneous equations is based on the elimination idea that we described in Section 1.4. This is easily programmed, and a computer can solve large systems of equations in a matter of seconds.

Key Terms

Cofactor The cofactor of the element, a_{ij}, is the determinant of the matrix left when row i and column j are deleted, multiplied by $+1$ or -1, depending on whether $i + j$ is even or odd, respectively.

Determinant A determinant can be expanded as the sum of the products of the elements in any one row or column and their respective cofactors.

Identity matrix An $n \times n$ matrix, $\mathbf{I}$, in which every element on the main diagonal is 1 and the other elements are all 0. If $\mathbf{A}$ is any $n \times n$ matrix, then $\mathbf{AI} = \mathbf{A} = \mathbf{IA}$.

Inverse matrix A matrix, $\mathbf{A}^{-1}$, with the property that $\mathbf{A}^{-1}\mathbf{A} = \mathbf{I} = \mathbf{AA}^{-1}$.

Minor The name given to the cofactor before the '$\pm$' pattern is imposed.

Non-singular matrix A square matrix with a non-zero determinant.

Singular matrix A square matrix with a zero determinant. A singular matrix fails to possess an inverse.

Square matrix A matrix with the same number of rows as columns.

Exercise 7.2

1. **(a)** Find the determinant of

   (i) $\begin{bmatrix} 2 & 7 \\ 1 & 4 \end{bmatrix}$ (ii) $\begin{bmatrix} 5 & 6 \\ 3 & 4 \end{bmatrix}$ (iii) $\begin{bmatrix} -2 & -10 \\ 1 & 4 \end{bmatrix}$ (iv) $\begin{bmatrix} -6 & -4 \\ -8 & -7 \end{bmatrix}$

   (b) Find the inverse of each matrix in part (a).

2. Let

   $$\mathbf{A} = \begin{bmatrix} 2 & 1 \\ 5 & 1 \end{bmatrix} \quad \text{and} \quad \mathbf{B} = \begin{bmatrix} 1 & 0 \\ 2 & 4 \end{bmatrix}$$

   (1) Find

   (a) $|\mathbf{A}|$ **(b)** $|\mathbf{B}|$ **(c)** $|\mathbf{AB}|$

   Do you notice any connection between $|\mathbf{A}|$, $|\mathbf{B}|$ and $|\mathbf{AB}|$?

   (2) Find

   (a) $\mathbf{A}^{-1}$ **(b)** $\mathbf{B}^{-1}$ **(c)** $(\mathbf{AB})^{-1}$

   Do you notice any connection between $\mathbf{A}^{-1}$, $\mathbf{B}^{-1}$ and $(\mathbf{AB})^{-1}$?

3. If the matrices

   $$\begin{bmatrix} 2 & -1 \\ 3 & a \end{bmatrix} \quad \text{and} \quad \begin{bmatrix} 2 & b \\ 3 & -4 \end{bmatrix}$$

   are singular, find the values of a and b.

4. Evaluate the matrix product, $\begin{bmatrix} 5 & -3 \\ -10 & 8 \end{bmatrix}\begin{bmatrix} 8 & 3 \\ 10 & 5 \end{bmatrix}$.

   Hence, or otherwise, write down the inverse of $\begin{bmatrix} 8 & 3 \\ 10 & 5 \end{bmatrix}$.

5. Use matrices to solve the following pairs of simultaneous equations:

(a) $3x + 4y = -1$ (b) $x + 3y = 8$

      $5x - y = 6$ $4x - y = 6$

6. The demand and supply functions for two interdependent goods are given by

$$Q_{D_1} = 50 - 2P_1 + P_2$$
$$Q_{D_2} = 10 + P_1 - 4P_2$$
$$Q_{S_1} = -20 + P_1$$
$$Q_{S_2} = -10 + 5P_2$$

(a) Show that the equilibrium prices satisfy

$$\begin{bmatrix} 3 & -1 \\ -1 & 9 \end{bmatrix} \begin{bmatrix} P_1 \\ P_2 \end{bmatrix} = \begin{bmatrix} 70 \\ 20 \end{bmatrix}$$

(b) Find the inverse of the 2×2 matrix in part (a) and hence find the equilibrium prices.

7. If a, b and k are non-zero, show that

(a) each of these 2×2 matrices is singular:

(i) $\begin{bmatrix} a & 0 \\ b & 0 \end{bmatrix}$ (ii) $\begin{bmatrix} a & b \\ ka & kb \end{bmatrix}$ (iii) $\begin{bmatrix} a & b \\ \dfrac{1}{b} & \dfrac{1}{a} \end{bmatrix}$

(b) each of these 2×2 matrices is non-singular:

(i) $\begin{bmatrix} a & b \\ 0 & k \end{bmatrix}$ (ii) $\begin{bmatrix} 0 & a \\ -a & 0 \end{bmatrix}$ (iii) $\begin{bmatrix} a & b \\ -b & a \end{bmatrix}$

Exercise 7.2*

1. If the matrices

$$\mathbf{A} = \begin{bmatrix} 1 & 2 \\ a & b \end{bmatrix} \quad \text{and} \quad \mathbf{B} = \begin{bmatrix} a & 4 \\ 2 & b \end{bmatrix}$$

are both singular, determine all possible values of a and b.

2. (a) If

$$\mathbf{A} = \begin{bmatrix} a & b \\ c & d \end{bmatrix} \quad \text{and} \quad \mathbf{B} = \begin{bmatrix} e & f \\ g & h \end{bmatrix}$$

work out the matrix product, $\mathbf{AB}$.

(b) Hence, show that $\det(\mathbf{AB}) = \det(\mathbf{A}) \times \det(\mathbf{B})$

(c) If **A** is singular and **B** is non-singular, what, if anything, can be deduced about **AB**? Give a brief reason for your answer.

3. Which one of the following matrices has an inverse which is not listed?

$$\mathbf{A} = \begin{bmatrix} 1 & 1 \\ 1 & 0 \end{bmatrix}, \quad \mathbf{B} = \begin{bmatrix} 1 & 0 \\ 0 & 1 \end{bmatrix}, \quad \mathbf{C} = \begin{bmatrix} 0 & 1 \\ 1 & -1 \end{bmatrix}, \quad \mathbf{D} = \begin{bmatrix} 1 & -1 \\ -1 & 0 \end{bmatrix}, \quad \mathbf{E} = \begin{bmatrix} -1 & 0 \\ 0 & 1 \end{bmatrix}$$

4. Find the determinant of the matrix

$$\begin{bmatrix} 5 & -2 & 3 \\ 4 & -1 & -5 \\ 6 & 7 & 9 \end{bmatrix}$$

5. Find the cofactor, A_{23}, of the matrix

$$\mathbf{A} = \begin{bmatrix} 5 & -2 & 7 \\ 6 & 1 & -9 \\ 4 & -3 & 8 \end{bmatrix}$$

6. Find (where possible) the inverse of the matrices

$$\mathbf{A} = \begin{bmatrix} 2 & 1 & -1 \\ 1 & 3 & 2 \\ -1 & 2 & 1 \end{bmatrix} \quad \text{and} \quad \mathbf{B} = \begin{bmatrix} 1 & 4 & 5 \\ 2 & 1 & 3 \\ -1 & 3 & 2 \end{bmatrix}$$

Are these matrices singular or non-singular?

7. For the commodity market

$$C = aY + b \quad (0\, a < 1, b > 0)$$
$$I = cr + d \quad (c < 0, d > 0)$$

For the money market

$$M_S = M_S^*$$
$$M_D = k_1 Y + k_2 r + k_3 \ (k_1, k_3 > 0, k_2 < 0)$$

Show that when the commodity and money markets are both in equilibrium, the income, Y, and interest rate, r, satisfy the matrix equation

$$\begin{bmatrix} 1 - a & -c \\ k_1 & k_2 \end{bmatrix} \begin{bmatrix} Y \\ r \end{bmatrix} = \begin{bmatrix} b + d \\ M_s^* - k_3 \end{bmatrix}$$

and solve this system for Y and r. Write down the multiplier for r due to changes in M_S^* and deduce that interest rates fall as the money supply grows.

8. Find the determinant of the matrix

$$\mathbf{A} = \begin{bmatrix} 2 & 1 & 3 \\ 1 & 0 & a \\ 3 & 1 & 4 \end{bmatrix}$$

in terms of a. Deduce that this matrix is non-singular provided $a \neq 1$ and find $\mathbf{A}^{-1}$ in this case.

9. Find the inverse of

$$\begin{bmatrix} -2 & 2 & 1 \\ 1 & -5 & -1 \\ 2 & -1 & -6 \end{bmatrix}$$

Hence find the equilibrium prices of the three-commodity market model given in Question 6 of Exercise 1.5*.

10. Find the inverse of the matrix

$$\mathbf{A} = \begin{bmatrix} 6 & 3 & a \\ 5 & 4 & 2 \\ 7 & 2 & 3 \end{bmatrix}$$

in terms of a.

For what value of a will simultaneous equations of the form

$$6x + 3y + az = b$$
$$5x + 4y + 2z = c$$
$$7x + 2y + 3z = d$$

fail to possess a unique solution?

11. (a) Multiply out the brackets in the expression $(a - b)(a - c)(c - b)$.

(b) Show that the determinant of the matrix

$$\mathbf{A} = \begin{bmatrix} 1 & 1 & 1 \\ a & b & c \\ a^2 & b^2 & c^2 \end{bmatrix}$$

is $(a - b)(a - c)(c - b)$ and deduce that the simultaneous equations

$$x + y + z = l$$
$$ax + by + cz = m$$
$$a^2x + b^2y + c^2z = n$$

have a unique solution provided, a, b, and c are distinct.

SECTION 7.3
Cramer's rule

Objectives

At the end of this section you should be able to:

- Appreciate the limitations of using inverses to solve systems of linear equations.
- Use Cramer's rule to solve systems of linear equations.
- Apply Cramer's rule to analyse static macroeconomic models.
- Apply Cramer's rule to solve two-country trading models.

In Section 7.2 we described the mechanics of calculating the determinant and inverse of 2×2 and 3×3 matrices. These concepts can be extended to larger systems in an obvious way, although the amount of effort needed rises dramatically as the size of the matrix increases. For example, consider the work involved in solving the system

$$\begin{bmatrix} 1 & 0 & 2 & 3 \\ -1 & 5 & 4 & 1 \\ 0 & 7 & -3 & 6 \\ 2 & 4 & 5 & 1 \end{bmatrix} \begin{bmatrix} x_1 \\ x_2 \\ x_3 \\ x_4 \end{bmatrix} = \begin{bmatrix} -1 \\ 1 \\ -24 \\ 15 \end{bmatrix}$$

using the method of matrix inversion. In this case the coefficient matrix has order 4×4 and so has 16 elements. Corresponding to each of these elements is a cofactor. This is defined to be the 3×3 determinant obtained by deleting the row and column containing the element, prefixed by a '+' or '−' according to the following pattern:

$$\begin{bmatrix} + & - & + & - \\ - & + & - & + \\ + & - & + & - \\ - & + & - & - \end{bmatrix}$$

Determinants are found by expanding along any one row or column, and inverses are found by stacking cofactors as before. However, given that there are 16 cofactors to be calculated, even the most enthusiastic student is likely to view the prospect with some trepidation. To make matters worse, it frequently happens in economics that only a few of the variables x_i are actually needed. For instance, it could be that the variable x_3 is the only one of interest. Under these circumstances, it is clearly wasteful expending a large amount of effort calculating the inverse matrix, particularly since the values of the remaining variables, x_1, x_2 and x_4, are not required.

In this section we describe an alternative method that finds the value of one variable at a time. This new method requires less effort if only a selection of the variables is required. It is known as Cramer's rule and makes use of matrix determinants. **Cramer's rule** for solving any $n \times n$ system, $\mathbf{Ax} = \mathbf{b}$, states that the ith variable, x_i, can be found from

$$x_i = \frac{\det(\mathbf{A}_i)}{\det(\mathbf{A})}$$

where $\mathbf{A}_i$ is the $n \times n$ matrix found by replacing the ith column of $\mathbf{A}$ by the right-hand-side vector $\mathbf{b}$. To understand this, consider the simple 2×2 system

$$\begin{bmatrix} 7 & 2 \\ 4 & 5 \end{bmatrix} \begin{bmatrix} x_1 \\ x_2 \end{bmatrix} = \begin{bmatrix} -6 \\ 12 \end{bmatrix}$$

and suppose that we need to find the value of the second variable, x_2, say. According to Cramer's rule, this is given by

$$x_2 = \frac{\det(\mathbf{A}_2)}{\det(\mathbf{A})}$$

where

$$\mathbf{A} = \begin{bmatrix} 7 & 2 \\ 4 & 5 \end{bmatrix} \quad \text{and} \quad \mathbf{A}_2 = \begin{bmatrix} 7 & -6 \\ 4 & 12 \end{bmatrix}$$

Notice that x_2 is given by the quotient of two determinants. The one on the bottom is that of the original coefficient matrix $\mathbf{A}$. The one on the top is that of the matrix found from $\mathbf{A}$ by replacing the second column (since we are trying to find the second variable) by the right-hand-side vector

$$\begin{bmatrix} -6 \\ 12 \end{bmatrix}$$

In this case the determinants are easily worked out to get

$$\det(\mathbf{A}_2) = \begin{vmatrix} 7 & -6 \\ 4 & 12 \end{vmatrix} = 7(12) - (-6)(4) = 108$$

$$\det(\mathbf{A}) = \begin{vmatrix} 7 & 2 \\ 4 & 5 \end{vmatrix} = 7(5) - 2(4) = 27$$

Hence

$$x_2 = \frac{108}{27} = 4$$

Example

Solve the system of equations

$$\begin{bmatrix} 1 & 2 & 3 \\ -4 & 1 & 6 \\ 2 & 7 & 5 \end{bmatrix} \begin{bmatrix} x_1 \\ x_2 \\ x_3 \end{bmatrix} = \begin{bmatrix} 9 \\ -9 \\ 13 \end{bmatrix}$$

using Cramer's rule to find x_1.

Solution

Cramer's rule gives

$$x_1 = \frac{\det(\mathbf{A}_1)}{\det(\mathbf{A})}$$

where $\mathbf{A}$ is the coefficient matrix

$$\begin{bmatrix} 1 & 2 & 3 \\ -4 & 1 & 6 \\ 2 & 7 & 5 \end{bmatrix}$$

and $\mathbf{A}_1$ is constructed by replacing the first column of $\mathbf{A}$ by the right-hand-side vector

$$\begin{bmatrix} 9 \\ -9 \\ 13 \end{bmatrix}$$

which gives

$$\mathbf{A}_1 = \begin{bmatrix} 9 & 2 & 3 \\ -9 & 1 & 6 \\ 13 & 7 & 5 \end{bmatrix}$$

If we expand each of these determinants along the top row, we get

$$\det(\mathbf{A}_1) = \begin{vmatrix} 9 & 2 & 3 \\ -9 & 1 & 6 \\ 13 & 7 & 5 \end{vmatrix}$$

$$= 9\begin{vmatrix} 1 & 6 \\ 7 & 5 \end{vmatrix} - 2\begin{vmatrix} -9 & 6 \\ 13 & 5 \end{vmatrix} + 3\begin{vmatrix} -9 & 1 \\ 13 & 7 \end{vmatrix}$$

$$= 9(-37) - 2(-123) + 3(-76)$$

$$= -315$$

and

$$\det(\mathbf{A}) = \begin{vmatrix} 1 & 2 & 3 \\ -4 & 1 & 6 \\ 2 & 7 & 5 \end{vmatrix}$$

$$= 1\begin{vmatrix} 1 & 6 \\ 7 & 5 \end{vmatrix} - 2\begin{vmatrix} -4 & 6 \\ 2 & 5 \end{vmatrix} + 3\begin{vmatrix} -4 & 1 \\ 2 & 7 \end{vmatrix}$$

$$= 1(-37) - 2(-32) + 3(-30)$$

$$= -63$$

Hence

$$x_1 = \frac{\det(\mathbf{A}_1)}{\det(\mathbf{A})} = \frac{-315}{-63} = 5$$

Practice Problem

1. **(a)** Solve the system of equations

$$2x_1 + 4x_2 = 16$$
$$3x_1 - 5x_2 = -9$$

using Cramer's rule to find x_2.

(b) Solve the system of equations

$$4x_1 + x_2 + 3x_3 = 8$$
$$-2x_1 + 5x_2 + x_3 = 4$$
$$3x_1 + 2x_2 + 4x_3 = 9$$

using Cramer's rule to find x_3.

We now illustrate the use of Cramer's rule to analyse economic models. We begin by considering the three-sector macroeconomic model involving government activity.

Advice

The incorporation of government expenditure and taxation into the model has already been considered in Section 5.3, and you might like to compare the working involved in the two approaches.

Example

The equilibrium levels of income, Y, disposable income, Y_d, and taxation, T, for a three-sector macroeconomic model satisfy the structural equations

$$Y = C + I^* + G^*$$
$$C = aY_d + b \qquad (0 < a < 1, b > 0)$$
$$Y_d = Y - T$$
$$T = tY + T^* \qquad (t < 1, T^* > 0)$$

Show that this system can be written as $\mathbf{Ax} = \mathbf{b}$, where

$$\mathbf{A} = \begin{bmatrix} 1 & -1 & 0 & 0 \\ 0 & 1 & -a & 0 \\ -1 & 0 & 1 & 1 \\ -t & 0 & 0 & 1 \end{bmatrix} \quad \mathbf{x} = \begin{bmatrix} Y \\ C \\ Y_d \\ T \end{bmatrix} \quad \mathbf{b} = \begin{bmatrix} I^* + G^* \\ b \\ 0 \\ T^* \end{bmatrix}$$

Use Cramer's rule to solve this system for Y.

Solution

In this model the endogenous variables are Y, C, Y_d and T, so we begin by manipulating the equations so that these variables appear on the left-hand sides. Moreover, since the vector of 'unknowns', $\mathbf{x}$, is given to be

$$\begin{bmatrix} Y \\ C \\ Y_d \\ T \end{bmatrix}$$

we need to arrange the equations so that the variables appear in the order Y, C, Y_d, T. For example, in the case of the third equation

$$Y_d = Y - T$$

we first subtract Y and add T to both sides to get

$$Y_d - Y + T = 0$$

but then reorder the terms to obtain

$$-Y + Y_d + T = 0$$

Performing a similar process with the remaining equations gives

$$\begin{aligned} Y - C &= I^* + G^* \\ C - aY_d &= b \\ -Y + Y_d + T &= 0 \\ -tY + T &= T^* \end{aligned}$$

so that in matrix form they become

$$\begin{bmatrix} 1 & -1 & 0 & 0 \\ 0 & 1 & -a & 0 \\ -1 & 0 & 1 & 1 \\ -t & 0 & 0 & 1 \end{bmatrix} \begin{bmatrix} Y \\ C \\ Y_d \\ T \end{bmatrix} = \begin{bmatrix} I^* + G^* \\ b \\ 0 \\ T^* \end{bmatrix}$$

The variable Y is the first, so Cramer's rule gives

$$Y = \frac{\det(\mathbf{A_1})}{\det(\mathbf{A})}$$

where

$$\mathbf{A_1} = \begin{bmatrix} I^* + G^* & -1 & 0 & 0 \\ b & 1 & -a & 0 \\ 0 & 0 & 1 & 1 \\ T^* & 0 & 0 & 1 \end{bmatrix}$$

and

$$\mathbf{A} = \begin{bmatrix} 1 & -1 & 0 & 0 \\ 0 & 1 & -a & 0 \\ -1 & 0 & 1 & 1 \\ -t & 0 & 0 & 1 \end{bmatrix}$$

The calculations are fairly easy to perform, in spite of the fact that both matrices are 4×4, because they contain a high proportion of zeros. Expanding $\mathbf{A}_1$ along the first row gives

$$\det(\mathbf{A}_1) = (I^* + G^*) \begin{vmatrix} 1 & -a & 0 \\ 0 & 1 & 1 \\ 0 & 0 & 1 \end{vmatrix} - (-1) \begin{vmatrix} b & -a & 0 \\ 0 & 1 & 1 \\ T^* & 0 & 1 \end{vmatrix}$$

along the first row the pattern is + − + −

Notice that there is no point in evaluating the last two cofactors in the first row, since the corresponding elements are both zero.

For the first of these 3×3 determinants we choose to expand down the first column, since this column has only one non-zero element. This gives

$$\begin{vmatrix} 1 & -a & 0 \\ 0 & 1 & 1 \\ 0 & 0 & 1 \end{vmatrix} = (1) \begin{vmatrix} 1 & 1 \\ 0 & 1 \end{vmatrix} = 1$$

It is immaterial which row or column we choose for the second 3×3 determinant, since they all contain two non-zero elements. Working along the first row gives

$$\begin{vmatrix} b & -a & 0 \\ 0 & 1 & 1 \\ T^* & 0 & 1 \end{vmatrix} = b \begin{vmatrix} 1 & 1 \\ 0 & 1 \end{vmatrix} - (-a) \begin{vmatrix} 0 & 1 \\ T^* & 1 \end{vmatrix} = b - aT^*$$

Hence

$$\det(\mathbf{A}_1) = (I^* + G^*)(1) - (-1)(b - aT^*) = I^* + G^* + b - aT^*$$

A similar process can be applied to matrix $\mathbf{A}$. Expanding along the top row gives

$$\det(\mathbf{A}) = (1) \begin{vmatrix} 1 & -a & 0 \\ 0 & 1 & 1 \\ 0 & 0 & 1 \end{vmatrix} - (-1) \begin{vmatrix} 0 & -a & 0 \\ -1 & 1 & 1 \\ -t & 0 & 1 \end{vmatrix}$$

The first of these 3×3 determinants has already been found to be 1 in our previous calculations. The second 3×3 determinant is new, and if we expand this along the first row, we get

$$\begin{vmatrix} 0 & -a & 0 \\ -1 & 1 & 1 \\ -t & 0 & 1 \end{vmatrix} = -(-a) \begin{vmatrix} -1 & 1 \\ -t & 1 \end{vmatrix} = a(-1 + t)$$

Hence

$$\det(\mathbf{A}) = (1)(1) - (-1)a(-1 + t) = 1 - a + at$$

Finally, we use Cramer's rule to deduce that

$$Y = \frac{I^* + G^* + b - aT^*}{1 - a + at}$$

Practice Problem

2. Use Cramer's rule to solve the following system of equations for Y_d.

$$
\begin{bmatrix}
1 & -1 & 0 & 0 \\
0 & 1 & -a & 0 \\
-1 & 0 & 1 & 1 \\
-t & 0 & 0 & 1
\end{bmatrix}
\begin{bmatrix}
Y \\
C \\
Y_d \\
T
\end{bmatrix}
=
\begin{bmatrix}
I^* + G^* \\
b \\
0 \\
T^*
\end{bmatrix}
$$

[Hint: the determinant of the coefficient matrix has already been evaluated in the previous worked example.]

We conclude this section by introducing foreign trade into our model. In all of our previous macroeconomic models we have implicitly assumed that the behaviour of different countries has no effect on the national income of the other countries. In reality this is clearly not the case, and we now investigate how the economies of trading nations interact. To simplify the situation we shall ignore all government activity and suppose that there are just two countries, labelled 1 and 2, trading with each other but not with any other country. We shall use an obvious subscript notation so that Y_1 denotes the national income of country 1, C_2 denotes the consumption of country 2 and so on. In the absence of government activity, the equation defining equilibrium in country i is

$$Y_i = C_i + I_i + X_i - M_i$$

where I_i is the investment of country i, X_i is the exports of country i and M_i is the imports of country i. As usual, we shall assume that I_i is determined exogenously and takes a known value I_i^*.

Given that there are only two countries, which trade between themselves, the exports of one country must be the same as the imports of the other. In symbols we write

$$X_1 = M_2 \quad \text{and} \quad X_2 = M_1$$

We shall assume that imports are a fraction of national income, so that

$$M_i = m_i Y_i$$

where the marginal propensity to import, m_i, satisfies $0 < m_i < 1$.

Once expressions for C_i and M_i are given, we can derive a system of two simultaneous equations for the two unknowns, Y_1 and Y_2, which can be solved either by using Cramer's rule or by using matrix inverses.

Example

The equations defining a model of two trading nations are given by

$$Y_1 = C_1 + I_1^* + X_1 - M_1 \quad Y_2 = C_2 + I_2^* + X_2 - M_2$$
$$C_1 = 0.8Y_1 + 200 \qquad\qquad C_2 = 0.9Y_2 + 100$$
$$M_1 = 0.2Y_1 \qquad\qquad\qquad M_2 = 0.1Y_2$$

Express this system in matrix form and hence write Y_1 in terms of I_1^* and I_2^*.

Write down the multiplier for Y_1 due to changes in I_2^* and hence describe the effect on the national income of country 1 due to changes in the investment in country 2.

Solution

In this problem there are six equations for six endogenous variables, Y_1, C_1, M_1 and Y_2, C_2, M_2. However, rather than working with a 6×6 matrix, we perform some preliminary algebra to reduce it to only two equations in two unknowns. To do this we substitute the expressions for C_1 and M_1 into the first equation to get

$$Y_1 = 0.8Y_1 + 200 + I_1^* + X_1 - 0.2Y_1$$

Also, since $X_1 = M_2 = 0.1Y_2$, this becomes

$$Y_1 = 0.8Y_1 + 200 + I_1^* + 0.1Y_2 - 0.2Y_1$$

which rearranges as

$$0.4Y_1 - 0.1Y_2 = 200 + I_1^*$$

A similar procedure applied to the second set of equations for country 2 gives

$$-0.2Y_1 + 0.2Y_2 = 100 + I_2^*$$

In matrix form this pair of equations can be written as

$$\begin{bmatrix} 0.4 & -0.1 \\ -0.2 & 0.2 \end{bmatrix} \begin{bmatrix} Y_1 \\ Y_2 \end{bmatrix} = \begin{bmatrix} 200 + I_1^* \\ 100 + I_2^* \end{bmatrix}$$

Cramer's rule gives

$$Y_1 = \frac{\begin{vmatrix} 200 + I_1^* & -0.1 \\ 100 + I_2^* & 0.2 \end{vmatrix}}{\begin{vmatrix} 0.4 & -0.1 \\ -0.2 & 0.2 \end{vmatrix}} = \frac{50 + 0.2I_1^* + 0.1I_2^*}{0.06}$$

To find the multiplier for Y_1 due to changes in I_2^* we consider what happens to Y_1 when I_2^* changes by an amount ΔI_2^*. The new value of Y_1 is obtained by replacing I_2^* by $I_2^* + \Delta I_2^*$ to get

$$\frac{50 + 0.2I_1^* + 0.1(I_2^* + \Delta I_2^*)}{0.06}$$

so the corresponding change in Y_1 is

$$\Delta Y_1 = \frac{50 + 0.2I_1^* + 0.1(I_2^* + \Delta I_2^*)}{0.06} - \frac{50 + 0.2I_1^* + 0.1I_2^*}{0.06}$$

$$= \frac{0.1}{0.06} \Delta I_2^*$$

$$= \frac{5}{3} \Delta I_2^*$$

We deduce that any increase in investment in country 2 leads to an increase in the national income in country 1. Moreover, because $^5/_3 > 1$, the increase in national income is greater than the increase in investment.

Practice Problem

3. The equations defining a model of two trading nations are given by

$$Y_1 = C_1 + I_1^* + X_1 - M_1 \quad Y_2 = C_2 + I_2^* + X_2 - M_2$$
$$C_1 = 0.7Y_1 + 50 \qquad\qquad C_2 = 0.8Y_2 + 100$$
$$I_1^* = 200 \qquad\qquad\qquad I_2^* = 300$$
$$M_1 = 0.3Y_1 \qquad\qquad\quad M_2 = 0.1Y_2$$

Express this system in matrix form and hence find the values of Y_1 and Y_2. Calculate the balance of payments between these countries.

Key Term

Cramer's rule   A method of solving simultaneous equations, $Ax = b$, by the use of determinants. The ith variable x_i can be computed using $\det(A_i)/\det(A)$ where A_i is the determinant of the matrix obtained from A by replacing the ith column by b.

Exercise 7.3

1. **(a)** Evaluate each of these determinants.

   (i) $\begin{vmatrix} 4 & 2 \\ 1 & 3 \end{vmatrix}$ (ii) $\begin{vmatrix} -7 & 2 \\ 5 & 3 \end{vmatrix}$ (iii) $\begin{vmatrix} 4 & -7 \\ 1 & 5 \end{vmatrix}$

   (b) Use your answers to part (a) to write down the solution of the simultaneous equations

   $$4x + 2x = -7$$
   $$x + 3y = 5$$

2. Use Cramer's rule to find the value of x which satisfies each of the following pairs of simultaneous equations:

   (a) $7x - 3y = 4$ **(b)** $-3x + 4y = 5$ **(c)** $x + 4y = 9$
   $\quad\;\; 2x + 5y = 7$ $\qquad\quad\;\; 2x + 5y = 12$ $\qquad\quad\; 2x - 7y = 3$

3. Use Cramer's rule to find the value of y which satisfies each of the following pairs of simultaneous equations:

   (a) $x + 3y = 9$ **(b)** $5x - 2y = 7$ **(c)** $2x + 3y = 7$
   $\quad\;\, 2x - 4y = -2$ $\qquad\;\; 2x + 3y = -1$ $\qquad\;\; 3x - 5y = 1$

4. Use Cramer's rule to solve the following sets of simultaneous equations:

   (a) $4x + 3y = 1$ **(b)** $4x + 3y = 1$ **(c)** $4x + 3y = -2$
   $\quad\;\; 2x + 5y = -3$ $\qquad\quad 2x + 5y = 11$ $\qquad\quad 2x + 5y = -36$

5. The demand and supply functions for two interdependent goods are given by

$$Q_{D_1} = 400 - 5P_1 - 3P_2$$
$$Q_{D_2} = 300 - 2P_1 - 3P_2$$
$$Q_{S_1} = -60 + 3P_1$$
$$Q_{S_2} = -100 + 2P_2$$

   (a) Show that the equilibrium prices satisfy

$$\begin{bmatrix} 8 & 3 \\ 2 & 5 \end{bmatrix} \begin{bmatrix} P_1 \\ P_2 \end{bmatrix} = \begin{bmatrix} 460 \\ 400 \end{bmatrix}$$

   (b) Use Cramer's rule to find the equilibrium price of good 1.

6. Consider the two-sector macroeconomic model

$$Y = C + I^*$$
$$C = aY + b$$

   (a) Express this system in the form

   $$\mathbf{Ax = b}$$

   where $\mathbf{x} = \begin{pmatrix} Y \\ C \end{pmatrix}$ and $\mathbf{A}$ and $\mathbf{b}$ are 2×2 and 2×1 matrices to be stated.

   (b) Use Cramer's rule to solve this system for C.

7. A total revenue function may be modelled by $TR = aQ + bQ^2$.

   (a) If $TR = 14$ when $Q = 2$ and $TR = 9$ when $Q = 3$, write down a pair of simultaneous equations for the parameters a and b.

   (b) Use Cramer's rule to solve the equations in part (a) and hence find the total revenue when $Q = 1$.

Exercise 7.3*

1. Use Cramer's rule to solve

   (a) $\begin{bmatrix} 3 & -2 & 4 \\ 1 & 4 & 0 \\ 5 & 7 & 0 \end{bmatrix} \begin{bmatrix} x \\ y \\ z \end{bmatrix} = \begin{bmatrix} 11 \\ 9 \\ 19 \end{bmatrix}$

   for x.

   (b) $\begin{bmatrix} 4 & 5 & 0 \\ -1 & 2 & 3 \\ 6 & -1 & 2 \end{bmatrix} \begin{bmatrix} x \\ y \\ z \end{bmatrix} = \begin{bmatrix} 0 \\ 19 \\ -30 \end{bmatrix}$

   for y.

(c) $\begin{bmatrix} 4 & -8 & 2 \\ 1 & 0 & 6 \\ -3 & 6 & 2 \end{bmatrix} \begin{bmatrix} x \\ y \\ z \end{bmatrix} = \begin{bmatrix} -43 \\ 0 \\ 34 \end{bmatrix}$

for z.

2. The matrix $\begin{bmatrix} 1 & -1 & 0 & 0 \\ 0 & 1 & -a & 0 \\ -1 & 0 & 1 & 1 \\ -t & 0 & 0 & 1 \end{bmatrix}$ has determinant, $1 - a + at$.

Use Cramer's rule to solve the following system of equations for C:

$$\begin{bmatrix} 1 & -1 & 0 & 0 \\ 0 & 1 & -a & 0 \\ -1 & 0 & 1 & 1 \\ -t & 0 & 0 & 1 \end{bmatrix} \begin{bmatrix} Y \\ C \\ Y_d \\ T \end{bmatrix} = \begin{bmatrix} I^* + G^* \\ b \\ 0 \\ T^* \end{bmatrix}$$

3. Consider the three-sector macroeconomic model:

$Y = C + I^* + G^*$

$C = a(Y - T) + b$

$T = tY + T^*$

(a) Express this system in the form

$\mathbf{Ax = b}$

where $\mathbf{x} = \begin{bmatrix} Y \\ C \\ T \end{bmatrix}$ and $\mathbf{A}$ and $\mathbf{b}$ are 3×3 and 3×1 matrices to be stated.

(b) Use Cramer's rule to solve this system for Y.

4. Consider the macroeconomic model defined by

$Y = C + I^* + G^* + X^* - M$

$C = aY + b$ $\qquad (0 < a < 1, b > 0)$

$M = mY + M^*$ $\qquad (0 < m < 1, M^* > 0)$

Show that this system can be written as $\mathbf{Ax = b}$, where

$$\mathbf{A} = \begin{bmatrix} 1 & -1 & 1 \\ -a & 1 & 0 \\ -m & 0 & 1 \end{bmatrix} \quad \mathbf{x} = \begin{bmatrix} Y \\ C \\ M \end{bmatrix} \quad \mathbf{b} = \begin{bmatrix} I^* + G^* + X^* \\ b \\ M^* \end{bmatrix}$$

Use Cramer's rule to show that

$$Y = \frac{b + I^* + G^* + X^* - M^*}{1 - a + m}$$

Write down the autonomous investment multiplier for Y and deduce that Y increases as I^* increases.

5. Consider the macroeconomic model defined by

national income: $Y = C + I + G^*$ $(G^* > 0)$

consumption: $C = aY + b$ $(0 < a < 1, b > 0)$

investment: $I = cr + d$ $(c < 0, d > 0)$

money supply: $M_s^* = k_1Y + k_2r$ $(k_1 > 0, k_2 < 0, M_s^* > 0)$

Show that this system can be written as $\mathbf{Ax} = \mathbf{b}$, where

$$\mathbf{A} = \begin{bmatrix} 1 & -1 & -1 & 0 \\ -a & 1 & 0 & 0 \\ 0 & 0 & 1 & -c \\ k_1 & 0 & 0 & k_2 \end{bmatrix} \quad \mathbf{x} = \begin{bmatrix} Y \\ C \\ I \\ r \end{bmatrix} \quad \mathbf{b} = \begin{bmatrix} G^* \\ b \\ d \\ M_s^* \end{bmatrix}$$

Use Cramer's rule to show that

$$r = \frac{M_s^*(1 - a) - k_1(b + d + G^*)}{k_2(1 - a) + ck_1}$$

Write down the government expenditure multiplier for r and deduce that the interest rate, r, increases as government expenditure, G^*, increases.

6. The equations defining a model of two trading nations are given by

$Y_1 = C_1 + I_1^* + X_1 - M_1$ $Y_2 = C_2 + I_2^* + X_2 - M_2$

$C_1 = 0.6Y_1 + 50$ $C_2 = 0.8Y_2 + 80$

$M_1 = 0.2Y_1$ $M_2 = 0.1Y_2$

If $I_2^* = 70$, find the value of I_1^* if the balance of payments is zero.

[Hint: construct a system of three equations for the three unknowns, Y_1, Y_2 and I_1^*.]

7. The equations defining a general model of two trading countries are given by

$Y_1 = C_1 + I_1^* + X_1 - M_1$ $Y_2 = C_2 + I_2^* + X_2 - M_2$

$C_1 = a_1Y_1 + b_1$ $C_2 = a_2Y_2 + b_2$

$M_1 = m_1Y_1$ $M_2 = m_2Y_2$

where $0 < a_i < 1$, $b_i > 0$ and $0 < m_i < 1$ $(i = 1, 2)$. Express this system in matrix form and use Cramer's rule to solve this system for Y_1. Write down the multiplier for Y_1 due to changes in I_2^* and hence give a general description of the effect on the national income of one country due to a change in investment in the other.

Formal mathematics

In Chapter 3 we introduced the sigma notation as a convenient shorthand for the summation of series. This notation has an obvious use in matrices where we naturally identify the elements of a matrix using a double subscript notation. In particular it is possible to formally define the operation of matrix multiplication. To motivate this, consider forming the matrix product $C = AB$ where A and B are general 2×3 and 3×3 matrices with elements, a_{ij} and b_{ij}, respectively:

$$\begin{bmatrix} c_{11} & c_{12} & c_{13} \\ c_{21} & c_{22} & c_{23} \end{bmatrix} = \begin{bmatrix} a_{11} & a_{12} & a_{13} \\ a_{21} & a_{22} & a_{23} \end{bmatrix} \begin{bmatrix} b_{11} & b_{12} & b_{13} \\ b_{21} & b_{22} & b_{23} \\ b_{31} & b_{32} & b_{33} \end{bmatrix}$$

If we equate entries in the first row, first column, we get:

$$c_{11} = a_{11}b_{11} + a_{12}b_{21} + a_{13}b_{31}$$

In sigma notation this could be written as $c_{11} = \sum_{k=1}^{3} a_{1k}b_{k1}$

Similarly, for the second row, third column, we get:

$$c_{23} = a_{21}b_{13} + a_{22}b_{23} + a_{23}b_{33}$$

which can be written as $c_{23} = \sum_{k=1}^{3} a_{2k}b_{k3}$.

In general, if A is an $m \times s$ matrix and B is an $s \times n$ matrix, then $C = AB$ is defined to be an $m \times n$ matrix with

$$c_{ij} = a_{i1}b_{1j} + a_{i2}b_{2j} + a_{i3}b_{3j} + \ldots + a_{is}b_{sj} = \sum_{k=1}^{s} a_{ik}b_{kj}$$

Multiple choice questions

Question 1

If **A**, **B**, **C** and **D** are 3×4, 2×3, 4×2 and 3×3 matrices, which one of the following matrix calculations is possible?

A. $(\mathbf{AC})^{-1}$

B. $\mathbf{DA} + \mathbf{BD}$

C. $\mathbf{D}^{-1}\mathbf{B}$

D. $5\mathbf{CB} - 4\mathbf{D}^{-1}$

E. $\mathbf{BD} + (\mathbf{AC})^{\mathrm{T}}$

Question 2

Find the inverse of the matrix $\begin{bmatrix} 5 & 3 \\ 2 & 1 \end{bmatrix}$.

A. $\begin{bmatrix} -5 & 3 \\ 2 & -1 \end{bmatrix}$

B. $\begin{bmatrix} 1 & -3 \\ -2 & 5 \end{bmatrix}$

C. $\begin{bmatrix} -1 & -3 \\ -2 & -5 \end{bmatrix}$

D. $\begin{bmatrix} -1 & 3 \\ 2 & -5 \end{bmatrix}$

E. $\begin{bmatrix} -1 & 2 \\ 3 & -5 \end{bmatrix}$

Question 3

For what value of a does the following matrix fail to possess an inverse?

$$\begin{bmatrix} -1 & 2 & 1 \\ -2 & 3 & a \\ 0 & 4 & 6 \end{bmatrix}$$

A. $7/2$

B. $3/2$

C. $17/2$

D. $23/2$

E. $1/2$

Question 4

Find the inverse of $\begin{bmatrix} 3 & 3 & -1 \\ 5 & 4 & 0 \\ 0 & 2 & -3 \end{bmatrix}$

A. $\begin{bmatrix} 12 & -7 & -3 \\ -15 & 9 & -5 \\ -10 & 6 & 3 \end{bmatrix}$

B. $\begin{bmatrix} 12 & -15 & -10 \\ -7 & 9 & 6 \\ -3 & -5 & 3 \end{bmatrix}$

C. $\begin{bmatrix} 12 & -7 & -4 \\ -15 & 9 & 5 \\ -10 & 6 & 3 \end{bmatrix}$

D. $\begin{bmatrix} -12 & 7 & 4 \\ 15 & -9 & -5 \\ 10 & -6 & -3 \end{bmatrix}$

E. $\begin{bmatrix} -12 & 15 & 10 \\ 7 & -9 & -6 \\ 4 & -5 & -3 \end{bmatrix}$

Question 5

The IS-LM model for a two-sector economy is given by

$$0.25Y + 10r - 1040 = 0$$
$$0.10Y - 36r - 256 = 0$$

where Y and r denote the equilibrium values of national income and interest rate, respectively.

If these equations are written in the form $\mathbf{A}x = b$ where $x = \begin{bmatrix} Y \\ r \end{bmatrix}$, work out the inverse of $\mathbf{A}$ and deduce the equilibrium value of r.

A. $\mathbf{A}^{-1} = \begin{bmatrix} 36 & -10 \\ -0.001 & 0.025 \end{bmatrix}, r = 5.36$

B. $\mathbf{A}^{-1} = \begin{bmatrix} 3.6 & 1 \\ 0.01 & -0.025 \end{bmatrix}, r = 2.8$

C. $\mathbf{A}^{-1} = \begin{bmatrix} 3.6 & 1 \\ 0.01 & -0.025 \end{bmatrix}, r = 4$

D. $\mathbf{A}^{-1} = \begin{bmatrix} 3.6 & -1 \\ 0.001 & 0.025 \end{bmatrix}, r = 7.44$

E. $\mathbf{A}^{-1} = \begin{bmatrix} 3.6 & -1 \\ 0.001 & 0.025 \end{bmatrix}, r = 3.4$

Question 6

If $\mathbf{A} = \begin{bmatrix} 1 & -3 \\ 2 & 1 \\ 0 & -3 \end{bmatrix}$ and $\mathbf{B} = \begin{bmatrix} 3 & 4 & 1 \\ 0 & -1 & 2 \end{bmatrix}$, work out $\mathbf{BA}$.

A. $\begin{bmatrix} 11 & -8 \\ -2 & -6 \end{bmatrix}$

B. $\begin{bmatrix} 11 & -8 \\ -2 & -7 \end{bmatrix}$

C. $\begin{bmatrix} 11 & 8 \\ -2 & -7 \end{bmatrix}$

D. $\begin{bmatrix} 9 & -8 \\ -2 & -7 \end{bmatrix}$

E. $\begin{bmatrix} 11 & -8 \\ 1 & -7 \end{bmatrix}$

Question 7

If $\mathbf{A} = \begin{bmatrix} 3 \\ 2 \\ 0 \\ -1 \end{bmatrix}$ and $\mathbf{B} = [1 \quad 0 \quad -2 \quad 3]$, work out $\mathbf{B}^{\mathrm{T}}\mathbf{A}^{\mathrm{T}}$.

A. $\begin{bmatrix} 3 & 2 & 0 & -1 \\ 0 & 0 & 0 & 0 \\ -6 & -4 & 0 & 2 \\ 9 & 6 & 0 & -3 \end{bmatrix}$

B. $[3 \quad 0 \quad 0 \quad -3]$

C. $[0]$

D. $\begin{bmatrix} 3 & 0 & -6 & 9 \\ 2 & 0 & -4 & 6 \\ 0 & 0 & 0 & 0 \\ -1 & 0 & 2 & -3 \end{bmatrix}$

E. $\begin{bmatrix} 3 \\ 0 \\ 0 \\ -3 \end{bmatrix}$

Question 8

In a macroeconomic model, $\mathbf{A}x = b$ where

$$\mathbf{A} = \begin{bmatrix} 1 & -1 & 0 & 0 \\ 0 & 1 & -a & 0 \\ -1 & 0 & 1 & 1 \\ -t & 0 & 0 & 1 \end{bmatrix}, x = \begin{bmatrix} Y \\ C \\ Y_d \\ T \end{bmatrix}, b = \begin{bmatrix} I^* + G^* \\ b \\ 0 \\ T^* \end{bmatrix} \text{ and } \det(\mathbf{A}) = 1 - a + at.$$

Use Cramer's rule to find C.

A. $\dfrac{b - aT^* - a(I^* + G^*)(1 - t)}{1 - a + at}$

B. $\dfrac{b - aT^* - a(I^* + G^*)(t - 1)}{1 - a + at}$

C. $\dfrac{b + aT^* + a(I^* + G^*)(t - 1)}{1 - a + at}$

D. $\dfrac{b - aT^* - at(I^* + G^*)}{1 - a + at}$

E. $\dfrac{(b - aT^*)t - a(I^* + G^*)}{1 - a + at}$

Question 9

Which one of these 2×2 matrices is not an inverse of any other matrix in the list?

A. $\begin{bmatrix} 4 & 5 \\ 5 & 6 \end{bmatrix}$

B. $\begin{bmatrix} -5 & 6 \\ 4 & -5 \end{bmatrix}$

C. $\begin{bmatrix} -5 & -6 \\ -4 & -5 \end{bmatrix}$

D. $\begin{bmatrix} 4 & -5 \\ -5 & 6 \end{bmatrix}$

E. $\begin{bmatrix} -6 & 5 \\ 5 & -4 \end{bmatrix}$

Question 10

If $\mathbf{A} = \begin{bmatrix} a & b \\ c & d \end{bmatrix}$ and $\mathbf{B} = \begin{bmatrix} p & q \\ r & s \end{bmatrix}$ work out $\mathbf{A}^{\mathrm{T}}\mathbf{B}$

A. $\begin{bmatrix} ap + bs & aq + br \\ cp + ds & cq + dr \end{bmatrix}$

B. $\begin{bmatrix} ap + br & aq + bs \\ cp + dr & cq + ds \end{bmatrix}$

C. $\begin{bmatrix} ap + cr & aq + cs \\ bp + dr & bq + ds \end{bmatrix}$

D. $\begin{bmatrix} ar + cp & aq + cs \\ br + dp & bq + ds \end{bmatrix}$

E. $\begin{bmatrix} ap + cr & as + cq \\ bp + dr & bs + dq \end{bmatrix}$

Examination questions

Question 1

If $\mathbf{A} = \begin{bmatrix} 1 & -2 \\ 0 & 4 \end{bmatrix}$ and $\mathbf{B} = \begin{bmatrix} 6 & -3 \\ -4 & 2 \end{bmatrix}$, work out, where possible:

(a) $\mathbf{A}^{\mathrm{T}} + 2\mathbf{B}$ (b) $\mathbf{AB}$ (c) $\mathbf{A}^{-1}$ (d) $\mathbf{B}^{-1}\mathbf{A}$

Question 2

The demand and supply functions of a good are given by

$$P + 4Q_{\mathrm{D}} = 61$$
$$3P - Q_{\mathrm{S}} = 14$$

Find the equilibrium price and quantity using

(a) the inverse matrix method;

(b) Cramer's rule.

Question 3

$$\mathbf{A} = \begin{bmatrix} 3 & -1 & 0 & 6 \\ -4 & 5 & 2 & 2 \end{bmatrix}, \mathbf{B} = \begin{bmatrix} 4 & -3 \\ 2 & 5 \end{bmatrix}, \mathbf{C} = \begin{bmatrix} 1 & 6 \\ 3 & 0 \\ -2 & 4 \\ -1 & -2 \end{bmatrix}$$

(a) Work out each of the following, where possible:

    (i) $\mathbf{A} + \mathbf{C}$ (ii) $2\mathbf{A} - \mathbf{C}^{\mathrm{T}}$ (iii) $\mathbf{AB}$ (iv) $\mathbf{BA}$

(b) Solve each of the following equations for $\mathbf{X}$:

    (i) $2\mathbf{X} + \mathbf{A}^{\mathrm{T}} = \mathbf{C}$ (ii) $\mathbf{BX} = \mathbf{A}$

Question 4

(a) The demand and supply functions of two interdependent commodities are given by

$$Q_{\mathrm{D}_1} = 40 - 3P_1 - P_2$$
$$Q_{\mathrm{D}_2} = 30 - 4P_1 - 0.5P_2$$
$$Q_{\mathrm{S}_1} = -6 + 5P_1$$
$$Q_{\mathrm{S}_2} = -5 + 2P_2$$

Show that the equilibrium prices satisfy

$$\begin{bmatrix} 8 & 1 \\ 4 & 2.5 \end{bmatrix} \begin{bmatrix} P_1 \\ P_2 \end{bmatrix} = \begin{bmatrix} 46 \\ 35 \end{bmatrix}$$

Solve this system by calculating the inverse of the coefficient matrix.

(b) Use Cramer's rule to find the value of y in the system:

$$\begin{bmatrix} 3 & 5 & 4 \\ 0 & 2 & 7 \\ 1 & 3 & -2 \end{bmatrix} \begin{bmatrix} x \\ y \\ z \end{bmatrix} = \begin{bmatrix} -12 \\ 0 \\ -20 \end{bmatrix}$$

Question 5

Airme and Blight are the only two airlines allowed to operate on the same route. The market share of regular business travellers changes from month to month. Airme retains four-fifths of its customers whilst Blight retains only three-quarters of its customers.

(a) If A_t and B_t, denote the number of customers who fly Airme and Blight in month t explain why

$$\begin{bmatrix} A_t \\ B_t \end{bmatrix} = \begin{bmatrix} 0.8 & 0.25 \\ 0.2 & 0.75 \end{bmatrix} \begin{bmatrix} A_{t-1} \\ B_{t-1} \end{bmatrix}$$

(b) If the number of customers who fly Airme and Blight in the first month are 10 000 and 16 000, respectively use matrix multiplication to work out the number of people who fly Airme

(i) one month later;

(ii) three months later.

(c) If the number of customers flying on Airme and Blight in any month had been 7300 and 5400, respectively, work out how many people flew by each airline the previous month.

Question 6

(a) Find the inverse of the following matrix, in terms of a.

$$\begin{bmatrix} 4 & -2 & -1 \\ -2 & 5 & 1 \\ -4 & 1 & a \end{bmatrix}$$

For what value of a is this matrix singular?

(b) Consider the three-commodity market model defined by:

$$Q_{S_1} = 2P_1 - 7; \quad Q_{D_1} = -2P_1 + 2P_2 + P_3 + 16$$
$$Q_{S_2} = 4P_2 - 4; \quad Q_{D_2} = 2P_1 - P_2 - P_3 + 8$$
$$Q_{S_3} = 2P_3 - 3; \quad Q_{D_3} = 4P_1 - P_2 - 4P_3 + 4$$

By making use of your answer to part (a), or otherwise, find the equilibrium prices.

Question 7

The supply and demand equations of two interdependent commodities are

$$Q_{S_1} = 4(P_1 - t) - 5, \qquad Q_{D_1} = 27 - 3P_1 + P_2$$
$$Q_{S_2} = P_2 - 3, \qquad Q_{D_2} = 25 + 2P_1 - 3P_2$$

where t is the unit tax imposed on good 1.

Show that the market equilibrium prices satisfy a matrix equation of the form $\mathbf{A}x = b$ where $x = \begin{bmatrix} P_1 \\ P_2 \end{bmatrix}$.

Find the inverse of $\mathbf{A}$ and hence solve this system to find P_1 and P_2.

Write down the taxation multiplier for P_2.

Question 8

Consider the following macroeconomic model:

$$Y = C + I^* + G^* + X^* - M^* \quad \text{(equilibrium of national income)}$$
$$C = aY_d + b \quad \text{(consumption; } 0 < a < 1; b > 0)$$
$$T = tY \quad \text{(taxation; } 0 < t < 1)$$

where I^*, G^*, X^*, M^* and Y_d denote investment, government expenditure, exports, imports and disposable income, respectively.

(a) Show that this system can be expressed as $\mathbf{A}x = b$ where

$$\mathbf{A} = \begin{bmatrix} 1 & -1 & 0 \\ -a & 1 & a \\ -t & 0 & 1 \end{bmatrix}, b = \begin{bmatrix} I + G^* + X^* - M^* \\ b \\ 0 \end{bmatrix} \text{ and } x = \begin{bmatrix} Y \\ C \\ T \end{bmatrix}.$$

(b) Show that the determinant of $\mathbf{A}$ is $1 - a(1 - t)$

(c) By using Cramer's rule, or otherwise, show that $Y = \dfrac{b + I^* + G^* + X^* - M^*}{1 - a(1 - t)}$.

(d) Write down the autonomous investment multiplier for Y and deduce that the change in national income exceeds any increase in investment.

(e) Work out the marginal propensity to consume multiplier for Y and hence state the direction of change in Y due to an increase in a.

Question 9

The trace of a 2×2 matrix $\mathbf{A} = \begin{bmatrix} a & b \\ c & d \end{bmatrix}$ is defined to be $\text{tr}(\mathbf{A}) = a + d$.

(a) Work out the trace of $\begin{bmatrix} 7 & 4 \\ -2 & -5 \end{bmatrix}$

(b) Prove that if $\mathbf{A}$ and $\mathbf{B}$ are any 2×2 matrices, then $\text{tr}(\alpha\mathbf{A} + \beta\mathbf{B}) = \alpha\,\text{tr}(\mathbf{A}) + \beta\,\text{tr}(\mathbf{B})$ for any numbers α and β.

(c) Decide whether following results are true or false for general 2×2 matrices. If the result is true, prove it, and if the result is false, provide a counter-example.

(i) $\text{tr}(\mathbf{A}^{-1}) = (\text{tr}(\mathbf{A}))^{-1}$

(ii) $\text{tr}(\mathbf{A}\mathbf{B}) = \text{tr}(\mathbf{B}\mathbf{A})$

CHAPTER 8
Linear Programming

Several methods were described in Chapter 5 for optimising functions of two variables subject to constraints. In economics not all relationships between variables are represented by equations, and we now consider the case when the constraints are given by inequalities. Provided the function to be optimised is linear and the inequalities are all linear, the problem is said to be one of linear programming. For simplicity we concentrate on problems involving just two unknowns and describe a graphical method of solution.

There are two sections, which should be read in the order that they appear. Section 8.1 describes the basic mathematical techniques and considers special cases when problems have either no solution or infinitely many solutions. Section 8.2 shows how an economic problem, initially given in words, can be expressed as a linear programming problem and hence solved.

The material in this chapter can be read at any stage, since it requires only an understanding of how to sketch a straight line on graph paper.

Graphical solution of linear programming problems

Objectives

At the end of this section you should be able to:

- Identify the region defined by a linear inequality.
- Sketch the feasible region defined by simultaneous linear inequalities.
- Solve linear programming problems graphically.
- Appreciate that a linear programming problem may have infinitely many solutions.
- Appreciate that a linear programming problem may have no finite solution.

In this and the following section we show you how to set up and solve linear programming problems. This process falls naturally into two separate phases. The first phase concerns problem formulation; a problem, initially given in words, is expressed in mathematical symbols. The second phase involves the actual solution of such a problem. Experience indicates that students usually find the first phase the more difficult. For this reason, we postpone consideration of problem formulation until Section 8.2 and begin by investigating techniques for their mathematical solution.

Advice

You may like to glance at one or two of the examples given in Section 8.2 now to get a feel for the type of problem that can be solved using these techniques.

Before you can consider linear programming it is essential that you know how to sketch linear inequalities. In Section 1.1 we discovered that a linear equation of the form

$$dx + ey = f$$

can be represented by a straight line on graph paper. We can give a similar graphical interpretation for linear inequalities involving two variables when the equals sign is replaced by one of

$<$ (less than)
$\leq$ (less than or equal to)
$>$ (greater than)
$\geq$ (greater than or equal to)

To illustrate this, consider the simple inequality

$$y \geq x$$

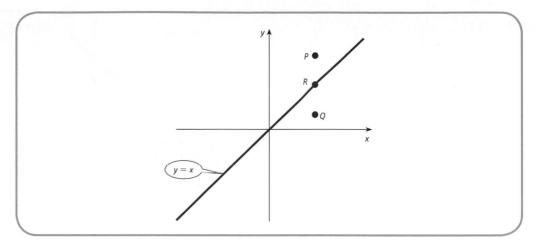

Figure 8.1

We would like to identify those points with coordinates (x, y) for which this inequality is true. Clearly, this has something to do with the straight line

$$y = x$$

sketched in Figure 8.1.

If a point P lies above the line, then the y coordinate is greater than the x coordinate, so that

$$y > x$$

Similarly, if a point Q lies below the line, then the y coordinate is less than the x coordinate, so that

$$y < x$$

Of course, the coordinates of a point R which actually lies on the line satisfy

$$y = x$$

Hence we see that the inequality

$$y \geq x$$

holds for any point that lies on or above the line $y = x$.

It is useful to be able to indicate this region pictorially. We do this by shading one half of the coordinate plane. There are actually two schools of thought here. Some people like to shade the region containing the points for which the inequality is true. Others prefer to shade the region for which it is false. In this text we adopt the latter approach and always shade the region that we are *not* interested in, as shown in Figure 8.2. This may seem a strange choice, but the reason for making it will soon become apparent.

In general, to sketch an inequality of the form

$$dx + ey < f$$
$$dx + ey \leq f$$
$$dx + ey > f$$
$$dx + ey \geq f$$

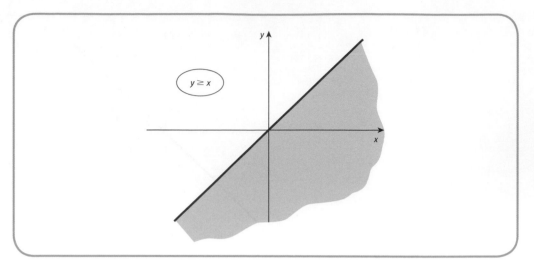

Figure 8.2

we first sketch the corresponding line

$$dx + ey = f$$

and then decide which side of the line to deal with. An easy way of doing this is to pick a 'test point', (x, y). It does not matter what point is chosen, provided it does not actually lie on the line itself. The numbers x and y are then substituted into the original inequality. If the inequality is satisfied, then the side containing the test point is the region of interest. If not, then we go for the region on the other side of the line.

For the region

$$2x + y < 4$$

we first sketch the line

$$2x + y = 4$$

When $x = 0$, we get

$$y = 4$$

When $y = 0$, we get

$$2x = 4$$

and so $x = 4/2 = 2$.

The line passes through $(0, 4)$ and $(2, 0)$ and is shown in Figure 8.3. For a test point let us take $(3, 2)$, which lies above the line. Substituting $x = 3$ and $y = 2$ into the expression $2x + y$ gives

$$2(3) + 2 = 8$$

This is *not* less than 4, so the test point does not satisfy the inequality. It follows that the region of interest lies below the line. This is illustrated in Figure 8.4. In this example the symbol $<$ is used rather than $\leq$. Hence the points on the line itself are not included in the region of interest. We have chosen to indicate this by using a broken line for the boundary.

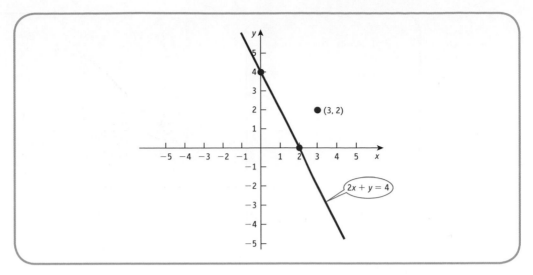

Figure 8.3

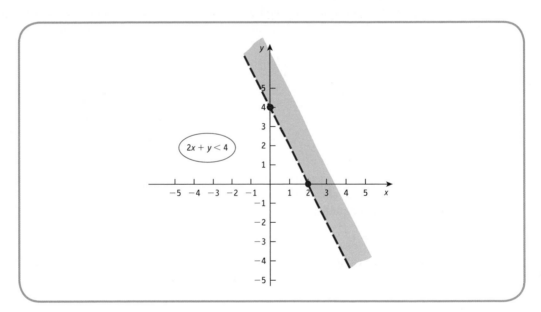

Figure 8.4

Practice Problem

1. Sketch the straight line

    $$-x + 3y = 6$$

    on graph paper. By considering the test point $(1, 4)$, indicate the region

    $$-x + 3y > 6$$

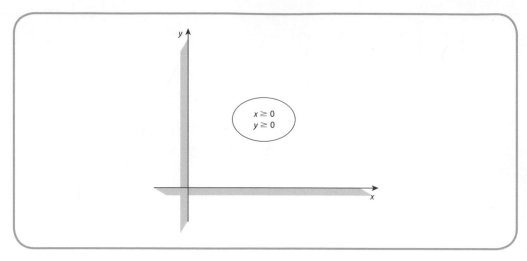

Figure 8.5

We now consider the region defined by simultaneous linear inequalities. This is known as a **feasible region**. It consists of those points (x, y) which satisfy several inequalities at the same time. We find it by sketching the regions defined by each inequality in turn. The feasible region is then the unshaded part of the plane corresponding to the intersection of all of the individual regions.

To illustrate this, consider the feasible region defined by

$$x + 2y \leq 12$$
$$-x + y \leq 3$$
$$x \geq 0$$
$$y \geq 0$$

In this problem the easiest inequalities to handle are the last two. These merely indicate that x and y are non-negative, and so we need only consider points in the top right-hand quadrant of the plane, as shown in Figure 8.5.

For the inequality

$$x + 2y \leq 12$$

we need to sketch the line

$$x + 2y = 12$$

When $x = 0$, we get

$$2y = 12$$

and so $y = 12/2 = 6$.

When $y = 0$, we get

$$x = 12$$

The line passes through $(0, 6)$ and $(12, 0)$.

For a test point let us take $(0, 0)$, since such a choice minimises the amount of arithmetic that we have to do. Substituting $x = 0$ and $y = 0$ into the inequality gives

$$0 + 2(0) \leq 12$$

which is obviously true. Now the region containing the origin lies below the line, so we shade the region that lies above it. This is indicated in Figure 8.6.

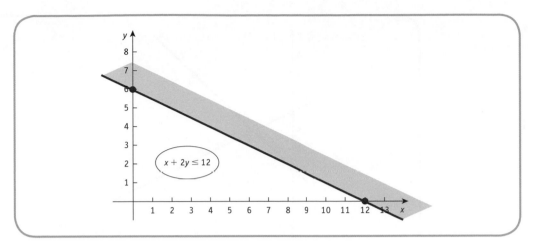

Figure 8.6

For the inequality

$$-x + y \leq 3$$

we need to sketch the line

$$-x + y = 3$$

When $x = 0$, we get

$$y = 3$$

When $y = 0$, we get

$$-x = 3$$

and so $x = 3/(-1) = -3$.

The line passes through $(0, 3)$ and $(-3, 0)$. Unfortunately, the second point does not lie on the diagram as we have drawn it. At this stage we can either redraw the x axis to include -3, or we can try finding another point on the line which does fit on the graph. For example, putting $x = 5$ gives

$$-5 + y = 3$$

so $y = 3 + 5 = 8$. Hence the line passes through $(5, 8)$, which can now be plotted along with $(0, 3)$ to sketch the line. At the test point $(0, 0)$ the inequality reads

$$-0 + 0 \leq 3$$

which is obviously true. We are therefore interested in the region below the line, since this contains the origin. As usual, we indicate this by shading the region on the other side. The complete picture is shown in Figure 8.7.

Points (x, y) which satisfy all four inequalities must lie in the unshaded 'hole' in the middle. Incidentally, this explains why we did not adopt the convention of shading the region of interest. Had we done so, our task would have been to identify the most heavily shaded part of the diagram, which is not so easy.

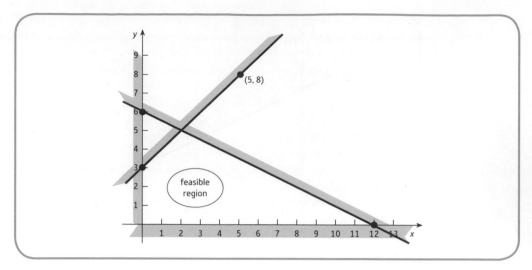

Figure 8.7

Practice Problem

2. Sketch the feasible region

$$x + 2y \leq 10$$
$$3x + y \leq 10$$
$$x \geq 0$$
$$y \geq 0$$

We are now in a position to explain exactly what we mean by a linear programming problem and how such a problem can be solved graphically. We actually intend to describe two slightly different methods of solution. One of these is fairly sophisticated and difficult to use, while the other is more straightforward. The justification for bothering with the 'harder' method is that it provides the motivation for the 'easier' method. It also helps us to handle one or two trickier problems that sometimes arise. We shall introduce both methods by concentrating on a specific example:

Solve the linear programming problem:

Minimise $-2x + y$

subject to the constraints

$$x + 2y \leq 12$$
$$-x + y \leq 3$$
$$x \geq 0$$
$$y \geq 0$$

In general, three ingredients make up a linear programming problem. First, there are several unknowns to be determined. In this example there are just two unknowns, x and y. Secondly, there is a mathematical expression of the form

$$ax + by$$

which we want to either maximise or minimise. Such an expression is called an **objective function**. In this example, $a = -2, b = 1$ and the problem is one of minimisation. Finally, the unknowns x and y are subject to a collection of linear inequalities. Quite often (but not always) two of the inequalities are $x \geq 0$ and $y \geq 0$. These are referred to as **non-negativity constraints**. In this example there are a total of four constraints including the non-negativity constraints.

Geometrically, points (x, y) which satisfy simultaneous linear inequalities define a feasible region in the coordinate plane. In fact, for this particular problem, the feasible region has already been sketched in Figure 8.7.

The problem now is to try to identify that point inside the feasible region which minimises the value of the objective function. One naïve way of doing this might be to use trial and error: that is, we could evaluate the objective function at every point within the region and choose the point which produces the smallest value. For instance, $(1, 1)$ lies in the region, and when the values $x = 1$ and $y = 1$ are substituted into

$$-2x + y$$

we get

$$-2(1) + 1 = -1$$

Similarly we might try $(3.4, 2.1)$, which produces

$$-2(3.4) + 2.1 = -4.7$$

which is an improvement, since $-4.7 < -1$.

The drawback of this approach is that there are infinitely many points inside the region, so it is going to take a very long time before we can be certain of the solution! A more systematic approach is to superimpose, on top of the feasible region, the family of straight lines,

$$-2x + y = c$$

for various values of the constant c. Looking back at the objective function, you will notice that the number c is precisely the thing that we want to minimise. That such an equation represents a straight line should come as no surprise to you by now. Indeed, we know from the rearrangement

$$y = 2x + c$$

that the line has a slope of 2 with a y intercept of c. Consequently, all of these lines are parallel to each other, their precise location being determined from the number c.

Now, when $y = 0$, the equation reads

$$0 = 2x + c$$

and so has solution $x = -c/2$. Hence the line passes through the point $(-c/2, 0)$. A selection of lines is sketched in Figure 8.8 for values of c in the range 0 to -24. These have been sketched using the information that they pass through $(-c/2, 0)$ and have a slope of 2. Note that as c decreases from 0 to -24, the lines sweep across the feasible region from left to right. Also, once c goes below -24, the lines no longer intersect this region. The minimum value of c (which, you may remember, is just the value of the objective function) is therefore -24. Moreover, when $c = -24$, the line

$$-2x + y = c$$

intersects the feasible region in exactly one point, namely $(12, 0)$. This, then, must be the solution of our problem. The point $(12, 0)$ lies in the feasible region as required and because it also lies on the line

$$-2x + y = -24$$

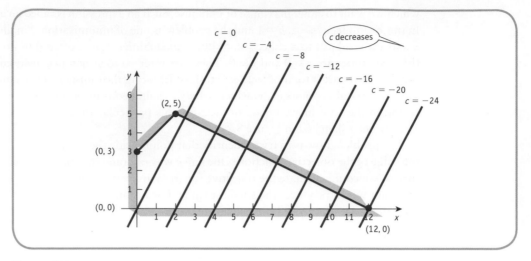

Figure 8.8

we know that the corresponding value of the objective function is -24, which is the minimum value. Other points in the feasible region also lie on lines

$$-2x + y = c$$

but with larger values of c.

Practice Problem

3. Consider the linear programming problem

   Maximise $-x + y$

   subject to the constraints

   $$3x + 4y \leq 12$$
   $$x \geq 0$$
   $$y \geq 0$$

   (a) Sketch the feasible region.

   (b) Sketch, on the same diagram, the five lines

   $$y = x + c$$

   for $c = -4, -2, 0, 1$ and 3.

   [Hint: lines of the form $y = x + c$ have a slope of 1 and pass through the points $(0, c)$ and $(-c, 0)$.]

   (c) Use your answers to part (b) to solve the given linear programming problem.

In the previous problem, and in Practice Problem 3, the optimal value of the objective function is attained at one of the corners of the feasible region. This is not simply a coincidence. It can be shown that the solution of any linear programming problem always occurs at one of the corners. Consequently, the trial-and-error approach suggested earlier is not so naïve after all. The only possible candidates for the answer are the corners, and so only a finite number of points need ever be examined. This method may be summarised:

Step 1

Sketch the feasible region.

Step 2

Identify the corners of the feasible region and find their coordinates.

Step 3

Evaluate the objective function at the corners and choose the one which has the maximum or minimum value.

Returning to the previous example, we work as follows:

Step 1

The feasible region has already been sketched in Figure 8.7.

Step 2

There are four corners with coordinates $(0, 0)$, $(0, 3)$, $(2, 5)$ and $(12, 0)$.

Step 3

Corner	Objective function
$(0, 0)$	$-2(0) + 0 = 0$
$(0, 3)$	$-2(0) + 3 = 3$
$(2, 5)$	$-2(2) + 5 = 1$
$(12, 0)$	$-2(12) + 0 = -24$

From this we see that the minimum occurs at $(12, 0)$, at which the objective function is -24. Incidentally, if we also require the maximum, then this can be deduced without further effort. From the table the maximum is 3, which occurs at $(0, 3)$.

Example

Solve the linear programming problem

   Maximise $5x + 3y$

subject to

   $2x + 4y \leq 8$
   $x \geq 0$
   $y \geq 0$

Solution

Step 1

The non-negativity constraints $x \geq 0$ and $y \geq 0$ indicate that the region is bounded by the coordinate axes in the positive quadrant.

The line $2x + 4y = 8$ passes through $(0, 2)$ and $(4, 0)$. Also, at the test point $(0, 0)$, the inequality

   $2x + 4y \leq 8$

reads

   $0 \leq 8$

which is true. We are therefore interested in the region below the line, since this region contains the test point, $(0, 0)$. The feasible region is sketched in Figure 8.9.

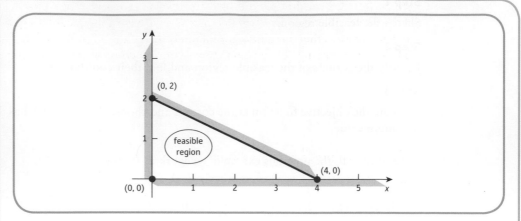

Figure 8.9

Step 2

The feasible region is a triangle with three corners, $(0, 0)$, $(0, 2)$ and $(4, 0)$.

Step 3

Corner	Objective function
$(0, 0)$	$5(0) + 3(0) = 0$
$(0, 2)$	$5(0) + 3(2) = 6$
$(4, 0)$	$5(4) + 3(0) = 20$

The maximum value of the objective function is 20, which occurs when $x = 4$ and $y = 0$.

Practice Problems

4. Solve the linear programming problem

Minimise $x - y$

subject to

$2x + y \le 2$
$x \ge 0$
$y \ge 0$

5. Solve the linear programming problem

Maximise $3x + 5y$

subject to

$x + 2y \le 10$
$3x + y \le 10$
$x \ge 0$
$y \ge 0$

[Hint: you might find your answer to Practice Problem 2 useful.]

In Section 1.4 we showed you how to solve a system of simultaneous linear equations. We discovered that such a system does not always have a unique solution. It is possible for a problem to have either no solution or infinitely many solutions. An analogous situation arises in linear programming. We conclude this section by considering two examples that illustrate these special cases.

Example

Solve the linear programming problem

   Maximise $x + 2y$

subject to

$$2x + 4y \leq 8$$
$$x \geq 0$$
$$y \geq 0$$

Solution

Step 1

The feasible region is identical to the one sketched in Figure 8.9 for the previous worked example.

Step 2

As before, the feasible region has three corners, $(0, 0)$, $(0, 2)$ and $(4, 0)$.

Step 3

Corner	Objective function
$(0, 0)$	$0 + 2(0) = 0$
$(0, 2)$	$0 + 2(2) = 4$
$(4, 0)$	$4 + 2(0) = 4$

This time, however, the maximum value is 4, which actually occurs at two corners, $(0, 2)$ and $(4, 0)$. This shows that the problem does not have a unique solution. To explain what is going on here, we return to the method introduced at the beginning of this section. We superimpose the family of lines obtained by setting the objective function equal to some constant, c. The parallel lines

   $x + 2y = c$

pass through the points $(0, c/2)$ and $(c, 0)$.

   A selection of lines is sketched in Figure 8.10 for values of c between 0 and 4. These particular values are chosen since they produce lines that cross the feasible region. As c increases, the lines sweep across the region from left to right. Moreover, when c goes above 4, the lines no longer intersect the region. The maximum value that c (that is, the objective function) can take is therefore 4. However, instead of the line

   $x + 2y = 4$

intersecting the region at only one point, it intersects along a whole line segment of points. Any point on the line joining the two corners $(0, 2)$ and $(4, 0)$ will be a solution. This follows because any point on this line segment lies in the feasible region, and the corresponding value of the objective function on this line is 4, which is the maximum value.

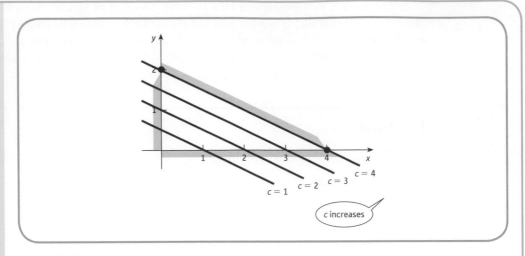

Figure 8.10

This example suggests the general result. If, in step 3, the maximum (or minimum) occurs at *two* corners, then the problem has infinitely many solutions. Any point on the line segment joining these corners, including the two corners themselves, is also a solution.

Example

Solve the linear programming problem

   Maximise $3x + 2y$

subject to

$$x + 4y \geq 8$$
$$x + y \geq 5$$
$$2x + y \geq 6$$
$$x \geq 0$$
$$y \geq 0$$

What can you say about the solution if this problem is one of minimisation rather than maximisation?

Solution

Step 1

As usual, the non-negativity constraints indicate that we need only consider the positive quadrant.
   The line $x + 4y = 8$ passes through $(0, 2)$ and $(8, 0)$.
   The line $x + y = 5$ passes through $(0, 5)$ and $(5, 0)$.
   The line $2x + y = 6$ passes through $(0, 6)$ and $(3, 0)$.

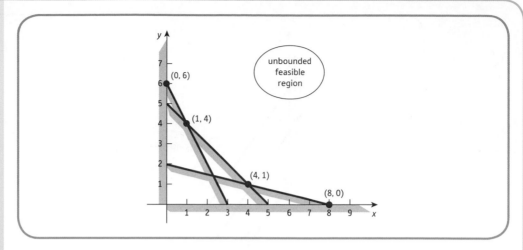

Figure 8.11

Also, the test point $(0, 0)$ does not satisfy any of the corresponding constraints because the three inequality signs are all '$\geq$'. We are therefore interested in the region *above* all of these lines, as shown in Figure 8.11.

Step 2

The feasible region has four corners, $(0, 6)$, $(1, 4)$, $(4, 1)$ and $(8, 0)$.

Step 3

Corner	Objective function
$(0, 6)$	$3(0) + 2(6) = 12$
$(1, 4)$	$3(1) + 2(4) = 11$
$(4, 1)$	$3(4) + 2(1) = 14$
$(8, 0)$	$3(8) + 2(0) = 24$

From the table, the minimum and maximum values of the objective function are 11 and 24, which occur at $(1, 4)$ and $(8, 0)$, respectively. However, we do have a slightly unusual situation in that the feasible region is not enclosed on all sides. We describe this by saying that the feasible region is **unbounded**. It is open at the top and, strictly speaking, it does not make sense to talk about the corners of such a region. Are we therefore justified in applying the 'easy' method in this case? To answer this question we superimpose the family of lines

$$3x + 2y = c$$

representing the objective function, as shown in Figure 8.12.

When $c = 11$, the line intersects the region at only one point $(1, 4)$. However, as c increases from this value, the lines sweep across the feasible region and never leave it, no matter how large c becomes. Consequently, if the problem is one of maximisation, we conclude that it does not have a finite solution. We can substitute huge values of x and y into $3x + 2y$ and get an ever-increasing result. On the other hand, if the problem is one of minimisation, then it does have a solution at the corner $(1, 4)$. This, of course, is the answer obtained previously using the 'easy' method.

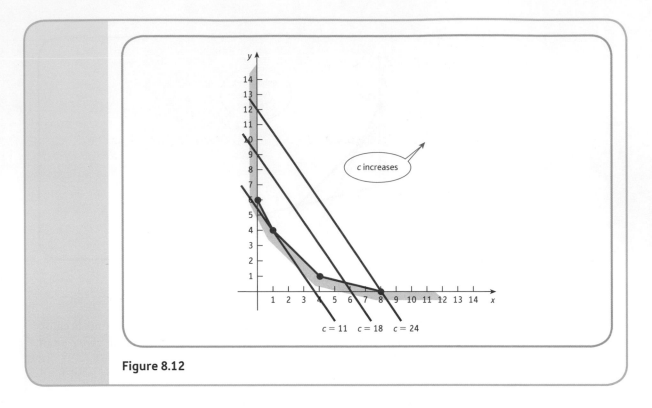

Figure 8.12

This example shows that a linear programming problem may not have a finite solution when the feasible region is unbounded. However, when a solution does exist, it may be found simply by inspecting the corners in the normal way. In practice, linear programming problems arise from realistic economic situations. We would therefore expect the problem to possess a sensible (that is, finite) answer, and so the difficulty of the non-existence of a solution rarely occurs.

Key Terms

Feasible region   The set of points which satisfy all of the constraints in a linear programming problem.

Non-negativity constraints   The constraints $x \geq 0$, $y \geq 0$, etc.

Objective function   The function that is optimised in a linear programming problem.

Unbounded region   A feasible region that is not completely enclosed by a polygon. The associated linear programming problem may not have a finite solution.

Exercise 8.1

1. Which of the following points satisfy the inequality

    $2x - 3y > -5$?

    $(1, 1), (-1, 1), (1, -1), (-1, -1), (-2, 1), (2, -1), (-1, 2)$ and $(-2, -1)$

2. How many points with integer coordinates lie in the feasible region defined by

    $3x + 4y \leq 12, \quad x \geq 0 \quad$ and $\quad y \geq 1$?

3. Sketch the feasible regions defined by the following sets of inequalities:

    (a) $5x + 3y \leq 30$ **(b)** $2x + 5y \leq 20$ **(c)** $x - 2y \leq 3$
    $\ \, 7x + 2y \leq 28$ $\ \ \, x + y \leq 5$ $\ \ \, x - y \leq 4$
    $\ \ \ \ \ \ \, x \geq 0$ $\ \ \ \ \ \ \ \, x \geq 0$ $\ \ \ \ \ \ \ \, x \geq 1$
    $\ \ \ \ \ \ \, y \geq 0$ $\ \ \ \ \ \ \ \, y \geq 0$ $\ \ \ \ \ \ \ \, y \geq 0$

4. Use your answers to Question 3 to solve the following linear programming problems:

    (a) Maximise $\quad 4x + 9y$

    subject to

    $\begin{aligned} 5x + 3y &\leq 30 \\ 7x + 2y &\leq 28 \\ x &\geq 0 \\ y &\geq 0 \end{aligned}$

    (b) Maximise $\quad 3x + 6y$

    subject to

    $\begin{aligned} 2x + 5y &\leq 20 \\ x + y &\leq 5 \\ x &\geq 0 \\ y &\geq 0 \end{aligned}$

    (c) Minimise $\quad x + y$

    subject to

    $\begin{aligned} x - 2y &\leq 3 \\ x - y &\leq 4 \\ x &\geq 1 \\ y &\geq 0 \end{aligned}$

5. What can you say about the solution to Question 4(c) if the problem is one of maximisation rather than minimisation? Explain your answer by superimposing the family of lines

    $x + y = c$

    on the feasible region.

6. Find, if possible, the minimum value of the objective function $3x - 4y$ subject to the constraints,

    $-2x + y \leq 12, \quad x - y \leq 2, \quad x \geq 0 \quad$ and $\quad y \geq 0$

7. What can you say about the solution of the linear programming problem specified in Question 6, if the

(a) objective function is to be maximised instead of minimised?

(b) second constraint is changed to $x + y \leq 2$ and the problem is one of minimisation?

(c) second constraint is changed to $3x - 4y \leq 24$, and the problem is one of maximisation?

Exercise 8.1*

1. The point $(x, 3)$ satisfies the inequality, $-5x - 2y \leq 13$. Find the smallest possible value of x.

2. The following five inequalities define a feasible region. Which one of these could be removed from the list without changing the region?

    A: $-x + y \leq 10$

    B: $x + y \leq 20$

    C: $x - 2y \geq -8$

    D: $\quad x \geq 0$

    E: $\quad y \geq 0$

3. Solve the following linear programming problems:

    (a) Maximise $\quad 2x + 3y$

    subject to

    $$2x + y \leq 8$$
    $$x + y \leq 6$$
    $$x + 2y \leq 10$$
    $$x \geq 0$$
    $$y \geq 0$$

    (b) Maximise $\quad -8x + 4y$

    subject to

    $$x - y \leq 2$$
    $$2x - y \geq -3$$
    $$x - y \geq -4$$
    $$x \geq 0$$
    $$y \geq 0$$

4. Explain why each of the following problems fails to possess a solution:

    (a) Maximise $\quad x + y$

    subject to

    $$y \geq 2$$
    $$x \leq 2$$
    $$x - y \leq 1$$
    $$x \geq 0$$
    $$y \geq 0$$

    (b) Maximise $\quad x + y$

    subject to

    $$2x - y \geq -1$$
    $$x - 2y \leq 2$$
    $$x \geq 0$$
    $$y \geq 0$$

5. Solve the linear programming problem

    Maximise $\quad 6x + 2y$

    subject to

    $$x - y \geq 0$$
    $$3x + y \geq 8$$
    $$x \geq 0$$
    $$y \geq 0$$

6. Show that the linear programming problem given in Question 3(a) can be expressed in matrix notation as

   Maximise $\mathbf{c}^T\mathbf{x}$

   subject to

   $$\mathbf{Ax} \leq \mathbf{b}$$
   $$\mathbf{x} \geq \mathbf{0}$$

   where $\mathbf{c}$, $\mathbf{x}$, and $\mathbf{0}$ are 2×1 matrices, $\mathbf{A}$ is a 3×2 matrix and $\mathbf{b}$ is a 3×1 matrix, which should be stated.

7. **(a)** Consider the linear programming problem

   Minimise $x + y$

   subject to

   $$2x + y \geq 16$$
   $$2x + 3y \geq 24$$
   $$-x + y \leq 12$$
   $$x \geq 0$$
   $$y \geq 0$$

   (i) Sketch the feasible region and find the exact coordinates of the corners.
   (ii) Tabulate the values of the objective function at each of the corners and hence state the coordinates of the optimal point.
   (iii) One of the five constraints is not needed for drawing the feasible region. State the redundant constraint.

   (b) What can you say about the solution if the problem is changed to one of

   (i) maximising $x + y$
   (ii) minimising $2x + y$

   and is subject to the same constraints as part (a)? Give reasons for your answers.

   (c) The objective function in part (a) is changed to

   $$ax + 2y$$

   where a is a positive constant. The problem remains one of minimisation subject to the same constraints as before.

   Find the largest value of a for which the linear programming problem has solution $x = 12$, $y = 0$. Explain your reasoning carefully.

Applications of linear programming

Objectives

At the end of this section you should be able to:

- Identify the decision variables in a linear programming problem.
- Find an expression for the objective function and decide whether it should be maximised or minimised.
- Write down all of the constraints in the problem specification.
- Solve linear programming problems expressed in words, remembering to confirm that the answer makes sense.
- Work out and interpret shadow prices.

The impression possibly given so far is that linear programming is a mathematical technique designed to solve rather abstract problems. This is misleading, since linear programming problems do arise from concrete situations.

In fact, linear programming is a vital tool for business managers who need to allocate finite resources such as labour, machine time or raw materials to maximise profits or minimise costs. The word 'programming' is used in the sense of scheduling or management planning. In this section we develop an important skill that can loosely be called problem formulation. Here we start with information, perhaps only vaguely given in words, and try to express it using the more precise language of mathematics. If the linear programming problem involves just two variables we can then use the graphical technique described in Section 8.1 to solve it. In the real world a problem could involve many more variables. Under these circumstances we would use a specialist computer package based on the simplex method to solve it. However, in order to describe problem formulation, we begin with an example involving just two variables.

A craft studio makes glass bowls and plates, and it can sell all of the products that it makes each week. Glassware is made in two stages. In the first stage molten glass is taken from a furnace and placed at the end of a blowpipe. Skilled glassblowers then mould the glass into the desired shape. During the second stage the glass is allowed to cool in a controlled way inside a second furnace (called an annealer) which helps to reduce stress and prevent the glass from cracking. The studio employs two glassblowers who each work a 35-hour week, and the total time available each week for annealing is 130 hours. The main raw material used in glassmaking is silica sand, and the studio orders 45 kg each week. A glass bowl and plate each require 1 kg of sand. It takes a glassblower two hours to make a bowl and one hour to make a plate. The time needed to cool a bowl in an annealer is four hours and a plate requires one hour. The profit made from selling a bowl and a plate is $150 and $100, respectively. Of course, if there were no restrictions on either time or materials, the studio would be able to maximise weekly profit by making only glass bowls. However, with limited resources, we use linear programming to decide on the best combination.

As mentioned in Section 8.1, there are three things constituting a linear programming problem: unknowns, an objective function which needs maximising or minimising, and some constraints. We consider each of these in turn.

The studio needs to decide how many bowls and plates to make each week. These are therefore the unknowns (called the **decision variables**) of this problem, and we denote these by the letters, x and y: that is, we let

- x = number of bowls
- y = number of plates

The object is to maximise profit, so we need to find an expression for this in terms of x and y. The studio makes a profit of \$150 for every bowl and, since it makes x of these, the total profit made is $150x$. Similarly, the profit made from sales of the plates is $100y$, so the combined profit made from both bowls and plates is

$$150x + 100y$$

This is the objective function that we want to maximise.

We now consider the limited resources available and use the information provided to obtain the constraints. The total amount of time available each week for glassblowing is 70 hours, and the time needed to make a bowl and a plate is two hours and one hour, respectively. Hence if x bowls and y plates are made, the total time needed is

$$2x + y$$

so we require

$$2x + y \leq 70$$

The total amount of time needed for annealing is

$$4x + y$$

and since this must not exceed the 130 hours available, we need

$$4x + y \leq 130$$

Similarly, the amount of sand ordered is 45 kg, so

$$x + y \leq 45$$

On the face of it there appears to be no further constraints given in the problem. However, a moment's thought should convince you that we are missing two important constraints, namely the non-negativity constraints

$$x \geq 0, \quad y \geq 0$$

Although these are not mentioned explicitly, it is obviously not possible to make a negative number of goods. The complete statement of the problem may now be stated:

Maximise $150x + 100y$ (profit)

subject to

$$2x + y \leq 70 \qquad \text{(glassblowing time)}$$
$$4x + y \leq 130 \qquad \text{(annealing time)}$$
$$x + y \leq 45 \qquad \text{(mass of silica sand)}$$
$$x \geq 0$$
$$y \geq 0$$

The problem can now be solved using the method described in Section 8.1.

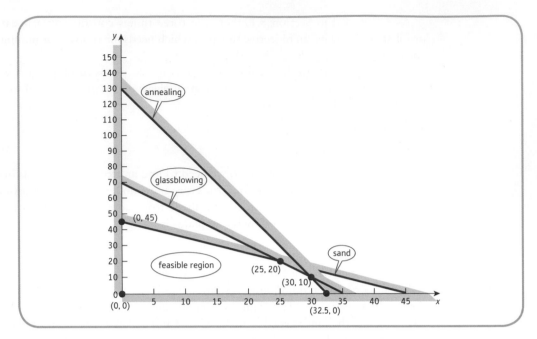

Figure 8.13

Step 1

As usual, the non-negativity constraints indicate that we need only consider points in the positive quadrant.

The line $2x + y = 70$ passes through $(0, 70)$ and $(35, 0)$
The line $4x + y = 130$ passes through $(0, 130)$ and $(32.5, 0)$
The line $x + y = 45$ passes through $(0, 45)$ and $(45, 0)$

Also, using the origin as the test point reveals that the region of interest lies below all three lines. It is sketched in Figure 8.13.

Step 2

The feasible region has five corners: $(0, 0)$, $(0, 45)$, $(25, 20)$, $(30, 10)$ and $(32.5, 0)$.

Step 3

Corner	Profit
(0, 0)	0
(0, 45)	4500
(25, 20)	5750
(30, 10)	5500
(32.5, 0)	4875

The maximum weekly profit is \$5750, which occurs when 25 bowls and 20 plates are made.

The corner giving the optimal solution, $(25, 20)$, is the point of the intersection of the lines $x + y = 45$ and $2x + y = 70$ which correspond to the constraints arising from sand and glassblowing. Mathematically, for these two resources the inequality '$\leq$' has been replaced by equality, '$=$', so the glassblowing time and the quantity of sand are fully utilised. On the other hand, the line for annealing does not pass through the optimum, so there is some slack in this constraint. Substituting $x = 25$ and $y = 20$ into the expression for the annealing time gives

$$4x + y = 4 \times 25 + 20 = 120$$

There were 130 hours available, so 10 of these hours are unused.

> ## Advice
>
> It is impossible to give a precise description of problem formulation. Each case has to be considered on its own merits. However, you might like to try the following general strategy:
>
> (1) Identify the decision variables and label them x and y.
>
> (2) Write down an expression for the objective function in terms of x and y, and decide whether it needs maximising or minimising.
>
> (3) Write down all constraints on the variables x and y, including the non-negativity constraints.

Practice Problem

1. An electronics firm decides to launch two models of a tablet, TAB1 and TAB2. The cost of making each device of type TAB1 is $120 and the cost for TAB2 is $160. The firm recognises that this is a risky venture, so it decides to limit the total weekly production costs to $4000. Also, due to a shortage of skilled labour, the total number of tablets that the firm can produce in a week is at most 30. The profit made on each device is $600 for TAB1 and $700 for TAB2. How should the firm arrange production to maximise profit?

One important task when planning business projects is to decide whether it is worthwhile buying in extra resources. For the glassmaking problem the studio might consider the option of increasing the number of hours available for glassblowing or annealing. It might also investigate what happens to the maximum profit if it buys an extra kilogram of sand. Do these changes make any difference to the number of bowls and plates that the studio should make to maximise profit? These questions can be answered by reworking the problem changing one constraint at a time. Most software packages provide this information automatically so that management can see at a glance how sensitive the optimal solution is to small changes in resources.

To illustrate this idea let us consider the case when one of the glassblowers works for an extra hour a week but all other resources are unchanged. The only difference to the problem specification is that the glassblowing constraint changes from

$$2x + y \leq 70 \quad \text{to} \quad 2x + y \leq 71$$

All that happens is that the line joining $(0, 70)$ and $(35, 0)$ moves to a line joining $(0, 71)$ and $(35.5, 0)$. The feasible region is barely altered, so the optimal point will still be at the intersection of the lines representing the boundaries of the glassblowing and sand constraints. Rather than attempt to draw these accurately on a diagram, it is easier to find the new point by solving the simultaneous equations

$$x + y = 45$$
$$2x + y = 71$$

Subtracting the first equation from the second gives $x = 26$. If this value is substituted into either equation, it is easy to see that $y = 19$. The new profit is worked out to be

$$150 \times 26 + 100 \times 19 = \$5800$$

This compares with a previous profit of $5750, so a 1-unit increase in the number of hours available for glassblowing results in a $50 increase in profit. This value is called the **shadow price** and is similar to the marginal concepts that we have met before. The shadow price represents the maximum premium that a firm would be willing to pay for 1 extra unit of that resource. The studio will welcome the extra hour of glassblowing provided it costs less than $50 to provide it. In this example the shadow price of annealing is obviously zero because we already know that 10 hours of annealing time is unused, so providing an extra hour for this would have no impact on the overall profit. This is the case for any resource when there is slack in the constraint (provided that the change is not so great that the optimum point in the feasible region moves from one corner to a different corner.)

Practice Problem

2. For the glass studio problem find the coordinates of the optimal corner of the feasible region when an extra kilogram of sand becomes available, and hence work out the shadow price of sand.

Example

An insurance company employs full- and part-time staff, who work 40 and 20 hours per week, respectively. Full-time staff are paid $800 per week and part-time staff $320. In addition, it is company policy that the number of part-time staff should not exceed one-third of the number of full-time staff.

If the number of worker-hours per week required to deal with the company's work is 900, how many workers of each type should be employed in order to complete the workload at minimum cost?

Solution

If the company employs x full-time staff and y part-time staff, then the company would like to choose x and y to minimise its weekly salary costs. Also, since full- and part-time staff are paid $800 and $320 per week, respectively, the total wage bill is then

$$800x + 320y$$

which is the objective function that needs to be minimised.

Full- and part-time staff work 40 and 20 hours per week, respectively, so the total number of worker-hours available is

$$40x + 20y$$

It is required that this is at least 900, so we obtain the constraint

$$40x + 20y \geq 900$$

A further constraint on the company arises from the fact that the number of part-time staff cannot exceed one-third of the number of full-time staff. This means, for example, that if the company employs 30 full-time staff, then it is not allowed to employ more than 10 part-time staff because

$1/3 \times 30 = 10$

In general, if x denotes the number of full-time staff, then the number of part-time staff, y, cannot exceed $x/3$: that is,

$y \leq x/3$

In addition, we have the obvious non-negativity constraints

$x \geq 0$ and $y \geq 0$

The complete problem may now be stated:

Minimise $800x + 320y$

subject to

$40x + 20y \geq 900$

$\qquad\quad y \leq x/3$

$\qquad\quad x \geq 0$

$\qquad\quad y \geq 0$

It can now be solved by applying the method described in Section 8.1.

Step 1

The feasible region can be sketched in the usual way. The line $y = x/3$ passes through $(0, 0)$, $(3, 1)$, $(6, 2)$ and so on. Unfortunately, because the origin actually lies on the line, it is necessary to use some other point as a test point. For example, substituting $x = 30$, $y = 5$ into the inequality

$y \leq x/3$

gives

$5 \leq (30)/3$

This inequality is clearly true, indicating that $(30, 5)$, which lies below the line, is in the region of interest. The constraint

$40x + 20y \geq 900$

is easier to handle. The corresponding line passes through $(0, 45)$ and $(22^1/_2, 0)$, and using the origin as a test point shows that we need to shade the region below the line. The feasible region is sketched in Figure 8.14.

Step 2

The feasible region has two corners. One of these is obviously $(22^1/_2, 0)$. However, it is not possible to write down directly from the diagram the coordinates of the other corner. This is formed by the intersection of the two lines

$\qquad\quad y = x/3$ \hfill (1)

$40x + 20y = 900$ \hfill (2)

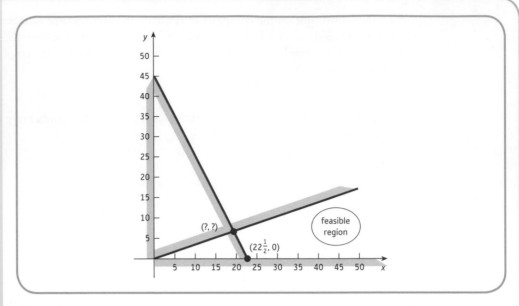

Figure 8.14

and so we must solve this system algebraically. In this case the easiest thing to do is to substitute equation (1) into equation (2) to eliminate y immediately. This gives

$$40x + \frac{20}{3}x = 900$$

that is,

$$\frac{140}{3}x = 900$$

which has the solution

$$x = \frac{2700}{140} = \frac{135}{7} = 19^2/_7$$

Finally, from equation (1),

$$y = \frac{1}{3}x = \frac{1}{3} \times \frac{135}{7} = \frac{45}{7} = 6\frac{3}{7}$$

The feasible region therefore has coordinates $(19^2/_7, 6^3/_7)$ and $(22^1/_2, 0)$.

Step 3

Corner	Objective function
$(19^2/_7, 6^3/_7)$	17 485$^5/_7$
$(22^1/_2, 0)$	18 000

The minimum cost is $17 485.71, which occurs when $x = 19^2/_7$ and $y = 6^3/_7$.

It might appear that this is the solution to our original problem. This is certainly mathematically correct, but it cannot possibly be the solution that we are looking for, since it does not make sense, for example, to employ $^2/_7$ of a worker. We are interested only in

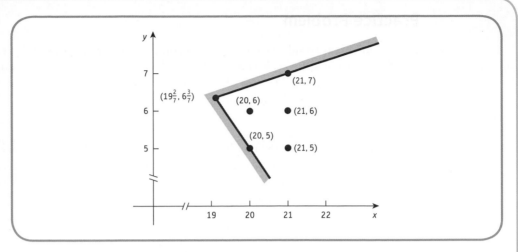

Figure 8.15

points whose coordinates are whole numbers. A problem such as this is referred to as an **integer programming** problem. We need to find that point (x, y) inside the feasible region where both x and y are whole numbers which minimises the objective function. A 'blow-up' picture of the feasible region near the minimum cost corner is shown in Figure 8.15, and the following table indicates that the optimal solution is $(20, 5)$.

Corner	Objective function
(20, 5)	17 600
(20, 6)	17 920
(21, 5)	18 400
(21, 6)	18 720

Other points in the neighbourhood with whole-number coordinates are $(20, 6)$, $(20, 7)$, $(21, 5)$ and so on. However, all of these have either a larger value of x or a larger value of y (or both) and so must produce a larger total cost. The company should therefore employ 20 full- and 5 part-time staff to minimise its salary bill.

Advice

This example highlights the need to look back at the original problem to make sure that the final answer makes sense. It is very tempting when solving linear programming problems just to write down the solution without thinking, neatly underline it and then go on to another problem. Unfortunately, it is all too easy to make mistakes, both in formulating the problem and in sketching the feasible region. Spending a few moments checking the validity of your solution may well help you to discover any blunders that you have made and may suggest possible modifications to the solution procedure, as in the previous example. We might, therefore, conclude the general strategy with the following step:

(4) Check that the final answer makes sense as a solution to the original problem.

Practice Problem

3. An individual spends 95% of earned income on essential goods and services, leaving only 5% to be spent on luxury goods, which is subdivided between trendy clothes and visits to the theatre. The cost of each item of clothing is $150 and a trip to the theatre costs $70. The corresponding utility function is

$$U = 3x + 7y$$

where x and y denote the number of trendy clothes and theatre visits per year, respectively. In order to maintain a reasonable appearance throughout the year, it is vital that at least nine new items of clothing are purchased each year. Given that annual earned income is $42 000, find the values of x and y which maximise utility.

Key Terms

Decision variable   The unknowns in a linear programming problem which can be controlled.

Integer programming   A linear programming problem in which the search for solution is restricted to points in the feasible region with whole-number coordinates.

Shadow price   The change in the optimal value of the objective function due to a 1-unit increase in one of the available resources.

Exercise 8.2

1. A manufacturer produces two models of racing bike, B and C, each of which must be processed through two machine shops. Machine shop 1 is available for 120 hours per month and machine shop 2 for 180 hours per month. The manufacture of each bike of type B takes six hours in shop 1 and three hours in shop 2. The corresponding times for C are 4 and 10 hours, respectively. If the profit is $180 and $220 per bike of type B and C, respectively, how should the manufacturer arrange production to maximise total profit?

2. A small firm manufactures and sells litre cartons of non-alcoholic cocktails, 'The Caribbean' and 'Mr Fruity', which sell for $1 and $1.25, respectively. Each is made by mixing fresh orange, pineapple and apple juices in different proportions. The Caribbean consists of one part orange, six parts pineapple and one part apple. Mr Fruity consists of two parts orange, three parts pineapple and one part apple. The firm can buy up to 300 litres of orange juice, up to 1125 litres of pineapple juice and up to 195 litres of apple juice each week at a cost of $0.72, $0.64 and $0.48 per litre, respectively.

   Find the number of cartons of 'The Caribbean' and 'Mr Fruity' that the firm should produce to maximise profits. You may assume that non-alcoholic cocktails are so popular that the firm can sell all that it produces.

3. In a student's diet a meal consists of beefburgers and chips. Beefburgers have 1 unit of nutrient N1, 4 units of N2 and 125 calories per ounce. The figures for chips are $1/2$ unit of N1, 1 unit of N2 and 60 calories per ounce. In the interests of the student's health it is essential for the meal to contain at least 7 units of N1 and 22 units of N2.

What should the student ask for on the next visit to the refectory to satisfy the nutrient requirements and minimise the number of calories?

4. An Italian restaurant offers a choice of pasta or pizza meals. It costs $3 to make a pasta dish, which it sells for $13. The corresponding figures for pizzas are $2 and $10, respectively. The maximum number of meals that can be cooked in a week is 1200 and the restaurant has a weekly cost budget of $3000. How many pasta and pizza dishes should be cooked each week to maximise profit?

5. A small manufacturer produces two kinds of good, A and B, for which demand exceeds capacity. The production costs for each item of A and B are $6 and $3, respectively, and the corresponding selling prices are $7 and $4. In addition, transport costs are 20 cents and 30 cents for each good of type A and B, respectively. The conditions of a bank loan limit the manufacturer to maximum weekly production costs of $2700 and maximum weekly transport costs of $120. How should the manufacturer arrange production to maximise profit?

6. A publisher decides to use one section of its plant to produce two textbooks called *Microeconomics* and *Macroeconomics*. The profit made on each copy is $12 for *Microeconomics* and $18 for *Macroeconomics*. Each copy of *Microeconomics* requires 12 minutes for printing and 18 minutes for binding. The corresponding figures for *Macroeconomics* are 15 and 9 minutes, respectively. There are 10 hours available for printing and 10.5 hours available for binding. How many of each should be produced to maximise profit?

7. A food producer uses two processing plants, P1 and P2, that operate seven days a week. After processing, beef is graded into high-, medium- and low-quality foodstuffs. High-quality beef is sold to butchers, medium-quality beef is used in supermarket ready-meals and the low-quality beef is used in dog food. The producer has contracted to provide 120 kg of high-, 80 kg of medium- and 240 kg of low-quality beef each week. It costs $4000 per day to run plant P1 and $3200 per day to run plant P2. Each day P1 processes 60 kg of high-quality beef, 20 kg of medium-quality beef and 40 kg of low-quality beef. The corresponding quantities for P2 are 20 kg, 20 kg and 120 kg, respectively. How many days each week should the plants be operated to fulfil the beef contract most economically?

8. [In this question, you are asked to formulate a linear programming problem. You are NOT expected to solve it.]

    An American university has enough places for 9000 students. Government restrictions mean that at least 75% of the places must be given to US students but the remainder may be given to non-US citizens. There are 5000 residential places available on campus.

    All overseas students and at least one-quarter of the US students must be given places on campus. The university gets $12 000 in tuition fees for each US student and $15 000 for each overseas student. It wants to maximise the fees received.

    Using the letter x for the number of places given to US students and y for the number of places for overseas students,

    (a) write down an expression for the objective function and state whether it is to be maximised or minimised;

    (b) write down the five constraints that define the feasible region and explain your reasoning carefully;

    (c) identify which aspect of the original problem has been overlooked in parts (a) and (b).

Exercise 8.2*

1. Leo has $12.50 to spend on his weekly supply of sweets, crisps and apples. A bag of crisps costs $0.65, a bag of sweets costs $0.85, and one apple costs $0.50. The total number of packets of crisps, sweets and apples consumed in a week must be at least seven, and he eats at least twice as many packets of sweets as crisps. His new healthy diet also means that total number of packets of sweets and crisps must not exceed one-third of the number of apples. If s, c and a denote the number of packets of sweets, packets of crisps, and apples, respectively, which **two** of the following represent the constraints defining the feasible region?

   (1) $3c + 3s \leq a$

   (2) $s \geq 0.5c$

   (3) $0.65s + 0.85c + 0.5a \geq 12.5$

   (4) $a + c + s > 7$

   (5) $s \leq c - a$

   (6) $17s + 10a + 13c \leq 250$

   (7) $c \leq 2s$

   (8) $a + c + s \leq 7$

   (9) $3c + 3s + a \leq 0$

   (10) $3s - 3c + a \geq 0$

2. A private hospital specialises in cosmetic and orthopaedic surgery. The profit made on each patient undergoing cosmetic surgery is $12 000, and for orthopaedic surgery the profit is $14 000. Each patient undergoing cosmetic surgery needs 1.5 hours of surgery followed by 12 hours of post-operative care. Orthopaedic surgery takes 2 hours with 10 hours of post-operative care. Each week the hospital can provide a total of 18 hours of surgical time and 120 hours of post-operative care. How many cosmetic and ortho-paedic patients should the hospital accept each week to maximise total profit?

3. A firm manufactures two products, X and Y. To make 1 unit of product X requires 3 units of raw materials and 2 units of labour. To make 1 unit of product Y requires 5 units of raw materials and 2 units of labour. The total number of units available for raw materials and labour is 31 500 and 17 000, respectively. The firm makes a profit of $15 for making and selling product X. The corresponding profit for Y is $20.

   (a) Formulate a linear programming problem to maximise the firm's profits.

   (b) Solve the linear programming problem graphically.

   (c) Find the shadow price of raw materials and give an interpretation of its value.

4. A manufacturer of outdoor clothing makes wax jackets and trousers. Each jacket requires one hour to make, whereas each pair of trousers takes 40 minutes. The materials for a jacket cost $32 and those for a pair of trousers cost $40. The company can devote only 34 hours per week to the production of jackets and trousers, and the firm's total weekly cost for materials must not exceed $1200. The company sells the jackets at a profit of $12 each and the trousers at a profit of $14 per pair. Market research indicates

that the firm can sell all of the jackets that are produced, but that it can sell at most half as many pairs of trousers as jackets.

(a) How many jackets and trousers should the firm produce each week to maximise profit?

(b) Due to the changes in demand, the company has to change its profit margin on a pair of trousers. Assuming that the profit margin on a jacket remains at \$12 and the manufacturing constraints are unchanged, find the minimum and maximum profit margins on a pair of trousers which the company can allow before it should change its strategy for optimum output.

5. A farmer wishes to feed pigs with minimum cost but needs to ensure that each receives at least 1.6 kg of protein, at least 0.3 kg of amino acid and no more than 0.3 kg of calcium per day. Foods available are fish meal and meat scraps, which contain protein, calcium and amino acid according to the following table:

	Kg protein per kg feed	Kg calcium per kg feed	Kg amino acid per kg feed
Fish meal	0.60	0.05	0.18
Meat scraps	0.50	0.11	0.05

Fish meal costs \$0.65 per kg, whereas meat scraps cost \$0.52 per kg. Determine a minimum-cost feeding programme.

6. A individual has \$300 000 to invest across a range of companies, A, B and C. The table shows the expected percentage risk, dividend and growth in each company.

Company	% risk	% dividend	% growth
A	10	15	10
B	15	5	25
C	5	5	15

The individual wants to invest all of the \$300 000 with minimum risk, but wants to make sure that the expected dividend is at least 10% and growth is at least 15% of the investment.

(a) If x and y denote the amount invested in company A and company B, respectively, show that the problem may be formulated as:

Minimise $0.05x + 0.1y + 15\ 000$

subject to $0.1x \geq 15\ 000$

$-0.05x + 0.1y \geq 0$

$x + y \leq 300\ 000$

$x \geq 0, y \geq 0$

(b) Solve the linear programming problem in part (a) to work out the optimal investment in companies A, B and C.

7. A supplier of computer games has two warehouses, A and B, which are located in different parts of the country. Warehouse A has 90 copies of a new computer game in stock, whereas B has 60 copies. Customers in town C request 50 copies and those in town D request 80 copies. The costs of delivering a copy to customers in towns C and D are shown in the table.

From/To	C	D
A	$1	$1.30
B	$0.90	$1.10

(a) If the supplier wishes to arrange delivery to minimise costs, show that the problem can be written as a linear programming problem involving two variables.

(b) Draw the feasible region for the problem in part (a) and hence determine the optimal delivery arrangements.

8. A company makes and sells two products, X and Y. The selling prices of each product are $120 and $258, respectively. The resource requirements for making 1 item of each product are listed in the table:

Product	X	Y
Raw material 1	5 kg	8 kg
Raw material 2	1 kg	1 kg
Machine time	3 hours	8 hours
Labour time	3 hours	10 hours

The unit cost of each resource and the maximum resource availability is shown in the table:

Resource	Cost	Total available
Raw material 1	$3 per kg	6150 kg
Raw material 2	$5 per kg	1086 kg
Machine time	$8 per hour	5190 hours
Labour time	$12 per hour	5250 hours

(a) Formulate and solve a linear programming problem which will maximise profit.

(b) State the shadow price of machine time. Would you advise the company to increase this resource?

Formal mathematics

We conclude this chapter by stating the general linear programming problem for n variables. The problem involves maximising or minimising the objective function:

$$z = c_1 x_1 + c_2 x_2 + \ldots + c_n x_n$$

subject to m linear constraints:

$$a_{11} x_1 + a_{12} x_2 + \ldots + a_{1n} x_n \leq b_1$$
$$a_{21} x_1 + a_{22} x_2 + \ldots + a_{2n} x_n \leq b_2$$
$$\ldots$$
$$a_{m1} x_1 + a_{m2} x_2 + \ldots + a_{mn} x_n \leq b_m$$

and non-negativity constraints:

$$x_1 \geq 0, \, x_2 \geq 0, \ldots \ldots, \, x_n \geq 0$$

where c_i, a_{ij} and b_j are given constants.

If any of the linear constraints in a given problem are presented with a '≥' sign, they can always be re-cast in the above form by simply multiplying both sides by the number -1.

Two other formulations are possible. In sigma notation the problem is to maximise or minimise

$$z = \sum_{i=1}^{n} c_i x_i \quad \text{subject to} \quad \sum_{j=1}^{n} a_{ij} x_j \leq b_i \quad \text{with} \quad x_j \geq 0$$

and in matrix notation we maximise or minimise

$$\mathbf{c}^{\mathrm{T}} \mathbf{x} \text{ subject to } \mathbf{Ax} \leq \mathbf{b} \text{ with } \mathbf{x} \geq \mathbf{0}$$

Multiple choice questions

Question 1

Show the set of points in the (x, y) plane which satisfy the inequality $3x - 4y \geq 12$. Use the convention of shading the unwanted region.

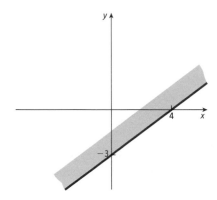

A.

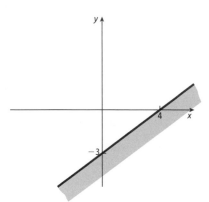

B.

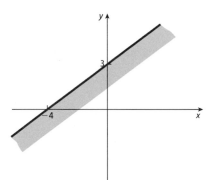

C.

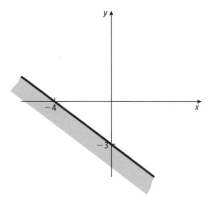

D.

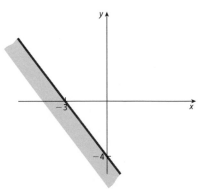

E.

Question 2

The diagram shows the feasible region defined by

$$3x + 2y \geq 22$$
$$5x + 9y \geq 55$$
$$6x + 2y \geq 27$$
$$x \geq 0$$
$$y \geq 0$$

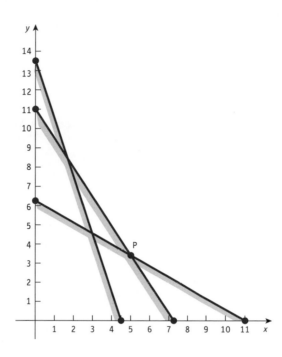

Find the exact coordinates of the point labelled P on the diagram.

A. $\left(\dfrac{88}{17}, \dfrac{55}{17} \right)$

B. $\left(\dfrac{26}{5}, \dfrac{16}{5} \right)$

C. $\left(\dfrac{53}{10}, \dfrac{61}{20} \right)$

D. $\left(\dfrac{68}{13}, \dfrac{125}{39} \right)$

E. $\left(\dfrac{646}{125}, \dfrac{81}{25} \right)$

Question 3

Find the number of points with *integer* coordinates which lie in the feasible region defined by:

$$3x + 8y \leq 24$$
$$x + y \leq 5$$
$$x \geq 1$$
$$y \geq 0$$

A. 8

B. 9

C. 10

D. 11

E. 12

Questions 4–6 all relate to the following diagram which shows the feasible region defined by the following inequalities:

$$x + 2y \leq 17$$
$$5x + 3y \leq 36$$
$$x \leq 6$$
$$y \leq 8$$
$$x \geq 0$$
$$y \geq 0$$

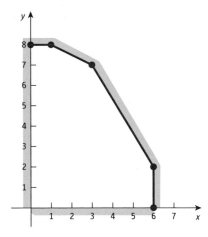

Question 4

Find the maximum value of the objective function $x + y$ in the feasible region.

A. 8

B. 9

C. 10

D. 11

E. 12

Question 5

Find the minimum value of the objective function, $-x - 1.5y$ in the feasible region.

A. -13

B. -15.5

C. -13.5

D. -12

E. -14

Question 6

The linear programming problem is to maximise $2x + ay$ in the feasible region and the solution set consists of all points on the line segment joining $(1, 8)$ and $(3, 7)$. Find the value of a.

A. 0

B. 1

C. 2

D. 3

E. 4

Questions 7–10 relate to the following linear programming problem:

A dietician recommends that a particular individual must consume a minimum of 18 units of calcium, 16 units of iron and 14 units of zinc each week. The person would like to make sure that she complies with the diet by buying some food supplements containing all the nutrients she needs from her local health shop which sells packets of 'VitaPlus' and 'BeHealthy'. She would like to choose a viable combination of these supplements at minimal cost. VitaPlus costs $3 a packet and contains 1 unit of calcium, 4 units of iron and 1 unit of zinc. A packet of BeHealthy costs $4 and contains 1.5 units of calcium, 1 unit of iron and 1 unit of zinc.

Letters x and y denote the number of packets of VitaPlus and BeHealthy, respectively.

Question 7

Write down the objective function and state whether it is to be maximised or minimised.

A. Minimise $4x + 3y$

B. Maximise $3x + 4y$

C. Minimise $3x - 4y$

D. Minimise $3x + 4y$

E. Maximise $4x + 3y$

Question 8

Write down the inequalities defining the constraints

A. $2x + 3y \geq 36, 4x + y \geq 16, x + y \geq 14, x \geq 0, y \geq 0$

B. $2x + 3y \leq 36, 4x + y \leq 16, x + y \leq 14, x \geq 0, y \geq 0$

C. $3x + 2y \geq 36, x + 4y \geq 16, x + y \geq 14, x \geq 0, y \geq 0$

D. $3x + 2y \leq 36, 4x + y \leq 16, x + y \leq 14, x \geq 0, y \geq 0$

E. $2x + 3y \leq 36, x + 4y \geq 16, x + y \geq 14, x \geq 0, y \geq 0$

Question 9

Use the feasible region sketched in the diagram below to work out the number of packets of VitaPlus and BeHealthy that need to be bought.

A. 18 packets of VitaPlus and 0 packets of BeHealthy

B. 1 packet of VitaPlus and 13 packets of BeHealthy

C. 1 packet of VitaPlus and 14 packets of BeHealthy

D. 0 packets of VitaPlus and 16 packets of BeHealthy

E. 6 packets of VitaPlus and 8 packets of BeHealthy

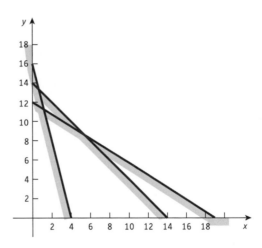

Question 10

Calculate the shadow price of iron.

A. 1/3

B. 5/3

C. 3/5

D. 0

E. 3

Examination questions

Question 1

(a) Solve the linear programming problem:

Maximise $x + y$

subject to

$$x + 4y \leq 12$$
$$2x + y \leq 10$$
$$x \geq 0$$
$$y \geq 0$$

(b) Find the solution if the objective is to

(i) minimise $x - 3y$

(ii) maximise $x + \dfrac{1}{2}y$

subject to the same constraints as before.

Question 2

Solve the linear programming problem:

Minimise $\quad 6x + 5y$

subject to

$$x + y \geq 8$$
$$x + 2y \geq 10$$
$$3x + y \geq 12$$
$$x \geq 0$$
$$y \geq 0$$

What can you say about the solution if the objective is to maximise $5x + 2y$?

Question 3

A designer clothing firm makes ladies' scarves and blouses using a blend of wool and silk fibres. The quantity of fibre (in grams) required for a scarf and a blouse, and the profit (in $s) made from the sale of each item are shown in the table below:

	Silk	Wool	Profit
Scarf	12	24	70
Blouse	18	12	84

(a) Write down an expression for the total profit if the firm makes x scarves and y blouses.

(b) If the firm has a weekly supply of 10.8 kg of silk and 19.2 kg of wool available, write down four constraints on the variables x and y.

(c) Show the feasible region on a sketch graph.

(d) How many scarves and blouses should the firm make each week to maximise profit?

Question 4

A specialist bakery makes two types of cakes, chocolate and fruit. Each chocolate cake uses 600 grams of flour, 100 grams of butter and 200 grams of sugar. The corresponding figures for a fruit cake are 300 grams, 100 grams and 300 grams. The bakery makes a profit of $20 and $24 for each chocolate and fruit cake sold. The bakery wants to make as many cakes of each type that it can to maximise total profit. However, it only has 96 kg flour, 20 kg butter and 52 kg sugar available each week. You may assume that there are no other restrictions and that the bakery can sell all cakes that it makes.

(a) Give a precise description of the two decision variables, x and y.

(b) Write down an expression in terms of x and y for the weekly profit.

(c) Write down inequalities for all constraints in the problem.

(d) Draw the feasible region and identify the coordinates of all of its corners.

(e) How many cakes of each type should be baked each week to maximise profit?

Question 5

I decide to extend my investment portfolio by spending no more than $5000 on shares in companies A and B. The cost of each share is $5 and $10, respectively, and my financial advisor estimates that I can expect to make a profit of 80 cents and 65 cents on each share. Due to environmental concerns, I decide to buy at least twice as many shares in company B as in company A.

(a) Formulate this as a linear programming problem.

(b) Sketch the feasible region.

(c) Write down the coordinates of the corners of the feasible region.

(d) How many of each type of share should I buy? State the corresponding profit.

Question 6

A fruit farmer supplies raspberries and blueberries to a leading supermarket. She is contracted to supply at least 100 kg of raspberries and 50 kg blueberries each week. The supermarket requires that the total weight of fruit delivered must be at least 200 kg. In a typical week she can harvest a maximum of 200 kg of raspberries and 300 kg of blueberries.

The cost of supplying a kilo of raspberries is $4.40, and the corresponding figure for blueberries is $3.10.

(a) Formulate this as a linear programming problem if the farmer's strategy is to minimise total cost.

(b) Sketch the feasible region.

(c) Write down the coordinates of the corners of the feasible region.

(d) How many kilos of raspberries and blueberries should the farmer supply each week to the supermarket?

(e) The selling prices of a kilo of raspberries and a kilo of blueberries are $8 and $10, respectively. Work out the maximum weekly profit that the supermarket could make.

Question 7

(a) Find the inverse of the matrix $\begin{bmatrix} 4 & 3 \\ 5 & 7 \end{bmatrix}$.

Hence find the exact solution of the simultaneous equations

$$4x + 3y = 900$$
$$5x + 7y = 1750$$

(b) A food supplier makes two different varieties of smoothie, 'Exotic' and 'Floridian', which it sells in 2-litre cartons. The main ingredients and the profit made on each carton are as follows:

	Banana	Mango	Orange	Profit
Exotic	4	2	5	$4.50
Floridian	3	1	7	$4.00

The company has 900 bananas, 400 mangoes and 1750 oranges available and wishes to arrange production to maximise total profit. It can sell all of the smoothies that it produces.

(i) Formulate this as a linear programming problem.

(ii) Sketch the feasible region.

(iii) Write down the exact coordinates of the corners of the feasible region.

(iv) Find the optimising production levels of each type of smoothie.

CHAPTER 9
Dynamics

This chapter provides a simple introduction to the dynamics of economic systems. So far, all of our models have been static. We have implicitly assumed that equilibrium prices and incomes are somehow attained instantaneously, as if by magic. In practice, economic variables take time to vary. The incorporation of time into economic models is known as **dynamics**, and it enables us to decide whether equilibrium values are actually achieved and, if so, exactly how individual variables approach these values. There are two sections that can be read in either order.

In Section 9.1 we consider the case when time, t, is a discrete variable taking whole number values. This describes the situation in which variables change only after fixed periods. For example, the prices of certain agricultural products change from one season to the next but are fixed throughout each season. We express this time dependence using an obvious subscript notation. The price during the first period is denoted by P_1, the price during the second period is P_2 and so on. Equations that relate the price in one period, P_t, to that of the previous period, P_{t-1}, are called difference equations, and a method is described for the solution of such equations.

In Section 9.2 we consider the case when time is a continuous variable taking all possible values in a certain interval. This describes the situation in which variables change from one moment to the next. For example, the prices of certain commodities, such as oil, effectively change instantaneously and are not fixed on a seasonal basis. We express this time dependence using the usual function notation, $P(t)$. It is appropriate to model the rate of change of P with respect to t using the derivative, $P'(t)$. Equations that involve the derivatives of an unknown function are called differential equations, and a method is described for solving such equations.

It is not possible in an introductory text such as this to give you more than a flavour of the mathematics of dynamics. However, in spite of this, we show you how to solve dynamic systems in both macroeconomics and microeconomics. Also, we hope that this chapter will encourage you to read other texts that describe more advanced methods and models.

Difference equations

CHAPTER 9

> ## Objectives
>
> At the end of this section you should be able to:
>
> - Find the complementary function of a difference equation.
> - Find the particular solution of a difference equation.
> - Analyse the stability of economic systems.
> - Solve lagged national income determination models.
> - Solve single-commodity-market models with lagged supply.

A **difference equation** (sometimes called a **recurrence relation**) is an equation that relates consecutive terms of a sequence of numbers. For example, the equation

$$Y_t = 2Y_{t-1}$$

describes sequences in which one number is twice its predecessor. There are obviously many sequences that satisfy this requirement, including

$2, 4, 8, 16, \ldots$

$5, 10, 20, 40, \ldots$

$-1, -2, -4, -8, \ldots$

In order to determine the sequence uniquely, we need to be given some additional information, such as the first term. It is conventional to write the first term as Y_0, and once this is given a specific value, all remaining terms are known.

If $Y_0 = 3$, then

$$Y_1 = 2Y_0 = 2 \times 3 = 6$$
$$Y_2 = 2Y_1 = 2 \times 6 = 12$$
$$Y_3 = 2Y_2 = 2 \times 12 = 24$$

If we write these terms as

$$Y_1 = 2Y_0 = 2^1 \times 3$$
$$Y_2 = 2Y_1 = 2^2 \times 3$$
$$Y_3 = 2Y_2 = 2^3 \times 3$$

we can see that the general term may be expressed as

$$Y_t = 3(2^t)$$

This is the solution of the difference equation

$$Y_t = 2Y_{t-1}$$

with **initial condition** $Y_0 = 3$.

The following problem gives you an opportunity to solve difference equations for yourself.

Practice Problem

1. Starting with the given initial conditions, write down the first four terms of each of the following sequences. By expressing these as an appropriate power, write down a formula for the general term Y_t in terms of t.

   (1) (a) $Y_t = 3Y_{t-1}$; $Y_0 = 1$ **(b)** $Y_t = 3Y_{t-1}$; $Y_0 = 7$ **(c)** $Y_t = 3Y_{t-1}$; $Y_0 = A$

   (2) (a) $Y_t = \dfrac{1}{2}Y_{t-1}$; $Y_0 = 1$ **(b)** $Y_t = \dfrac{1}{2}Y_{t-1}$; $Y_0 = 7$ **(c)** $Y_t = \dfrac{1}{2}Y_{t-1}$; $Y_0 = A$

   (3) $Y_t = bY_{t-1}$; $Y_0 = A$

The result of the last part of Practice Problem 1 shows that the solution of the general equation

$$Y_t = bY_{t-1} \tag{1}$$

with initial condition

$$Y_0 = A$$

is given by

$$Y_t = A(b^t)$$

Before we can consider the use of difference equations in economic models, we must examine the solution of more general equations of the form

$$Y_t = bY_{t-1} + c \tag{2}$$

where the right-hand side now includes a non-zero constant, c. We begin by defining some terminology. The **general solution** of equation (2) can be written as the sum of two separate expressions known as the complementary function (CF) and the particular solution (PS). The **complementary function** is the name that we give to the solution of equation (2) when the constant, c, is zero. In this case, equation (2) reduces to equation (1), and so

$$\text{CF} = A(b^t)$$

The **particular solution** is the name that we give to any solution of equation (2) that we are clever enough to 'spot'. This turns out to be easier to do than might at first appear, and we will see how this can be done in a moment. Finally, once CF and PS have been found, we can write down the general solution of equation (2) as

$$Y_t = \text{CF} + \text{PS} = A(b^t) + \text{PS}$$

The letter A is no longer equal to the first term, Y_0, although it can easily be calculated, as the following example demonstrates.

Example

Solve the following difference equations with the specified initial conditions. Comment on the qualitative behaviour of the solution in each case.

(a) $Y_t = 4Y_{t-1} + 21$; $Y_0 = 1$

(b) $Y_t = \dfrac{1}{3}Y_{t-1} + 8$; $Y_0 = 2$

Solution

(a) The difference equation

$$Y_t = 4Y_{t-1} + 21$$

is of the standard form

$$Y_t = bY_{t-1} + c$$

and so can be solved using the complementary function and particular solution. The complementary function is the general solution of the equation when the constant term on the right-hand side is replaced by zero: that is, it is the solution of

$$Y_t = 4Y_{t-1}$$

which is $A(4^t)$.

The particular solution is any solution of the original equation

$$Y_t = 4Y_{t-1} + 21$$

that we are able to find. In effect, we need to think of a sequence of numbers, Y_t, such that when this is substituted into

$$Y_t - 4Y_{t-1}$$

we obtain the constant value of 21. One obvious sequence likely to work is a constant sequence,

$$Y_t = D$$

for some number, D. If this is substituted into

$$Y_t = 4Y_{t-1} + 21$$

we obtain

$$D = 4D + 21$$

(Note that $Y_t = D$ whatever the value of t, so Y_{t-1} is also equal to D.) This algebraic equation can be rearranged to get

$$-3D = 21$$

and so $D = -7$.

We have therefore shown that the complementary function is given by

$$CF = A(4^t)$$

and that the particular solution is

$$PS = -7$$

Hence

$$Y_t = \text{CF} + \text{PS} = A(4^t) - 7$$

which is the general solution of the difference equation

$$Y_t = 4Y_{t-1} + 21$$

To find the specific solution that satisfies the initial condition

$$Y_0 = 1$$

we simply put $t = 0$ in the general solution to get

$$Y_0 = A(4^0) - 7 = 1$$

that is,

$$A - 7 = 1$$

which gives

$$A = 8$$

The solution is

$$Y_t = 8(4^t) - 7$$

A graphical interpretation of this solution is shown in Figure 9.1, where Y_t is plotted against t. It is tempting to join the points up with a smooth curve. However, this does

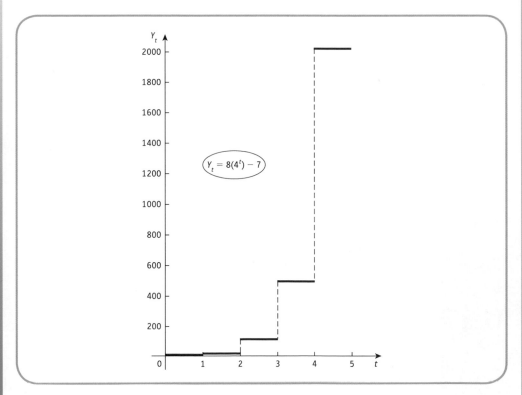

Figure 9.1

not make sense because t is allowed to take only whole number values. Consequently, we join up the points with horizontal lines to create the 'staircase' which more properly reflects the fact that t is discrete. Figure 9.1 shows that the values of Y_t increase without bound as t increases. This is also apparent from the formula for Y_t because the numbers 4^t get ever larger as t increases. We describe this by saying that the time path **diverges uniformly** or *explodes*. This sort of behaviour can be expected to occur for any solution

$$Y_t = A(b^t) + \text{PS}$$

where $b > 1$.

(b) The difference equation

$$Y_t = \frac{1}{3}Y_{t-1} + 8$$

can be solved in a similar way to that of part (a). The complementary function is given by

$$\text{CF} = A\left(\frac{1}{3}\right)^t$$

and for a particular solution we try

$$Y_t = D$$

for some constant D. Substituting this into the difference equation gives

$$D = \frac{1}{3}D + 8$$

which has solution $D = 12$, so

$$\text{PS} = 12$$

The general solution is therefore

$$Y_t = \text{CF} + \text{PS} = A\left(\frac{1}{3}\right)^t + 12$$

Finally, the specific value of A can be found from the initial condition

$$Y_0 = 2$$

Setting $t = 0$ in the general solution gives

$$2 = A\left(\frac{1}{3}\right)^0 + 12 = A + 12$$

and so A is -10. The solution is

$$Y_t = -10\left(\frac{1}{3}\right)^t + 12$$

This solution is sketched in Figure 9.2, which shows that the values of Y_t increase but eventually settle down at 12. We describe this by saying that the time path **converges uniformly** to the value of 12, which is referred to as the **equilibrium value**. This

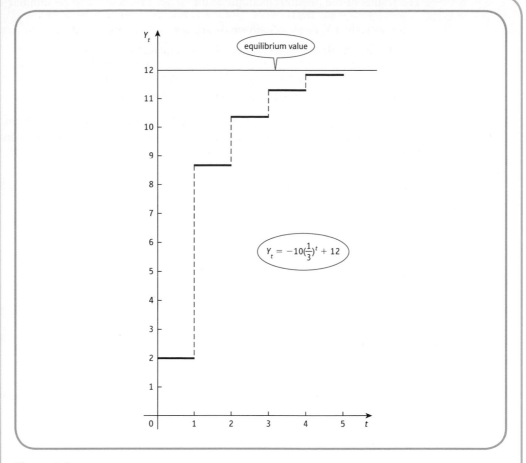

Figure 9.2

behaviour is also apparent from the formula for Y_t because the number $(1/3)^t$ gets ever smaller as t increases. In effect, the complementary function disappears, leaving just the particular solution. The particular solution is the equilibrium value of Y_t, whereas the complementary function measures the deviation from the equilibrium which, in this case, converges to zero as t increases. This sort of behaviour can be expected to occur for any solution

$$Y_t = A(b^t) + \text{PS}$$

when $0 < b < 1$.

Practice Problem

2. Solve the following difference equations with the specified initial conditions:

(a) $Y_t = -\frac{1}{2}Y_{t-1} + 6;\ Y_0 = 0$ (b) $Y_t = -2Y_{t-1} + 9;\ Y_0 = 4$

In each case, sketch the corresponding 'staircase' diagram and comment on the qualitative behaviour of the solution as t increases.

The results of the previous example and Practice Problem 2 can be summarised:

If $b > 1$, then Y_t displays uniform divergence.

If $0 < b < 1$, then Y_t displays uniform convergence.

If $-1 < b < 0$, then Y_t displays oscillatory convergence.

If $b < -1$, then Y_t displays oscillatory divergence.

The remaining possibilities, $b = 1$, $b = -1$ and $b = 0$, are considered in Problem 1 of Exercise 9.1 at the end of this section, which shows that Y_t converges when b is 0 but diverges when b is 1 or -1. We conclude that the solution of the difference equation eventually settles down to an equilibrium state only when b lies in the range $-1 < b < 1$.

If convergence does occur in an economic model, the model is said to be **stable**. If the variables diverge, it is said to be **unstable**.

We now investigate two applications of difference equations taken from macroeconomics and microeconomics, respectively:

- national income determination;
- supply and demand analysis.

We consider each of these in turn.

9.1.1 National income determination

In Section 1.7 we introduced a simple two-sector model with structural equations

$$Y = C + I$$
$$C = aY + b$$
$$I = I^*$$

where b and I^* denote autonomous consumption and investment, and a is the marginal propensity to consume, which lies in the range $0 < a < 1$. In writing down the equations in this form, we are implicitly assuming that only one time period is involved, that consumption depends on national income within this time period and that equilibrium values are attained instantaneously. In practice, there is a time lag between consumption and national income. Consumption, C_t, in period t depends on national income, Y_{t-1}, in the previous period, $t - 1$. The corresponding consumption function is given by

$$C_t = aY_{t-1} + b$$

If we assume that investment is the same in all time periods, then

$$I_t = I^*$$

for some constant, I^*. Finally, if the flow of money is in balance in each time period, we also have

$$Y_t = C_t + I_t$$

Substituting the expressions for C_t and I_t into this gives

$$Y_t = aY_{t-1} + b + I^*$$

which we recognise as a difference equation of the standard form given in this section. This equation can therefore be solved and the time path analysed.

Example

Consider a two-sector model:

$$Y_t = C_t + I_t$$
$$C_t = 0.8Y_{t-1} + 100$$
$$I_t = 200$$

Find an expression for Y_t when $Y_0 = 1700$. Is this system stable or unstable?

Solution

Substituting the expressions for C_t and I_t into

$$Y_t = C_t + I_t$$

gives

$$Y_t = (0.8Y_{t-1} + 100) + 200$$
$$= 0.8Y_{t-1} + 300$$

The complementary function is given by

$$CF = A(0.8)^t$$

and for a particular solution we try

$$Y_t = D$$

for some constant D. Substituting this into the difference equation gives

$$D = 0.8D + 300$$

which has solution $D = 1500$. The general solution is therefore

$$Y_t = A(0.8)^t + 1500$$

The initial condition,

$$Y_0 = 1700$$

gives

$$1700 = A(0.8)^0 + 1500 = A + 1500$$

and so A is 200. The solution is

$$Y_t = 200(0.8^t) + 1500$$

As t increases, $(0.8)^t$ converges to zero, and so Y_t eventually settles down at the equilibrium level of 1500. The system is therefore stable. Note also that because 0.8 lies between 0 and 1, the time path displays uniform convergence.

Practice Problem

3. Consider the two-sector model:

$$Y_t = C_t + I_t$$
$$C_t = 0.9Y_{t-1} + 250$$
$$I_t - 350$$

Find an expression for Y_t when $Y_0 = 6500$. Is this system stable or unstable?

In the previous example and again in Practice Problem 3, we noted that the model is stable and that it displays uniform convergence. If we return to the general equation

$$Y_t = aY_{t-1} + b + I^*$$

it is easy to see that this is always the case for the simple two-sector model because the coefficient of Y_{t-1} is the marginal propensity to consume, which is known to lie between 0 and 1.

9.1.2 Supply and demand analysis

In Section 1.5 we introduced a simple model of supply and demand for a single good in an isolated market. If we assume that the supply and demand functions are both linear, then we have the relations

$$Q_S = aP - b$$
$$Q_D = -cP + d$$

for some positive constants, a, b, c and d. (Previously, we have written P in terms of Q and have sketched the supply and demand curves with Q on the horizontal axis and P on the vertical axis. It turns out that it is more convenient in the present context to work the other way round and to write Q as a function of P.) In writing down these equations, we are implicitly assuming that only one time period is involved, that supply and demand are dependent only on the price in this time period and that equilibrium values are attained instantaneously. However, for certain goods, there is a time lag between supply and price. For example, a farmer needs to decide precisely how much of any crop to sow well in advance of the time of sale. This decision is made on the basis of the price at the time of planting and not on the price prevailing at harvest time, which is unknown. In other words, the supply, Q_S, in period t depends on the price, P_{t-1}, in the preceding period $t - 1$. The corresponding time-dependent supply and demand equations are

$$Q_{S_t} = aP_{t-1} - b$$
$$Q_{D_t} = -cP_t + d$$

If we assume that, within each time period, demand and supply are equal, so that all goods are sold, then

$$Q_{D_t} = Q_{S_t}$$

that is,

$$-cP_t + d = aP_{t-1} - b$$

This equation can be rearranged as

$$-cP_t = aP_{t-1} - b - d \quad \text{(subtract } d \text{ from both sides)}$$

$$P_t = \left(-\frac{a}{c}\right)P_{t-1} + \frac{b + d}{c} \quad \text{(divide both sides by } -c)$$

which is a difference equation of the standard form. The equation can therefore be solved in the usual way and the time path analysed. Once a formula for P_t is obtained, we can use the demand equation

$$Q_t = -cP_t + d$$

to deduce a corresponding formula for Q_t by substituting the expression for P_t into the right-hand side.

Example

Consider the supply and demand equations

$$Q_{S_t} = 4P_{t-1} - 10$$
$$Q_{D_t} = -5P_t + 35$$

Assuming that the market is in equilibrium, find expressions for P_t and Q_t when $P_0 = 6$. Is the system stable or unstable?

Solution

If

$$Q_{D_t} = Q_{S_t}$$

then

$$-5P_t + 35 = 4P_{t-1} - 10$$

which rearranges to give

$$-5P_t = 4P_{t-1} - 45 \qquad \text{(subtract 35 from both sides)}$$
$$P_t = -0.8P_{t-1} + 9 \quad \text{(divide both sides by } -5)$$

The complementary function is given by

$$\text{CF} = A(-0.8)^t$$

and for a particular solution we try

$$P_t = D$$

for some constant D. Substituting this into the difference equation gives

$$D = -0.8D + 9$$

which has solution $D = 5$. The general solution is therefore

$$P_t = A(-0.8)^t + 5$$

The initial condition, $P_0 = 6$, gives

$$6 = A(-0.8)^0 + 5 = A + 5$$

and so A is 1. The solution is

$$P_t = (-0.8)^t + 5$$

An expression for Q_t can be found by substituting this into the demand equation

$$Q_t = -5P_t + 35$$

to get

$$Q_t = -5[(-0.8)^t + 5] + 35$$
$$= -5(-0.8)^t + 10$$

As t increases, $(-0.8)^t$ converges to zero, and so P_t and Q_t eventually settle down at the equilibrium levels of 5 and 10, respectively. The system is therefore stable. Note also that because -0.8 lies between -1 and 0, the time paths display oscillatory convergence.

Practice Problems

4. Consider the supply and demand equations

   $$Q_{S_t} = P_{t-1} - 8$$
   $$Q_{D_t} = -2P_t + 22$$

   Assuming equilibrium, find expressions for P_t and Q_t when $P_0 = 11$. Is the system stable or unstable?

5. Consider the supply and demand equations

   $$Q_{S_t} = 3P_{t-1} - 20$$
   $$Q_{D_t} = -2P_t + 80$$

   Assuming equilibrium, find expressions for P_t and Q_t when $P_0 = 8$. Is the system stable or unstable?

Two features emerge from the previous example and Practice Problems 4 and 5. Firstly, the time paths are always oscillatory. Secondly, the system is not necessarily stable, and so equilibrium might not be attained. These properties can be explained if we return to the general equation

$$P_t = \left(-\frac{a}{c}\right)P_{t-1} + \frac{b+d}{c}$$

The coefficient of P_{t-1} is $-a/c$. Given that a and c are both positive, it follows that $-a/c$ is negative and so oscillations will always be present. Moreover,

- if $a > c$, then $-a/c < -1$ and P_t diverges
- if $a < c$, then $-1 < -a/c < 0$ and P_t converges.

We conclude that stability depends on the relative sizes of a and c, which govern the slopes of the supply and demand curves. Bearing in mind that we have chosen to consider supply and demand equations in which Q is expressed in terms of P, namely

$$Q_S = aP - b$$
$$Q_D = -cP + d$$

we deduce that the system is stable whenever the supply curve is flatter than the demand curve when P is plotted on the horizontal axis.

Throughout this section we have concentrated on linear models. An obvious question to ask is whether we can extend these to cover the case of non-linear relationships. Unfortunately, the associated mathematics gets hard very quickly, even for mildly non-linear problems. It is usually impossible to find an explicit formula for the solution of such difference equations. Under these circumstances, we fall back on the tried and trusted approach of actually calculating the first few values until we can identify its behaviour. A spreadsheet provides an ideal way of doing this, since the parameters in the model can be easily changed.

Key Terms

Complementary function of a difference equation   The solution of the difference equation $Y_t = bY_{t-1} + c$ when the constant c is replaced by zero.

Difference equation   An equation that relates consecutive terms of a sequence of numbers.

Dynamics   Analysis of how equilibrium values vary over time.

Equilibrium value of a difference equation   A solution of a difference equation that does not vary over time; it is the limiting value of Y_n as n tends to infinity.

General solution of a difference equation   The solution of a difference equation that contains an arbitrary constant. It is the sum of the complementary function and a particular solution.

Initial condition   The value of Y_0 that needs to be specified to obtain a unique solution of a difference equation.

Particular solution of a difference equation   Any one solution of a difference equation such as $Y_t = bY_{t-1} + c$.

Recurrence relation   An alternative term for a difference equation. It is an expression for Y_n in terms of Y_{n-1} (and possibly Y_{n-2}, Y_{n-3}, etc.).

Stable (unstable) equilibrium   An economic model in which the solution of the associated difference equation converges (diverges).

Uniformly convergent sequence   A sequence of numbers which progressively increases (or decreases) to a finite limit.

Uniformly divergent sequence   A sequence of numbers which progressively increases (or decreases) without a finite limit.

Exercise 9.1

1. Calculate the first four terms of the sequences defined by the following difference equations. Hence write down a formula for Y_t in terms of t. Comment on the qualitative behaviour of the solution in each case.

   (a) $Y_t = Y_{t-1} + 2$; $Y_0 = 0$ **(b)** $Y_t = -Y_{t-1} + 6$; $Y_0 = 4$ **(c)** $Y_t = 0Y_{t-1} + 3$; $Y_0 = 3$

2. Solve the following difference equations with the specified initial conditions:

   (a) $Y_t = \dfrac{1}{4}Y_{t-1} + 6$; $Y_0 = 1$ **(b)** $Y_t = -4Y_{t-1} + 5$; $Y_0 = 2$

   Comment on the qualitative behaviour of the solution as t increases.

3. Consider the two-sector model:

   $$Y_t = C_t + I_t$$
   $$C_t = 0.7Y_{t-1} + 400$$
   $$I_t = 0.1Y_{t-1} + 100$$

   Given that $Y_0 = 3000$, find an expression for Y_t. Is this system stable or unstable?

4. Consider the supply and demand equations

   $$Q_{S_t} = 0.4P_{t-1} - 12$$
   $$Q_{D_t} = -0.8P_t + 60$$

→

Assuming that equilibrium conditions prevail, find an expression for P_t when $P_0 = 70$. Is the system stable or unstable?

5. Consider the two-sector model:

$$Y_t = C_t + I_t$$
$$C_t = 0.75Y_{t-1} + 400$$
$$I_t = 200$$

Find the value of C_2, given that, $Y_0 = 400$.

6. The Harrod–Domar model of the growth of an economy is based on three assumptions.

(1) Savings, S_t, in any time period are proportional to income, Y_t, in that period, so that

$$S_t = \alpha Y_t \qquad (\alpha > 0)$$

(2) Investment, I_t, in any time period is proportional to the change in income from the previous period to the current period so that

$$I_t = \beta(Y_t - Y_{t-1}) \quad (\beta > 0)$$

(3) Investment and savings are equal in any period so that

$$I_t = S_t$$

Use these assumptions to show that

$$Y_1 = \left(\frac{\beta}{\beta - \alpha}\right)Y_{t-1}$$

and hence write down a formula for Y_t in terms of Y_0. Comment on the stability of the system in the case when $\alpha = 0.1$ and $\beta = 1.4$.

Exercise 9.1*

1. Describe the qualitative behaviour of the sequence of numbers which satisfy

$$Y_t = -\frac{1}{2}Y_{t-1}^2$$

with initial condition $Y_0 = -1$.

2. (a) Write down the next four terms of the sequence defined by

$$Y_t = \frac{1}{1 - Y_{t-1}}; Y_0 = 2$$

Deduce the value of Y_{200}.

(b) Write down the next four terms of the sequence defined by

$$Y_t = Y_{t-1} + 4; Y_0 = 3$$

Write down a formula for Y_t in terms of t.

3. Find the solution of the difference equation

$$Y_t = bY_{t-1} + c$$

with initial condition, $Y_0 = a$.

4. Consider the two-sector model:

$$Y_t = C_t + I_t$$
$$C_t = 0.85Y_{t-1} + 300$$
$$I_t = 0.15Y_{t-1} + 100$$

Given that $Y_0 = 4000$, find an expression for Y_t. Is this system stable or unstable?

5. Consider the supply and demand equations

$$Q_{S_t} = aP_{t-1} - b$$
$$Q_{D_t} = -cP_t + d$$

where the constants a, b, c and d are all positive.

(a) Assuming that the market is in equilibrium, show that

$$P_t = \left(-\frac{a}{c}\right)P_{t-1} + \frac{b+d}{c}$$

(b) Show that $\dfrac{b+d}{a+c}$ is a particular solution of the difference equation in part (a), and write down an expression for the general solution.

(c) State the conditions under which the solution in part (a) is guaranteed to converge, and state the equilibrium price and quantity. Simplify your answers.

6. Find the reduced form connecting P_t and P_{t-1} for the market model:

$$Q_{S_t} = aP_t - b$$
$$Q_{D_t} = -cP_t + d$$
$$P_t = P_{t-1} - e(Q_{S_{t-1}} - Q_{D_{t-1}})$$

7. A bank offers an individual a loan of $\$A$ at a rate of interest of $r\%$ compounded monthly. The individual pays off the loan by monthly instalments of $\$a$. If u_t denotes outstanding balance after t months, explain why

$$u_t = \left(1 + \frac{r}{1200}\right)u_{t-1} - a$$

and show that

$$u_t = \left(A - \frac{1200a}{r}\right)\left(1 + \frac{r}{1200}\right)^t + \frac{1200a}{r}$$

Hence write down an expression for the monthly repayment if the loan is paid off after N months.

8. Consider the difference equation

    $$Y_t = 0.1Y_{t-1} + 5(0.6)^t$$

    (a) Write down the complementary function.

    (b) By substituting $Y_t = D(0.6)^t$ into this equation, find a particular solution.

    (c) Use your answers to parts (a) and (b) to write down the general solution and hence find the specific solution that satisfies the initial condition, $Y_0 = 9$.

    (d) Is the solution in part (c) stable or unstable?

9. Consider the difference equation

    $$Y_t = 0.2Y_{t-1} + 0.8t + 5$$

    (a) Write down the complementary function.

    (b) By substituting $Y_t = Dt + E$ into this equation, find a particular solution.

    (c) Use your answers to parts (a) and (b) to write down the general solution and hence find the specific solution that satisfies the initial condition, $Y_0 = 10$.

    (d) Is the solution in part (c) stable or unstable?

SECTION 9.2
Differential equations

Objectives

At the end of this section you should be able to:

- Find the complementary function of a differential equation.
- Find the particular solution of a differential equation.
- Analyse the stability of economic systems.
- Solve continuous time national income determination models.
- Solve continuous time supply and demand models.

A **differential equation** is an equation that involves the derivative of an unknown function. Several examples have already been considered in Chapter 6. For instance, in Section 6.2 we noted the relationship

$$\frac{dK}{dt} = I$$

where K and I denote capital stock and net investment, respectively. Given any expression for $I(t)$, this represents a differential equation for the unknown function, $K(t)$. In such a simple case as this, we can solve the differential equation by integrating both sides with respect to t. For example, if $I(t) = t$, the equation becomes

$$\frac{dK}{dt} = t$$

and so

$$K(t) = \int t\,dt = \frac{t^2}{2} + c$$

where c is a constant of integration. The function $K(t)$ is said to be the **general solution** of the differential equation, and c is referred to as an **arbitrary constant**. Some additional information is needed if the solution is to be pinned down uniquely. This is usually provided in the form of an **initial condition** in which we specify the value of K at $t = 0$. For example, the capital stock may be known to be 500 initially. Substituting $t = 0$ into the general solution

$$K(t) = \frac{t^2}{2} + c$$

gives

$$K(0) = \frac{0^2}{2} + c = 500$$

and so c is 500. Hence the solution is

$$K(t) = \frac{t^2}{2} + 500$$

In this section we investigate more complicated equations where the right-hand sides of these equations are given in terms of y such as

$$\frac{dy}{dt} = 3y$$

The solution of this equation is any function, $y(t)$, which differentiates to three times itself. We have seen in Section 4.8 that e^{mt} differentiates to m times itself, so an obvious candidate for the solution is

$$y = e^{3t}$$

However, there are many functions with the same property, including

$$y = 2e^{3t}, y = 5e^{3t} \quad \text{and} \quad y = -7.52e^{3t}$$

Indeed, any function of the form

$$y = Ae^{3t}$$

satisfies this differential equation because

$$\frac{dy}{dt} = 3(Ae^{3t}) = 3y$$

The precise value of the constant A is determined from an initial condition such as

$$y(0) = 5$$

If we substitute $t = 0$ into the general solution

$$y(t) = Ae^{3t}$$

we get

$$y(0) = Ae^0 = A$$

and so A is 5. The solution is

$$y(t) = 5e^{3t}$$

Practice Problem

1. (a) Find the solution of the differential equation

$$\frac{dy}{dt} = 4y$$

which satisfies the initial condition, $y(0) = 6$.

(b) Find the solution of the differential equation

$$\frac{dy}{dt} = -5y$$

which satisfies the initial condition, $y(0) = 2$.

Consider the differential equation

$$\frac{dy}{dt} = my + c \qquad (1)$$

where m and c are constants. The general solution of equation (1) is the sum of two separate functions, known as the complementary function (CF) and particular solution (PS). These are defined in much the same way as their counterparts for difference equations discussed in the previous section. The **complementary function** is the solution of equation (1) when the constant term on the right-hand side is replaced by zero. In other words, the complementary function is the solution of

$$\frac{dy}{dt} = my$$

The results of Practice Problem 1 show that this is given by

$$CF = Ae^{mt}$$

The **particular solution** is any solution that we are able to find of the original equation (1). This can be done by 'guesswork', just as we did in Section 9.1. Finally, once CF and PS have been determined, the general solution of equation (1) can be written down as

$$y = CF + PS = Ae^{mt} + PS$$

As usual, the specific value of A can be worked out at the very end of the calculations via an initial condition.

Example

Solve the differential equation

$$\frac{dy}{dt} = -2y + 100$$

in the case when the initial condition is

(a) $y(0) = 10$ **(b)** $y(0) = 90$ **(c)** $y(0) = 50$

Comment on the qualitative behaviour of the solution in each case.

Solution

The differential equation

$$\frac{dy}{dt} = -2y + 100$$

is of the standard form

$$\frac{dy}{dt} = my + c$$

and so can be solved using the complementary function and particular solution.

The complementary function is the general solution of the equation when the constant term is taken to be zero: that is, it is the solution of

$$\frac{\mathrm{d}y}{\mathrm{d}t} = -2y$$

which is Ae^{-2t}. The particular solution is any solution of the original equation

$$\frac{\mathrm{d}y}{\mathrm{d}t} = -2y + 100$$

that we are able to find. In effect, we need to think of a function, $y(t)$, such that when it is substituted into

$$\frac{\mathrm{d}y}{\mathrm{d}t} + 2y$$

we obtain the constant value of 100. One obvious function likely to work is a constant function,

$$y(t) = D$$

for some constant D. If this is substituted into

$$\frac{\mathrm{d}y}{\mathrm{d}t} = -2y + 100$$

we obtain

$$0 = -2D + 100$$

(Note that $\mathrm{d}y/\mathrm{d}t = 0$ because constants differentiate to zero.) This algebraic equation can be rearranged to get

$$2D = 100$$

and so $D = 50$.

We have therefore shown that the complementary function is given by

$$\mathrm{CF} = Ae^{-2t}$$

and that the particular solution is

$$\mathrm{PS} = 50$$

Hence

$$y(t) = \mathrm{CF} + \mathrm{PS} = Ae^{-2t} + 50$$

This is the general solution of the differential equation

$$\frac{\mathrm{d}y}{\mathrm{d}t} = -2y + 100$$

(a) To find the specific solution that satisfies the initial condition

$$y(0) = 10$$

we simply put $t = 0$ into the general solution to get

$$y(0) = Ae^0 + 50 = 10$$

that is

$$A + 50 = 10$$

which gives

$$A = -40$$

The solution is

$$y(t) = -40e^{-2t} + 50$$

A graph of y against t is sketched as the bottom graph in Figure 9.3. This shows that $y(t)$ increases from its initial value of 10 and settles down at the value of 50 for sufficiently large t. As usual, this limit is called the **equilibrium value** and is equal to the particular solution. The complementary function measures the deviation from the equilibrium.

(b) If the initial condition is

$$y(0) = 90$$

then we can substitute $t = 0$ into the general solution

$$y(t) = Ae^{-2t} + 50$$

to get

$$y(0) = Ae^0 + 50 = 90$$

which has solution $A = 40$. Hence

$$y(t) = 40e^{-2t} + 50$$

A graph of y against t is sketched as the top curve in Figure 9.3. In this case $y(t)$ decreases from its initial value of 90 but again settles down at the equilibrium level of 50.

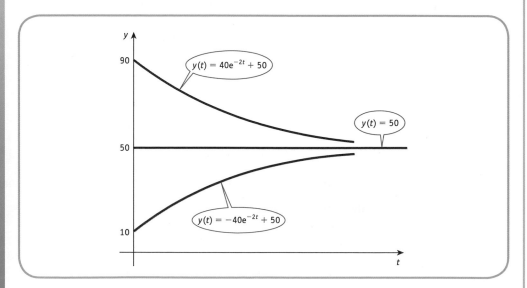

Figure 9.3

(c) If the initial condition is

$$y(0) = 50$$

then we can substitute $t = 0$ into the general solution

$$y(t) = Ae^{-2t} + 50$$

to get

$$y(0) = Ae^0 + 50 = 50$$

which has solution $A = 0$. Hence

$$y(t) = 50$$

A graph of y against t is sketched as the horizontal line in Figure 9.3. In this case, y is initially equal to the equilibrium value and y remains at this constant value for all time.

Notice that the solution $y(t)$ eventually settles down at the equilibrium value irrespective of the initial conditions. This is because the coefficient of t in the expression

$$CF = Ae^{-2t}$$

is negative, causing CF to converge to zero as t increases. We would expect convergence to occur for any solution

$$y(t) = Ae^{mt} + D$$

when $m < 0$.

Practice Problem

2. Solve the following differential equation subject to the given initial condition. Comment on the qualitative behaviour of the solution as t increases.

$$\frac{dy}{dt} = 3y - 60; \quad y(0) = 30$$

The results of the previous example and Practice Problem 2 can be summarised as:

- if $m < 0$ then $y(t)$ converges;
- if $m > 0$ then $y(t)$ diverges.

We say that an economic model is **stable** whenever the variables converge as t increases. The above results indicate that an economic system represented by

$$\frac{dy}{dt} = my + c$$

is stable if the coefficient of y is negative and unstable if it is positive. Of course, it could happen that m is zero. The differential equation then becomes

$$\frac{dy}{dt} = c$$

which can be integrated directly to get

$$y(t) = \int c\,dt = ct + d$$

for some arbitrary constant d. The corresponding model is therefore unstable unless c is also zero, in which case $y(t)$ takes the constant value of d for all t.

We now investigate two applications of differential equations taken from macroeconomics and microeconomics, respectively:

- national income determination;
- supply and demand analysis.

We consider each of these in turn.

9.2.1 National income determination

The defining equations of the usual two-sector model are

$$Y = C + I \tag{1}$$
$$C = aY + b \tag{2}$$
$$I = I* \tag{3}$$

The first of these is simply a statement that the economy is already in balance. The left-hand side of equation (1) is the flow of money from firms to households given as payment for the factors of production. The right-hand side is the total flow of money received by firms, either in the form of investment or as payment for goods bought by households. In practice, the equilibrium values are not immediately attained, and we need to make an alternative assumption about how national income varies with time. It seems reasonable to suppose that the rate of change of Y is proportional to the excess expenditure, $C + I - Y$: that is,

$$\frac{dY}{dt} = \alpha(C + I - Y) \tag{1$'$}$$

for some positive **adjustment coefficient**, α. This makes sense because

- if $C + I > Y$, it gives $dY/dt > 0$, and so Y rises in order to achieve a balance between expenditure and income
- if $C + I = Y$, it gives $dY/dt = 0$, and so Y is held constant at the equilibrium level
- if $C + I < Y$, it gives $dY/dt < 0$, and so Y falls in order to achieve a balance between expenditure and income.

The usual relations (2) and (3) can be substituted into the new equation (1$'$) to obtain

$$\frac{dY}{dt} = \alpha(aY + b + I* - Y)$$
$$= \alpha(a - 1)Y + \alpha(b + I*)$$

which we recognise as a differential equation of the standard form given in this section.

Example

Consider the two-sector model

$$\frac{dY}{dt} = 0.5(C + I - Y)$$

$$C = 0.8Y + 400$$

$$I = 600$$

Find an expression for $Y(t)$ when $Y(0) = 7000$. Is this system stable or unstable?

Solution

Substituting the expressions for C and I into

$$\frac{dY}{dt} = 0.5(C + I - Y)$$

gives

$$\frac{dY}{dt} = 0.5(0.8Y + 400 + 600 - Y)$$

$$= -0.1Y + 500$$

The complementary function is given by

$$CF = Ae^{-0.1t}$$

and for a particular solution we try

$$Y(t) = D$$

for some constant, D. Substituting this into the differential equation gives

$$0 = -0.1D + 500$$

which has solution $D = 5000$. The general solution is therefore

$$Y(t) = Ae^{-0.1t} + 5000$$

The initial condition

$$Y(0) = 7000$$

gives

$$A + 5000 = 7000$$

and so A is 2000. The solution is

$$Y(t) = 2000e^{-0.1t} + 5000$$

The first term is a negative exponential, so it converges to zero as t increases. Consequently, $Y(t)$ eventually settles down to an equilibrium value of 5000 and the system is stable.

Practice Problem

3. Consider the two-sector model

$$\frac{dY}{dt} = 0.1(C + I - Y)$$

$$C = 0.9Y + 100$$

$$I = 300$$

Find an expression for $Y(t)$ when $Y(0) = 2000$. Is this system stable or unstable?

In the previous example and again in Practice Problem 3, we noted that the macroeconomic system is stable. If we return to the general equation

$$\frac{dY}{dt} = \alpha(a - 1)Y + \alpha(b + I^*)$$

it is easy to see that this is always the case for the simple two-sector model, since the coefficient of Y is negative. This follows because, as previously stated, $\alpha > 0$, and because the marginal propensity to consume, a, is less than 1.

9.2.2 Supply and demand analysis

The equations defining the usual linear single-commodity market model are

$$Q_S = aP - b \tag{1}$$
$$Q_D - -cP + d \tag{2}$$

for some positive constants a, b, c and d. As in Section 9.1, we have written Q in terms of P for convenience. Previously, we have calculated the equilibrium price and quantity simply by equating supply and demand: that is, by putting

$$Q_S = Q_D$$

In writing down this relation, we are implicitly assuming that equilibrium is immediately attained and, in doing so, we fail to take into account the way in which this is achieved. A reasonable assumption to make is that the rate of change of price is proportional to excess demand, $Q_D - Q_S$: that is,

$$\frac{dP}{dt} = \alpha(Q_D - Q_S)$$

for some positive adjustment coefficient, α. This makes sense because

- if $Q_D > Q_S$, it gives $dP/dt > 0$, and so P increases in order to achieve a balance between supply and demand;
- if $Q_S = Q_D$, it gives $dP/dt = 0$, and so P is held constant at the equilibrium level;
- if $Q_D < Q_S$, it gives $dP/dt < 0$, and so P decreases in order to achieve a balance between supply and demand.

Substituting equations (1) and (2) into equation (3) gives

$$\frac{dP}{dt} = \alpha[(-cP + d) - (aP - b)] = -\alpha(a + c)P + \alpha(d + b)$$

which is a differential equation of the standard form.

Example

Consider the market model

$$Q_S = 3P - 4$$

$$Q_D = -5P + 20$$

$$\frac{dP}{dt} = 0.2(Q_D - Q_S)$$

Find expressions for $P(t)$, $Q_S(t)$ and $Q_D(t)$ when $P(0) = 2$. Is this system stable or unstable?

Solution

Substituting the expressions for Q_D and Q_S into

$$\frac{dP}{dt} = 0.2(Q_D - Q_S)$$

gives

$$\frac{dP}{dt} = 0.2[(-5P + 20) - (3P - 4)] = -1.6P + 4.8$$

The complementary function is given by

$$CF = Ae^{-1.6t}$$

and for a particular solution we try

$$P(t) = D$$

for some constant D. Substituting this into the differential equation gives

$$0 = -1.6D + 4.8$$

which has solution $D = 3$. The general solution is therefore

$$P(t) = Ae^{-1.6t} + 3$$

The initial condition

$$P(0) = 2$$

gives

$$A + 3 = 2$$

and so A is -1. The solution is

$$P(t) = -e^{-1.6t} + 3$$

Corresponding expressions for $Q_S(t)$ and $Q_D(t)$ can be found from the supply and demand equations, which give

$$Q_S(t) = 3P - 4 = 3(-e^{-1.6t} + 3) - 4 = -3e^{-1.6t} + 5$$

$$Q_D(t) = -5P + 20 = -5(-e^{-1.6t} + 3) + 20 = 5e^{-1.6t} + 5$$

Note that all three expressions involve a negative exponential that converges to zero as t increases, so the system is stable. The price $P(t)$ eventually settles down to the equilibrium price, 3, and $Q_S(t)$ and $Q_D(t)$ both approach the equilibrium quantity, 5.

Practice Problem

4. Consider the market model

$$Q_S = 2P - 2$$

$$Q_D = -P + 4$$

$$\frac{dP}{dt} = \frac{1}{3}(Q_D - Q_S)$$

Find expressions for $P(t)$, $Q_S(t)$ and $Q_D(t)$ when $P(0) = 1$. Is this system stable or unstable?

In the previous example and again in Practice Problem 4, we noted that the single commodity market model is stable. If we return again to the general equation

$$\frac{dP}{dt} = -\alpha(a + c)P + \alpha(d + b)$$

it is easy to see that this is always the case, since the coefficient of P is negative. This follows because, as previously stated, α, a and c are all positive.

Key Terms

Adjustment coefficient The constant of proportionality in the simple macroeconomic model, in which the rate of change of national income is assumed to be proportional to excess expenditure.

Arbitrary constant A letter representing an unspecified constant in the general solution of a differential equation.

Complementary function of a differential equation The solution of the differential equation $\dfrac{dy}{dt} = my + c$ when the constant c is replaced by zero.

Differential equation An equation connecting derivatives of an unknown function.

Equilibrium value of a differential equation A solution of a differential equation that does not vary over time; it is the limiting value of $y(t)$ as t tends to infinity.

General solution of a differential equation The solution of a differential equation that contains an arbitrary constant. It is the sum of the complementary function and a particular solution.

Initial condition The value of $y(0)$ that needs to be specified to obtain a unique solution of a differential equation.

Particular solution of a differential equation Any one solution of a differential equation such as $\dfrac{dy}{dt} = my + c$.

Stable equilibrium An economic model in which the solution of the associated differential equation converges.

Exercise 9.2

1. Use integration to solve each of the following differential equations subject to the given initial conditions:

   (a) $\dfrac{dy}{dt} = 2t;\ y(0) = 7$ **(b)** $\dfrac{dy}{dt} = e^{-3t};\ y(0) = 0$ **(c)** $\dfrac{dy}{dt} = t^2 + 3t - 5;\ y(0) = 1$

2. Solve the differential equation

   $$\frac{dy}{dt} = -3y + 180$$

   in the case when the initial condition is

   (a) $y(0) = 40$ **(b)** $y(0) = 80$ **(c)** $y(0) = 60$

   Comment on the qualitative behaviour of the solution in each case.

3. A principal of \$60 is invested. The value, $I(t)$, of the investment, t days later, satisfies the differential equation

   $$\frac{dI}{dt} = 0.002I + 5$$

   Find the value of the investment after 27 days, correct to 2 decimal places.

4. Consider the two-sector model

   $$\frac{dY}{dt} = 0.5(C + I - Y)$$

   $$C = 0.7Y + 500$$

   $$I = 0.2Y + 500$$

   Find an expression for $Y(t)$ when $Y(0) = 15\,000$. Is the system stable or unstable?

5. Consider the two-sector model

   $$\frac{dY}{dt} = 0.3(C + I - Y)$$

   $$C = 0.8Y + 300$$

   $$I = 0.7Y + 600$$

   Find an expression for $Y(t)$ when $Y(0) = 200$. Is this system stable or unstable?

6. Consider the market model

   $$Q_S = 3P - 1$$

   $$Q_D = -2P + 9$$

   $$\frac{dP}{dt} = 0.5(Q_D - Q_S)$$

   Find expressions for $P(t)$, $Q_S(t)$ and $Q_D(t)$ when $P(0) = 1$. Is this system stable or unstable?

7. Oil reserves decrease at a constant proportional rate, $k > 0$, so that

$$\frac{dN}{dt} = -kN$$

where N denotes the number of barrels of oil remaining in t years' time.

(a) Write down an expression for $N(t)$ when current oil reserves are A barrels.

(b) Show that the time taken for oil reserves to fall to half their current levels is $(\ln 2)/k$.

Exercise 9.2*

1. Find the solution of the differential equation

$$\frac{dy}{dt} = 3t^2 - \frac{4}{\sqrt{t}}$$

with initial condition, $y(0) = 4$.

2. Consider the market model

$$Q_S = 4P - 3$$

$$Q_D = -2P + 13$$

$$\frac{dP}{dt} = 0.4(Q_D - Q_S)$$

Find an expression for $Q_D(t)$ when $P(0) = 2$.

3. A principal of \$4000 is invested at an annual interest rate of 6%, and the future value of this investment t years later is $S(t)$, which satisfies

$$\frac{dS}{dt} = 0.06S$$

(a) Solve this equation to express S in terms of t.

(b) What type of compounding is represented by this model?

4. Solve the differential equation

$$\frac{dy}{dt} = 8e^{-2t}$$

with initial condition $y(0) = 10$.
  Sketch the graph of y against t.

5. Consider the two-sector model

$$\frac{dY}{dt} = 0.4(C + I - Y)$$

$$C = 0.6Y + 400$$

$$I = 0.8Y + 500$$

Given that $Y(0) = 100$, find the value, correct to the nearest whole number, of $Y(2.4)$.

6. Consider the two-sector macroeconomic model

$$\frac{dY}{dt} = 0.2(C + I - Y)$$

$$C = 0.8Y + 420$$

$$I = 300$$

(a) Find an expression for $Y(t)$ when $Y(0) = 8000$.

(b) Hence find an expression for the savings function, $S(t)$.

(c) Find the time taken for income to fall to 4150, and find the rate of change of income at this time. Give your answers to the nearest whole number.

7. The value of an economic variable over time satisfies the relation

$$R(t) = \frac{6}{1 + t^2} + 3e^{-0.4t}$$

Find the equilibrium value of R.

8. A simple model of the growth of an economy is based on three assumptions.

(1) Savings, S, are proportional to income, Y, so that

$$S = \alpha Y \quad (\alpha > 0)$$

(2) Investment, I, is proportional to the rate of change of Y so that

$$I = \beta\frac{dy}{dt} \quad (\beta > 0)$$

(3) Investment and savings are equal so that

$$I = S$$

Use these assumptions to show that

$$\frac{dY}{dt} = \frac{\alpha}{\beta}Y$$

and hence write down a formula for $Y(t)$ in terms of $Y(0)$. Is this system stable or unstable?

9. A model predicts that monthly sales, $S(t)$, of a new product after t months satisfy the differential equation

$$\frac{dS}{dt} = k(M - S) \text{ with initial condition } S(0) = C$$

where k, M and C are positive constants.

(a) Show that $S(t) = M(1 - e^{-kt}) + Ce^{-kt}$.

(b) Sketch a graph of S against t and comment on the forecast for sales in the long run.

(c) If $S(0) = 100$, $S(6) = 2000$ and $M = 5000$, what does the model predict that monthly sales will be after one year of trading?

10. Show, by substituting into the differential equation, that

$$y(t) = Ae^{mt} - \frac{c}{m}$$

is a solution of

$$\frac{dy}{dt} = my + c$$

11. Consider the differential equation

$$\frac{dy}{dt} = -2y + 5e^{3t}$$

(a) Find the complementary function.

(b) By substituting $y = De^{3t}$ into this equation, find a particular solution.

(c) Use your answers to parts (a) and (b) to write down the general solution and hence find the specific solution that satisfies the initial condition, $y(0) = 7$.

(d) Is the solution in part (c) stable or unstable?

12. Consider the differential equation

$$\frac{dy}{dt} = -y + 4t - 3$$

(a) Find the complementary function.

(b) By substituting $y = Dt + E$ into this equation, find a particular solution.

(c) Use your answers to parts (a) and (b) to write down the general solution and hence find the specific solution that satisfies the initial condition, $y(0) = 1$.

(d) Is the solution in part (c) stable or unstable?

Formal mathematics

We conclude this chapter with a formal derivation of the solution of the general difference equation considered in Section 9.1:

$$Y_t = bY_{t-1} + c \text{ with } Y_0 = a.$$

Setting $t = 1, 2$ and 3 in turn gives

$$Y_1 = bY_0 + c = ab + c$$
$$Y_2 = bY_1 + c = b(ab + c) + c = ab^2 + bc + c$$
$$Y_3 = bY_2 + c = b(ab^2 + bc + c) + c = ab^3 + b^2c + bc + c$$

Continuing gives

$$Y_t = ab^t + b^{t-1}c + b^{t-2}c + \ldots + b^2c + bc + c$$
$$= ab^t + c(1 + b + b^2 + \ldots + b^{t-1})$$

The expression in the brackets is the first t terms of a geometric series with ratio b. If we assume that $b \neq 1$, we can write

$$Y_t = ab^t + c\left(\frac{b^t - 1}{b - 1}\right)$$

$$= \left(a + \frac{c}{b - 1}\right)b^t - \frac{c}{b - 1}$$

which confirms the '$Y_t = Ab^t + PS$' form used in Section 9.1.

Example

Solve the difference equation $Y_t = -2Y_{t-1} + 9;\ Y_0 = 4$

Solution

Substituting $a = 4$, $b = -2$ and $c = 9$ into the general solution gives

$$Y_t = \left(4 + \frac{9}{-2 - 1}\right)(-2)^t - \frac{9}{-2 - 1} = (-2)^t + 3$$

[This is the same difference equation considered in Practice Problem 2 (b) in Section 9.1.]

Multiple choice questions

Question 1

The variation of capital stock, K, satisfies the differential equation $\dfrac{\mathrm{d}K}{\mathrm{d}t} = 3\sqrt{t} + 2$ where $K = 25$ when $t = 1$. Work out the capital stock when $t = 4$.

A. 40   B. 20   C. 25   D. 30   E. 45

Question 2

Consider the two-sector model:

$$Y_t = C_t + 400$$
$$C_t = 0.8Y_{t-1} + 100$$

If $Y_0 = 450$, work out the value of C_2.

A. 860

B. 788

C. 708

D. 786

E. 888

Question 3

Solve the differential equation $\dfrac{\mathrm{d}y}{\mathrm{d}t} = 0.6y$ with initial condition $y(0) = 4$ to find $y(6)$ correct to the nearest whole number.

A. 2

B. 3

C. 146

D. 72

E. 36

Question 4

Find the complementary function of the difference equation, $Y_t - 3Y_{t-1} = 18$

A. $A(-3)^t$

B. -2

C. -9

D. $A(3^t)$

E. $-9 + A(-3)^t$

Question 5

Find the particular solution of the differential equation, $\dfrac{dy}{dt} = -3y + 6e^t$

A. $6e^{-3t}$

B. $1.5e^t$

C. Ae^{-3t}

D. $6e^t$

E. $Ae^{-3t} + 6e^t$

Question 6

Describe the qualitative behaviour of the solution of the difference equation

$Y_t = -\dfrac{3}{4}Y_{t-1}; \; Y_0 = 10$

A. Oscillatory convergence

B. Oscillatory divergence

C. Uniform convergence

D. Unstable convergence

E. Stable divergence

Question 7

Find the solution of the differential equation $\dfrac{dy}{dt} + 4y = 200$ with initial condition, $y(0) = 30$

A. $50 + 20e^{4t}$

B. $50 - 20e^{-4t}$

C. $-50 - 20e^{-4t}$

D. $-50 - 20e^{4t}$

E. $50 + 20e^{-4t}$

Question 8

Consider the supply and demand equations

$$Q_{S_t} = 2P_{t-1} - 10$$
$$Q_{D_t} = -4P_t + 40$$

Assuming that the market is in equilibrium, find an expression for Q_t when $P_0 = 4$.

A. $-\dfrac{8}{3}\left(-\dfrac{1}{2}\right)^t + \dfrac{20}{3}$

B. $-\dfrac{13}{3}\left(-\dfrac{1}{2}\right)^t + \dfrac{25}{3}$

C. $\dfrac{52}{3}\left(-\dfrac{1}{2}\right)^t + \dfrac{20}{3}$

D. $-\dfrac{13}{3}\left(\dfrac{1}{2}\right)^t + \dfrac{25}{3}$

E. $-\dfrac{8}{3}\left(\dfrac{1}{2}\right)^t + \dfrac{20}{3}$

Question 9

Consider the two-sector model:

$$\frac{dY}{dt} = 0.6(C + I - Y)$$

$$C = 0.9Y + 600$$

$$I = 400$$

Find an expression for $Y(t)$ when $Y(0) = 9000$.

A. $8000e^{-0.06t} + 10000$

B. $10000 - 1000e^{-0.06t}$

C. $8000e^{-0.6t} + 1000$

D. $1000e^{-0.1t} + 1000$

E. $10000 - 8000e^{-0.6t}$

Question 10

Consider the general supply and demand model:

$Q_S = aP - b$

$Q_D = -cP + d$

$\dfrac{dP}{dt} = \alpha(Q_D - Q_S)$

where a, b, c, d and α are all positive constants.

Find an expression for $P(t)$ when $P(0) = \beta$.

A. $\dfrac{(a + c + \beta(b + d))e^{-\alpha(a+c)t} + b + d}{a + c}$

B. $\dfrac{(b + d)\,(e^{-\alpha(a+c)t} - 1) + \beta(a + c)e^{-\alpha(a+c)t}}{a + c}$

C. $\dfrac{(b + d + \beta(a + c))e^{-\alpha(a+c)t} + b + d}{a + c}$

D. $\dfrac{(b + d - \beta(a + c))e^{-\alpha(a+c)t} - (b + d)}{a + c}$

E. $\dfrac{(b + d)\,(1 - e^{-\alpha(a+c)t}) + \beta(a + c)e^{-\alpha(a+c)t}}{a + c}$

Examination questions

Question 1

Find the equilibrium price and quantity given the following static supply and demand equations:

$$Q_S = 6P - 10$$
$$Q_D = -4P + 45$$

The equations for the corresponding dynamic model are:

$$Q_{S_t} = 6P_{t-1} - 10$$
$$Q_{D_t} = -4P_t + 45$$

Find an expression for P_t in terms of t given the initial condition, $P_0 = 8$ and describe the behaviour of P_t as t increases.

Question 2

(a) Solve the differential equation $\dfrac{dy}{dx} = \dfrac{4}{\sqrt{x}} + 6x^2$ given the condition, $y(4) = 3$.

(b) The population, N, of a small country is currently 5 million. It is expected that this population will grow according to the differential equation.

$$\frac{dN}{dt} = 0.015N$$

where t is measured in years.

Solve this equation to express N in terms of t and hence predict how many years it will take for the population to double. Give your answer to one decimal place.

Question 3

Government expenditure, G, satisfies the differential equation

$$\frac{dG}{dt} = -0.05G$$

where G is measured in billions of dollars and time t is in years. The initial condition is $G(0) = 500$.

(a) Solve this equation to express G in terms of t.

(b) Find the value of (i) G when $t = 6$; (ii) t when $G = 125$. Round your answers to three significant figures.

Question 4

A two sector lagged-income model is defined by

$$Y_t = C_t + I_t$$
$$C_t = 0.8Y_{t-1} + 200$$
$$I_t = 1000$$

where Y_t, C_t and I_t denote national income, consumption and planned investment in time period t. The initial value of national income is $Y_0 = 5000$.

(a) Use these relations to work out Y_2 and C_2.

(b) Derive a first-order difference equation relating Y_t and Y_{t-1}.

(c) Solve the difference equation to express Y_t in terms of t.

(d) Verify that your general formula in part (c) agrees with the value of Y_2 calculated in part (a).

(e) Find an expression for C_t in terms of t and hence determine the time period in which the consumption first exceeds 4750.

Question 5

National income Y varies over time t according to the following model:

$$\frac{dY}{dt} = 0.6(C + I - Y)$$
$$C = 0.8Y + 600$$
$$I = 800$$

where C is consumption and I is planned investment. Initially, $Y = 2000$.

(a) Find an expression for $Y(t)$ and deduce that the system is stable.

(b) Sketch a graph of Y against t.

(c) Find the time taken for national income to rise to 90% of its equilibrium value. Round your answer to one decimal place.

(d) Find an expression for $C(t)$.

Question 6

Consider the supply and demand equations:

$$Q_{S_t} = 2P_t + aP_{t-1} - 20$$
$$Q_{D_t} = 100 - 8P_t$$

for some parameter, a.

Assuming that the market is in equilibrium, show that $P_t = 12 - 0.1aP_{t-1}$.

If $P_0 = 10$, find an expression for P_t in terms of t and a.

If the solution displays oscillatory convergence, state the range of values of a and find the particular value of a if $P_1 = 9.5$.

ANSWERS

CHAPTER 1

Section 1.1

Practice Problems

1 (a) -30 (b) 2   (c) -5
   (d) 5   (e) 36   (f) -1

2 (a) -1 (b) -7 (c) 5
   (d) 0   (e) -91 (f) -5

3 (a) 19   (b) 1500   (c) 32   (d) 35

4 (a) $x + 9y$ (b) $2y + 4z$ (c) not possible
   (d) $8r^2 + s + rs - 3s^2$ (e) $-4f$
   (f) not possible   (g) 0

5 (a) $5z - 2z^2$ (b) $-3y$ (c) $z - x^2$

6 (a) $7(d + 3)$ (b) $4(4w - 5q)$
   (c) $3(2x - y + 3z)$ (d) $5Q(1 - 2Q)$

7 (a) $x^2 + x - 6$ (b) $x^2 - y^2$
   (c) $x^2 + 2xy + y^2$
   (d) $5x^2 - 3xy + 5x - 2y^2 + 2y$

8 (a) $(x + 8)(x - 8)$
   (b) $(2x + 9)(2x - 9)$

Exercise 1.1

1 (a) -20 (b) 3   (c) -4 (d) 1
   (e) -12 (f) 50   (g) -5 (h) 3
   (i) 30   (j) 4

2 (a) -1 (b) -3 (c) -11 (d) 16
   (e) -1 (f) -13 (g) 11   (h) 0
   (i) -31 (j) -2

3 (a) -3 (b) 2   (c) 18   (d) -15
   (e) -41 (f) -3 (g) 18   (h) -6
   (i) -25 (j) -6

4 (a) $2PQ$ (b) $8I$ (c) $3xy$
   (d) $4qwz$ (e) b^2 (f) $3k^2$

5 (a) $19w$ (b) $4x - 7y$ (c) $9a + 2b - 2c$
   (d) $x^2 + 2x$ (e) $4c - 3cd$ (f) $2st + s^2 + t^2 + 9$

6 (a) 10   (b) 18   (c) 2000
   (d) 96   (e) 70

7 (a) 1   (b) 5   (c) -6 (d) -6
   (e) -30 (f) 44

8 (a) 16
   (b) Presented with the calculation, -4^2, your calculator uses BIDMAS, so squares first to get 16 and then subtracts from zero to give a final answer, -16. To obtain the correct answer you need to use brackets:

   $($ $-$ 4 $)$ x^2 $=$

9 (a) 9   (b) 21; no

10 (a) 43.96   (b) 1.13   (c) 10.34   (d) 0.17
    (e) 27.38   (f) 3.72   (g) 62.70   (h) 2.39

11 (a) $7x - 7y$ (b) $15x - 6y$ (c) $4x + 12$
    (d) $21x - 7$ (e) $3x + 3y + 3z$ (f) $3x^2 - 4x$
    (g) $-2x - 5y + 4z$

12 (a) $5(5c + 6)$ (b) $9(x - 2)$ (c) $x(x + 2)$
    (d) $4(4x - 3y)$ (e) $2x(2x - 3y)$ (f) $5(2d - 3e + 10)$

13 (a) $x^2 + 7x + 10$ (b) $a^2 + 3a - 4$ (c) $d^2 - 5d - 24$
    (d) $6s^2 + 23s + 21$ (e) $2y^2 + 5y + 3$ (f) $10t^2 - 31t - 14$
    (g) $9n^2 - 4$ (h) $a^2 - 2ab + b^2$

14 (a) $6x + 2y$ (b) $11x^2 - 3x - 3$ (c) $14xy + 2x$
    (d) $6xyz + 2xy$ (e) $10a - 2b$ (f) $17x + 22y$
    (g) $11 - 3p$ (h) $x^2 + 10x$

15 (a) $(x + 2)(x - 2)$ (b) $(Q + 7)(Q - 7)$
    (c) $(x + y)(x - y)$ (d) $(3x + 10y)(3x - 10y)$

16 (a) $4x^2 + 8x - 2$ (b) $-13x$

17 $S = 1.2N + 3000E + 1000(A - 21)$;   \$204 000

18 (a) $C = 80 + 60L + K$ (b) $C = 10 + 1.25x$
    (c) $H = 5a + 10b$ (d) $X = Cd + cm$

Exercise 1.1*

1 (a) 3   (b) 5   (c) -7

2 (a) $2 - 7 - (9 + 3) = -17$
   (b) $8 - (2 + 3) - 4 = -1$
   (c) $7 - (2 - 6 + 10) = 1$

3 (a) -6 (b) 6   (c) -5 (d) -96
   (e) -1 (f) 6   (g) $\dfrac{5}{4}$ (h) 63

4 (a) 6   (b) 2   (c) 5

5 $-y^2 + xy - 5x + 2y - 6$

6 (a) $2x - 2y$ (b) $2x$ (c) $-2x + 3y$

7 (a) $x^2 - 2x - 24$ (b) $6x^2 - 29x + 35$

(c) $6x^2 + 2xy - 4x$ (d) $12 - 2g + 3h - 2g^2 + gh$

(e) $2x - 2x^2 - 3xy + y - y^2$ (f) $a^2 - b^2 - c^2 - 2bc$

8 (a) $3(3x - 4y)$ (b) $x(x - 6)$

(c) $5x(2y + 3x)$ (d) $3xy(y - 2x + 4)$

(e) $x^2(x - 2)$ (f) $5xy^3(12x^3y^3 - 3xy + 4)$

9 (a) $(p + 5)(p - 5)$ (b) $(3c + 8)(3c - 8)$

(c) $2(4v + 5d)(4v - 5d)$ (d) $(4x^2 + y^2)(2x + y)(2x - y)$

10 (a) $112\,600\,000$ (b) 1.7999

(c) $283\,400$ (d) $246\,913\,577$

11 (a) $\pi = 12y - 3x - 800$ (b) $\$5800$

(c) $0 \le y \le x$ (d) $\pi = 9x - 800$

12 (a) $2KL(L + 2)$ (b) $(L - 0.2K)(L + 0.2K)$

(c) $(K + L)^2$

Section 1.2

Practice Problems

1 (a) $\dfrac{3}{5}$ (b) $\dfrac{4}{5}$ (c) $\dfrac{1}{2y}$ (d) $\dfrac{1}{2 + 3x}$ (e) $\dfrac{1}{x - 4}$

2 (a) $\dfrac{3}{8}$ (b) $\dfrac{7}{4}$ (c) $\dfrac{3}{4}$ (d) $\dfrac{1}{18}$

3 (a) $\dfrac{2}{7}$ (b) $\dfrac{11}{15}$ (c) $\dfrac{5}{36}$

4 (a) $\dfrac{5}{x + 2}$ (b) $\dfrac{x(x + 1)}{x + 10}$

(c) $\dfrac{5}{x + 1}$ (d) $\dfrac{x + 3}{(x + 1)(x + 2)}$

5 (a) 6 (b) 12 (c) $-\dfrac{3}{4}$ (d) $\dfrac{9}{5}$ (e) $-\dfrac{3}{2}$

6 (a) $12 > 9$ (true)   (b) $12 > 6$ (true)

(c) $3 > 0$ (true)   (d) same as (c)

(e) $2 > 1$ (true)   (f) $-24 > -12$ (false)

(g) $-6 > -3$ (false)   (h) $-2 > -1$ (false)

(i) $-4 > -7$ (true)

7 (a) $x > -7$ (b) $x \ge 2$

Exercise 1.2

1 (a) $\dfrac{1}{2}$ (b) $\dfrac{3}{4}$ (c) $\dfrac{3}{5}$ (d) $\dfrac{1}{3}$ (e) $\dfrac{4}{3} = 1\dfrac{1}{3}$

2 (a) $\dfrac{7}{20}; \dfrac{14}{25}$ (b) $1\dfrac{3}{5}$

3 (a) $\dfrac{2x}{3}$ (b) $\dfrac{1}{2x}$ (c) $\dfrac{1}{ac}$ (d) $\dfrac{2}{3xy}$ (e) $\dfrac{3a}{4b}$

4 (a) $\dfrac{p}{2q + 3r}$ (b) $\dfrac{1}{x - 4}$ (c) $\dfrac{b}{2a + 1}$

(d) $\dfrac{2}{3 - e}$ (e) $\dfrac{1}{x - 2}$

5 $\dfrac{x - 1}{2x - 2} = \dfrac{x - 1}{2(x - 1)} = \dfrac{1}{2}$; other two have no common

factors on top and bottom.

6 (a) $\dfrac{3}{7}$ (b) $-\dfrac{1}{3}$ (c) $\dfrac{5}{6}$ (d) $\dfrac{7}{20}$

(e) $\dfrac{7}{18}$ (f) $\dfrac{5}{6}$ (g) $\dfrac{5}{8}$ (h) $\dfrac{2}{5}$

(i) $\dfrac{7}{12}$ (j) $\dfrac{1}{30}$ (k) $\dfrac{2}{27}$ (l) $\dfrac{21}{2} = 10\dfrac{1}{2}$

7 38

8 (a) $\dfrac{1}{x}$ (b) $\dfrac{2}{5}$ (c) $\dfrac{3x - 2}{x^2}$

(d) $\dfrac{7y + 2x}{xy}$ (e) 3 (f) $\dfrac{15c + 10d}{36}$

(g) $\dfrac{x + 2}{x + 3}$ (h) $\dfrac{18h^2}{7}$ (i) $\dfrac{t}{20}$ (j) 1

9 (a) 5 (b) 6 (c) 18 (d) 2

(e) 10 (f) -1 (g) 60 (h) $1\dfrac{2}{3}$

(i) -5 (j) -3 (k) -2 (l) $-3\dfrac{2}{3}$

(m) $3\dfrac{1}{4}$ (n) 3 (o) $\dfrac{1}{4}$

10 (a), (d), (e), (f)

11 (a) $x > 1$ (b) $x \le 3$ (c) $x < -3$ (d) $x > 2$

12 $\dfrac{2}{x^3}$

13 (a) $-\dfrac{7}{26}$ (b) $x \le 10$

Exercise 1.2*

1 (a) $\dfrac{x - 3}{2}$ (b) $\dfrac{3}{2x - 1}$ (c) 4

(d) -1 (e) $\dfrac{1}{x - 6}$ (f) $\dfrac{x + 3}{x + 4}$

(g) $\dfrac{1}{2x^2 - 5x + 3}$ (h) $\dfrac{2x + 5y}{3}$

2 (a) $\dfrac{5}{7}$ (b) $\dfrac{1}{10}$ (c) $\dfrac{3}{2}$ (d) $\dfrac{5}{48}$

(e) $\dfrac{-2}{13}$ (f) $\dfrac{11}{9}$ (g) $\dfrac{141}{35}$ (h) $\dfrac{34}{5}$

(i) 6 (j) $\dfrac{17}{10}$ (k) $\dfrac{7}{9}$ (l) 4

3 (a) $x + 6$ (b) $\dfrac{x+1}{x}$ or equivalently $1 + \dfrac{1}{x}$

(c) $\dfrac{5}{xy}$ (d) $\dfrac{5x+2}{6}$ (e) $\dfrac{7x+3}{x(x+1)}$ (f) $\dfrac{3x+5}{x^2}$

(g) $\dfrac{x^2+x-2}{x+1}$ (h) $\dfrac{x+3}{x(x+1)}$

4 (a) $-\dfrac{11}{7}$ (b) 1 (c) $-\dfrac{35}{9}$ (d) 8

(e) $\dfrac{4}{5}$ (f) $\dfrac{1}{4}$ (g) $-\dfrac{11}{7}$ (h) 8

(i) 9 (j) $\dfrac{71}{21}$ (k) 7 (l) -9

(m) 1 (n) -5 (o) 3 (p) 5

5 $1.6 + \dfrac{5x}{7} = 6.75$; $\$7.21$

6 (a) $\$3221.02$ (b) $\$60\,000$ (c) 10

7 (a) $x < -8\dfrac{3}{5}$ (b) $x > -\dfrac{12}{13}$ (c) $x \le 13$

(d) $x > -3$ (e) $-1 < x \le 3$

8 (a) $9000 + 50x$

(b) $10\,800 \le 9000 + 50x \le 12\,500$; $36 \le x \le 70$

9 $-3, -2, -1, 0$

10 (a) $\dfrac{3}{2x-1}$ (b) -1 (c) $x \ge \dfrac{11}{5}$

11 $\dfrac{x(x-1)}{2}$

Section 1.3

Practice Problems

1 From Figure S1.1, note that all five points lie on a straight line.

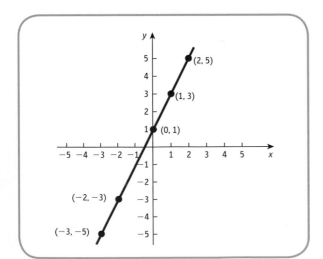

Figure S1.1

2

Point	Check	
$(-1, 2)$	$2(-1) + 3(2) = -2 + 6 = 4$	✓
$(-4, 4)$	$2(-4) + 3(4) = -8 + 12 = 4$	✓
$(5, -2)$	$2(5) + 3(-2) = 10 - 6 = 4$	✓
$(2, 0)$	$2(2) + 3(0) = 4 + 0 = 4$	✓

The graph is sketched in Figure S1.2.
The graph shows that $(3, -1)$ does not lie on the line.

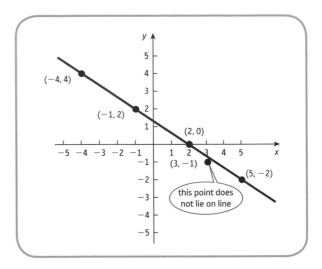

Figure S1.2

3 $(2, 1)$ and $(-2, -5)$ lie on the line.

The line is sketched in Figure S1.3.

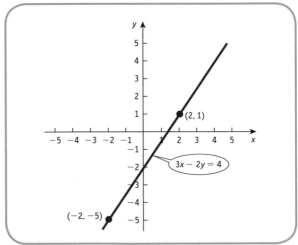

Figure S1.3

4 $(0, -1)$ and $(2, 0)$ lie on the line.

The graph is sketched in Figure S1.4.

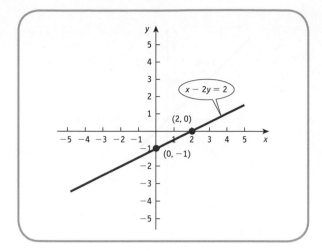

Figure S1.4

5 From Figure S1.5, the point of intersection is $(1, -\frac{1}{2})$.

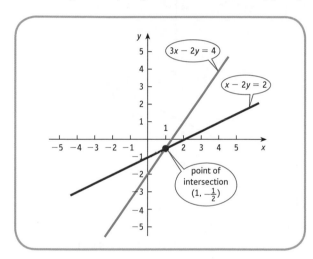

Figure S1.5

6 (a) $a = 1, b = 2$. The graph is sketched in Figure S1.6.

   (b) $a = -2, b = \frac{1}{2}$. The graph is sketched in Figure S1.7.

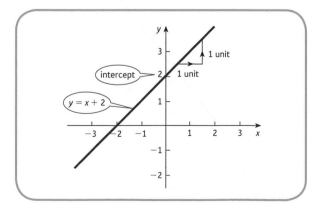

Figure S1.6

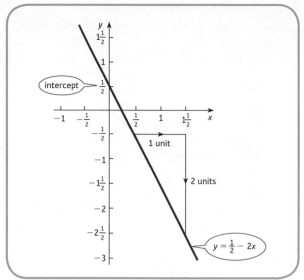

Figure S1.7

Exercise 1.3

1 From Figure S1.8, the point of intersection is $(2, 3)$.

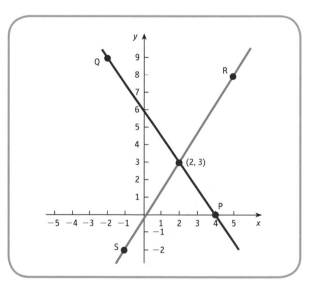

Figure S1.8

2 (a) The graph is sketched in Figure S1.9.

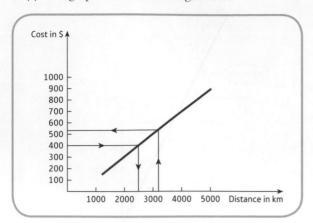

Figure S1.9

(b) (i) $540 (ii) 2500 km

3 A, C, D, E

4 (a) 6   (b) −1;   (6, 2), (1, −1)

5

x	y
0	8
6	0
3	4

The graph is sketched in Figure S1.10.

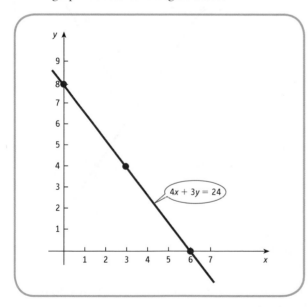

Figure S1.10

6 (a) (−2, −2) (b) (2, 1½)   (c) (1½, 1)   (d) (10, −9)

7 (a) 5, 9   (b) 3, −1   (c) −1, 13   (d) 1, 4

(e) −2, $\dfrac{5}{2}$ (f) 5, −6

8 (a) The graph is sketched in Figure S1.11.

(b) The graph is sketched in Figure S1.12.

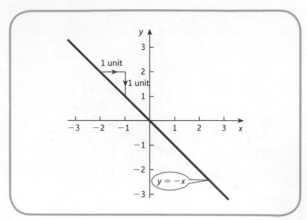

Figure S1.11

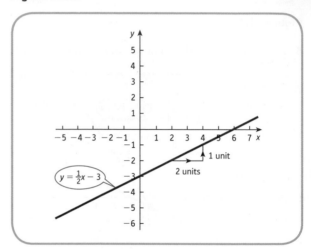

Figure S1.12

9 (a) $C = 4 + 2.5x$

(b) The graph is sketched in Figure S1.13.

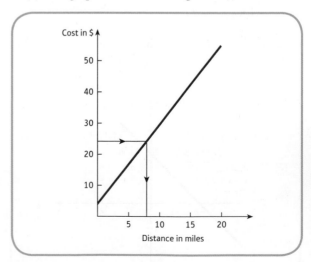

Figure S1.13

(c) 8 miles

10 (a) The graph is sketched in Figure S1.14.

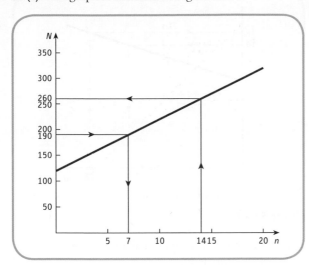

Figure S1.14

(b) (i) $N = 260$ (ii) $n = 7$

(c) Slope $= 10$; this is the number of staff employed in each café. Intercept $= 120$; number of staff employed managing the company.

11 (a) $9000   **(b)** $18\,600   **(c)** $500   **(d)** $12

Exercise 1.3*

1 $(5, -2), (10, 1), (0, -5)$

2 (a) $(2, 5)$ **(b)** $(1, 4)$ **(c)** $(-2, 3)$ **(d)** $(-8, 3)$

3 (a) $7, -34$ **(b)** $-1, 1$ **(c)** $\dfrac{3}{2}, \; -3$ **(d)** $2, \; \dfrac{5}{2}$

(e) $\dfrac{1}{5}, \; 0$ (f) $0, 2$

(g) The vertical line, $x = 4$, has no gradient and does not intercept the y-axis.

4 (b) and (d)

5 (a) $x + 100$ **(b)** $3.5x + 35$ **(c)** 26

6 (a) -12 **(b)** 408 **(c)** 300 **(d)** $20

7 (1) Gradients are $-\dfrac{a}{b}$ and $-\dfrac{d}{e}$, respectively, so the lines are parallel when $\dfrac{a}{b} = \dfrac{d}{e}$ which gives $ae = bd$.

(2) Parallel lines so no solution.

8 $\left(0, \dfrac{c}{b}\right), \left(\dfrac{c}{a}, 0\right)$

Section 1.4

Practice Problems

1 (a) $x = 1, y = -\dfrac{1}{2}$ **(b)** $x = 3, y = 2$

2 (a) There are no solutions.

(b) There are infinitely many solutions.

3 $x = 1, y = -1, z = 1$

Exercise 1.4

1 (a) $x = -2, y = -2$ **(b)** $x = 2, y = 3/2$

    (c) $x = 3/2, y = 1$ **(d)** $x = 10, y = -9$

2 (a) $x + y = 3500$

     $30x + 25y = 97\,500$

(b) 1500

3 The lines are sketched in Figure S1.15.

(a) Infinitely many

(b) No solution

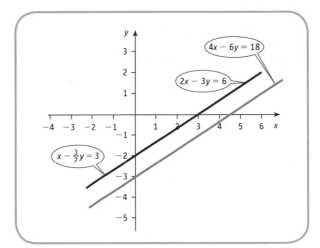

Figure S1.15

4 (a) Infinitely many

(b) No solution

5 $k = -1$

Exercise 1.4*

1 (a) $x = 2, y = 5$ **(b)** $x = 1, y = 4$

    (c) $x = -2, y = 3$ **(d)** $x = -8, y = 3$

2 (a) $a = 4, b = 8$ **(b)** $a = -3, b \neq \dfrac{1}{2}$

3 Multiply the first equation by d, the second by a and subtract to eliminate x.

4 (a) $x = 3, y = -2, z = -1$

(b) $x = -1, y = 3, z = 4$

5 (a) No solution.

(b) Infinitely many solutions.

6 $k = 6$; no solutions otherwise.

7 $98.85

Section 1.5

Practice Problems

1 (a) 0 (b) 48 (c) 16 (d) 25 (e) 1 (f) 17

The function g reverses the effect of f and takes you back to where you started. For example, when 25 is put into the function f, the outgoing number is 0; and when 0 is put into g, the original number, 25, is produced. We describe this by saying that g is the inverse of f (and vice versa).

2 The demand curve that passes through $(0, 75)$ and $(25, 0)$ is sketched in Figure S1.16. From this diagram we see that

(a) $P = 6$ when $Q = 23$

(b) $Q = 19$ when $P = 18$

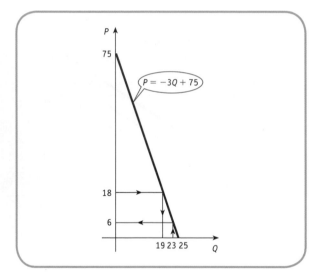

Figure S1.16

3 (a) $Q = 21$ and $P = 36$

(b) $Q = 18$ and $P = 48$. The consumer pays an additional \$12. The remaining \$1 of the tax is paid by the firm.

4 $P_1 = 4, P_2 = 7, Q_1 = 13, Q_2 = 14$.

The goods are complementary.

Exercise 1.5

1 (a) 21   (b) 45

   (c) 15   (d) 2

   (e) 10   (f) 0; inverse

2 The supply curve is sketched in Figure S1.17.

   (a) 11   (b) 9

   (c) 0; once the price falls below 7, the firm does not plan to produce any goods.

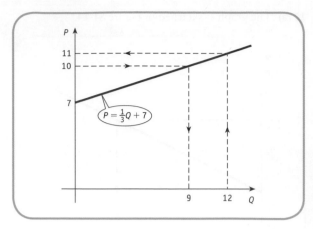

Figure S1.17

3 (a) Demand is 173. Additional advertising expenditure is 12.

(b) Normal

4 (a) 23

(b) Substitutable; a rise in P_A leads to an increase in Q.

(c) 6

5 $a = -6, b = 720$

6 (a) 20, 10, 45; line passes through these three points.

(b) Line passing through $(50, 0)$ and $(0, 50)$

$$Q = 20, P = 30$$

(c) Price increases; quantity increases.

7 6

8 $P_1 = 40, P_2 = 10; Q_1 = 30, Q_2 = 55$

9 (a) $Q = 30$

(b) Substitutable; e.g. since coefficient of P_r is positive.

(c) $P = 14$

(d) (i) slope $= -20$, intercept $= 135$

(ii) slope $= -\dfrac{1}{20}$, intercept $= 6.75$

Exercise 1.5*

1 (a) As P_S rises, consumers are likely to switch to the good under consideration, so demand for this good also rises: that is, the graph shifts to the right.

(b) As P_C rises, demand for the bundle of goods as a whole is likely to fall, so the graph shifts to the left.

(c) Assuming that advertising promotes the good and is successful, demand rises and the graph shifts to the right. For some goods, such as drugs, advertising campaigns are intended to discourage consumption, so the graph shifts to the left.

2 $m = -\dfrac{3}{2}, \quad c = 9$

3 0 and 30

4 (1) $P = 30, Q = 10$

   (2) New supply equation is $0.85P = 2Q_S + 10$;
     $P = 33.6, Q = 9.28$.

5 (a) 53, 9   (b) \$324

6 $P_1 = 20, P_2 = 5, P_3 = 8; Q_1 = 13, Q_2 = 16, Q_3 = 11$

7 Change supply equation to $P = 2Q_S + 40 + t$.

   In equilibrium

$$-3Q + 60 = 2Q + 40 + t$$
$$-5Q = -20 + t$$
$$Q = 4 - \frac{t}{5}$$

   Substitute to get $P = 48 + \dfrac{3}{5}t$.

   (a) $t = 5$; firm pays \$2   (b) $P = 45, Q = 5$

8 (a) $a > 0, b > 0, c < 0, d > 0$

   (b) $Q = \dfrac{d - b}{a - c}$ and $P = \dfrac{ad - bc}{a - c}$

Section 1.6

Practice Problems

1 (a) $Q = 8$

   (b) $Q = 2P - 26$ (multiply out brackets)

   (c) $Q = 2 \times 17 - 26 = 8$

2 (a) $x = \sqrt{\dfrac{y}{6}}$ (b) $x = \dfrac{1}{7}\left(\dfrac{1}{y} + 1\right) = \dfrac{1 + y}{7y}$

3 (a) $x = \left(\dfrac{1 + a}{1 - c}\right)y$ (b) $x = \dfrac{-2 - 4y}{y - 1}$

Exercise 1.6

1 $Q = \dfrac{1}{2}P - 4; 22$

2 (a) $y = 2x + 5$ (b) $y = 2(x + 5)$

   (c) $y = \dfrac{5}{x^2}$ (d) $y = 2(x + 4)^2 - 3$

3 (a) multiply by 5   add 3

   (b) add 3   multiply by 5

   (c) multiply by 6   subtract 9

   (d) square   multiply by 4   subtract 6

   (e) divide by 2   add 7

   (f) reciprocate   multiply by 2

   (g) add 3   reciprocate

4 (a) $x = \dfrac{1}{9}(y + 6)$ (b) $x = 3y - 4$

   (c) $x = 2y$ (d) $x = 5(y - 8)$

   (e) $x = \dfrac{1}{y} - 2$ (f) $x = \dfrac{1}{3}\left(\dfrac{4}{y} + 7\right)$

5 (a) $P = \dfrac{Q}{a} - \dfrac{b}{a}$ (b) $Y = \dfrac{b + I}{1 - a}$

   (c) $P = \dfrac{1}{aQ} - \dfrac{b}{a}$

6 $x = \dfrac{3}{y + 2}$

7 (a) $D = \dfrac{HQ^2}{2R}$ (b) $H = \dfrac{2DR}{Q^2}$

Exercise 1.6*

1 (1) (a) multiply by 9   add 1

      (b) multiply by -1 add 3

      (c) square   multiply by 5   subtract 8

      (d) multiply by 3   add 5   square root

      (e) square   add 8   reciprocate   multiply by 4

   (2) (a) $x = \dfrac{y - 1}{9}$ (b) $x = 3 - y$

      (c) $x = \pm\sqrt{\dfrac{y + 8}{5}}$ (d) $x = \dfrac{y^2 - 5}{3}$

      (e) $x = \pm\sqrt{\dfrac{4}{y} - 8}$

2 (a) $x = \dfrac{c - a}{b}$ (b) $x = \dfrac{a^2 + b}{a + 1}$

   (c) $x = (g - e)^2 - f$ (d) $x = \dfrac{ma^2}{b^2} + n$

   (e) $x = \dfrac{n^2}{m^2} + m$ (f) $x = \left(\dfrac{a^2 + b^2}{b - a}\right)^2$

3 $t = \dfrac{V + 1}{V - 5}; 11$

4 $r = 100\left(\sqrt[n]{\dfrac{S}{P}} - 1\right)$

5 (a) $G = Y(1 - a + at) + aT - b - I$

   (b) $T = \dfrac{G + b + I - Y(1 - a + at)}{a}$

   (c) $t = \dfrac{G + b + I - Y + aY - aT}{aY}$

   (d) $a = \dfrac{G + b + I - Y}{T - Y + tY}$

Section 1.7

Practice Problems

1 $S = 0.2Y - 25$

2 $Y = 210; Y = 215$

3 $Y = 400$

4 $Y = 2950; r = 8$

The IS and LM curves shown in Figure S1.18 confirm this, since the point of intersection has coordinates (8, 2950). A change in I does not affect the LM schedule. However, if the autonomous level of investment increases from its current level of 1200, the IS curve moves upwards, causing both r and Y to increase.

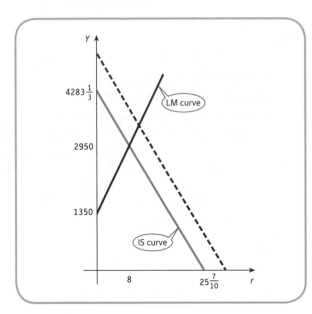

Figure S1.18

Exercise 1.7

1 MPC $= 0.75$; MPS $= 0.25$

2 (a) MPC $= 0.7$; MPS $= 0.3$

   (b) $C = 0.7Y + 100$

3 (a) 40

   (b) $0.7; Y = \dfrac{10}{7}(C - 40); 100$

4 (a) $S = 0.1Y - 72$ (b) $S = 0.2Y - 100$

5 (a) 325   (b) 225   (c) 100

6 $10a + b = 28$

   $30a + b = 44$

   $a = 0.8, b = 20; Y = 165$

7 187.5

Exercise 1.7*

1 (a) $S = 0.3Y - 30$ (b) $S = \dfrac{10Y - 500}{Y + 10}$

2 $C = \dfrac{aI^* + b}{1 - a}$

3 $a = \dfrac{Y - b - I^*}{Y}$

4 825

5 $Y = 2500, r = 10$

6 $a = \dfrac{Y - 74}{Y - 20}; a = 0.6, C = 131$

7 (a) increases   (b) decreases

Multiple Choice Questions

1 E	2 B	3 C
4 D	5 A	6 A
7 E	8 B	9 D
10 A	11 D	12 D
13 C	14 E	15 A
16 A	17 D	18 C

Examination Questions

1 (a) The graphs are sketched in Figure S1.19.

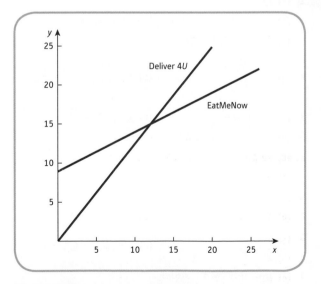

Figure S1.19

(b) 12 miles

(c) EatMeNow: $y = 0.5x + 9$, Deliver4U: $y = 1.25x$

2 (a)

P	5	10	15	20	25
Q_D	325	250	175	100	25
Q_S	0	50	100	150	200

The graphs are sketched in Figure S1.20.

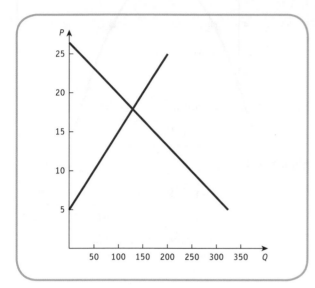

Figure S1.20

(b) $P = 18$, $Q = 130$

(c) $P < 18$

(d) The demand curve is unchanged and the supply curve shifts upwards by 5 units.

$P = 20$, $Q = 100$

3 (a) (1) is demand and (2) is supply.

(b) slope $= -1/3$, vertical intercept $= 16$

(c) $P = 3.6$, $Q = 37.2$

4 (a) 1850

(b) 5

5 (a) 12

(b) 20

(c) $K = \dfrac{2QL}{L - Q}$

6

Y	0	100	200
$C + I$	40	115	190

The lines are sketched in Figure S1.21.

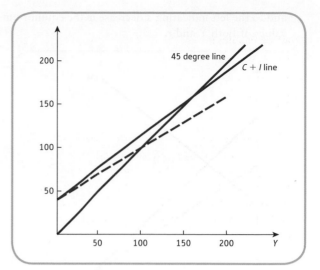

Figure S1.21

$Y = 160$

If MPC decreases, the slope decreases as indicated by the dashed line. The point of intersection shifts down the 45° line, showing that the equilibrium value of Y decreases.

7 (a) The coefficient of P_2 in the demand equation for good 1 is positive, indicating that demand for good 1 rises as the price of good 2 goes up. Similarly, for the second equation. Hence the goods are substitutable.

(b) $P_1 = 15$, $P_2 = 8$; $Q_1 = 98$, $Q_2 = 157$

(c) The price of good 1 reduces by $3.15 and the price of good 2 reduces by $0.35.

8 (a) $3f + 4s \leq 3000$; 640 kg

(b) (i) 3

(ii) 5

(iii) $Q = \dfrac{36 - 5P}{2P}$

(c) $S = \dfrac{2Y - 100}{Y + 2}$

9 (a) $x = \dfrac{6n - m}{2(9 - m)}$, $y = \dfrac{3 - 2n}{2(9 - m)}$; $m = 9$

(i) Infinitely many solutions

(ii) No solutions

(b) $P_1 = 12$, $P_2 = 7$, $P_3 = 8$

10 $Y = 3160$, $r = 2.4$

Figure S1.22 (not to scale) shows the IS and LM curves intersecting at the equilibrium point (2.4, 3160). The dashed line shows the new IS curve after a reduction in MPC. The point of intersection has moved down and to the left indicating a decrease in the equilibrium values of both Y and r.

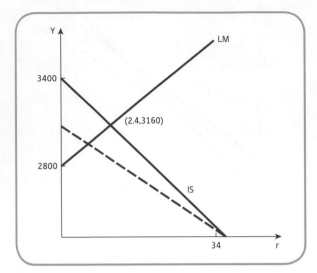

Figure S1.22

CHAPTER 2

Section 2.1

Practice Problems

1 (a) $x = \pm10$ (b) $x = \pm2$

  (c) $x = \pm1.73$ (d) $x = \pm2.39$

  (e) No solution   (f) No solution

  (g) $x = 0$

2 (a) $x = 10$ and $-\dfrac{1}{2}$ (b) $x = -\dfrac{3}{2}$

  (c) No solution   (d) $x = 2$ and 3

3 (a)

x	-1	0	1	2	3	4
$f(x)$	21	5	-3	-3	5	21

The graph is sketched in Figure S2.1.

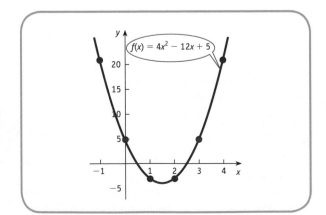

Figure S2.1

(b)

x	0	1	2	3	4	5	6
$f(x)$	-9	-4	-1	0	-1	-4	-9

The graph is sketched in Figure S2.2.

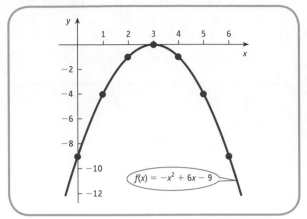

Figure S2.2

(c)

x	-2	-1	0	1	2	3	4
$f(x)$	-22	-12	-6	-4	-6	-12	-22

The graph is sketched in Figure S2.3.

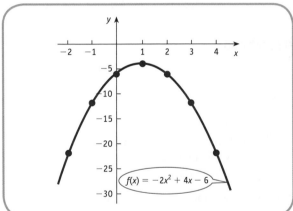

Figure S2.3

4 (a) The graph is sketched in Figure S2.4.

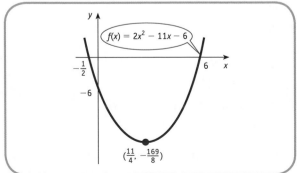

Figure S2.4

(b) The graph is sketched in Figure S2.5.

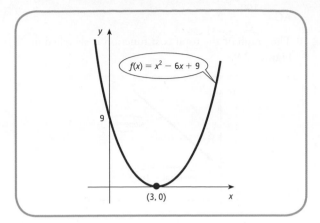

Figure S2.5

5 (a) $-\dfrac{1}{2} \le x \le 6$

(b) The solution consists of all values of x except for $x = 3$.

6 (a) $1 \le x \le 4$

(b) $x < -2, x \ge 1$

7 $Q = 2$ and $P = 38$

Exercise 2.1

1 (a) ± 9

(b) ± 6

(c) ± 2

(d) $-2, 4$

(e) $-9, -1$

2 (a) $1, -3$

(b) $\frac{1}{2}, -10$

(c) $0, -5$

(d) $-\frac{5}{3}, \frac{9}{4}$

(e) $\frac{5}{4}, 5$

3 (a) $0.44, 4.56$

(b) $-2.28, -0.22$

(c) $-0.26, 2.59$

(d) $-0.30, 3.30$

(e) -2

(f) No solutions

4 (a) $-4, 4$

(b) $0, 100$

(c) $5, 17$

(d) 9

(e) No solution

5 The graphs are sketched in Figure S2.6.

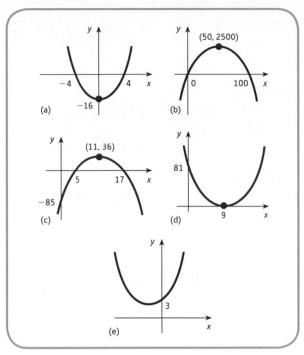

Figure S2.6

6 (a) $x \le -4, x \ge 4$ (b) $0 < x < 100$

(c) $5 \le x \le 17$ (d) $x = 9$

(e) all values of x

7 (a) $56.166, 56.304, 56.35, 56.304, 56.166, 55.936, 55.614, 55.2$

The graph is sketched in Figure S2.7.

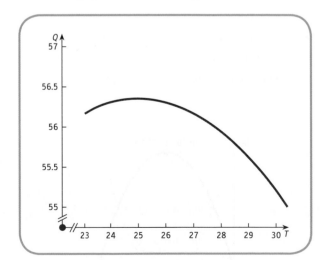

Figure S2.7

(b) The production level is a maximum at 25°C, so as temperature increases, output will fall.

8 (a) $x < 0, x > 3$ (b) $x \leq -1, x \geq 1$

   (c) $-4 < x < 2$

9 $Q = 4, P = 36$

10 $P = 22, Q = 3$

11 (a) \$277   (b) 85

Exercise 2.1*

1 (a) ± 13 (b) $-3, 13$ (c) $-2, 9$

2 $-7d, d$

3 (a) $3, -8$ (b) $\dfrac{2}{3}, -\dfrac{9}{2}$ (c) $0, \dfrac{3}{4}$ (d) $\dfrac{1}{6}$ (twice)

   (e) $2, -1, 4$

4 (a) $7, 8$ (b) $0.22, 2.28$

   (c) ± 3 (d) 7 (twice)

   (e) No solutions   (f) $10, 19$

5 (a) $x \leq -8, x \geq 8$ (b) $1 \leq x \leq 9$

   (c) $-7 < x < -\dfrac{1}{2}$ (d) $-1 \leq x \leq \dfrac{5}{3}$

   (e) $x = -1$

6 $c = 12; 6$

7 $k = 27$

8 (a) $x \leq -3, x \geq 4$ (b) $-1 < x < 2$

   (c) $x \leq 1, 2 \leq x \leq 3$ (d) $2 \leq x < 3, x > 5$

9 \$2250

10 120.76

11 (a) $P = 18$ (b) $B = 15$

12 (b) between \$18 and \$40   (c) \$29

13 $P = 5, Q = 65$

Section 2.2

Practice Problems

1 $TR = 1000Q - Q^2$

   The graph is sketched in Figure S2.8.

   $Q = 500$ and $P = 500$

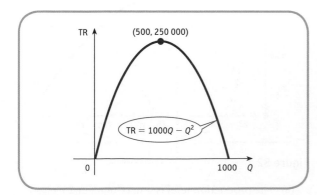

Figure S2.8

2 $TC = 100 + 2Q$

   $AC = \dfrac{100}{Q} + 2$

   The graph of the total cost function is sketched in Figure S2.9.

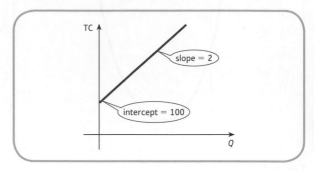

Figure S2.9

The graph of the average cost function is sketched in Figure S2.10.

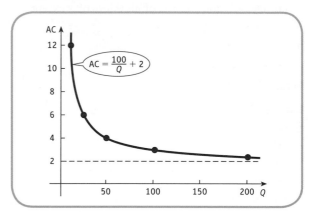

Figure S2.10

3 $\pi = -Q^2 + 18Q - 25$

   The graph of the profit function is sketched in Figure S2.11.

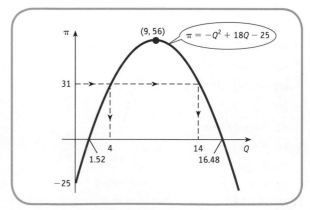

Figure S2.11

(a) $Q = 4$ and 14 (b) $Q = 9$; $\pi = 56$

Exercise 2.2

1 (a) $P = 50$; $TR = 500$

(b) $TC = 150$

(c) $\pi = 350$

2 (a) $4Q$

(b) 7

(c) $10Q - 4Q^2$

The graphs are sketched in Figures S2.12, S2.13 and S2.14.

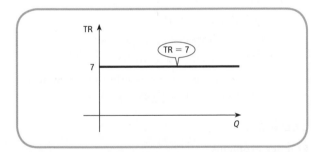

Figure S2.12

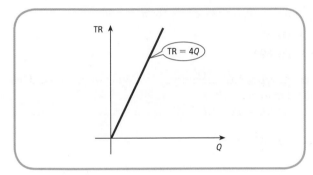

Figure S2.13

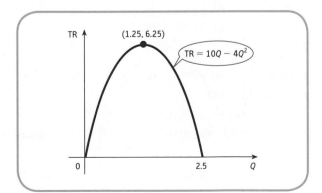

Figure S2.14

3 (a) $P = 50 - 4Q$

(b) $P = \dfrac{10}{Q}$

4 $TC = 500 + 10Q$; $AC = \dfrac{500}{Q} + 10$

The graphs are sketched in Figures S2.15 and S2.16.

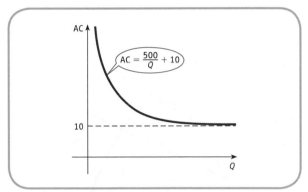

Figure S2.15

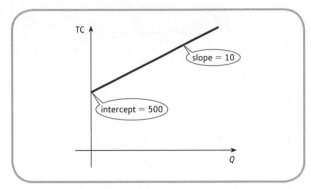

Figure S2.16

5 $TC = Q^2 + Q + 1$; $AC = Q + 1 + \dfrac{1}{Q}$

The graphs are sketched in Figures S2.17 and S2.18.

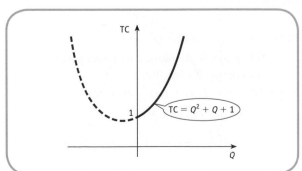

Figure S2.17

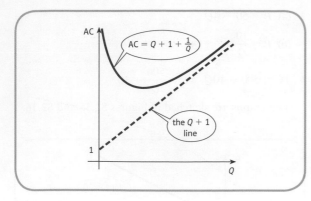

Figure S2.18

6 TC $= 5Q + 100$

7 (a) VC $= \$76$ (b) $47 600

8 (a) $5.50   (b) $x > 40$

9 $\pi = -2Q^2 + 20Q - 32$

   (a) 2, 8   (b) 20   (c) 5

10 The graphs of TR and TC are sketched in Figure S2.19.

   (a) 1, 5   (b) 3

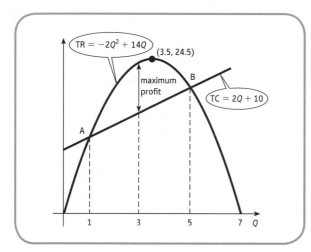

Figure S2.19

11 (a) TR $= PQ = 60Q - Q^2$

    The graph is an inverted parabola passing through $(0, 0)$, $(60, 0)$.

   (b) TC $= 100 + (Q + 6)Q = Q^2 + 6Q + 100$

    Divide by Q to find AC.

    $31, 26, 27\frac{2}{3}, 31$; $Q = 10$

(c) $\pi =$ TR $-$ TC $= 60Q - Q^2 - (Q^2 + 6Q + 100)$
$$= -2Q^2 + 54Q - 100$$

e.g. multiply out brackets

    $Q = 2, 25$

    When $Q = 13.5$, $\pi = 264.5$.

Exercise 2.2*

1 15 and $\frac{2}{3}$; max profit is $154\frac{1}{12}$ which occurs at $Q = 7\frac{5}{6}$.

2 $a + b + c = 9$

   $4a + 2b + c = 34$

   $9a + 3b + c = 19$

   $a = -20, b = 85, c = -56; \pi = -36$

3 (a) 20

   (b) 800

4 (a) TR $= \dfrac{cQ - bQ^2}{a}$

   (b) TC $= eQ + d$

   (c) AC $= e + \dfrac{d}{Q}$

   (d) $\pi = \dfrac{-bQ^2 + (c - ae)Q - ad}{a}$

5 (a) Ennerdale: $0.5aN + 0.25(1 - a)N$

    North Borsetshire: $15 + 0.3N$

    Equate two expressions to get result.

    L-shaped curve, tending to 1/5.

   (b) $a < 0.4$ leads to $N > 300$, so choose Ennerdale if number of withdrawals exceeds 300.

Section 2.3

Practice Problems

1 (a) 100   (b) 10   (c) 1   (d) 1/10

   (e) 1/100   (f) 1   (g) -1 (h) 1/343

   (i) 81   (j) 72 101   (k) 1

2 (a) 4   (b) 3   (c) 32   (d) $\dfrac{1}{4}$ (e) 1

3 (a) x^6 (b) $x^{1/2}$ (c) $x^6 y^{12}$ (d) $x^3 + x^{1/2} y^3$

4 (a) $f(K, L) = 7KL^2$

    $f(\lambda K, \lambda L) = 7(\lambda K)(\lambda L)^2$

             $= 7\lambda K \lambda^2 L^2$ (rule 4)

             $= (\lambda \lambda^2)(7KL^2)$

             $= \lambda^3 f(K, L)$ (rule 1)

    Increasing returns to scale because $3 > 1$.

(b) $f(K, L) = 50K^{1/4}L^{3/4}$

$f(\lambda K, \lambda L) = 50(\lambda K)^{1/4}(\lambda L)^{3/4}$

$\qquad = 50\lambda^{1/4}K^{1/4}\lambda^{3/4}L^{3/4}$ （rule 4）

$\qquad = (\lambda^{1/4}\lambda^{3/4})(50K^{1/4}L^{3/4})$

$\qquad = \lambda^1 f(K, L)$ （rule 1）

Constant returns to scale.

5 (1) (a) 3　(b) 2　(c) 1　(d) 0

(e) −1　(f) −2

(2) Same as part (1).

6 (a) $\log_b\left(\dfrac{xz}{y}\right)$

(b) $\log_b(x^4y^2)$

7 (a) $x = 1.77$　(b) $x = 1$

Exercise 2.3

1 (a) 64　(b) 2　(c) 1/3　(d) 1

(e) 1　(f) 6　(g) 4　(h) 1/343

2 (a) a^{11}　(b) b^5　(c) c^6　(d) x^2y^2

(e) x^3y^6　(f) y^{-4}　(g) x^4　(h) f^7

(i) y^3　(j) x^5

3 (a) $x^{\frac{1}{2}}$　(b) x^{-2}　(c) $x^{\frac{1}{3}}$　(d) x^{-1}

(e) $x^{-\frac{1}{2}}$　(f) $x^{\frac{3}{2}}$

4 (a) 3600　(b) 200 000

5 The functions in parts (a) and (b) are homogeneous of degree 7/12 and 2, respectively, so (a) displays decreasing returns to scale and (b) displays increasing returns to scale. The function in part (c) is not homogeneous.

6 (a) 2　(b) −1　(c) −3　(d) 6　(e) ½　(f) 0

7 (a) 2　(b) 1　(c) 0　(d) ½　(e) −1

8 (a) $\log_b(xz)$　(b) $\log_b\left(\dfrac{x^3}{y^2}\right)$　(c) $\log_b\left(\dfrac{y}{z^3}\right)$

9 (a) $2\log_b x + \log_b y$　(b) $\log_b x - 2\log_b y$

(c) $2\log_b x + 7\log_b y$

10 (a) 1.29　(b) 1.70　(c) 6.03　(d) 8.31

11 (1) (a) 5　(b) $-\dfrac{1}{2}$

(2) $\log_b\left(\dfrac{x^2}{y^4}\right)$

(3) 69.7

12 (1) (a) 4　(b) −2　(c) 2

(2) (a) x^3y　(b) $x^{15}y^5$　(c) x^2y^2

13 (a) 98, 115, 125, 134, 140, 146

(b) The graph is sketched in Figure S2.20.

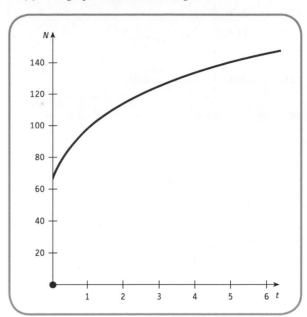

Figure S2.20

The number of complaints increases but at a decreasing rate.

14 9

Exercise 2.3*

1 (a) 8　(b) 1/32　(c) 625　(d) $2\dfrac{1}{4}$　(e) 2/3

2 (a) y^2　(b) xy^2　(c) x^4y^2　(d) 1

(e) 2　(f) $5pq^2$

3 (a) x^{-7}　(b) $x^{1/4}$　(c) $x^{-3/2}$　(d) $2x^{11/2}$　(e) $8x^{-4/3}$

4 $3x^3y^7$

5 $A[b(\lambda K)^\alpha + (1 - b)(\lambda L)^\alpha]^{1/\alpha}$

$\qquad = A[b\lambda^\alpha K^\alpha + (1 - b)\lambda^\alpha L^\alpha]^{1/\alpha}$ （rule 4）

$\qquad = A[(\lambda^\alpha)(bK^\alpha + (1 - b)L^\alpha)]^{1/\alpha}$ （factorise）

$\qquad = A(\lambda^\alpha)^{1/\alpha}[bK^\alpha + (1 - b)L^\alpha]^{1/\alpha}$ （rule 4）

$\qquad = \lambda A[bK^\alpha + (1 - b)L^\alpha]^{1/\alpha}$ （rule 3）

so $f(\lambda K, \lambda L) = \lambda^1 f(K, L)$ as required.

6 (a) 2/3　(b) 3　(c) ¼

7 (a) $\log_b(1)$　(b) $\log_b\left(\dfrac{x^3}{y^2}\right)$　(c) $\log_b\left(\dfrac{x^5y}{z^2}\right)$

(d) $\log_b(b^2x^3)$

8 (a) $2\log_b x + 3\log_b y + 4\log_b z$

(b) $4\log_b x - 2\log_b y - 5\log_b z$

(c) $\log_b x - \dfrac{1}{2}\log_b y - \dfrac{1}{2}\log_b z$

9 (a) $-q$ (b) $2p + q$ (c) $q - 4r$ (d) $p + q + 2r$

10 (a) 78.31   (b) 1.48   (c) 3   (d) 0.23

11 (a) $x \le 0.386$ (3 dp)

  (b) $x > 14.425$

12 $x = 3$

13 (2) $\dfrac{2}{3}$; constant returns to scale.

14 (1) (a) $\dfrac{2}{3}$ (b) $-\dfrac{1}{2}$

  (2) $y = \dfrac{1}{7}x^2$

15 $\log_{10} x^2 - \log_{10} \sqrt{y} - \log_{10} 10$

$$= \log_{10}\left(\frac{x^2}{\sqrt{y}}\right) - 1$$

$$= \log_{10}\left(\sqrt{\frac{x^4}{y}}\right) - 1$$

16 (a) $L = \left(\dfrac{Q}{AK^{\alpha}}\right)^{1/\beta}$ (b) $L = \left(\dfrac{(Q/A)^{\alpha} - bK^{\alpha}}{1 - b}\right)^{1/\alpha}$

17 (a) 1   (b) 2   (c) n   (d) 3

Section 2.4

Practice Problems

1

x	-3	-2	-1	0	1	2	3
3^x	0.04	0.11	0.33	1	3	9	27
3^{-x}	27	9	3	1	0.33	0.11	0.04

The graphs of 3^x and 3^{-x} are sketched in Figures S2.21 and S2.22, respectively.

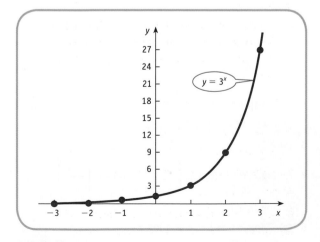

Figure S2.21

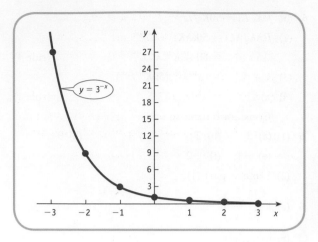

Figure S2.22

2 (a) 2.718 145 927, 2.718 268 237, 2.718 280 469

  (b) 2.718 281 828; values in part (a) are getting closer to that of part (b).

3 (1) (a) 0.07%   (b) 1.35%   (c) 18.44%   (d) 50.06%

  (2) 55%

  (3) A graph of y against t, based on the information obtained in parts (1) and (2), is sketched in Figure S2.23. This shows that, after a slow start, microwave ownership grows rapidly between $t = 10$ and 30. However, the rate of growth then decreases as the market approaches its saturation level of 55%.

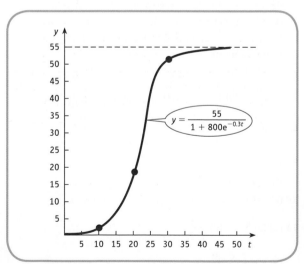

Figure S2.23

4 (a) $2 \ln a + 3 \ln b$ (b) $\ln\left(\dfrac{x^{1/2}}{y^3}\right)$

5 (a) \$5 million and \$3.7 million

  (b) 4 years

6 (1) Missing numbers are 0.99 and 2.80.

(2) The graph is sketched in Figure S2.24.

Intercept, 0.41; slope, 0.20.

(3) $A = 0.2$, $B = e^{0.41} = 1.5$

(4) (a) 9100

(b) 2.4×10^8; answer to part (b) is unreliable since $t = 60$ is well outside the range of given data.

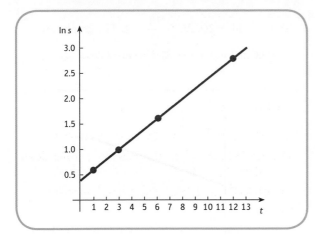

Figure S2.24

Exercise 2.4

1 (1) (a) 33 (b) 55 (c) 98

(2) 100

(3) The graph of N against t is sketched in Figure S2.25.

The graph sketched in Figure S2.25 is called a **learning curve**. It shows that immediately after training the worker can produce only a small number of items. However, with practice, output quickly increases and finally settles down at a daily rate of 100 items.

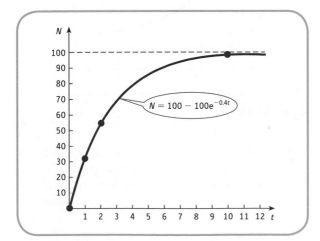

Figure S2.25

2 (a) $\ln x + \ln y$ (b) $\ln x + 4 \ln y$ (c) $2 \ln x + 2 \ln y$

(d) $5 \ln x - 7 \ln y$ (e) $\frac{1}{2} \ln x - \frac{1}{2} \ln y$

(f) $\frac{1}{2} \ln x + \frac{3}{2} \ln y - \frac{1}{2} \ln z$

3 (a) $\ln x^3$ (b) $\ln\left(\dfrac{x^4 z^5}{y^3}\right)$

4 (a) 1.77 (b) -0.80 (c) no solution

(d) 0.87 (e) 0.22 (f) 0.35

5 $A = 50\,000$, $a = 0.137$ (a) \$25 205 (b) \$0

6 (a) e^5 (b) 1

7 91.6

8 Increasing returns to scale.

Exercise 2.4*

1 \$162.19

2 (a) 1.13 (b) 1.79 (c) 8.77

3 The equation

$$N = c(1 - e^{-kt}) = c - ce^{-kt}$$

rearranges as

$$e^{-kt} = \frac{c - N}{c}$$

Taking logarithms gives

$$-kt = \ln\left(\frac{c - N}{c}\right)$$

$$t = -\frac{1}{k}\ln\left(\frac{c - N}{c}\right)$$

$$= \frac{1}{k}\ln\left(\frac{c - N}{c}\right)^{-1} = \frac{1}{k}\ln\left(\frac{c}{c - N}\right)$$

(a) 350 000

(b) 60 days

(c) Market saturation level is 700 000, which is less than the three-quarters of a million copies needed to make a profit, so the proprietor should sell.

4 $\ln Q = \ln 3 + \dfrac{1}{2}\ln L + \dfrac{1}{3}\ln K$

Putting $y = \ln Q$, $x = \ln K$ gives

$$y = \frac{1}{3}x + (\ln 3 + \frac{1}{2}\ln L)$$

which is of the form '$y = ax + b$'.

Slope $= \frac{1}{3}$, intercept $= \ln 3 + \frac{1}{2}\ln L$.

5 (a) $\ln Q = \ln(AL^n) = \ln A + \ln L^n = \ln A + n \ln L$

(b)

$\ln L$	0	0.69	1.10	1.39	1.61
$\ln Q$	-0.69	-0.46	-0.33	-0.22	-0.16

(c) $n = 0.34$, $A = 0.50$

6 (a) $3y^2 + 13y - 10$

(b) Put $y = e^x$ in part (a) to deduce -0.405.

7 (a) $y = \dfrac{1}{b}\ln\left(\dfrac{x}{a}\right)$ (b) $x = \dfrac{1}{2}\ln(e^y - 3)$

8 (a) 6   (b) -1 or 2   (c) 25   (d) 0.26   (e) ± 1.655

9 $P = \dfrac{\ln(A/B)}{k_1 + k_2}$

Multiple Choice Questions

1 B	**2** D	**3** C
4 B	**5** C	**6** D
7 C	**8** A	**9** A
10 B	**11** D	**12** E
13 D	**14** B	**15** A

Examination Questions

1 (a) 2000

(b) 100

(c) 64

(d) Show $f(\lambda K, \lambda L) = \lambda^{7/6} f(K, L)$; increasing returns to scale

2 $\pi = -Q^2 + 6Q - 8$. A graph of the profit function is sketched in Figure S2.26

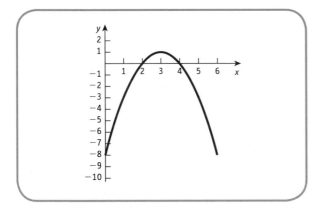

Figure S2.26

(a) $Q = 2, 4$

(b) 1

(c) Shifts vertically upwards

3 (a) $P = 100, Q = 6$

(b) $P = 101.79, Q = 5.88$; consumer pays $1.79 and producer pays $3.21

4 (a) TR $= 10Q - Q^2$

(b) $5 \le P \le 7$

5 (a) (i) $\log_a\left(\dfrac{x^6}{y}\right)$

(ii) -2

(b) Each year the price is multiplied by the same factor, 1.1; $A = 1000$; $b = 1.1$

(i) $2594

(ii) At the beginning of Year 22

6 (a) TC $= 14 + 2Q$; AC $= \dfrac{14}{Q} + 2$. The graphs are sketched in Figures S2.27 and S2.28.

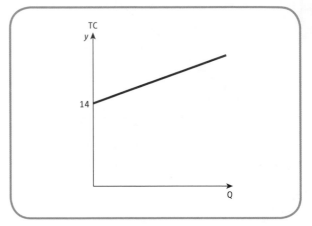

Figure S2.27

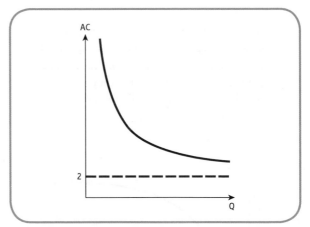

Figure S2.28

(b) When $Q = 0$, there is no revenue and the only costs are the fixed ones which are given to be 14, so the profit is $0 - 14 = -14$. Substituting $Q = 0$ into $\pi = aQ^2 + bQ + c$ gives $\pi = c$, so c must equal -14.

(c) $a + b = 8$, $6a + b = 3$; $a = -1$, $b = 9$

(d) $Q = 2, 7$; max profit is 6.25

(e) TR $= -Q^2 + 11Q$; $P + Q = 11$

7 (a) (i) $\dfrac{a^5 b^3}{2}$

(ii) $4x^2 y^4$

(iii) 6

(iv) $\log_b(xy^2 z^2)$

(b) -1.36

(c) (i) 659,360

(ii) 3.5

(iii) The sales graph is sketched in Figure S2.29.

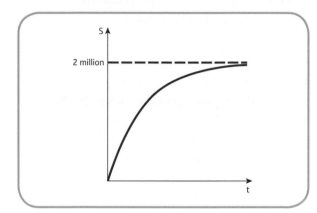

Figure 2.29

8 (a) $A = 50{,}000$; $b = 0.95$; A is the initial price

(b) $r = -0.0513$

(c) Use rules to logs to obtain $\ln V = -0.0513t + \ln 50000$ so it is a line with gradient -0.0513 and vertical intercept 10.8.

9 (a) $\dfrac{1}{Q} + 0.5 + 0.04Q$; $\dfrac{5}{Q} + 0.5$; 1

(b) A = IT; B = Printing; C = Retail

(c) $2.5 < Q < 10$

CHAPTER 3

Section 3.1

Practice Problems

1 (a) $0.29 (b) $937.50 (c) $139.20

2 (a) 10% (b) $1564 (c) $8835

3 (a) $7.345 million (b) $76 billion (c) 7%

4 (a) 8750 (b) 750 (c) 80%

5 (a) 82% increase (b) 58% decrease

(c) 45% decrease

6 100, 101.5, 105.4, 104.3, 106.9

7 (a) 5.7% increase (b) 18.4% increase

(c) 12.0% increase

8 The complete set of 'constant Year 2 prices' is listed in Table S3.1.

During Year 1/2 salaries remain unchanged in real terms. However, since Year 2 salaries have outpaced inflation with steady increases in real terms.

Table S3.1

	Year				
	1	2	3	4	5
Real salaries	18.1	18.1	19.0	21.7	23.2

Exercise 3.1

1 (a) $\dfrac{7}{20}$ (b) $\dfrac{22}{25}$ (c) $2\dfrac{1}{2}$ (d) $\dfrac{7}{40}$ (e) $\dfrac{1}{500}$

2 (a) 1.2 (b) 7.04 (c) 2190.24 (d) 62.72

3 (a) 60% (b) 22

4 (a) 1.19 (b) 3.5 (c) 0.98 (d) 0.57

5 (a) 4% increase (b) 42% increase

(c) 14% decrease (d) 245% increase

(e) 0.25% increase (f) 96% decrease

6 (a) $18.20 (b) 119 244 (c) $101.09

(d) $1610 (e) $15 640

7 35%

8 (a) $15.50 (b) $10.54 (c) 32%

9 $862.50

10 (a) $26 100 (b) 31% (nearest percentage)

11 (a) 37.5% increase (b) 8.9% increase

(c) 6.25% decrease

12 $11.6 million

13 50 60 72 86 100

Prices rise consistently over the past five years at an steadily increasing rate.

14 (a) Jan (b) 4800 (c) 133

15 (1) 1995

(2) (a) 30% (b) 52.3% (c) 13.1% (d) 9.4%

(3) (a) 25% (b) 44% (c) 10.6% (d) 11.1%

(4) Public transport costs have risen at a faster rate than private transport throughout the period 1995–2010. However, for the final five years there are signs that the trend has stopped and has possibly reversed.

16 964, 100, 179, 750; e.g. seasonal variations.

17 (a) 83.3, 100, 91.7, 116.7, 125, 147.9

(b) 64.8 (c) Year 5

Exercise 3.1*

1 $140

2 $5875

3 (a) $90

(b) 40%; the 20% discount is applied to the price after the first reduction not the original.

4 (a) $720

(b) 40% of the new price is less than 40% of the original.

(c) Divide by 0.6.

5 (a) $850   (b) 19% decrease   (c) 23.5% increase

6 (a) 100, 101.7, 113.1, 116.9

(b) Real output: 236, 229.2, 244.7, 244.7

Index: 100, 97.1, 103.7, 103.7

(c) In real terms, spending on education fell by 2.9% in Year 2, increased by 6.8% in Year 3 and remained unchanged in Year 4.

7 (a) 1 and 6, respectively

(b) 142, 150

(c) 94, 87, 83, 75, 79

(d) 1.1 million and 1.6 million

8 (a) 239.2, 242, 243.69, 243.43, 250.73, 258.56

98.8, 100, 100.7, 100.6, 103.6, 106.8

(b) 297   (c) 3.5%

9 (a) 100, 97, 112

(b) Although the price changes to goods A and C in Year 2 appear to cancel each other out, the firm buys more of C, so this has the greater impact on the index. In Year 3, there is a slight fall in the price of good B. However, the firm buys relatively few items of good B and the prices of the other two goods have increased significantly.

10 (a) 100, 107, 146

(b) No change in Year 1 since this is the base year.

In Year 2 the firm has bought more of each good so the index has increased.

In Year 3 the firm has nearly doubled its order for good A which has also increased markedly in price. This is reflected in a much higher index than before.

Section 3.2

Practice Problems

1 $S = 1000(1.08)^{10} = \$2158.92$

2 Four years

3 (1) (a) $33.71   (b) $33.77   (c) $33.79

(d) $33.81   (e) $33.82   (f) $33.82

(2) $33.82

4 13.86%

5 12.55%

6 Nine years

Exercise 3.2

1 $6753.29; 50%

2 $23 433.19

3 (a) $619 173.64   (b) 13

4 15 years

5 $42 868.75

6 (a) $13 947.94   (b) $14 156.59

(c) $14 342.45   (d) $14 381.03

7 Account B has the greater return.

8 $205.44

9 36.6 years

10 17.0 years

11 We are charged interest on the interest; 26.82%.

12 7.25%

13 (a) Six years (b) 5.19%

14 $4410; $5143.82; 28.60%

15 21.70%

16 $P = S\left(1 + \dfrac{r}{100}\right)^{-n}$

17 5.75%

18 (a) $28 000 (b) $25 920 (c) Year 5

Exercise 3.2*

1 13 years

2 $158.45

3 (a) Midwest (b) BFB

4 (a) $35 000   (b) Seven years

5 7.67%

6 Store B

7 (a) Interest is $(r/k)\%$ per period and there are kt periods in t years, so $S = P\left(1 + \dfrac{r}{100k}\right)^{kt}$.

(b) If $m = \dfrac{100k}{r}$ then $\dfrac{r}{100k} = \dfrac{1}{m}$ and

$kt = \dfrac{mrt}{100k}$ so

$$S = P\left(1 + \frac{1}{m}\right)^{rtm/100} = P\left[\left(1 + \frac{1}{m}\right)^{m}\right]^{rt/100}$$

by rule 3 of indices.

(c) Now, since $m = 100k/r$, we see that if the frequency increases (i.e. if $k \rightarrow \infty$), then $m \rightarrow \infty$, causing

$$\left(1 + \frac{1}{m}\right)^m$$

to approach e. Substituting this into the result of part (b) gives

$$S = Pe^{rt/100}$$

8 22 years

9 (a) 1.5%   (b) 17.87%

10 $100(g^{1/n} - 1)$

11 (b) $100e^{rt/100} - 100$

Section 3.3

Practice Problems

1 The geometric ratios of (a), (c), (d) and (e) are 2, -3, $^1/_2$ and 1.07, respectively.

Sequence (b) is not a geometric progression.

2 (a) 16; 31   (b) 4386.52

3 (a) $15 645.49   (b) 12 years

4 $177.69

5 36 years

Exercise 3.3

1 11 463.88

2 (a) $78 227.44   (b) $78 941.10

3 $983.26

4 17 years

5 200 million tonnes

6 $19 053.06

7 (a) $13 586.80

  (b) $35 868; $18 698.20

8 $966.43

Exercise 3.3*

1 $-16\,777\,215$

2 (a) $9280.71   (b) $9028.14

3 140 040

4 $424.19

  (a) $459.03   (b) $456.44

5 $313 238

6 $31 876.08

7 $rS_n = r(a + ar + ar^2 + \ldots + ar^{n-1})$

     $= ar + ar^2 + ar^3 + \ldots + ar^n$

which is very similar to the given expression for S_n except that the first term, a, is missing and we

have the extra term, ar^n. Consequently, when S_n is subtracted from rS_n, the rest of the terms cancel, leaving

$$rS_n - S_n \quad = ar^n - a$$
$$(r - 1)S_n \quad = a(r^n - 1)$$

(factorise both sides)

$$S_n = a\left(\frac{r^n - 1}{r - 1}\right)$$

(divide through by $r - 1$)

The expression for S_n denotes the sum of the first n terms of a geometric series because the powers of r run from 0 to $n - 1$, making n terms in total. Notice that we are not allowed to divide by zero, so the last step is not valid for $r = 1$.

8 (a) $480

  (b) $3024.52

  (c) After n payments, debt is

$$((((8480 - A)R - A)R - A)R \ldots - A)$$
$$= 8480R^{n-1} - A(1 + R + R^2 + \ldots + R^{n-1})$$
$$= 8480R^{n-1} - A\left(\frac{R^n - 1}{R - 1}\right)$$

Finally, setting this expression equal to zero gives the desired formula for A.

  (d) $637.43

Section 3.4

Practice Problems

1 (a) $55 839.48

  (b) $54 881.16

2 (a) NPV = $452; worthwhile since this is positive.

  (b) $r = 16\%$; worthwhile since the IRR exceeds the market rate.

3 NPV of Project A is $2221.90; NPV of Project B is $2354.70, so Project B is to be preferred.

4 $180 146.91

5 The results are given in Table S3.2.

There is very little to choose between these two projects. Both present values are considerably less than the original expenditure of $10 000. Consequently, neither project is to be recommended, since the net present values are negative. The firm would be better off just investing the $10 000 at 15% interest!

Table S3.2

	Discounted revenue	
	($)	
End of year	Project 1	Project 2
1	1739.13	869.57
2	1512.29	756.14
3	1972.55	1315.03
4	1715.26	3430.52
5	1491.53	1988.71
Total	8430.76	8359.97

6 9%; this exceeds the market rate, so the project is worthwhile.

7 The present values of the income stream are listed in Table S3.3.

Table S3.3

End of year	Cash flow ($)	Present value ($)
1	70	64.81
2	70	60.01
3	1070	849.40
Total present vlaue		974.22

Exercise 3.4

1 (a) $5974.43

(b) $5965.01

2 (a) 7%

(b) Yes, provided there are no risks.

3 Project 2

4 $4 567 138.81

5 Option 2

6 6.27%

7 (a) The discount rate is certainly between 4% and 5%. An estimate of about 4.1% or 4.2% is sensible.

(b) No

8 Project B is best.

9 (a) $379.08

(b) $1000

10 Project A $PV = 626.38$

Project B $PV = 1248.28$

Choose B

11 20.3%

Exercise 3.4*

1 $257.85

2 $5000

3 $31 250

4 $61 672.67

5 $38 887.69

6 27%

7 $349.15

8 (a) $400 000

(b) $92 550.98

(c) $307 449.02

9 (a) $333 million

(b) $5\left(\dfrac{1 - (1.06)^{1-n}}{1.06^2 - 1.06}\right)$

(c) Same expression as (b) but with 5 replaced by 50.

(d) 12

10 $49 280

11 $R(1 + r/100)^{-1} + R(1 + r/100)^{-2} + \ldots + R(1 + r/100)^{-n}$

$= \dfrac{R}{1 + r/100}\left(\dfrac{1 - (1 + r/100)^{-n}}{1 - (1 + r/100)^{-1}}\right)$

$= R\left(\dfrac{1 - (1 + r/100)^{-n}}{1 + r/100 - 1}\right)$

$= 100R\left(\dfrac{1 - (1 + r/100)^{-n}}{r}\right)$

(a) $1488.94 (b) $\dfrac{100R}{r}$

12 (b) 1%

Multiple Choice Questions

1 A	**2** D	**3** E
4 D	**5** B	**6** C
7 E	**8** D	**9** C
10 C	**11** E	**12** D
13 C	**14** E	**15** E
16 D		

Examination Questions

1 (a) $4880.76

(b) $4885.61

(c) 4.06%, 4.08%

(d) 2.94

2 (a) 2.62% decrease

(b) $607.15

(c) $230,000

3 (a) (i) 3950

(ii) 3905

(c) Decreases but settles down to 3500

4 (a) 122.54

(b) 135.21

(c) Paasche has the advantage of reflecting changes in actual purchases made. However, the amounts bought in Year 2 may be unavailable, and you are not really comparing like with like in the Paasche index.

5 4.77% and 4.88%. Very little to choose between these two projects which are both close to the prevailing rate. Other considerations such as project viability and access arrangements need to be considered in order to make an informed decision.

6 (a) 24

(b) (i) 44

(ii) $324.06

(iii) Remains at $4000

7 (a) (i) $4776.21

(ii) $2500

(iii) 2.8%

(iv) 5

(b) (i) $40,554.48

(ii) $125,000

8 (a) $24 464.35

(b) $11 876.26

CHAPTER 4

Section 4.1

Practice Problems

1 (a) 2 (b) −1 (c) 0

2 Using a calculator, the values of the cube function, correct to two decimal places, are

x	−1.50	−1.25	−1.00	−0.75	
$f(x)$	−3.38	−1.95	−1.00	−0.42	
x	−0.50	−0.25	0.00	0.25	0.50
$f(x)$	−0.13	−0.02	0.00	0.02	0.13
x	0.75	1.00	1.25	1.50	
$f(x)$	0.42	1.00	1.95	3.38	

The graph of the cube function is sketched in Figure S4.1.

$$f'(-1) = 3.0; f'(0) = 0; f'(1) = 3.0$$

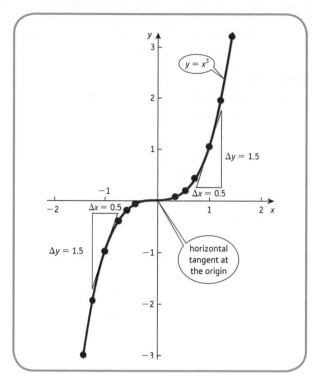

Figure S4.1

3 $f'(x) = 3x^2$

Hence $f'(-1) = 3; f'(0) = 0; f'(1) = 3$.

4 (a) $5x^4$ (b) $6x^5$ (c) $100x^{99}$

(d) $-x^{-2}$ (e) $-2x^{-3}$

Exercise 4.1

1 (a) 2 (b) −1 (c) 0

2 $-^2/_3$; downhill.

3 The graph of $f(x) = 5$ is sketched in Figure S4.2. The graph is horizontal, so it has zero slope at all values of x.

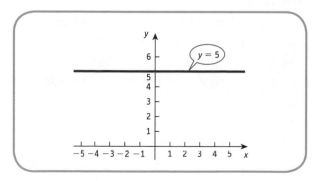

Figure S4.2

4 $7x^6$; 448

5 (a) $8x^7$ (b) $50x^{49}$ (c) $19x^{18}$ (d) $999x^{998}$

6 (a) $-\dfrac{3}{x^4}$ (b) $\dfrac{1}{2\sqrt{x}}$ (c) $-\dfrac{1}{2x\sqrt{x}}$ (d) $\dfrac{3\sqrt{x}}{2}$

7 3, 1.25, 0, −0.75, −1, −0.75, 0, 1.25

   (a) −3   (b) 0   (c) 1

Exercise 4.1*

1 When $x = 0$, $y = a(0) + b = b$.   ✓

   When $x = 1$, $y = a(1) + b = a + b$.   ✓

$$\text{Slope} = \frac{(a + b) - b}{1 - 0} = a$$

2 (a) $15x^{14}$ (b) $\dfrac{9x^3\sqrt{x}}{2}$ (c) $\dfrac{\sqrt[3]{x}}{3x}$ (d) $-\dfrac{1}{4\sqrt[4]{x}x}$

   (e) $-\dfrac{13\sqrt{x}}{2x^8}$

3 (a) (i) 2, 2.0248...   (ii) 0.24845...   (iii) 0.25

   (b) (i) 8, 8.3018...   (ii) 3.01867...   (iii) 3

   (c) (i) 0.5, 0.4938...   (ii) −0.06135...   (iii) −0.0625

   In all three cases the gradient of the chord gives a good approximation to that of the tangent.

4 (a) (8, 4)   (b) (±3, ±243)

   (c) $\left(-\dfrac{1}{2}, 4\right)$ (d) $\left(4, \dfrac{1}{8}\right)$

Section 4.2

Practice Problems

1 (a) $12x^2$ (b) $-2/x^2$

2 (a) $5x^4 + 1$ (b) $2x$

3 (a) $2x - 3x^2$ (b) $\dfrac{3}{x^4}$

4 (a) $45x^4 + 4x$ (b) $40x^7 + 3/x^2$

   (c) $2x + 6$ (d) $8x^3 + 36x^2 - 8x + 7$

5 134

Exercise 4.2

1 (a) $10x$ (b) $-3/x^2$ (c) 2   (d) $2x + 1$

   (e) $2x - 3$ (f) $3 + 7/x^2$ (g) $6x^2 - 12x + 49$

   (h) a (i) $2ax + b$ (j) $4 + 3/x^2 - 14/x^3$

2 (a) 27   (b) 4   (c) 2   (d) −36

   (e) 3/8

3 $4x^3 + 6x^2$

   (a) $9x^2 - 8x$ (b) $12x^3 - 6x^2 + 12x - 7$ (c) $2x - 5$

   (d) $1 + \dfrac{3}{x^2}$ (e) $-\dfrac{2}{x^3} + \dfrac{4}{x^2}$ (f) $\dfrac{3}{x^2} - \dfrac{10}{x^3}$

4 (a) 14   (b) $6/x^4$ (c) 0

5 4.

6 0; horizontal tangent, i.e. vertex of parabola must be at $x = 3$.

7 $\dfrac{1}{\sqrt{x}}$ (a) $\dfrac{5}{2\sqrt{x}}$ (b) $x^{-2/3}$ (c) $\dfrac{3}{2}x^{-1/4}$ (d) $-\dfrac{5}{2}x^{-3/2}$

8 (a) $2P + 1$ (b) $50 - 6Q$ (c) $-30/Q^2$

   (d) 3   (e) $5/\sqrt{L}$ (f) $-6Q^2 + 30Q - 24$

Exercise 4.2*

1 $\dfrac{3}{2}$

2 (a) $4P + 1$ (b) $40 - \dfrac{9}{2}\sqrt{Q}$ (c) $-\dfrac{20}{Q^2} + 7$

   (d) $4Y + 3$ (e) $200 - \dfrac{1}{L\sqrt[4]{L}}$ (f) $-3Q^2 + 40Q - 7$

3 −40; concave

4 (a) uphill; $f'(-1) = 1 > 0$

   (b) concave; $f''(-1) = -72 < 0$

5 $f''(x) = 6ax + 2b > 0$ gives $x > -b/3a$

   $f''(x) = 6ax + 2b < 0$ gives $x < -b/3a$

6 $y = x - 3$

7 (a) $f'(x) = -\dfrac{aA}{x^{a+1}} < 0$ so the function is decreasing.

   (b) $f''(x) = \dfrac{a(a + 1)A}{x^{a+2}} > 0$ so the function is convex.

   (c) The graph is sketched in Figure S4.3.

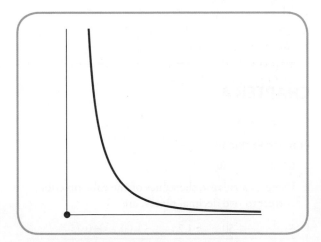

Figure S4.3

   (d) For salaries over $100 000, the proportion of people who earn a fixed range of salaries decreases as income rises so, for example, there are fewer people earning between $150 000 and $200 000 than between $100 000 and $150 000.

8 $r = \gamma$ which is a constant

Section 4.3

Practice Problems

1 $TR = 60Q - Q^2$

(1) $MR = 60 - 2Q$; -40

(2) (a) 500   (b) 459

so TR changes by -41, which is approximately the same as the exact value obtained in part (1).

2 $MR = 1000 - 8Q$

(a) Total revenue rises by about 2280.

(b) Total revenue falls by about 1520.

3 $MC = 2$, so a 1-unit increase in Q always leads to a 2-unit increase in TC irrespective of the level of output.

4 $Q = 50L^{1/2}$

(a) 25   (b) $\dfrac{25}{3}$ (c) 0.25

The fact that these values decrease as L increases suggests that the law of diminishing marginal productivity holds for this function.

5 $MPS = 0.6$; $MPC = 0.4$

This indicates that, at the current level of income, a 1-unit increase in national income causes a rise of about 0.6 units in savings and 0.4 units in consumption.

Exercise 4.3

1 $TR = 100Q - 4Q^2$, $MR = 100 - 8Q$; 1.2

2 $TR = 80Q - 3Q^2$, so $MR = 2P - 80$

3 $TR = 100Q - Q^2$; $MR = 100 - 2Q$. Graphs of TR and MR are sketched in Figures S4.4 and S4.5, respectively. $MR = 0$ when $Q = 50$. This is the value of Q at which TR is a maximum.

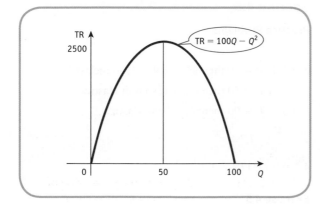

Figure S4.4

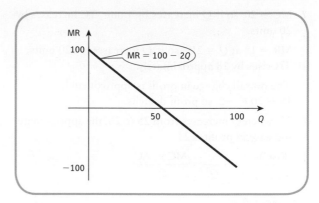

Figure S4.5

4 $TC = 15 + 2Q^2 + 9Q$; 15; $4Q + 9$

5 (a) 49.98

(b) 49.8

(c) 48

(d) 30. Yes, because $d^2Q/dL^2 = -0.02 < 0$.

6 $MPC = 1/6$ and $MPS = 5/6$. If national income rises by 1 unit, the approximate increase in consumption and savings is 1/6 and 5/6, respectively.

7 13

8 At midday on 6 January, the company's share price is increasing at a rate of 25 cents a day.

By 7 January shares will have risen by 25 cents (approximately).

9 $TR = 3000Q - 2Q^{3/2}$; $MR = 3000 - 3\sqrt{Q}$

$MR = 2991$; if Q rises from 9 to 10 the approximate change in TR is 2991.

Exercise 4.3*

1 (a) $TR = 100Q - 4Q^{3/2} - 3Q^2$

(b) $MR = 100 - 6Q^{1/2} - 6Q$; $MR = 28$

(c) 7 compared to 6.78

2 (a) $MPC = 0.96$, $MPS = 0.04$

(b) $S = 0.2Y - 100 - 0.01Y^2$

3 (a) $TC = 100 + 2Q + Q^2/10$ $MC = 2 + Q/5$

(b) $MC = 8$; $\Delta(TC) \cong 16$

(c) 100

4 $\dfrac{d^2Q}{dL^2} = 12 - 1.2L < 0$ for all $L > 10$

5 (a) $MP_L = \dfrac{5}{2}L^{-1/2} - 0.1$

(b) $L = 625$; output is maximised when $L = 625$.

(c) $\dfrac{d^2Q}{dL^2} = -\dfrac{5}{4}L^{-3/2} < 0$

6 36

7 MC = 20, so if Q increases by 1 unit, TC increases by 20 units.

MR = 18 at Q = 219, so if Q increases to 220 units, TR rises by 18 approximately.

The overall change in profit is approximately $18 - 20 = -2$, so profit decreases.

8 25; when Q increases from 25 to 26, the approximate increase in profit is 25.

9 $\dfrac{d(AC)}{dQ} = a - \dfrac{c}{Q^2} = \dfrac{MC - AC}{Q}$

Section 4.4

Practice Problems

1 (a) $15(3x - 4)^4$ (b) $3(x^2 + 3x + 5)^2(2x + 3)$

(c) $\dfrac{-2}{(2x - 3)^2}$ (d) $\dfrac{2}{\sqrt{(4x - 3)}}$

2 (a) $(3x - 1)^5(21x - 1)$

(b) $\dfrac{x^3}{\sqrt{(2x + 3)}} + 3x^2\sqrt{(2x + 3)} = \dfrac{x^2(7x + 9)}{\sqrt{(2x + 3)}}$

(c) $\dfrac{-2}{(x - 2)^2}$

3 (a) $\dfrac{-2}{(x - 2)^2}$ (b) $\dfrac{2}{(x + 1)^2}$

Exercise 4.4

1 (a) $15(5x + 1)^2$ (b) $16(2x - 7)^7$ (c) $5(x + 9)^4$

(d) $24x(4x^2 - 7)^2$ (e) $8(x + 2)(x^2 + 4x - 3)$

(f) $\dfrac{1}{\sqrt{2x + 1}}$ (g) $\dfrac{-3}{(3x + 1)^2}$ (h) $\dfrac{-8}{(4x - 3)^3}$

(i) $\dfrac{-1}{(2x + 3)\sqrt{(2x + 3)}}$

2 (a) $(9x + 4)(3x + 4)$ (b) $x(5x - 4)(x - 2)^2$

(c) $\dfrac{3x + 4}{2\sqrt{x + 2}}$ (d) $(4x + 3)(x + 6)^2$

(e) $(8x + 13)(x + 5)^2$ (f) $x^2(14x - 15)(2x - 5)^3$

3 (a) $\dfrac{-5}{(x - 5)^2}$ (b) $\dfrac{7}{(x + 7)^2}$ (c) $\dfrac{-5}{(x - 2)^2}$

(d) $\dfrac{-25}{(3x + 1)^2}$ (e) $\dfrac{6}{(5x + 6)^2}$ (f) $\dfrac{-19}{(3x - 7)^2}$

4 $10(5x + 7) = 50x + 70$

5 $7x^6 + 24x^5 + 20x^4$

6 (a) $(100 - 4Q)(100 - Q)^2$ (b) $\dfrac{4000}{(Q + 4)^2}$

7 MPC = 1.78, MPS = -0.78. If national income rises by 1 unit, consumption rises by 1.78 units, whereas savings actually fall by 0.78 units.

Exercise 4.4*

1 (a) $20(2x + 1)^9$

(b) $3(x^2 + 3x - 5)^2(2x + 3)$

(c) $-7/(7x - 3)^2$

(d) $-2x/(x^2 + 1)^2$

(e) $4/\sqrt{(8x - 1)}$

(f) $-2(6x - 5)^{-\frac{4}{3}} = \dfrac{-2}{(6x - 5)\sqrt[3]{(6x - 5)}}$

2 (a) $5x(x + 2)(x + 5)^2$

(b) $x^4(4x + 5)(28x + 25)$

(c) $\dfrac{x^3(9x + 8)}{2\sqrt{(x + 1)}}$

3 (a) $\dfrac{x(x + 8)}{(x + 4)^2}$ (b) $\dfrac{3}{(x + 1)^2}$ (c) $\dfrac{x^2(5x - 6)}{2(x - 1)^{3/2}}$

4 (a) $(x - 3)^3(5x - 3)$ (b) $\dfrac{3(x - 1)}{\sqrt{2x - 3}}$ (c) $\dfrac{3x^2(x + 5)}{(3x + 5)^3}$

(d) $\dfrac{1 - x^2}{(x^2 + 1)^2}$ (e) $\dfrac{ad - bc}{(cx + d)^2}$

(f) $[ac(m + n)x + mad + ncb](ax + b)^{m-1}(cx + d)^{n-1}$

(g) $(6x^2 + 17x + 6)(x + 2)(x + 3)^2$

5 $\dfrac{-4}{(2x + 1)^3}$

6 (a) $\dfrac{100 - 3Q}{\sqrt{(100 - 2Q)}}$ (b) $\dfrac{200 + 50Q}{(2 + Q)^{3/2}}$

7 1.098; -0.098; if income rises by 1 unit, consumption goes up by more than this, with the excess taken out of savings.

8 Use the quotient rule. As Q increases, MC decreases and converges to 2.

9 Use the product rule to differentiate TR = $aQ - Q(bQ + c)^{1/2}$.

Section 4.5

Practice Problems

1 -0.26

2 (a) If $P = 10$ then $|E| = 1/9 < 1$, so inelastic.

(b) If $P = 50$ then $|E| = 1$, so unit elastic.

(c) If $P = 90$ then $|E| = 9$, so elastic.

3 $-\dfrac{47}{36}$;   7.7%

4 (a) 0.333175   (b) $\dfrac{1}{3}$

Exercise 4.5

1 $-43/162 = -0.27$

2 $-22/81 = -0.27$; agree to two decimal places.

3 (a) $-1/4$ (b) $-1/4$ (c) $-9/8$

4 (a) −0.3125, so inelastic.

   (b) Would expect demand for economy class flights to be more sensitive to price rises, so the magnitude of E would be larger.

5 (a) −2, so when price rises by 2%, demand falls by 4%.

   (b) −3.88%

6 (a) $1 - \dfrac{400}{Q}$ (b) 200   (c) MR = $20 - 0.1Q$

7 (a) $0.2P$

   (b) $0.1P^2 = Q - 4$

   (subtract 4 from both sides)

   $\qquad P^2 = 10(Q - 4) = 10Q - 40$

   (multiply both sides by 10)

   $\qquad P = \sqrt{(10Q - 40)}$

   (square root both sides)

   $\qquad \dfrac{dP}{dQ} = \dfrac{5}{\sqrt{(10Q - 40)}}$

   (c) $\dfrac{1}{dP/dQ} = \dfrac{\sqrt{(10Q - 40)}}{5}$

   $\qquad\qquad = \dfrac{P}{5} = 0.2P = \dfrac{dQ}{dP}$

   (d) $E = 10/7$

8 1.46;   (a) elastic   (b) 7.3%

Exercise 4.5*

1 −1.54

2 3.75%

3 $4P/(4P - 60)$; 7.5

4 $E = -\dfrac{1}{n}$ which is a constant.

5 $\dfrac{aP}{aP + b}$

   (a) If $b = 0$, then $E = \dfrac{\cancel{P}\cancel{a}}{\cancel{P}\cancel{a}} = 1$.

   (b) If $b < 0$, then $aP + b < aP$, so $E = \dfrac{aP}{aP + b} > 1$.

   Assuming that the line is sketched with quantity on the horizontal axis and price on the vertical axis, supply is unit elastic when the graph passes through the origin, and elastic when the vertical intercept is negative.

6 (1) 0.528

   (2) $\dfrac{0.2P^2}{40 + 0.1P^2}$ (a) 4.2%   (b) 20

7 (a) $Q = \dfrac{P - b}{a} \Rightarrow \dfrac{dQ}{dP} = \dfrac{1}{a}$

   $E = P \times \dfrac{\cancel{a}}{P - b} \times \dfrac{1}{\cancel{a}} = \dfrac{P}{P - b}$

   (b) $a = \dfrac{2}{5}, b = 9$

8 (b) (i) 3   (ii) 1.5   (iii) $\dfrac{5\sqrt{P}}{10\sqrt{P} - 4}$

Section 4.6

Practice Problems

1 (a) There is one minimum point at $(-2, -47)$.

   A graph is sketched in Figure S4.6.

   (b) Minimum at $(2, -1)$ and maximum at $(3, 0)$.

   A graph is sketched in Figure S4.7 based on the following table of function values:

x	−10	0	2	3	10
$f(x)$	3887	27	−1	0	−833

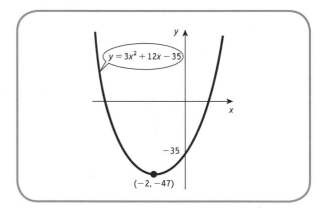

Figure S4.6

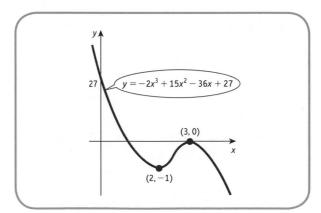

Figure S4.7

2 $L = 10$; $MP_L = AP_L = 2000$

3 (a) $Q = 5$

(b) $Q = 4$ gives the maximum profit, $\pi = 30$;
$MR = MC = 4$

4 $Q = 6$; $AC = MC5$ $\qquad$ $t = 12.5$

Exercise 4.6

1 (a) Maximum at $(1/2, 5/4)$; graph is sketched in
Figure S4.8.

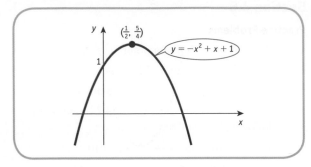

Figure S4.8

(b) Minimum at $(2, 0)$; graph is sketched in
Figure S4.9.

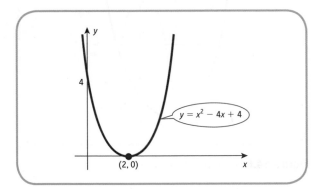

Figure S4.9

(c) Minimum at $(10, 5)$; graph is sketched in
Figure S4.10.

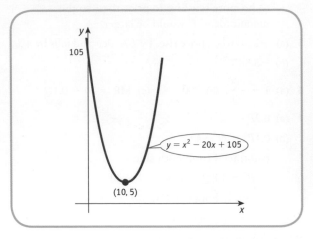

Figure S4.10

(d) Maximum at $(1, 2)$, minimum at $(-1, -2)$; graph
is sketched in Figure S4.11.

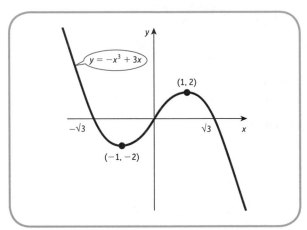

Figure S4.11

2 10

3 30; $MP_L = 450 = AP_L$

4 (a) $TC = 13 + (Q + 2)Q$
$\qquad = 13 + Q^2 + 2Q$

$$AC = \frac{TC}{Q} = \frac{13}{Q} + Q + 2$$

Q	1	2	3	4	5	6
AC	16	10.5	9.3	9.3	9.6	10.2

The graph of AC is sketched in Figure S4.12.

(b) From Figure S4.12 minimum average cost is 9.2.

(c) Minimum at $Q = \sqrt{13}$, which gives $AC = 9.21$.

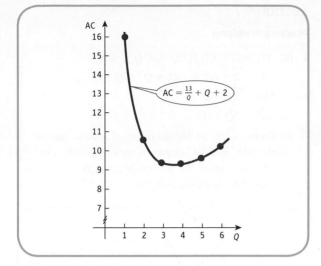

Figure S4.12

5 (a) $TR = 4Q - \dfrac{Q^2}{4}$

$\pi = \dfrac{-Q^3}{20} + \dfrac{Q^2}{20} + 2Q - 4$

$MR = 4 - \dfrac{Q}{2}$

$MC = 2 - \dfrac{3Q}{5} + \dfrac{3Q^2}{20}$

(b) 4   (c) MR = 2 = MC

6 $3

7 (a) $TC = 2Q^2 - 36Q + 200$

$AC = \dfrac{TC}{Q} = 2Q - 36 + \dfrac{200}{Q}$

(b) $Q = 10 \implies AC = 4$

At $Q = 10$, $\dfrac{d^2(AC)}{dQ^2} = 0.4 > 0 \implies$ min.

(c) $Q = 10 \implies MC = 4 = AC$

8 56.25

9 $440

10 37 037

Exercise 4.6*

1 531.5

2 Graphs of the three functions are sketched in Figure S4.13, which shows that the stationary points in (a), (b) and (c) are a point of inflection, minimum and maximum, respectively.

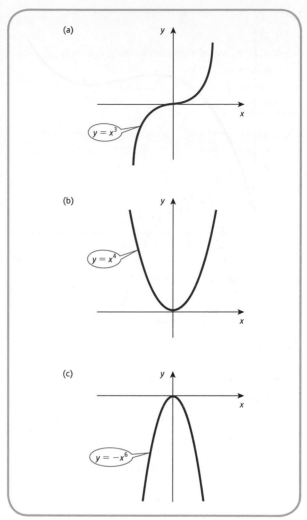

Figure S4.13

3 $TC = 2Q^2 + 15$, $AC = 2Q + \dfrac{15}{Q}$,

$MC = 4Q$; $\sqrt{7.5}$; $AC = 11 = MC$

4 (a) (6, 492) is a maximum and (10, 460) is a minimum.

(b) The graph is sketched in Figure S4.14.

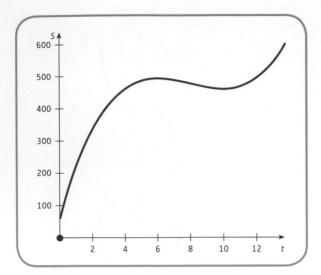

Figure S4.14

(c) 492 and 465

5 167

6 (a) 15

(b) $Q = 15 - \dfrac{t}{10}$ gives $P = 140 + \dfrac{2t}{5}$

P rises from 140 to $140 + \dfrac{2t}{5}$, so the increase is $\dfrac{2}{5}t$.

7 $a = -7, b = 16, c = -7$

8 (a) The graph is sketched in Figure S4.15.

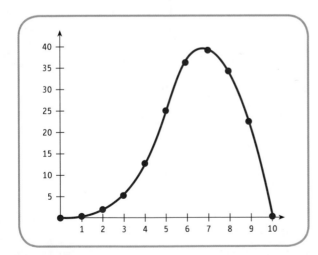

Figure S4.15

(b) TR $= 39.0625$, $Q = 6.875$

(c) 5

Section 4.7

Practice Problems

1 (a) TR $= (25 - 0.5Q)Q = 25Q - 0.5Q^2$

TC $= 7 + (Q + 1)Q = Q^2 + Q + 7$

MR $= 25 - Q$

MC $= 2Q + 1$

(b) From Figure S4.16, the point of intersection of the MR and MC curves occurs at $Q = 8$. The MC curve cuts the MR curve from below, so this must be a maximum point.

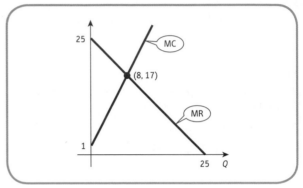

Figure S4.16

2 MC $= 100$

(a) $P_1 = \$200$ and $P_2 = \$150$

(b) $P = \$500/3$

With discrimination, profit is \$10 000.

Without discrimination, profit is \$8333.

3 *Domestic market*: $|E| = 2$

Foreign market: $|E| = 3$

We see that the firm charges the higher price in the domestic market, which has the lower value of $|E|$.

Exercise 4.7*

1 (a) TR $= aQ^2 + bQ$, TC $= dQ + c$

(b) MR $= 2aQ + b$, MC $= d$

(c) The equation $2aQ + b = d$ has solution

$$Q = \frac{d - b}{2a}$$

2 (a) At the point of maximum total revenue

$$MR = \frac{d(TR)}{dQ} = 0$$

so $E = -1$

(b) Maximum occurs when $Q = 10$.

3 (a) $P_1 = \$30$, $P_2 = \$20$ (b) $P = \$24.44$

The profits in parts (a) and (b) are $95 and $83.89, respectively.

4 Argument is similar to that given in text but with < replaced by >.

5 (a) $\dfrac{d^2C}{dQ^2} = 2DRQ^{-3} > 0$ (b) $\sqrt{2DRH}$

6 (a) EOQ = 40 with $C = \$4000$

(b) EOQ = 50 with $C = \$3200$

(c) EOQ = 80 with $C = \$8000$

(d) Reducing (increasing) the order costs by a factor of k reduces (increases) the minimum total cost by a factor of $\sqrt{k}$. The same applies to changes in the holding costs.

7 $AC = aQ + b + \dfrac{c}{Q}$; $2\sqrt{ac} + b$

8 The argument is similar to that given in the text for AP_L.

9 The new supply equation is

$$P = aQ_S + b + t$$

In equilibrium

$$aQ + b + t = -cQ + d$$

which has solution

$$Q = \frac{d - b - t}{a + c}$$

Hence

$$tQ = \frac{(d - b)t - t^2}{a + c}$$

which differentiates to give

$$\frac{d - b - 2t}{a + c}$$

This is zero when

$$t = \frac{d - b}{2}$$

Also the second derivative is

$$\frac{-2}{a + c} < 0 \quad \text{(since } a \text{ and } c \text{ are both positive)}$$

which confirms that the stationary point is a maximum.

Section 4.8

Practice Problems

1

x	0.50	1.00	1.50	2.00
$f(x)$	−0.69	0.00	0.41	0.69

x	2.50	3.00	3.50	4.00
$f(x)$	0.92	1.10	1.25	1.39

The graph of the natural logarithm function is sketched in Figure S4.17.

$$f'(1) = 1$$

$$f'(2) = \frac{1}{2}$$

$$f'(3) = \frac{1}{3}$$

These results suggest that $f'(x) = 1/x$.

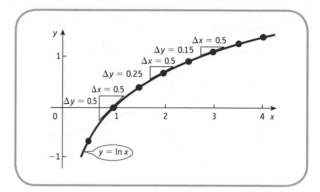

Figure S4.17

2 (a) $3e^{3x}$ (b) $-e^{-x}$ (c) $1/x$ (d) $1/x$

3 (a) $x^3(1 + 4\ln x)$ (b) $2xe^{x^2}$ (c) $\dfrac{x + 2 - x\ln x}{x(x+2)^2}$

4 (a) $\dfrac{7x + 6}{x(x + 2)}$ (b) $\dfrac{2x + 6}{x(2x + 3)}$

5 In terms of P the total revenue function is given by

$$TR = PQ = 1000Pe^{-0.2P}$$

and the total cost function is

$$TC = 100 + 2Q = 100 + 2000e^{-0.2P}$$

Hence

$$\pi = TR - TC$$
$$= 1000Pe^{-0.2P} - 2000e^{-0.2P} - 100$$

For maximum profit, $P = 7$.

6 $E = -2.05$

Exercise 4.8

1 (a) $6e^{6x}$ (b) $-342e^{-342x}$

(c) $-2e^{-x} + 4e^x$ (d) $40e^{4x} - 4x$

2 (1) (a) $4885.61   (b) $4887.57;   196

(2) $160e^{0.04t}$; 195.42

3 (a) $\dfrac{1}{x}$ (b) $\dfrac{1}{x}$

4 (a) $3x^2e^{x^3}$ (b) $\dfrac{4x^3 + 6x}{x^4 + 3x^2}$

5 (a) $(4x^3 + 2x^4)e^{2x}$

(b) $1 + \ln x$

6 (a) $\dfrac{2e^{4x}(2x^2 - x + 4)}{(x^2 + 2)^2}$

(b) $\dfrac{e^x(x\ln x - 1)}{x(\ln x)^2}$

7 (a) Maximum at $(1, e^{-1})$; the graph is sketched in Figure S4.18.

(b) Maximum at $(1, -1)$; the graph is sketched in Figure S4.19.

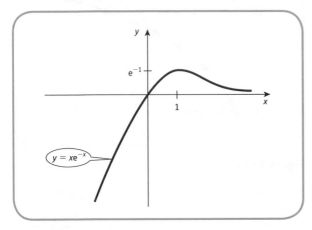

Figure S4.18

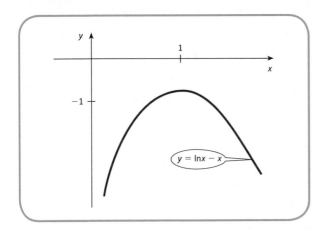

Figure S4.19

8 (a) 2359.88, 2313.15 so the decrease is 46.7.

(b) $\dfrac{dS}{dt} = -47.2$ so is a good approximation.

9 49

10 50

11 $E = -\dfrac{10}{Q}$, which is -1 when $Q = 10$.

Exercise 4.8*

1 (a) $2e^{2x} + 12e^{-4x}$ (b) $(4x + 1)e^{4x}$ (c) $\dfrac{-(x + 2)e^{-x}}{x^3}$

(d) $(m\ln x + 1)x^{m-1}$ (e) $\ln x$ (f) $\dfrac{(n\ln x - 1)x^{n-1}}{(\ln x)^2}$

(g) $\dfrac{(amx + bm - an)e^{mx}}{(ax + b)^{n+1}}$ (h) $\dfrac{(ax\ln bx - n)e^{ax}}{x(\ln bx)^{n+1}}$

(i) $\dfrac{2e^x}{(e^x + 1)^2}$

2 (a) $\dfrac{1}{x(1 + x)}$ (b) $\dfrac{9x - 2}{2x(3x - 1)}$ (c) $\dfrac{1}{1 - x^2}$

3 (a) $\dfrac{dy}{dx} \div y = Ake^{kt} \div Ae^{kt} = k$

(b) (i) a and b

(ii) $\dfrac{\text{GDP}}{N} = \dfrac{A}{B}e^{(a - b)t}$ which is exponential with a growth rate of $(a - b)$.

4 (a) $4x^3(1 - x^2)e^{-2x^2}$ (b) $\dfrac{1 - x}{x(x + 1)}$

5 (a) Maximum at $\left(-\dfrac{1}{a}, \dfrac{-e^{-1}}{a}\right)$.

(b) Maximum at $\left(-\dfrac{b}{2a}, \ln\left(-\dfrac{b^2}{4a}\right)\right)$.

6 (b) $\dfrac{4(x + 1)}{(2x + 1)(4x + 3)}$

7 100

8 $\dfrac{(2Q + 1)(3\ln(2Q + 1) - 20)}{6Q}$

9 (a) $\dfrac{(2Q^2 - 1)e^{Q^2}}{Q^2}$ (b) $\dfrac{1}{3Q + 1} + \ln\left(\dfrac{2Q}{3Q + 1}\right)$

10 (a) $E = \dfrac{-P}{100}$ so demand is inelastic when $0 \le P < 100$.

(b) 100

11 2

12 (a) $\dfrac{dy}{dt} = \dfrac{abke^{-at}}{(1 + be^{-at})^2} > 0$ so the gradient is positive.

(b) $\dfrac{d^2y}{dt^2} = \dfrac{a^2bke^{-at}(-1 + be^{-at})}{(1 + be^{-at})^3}$

All of the factors are positive for all values of t except for the factor $-1 + be^{-at}$ which is positive when $t < \dfrac{\ln b}{a}$ and negative when $t > \dfrac{\ln b}{a}$.

(c) The curve crosses the y axis at $\left(0, \dfrac{k}{1 + b}\right)$ and approaches k as $t \to \infty$ because $e^{-at} \to 0$.

(d) The graph is sketched in Figure S4.20.

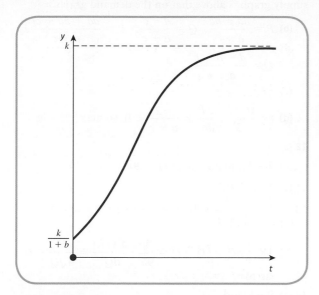

Figure S4.20

13 (a) $PV = Ve^{-0.1t} = 2e^{\sqrt{t}} \times e^{-0.1t}$ (b) 25

Multiple Choice Questions

1 E	**2** A	**3** B
4 A	**5** A	**6** E
7 C	**8** A	**9** E
10 D	**11** A	**12** A
13 B	**14** C	**15** B
16 D	**17** E	**18** B
19 B	**20** E	**21** C
22 D	**23** A	**24** C

Examination Questions

1 MR $= \dfrac{35}{2} - \dfrac{Q}{2}$;

(a) An increase of 0.625

(b) 35

2 (b) $-6x^2 + 10x + 24$; $(3, 36)$, $\left(-\dfrac{4}{3}, -\dfrac{1225}{27}\right)$

(c) $-12x + 10$; max at $x = 3$ and min at $x = -\dfrac{4}{3}$

(d) The graph is sketched in Figure S4.21. It crosses the x-axis at -3, 1 and 4.5, and it crosses the y-axis at -27.

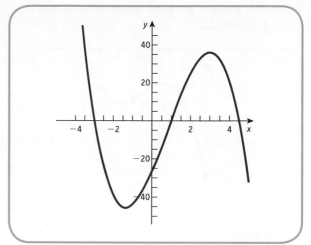

Figure S4.21

3 (a) (i) 90

(ii) $-1/3$

(iii) 1

(b) (i) $25/41 = 0.610$

(ii) $30/49 = 0.612$

4 (a) (i) 31, 34.222; 32.22

(ii) 31

(iii) Gradients of chord and tangent very similar with the chord slightly steeper

(b) (i) MC $= 6Q + 8$

(ii) 94 versus 94.75 so the % error in the estimate is 0.79%

5 (a) 7

(b) 7/3

(c) 6/7%, elastic

6 (a) (i) $12e^2x$

(ii) $\dfrac{2x}{x^2 + 1}$

(b) 14, 16;

(i) increasing

(ii) convex

7 (i) 48

(ii) 294

(iii) 1/2

(iv) 3/8

(v) 0; output maximised at $L = 50$

8 (a) $\pi(0) = -16 < 0$; $\pi(1) = 1 - 9 + 24 - 16 = 0$

(b) $(2,4)$, $(4,0)$

(c) Max and min, respectively

(d) The graph of the profit function is sketched in Figure S4.22.

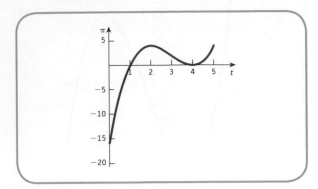

Figure S4.22

(e) increasing on $0 \le t < 2$, $t > 4$ and decreasing on $2 < x < 4$

(f) $t < 3$, $t > 3$

(g) After an initial loss of 16, the profit increases so that it breaks even after one year and reaches a local maximum of 4 after two years. The profit then declines so that the firm breaks even again after four years. For the next year the profit rises at an increasing rate, reaching 4 at the end of the five-year period.

9 (a) $10 + 12L - 0.3L^2$; $10 + 6L - 0.1L^2$

(b) 30

(c) $\dfrac{d^2Q}{dL^2} > 0$ for $L > 20$

10 (a) $\dfrac{400 - 9Q}{\sqrt{400 - 6Q}}$

(b) $\dfrac{20Y + Y^2 - 200}{(10 + Y)^2}$

11 (a) The supply and demand curves are sketched in Figure S4.23.

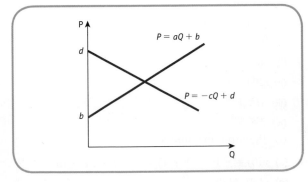

Figure S4.23

Lines intersect only if the vertical intercept on the supply graph is above that on the demand graph.

(b) $P = \dfrac{ad + bc}{a + c}$, $Q = \dfrac{d - c}{a + c}$; $P = \dfrac{ad + bc + ct}{a + c}$,

$Q = \dfrac{d - b - t}{a + c}$

(c) $c : a$

(d) $t = \dfrac{d - b}{2}$; $\dfrac{d^2T}{dt^2} = \dfrac{-2}{a + c} < 0$, so max

12 (a) 0

(b) 20; AC minimum at $Q = 20$

(c) 40; $-31/12$

13 (a) $E = \dfrac{2P}{P - a}$; solve $E = -1$ to get $P = a/3$

(b) $TR = aQ + bQ^{3/2}$; $Q = \dfrac{4a}{9b^2}$; $\dfrac{d^2(TR)}{dQ^2} = \dfrac{3b}{4\sqrt{Q}} < 0$, so max

14 (a) Bookwork

(b) $P_1 = 60$, $P_2 = 135$; $E_1 = -\dfrac{3}{2}$, $E_2 = -\dfrac{27}{23}$;

Bookwork

15 Bookwork

16 (a) 32/55; 32/11; inelastic

(b) $a = -4$, $b = 80$

CHAPTER 5

Section 5.1

Practice Problems

1 (a) -10 (b) -1 (c) 2   (d) 21   (e) 0   (f) 21

2 (a) $\dfrac{\partial f}{\partial x} = 20x^3 - 0 = 20x^3$; $\dfrac{\partial f}{\partial y} = 0 - 2y = -2y$

(b) $\dfrac{\partial f}{\partial x} = 2xy^3 - 10$; $\dfrac{\partial f}{\partial y} = 3x^2y^2 - 0 = 3x^2y^2$

3 (a) $f_{xx} = 60x^2$

$f_{yy} = -2$

$f_{yx} = f_{xy} = 0$

(b) $f_{xx} = 2y^3$

$f_{yy} = 6x^2y$

$f_{yx} = f_{xy} = 6xy^2$

4 $f_1 = \dfrac{\partial f}{\partial x_1} = x_2 + 5x_1^4$

$f_{11} = \dfrac{\partial^2 f}{\partial x_1^2} = 20x_1^3$

$f_{21} = \dfrac{\partial^2 f}{\partial x_2 \partial x_1} = 1$

5 $\dfrac{\partial z}{\partial x} = 1, \dfrac{\partial z}{\partial y} = 4$

(a) z increases by approximately 0.3.

(b) At $(2, 6)$, $z = 14$, and at $(1.9, 6.1)$, $z = 14.29$, so the exact increase is 0.29.

6 (a) $\dfrac{dy}{dx} = \dfrac{-y}{x - 3y^2 + 1}$ (b) $\dfrac{dy}{dx} = \dfrac{y^2}{5y^4 - 2xy}$

Exercise 5.1

1 324; 75; 0

2 (a) $f(a, a) = 2a^2 + aa = 3a^2$

(b) $f(b, -b) = 2b^2 + b(-b) = b^2$

3 $f(2x, 2y) = (2x)(2y)^2 + 4(2x)^3$

$= 2x \times 4y^2 + 4 \times 8x^3$

$= 8xy^2 + 32x^3$

$= 8(xy^2 + 4x^3)$

$= 8f(x, y)$

4 (a) $f_x = 2x, f_y = 20y^4$

(b) $f_x = 9x^2, f_y = -2e^y$

(c) $f_x = y, f_y = x + 6$

(d) $f_x = 6x^5y^2, f_y = 2x^6y + 15y^2$

5 $f_x = 4x^3y^5 - 2x$

$f_y = 5x^4y^4 + 2y$

$f_x(1, 0) = -2$

$f_y(1, 1) = 7$

6 (a) -0.6

(b) -2

(c) -2.6

7 (a) $f_x = -3x^2 + 2, f_y = 1$

$\dfrac{dy}{dx} = \dfrac{-(-3x^2 + 2)}{1} = 3x^2 - 2$

(b) $y = x^3 - 2x + 1$, so

$\dfrac{dy}{dx} = 3x^2 - 2$ ✓

8 (a) $\dfrac{\partial z}{\partial u} = 1 + 2v, \dfrac{\partial z}{\partial v} = 2v + 2u, \dfrac{\partial z}{\partial w} = -15w^2$

(b) $\dfrac{\partial z}{\partial u} = 3u^{-1/2}v^{1/3}w^{1/6}, \dfrac{\partial z}{\partial v} = 2u^{1/2}v^{-2/3}w^{1/6},$

$\dfrac{\partial z}{\partial w} = u^{1/2}v^{1/3}w^{-5/6}$

9 (a) 21.5

(b) 24.575; 12.5%

Exercise 5.1*

1 $85 \neq 91$; $(0, y)$ for any y.

2 $f(kw, kx, ky) = 5(kw)^{0.34}(kx)^{0.25}(ky)^{0.41}$

$= 5k^{0.34}w^{0.34}k^{0.25}x^{0.25}k^{0.41}y^{0.41}$

$= 5k^{0.34+0.25+0.41}w^{0.34}x^{0.25}y^{0.41}$

$= 5kf(w, x, y)$

3

	f_x	f_y	f_{xx}	f_{yy}	f_{yx}	f_{xy}
(a)	y	x	0	0	1	1
(b)	e^xy	e^x	e^xy	0	e^x	e^x
(c)	$2x + 2$	1	2	0	0	0
(d)	$4x^{-3/4}y^{3/4}$	$12x^{1/4}y^{-1/4}$	$-3x^{-7/4}y^{3/4}$	$-3x^{1/4}y^{-5/4}$	$3x^{-3/4}y^{-1/4}$	$3x^{-3/4}y^{-1/4}$
(e)	$\dfrac{-2y}{x^3} + \dfrac{1}{y}\dfrac{1}{x^2}$	$-\dfrac{x}{y^2}\dfrac{6y}{x^4}$	$\dfrac{2x}{y^3}$	$\dfrac{-2}{x^3} - \dfrac{1}{y^2}\dfrac{-2}{x^3}$	$-\dfrac{1}{y^2}$	

4 78; 94; 6.2

5 (a) $\dfrac{\partial z}{\partial u} = 24(6u + vw^3)^3, \dfrac{\partial z}{\partial v} = 4w^3(6u + vw^3)^3,$

$\dfrac{\partial z}{\partial w} = 12vw^2(6u + vw^3)^3$

(b) $\dfrac{\partial z}{\partial u} = \sqrt{w}e^{-vw}, \dfrac{\partial z}{\partial v} = -uw\sqrt{w}e^{-vw},$

$\dfrac{\partial z}{\partial w} = \dfrac{u}{2\sqrt{w}}e^{-vw} - uv\sqrt{w}e^{-vw}$

6 $f_x(e, 1) = 3; f_y(e, 1) = -2e; f_{xx}(e, 1) = 6e^{-1}; f_{yy}(e, 1) = 4e;$
$f_{xy}(e, 1) = -6$

7 1/3

8 $f_1 = \dfrac{x_3^2}{x_2}; f_2 = -\dfrac{x_1x_3^2}{x_2^3} + \dfrac{1}{x_2}; f_3 = \dfrac{2x_1x_3}{x_2} + \dfrac{1}{x_3};$

$f_{11} = 0; f_{22} = \dfrac{2x_1x_3^2}{x_2^3} - \dfrac{1}{x_2^2}; f_{33} = \dfrac{2x_1}{x_2} - \dfrac{1}{x_3^2};$

$f_{12} = \dfrac{-x_3^2}{x_2^2} = f_{21}; f_{13} = \dfrac{2x_3}{x_2} = f_{31};$

$f_{23} = \dfrac{-2x_1x_3}{x_2^2} = f_{32}$

9 e.g. $f(x, y) = x^3y^2 + 3x^2y$

10 5

11 2.5

12 (a) $\dfrac{-3x^2y - 4y^2}{x^3 + 8xy}$ (b) $\dfrac{-4x^{-2/3}y^{1/4} - 1}{3x^{1/3}y^{-3/4}}$

(c) $\dfrac{-y^2}{1 + xy}$ (d) $\dfrac{-x^2 - 2xy + y^2}{-x^2 + 2xy + y^2}$

Section 5.2

Practice Problems

1 (a) -0.14 (b) -0.14 (c) 0.12

0.6%. A rise in income causes a rise in demand. Normal.

2 $\dfrac{\partial U}{\partial x_1} = 2948$ and $\dfrac{\partial U}{\partial x_2} = 140$

$\Delta U = -848$

The law of diminishing marginal utility holds for both x_1 and x_2.

3 21.06; \$42.12

4 $MP_K = 2K$ and $MP_L = 4L$

(a) $MRTS = \dfrac{MP_L}{MP_K} = \dfrac{4L}{2K} = \dfrac{2L}{K}$

(b) $K\dfrac{\partial Q}{\partial K} + L\dfrac{\partial Q}{\partial L} = K(2K) + L(4L)$

$= 2(K^2 + 2L^2) = 2Q$ ✓

Exercise 5.2

1 2.71. This is greater than 1, so the good is superior.

2 (a) $-4/233$ (b) $-3/233$

(c) $40/233$; -0.04%; complementary

3 (a) $2x^2 + y^2 = 36$

(b) 16 and 4 so the gradient is -4.

4 (a) 80   (b) 960

5 1

6 $\dfrac{\partial U}{\partial x_1} = \dfrac{1}{5}$ and $\dfrac{\partial U}{\partial x_2} = \dfrac{5}{12}$

(a) 37/60   (b) 12/25

7 $MP_K = 8$, $MP_L = 14\tfrac{1}{4}$ (a) $1^{25}/_{32}$ (b) $1^{25}/_{32}$

8 $K(6K^2 + 3L^2) + L(6LK) = 6K^3 + 9L^2K = 3(2K^3 + 3L^2K)$

9 (a) -0.5; -1.5 so A is inelastic and B is elastic, so B is more sensitive to a change in price.

(b) 0.5; 1.5

A is normal because income elasticity is positive and is less than one.

B is superior because income elasticity of demand exceeds one.

10 (a) $18(\lambda K)^{1/6}(\lambda L)^{5/6} = 18\lambda^{1/6}K^{1/6}\lambda^{5/6}L^{5/6} = \lambda(18K^{1/6}L^{5/6}) = \lambda Q$

(b) $MP_K = 3K^{-5/6}L^{5/6}$; $MP_L = 15K^{1/6}L^{-1/6}$

(c) (i) decreases   (ii) increases

Exercise 5.2*

1 (a) 0.4   (b) 3.2%

Since $E < 1$, the good is income-inelastic. The relative market share of the good decreases as the economy expands.

2 0.5

3 16

4 $A(\lambda K)^\alpha(\lambda L)^\beta = A\lambda^\alpha K^\alpha \lambda^\beta L^\beta = \lambda^{\alpha+\beta}Q$

---

5 (a) $\dfrac{\partial U}{\partial x_1} = 0.7Ax_1^{-0.3}x_2^{0.5} > 0$ since it is the product of four positive numbers.

Utility increases as more units of good 1 are consumed.

(b) $\dfrac{\partial^2 U}{\partial x_1 \partial x_2} = 0.35\,Ax_1^{-0.3}x_2^{-0.5} > 0$ since it is the product of four positive numbers.

Consuming more of one good increases the marginal utility of the other good.

(c) $\dfrac{\partial^2 U}{\partial x_1^2} = -0.21Ax_1^{-1.3}x_2^{0.5} < 0$ since it is the product of three positive numbers and one negative number.

Consuming more of good 1 decreases the marginal utility of good 1; there is diminishing marginal utility of good 1.

6 The graph is sketched in Figure S5.1, which shows that MRTS $= -(-5/7) = 5/7$.

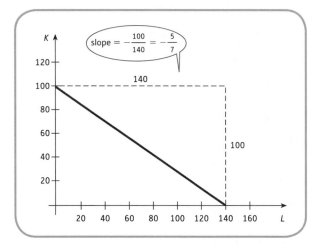

Figure S5.1

7 (a) $MP_K = \dfrac{10}{3}$; $MP_L = \dfrac{21}{2}$

(b) $\Delta Q \approx -11$

(c) 3.15; e.g. a 1-unit increase in labour and a 3.15 decrease in capital maintains a constant level of output.

8 (a) $MP_K = AbK^{\alpha-1}[\ ]^{\frac{1}{\alpha}-1}$; $MP_L = A(1-b)L^{\alpha-1}[\ ]^{\frac{1}{\alpha}-1}$

$MRTS = \dfrac{MP_L}{MP_K} = \dfrac{1-b}{b} \times \dfrac{L^{\alpha-1}}{K^{\alpha-1}} = \dfrac{1-b}{b}\left(\dfrac{K}{L}\right)^{1-\alpha}$

(b) $KAbK^{\alpha-1}[\ ]^{\frac{1}{\alpha}-1} + LA(1-b)L^{\alpha-1}[\ ]^{\frac{1}{\alpha}-1}$

$= A(bK^\alpha + (1-b)L^\alpha)[\ ]^{\frac{1}{\alpha}-1}$

$= A[\ ]^{\frac{1}{\alpha}}$

$= Q$

9 (a) Complementary; coefficient of P_A is negative.

(b) (i) $E_P = \dfrac{-b}{100}$

(ii) $E_{P_A} = -\dfrac{3c}{500}$

(iii) $E_Y = \dfrac{d}{5}$

(c) $a = 4310, b = 5, c = 2, d = 1$

10 (a) $\dfrac{\partial Q}{\partial P_A} = kbP^{-a}P_A^{b-1}Y^c > 0$; as the price of the alternative good increases, demand for the good increases.

(c) The partial derivative of this proportion with respect to Y is $k(c-1)P^{1-a}P_A^bY^{c-2} > 0$.

11 (a) MRCS $= \dfrac{2}{3}$; constant so the indifference map consists of straight lines.

(b) MRCS $= \dfrac{3x_2}{x_1}$; decreases as x_1 increases so the indifference curve is convex.

(c) MRCS $= \dfrac{1}{3}\sqrt{\dfrac{x_2}{x_1}}$; decreases as x_1 increases so the indifference curve is convex.

Section 5.3

Practice Problems

1 $C = a\left(\dfrac{b + I^*}{I - a}\right) + b$

$\dfrac{\partial C}{\partial I^*} = \dfrac{a}{1 - a} > 0$

because $0 < a < 1$

Hence an increase in I^* leads to an increase in C.

Change in C is 2.

2 (a) Substitute C, I, G, X and M into the Y equation to get

$Y = aY + b + I^* + G^* + X^* - (mY + M^*)$

Collecting like terms gives

$(1 - a + m)Y = b + I^* + G^* + X^* - M^*$

so

$Y = \dfrac{b + I^* + G^* + X^* - M^*}{1 - a + m}$

(b) $\dfrac{\partial Y}{\partial X^*} = \dfrac{1}{1 - a + m}$

$\dfrac{\partial Y}{\partial m} = -\dfrac{b + I^* + G^* + X^* - M^*}{(1 - a + m)^2}$

An increase in X^* leads to an increase in Y. An increase in m leads to a decrease in Y.

(c) $Y = 2100; \Delta Y = \dfrac{100}{3}$

3 If d increases by a small amount, then the intercept increases and the demand curve shifts upwards slightly. Figure S5.2 shows that the effect is to increase the equilibrium quantity from Q_1 to Q_2, confirming that $\partial Q/\partial d > 0$.

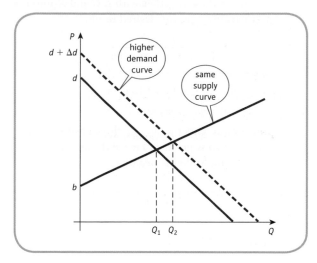

Figure S5.2

Exercise 5.3*

1 (a) Substituting equations (3) and (4) into (2) gives

$C = a(Y - T^*) + b = aY - aT^* + b$ (7)

Substituting (5), (6) and (7) into (1) gives

$Y = aY - aT^* + b + I^* + G^*$

so that

$Y = \dfrac{-aT^* + b + I^* + G^*}{1 - a}$

Finally, from (7), we see that

$C = a\left(\dfrac{-aT^* + b + I^* + G^*}{1 - a}\right) - aT^* + b$

$= \dfrac{a(-aT^* + b + I^* + G^*) + (1 - a)(-aT^* + b)}{1 - a}$

$= \dfrac{aI^* + aG^* - aT^* + b}{1 - a}$

(b) $\dfrac{a}{1 - a} > 0$; C increases   (c) 1520; rise of 18

2 $\dfrac{-a(b + I^* + G^* - aT^*}{(1 - a - at)^2}$

3 (1) From the relations

$$C = aY_d + b$$

$$Y_d = Y - T$$

$$T = tY + T^*$$

we see that

$$C = a(Y - tY - T^*) + b$$

Similarly,

$$M = m(Y - tY - T^*) + M^*$$

Substitute these together with I, G and X into the Y equation to get the desired result.

(2) (a) $$\frac{\partial Y}{\partial T^*} = \frac{m - a}{1 - a + at + m - mt}$$

Numerator is negative because $m < a$.
Denominator can be written as

$$(1 - a) + at + m(1 - t)$$

which represents the sum of three positive numbers, so is positive. Hence the autonomous taxation multiplier is negative.

(b) $$\frac{\partial Y}{\partial G^*} = \frac{1}{1 - a + at + m - mt} > 0$$

(3) (a) 1000

(b) $\Delta Y = 20$

(c) $\Delta T^* = 18^1/_3$

4 From text, equilibrium quantity is

$$\frac{d - b}{a + c}$$

Substituting this into either the supply or demand equation gives the desired result.

$$\frac{\partial P}{\partial a} = \frac{c(d - b)}{(a + c)^2} > 0, \quad \frac{\partial P}{\partial b} = \frac{c}{a + c} > 0$$

$$\frac{\partial P}{\partial c} = \frac{a(b - d)}{(a + c)^2} < 0, \quad \frac{\partial P}{\partial d} = \frac{a}{a + c} > 0$$

where the quotient rule is used to obtain $\partial P/\partial a$ and $\partial P/\partial c$. An increase in a, b or d leads to an increase in P, whereas an increase in c leads to a decrease in P.

5 (a) $C = aY_d + b = a(Y - T) + b = a(Y - T^*) + b$

$$Y = C + I + G = a(Y - T^*) + b + I^* + G^*$$

$$(1 - a)Y = -aT^* + b + I^* + G^* \Rightarrow$$

$$Y = \frac{1}{1 - a}(b - aT^* + I^* + G^*)$$

(b) $$\frac{\partial Y}{\partial G^*} = \frac{1}{1 - a}; \quad \frac{\partial Y}{\partial T^*} = -\frac{a}{1 - a};$$

$$\Delta Y = \frac{1 - a}{1 - a} = 1$$

(c) 1

6 (1) Substituting second and third equations into first gives

$$Y = aY + b + cr + d$$

so that

$$(1 - a)Y - cr = b + d \qquad (1)$$

(2) Substituting first and second equations into third gives

$$k_1Y + k_2r + k_3 = M_S^*$$

so that

$$k_1Y + k_2r = M_S^* - k_3 \qquad (2)$$

(3) (a) Working out $c \times (2) + k_2 \times (1)$ eliminates r to give

$$ck_1Y + k_2(1 - a)Y = c(M_S^* - k_3) + k_2(b + d)$$

Dividing both sides by $ck_1 + k_2(1 - a)$ gives result.

(b) $$\frac{c}{(1 - a)k_2 + ck_1},$$ which is positive because the top and bottom of this fraction are both negative.

7 (a) $Y_d = Y - T = Y - (tY = T^*) = (1 - t)Y - T^*$

$C = aY_d + b = a[(1 - t)Y - T^*] + b = a(1 - t)Y - aT^* + b$

$Y = C + I = a(1 - t)Y - aT^* + b + cr + d$

$(1 - a(1 - t))Y = -aT^* + b + cr + d \Rightarrow$

$$Y = \frac{b + d - aT^* + cr}{1 - a(1 - t)}$$

(b) $$\frac{\partial Y}{\partial c} = \frac{r}{1 - a(1 - t)};$$

$$\frac{\partial Y}{\partial a} = \frac{-T^* + (1 - t)(b + d) + cr)}{(1 - a(1 - t))^2}$$

(c) $0 < t < 1$ and $0 < a < 1 \Rightarrow$
$0 < a(1 - t) < 1 \Rightarrow 1 - a(1 - t) > 0$

$$r > 0 \Rightarrow \frac{\partial Y}{\partial c} > 0 \Rightarrow Y \text{ increases}$$

(d) $Y = 2800; \Delta Y = 46.25$

8 (a) $\pi = (a - bQ)Q - (f + vQ) = -bQ^2 + (a - v)Q - f$

At the stationary point, $Q = \dfrac{a - v}{2b}$.

(b) $$\frac{\partial \pi}{\partial a} = \frac{a - v}{2b}, \frac{\partial \pi}{\partial b} = -\frac{(a - v)^2}{4b^2}, \frac{\partial \pi}{\partial f} = -1,$$

$$\frac{\partial \pi}{\partial v} = -\frac{a - v}{2b}$$

(c) From (a), $Q = \dfrac{a - v}{2b}$ so $a - v > 0$.

Hence all of the multipliers in (b) are negative except for the first one.

An increase in a causes maximum profit to rise, whereas an increase in b, f or v results in a decrease in maximum profit.

Section 5.4

Practice Problems

1 One saddle point at $(0, 1)$.

2 Total revenue from the sale of G1 is
$$\text{TR}_1 = P_1 Q_1 = (50 - Q_1)Q_1 = 50Q_1 - Q_1^2$$
Total revenue from the sale of G2 is
$$\text{TR}_2 = P_2 Q_2 = (95 - 3Q_2)Q_2$$
$$= 95Q_2 - 3Q_2^2$$
Total revenue from the sale of both goods is
$$\text{TR} = \text{TR}_1 + \text{TR}_2$$
$$= 50Q_1 - Q_1^2 + 95Q_2 - 3Q_2^2$$
Profit is
$$\pi = \text{TR} - \text{TC}$$
$$= (50Q_1 - Q_1^2 + 95Q_2 - 3Q_2^2) - (Q_1^2 + 3Q_1Q_2 + Q_2^2)$$
$$= 50Q_1 - 2Q_1^2 + 95Q_2 - 4Q_2^2 - 3Q_1Q_2$$
$$Q_1 = 5, Q_2 = 10; P_1 = 45 \text{ and } P_2 = 65$$

3 $P_1 = 200$, $P_2 = 150$ and $\pi = 10\,000$

Exercise 5.4

1 (a) $\dfrac{\partial z}{\partial x} = 4x - 12$, $\quad \dfrac{\partial z}{\partial y} = 2y - 8$; $(3, 4)$

(b) $\left(\dfrac{\partial^2 z}{\partial x^2}\right)\left(\dfrac{\partial^2 z}{\partial y^2}\right) - \left(\dfrac{\partial z}{\partial x \partial y}\right)^2 = 4 \times 2 - 0^2 > 0$ so the

point is not a saddle point.

Also $\dfrac{\partial^2 z}{\partial x^2} > 0$, $\dfrac{\partial^2 z}{\partial y^2} > 0$ so the point is a minimum.

2 (a) Minimum at $(1, 1)$, maximum at $(-1, -1)$, and saddle points at $(1, -1)$ and $(-1, 1)$.

(b) Minimum at $(2, 0)$, maximum at $(0, 0)$, and saddle points at $(1, 1)$ and $(1, -1)$.

3 $Q_1 = 9$, $Q_2 = 6$

$$\dfrac{\partial^2 \pi}{\partial Q_1^2} = -2 < 0, \quad \dfrac{\partial^2 \pi}{\partial Q_2^2} = -4 < 0, \quad \dfrac{\partial^2 \pi}{\partial Q_1 \partial Q_2} = -1$$

$$\left(\dfrac{\partial^2 \pi}{\partial Q_1^2}\right)\left(\dfrac{\partial^2 \pi}{\partial Q_2^2}\right) - \left(\dfrac{\partial^2 \pi}{\partial Q_1 \partial Q_2}\right)^2$$

$$= (-2)(-4) - (-1)^2 = 7 > 0 \Rightarrow \max$$

4 Maximum profit is $1300 when $Q_1 = 30$ and $Q_2 = 10$.

5 $x_1 = 138$, $x_2 = 500$; $16.67 per hour.

6 $Q_1 = 19$, $Q_2 = 4$

7 (a) $\pi = (32 - Q_1)Q_1 + (40 - 2Q_2)Q_2 - 4(Q_1 + Q_2)$
$$= 32Q_1 - Q_1^2 + 40Q_2 - 2Q_2^2 - 4Q_1 - 4Q_2$$
$$= 28Q_1 + 36Q_2 - Q_1^2 - 2Q_2^2$$

(b) $Q_1 = 14$; $Q_2 = 9$; $\pi = 358$
$$\left(\dfrac{\partial^2 \pi}{\partial Q_1^2}\right)\left(\dfrac{\partial^2 \pi}{\partial Q_2^2}\right) - \left(\dfrac{\partial \pi}{\partial Q_1 \partial Q_2}\right)^2 = (-2) \times (-4) - 0^2 > 0$$
so the point is not a saddle point.

Also $\dfrac{\partial^2 \pi}{\partial Q_1^2} < 0$, $\dfrac{\partial^2 \pi}{\partial Q_2^2} < 0$ so the point is a maximum.

8 (a) Add $Q_1 = 32 - P$; $Q_2 = 20 - \dfrac{1}{2}P$ to get result.

The demand equation can be transposed as
$$P = \dfrac{104}{3} - \dfrac{2}{3}Q.$$

$$\pi = \left(\dfrac{104}{3} - \dfrac{2}{3}Q\right)Q - 4Q = \dfrac{1}{3}(92Q - 2Q^2)$$

(b) $Q = 23$; new $\pi = 352\dfrac{2}{3}$ so the reduction in profit

is $5\dfrac{1}{3}$.

Exercise 5.4*

1 (a) Minimum at $(0, 0)$ and saddle point at $\left(-\dfrac{1}{2}, -\dfrac{1}{4}\right)$.

(b) Saddle point at $(0, 0)$ and minimum at $(-2, 2)$.

(c) Saddle point at $(0, 0)$ and minimum at $\left(-\dfrac{20}{3}, -\dfrac{10}{3}\right)$.

2 Maximum profit is $176 when $L = 16$ and $K = 144$.

3 $346\,500

4 Maximum profit is $95 when $P_1 = 30$ and $P_2 = 20$.

5 (a) $P_1 = 55$; $P_2 = 0.5a + 5$

(b) $P = 15 + 0.4a$

Profit under (a) is $\pi_a = 512.5 + 0.5(a - 10)^2$.

Profit under (b) is $\pi_b = -437.5 + 10a + 0.4a^2$.

$$\pi_a - \pi_b = 0.1(a - 100)^2 \geq 0$$

6 (a) At the maximum profit the marginal products equal their relative prices.

(b) $K = 4096$; $L = 512$

7 $Q_i = \dfrac{p_i}{2c_i}$; $\quad \pi = \dfrac{p_1^2}{4c_1} + \dfrac{p_2^2}{4c_2}$

8 $x = \dfrac{2p - q}{14}$; $\quad y = \dfrac{4q - p}{14}$

Section 5.5

Practice Problems

1 The constrained function has a maximum value of 11 at the point $(1, 1)$.

2 $x_1 = 100, x_2 = 20$

$$\frac{U_1}{P_1} = \frac{20}{2} = 10 \quad \text{and} \quad \frac{U_2}{P_2} = \frac{100}{10} = 10$$

3 $x_1 = 30, x_2 = 10$

Exercise 5.5

1 (a) $y = \frac{2}{3} - 3x$ (b) Maximum value of z is $\frac{1}{9}$ which occurs at $\left(\frac{1}{9}, \frac{1}{3}\right)$.

2 Maximum value of z is 13, which occurs at (3, 11).

3 27 000

4 $K = 6$ and $L = 4$

5 $x + y = 20$; 6 of product A and 14 of product B.

6 8100

7 (a) 1000

   (b) 15 985

8 (a) $2K + L = 1000$

   (b) $MP_K = AL, MP_L = AK$

   (c) $\frac{MP_K}{MP_L} = \frac{AL}{AK} = \frac{L}{K} \Rightarrow \frac{L}{K} = \frac{2}{1} \Rightarrow L = 2K$

   (d) $K = 250; L = 500$

Exercise 5.5*

1 (a) Minimum value of 1800 occurs at (10, 30).

   (b) Maximum value of 10 occurs at $\left(\frac{1}{2}, 2\right)$.

2 $K = 10$ and $L = 4$

3 Maximum profit is \$165, which is achieved when $K = 81$ and $L = 9$.

4 $x_1 = 3, x_2 = 4$

5 (a) $2x_1 + 4x_2 = 300$

   (b) $x_1 = 100; x_2 = 25$

   (c) The curves are sketched in Figure S5.3.

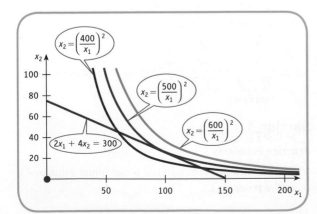

Figure S5.3

6 (a) $K = 200; L = 150$

   (b) The isoquant is sketched in Figure S5.4.

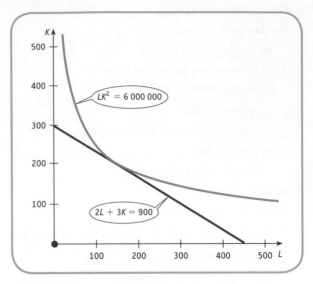

Figure S5.4

7 (a) $U = \sqrt{x_1} + x_2 = x_1^{1/2} + b - ax_1$ and at a stationary point, $x_1 = \frac{1}{4a^2}$.

   (b) $\frac{\partial U^*}{\partial a} = -\frac{1}{4a^2} < 0$ so an increase in a causes a decrease in optimal utility.

   $\frac{\partial U^*}{\partial b} = 1$ so a 1 unit increase in b, increases U^* by 1 unit.

Section 5.6

Practice Problems

1 Optimal point has coordinates (2, 10) and value of the objective function is -12.

2 The maximum value of U is 1849; 1892.

3 $x_1 = \frac{P_2 M}{P_1(P_1 + P_2)}; x_2 = \frac{P_1 M}{P_2(P_1 + P_2)}$

Exercise 5.6

1 9

2 (a) 800; $x = 20, y = 10, \lambda = 40$

   (b) 840.5; $x = 20.5, y = 10.25, \lambda = 41$

   (c) Change is 40.5 compared to a multiplier of 40.

3 4.5

4 (b) $\frac{\partial g}{\partial K} = 2 - \lambda L, \quad \frac{\partial g}{\partial L} = 1 - \lambda K, \quad \frac{\partial g}{\partial \lambda} = 50 - KL$

   (c) $L = 10$ and $K = 5$

5 (a) $\dfrac{\partial g}{\partial K} = 80L - 3\lambda, \quad \dfrac{\partial g}{\partial L} = 80K - 5\lambda,$

$\dfrac{\partial g}{\partial \lambda} = 1500 - 3K - 5L$

(b) $K = 250$ and $L = 150$ (c) 4000

6 Maximum profit is \$600 at $Q_1 = 10$, $Q_2 = 5$. Lagrange multiplier is 3, so profit rises to \$603 when total cost increases by 1 unit.

Exercise 5.6*

1 (a) $z = M + 1$

(b) If M increases by 1 unit then z goes up by 1 unit, which is the value of λ.

2 (a) 585 412   (b) 93.2

3 (a) 375.5   (b) doubles

4 There are two wheels per frame, so the constraint is $y = 2x$. Maximum profit is \$4800 at $x = 40$, $y = 80$.

5 40; 2.5

6 $x_1 = \dfrac{\alpha M}{(\alpha + \beta)P_1}$ and $x_2 = \dfrac{\beta M}{(\alpha + \beta)P_2}$

7 $x = \$6715.56$; $y = \$3284.44$

8 $x = 13$, $y = 17$, $z = 2$

9 $x = 6$, $y = 11$

10 $\dfrac{U_1}{P_1} = \lambda = \dfrac{U_2}{P_2}$

11 $x = \dfrac{a}{\sqrt{a^2 + b^2}}, \quad y = \dfrac{b}{\sqrt{a^2 + b^2}}$

Multiple Choice Questions

1 E	**2** E	**3** A
4 B	**5** C	**6** D
7 A	**8** E	**9** C
10 E	**11** A	**12** D
13 A	**14** C	

Examination Questions

1 (a) $f_x = 2 + 6xy, f_y = 3x^2 - 2y, f_{xx} = 6y,$
$f_{yy} = -2, f_{xy} = 6x$

(b) $f_x(1, 2) = 14, f_y(1, 2) = -1$; 2.9

(c) $2 + 6 - 4 = 4$; 14

2 $-1/2$, $3/80$

(a) Normal

(b) 4

3 (a) $x_1 + 2x_2 = 50$

(b) $x_1 = 26$, $x_2 = 12$

4 (a) $\mathrm{MP}_L = \dfrac{1}{2}\sqrt{\dfrac{K}{L}} + \dfrac{3}{4L}, \mathrm{MP}_K = \dfrac{1}{2}\sqrt{\dfrac{L}{K}} + \dfrac{1}{4K}$

(b) 0.3718

5 (a) Complementary

(c) $Q_1 = 60$, $Q_2 = 65$

(d) $P_1 = 240$, $P_2 = 195$

6 $K = 15$, $L = 60$

7 $K = 20.25$, $L = 25$

8 Saddle point at $(0,0)$, minimum at $(2,2)$

9 (a) Show that $f(\lambda K, \lambda L) = \lambda^2 f(K, L)$

(b) $\mathrm{MP}_K = \dfrac{KL(K + 8L)}{(K + 4L)^2}, \mathrm{MP}_L = \dfrac{K^3}{(K + 4L)^2}$; show that $K(\mathrm{MP}_K) + L(\mathrm{MP}_L) = 2Q$

(c) 2/3; if labour decreases by 1 unit, capital would need to rise by 2/3 to maintain output.

(d) 0.90625

10 Substituting $W = E/20$ into $W + F = 168$ gives the constraint $E + 20F = 3360$; 56; stay the same

11 (a) 7.5

(b) -1.5625

(c) 1.5625; Bookwork

12 (a) $-8 - 12 + 81 = 61$; $-9/52$;

(b) Minimum at $(1, 0)$

13 (a) $\dfrac{\partial U}{\partial x_1} = \dfrac{x_2^2}{(2x_1 + x_2)^2}, \dfrac{\partial U}{\partial x_2} = \dfrac{2x_1^2}{(2x_1 + x_2)^2};$

$\dfrac{\partial^2 U}{\partial x_1^2} = \dfrac{-4x_2^2}{(2x_1 + x_2)^3} < 0, \quad \dfrac{\partial^2 U}{\partial x_2^2} = \dfrac{-4x_1^2}{(2x_1 + x_2)^3} < 0$

(b) 4.5; 0.09

(c) $x_1 = 20$, $x_2 = 10$

14 $K = M/2$, $L = M/4$

(a) Both ratios are $2M$; last dollar spent on capital yields the same addition to output as the last dollar spent on labour.

(b) Check that $(M + 1)^2 - M^2 \approx \lambda$

(c) $K = \dfrac{M^2}{8L}$; check that they both have a slope of -2; Bookwork

15 (c) $\dfrac{\partial Y}{\partial b} = \dfrac{k_2}{(1 - a)k_2 + ck_1} > 0$ so Y increases as b increases

CHAPTER 6

Section 6.1

Practice Problems

1 (a) x^2 (b) x^4 (c) x^{100} (d) $\dfrac{1}{4}x^4$ (e) $\dfrac{1}{19}x^{19}$

2 (a) $\frac{1}{5}x^5 + c$ (b) $-\frac{1}{2x^2} + c$ (c) $\frac{3}{4}x^{4/3} + c$

(d) $\frac{1}{3}e^{3x} + c$ (e) $x + c$

(f) $\frac{x^2}{2} + c$ (g) $\ln x + c$

3 (a) $x^2 - x^4 + c$ (b) $2x^5 - \frac{5}{x} + c$

(c) $\frac{7}{3}x^3 - \frac{3}{2}x^2 + 2x + c$

4 (a) TC $= 2Q + 500$; TC $= 580$

(b) TR $= 100Q - 3Q^2$; $P = 100 - 3Q$

(c) $S = 0.4Y - 0.2Y^{1/2} - 38$

5 (a) $\frac{1}{20}(5x + 1)^4 + c$

(b) $\frac{1}{16}\left(1 + x^2\right)^8 + c$

(c) $\ln(2 + x^4) + c$

(d) $\frac{1}{4}\left(1 + e^x\right)^4 + c$

Exercise 6.1

1 (a) $x^6 + c$ (b) $\frac{1}{5}x^5 + c$ (c) $e^{10x} + c$ (d) $\ln x + c$

(e) $\frac{2}{5}x^{5/2} + c$ (f) $\frac{1}{2}x^4 - 3x^2 + c$

(g) $\frac{1}{3}x^3 - 4x^2 + 3x + c$ (h) $\frac{ax^2}{2} + bx + c$

(i) $\frac{7}{4}x^4 - 2e^{-2x} + \frac{3}{x} + c$

2 (a) TC $= \frac{Q^2}{2} + 5Q + 20$ (b) TC $= 6e^{0.5Q} + 4$

3 380

4 (a) TR $= 20Q - Q^2$; $P = 20 - Q$

(b) TR $= 12\sqrt{Q}$; $P = \frac{12}{\sqrt{Q}}$

5 $C = 0.6Y + 7$, $S = 0.4Y - 7$

6 (a) $1000L - L^3$ (b) $12\sqrt{L} - 0.01L$

7 6

8 (1) $F'(x) = 10(2x + 1)^4$, which is 10 times too big, so the integral is $\frac{1}{10}(2x + 1)^5 + c$.

(2) (a) $\frac{1}{24}(3x - 2)^8 + c$ (b) $-\frac{1}{40}(2 - 4x)^{10} + c$

(c) $\frac{1}{3}(2x + 1)^{3/2} + c$ (d) $\frac{1}{7}\ln(7x + 3) + c$

Exercise 6.1*

1 (a) $\frac{x^7}{7} - x^2 + c$ (b) $\frac{x^{11}}{11} - 2x\sqrt{x} - e^{-x} + c$

(c) $\frac{x^4}{4} + \frac{1}{x^5} + 2\ln x + e^{-4x} + c$

2 (a) $C = 20(Y + 2Y^{1/4} + 1)$ (b) VC $= 15 + Q^2$

3 (a) TC $= \frac{aQ^2}{2} + bQ + C$ (b) TC $= \frac{a}{b}(e^{bQ} - 1) + C$

4 (a) $\frac{1}{24}(4x - 7)^6$

(b) $\frac{1}{3}\ln(3x + 1) + c$

(c) $\sqrt{2x + 3} + c$

(d) $\frac{1}{10}\left(1 + x^2\right)^5 + c$

(e) $\frac{-1}{4\left(1 + x^4\right)}$

(f) $-\frac{1}{2}e^{-x^2} + c$

(g) $\frac{1}{3}(1 + \ln x)^3$

(h) $\frac{2\sqrt{x^3 + 5}}{3}$

5 (a) $\frac{1}{2}x^2 + \frac{2}{7}x^{7/2} + c$

(b) $\frac{1}{11}x^{11} + \frac{1}{3}x^3 + c$; $\frac{1}{5}e^{5x} + e^x + \frac{3}{2}e^{2x} + c$; $\frac{1}{3}x^3 - \frac{1}{2}x^2 + c$

6 (a) $\frac{1}{4}x^4 - \frac{1}{2}x^2 + 2x^{\frac{1}{2}} + c$

(b) $\ln x + \frac{1}{x} + c$; $-e^{-x} + \frac{1}{3}e^{-3x} + c$; $\ln x - x + \frac{2}{3}x^{3/2} + c$

7 $S = 0.6Y - 0.8\sqrt{Y} - 2$

8 $f(x) = x^3 - 4x + 2$

9 (a) $\ln x + 1$ (b) $x \ln x - x + c$

10 $N = 100(1 - e^{-0.1t})$; 55; 100

11 20

12 550

13 (a) $\frac{1}{a(n + 1)}(ax + b)^{n+1} + c$ (b) $\frac{1}{a}e^{ax+b} + c$

(c) $\frac{1}{a}\ln(ax + b) + c$

14 (a) $\frac{2}{2x + 3} - \frac{6}{(2x + 3)^2} = \frac{2(2x + 3) - 6}{(2x + 3)^2} = \frac{4x}{(2x + 3)^2}$

(b) $e^x(x^2 - 2x + 2) + e^x(2x - 2) = x^2e^x$

Section 6.2

Practice Problems

1 (a) $\dfrac{1}{4}$ (b) 24   (c) 16.5   (d) e − 1

2 341.33

3 (a) 100   (b) 100

4 (a) 9000   (b) 27

5 $37 599.03

Exercise 6.2

1 (a) $\dfrac{104}{3}$ (b) $\dfrac{5}{36}$ (c) 12   (d) 16

2 (a) $\dfrac{290}{3}$ (b) $\dfrac{1}{3}$ (c) 234   (d) e − 1   (e) 1

3 (a) 4

   (b) 0. The graph is sketched in Figure S6.1.
Integration gives a positive value when the graph
is above the x axis and a negative value when it
is below the x axis. In this case there are equal
amounts of positive and negative area which
cancel out. Actual area is twice that between 0
and 2, so is 8.

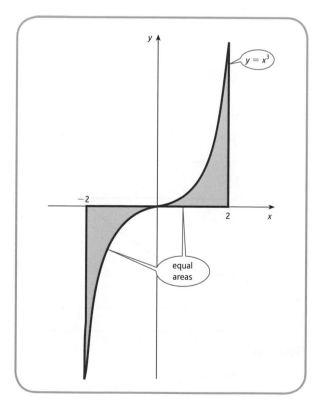

Figure S6.1

4 (a) 100   (b) 20

5 (a) 81   (b) 180

6 (a) $\dfrac{320}{3}$ (b) 129.87

7 (a) 74⅔   (b) 58⅔

8 $16 703

9 (a) 12 800   (b) $1600\left(N^{\frac{3}{2}} - (N-1)^{\frac{3}{2}} \right)$; fourth year

10 $72 190.14

11 384,000 barrels

Exercise 6.2*

1 (a) 27   (b) $\dfrac{2}{15}$

2 (a) 128   (b) 10

3 $83\dfrac{1}{3}$ and $133\dfrac{1}{3}$ respectively

4 $P = 80,\ Q = 30;\ CS = 1265.2;\ PS = 450$

5 $P = 58.48,\ Q = 2.682,\ CS = 50.7,\ PS = 60.7$

6 (a) $427.32   (b) During the 47th year

7 (a) $\dfrac{AT^{\alpha+1}}{\alpha + 1}$ (b) $\dfrac{A}{\alpha}(e^{\alpha T} - 1)$

8 (a) $2785.84   (b) $7869.39

   (c) $19 865.24   (d) $20 000

9 6.9 years

10 $5x^2 - 2x$

11 $\dfrac{100S}{r}(1 - e^{-nr/100})$

12 26.5

13 (a) $I(5) = 25 = J(5)$

   The graph is sketched in Figure S6.2

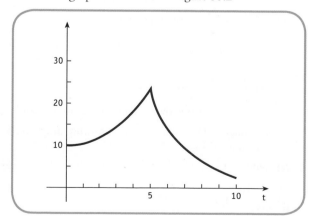

Figure S6.2

   (b) 7.1

14 (a) 74

(b) The graph is sketched in Figure S6.3

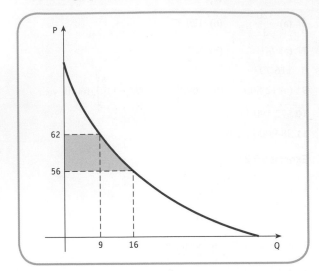

Figure S6.3

Multiple Choice Questions

1 B	**2** E	**3** B
4 D	**5** A	**6** A
7 D	**8** B	**9** A
10 D	**11** E	

Examination Questions

1 (a) $\pi = -3Q^3 - 3Q^2 + 255Q - 25$

(b) 5; $\dfrac{d^2\pi}{dQ^2} = -18Q - 6 < 0$, so max

2 (a) $8\dfrac{1}{3}$

(b) (i) $\dfrac{x^6}{6} - \dfrac{2x^3}{3} + 9x + c$

(ii) $e^x + 3\ln x + c$

(iii) $\dfrac{x^2}{2} - \dfrac{1}{x^2} - 6x\sqrt{x} + c$

(c) Put both fractions over a common denominator. Use $[\ln(x - 1) + 2\ln(x + 3)]_2^5$ substitute limits and use rules of logs.

3 (a) 4800

(b) 5011.15

(c) $600N^{3/2}$; 9

4 (a) TR $= 140Q - 3Q^2$; $P = 140 - 3Q$

(b) TC $= \dfrac{1}{3}Q^3 + \dfrac{1}{2}Q^2 + 20Q + 10$

(c) 8; $555\dfrac{1}{3}$

5 (a) The supply and demand curves are sketched in Figure S6.4.

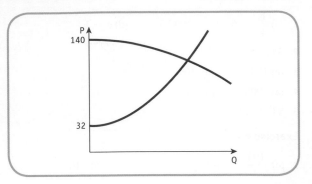

Figure S6.4

(b) 486, 162

(c) (i) Price increases and quantity decreases

(ii) Decreases

6 (a) \$27 385.10

(b) 15 years

7 (a) (i) $\dfrac{1}{3}\ln(1 + 6x) + c$

(ii) $\dfrac{1}{9}\left(1 + 3x^2\right)^{3/2} + c$

(b) $a = \dfrac{1}{6}, \quad b = -\dfrac{1}{6}$

8 (a) $Q^2 + 2Q\sqrt{Q} + 8$

(b) 4.05

9 $P = 35 - Q^2$

10 (a) (b) The graphs are sketched in Figure S6.5.

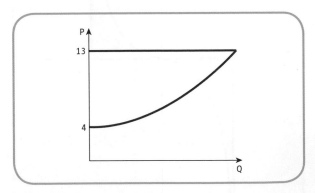

Figure S6.5

(c) 18; producer's surplus

11 (a) The graphs are sketched in Figure S6.6.

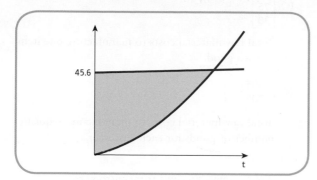

Figure S6.6

(b) 8

(c) $225 066.67

12 (a) E = −3

(b) The graph of the demand curve is sketched in Figure S6.7.

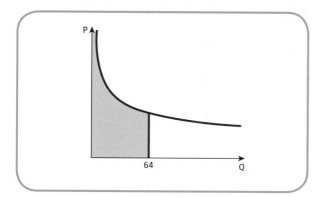

Figure S6.7

(c) 640

CHAPTER 7

Section 7.1

Practice Problems

1 (a) 2×2, 1×5, 3×5, 1×1

(b) 1, 4, 6, 2, 6, ?, 6; the value of c_{43} does not exist

2 $\mathbf{A}^{\mathrm{T}} = \begin{bmatrix} 1 & 3 & 2 & 2 \\ 4 & 7 & 1 & -5 \\ 0 & 6 & 3 & 1 \\ 1 & 1 & 5 & 8 \\ 2 & 4 & -1 & 0 \end{bmatrix}$

$\mathbf{B}^{\mathrm{T}} = \begin{bmatrix} 1 \\ 5 \\ 7 \\ 9 \end{bmatrix}$

$\mathbf{C}^{\mathrm{T}} = \begin{bmatrix} 1 & 2 & 3 \\ 2 & 4 & 5 \\ 3 & 5 & 6 \end{bmatrix} = \mathbf{C}$

3 (a) $\begin{bmatrix} 1 & 7 \\ 3 & -8 \end{bmatrix}$ (c) $\begin{bmatrix} 3 \\ 2 \end{bmatrix}$ (d) $\begin{bmatrix} 2 \\ 2 \end{bmatrix}$ (e) $\begin{bmatrix} 0 & 0 \\ 0 & 0 \end{bmatrix}$

Part (b) is impossible.

4 (1) (a) $\begin{bmatrix} 2 & -4 \\ 6 & 10 \\ 0 & 8 \end{bmatrix}$ (b) $\begin{bmatrix} 0 & -2 \\ 4 & 14 \\ 2 & 12 \end{bmatrix}$

(c) $\begin{bmatrix} 1 & -3 \\ 5 & 12 \\ 1 & 10 \end{bmatrix}$ (d) $\begin{bmatrix} 2 & -6 \\ 10 & 24 \\ 2 & 20 \end{bmatrix}$

From (a) and (b)

$$2\mathbf{A} + 2\mathbf{B} = \begin{bmatrix} 2 & -6 \\ 10 & 24 \\ 2 & 20 \end{bmatrix}$$

which is the same as (d), so

$$2(\mathbf{A} + \mathbf{B}) = 2\mathbf{A} + 2\mathbf{B}$$

(2) (a) $\begin{bmatrix} 3 & -6 \\ 9 & 15 \\ 0 & 12 \end{bmatrix}$ (b) $\begin{bmatrix} -6 & 12 \\ -18 & -30 \\ 0 & -24 \end{bmatrix}$

From (a)

$$-2(3\mathbf{A}) = \begin{bmatrix} -6 & 12 \\ -18 & -30 \\ 0 & -24 \end{bmatrix}$$

which is the same as (b), so

$$-2(3\mathbf{A}) = -6\mathbf{A}$$

5 (a) [8]

(b) [0]

(c) This is impossible.

6 Figure S7.1 shows that it is possible to perform the multiplication and that the order of the answer is 3×2.

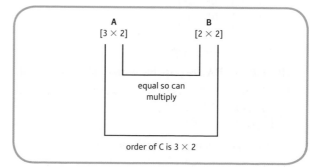

Figure S7.1

$$\mathbf{AB} = \begin{bmatrix} 7 & 10 \\ 3 & 4 \\ 6 & 10 \end{bmatrix}$$

7 (a) $\begin{bmatrix} 5 \\ 7 \\ 5 \end{bmatrix}$ (d) $\begin{bmatrix} 4 & 3 \\ 2 & -1 \\ 5 & 5 \end{bmatrix}$ (f) $\begin{bmatrix} 9 & 6 & 13 \\ 27 & 15 & 28 \end{bmatrix}$

(g) $\begin{bmatrix} 5 & 7 & 9 \\ 3 & 3 & 3 \\ 6 & 9 & 12 \end{bmatrix}$ (h) $\begin{bmatrix} 5 & 6 \\ 11 & 15 \end{bmatrix}$

Parts (b), (c) and (e) are impossible.

8 **Ax** is the 3×1 matrix

$$\begin{bmatrix} x + 4y + 7z \\ 2z + 6y + 5z \\ 8x + 9y + 5z \end{bmatrix}$$

However, $x + 4y + 7z = -3$, $2x + 6y + 5z = 10$ and $8x + 9y + 5z = 1$, so this matrix is just

$$\begin{bmatrix} -3 \\ 10 \\ 1 \end{bmatrix}$$

which is **b**. Hence **Ax** = **b**.

Exercise 7.1

1 (a) $\mathbf{J} = \begin{bmatrix} 35 & 27 & 13 \\ 42 & 39 & 24 \end{bmatrix}$ $\mathbf{F} = \begin{bmatrix} 31 & 17 & 3 \\ 25 & 29 & 16 \end{bmatrix}$

(b) $\begin{bmatrix} 66 & 44 & 16 \\ 67 & 68 & 40 \end{bmatrix}$

(c) $\begin{bmatrix} 4 & 10 & 10 \\ 17 & 10 & 8 \end{bmatrix}$

2 (a) $\begin{bmatrix} 4 & 6 & 2 & 18 \\ 2 & 0 & 10 & 0 \\ 12 & 14 & 16 & 8 \end{bmatrix}$

(b) $\begin{bmatrix} 2 & 14 & 18 & 12 \\ 4 & 2 & 0 & 10 \\ 12 & 8 & 10 & 6 \end{bmatrix}$

(c) $\begin{bmatrix} 6 & 20 & 20 & 30 \\ 6 & 2 & 10 & 10 \\ 24 & 22 & 26 & 14 \end{bmatrix}$

(d) Same answer as (c).

3 $4\mathbf{B}$, $(\mathbf{CB})^{\mathrm{T}}$, $\mathbf{CBA}$ are possible with order 2×3, 3×4, 4×3 respectively.

4 (a) $\begin{bmatrix} 5900 \\ 1100 \end{bmatrix}$

Total cost charged to each customer.

(b) $\begin{bmatrix} 13 & 7 & 23 & 22 \\ 3 & 1 & 4 & 5 \end{bmatrix}$

Amount of raw materials used to manufacture each customer's goods.

(c) $\begin{bmatrix} 35 \\ 75 \\ 30 \end{bmatrix}$

Total raw material costs to manufacture one item of each good.

(d) $\begin{bmatrix} 1005 \\ 205 \end{bmatrix}$

Total raw material costs to manufacture requisite number of goods for each customer.

(e) [7000]

Total revenue received from customers.

(f) [1210]

Total cost of raw materials.

(g) [5790]

Profit before deduction of labour, capital and overheads.

5 (a) $[8 \quad 30 \quad 15]\begin{bmatrix} 12 \\ 30 \\ 25 \end{bmatrix} = [1371]$

(b) 1300.2; 5.2% decrease

6 (1) (a) $\begin{bmatrix} 1 & 3 & 5 \\ 2 & 4 & 6 \end{bmatrix}$

(b) $\begin{bmatrix} 1 & 2 & -3 \\ -1 & 1 & 4 \end{bmatrix}$

(c) $\begin{bmatrix} 2 & 1 \\ 5 & 5 \\ 2 & 10 \end{bmatrix}$

(d) $\begin{bmatrix} 2 & 5 & 2 \\ 1 & 5 & 10 \end{bmatrix}$

$(\mathbf{A} + \mathbf{B})^{\mathrm{T}} = \mathbf{A}^{\mathrm{T}} + \mathbf{B}^{\mathrm{T}}$: that is, 'transpose of the sum is the sum of the transposes'.

(2) (a) $\begin{bmatrix} 1 & 5 \\ 4 & 9 \end{bmatrix}$

(b) $\begin{bmatrix} 2 & -1 \\ 1 & 0 \\ 0 & 1 \end{bmatrix}$

(c) $\begin{bmatrix} -2 & 1 & 4 \\ 1 & 5 & 9 \end{bmatrix}$

(d) $\begin{bmatrix} -2 & 1 \\ 1 & 5 \\ 4 & 9 \end{bmatrix}$

$(\mathbf{CD})^{\mathrm{T}} = \mathbf{D}^{\mathrm{T}}\mathbf{C}^{\mathrm{T}}$: that is, 'transpose of a product is the product of the transposes multiplied in reverse order'.

7 (a) $\mathbf{B} + \mathbf{C} = \begin{bmatrix} 0 & 6 \\ 5 & 2 \end{bmatrix}$

so $\mathbf{A}(\mathbf{B} + \mathbf{C}) = \begin{bmatrix} -15 & 24 \\ 5 & 14 \end{bmatrix}$

$\mathbf{AB} = \begin{bmatrix} -7 & 25 \\ 6 & 10 \end{bmatrix}$ and

$\mathbf{AC} = \begin{bmatrix} -8 & -1 \\ -1 & 4 \end{bmatrix}$, so $\mathbf{AB} + \mathbf{AC} = \begin{bmatrix} -15 & 24 \\ 5 & 14 \end{bmatrix}$

(b) $\mathbf{AB} = \begin{bmatrix} -7 & 25 \\ 6 & 10 \end{bmatrix}$, so

$(\mathbf{AB})\mathbf{C} = \begin{bmatrix} 32 & 43 \\ 4 & 26 \end{bmatrix}$

$\mathbf{BC} = \begin{bmatrix} 4 & 11 \\ -4 & 4 \end{bmatrix}$, so

$\mathbf{A}(\mathbf{BC}) = \begin{bmatrix} 32 & 43 \\ 4 & 26 \end{bmatrix}$

8 $\mathbf{AB} = [9];$ $\quad \mathbf{BA} = \begin{bmatrix} 1 & 2 & -4 & 3 \\ 7 & 14 & -28 & 21 \\ 3 & 6 & -12 & 9 \\ 2 & 4 & -8 & 6 \end{bmatrix}$

9 (a) $\begin{bmatrix} 7x + 5y \\ x + 3y \end{bmatrix}$

(b) $\mathbf{A} = \begin{bmatrix} 2 & 3 & -2 \\ 1 & -1 & 2 \\ 4 & 2 & 5 \end{bmatrix}, \quad \mathbf{x} = \begin{bmatrix} x \\ y \\ z \end{bmatrix}, \quad \mathbf{b} = \begin{bmatrix} 6 \\ 3 \\ 1 \end{bmatrix}$

Exercise 7.1*

1 (**a**), (**c**) and (**f**) are possible

with orders, $5 \times 2, 3 \times 5, 5 \times 5$, respectively.

2 $a = 2, b = 6, c = 4, d = 5$

3 (a) $\mathbf{A}^{\mathrm{T}} = \begin{bmatrix} a & d \\ b & e \\ c & f \end{bmatrix}, \quad \mathbf{B}^{\mathrm{T}} = \begin{bmatrix} g & i & k \\ h & j & l \end{bmatrix}$

(b) $\mathbf{AB} = \begin{bmatrix} ag + bi + ck & ah + bj + cl \\ dg + ei + fk & dh + ej + fl \end{bmatrix}$

$\mathbf{B}^{\mathrm{T}}\mathbf{A}^{\mathrm{T}} = \begin{bmatrix} ga + ib + kc & gd + ie + kf \\ ha + jb + lc & hd + je + lf \end{bmatrix}$

(c) $(\mathbf{AB})^{\mathrm{T}} = \mathbf{B}^{\mathrm{T}}\mathbf{A}^{\mathrm{T}}$

$(\mathbf{A}^{\mathrm{T}}\mathbf{B}^{\mathrm{T}}\mathbf{C}^{\mathrm{T}})^{\mathrm{T}} = \mathbf{CBA}$

4 (a) $a_{11} = 137.50$

It is the total weekly profit on T-shirts across all shops in the chain.

(b) $b_{33} = 1327.50$

It is the total weekly profit from Shop C for all three goods.

5 (a) At the end of one year, the market share of customers shopping in A, L, S and W is 29.5%, 25.5%, 33%, 12%.

(b) (i) 29.8% (ii) 33.2%

6 $\begin{bmatrix} 6 & 6 \\ 2 & 11 \\ 13 & 1 \end{bmatrix}$

7 -109

8 (a) $\mathbf{AI} = \begin{bmatrix} a & b \\ c & d \end{bmatrix}\begin{bmatrix} 1 & 0 \\ 0 & 1 \end{bmatrix} = \begin{bmatrix} a & b \\ c & d \end{bmatrix} = \mathbf{A}$

Similarly, $\mathbf{IA} = \mathbf{A}$.

(b) $\mathbf{A}^{-1}\mathbf{A}$

$= \dfrac{1}{ad - bc}\begin{bmatrix} d & -b \\ -c & a \end{bmatrix}\begin{bmatrix} a & b \\ c & d \end{bmatrix}$

$= \dfrac{1}{ad - bc}\begin{bmatrix} da - bc & db - bd \\ -ca + ac & -cb + ad \end{bmatrix}$

$= \dfrac{1}{ad - bc}\begin{bmatrix} ad - bc & 0 \\ 0 & ad - bc \end{bmatrix} = \begin{bmatrix} 1 & 0 \\ 0 & 1 \end{bmatrix}$

Similarly, $\mathbf{AA}^{-1} = \mathbf{I}$.

(c) $\mathbf{Ix} = \begin{bmatrix} 1 & 0 \\ 0 & 1 \end{bmatrix}\begin{bmatrix} x \\ y \end{bmatrix} = \begin{bmatrix} x \\ y \end{bmatrix} = \mathbf{x}$

9 $\begin{bmatrix} k_2 & k_1 \\ -c & 1 - a \end{bmatrix}$

Section 7.2

Practice Problems

1 **A** is non-singular and its inverse is given by

$\begin{bmatrix} 1/4 & -1/2 \\ -1/8 & 3/4 \end{bmatrix}$

B is singular so its inverse does not exist.

2 We need to solve $\mathbf{Ax} = \mathbf{b}$, where

$\mathbf{A} = \begin{bmatrix} 9 & 1 \\ 2 & 7 \end{bmatrix} \quad \mathbf{x} = \begin{bmatrix} P_1 \\ P_2 \end{bmatrix} \quad \mathbf{b} = \begin{bmatrix} 43 \\ 57 \end{bmatrix}$

$\begin{bmatrix} P_1 \\ P_2 \end{bmatrix} = \begin{bmatrix} 4 \\ 7 \end{bmatrix}$

3 In equilibrium, $Q_S = Q_D = Q$, say, so the supply equation becomes

$$P = aQ + b$$

Subtracting aQ from both sides gives

$$P - aQ = b \qquad (1)$$

Similarly, the demand equation leads to

$$P + cQ = d \qquad (2)$$

In matrix notation, equations (1) and (2) become

$$\begin{bmatrix} 1 & -a \\ 1 & c \end{bmatrix}\begin{bmatrix} P \\ Q \end{bmatrix} = \begin{bmatrix} b \\ d \end{bmatrix}$$

$$P = \frac{cb + ad}{c + a} \text{ and } Q = \frac{-b + d}{c + a}$$

The multiplier is $\dfrac{-1}{c + a}$.

Given that c and a are both positive, it follows that the multiplier is negative. Consequently, an increase in b leads to a decrease in Q.

4 $A_{11} = 7$

$A_{12} = -1$

$A_{13} = -1$

$A_{21} = -3$

$A_{22} = 1$

$A_{23} = 0$

$A_{31} = -3$

$A_{32} = 0$

$A_{33} = 1$

5 1 and 0

6 $\mathbf{A} = \begin{bmatrix} 7 & -3 & -3 \\ -1 & 1 & 0 \\ -1 & 0 & 1 \end{bmatrix}$

The determinant of $\mathbf{B}$ has already been found in Practice Problem 5 to be 0, so $\mathbf{B}$ is singular and does not have an inverse.

7 $\begin{bmatrix} P_1 \\ P_2 \\ P_3 \end{bmatrix} = \begin{bmatrix} 8 \\ 5 \\ 3 \end{bmatrix}$

Exercise 7.2

1 (a) (i) 1   (ii) 2   (iii) 2   (iv) 10

(b) (i) $\begin{bmatrix} 4 & -7 \\ -1 & 2 \end{bmatrix}$ (ii) $\begin{bmatrix} 2 & -3 \\ -1.5 & 2.5 \end{bmatrix}$

(iii) $\begin{bmatrix} 2 & 5 \\ -0.5 & -1 \end{bmatrix}$ (iv) $\begin{bmatrix} -0.7 & 0.4 \\ 0.8 & -0.6 \end{bmatrix}$

2 (1) (a) $|\mathbf{A}| = -3$ (b) $|\mathbf{B}| = 4$

(c) $\mathbf{AB} = \begin{bmatrix} 4 & 4 \\ 7 & 4 \end{bmatrix}$

so $|\mathbf{AB}| = -12$. These results give $|\mathbf{AB}| = |\mathbf{A}||\mathbf{B}|$: that is, 'determinant of a product is the product of the determinants'.

(2) (a) $\mathbf{A}^{-1} = \begin{bmatrix} -1/3 & 1/3 \\ 5/3 & -2/3 \end{bmatrix}$ (b) $\mathbf{B}^{-1} = \begin{bmatrix} 1 & 0 \\ -1/2 & -1/4 \end{bmatrix}$

(c) $(\mathbf{AB})^{-1} = \begin{bmatrix} -1/3 & 1/3 \\ 7/12 & -1/3 \end{bmatrix}$

These results give $(\mathbf{AB})^{-1} = \mathbf{B}^{-1}\mathbf{A}^{-1}$: that is, 'inverse of a product is the product of the inverses multiplied in reverse order'.

3 $a = -3/2, b = -8/3$

4 $\begin{bmatrix} 10 & 0 \\ 0 & 10 \end{bmatrix}$ so the inverse is $\dfrac{1}{10}\begin{bmatrix} 5 & -3 \\ -10 & 8 \end{bmatrix}$

5 (a) $x = 1, y = -1$ (b) $x = 2, y = 2$

6 (a) $50 - 2P_1 + P_2 = -20 + P_1 \Rightarrow 3P_1 - P_2 = 70$

$10 + P_1 - 4P_2 = -10 + 5P_2 \Rightarrow -P_1 + 9P_2 = 20$

(b) Inverse $= \dfrac{1}{26}\begin{bmatrix} 9 & 1 \\ 1 & 3 \end{bmatrix}$

$\dfrac{1}{26}\begin{bmatrix} 9 & 1 \\ 1 & 3 \end{bmatrix}\begin{bmatrix} 70 \\ 20 \end{bmatrix} = \begin{bmatrix} 25 \\ 5 \end{bmatrix}$

7 (a) (i) $a \times 0 - b \times 0 = 0$ (ii) $kab - kab = 0$

(iii) $\dfrac{a}{a} - \dfrac{b}{b} = 1 - 1 = 0$

(b) (i) $ak \neq 0$ (ii) $a^2 > 0$ (iii) $a^2 + b^2 > 0$

Exercise 7.2*

1 $a = \pm 2, b = \pm 4$

2 (a) $\begin{bmatrix} ae + bg & af + bh \\ ce + dg & cf + dh \end{bmatrix}$

(b) $\det(\mathbf{A}) = ad - bc; \det(\mathbf{B}) = eh - fg$

$\det(\mathbf{A}) \times \det(\mathbf{B}) = (ad - bc)(eh - fg)$

$\qquad = adeh - adfg - bceh + bcfg$

$\det(\mathbf{AB}) = (ae + bg)(cf + dh) - (af + bh)(ce + dg)$

$\qquad = acef + adeh + bcfg + bdgh - acef - adfg$

$\qquad - bceh - bdgh$

$\qquad = adeh + bcfg - adfg - bceh$

(c) $\mathbf{AB}$ singular;

$\det(\mathbf{AB}) = \det(\mathbf{A}) \times \det(\mathbf{B}) = 0 \times \det(\mathbf{B}) = 0$

3 D

4 364

5 7

6 The determinant of **A** is $-10 \neq 0$, so matrix is non-singular.

$$\mathbf{A}^{-1} = \begin{bmatrix} 1/10 & 3/10 & -1/2 \\ 3/10 & -1/10 & 1/2 \\ -1/2 & 1/2 & -1/2 \end{bmatrix}$$

It is interesting to notice that because the original matrix **A** is symmetric, so is $\mathbf{A}^{-1}$. The determinant of **B** is 0, so it is singular and does not have an inverse.

7 Commodity market is in equilibrium when $Y = C + I$, so $Y = aY + b + cr + d$, which rearranges as

$$(1 - a)Y - cr = b + d \tag{1}$$

Money market is in equilibrium when $M_S = M_D$, so $M_S^* = k_1Y + k_2r + k_3$, which rearranges as

$$k_1Y + k_2r = M_S^* - k_3 \tag{2}$$

In matrix notation, equations (1) and (2) become

$$\begin{bmatrix} 1 - a & -c \\ k_1 & k_2 \end{bmatrix} \begin{bmatrix} Y \\ r \end{bmatrix} = \begin{bmatrix} b + d \\ M_S^* - k_3 \end{bmatrix}$$

Using the inverse of the coefficient matrix,

$$\begin{bmatrix} Y \\ r \end{bmatrix} = \frac{1}{k_2(1 - a) + ck_1} \times \begin{bmatrix} k_2 & c \\ -k_1 & 1 - a \end{bmatrix} \begin{bmatrix} b + d \\ M_S^* - k_3 \end{bmatrix}$$

$$Y = \frac{k_2(b + d) + c(M_S^* - k_3)}{k_2(1 - a) + ck_1}$$

and

$$r = \frac{-k_1(b + d) + (1 - a)(M_S^* - k_3)}{k_2(1 - a) + ck_1}$$

The required multiplier is

$$\frac{\partial r}{\partial M_S^*} = \frac{1 - a}{k_2(1 - a) + ck_1}$$

Now $1 - a > 0$ since $a < 1$, so numerator is positive. Also $k_2 < 0$, $1 - a > 0$, gives $k_2(1 - a) < 0$ and $c < 0$, $k_1 > 0$ gives $ck_1 < 0$, so the denominator is negative.

8 $a - 1$, which is non-zero provided $a \neq 1$

$$\frac{1}{a - 1} \begin{bmatrix} -a & -1 & a \\ 3a - 4 & -1 & 3 - 2a \\ 1 & 1 & -1 \end{bmatrix}$$

9 $\mathbf{A}^{-1} = \frac{1}{-41} \begin{bmatrix} 29 & 11 & 3 \\ 4 & 10 & -1 \\ 9 & 2 & 8 \end{bmatrix}$; $\begin{bmatrix} P_1 \\ P_2 \\ P_3 \end{bmatrix} = \begin{bmatrix} 20 \\ 5 \\ 8 \end{bmatrix}$

10 $\mathbf{A}^{-1} = \frac{1}{45 - 18a} \begin{bmatrix} 8 & 2a - 9 & 6 - 4a \\ -1 & 18 - 7a & 5a - 12 \\ -18 & 9 & 9 \end{bmatrix}$ $a = 2.5$

11 (a) $a^2c - a^2b - ac^2 + ab^2 + bc^2 - b^2c$

(b) The factors in the expression $(a - b)(a - c)$ $(c - b)$ are all non-zero if the numbers, a, b and c are distinct.

Section 7.3

Practice Problems

1 (a) $x_2 = \frac{-66}{-22} = 3$ (b) $x_3 = \frac{26}{26} = 1$

2 $y_d = \dfrac{-T^* - (I^* + G^*)(-1 + t) - b(-1 + t)}{1 - a + at}$

3 $\begin{bmatrix} 0.6 & -0.1 \\ -0.3 & 0.3 \end{bmatrix} \begin{bmatrix} Y_1 \\ Y_2 \end{bmatrix} = \begin{bmatrix} 250 \\ 400 \end{bmatrix}$

$Y_1 = 766.67$ and $Y_2 = 2100$; 20

Exercise 7.3

1 (a) (i) 10 (ii) -31 (iii) 27
  (b) $x = -3.1$, $y = 2.7$

2 (a) 1 (b) 1 (c) 5

3 (a) 2 (b) -1 (c) 1

4 (a) $x = 1$, $y = -1$

  (b) $x = -2$, $y = 3$

  (c) $x = 7$, $y = -10$

5 (a) $400 - 5P_1 - 3P_2 = -60 + 3P_1 \Rightarrow 8P_1 + 3P_2 = 460$

  $300 - 2P_1 - 3P_2 = -100 + 2P_2 \Rightarrow 2P_1 + 5P_2 = 400$

  (b) $32\dfrac{6}{17}$

6 (a) $\begin{bmatrix} 1 & -1 \\ -a & 1 \end{bmatrix} \begin{bmatrix} Y \\ C \end{bmatrix} = \begin{bmatrix} I^* \\ b \end{bmatrix}$

  (b) $C = \dfrac{\begin{vmatrix} 1 & I^* \\ -a & b \end{vmatrix}}{\begin{vmatrix} 1 & -1 \\ -a & 1 \end{vmatrix}} = \dfrac{b + aI^*}{1 - a}$

7 (a) $\begin{pmatrix} 2 & 4 \\ 3 & 9 \end{pmatrix} \begin{pmatrix} a \\ b \end{pmatrix} = \begin{pmatrix} 14 \\ 9 \end{pmatrix}$

  (b) $a = 15$; $b = -4$; TR $= 11$

Exercise 7.3*

1 (a) 1 (b) 4 (c) 1/2

2 $\dfrac{b - aT^* + a(I^* + G^*)(t - 1)}{1 - a + at}$

3 (a) $\begin{bmatrix} 1 & -1 & 0 \\ -a & 1 & a \\ -t & 0 & 1 \end{bmatrix} \begin{bmatrix} Y \\ C \\ T \end{bmatrix} = \begin{bmatrix} I^* + G^* \\ b \\ T^* \end{bmatrix}$

  (b) $Y = \dfrac{I^* + G^* + b - aT^*}{1 - a + at}$

4 The equations can be rearranged as

$$Y - C + M = I^* + G^* + X^*$$

$$-aY + C + 0M = b$$

$$-mY + 0C + M = M^*$$

as required.

Autonomous investment multiplier, $\dfrac{1}{1 - a + m}$, is

positive because $1 - a$ and m are both positive.

5 The multiplier is

$$\frac{-k_1}{k_2(1 - a) + ck_1}$$

which is positive since the top and bottom of this fraction are both negative. To see that the bottom is negative, note that $k_2(1 - a) < 0$ because $k_2 < 0$ and $a < 1$, and $ck_1 < 0$ because $c < 0$ and $k_1 > 0$.

6 The equations are

$$0.6Y_1 - 0.1Y_2 - I_1^* = 50$$
$$-0.2Y_1 + 0.3Y_2 = 150$$
$$0.2Y_1 - 0.1Y_2 = 0$$

The third equation follows from the fact that if the balance of payments is 0, then $M_1 = X_1$, or equivalently, $M_1 = M_2$. Cramer's rule gives

$$I_1^* = \frac{\det(A_3)}{\det(A)} = \frac{4}{0.04} = 100$$

7 $\begin{bmatrix} 1 - a_1 + m_1 & -m_2 \\ -m_1 & 1 - a_2 + m_2 \end{bmatrix} \begin{bmatrix} Y_1 \\ Y_2 \end{bmatrix} = \begin{bmatrix} b_1 + I_1^* \\ b_2 + I_1^* \end{bmatrix}$

$$Y_1 = \frac{(b_1 + I_1^*)(1 - a_2 + m_2) + m_2(b_2 + I_2^*)}{(1 - a_1 + m_1)(1 - a_2 + m_2) - m_1 m_2}$$

The multiplier is

$$\frac{m_2}{(1 - a_1 + m_1)(1 - a_2 + m_2) - m_1 m_2}$$

which is positive since the top and bottom of the fraction are both positive. To see that the bottom is positive, note that since $a_i < 1$, $1 - a_i + m_i > m_i$, so that $(1 - a_1 + m_1)(1 - a_2 + m_2) > m_1 m_2$. Hence the national income of one country rises as the investment in the other country rises.

Multiple Choice Questions

1 E	**2** D	**3** E
4 C	**5** C	**6** B
7 A	**8** B	**9** D
10 C		

Examination Questions

1 (a) $\begin{bmatrix} 13 & -6 \\ -10 & 8 \end{bmatrix}$

(b) $\begin{bmatrix} 14 & -7 \\ -16 & 8 \end{bmatrix}$

(c) $\begin{bmatrix} 1 & 1/2 \\ 0 & 1/4 \end{bmatrix}$

(d) Impossible

2 $P = 9, Q = 13$

3 (a) (i) Impossible

(ii) $\begin{bmatrix} 5 & -5 & 2 & 13 \\ -14 & 10 & 0 & 6 \end{bmatrix}$

(iii) Impossible

(iv) $\begin{bmatrix} 24 & -19 & -6 & 18 \\ -14 & 23 & 10 & 22 \end{bmatrix}$

(b) (i) $\begin{bmatrix} -1 & 5 \\ 2 & -1 \\ -1 & 1 \\ -3.5 & -2 \end{bmatrix}$

(ii) $\dfrac{1}{26}\begin{bmatrix} 3 & 10 & 6 & 36 \\ -22 & 22 & 8 & -4 \end{bmatrix}$

4 (a) $P_1 = 5, P_2 = 6$

(b) -7

5 (a) Number of customers using Airme are made up of two types: those who used it the previous month which are 80% of A_{t-1}, and those switching airlines who are 25% of B_{t-1}. Likewise, for the numbers using Blight in month t.

(b) (i) 12000

(ii) 13705

(c) 7500 and 5200, respectively

6 (a) $\dfrac{1}{16a - 14}\begin{bmatrix} 5a - 1 & 2a - 1 & 3 \\ 2a - 4 & 4a - 4 & -2 \\ 18 & 4 & 16 \end{bmatrix}$; 7/8

(b) 10, 5, 7

7 $A^{-1} = \dfrac{1}{26}\begin{bmatrix} 4 & 1 \\ 2 & 7 \end{bmatrix}$; $P_1 = 6 + \dfrac{8t}{13}$, $P_2 = 10 + \dfrac{4t}{13}$; $\dfrac{4}{13}$

8 (d) $\dfrac{\partial Y}{\partial I^*} = \dfrac{1}{1 - a(1 - t)} > 1$

(e) $\dfrac{\partial Y}{\partial a} = \dfrac{Y(1 - a)}{1 - a(1 - t)} > 0$, so increases

9 (a) 2

(c) (i) False

(ii) True

CHAPTER 8

Section 8.1

Practice Problems

1 The line and region are shown in Figure S8.1.

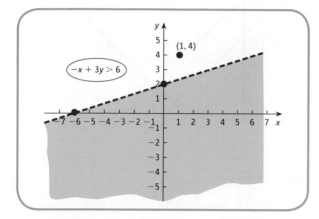

Figure S8.1

2 The feasible region is shown in Figure S8.2.

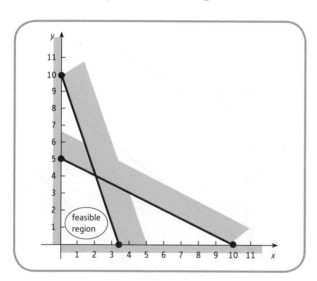

Figure S8.2

3 The answers to parts (a) and (b) are shown in Figure S8.3.

  (c) Once c becomes greater than 3, the lines no longer intersect the feasible region. The maximum value of c (that is, the objective function) is therefore 3, which occurs at the corner $(0, 3)$, when $x = 0$, $y = 3$.

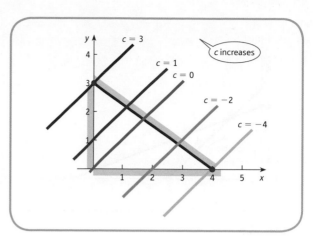

Figure S8.3

4 Minimum is -2, which occurs at $(0, 2)$.

5 Maximum is 26, which occurs at $(2, 4)$.

Exercise 8.1

1 $(1, 1), (1, -1), (-1, -1), (2, -1), (-2, -1)$

2 6

3 The feasible regions for parts (a), (b) and (c) are sketched in Figures S8.4, S8.5 and S8.6, respectively.

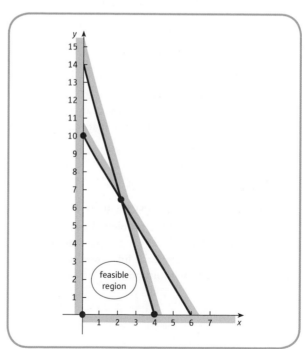

Figure S8.4

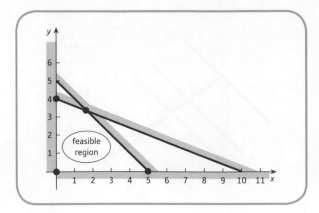

Figure S8.5

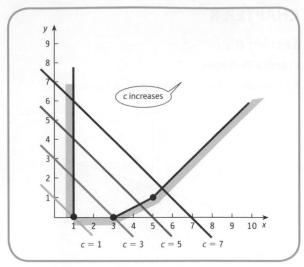

Figure S8.7

6 Figure S8.8 shows that the problem does not have a finite solution.

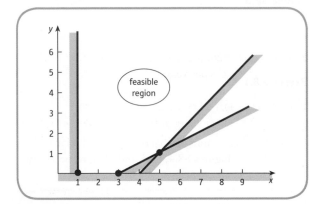

Figure S8.6

4 (a) Maximum is 90, which occurs at (0, 10).

(b) Maximum is 25, which occurs at $(^5/_3, {}^{10}/_3)$.
Note that the exact coordinates can be found by solving the simultaneous equations

$$2x + 5y = 20$$

$$x + y = 5$$

using an algebraic method.

(c) Minimum is 1, which occurs at (1, 0).

5 Figure S8.7 shows that the problem does not have a finite solution. The lines $x + y = c$ pass through $(c, 0)$ and $(0, c)$. As c increases, the lines move across the region to the right without bound.

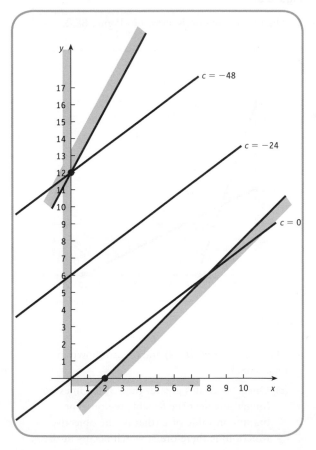

Figure S8.8

7 (a) Unique solution at (2, 0).

(b) Unique solution at (0, 2).

(c) Infinitely many solutions.

Exercise 8.1*

1 -3.8

2 A

3 (a) Maximum is 16, which occurs at (2, 4).

(b) Maximum is 12, which occurs at any point on the line joining (0, 3) and (1, 5).

4 (a) There is no feasible region, since the constraints are contradictory.

(b) The feasible region is unbounded and there is no limit to the values that the objective function can take in this region.

5 Maximum is 16, which occurs at the two corners (2, 2) and (8/3, 0), so any point on the line segment joining these two corners is also a solution.

6 $\mathbf{c} = \begin{bmatrix} 2 \\ 3 \end{bmatrix}$, $\mathbf{x} = \begin{bmatrix} x \\ y \end{bmatrix}$, $\mathbf{b} = \begin{bmatrix} 8 \\ 6 \\ 10 \end{bmatrix}$, $\mathbf{0} = \begin{bmatrix} 0 \\ 0 \end{bmatrix}$, $\mathbf{A} = \begin{bmatrix} 2 & 1 \\ 1 & 1 \\ 1 & 2 \end{bmatrix}$

7 (a) (i) Line 1: passing through (8, 0) and (0, 16).

Line 2: passing through (12, 0) and (0, 8).

Line 3: passing through (0, 12) and, for example, (8, 20).

Shade under the $y = 0$, line 1, line 2, but above line 3.

Corners: (12, 0), (6, 4).

For the third corner, solve simultaneous equations

$$2x + y = 16$$
$$-x + y = 12$$

to get $\left(1\frac{1}{3}, 13\frac{1}{3}\right)$.

(ii)

Corners	Objective function
(12, 0)	12
(6, 4)	10
$\left(1\frac{1}{3}, 13\frac{1}{3}\right)$	$14\frac{2}{3}$

Optimal point (6, 4).

(iii) $x \geq 0$

(b) (i) No solution since $x + y$ increases without bound as the lines $x + y = c$ sweep across the region to the right.

(ii) Infinitely many solutions; any point on the line segment between (6, 4) and $\left(1\frac{1}{3}, 13\frac{1}{3}\right)$ will be a solution.

(c) The line $2x + 3y = 24$ rearranges as $y = 8 - \frac{2}{3}x$, so has slope, $-\frac{2}{3}$.

The line $ax + 2y = c$ rearranges as $y = \frac{c}{2} - \frac{a}{2}x$, so has slope, $-\frac{a}{2}$.

$$\frac{a}{2} \leq \frac{2}{3} \Rightarrow a \leq \frac{4}{3}$$

Section 8.2

Practice Problems

1 The firm should produce 20 tablets of model TAB1 and 10 of model TAB2 to achieve a maximum profit of \$19 000.

2 (24, 22); \$50

3 We need to buy nine items of clothing and visit the theatre 10 times per year.

Exercise 8.2

1 The manufacturer should produce 10 bikes of type B and 15 of type C each month to achieve a maximum profit of \$5100.

2 The firm should produce 720 cartons of 'The Caribbean' and 630 cartons of 'Mr Fruity' each week to give a maximum profit of \$650.70.

3 The student should order a quarterpounder served with six oz chips to consume a minimum of 860 calories. Note that the unbounded feasible region causes no difficulty here, because the problem is one of minimisation.

4 600 of each

5 375 goods of type A and 150 goods of type B

6 40 copies of *Macro* and no copies of *Micro*

7 P1 for one day a week and P2 for three days a week

8 (a) $12\,000x + 15\,000y$; maximise

(b) Total number of students is $x + y$ and this must not exceed 9000, so

$$x + y \leq 9000$$

At least ¾ of the students are US citizens, so

$$\frac{3}{4}(x + y) \leq x \Rightarrow 3x + 3y \leq 4x \Rightarrow x \geq 3y$$

All non-US students together with a quarter of the US students must be given residential places, so

$$y + \frac{1}{4}x \leq 5000$$

$$x \geq 0; y \geq 0$$

(c) x and y must be whole numbers.

Exercise 8.2*

1 1 and 6

2 4 cosmetic and 6 orthopaedic patients

3 (a) If x and y denote the number of goods of type X and Y, then the problem is to

Maximise $15x + 20y$ (profit)

subject to $3x + 5y \leq 31\,500$ (raw materials)

$2x + 2y \leq 17\,000$ (labour)

$x \geq 0, y \geq 0$ (non-negativity)

(b) 5500 of type X and 3000 of type Y.

(c) \$2.50; it would be worthwhile providing an extra unit of raw materials provided the cost is less than \$2.50.

4 (a) The firm should make 30 jackets and 6 pairs of trousers each week to achieve a maximum profit of \$444.

(b) The profit margin on a pair of trousers should be between \$8 and \$15.

5 The optimal diet consists of 1.167 kg of fish meal and 1.800 kg of meat scraps, which gives a minimum cost of \$1.69 per pig per day.

6 (b) \$150 000 in A, \$75 000 in B and \$75 000 in C.

7 (a) If the number of copies sent from A to C is denoted by x and the number of copies sent from A to D is denoted by y, then the problem is to

Minimise $0.1x + 0.2y + 133$ (cost)

subject to $x + y \leq 90$ (warehouse A supplies)

$x + y \geq 70$ (warehouse B supplies)

$0 \leq x \leq 50, 0 \leq y \leq 80$

(b) The feasible region is sketched in Figure S8.9.

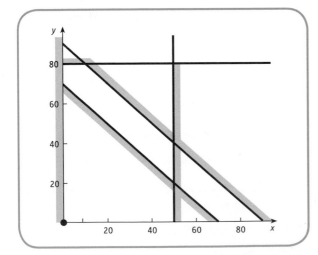

Figure S8.9

A sends 50 to C and 20 to D; B sends 60 to D.

8 (a) If x and y denote the number of goods of types X and Y then the problem is to

Maximise $40x + 45y$ (profit)

subject to $5x + 8y \leq 6150$ (raw material 1)

$x + y \leq 1086$ (raw material 2)

$3x + 8y \leq 5190$ (machine time)

$3x + 10y \leq 5250$ (labour)

$x \geq 0, y \geq 0$ (non-negativity)

846 of type X and 240 of type Y

(b) 0; no

Multiple Choice Questions

1 A	**2** A	**3** D
4 C	**5** C	**6** E
7 D	**8** A	**9** E
10 D		

Examination Questions

1 (a) 6 at (4, 2)

(b) (i) -9 at (0, 3)

(ii) 5 at any point on the line segment joining (5, 0) and (4, 2)

2 42 at (2, 6); no solution since the feasible region unbounded

3 (a) $70x + 84y$

(b) $x + 1.5y \leq 900, 2x + y \leq 1600, x \geq 0, y \geq 0$

(c) Feasible region has corners (0, 0), (0, 600), (750, 100) and (800, 0)

(d) 750 scarves and 100 blouses

4 (a) x and y are number of chocolate cakes and fruit cakes made each week.

(b) $20x + 24y$

(c) $2x + y \leq 320, x + y \leq 200, 2x + 3y \leq 520, x \geq 0, y \geq 0$

(d) $\left(0, 173\frac{1}{3}\right)$, (80, 120) (120, 80) (160, 0) (0, 0)

(e) 80 chocolate cakes and 120 fruit cakes

5 (a) Let x and y denote the number of shares in companies A and B.

Maximise $0.8x + 0.65y$ subject to $x + 2y \leq 1000$, $y \geq 2x, x \geq 0, y \geq 0$

(c) (0, 0), (0, 500), (200, 400)

(d) 200 of A and 400 of B; \$420

6 (a) x and y denote the number of kilos of raspberries and blueberries supplied to the supermarket.

Minimise $4.4x + 3.1y$ subject to $x + y \geq 200$, $100 \leq x \leq 200, 50 \leq y \leq 300$

(c) (100 100), (150 50), (200 50), (100 300), (200 300)

(d) 100 kg of each

(e) $2790

7 (a) $\dfrac{1}{13}\begin{bmatrix} 7 & -3 \\ -5 & 4 \end{bmatrix}$; $x = 80\dfrac{10}{13}$ $y = 192\dfrac{4}{13}$

(b) (i) Let x and y denote the number of cartons of Exotic and Floridian.

Maximise $4.5x + 4y$ subject to

$4x + 3y \le 900$, $2x + y \le 400$, $5x + 7y \le 1750$, $x \ge 0$, $y \ge 0$

(iii) (0, 0), (0, 250), (200, 0), (150, 100),

$$\left(80\dfrac{10}{13}, 192\dfrac{4}{13} \right)$$

(iv) 81 cartons of Exotic and 192 cartons of Floridian

CHAPTER 9

Section 9.1

Practice Problems

1 (1) (a) 1, 3, 9, 27; 3^t

(b) 7, 21, 63, 189; $7(3^t)$

(c) A, $3A$, $9A$, $27A$; $A(3^t)$

(2) (a) $1, \dfrac{1}{2}, \dfrac{1}{4}, \dfrac{1}{8}; \left(\dfrac{1}{2} \right)^t$

(b) $7, 7\left(\dfrac{1}{2} \right), 7\left(\dfrac{1}{4} \right), 7\left(\dfrac{1}{8} \right), 7\left(\dfrac{1}{2} \right)^t$

(c) $A, A\left(\dfrac{1}{2} \right), A\left(\dfrac{1}{4} \right), A\left(\dfrac{1}{8} \right), A\left(\dfrac{1}{2} \right)^t$

(3) $A, Ab, Ab^2, Ab^3; A(b^t)$

2 (a) $Y_t = -4\left(-\dfrac{1}{2} \right)^t + 4$

From the staircase diagram shown in Figure S9.1, we see that Y_t oscillates about $Y_t = 4$. Moreover, as t increases, these oscillations damp down and Y_t converges to 4. Oscillatory convergence can be expected for any solution.

$Y_t = A(b^t) + \text{PS}$

when $-1 < b < 0$.

(b) $Y_t = (-2)^t + 3$. From Figure S9.2, we see that Y_t oscillates about 3 and that these oscillations explode with increasing t. Oscillatory divergence can be expected for any solution

$Y_t = A(b^t) + \text{PS}$

when $b < -1$.

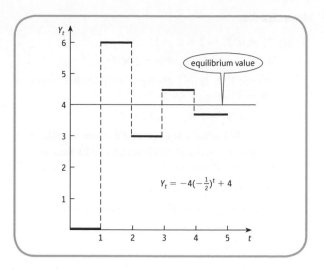

Figure S9.1

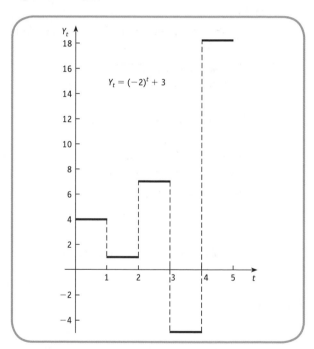

Figure S9.2

3 $Y_t = 500(0.9)^t + 6000$; stable.

4 $P_t = \left(-\dfrac{1}{2} \right)^t + 10$

$Q_t = -2\left(-\dfrac{1}{2} \right)^t + 2$

The system is stable.

5 $P_t = -12(-1.5)^t + 20$

$Q_t = 24(-1.5)^t + 40$

The system is unstable.

Exercise 9.1

1 (a) $Y_0 = 0$, $Y_1 = 2 = 2 \times 1$,

$Y_2 = 4 = 2 \times 2$, $Y_3 = 6 = 2 \times 3$, ...

Hence $Y_t = 2t$ and displays uniform divergence as shown in Figure S9.3.

(b) $Y_0 = 4$, $Y_1 = 2$, $Y_2 = 4$, $Y_3 = 2$, ...

So Y_t is 4 when t is even and 2 when t is odd. Hence Y_t oscillates with equal oscillations as shown in Figure S9.4.

(c) $Y_0 = 3$, $Y_1 = 3$, $Y_2 = 3$, $Y_3 = 3$, ...

Hence $Y_t = 3$ for all t and remains fixed at this value.

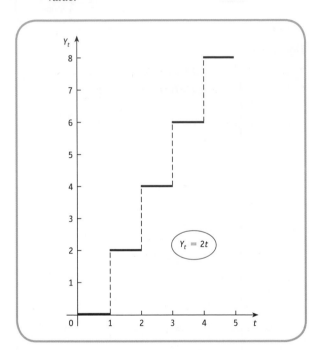

Figure S9.3

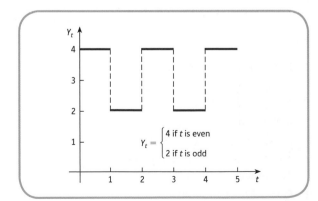

Figure S9.4

2 (a) $Y_t = -7\left(\dfrac{1}{4}\right)^t + 8$; uniform convergence to 8.

(b) $Y_t = (-4)^t + 1$; oscillatory divergence.

3 $Y_t = 500(0.8^t) + 2500$; stable.

4 $P_t = 10(-0.5)^t + 60$; stable.

5 1075

6 Substitute assumptions (1) and (2) into (3) to get

$$\beta(Y_t - Y_{t-1}) = \alpha Y_t$$

which rearranges as

$$Y_t = \left(\frac{\beta}{\beta - \alpha}\right) Y_{t-1}$$

with solution

$$Y_t = \left(\frac{\beta}{\beta - \alpha}\right)^t Y_0$$

If $\alpha = 0.1$ and $\beta = 1.4$ then $Y_t = (1.08)^t Y_0$.

As t increases, Y_t diverges uniformly, so unstable.

Exercise 9.1*

1 uniform convergence

2 (a) -1, $1/2$, 2, -1; $1/2$

(b) 7, 11, 15, 19; $Y_t = 4t + 3$

3 $Y_t = \dfrac{c(1 - b^t)}{1 - b} + ab^t$

4 $Y_t = 4000 + 400t$, so unstable

5 (a) $aP_{t-1} - b = -cP_t + d$

$\Rightarrow -cP_t = aP_{t-1} - (b + d) \Rightarrow P_t = -\dfrac{a}{c}P_{t-1} + \dfrac{b + d}{c}$

(b) $P_{t-1} = P_t = D$

$D = -\dfrac{aD}{c} + \dfrac{b + d}{c} \Rightarrow (a + c)D = b + d$

$\Rightarrow D = \dfrac{b + d}{a + c}$

$P_t = A\left(-\dfrac{a}{c}\right)^t + \dfrac{b + d}{a + c}$

(c) $a < c$

$P = \dfrac{b + d}{a + c}$

$Q = a\left(\dfrac{b + d}{a + c}\right) - b = \dfrac{a(b + d) - b(a + c)}{a + c} = \dfrac{ad - bc}{a + c}$

6 $P_t = (1 - ae - ce)P_{t-1} + e(b+d)$

7
$$\frac{rA}{1200\left[1 - \left(1 + \dfrac{r}{1200}\right)^{-N}\right]}$$

8 (a) $CF = A(0.1)^t$

(b) $PS = 6(0.6)^t$

(c) $Y_t = A(0.1)^t + 6(0.6)^t$, $Y_t = 3(0.1)^t + 6(0.6)^t$

(d) stable

9 (a) $CF = A(0.2)^t$

(b) $PS = t + 6$

(c) $Y_t = A(0.2)^t + t + 6$, $Y_t = 4(0.2)^t + t + 6$

(d) unstable

Section 9.2

Practice Problems

1 (a) $y = 6e^{4t}$

(b) $y = 2e^{-5t}$

2 $y(t) = 10e^{3t} + 20$

A graph of y against t is sketched in Figure S9.5, which indicates that $y(t)$ rapidly diverges. We would expect divergence to occur for any solution

$$y(t) = Ae^{mt} + D \; (A \neq 0)$$

when $m > 0$.

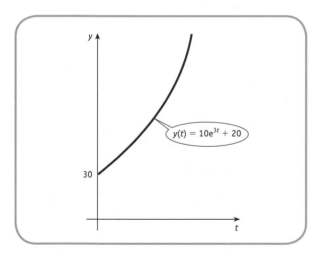

Figure S9.5

3 $Y(t) = -2000e^{-0.01t} + 4000$

This system is stable because the complementary function is a negative exponential and so $Y(t)$ converges to its equilibrium value of 4000 as t increases.

4 $P(t) = -e^{-t} + 2$

$Q_S(t) = -2e^{-t} + 2$

$Q_D(t) = e^{-t} + 2$

All three functions involve a negative exponential, so the system is stable.

Exercise 9.2

1 (a) $t^2 + 7$ (b) $-\frac{1}{3}e^{-3t} + \frac{1}{3}$ (c) $\frac{1}{3}t^3 + \frac{3}{2}t^2 - 5t + 1$

2 (a) $-20e^{-3t} + 60$; starting at 40, $y(t)$ increases uniformly to 60.

(b) $20e^{-3t} + 60$; starting at 80, $y(t)$ decreases uniformly to 60.

(c) 60; $y(t)$ remains at the equilibrium level of 60 for all time.

3 \$202.04

4 $Y(t) = 5000e^{-0.05t} + 10000$; stable.

5 $Y(t) = 2000e^{0.15t} - 1800$; unstable.

6 $P(t) = -e^{-2.5t} + 2$; $Q_S(t) = -3e^{-2.5t} + 5$; $Q_D(t) = 2e^{-2.5t} + 5$; stable.

7 (a) $N = Ae^{-kt}$

Exercise 9.2*

1 $t^3 - 8\sqrt{t} + 4$

2 $\dfrac{1}{3}(23 + 4e^{-2.4t})$

3 (a) $S = 4000e^{0.06t}$ (b) continuous

4 $y = 14 - 4e^{-2t}$; graph has a y-intercept of 10, increases and approaches 14.

5 1200

6 (a) $Y = 4400e^{-0.04t} + 3600$

(b) $S = 880e^{-0.04t} + 300$

(c) $t = 52$; $dY/dt = -22$

7 0

8 Substitute assumptions (1) and (3) into (2) to get

$$\beta\frac{dY}{dt} = \alpha Y$$

which rearranges as

$$\frac{dY}{dt} = \frac{\alpha}{\beta}Y$$

with solution

$$Y(t) = Y(0)e^{(\alpha/\beta)t}$$

This is unstable because $\alpha/\beta > 0$.

9 (b) The graph is sketched in Figure S9.6.

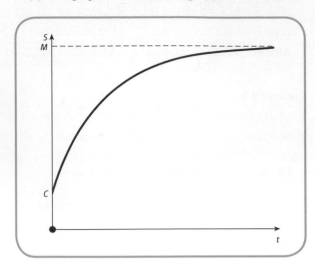

Figure S9.6

As $t \to \infty$, $S(t) \to M$

(c) 3164

10 The right-hand side is

$$my + c = m\left(Ae^{mt} - \frac{c}{m} \right) + c$$

$$= Ame^{mt} - c + c = Ame^{mt}$$

which we recognise as the derivative of $y(t)$.

11 (a) Ae^{-2t}

(b) e^{3t}

(c) $Ae^{-2t} + e^{3t}$; $6e^{-2t} + e^{3t}$

(d) unstable

12 (a) Ae^{-t}

(b) $4t - 7$

(c) $y = Ae^{-t} + 4t - 7$; $y = 8e^{-t} + 4t - 7$

(d) unstable

Multiple Choice Questions

1 E **2** B **3** C

4 D **5** B **6** A

7 B **8** C **9** B

10 E

Examination Questions

1 $P = 5.5$, $Q = 23$; $2.5(-1.5)^t + 5.5$; oscillatory divergence

2 (a) $y = 8\sqrt{x} + 2x^3 - 141$

(b) $N = 5\,000\,000e^{0.015t}$; 46.2 years

3 (a) $G = 500e^{-0.05t}$

(b) (i) \$370 billion
(ii) 27.7

4 (a) $Y_2 = 5360$, $C_2 = 4360$

(b) $Y_t = 0.8Y_{t-1} + 1200$

(c) $Y_t = 6000 - 1000(0.8)^t$

(e) $C_t = 5000 - 1000(0.8)^t$; 7

5 (a) $Y(t) = 7000 - 5000e^{-0.12t}$; negative exponential so $Y(t)$ converges at t increases

(b) The graph of Y against t is sketched in Figure S9.7

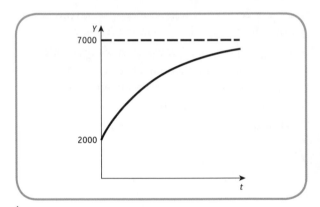

Figure S9.7

(c) 16.4

(d) $C(t) = 6{,}200 - 4{,}000e^{-0.12t}$

6 $P_t = \dfrac{(a-2)(-0.1a)^t + 12}{1 + 0.1a}$; $0 < a < 10$; $a = 2.5$

GLOSSARY

Absolute value The positive value or magnitude of a number.

Adjustment coefficient The constant of proportionality in the simple macroeconomic model in which the rate of change of national income is assumed to be proportional to excess expenditure.

Algebraic fraction Ratio of two expressions; $p(x)/q(x)$ where $p(x)$ and $q(x)$ are algebraic expressions such as $ax^2 + bx + c$ or $dx + e$.

Annual percentage rate (APR) The equivalent annual interest paid for a loan, taking into account the compounding over a variety of time periods.

Annuity A lump-sum investment designed to produce a sequence of equal regular payments over time.

Anti-derivative A function whose derivative is a given function.

Arbitrary constant A letter representing an unspecified constant in the general solution of a differential equation.

Arc elasticity Elasticity measured between two points on a curve.

Arithmetic progression A sequence of numbers with a constant difference between consecutive terms; the nth term takes the form $a + bn$.

Autonomous consumption The level of consumption when there is no income.

Autonomous consumption multiplier The number by which you multiply the change in autonomous consumption to deduce the corresponding change in, say, national income: $\partial Y/\partial b$.

Autonomous savings The withdrawals from savings when there is no income.

Average cost Total cost per unit of output: $AC = TC/Q$.

Average product of labour (labour productivity) Output per worker: $AP_L = Q/L$.

Average revenue Total revenue per unit of output: $AR = TR/Q = P$.

Balanced budget multiplier The number by which you multiply the change in government expenditure to deduce the corresponding change in, say, national income, $\partial Y/\partial G^*$, assuming that this change is financed entirely by a change in taxation.

Capital Man-made assets used in the production of goods and services.

Chord A straight line joining two points on a curve.

Closed interval The set of all real numbers between and including two given numbers: $a \leq x \leq b$.

Cobb–Douglas production function A production function of the form $Q = AK^\alpha L^\beta$.

Coefficient A numerical multiplier of the variables in an algebraic term, such as the numbers 4 and 7 in the expression $4x + 7yz^2$.

Cofactor The cofactor of the element a_{ij} is the determinant of the matrix left when row i and column j are deleted, multiplied by $+1$ or -1, depending on whether $i + j$ is even or odd, respectively.

Column vector A matrix with one column.

Comparative statics Examination of the effect on equilibrium values due to changes in the parameters of an economic model.

Complementary function of a difference equation The solution of the difference equation $Y_t = bY_{t-1} + c$ when the constant c is replaced by zero.

Complementary function of a differential equation The solution of the differential equation $\dfrac{dy}{dt} = my + c$ when the constant c is replaced by zero.

Complementary goods A pair of goods consumed together. As the price of either goes up, the demand for both goods goes down.

Compound interest The interest which is added on to the initial investment, so that this will itself gain interest in subsequent time periods.

Concave Graph bends downwards when $f''(x) < 0$.

Constant of integration The arbitrary constant that appears in an expression when finding an indefinite integral.

Constant returns to scale Exhibited by a production function when a given percentage increase in input leads to the same percentage increase in output: $f(\lambda K, \lambda L) = \lambda f(K, L)$.

Consumer's surplus The excess cost that a person would have been prepared to pay for goods over and above what is actually paid.

Consumption function The relationship between national income and consumption.

Continuous compounding The limiting value when interest is compounded with ever-increasing frequency.

Continuous The name given to a function which can be drawn without taking a pen off the paper. More formally, when $\lim_{x \to a} f(x) = f(a)$ at all points in the domain.

Convex Graph bends upwards when $f''(x) > 0$.

Coordinates A set of numbers that determine the position of a point relative to a set of axes.

Cramer's rule A method of solving simultaneous equations, $\mathbf{Ax} = \mathbf{b}$, by the use of determinants. The ith variable x_i can be computed using $\det(\mathbf{A}_i)/\det(\mathbf{A})$ where $\mathbf{A}_i$ is the determinant of the matrix obtained from $\mathbf{A}$ by replacing the ith column by $\mathbf{b}$.

Cross-price elasticity of demand The responsiveness of demand for one good to a change in the price of another: (percentage change in quantity) ÷ (percentage change in the price of the alternative good).

Decision variable The unknowns in a linear programming problem which can be controlled.

Decreasing function A function, $y = f(x)$, in which y decreases as x increases.

Decreasing returns to scale Exhibited by a production function when a given percentage increase in input leads to a smaller percentage increase in output: $f(\lambda K, \lambda L) = \lambda^n f(K, L)$ where $0 < n < 1$.

Definite integral The number $\int_a^b f(x)\mathrm{d}x$ which represents the area under the graph of $f(x)$ between $x = a$ and $x = b$.

Definite integration The process of finding the area under a graph by subtracting the values obtained when the limits are substituted into the anti-derivative.

Degree of homogeneity The number n in the relation $f(\lambda K, \lambda L) = \lambda^n f(K, L)$.

Degree The highest power in a polynomial.

Demand function A relationship between the quantity demanded and various factors that affect demand, including price.

Denominator The number (or expression) on the bottom of a fraction.

Dependent variable A variable whose value is determined by that taken by the independent variables; in $y = f(x)$, the dependent variable is y.

Derivative The gradient of the tangent to a curve at a point. The derivative at $x = a$ is written $f'(a)$.

Derived function The rule, f', which gives the gradient of a function, f, at a general point.

Determinant A determinant can be expanded as the sum of the products of the elements in any one row or column and their respective cofactors.

Difference equation An equation that relates consecutive terms of a sequence of numbers.

Difference of two squares The algebraic result which states that $a^2 - b^2 = (a + b)(a - b)$.

Differential equation An equation connecting derivatives of an unknown function.

Differentials Limiting values of incremental changes. In the limit the approximation $\Delta z \cong \dfrac{\partial z}{\partial x} \times \Delta x$ becomes $\mathrm{d}z = \dfrac{\partial z}{\partial x} \times \mathrm{d}x$ where $\mathrm{d}z$ and $\mathrm{d}x$ are the differentials.

Differentiation The process or operation of determining the first derivative of a function.

Discontinuous The name given to a function which is not continuous everywhere. The graph of the function has jumps or gaps.

Discount rate The interest rate that is used when going backwards in time to calculate the present value from a future value.

Discounting The process of working backwards in time to find the present values from a future value.

Discriminant The number $b^2 - 4ac$, which is used to indicate the number of solutions of the quadratic equation $ax^2 + bx + c = 0$.

Disposable income Household income after the deduction of taxes and the addition of benefits.

Distributive law The law of arithmetic which states that $a(b + c) = ab + ac$, for any numbers a, b and c.

Domain The numbers which are used as inputs to a function.

Dynamics Analysis of how equilibrium values vary over time.

Economic ordering quantity The quantity of a product that should be ordered so as to minimise the total cost that includes ordering costs and holding costs.

Elastic demand Where the percentage change in demand is more than the corresponding change in price: $|E| > 1$.

Elements The individual numbers inside a matrix. (Also called entries.)

Elimination method The method in which variables are removed from a system of simultaneous equations by adding (or subtracting) a multiple of one equation to (or from) a multiple of another.

Endogenous variable A variable whose value is determined within a model.

Equation Equality of two algebraic expressions which is true only for certain values of the variable.

Equilibrium (market) This state occurs when quantity supplied and quantity demanded are equal.

Equilibrium value of a difference equation A solution of a difference equation that does not vary over time; it is the limiting value of Y_n as n tends to infinity.

Equilibrium value of a differential equation A solution of a differential equation that does not vary over time; it is the limiting value of $y(t)$ as t tends to infinity.

Equivalent fractions Fractions which may appear different but which have the same numerical value.

Euler's theorem If each input is paid the value of its marginal product, the total cost of these inputs is equal to total output, provided there are constant returns to scale.

Exogenous variable A variable whose value is determined outside a model.

Exponent A superscript attached to a variable; the number 5 is the exponent in the expression, $2x^5$.

Exponential form A representation of a number which is written using powers. For example, 2^5 is the exponential form of the number 32.

Exponential function The function $f(x) = e^x$; an exponential function in which the base is the number $e = 2.718\,281\ldots$

Factor Part of an expression which, when multiplied by all the other factors, gives the complete expression.

Factorisation The process of writing an expression as a product of simpler expressions using brackets.

Factors of production The inputs into the production of goods and services: land, capital, labour and raw materials.

Feasible region The set of points which satisfy all of the constraints in a linear programming problem.

First-order derivative The rate of change of a function with respect to its independent variable. It is the same as the 'derivative' of a function, $y = f(x)$, and is written as $f'(x)$ or dy/dx.

Fixed costs Total costs that are independent of output.

Flow chart A diagram consisting of boxes of instructions indicating a sequence of operations and their order.

Function A rule that assigns to each incoming number, x, a uniquely defined outgoing number, y.

Function of two variables A rule which assigns to each pair of incoming numbers, x and y, a uniquely defined outgoing number, z.

Future value The final value of an investment after one or more time periods.

General solution of a difference equation The solution of a difference equation that contains an arbitrary constant. It is the sum of the complementary function and particular solution.

General solution of a differential equation The solution of a differential equation that contains an arbitrary constant. It is the sum of the complementary function and a particular solution.

Geometric progression A sequence of numbers with a constant ratio between consecutive terms; the nth term takes the form, ar^{n-1}.

Geometric ratio The constant multiplier in a geometric series.

Geometric series A sum of the consecutive terms of a geometric progression.

Government expenditure The total amount of money spent by government on defence, education, health, police, etc.

Gradient The gradient of a line measures steepness and is the vertical change divided by the horizontal change between any two points on the line. The gradient of a curve at a point is that of the tangent at that point.

Homogeneous function A function with the property that when all of the inputs are multiplied by a constant, l, the output is multiplied by ln where n is the degree of homogeneity.

Identity Equality of two algebraic expressions which is true for all values of the variable.

Identity matrix An $n \times n$ matrix, $\mathbf{I}$, in which every element on the main diagonal is 1 and the other elements are all 0. If $\mathbf{A}$ is any $n \times n$ matrix, then $\mathbf{AI} = \mathbf{I} = \mathbf{IA}$.

Implicit differentiation The process of obtaining dy/dx where the function is not given explicitly as an expression for y in terms of x.

Improper integral An definite integral representing the area of an unbounded region.

Income elasticity of demand The responsiveness of demand for one good to a change in income: (percentage change in quantity) ÷ (percentage change in income).

Increasing function A function, $y = f(x)$, in which y increases as x increases.

Increasing returns to scale Exhibited by a production function when a given percentage increase in input leads to a larger percentage increase in output: $f(\lambda K, \lambda L) = \lambda^n f(K, L)$ where $n > 1$.

Indefinite integration The process of obtaining an anti-derivative.

Independent variable A variable whose value determines that of the dependent variable; in $y = f(x)$, the independent variable is x.

Index Alternative word for exponent or power.

Index number The scale factor of a variable measured from the base year multiplied by 100.

Indifference curve A curve indicating all combinations of two goods which give the same level of utility.

Indifference map A diagram showing the graphs of a set of indifference curves. The further the curve is from the origin, the greater the level of utility.

Inelastic demand Where the percentage change in demand is less than the corresponding change in price: $|E| < 1$.

Inferior good A good whose demand decreases as income increases.

Inflation The percentage increase in the level of prices over a 12-month period.

Initial condition The value of Y_0 (or $y(0)$) which needs to be specified to obtain a unique solution of a difference (or differential) equation.

Integer programming A linear programming problem in which the search for solution is restricted to points in the feasible region with whole-number coordinates.

Integral The number $\int_a^b f(x)dx$ (definite integral) or the function $\int f(x)dx$ (indefinite integral).

Integration The generic name for the evaluation of definite or indefinite integrals.

Intercept The points where a graph crosses one of the co-ordinate axes.

Internal rate of return (IRR) The interest rate for which the net present value is zero.

Interval The set of all real numbers between (and possibly including) two given numbers.

Inverse (operation) The operation that reverses the effect of a given operation and takes you back to the original. For example, the inverse of halving is doubling.

Inverse function A function, written f^{-1}, which reverses the effect of a given function, f, so that $x = f^{-1}(y)$ when $y = f(x)$.

Inverse matrix A matrix $\mathbf{A}^{-1}$ with the property that $\mathbf{A}^{-1}\mathbf{A} = \mathbf{I} = \mathbf{A}\mathbf{A}^{-1}$.

Investment The creation of output not for immediate consumption.

Investment multiplier The number by which you multiply the change in investment to deduce the corresponding change in, say, national income: $\partial Y/\partial I^*$.

Isocost curve A line showing all combinations of two factors which can be bought for a fixed cost.

IS schedule The equation relating national income and interest rate based on the assumption of equilibrium in the goods market.

Isoquant A curve indicating all combinations of two factors which give the same level of output.

L-shaped curve A term used by economists to describe the graph of a function, such as $f(x) = a + \dfrac{b}{x}$, which bends roughly like the letter L.

Labour All forms of human input to the production process.

Labour productivity Average output per worker: Q/L

Lagrange multiplier The number λ which is used in the Lagrangian function. In economics this gives the approximate change in the value of the objective function when the value of the constraint is increased by 1 unit.

Lagrangian The function $f(x, y) + \lambda[M - \varphi(x, y)]$, where $f(x, y)$ is the objective function and $\varphi(x, y) = M$ is the constraint. The stationary point of this function is the solution of the associated constrained optimisation problem.

Laspeyre index An index number for groups of data which are weighted by the quantities used in the base year.

Law of diminishing marginal productivity (law of diminishing returns) Once the size of the workforce exceeds a particular value, the increase in output due to a 1-unit increase in labour will decline: $d^2Q/dL^2 < 0$ for sufficiently large L.

Law of diminishing marginal utility The law which states that the increase in utility due to the consumption of an additional good will eventually decline: $\partial^2U/\partial x_i^2 < 0$ for sufficiently large x_i.

Like terms Multiples of the same combination of algebraic symbols.

Limited growth Used to describe an economic variable which increases over time but which tends to a fixed quantity.

Limits of integration The numbers a and b which appear in the definite integral, $\int_a^b f(x)dx$.

Linear equation An equation of the form $y = dx + f$.

LM schedule The equation relating national income and interest rate based on the assumption of equilibrium in the money market.

Logarithm The power to which a base must be raised to yield a particular number.

Lower limit The number which appears at the bottom of the sigma notation to indicate the first term in a summation.

Marginal cost The cost of producing 1 more unit of output: $MC = d(TC)/dQ$.

Marginal product of capital The additional output produced by a 1-unit increase in capital: $MP_K = \partial Q/\partial K$.

Marginal product of labour The additional output produced by a 1-unit increase in labour: $MP_L = \partial Q/\partial L$.

Marginal propensity to consume The fraction of a rise in national income which goes into consumption: $MPC = dC/dY$.

Marginal propensity to consume multiplier The number by which you multiply the change in MPC to deduce the corresponding change in, say, national income: $\partial Y/\partial a$.

Marginal propensity to save The fraction of a rise in national income which goes into savings: $MPS = dS/dY$.

Marginal rate of commodity substitution (MRCS) The amount by which one input needs to increase to maintain a constant value of utility when the other input decreases by 1 unit: $MRTS = \partial U/\partial x_1 \div \partial U/\partial x_2$.

Marginal rate of technical substitution (MRTS) The amount by which capital needs to rise to maintain a constant level of output when labour decreases by 1 unit: $MRTS = MP_L/MP_K$.

Marginal revenue The extra revenue gained by selling 1 more unit of a good: $MR = d(TR)/dQ$.

Marginal utility The extra satisfaction gained by consuming 1 extra unit of a good: $\partial U/\partial x_i$.

Matrix A rectangular array of numbers, set out in rows and columns, surrounded by a pair of brackets. (Plural **matrices**.)

Maximum (local) point A point on a curve which has the highest function value in comparison with other values in its neighbourhood; at such a point the first-order derivative is zero and the second-order derivative is either zero or negative.

Maximum point (of a function of two variables) A point on a surface which has the highest function value in comparison with other values in its neighbourhood; at such a point the surface looks like the top of a mountain.

Method of substitution The method of solving constrained optimisation problems whereby the constraint is used to eliminate one of the variables in the objective function.

Minimum (local) point A point on a curve which has the lowest function value in comparison with other values in its neighbourhood; at such a point the first-order derivative is zero and the second-order derivative is either zero or positive.

Minimum point (of a function of two variables) A point on a surface which has the lowest function value in comparison with other values in its neighbourhood; at such a point the surface looks like the bottom of a valley or bowl.

Minor The name given to the cofactor before the '$\pm$' pattern is imposed.

Modelling The creation of a piece of mathematical theory which represents (a simplification of) some aspect of practical economics.

Modulus The positive value or magnitude of a number.

Money supply The notes and coins in circulation together with money held in bank deposits.

Monopolist The only firm in the industry.

Multiplier The number by which you multiply the change in an independent variable to find the change in the dependent variable.

National income The flow of money from firms to households.

Natural logarithm A logarithm to base e; if $M = e^n$ then n is the natural logarithm of M.

Net investment Rate of change of capital stock over time: $I = dK/dt$.

Net present value (NPV) The present value of a revenue flow minus the original cost.

Nominal data Monetary values prevailing at the time that they were measured.

Non-negativity constraints The constraints $x \geq 0$, $y \geq 0$, etc.

Non-singular matrix A square matrix with a non-zero determinant.

Normal good A good whose demand increases as income increases.

Number line An infinite line on which the points represent real numbers by their (signed) distance from the origin.

Numerator The number (or expression) on the top of a fraction.

Objective function A function that is optimised in a linear programming problem.

Open interval The set of all real numbers between but excluding two given numbers: $a < x < b$.

Optimisation The determination of the optimal (usually stationary) points of a function.

Order (of a matrix) The dimensions of a matrix. A matrix with m rows and n columns has order $m \times n$.

Origin The point where the coordinate axes intersect.

Paasche index An index number for groups of data which are weighted by the quantities used in the current year.

Parabola The shape of the graph of a quadratic function.

Parameter A constant whose value affects the specific values but not the general form of a mathematical expression, such as the constants a, b and c in $ax^2 + bx + c$.

Partial derivative The derivative of a function of two or more variables with respect to one of these variables, the others being regarded as constant.

Particular solution of a difference equation Any one solution of a difference equation such as $Y_t = B_{t-1} + c$.

Particular solution of a differential equation Any one solution of a differential equation such as $\dfrac{dy}{dt} = my + c$.

Perfect competition A situation in which there are no barriers to entry in an industry where there are many firms selling an identical product at the market price.

Point elasticity Elasticity measured at a particular point on a curve: $E = \dfrac{P}{Q} \times \dfrac{dQ}{dP}$.

Polynomial A function of the form $a_n x^n + a_{n-1} x^{n-1} + \ldots + a_0$.

Power Another word for exponent. If this is a positive integer, then it gives the number of times a number is multiplied by itself.

Precautionary demand for money Money held in reserve by individuals or firms to fund unforeseen future expenditure.

Present value The amount that is invested initially to produce a specified future value after a given period of time.

Price elasticity of demand A measure of the responsiveness of the change in demand due to a change in price: (percentage change in demand) ÷ (percentage change in price).

Price elasticity of supply A measure of the responsiveness of the change in supply due to a change in price: (percentage change in supply) ÷ (percentage change in price).

Primitive An alternative word for an anti-derivative.

Principal The value of the original sum invested.

Producer's surplus The excess revenue that a producer has actually received over and above the lower revenue that it was prepared to accept for the supply of its goods.

Production function The relationship between the output of a good and the inputs used to produce it.

Profit Total revenue minus total cost: $\pi = \text{TR} - \text{TC}$.

Quadratic function A function of the form $f(x) = ax^2 + bx + c$ where $a \neq 0$.

Range The numbers which form the set of outputs from a function.

Real data Monetary values adjusted to take inflation into account.

Rectangular hyperbola A term used by mathematicians to describe the graph of a function, such as $f(x) = a + \dfrac{b}{x}$, which is a hyperbola with horizontal and vertical asymptotes.

Recurrence relation An alternative term for a difference equation. It is an expression for Y_n in terms of Y_{n-1} (and possibly Y_{n-2}, Y_{n-3}, etc.).

Reduced form The final equation obtained when exogenous variables are eliminated in the course of solving a set of structural equations in a macroeconomic model.

Reverse flow chart A flow chart indicating the inverse of the original sequence of operations in reverse order.

Row vector A matrix with one row.

Saddle point A stationary point which is neither a maximum nor a minimum and at which the surface looks like the middle of a horse's saddle.

Scale factor The multiplier that gives the final value in percentage problems.

Second-order derivative The derivative of the first-order derivative. The expression obtained when the original function, $y = f(x)$, is differentiated twice in succession and is written as $f''(x)$ or d^2y/dx^2.

Second-order partial derivative The partial derivative of a first-order partial derivative. For example, f_{xy} is the second-order partial derivative when f is differentiated first with respect to y and then with respect to x.

Shadow price The change in the optimal value of the objective function due to a 1-unit increase in one of the available resources.

Simple interest The interest which is paid directly to the investor instead of being added to the original amount.

Simultaneous linear equations A set of linear equations in which there are (usually) the same number of equations and unknowns. The solution consists of values of the unknowns which satisfy all of the equations at the same time.

Singular matrix A square matrix with a zero determinant. A singular matrix fails to possess an inverse.

Sinking fund A fixed sum of money saved at regular intervals which is used to fund some future financial commitment.

Slope of a line Also known as the gradient, it is the change in the value of y when x increases by 1 unit.

Small increments formula The result
$$\Delta z \cong \frac{\partial z}{\partial x} \Delta x + \frac{\partial z}{\partial y} \Delta y.$$

Speculative demand for money Money held back by firms or individuals for the purpose of investing in alternative assets, such as government bonds, at some future date.

Square matrix A matrix with the same number of rows as columns.

Square root A number that when multiplied by itself equals a given number; the solutions of the equation $x^2 = c$ which are written $\pm\sqrt{x}$.

Stable (unstable) equilibrium An economic model in which the solution of the associated difference (or differential) equation converges (diverges).

Statics The determination of the equilibrium values of variables in an economic model which do not change over time.

Stationary point of inflection A stationary point that is neither a maximum nor a minimum; at such a point both first- and second-order derivatives are zero.

Stationary points (critical points, turning points, extrema) Points on a graph at which the tangent is horizontal; at a stationary point the first-order derivative is zero.

Structural equations A collection of equations that describe the equilibrium conditions of a macroeconomic model.

Substitutable goods A pair of goods that are alternatives to each other. As the price of one good goes up, the demand for the other rises.

Superior good A normal good for which the percentage rise in consumption exceeds the percentage increase in income.

Supply function A relationship between the quantity supplied and various factors that affect supply, including price.

Tangent A line that just touches a curve at a point.

Taxation Money paid to government based on an individual's income and wealth (direct taxation) together with money paid by suppliers of goods or services based on expenditure (indirect taxation).

Time series A sequence of numbers indicating the variation of data over time.

Total cost The sum of the total variable and fixed costs: TC = TVC + FC.

Total revenue A firm's total earnings from the sales of a good: TR = PQ.

Transactions demand for money Money used for everyday transactions of goods and services.

Transpose (of a matrix) The matrix obtained from a given matrix by interchanging rows and columns. The transpose of a matrix $\mathbf{A}$ is written $\mathbf{A}^\mathrm{T}$.

Transpose a formula The rearrangement of a formula to make one of the other letters the subject.

U-shaped curve A term used by economists to describe a curve, such as a parabola, which bends upwards, like the letter U.

Unbounded region A feasible region that is not completely enclosed by a polygon. The associated linear programming problem may not have a finite solution.

Uniformly convergent sequence A sequence of numbers which progressively increases (or decreases) to a finite limit.

Uniformly divergent sequence A sequence of numbers which progressively increases (or decreases) without a finite limit.

Unit elasticity of demand Where the percentage change in demand is the same as the percentage change in price: $|E| = 1$.

Unlimited growth Used to describe an economic variable which increases without bound.

Unstable equilibrium An economic model in which the solution of the associated difference (or differential) equation diverges.

Upper limit The number which appears at the top of the sigma notation to indicate the last term in a summation.

Utility The satisfaction gained from the consumption of a good.

Variable costs Total costs that change according to the amount of output produced.

x axis The horizontal coordinate axis pointing from left to right.

y axis The vertical coordinate axis pointing upwards.

Zero matrix A matrix in which every element is zero.

INDEX

Note: page numbers in **bold** refer to glossary entries.